"BEHOLD

A

PALE HORSE"

Milton William Cooper

Published by
Light Technology Publishing
P. O. Box 1495, Sedona, AZ 86336
ISBN 0-929385-22-5

Cover Art by Joanna Heikens

Printed by Mission Possible Commercial Printing
A Division of Light Technology Communication Services
Sedona, Arizona

And I looked,

and behold a pale horse:

and his name that sat upon him was Death,

and Hell followed with him.

And power was given unto them

over the fourth part of the earth,

to kill with sword,

and with hunger,

and with the beasts

of the earth.

The Holy Bible
The Book of Revelation
Chapter 6
Verse 8

The ideas and conclusions expressed in this work are mine alone. It is possible that one or more conclusions may be wrong. The purpose of this book is to convince you (the reader) that something is terribly wrong. It is my hope that this work will inspire you to begin an earnest search for the truth. Your conclusions may be different but together maybe we can build a better world.

One
basic
truth can
be used as
a foundation for
a mountain of lies,
and if we dig down deep
enough in the mountain of lies,
and bring out that truth, to set it
on top of the mountain of lies; the entire
mountain of lies will crumble under the weight of
that one truth, and there is nothing more devastating to a
structure of lies than the revelation of the truth upon which
the structure of lies was built, because the shock waves of
the revelation of the truth reverberate, and continue to
reverberate throughout the Earth for generations to
follow, awakening even those
people who had no
desire to be
awakened
to the
truth.

Delamer Duverus

Dedication

I dedicate this book to my children
Jenny
Tony
Jessica
and little Dorothy.

I love you every moment of every day.

Acknowledgment

My deepest appreciation and warmest friendship is extended to all those wonderful people who have helped to make this book a reality. I especially thank those listed below who made outstanding contributions. Some have taken great risks.

Annie, for your understanding, and for all the sandwiches. Little Dorothy, for the happiness.

Barbara Ann and husband; Ron and Karen Brown; Taryn Krive; Jane Drucker; The November 5th 1989 Volunteers; Ron Regehr; Keith Ranch; Gordon Davis; Billy Goodman; Stanley and Elma Barrington; Roger Scherrer; Glenn and Cheryl; the people who sent letters from Minnesota; Nancy Batchelder; Sal from Rhode Island; Mike Whelen; Joe Hysong; JMP; William Stienman; Tal Levesque; Pavel; Roger and Karen LaChance; O'Ryin Swanson; Jeanne Ann; Anthony Hilder; Leota Rinehart; Tim Bennett; all who are acknowledged in the text.

And all the others who have so freely given. I thank you.

Table Of Contents

INTRODUCTION

Sometime ago I had the opportunity to meet William Cooper and his wife Annie. It was part of my job to verify whether this man did indeed speak the truth or was just another person seeking fame and fortune. What I found was a rugged, bulldog, driven individual who was kind, thoughtful and tenderhearted. He was truly concerned about you and your welfare.

Bill knew that people were badly informed by a society which spoon-feeds you deception until there is no distinction between fiction and reality. He sees what many other[s] see happening, and he is not afraid to do something about it.

There are many who do not want you to know what Bill has to say. They have tried many times to stop him from saying it. The scars on his face and the loss of his leg are his badges of sincerity on your behalf.

No one becomes popular by telling people the truth. History records what happened to the true prophets of the past. However, some have listened to their warnings and were not caught off-guard. Others have put their heads in the sand and refused to listen.

Bill has it together, and has put it together for you so you can also be one of the informed of the world. A well informed person can make the right decision. William Cooper has my vote of approval because I cared enough to find out who the man is. Now is your opportunity.

Barbara Ann

There have been many related sequential coincidences all throughout my life, incidents that by themselves would have led nowhere. Statistically, the odds against the same or a related sequence of events happening to one individual are astronomically high. It is this series of incidents that have convinced me that God has had a hand in my life. I do not believe in fate. I do not believe in accidents.

I cannot and will not accept the theory that long sequences of unrelated accidents determine world events. It is inconceivable that those with power and wealth would *not* band together with a common bond, a common interest, and a long-range plan to decide and direct the future of the world. For those with the resources, to do otherwise would be totally irresponsible. I know that I would be the first to organize a conspiracy to control the outcome of the future, if I were such a person and a conspiracy did not yet exist. I would do it in an attempt to ensure the survival of the principles in which I believe, the survival of my family, my survival, and the survival of the human race, if for no other reason.

I believe, therefore, that a grand game of chess is being played on a level that we can barely imagine, and we are the pawns. Pawns are valuable only under certain circumstances and are frequently sacrificed to gain an advantage. Anyone who has studied military strategy is familiar with the concept of sacrifice. Those who have seriously studied history have probably discovered the real reason we go to war on a regularly scheduled basis.

Before reading this book I advise you to play at least two complete games of chess. You must learn the rules THEY play by. You must realize objectively that some pieces are more valuable than others and that the king is the most valuable of all. You cannot learn reality if you get caught up in the fantasy that "it's not fair." You must come to know that the ultimate outcome of the game is the only thing that counts. You were lied to when you were told that "it does not matter whether you win or lose, it's how you play the game." Winning in the world of the elite is everything. Indeed, it is the only thing. The power elite intend to win.

My research has shown, at this point, that the future laid out for us may be just about impossible to change. I do not agree with the means by which the powerful few have chosen for us to reach the end. I do not agree that the end is where we should end at all. But unless we can wake the people from their sleep, nothing short of civil war will stop the planned outcome. I base that statement not on defeatism but on the apathy of the majority of the American people. Twenty-five years ago I would have believed otherwise — but twenty-five years ago I was also sound asleep.

We have been taught lies. Reality is not at all what we perceive it to be.

INTRODUCTION

We cannot survive any longer by hanging onto the falsehoods of the past. Reality must be discerned at all costs if we are to be a part of the future. Truth must prevail in all instances, no matter who it hurts or helps, if we are to continue to live upon this earth. At this point, what we want may no longer matter. It is what we must do to ensure our survival that counts. The old way is in the certain process of destruction and a New World Order is beating down the door.

To cling to the past is guaranteed suicide. To remain apathetic is assured enslavement. To learn the truth and then act upon it is the only means of survival at this moment. To shrug off the information contained in this book and to disregard its warning will result in the complete destruction of the Republic of the United States of America. You will never get a second warning or a second chance. Like it or not, this is it, stark reality. You can no longer turn your head, ignore it, pretend it's not true, say "it can't happen to me," run, or hide. The wolf is at the door.

I fear for the little ones, the innocents, who are already paying for our mistakes. There exists a great army of occupationally orphaned children. They are attending government-controlled day-care centers. And latch-key kids who are running wild in the streets. And the lop-sided, emotionally wounded children of single welfare mothers, born only for the sake of more money in the monthly check. Open your eyes and look at them, for they are the future. In them I see the sure and certain destruction of this once-proud nation. In their vacant eyes I see the death of Freedom. They carry with them a great emptiness — and someone will surely pay a great price for their suffering.

If we do not act in concert with each other and ensure that the future becomes what we need it to be, then we will surely deserve whatever fate awaits us.

I believe with all my heart that God put me in places and in positions throughout my life so that I would be able to deliver this warning to His people. I pray that I have been worthy and that I have done my job.

THIS IS MY CREED

I believe first in God, the same God in which my ancestors believed. I believe in Jesus Christ and that he is my saviour. Second, I believe in the Constitution of the Republic of the United States of America, without interpretation, as it was written and meant to work. I have given my sacred oath "to protect and defend the Constitution of the United States of America against all enemies foreign and domestic." I intend to fulfill that oath. Third, I believe in the family unit and, in particular, my family unit. I have sworn that I will give my life, if it is required, in defense of God, the

Constitution, or my family. Fourth, I believe that any man without principles that he is ready and willing to die for at any given moment is already dead and is of no use or consequence whatsoever.

William Cooper
August 3, 1990
Camp Verde, Arizona

INTRODUCTION

FOREWORD

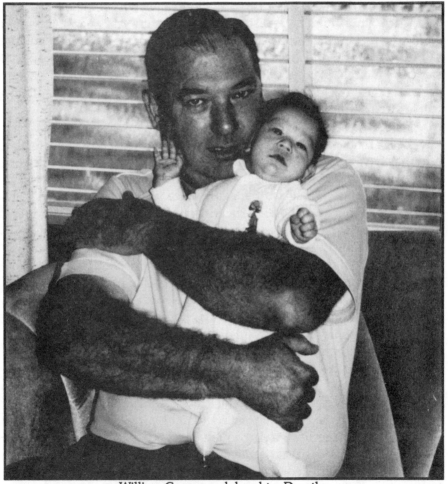

William Cooper and daughter Dorothy

The one thing that I find most difficult is to write about myself. It is hard to understand why some people thirst for knowledge about me. It was never my intention to be anyone's hero. I am certainly no great example upon which to base one's life. I consider myself a very average normal kind of guy. I have some pretty good points; I have some human failings. I am proud of some of my achievements, and there are things that I wish I had not done. I'm not perfect, and I am not sure that I ever want to be. But it is certain that I do not belong on anyone's pedestal. I am a man with a message. And the message will be accepted by only a few. To those few who will understand, I am your brother. Maybe...we can change the future for the better.

William Moore, in his disinformation publication entitled "Focus," said that I am a fundamentalist preacher. Twenty years ago that would have been a compliment, but today it implies sleaziness. That is why he said it. I am not, and have never been any kind of preacher. I am not starting a church. I am not developing a religion. I do not belong to any organizations. I do not have an entourage. There is no cult and I am not a cult leader. No one camps out around my house.

People have called radio talk shows claiming to have first-hand knowledge that I am a notorious radical right-wing extremist. Others have said they have proof that I belong to a white racist organization. Someone said that they found my name on a list of communist party members. A man in Los Angeles, always the same voice, calls when I am on radio claiming that I am an alcoholic. The truth is, most of my close friends and acquaintances consider themselves to be liberal democrats. My only political stance is Constitutional. My wife is Chinese. That rules out the racist propaganda. I fought the communists in Vietnam. I will fight them again, if necessary, but only on United States soil. I used to drink a lot of alcohol in my younger days. As I became older the booze dwindled to a trickle. Now I do not drink much at all. Most of my friends have never seen me take a drink. Annie and I are fond of using wine in our cooking. The lies, no doubt, will continue.

For the purpose of keeping everything in perspective, let's all understand that attempts to assassinate my character will continue and in all probability will become worse. Rather than let that get in the way, *I want you to believe everything bad that you ever hear about me.* See if that changes anything that I have been trying to tell you. See if it negates any of the proof. I believe that is the easiest way to handle those attacks. You who are sincerely interested in knowing will seek out me or those who are intimately close to me. Those who do are the only ones who will ever really know who and what I am.

FOREWORD

My ancestors came from England, Scotland, and Ireland. I had relatives who fought on both sides in the Civil War. And some who fought in the Indian Wars. One of my ancestors was a horse thief in Texas. I don't know for sure, but I think he got hung for it. When I was a little boy I heard whispers that there was some Cherokee blood in the family. Every time I asked about it I was told to shut up. I never could figure out why everyone was afraid to talk about the Indian blood. I thought, and still think, that it is something of which to be proud. I have since discovered that the old folks in my family, like the old folks in almost every family, thought there was some stigma attached to being part Indian. In the old days on the American frontier, people lived by hard rules. If you weren't accepted by your neighbors you were more than likely to end up dead.

My paternal grandmother's family, named Vance, traveled to Texas in a covered wagon and were some of the first settlers in the area of Odessa. My great grandfather Vance was a real cowboy who eventually became one of the first oil-field workers. My great grandmother Vance told me that one of their first homes was a dugout on the prairie. My great aunt Sister owned a photo of her father, my great grandfather Vance, standing in front of a saloon beside his friend. Both men had six-guns stuck in their belts.

When she was about 84 or so she told me that my great grandfather Vance had gone off to do some work for a rancher. It was during a particularly nasty Indian uprising. My great grandmother was a newly married young woman at the time. She rose early one morning and saw smoke rising from the direction of one of her neighbors. Soon a war party of five young braves rode up to her dugout. She told me that she was scared to death but knew if she showed it they would kill her for sure. The Indians were hungry. Great Grandma Vance made them get down off their ponies, dragged them inside and fed them. They didn't harm her. After filling their stomachs they rode off in the direction where she saw smoke rising later that afternoon. She said that she learned later that she was the only one in the area that had not been burned out or killed. She was a very brave woman.

Great Grandma Vance died in a car accident just a short time after telling me that story. I thought it was a very strange way for her to die. She went from covered wagons to Fords and Boeing 707s. Grandma Vance saw just about everything that ever was important in this world happen in her lifetime.

My paternal grandfather's family also rode across the country in a covered wagon. They strayed a little north, however, and ended up in the Indian territory now known as Oklahoma. They were on the front line during the Oklahoma land rush and succeeded in staking out 320 acres on

Big Bear Creek near what would eventually become Enid. A little town sprang up not too far away called Garber. They raised a lot of kids. I remember my great grandmother cooking the biggest breakfast I had ever seen. We slept in real feather beds that swallowed us up. We ran to the outhouse in the middle of the night because we were embarrassed to use the chamber pot that Great Grandma kept handy under every bed. In the morning everyone would crowd around the wood stove in the kitchen or the coal stove in the parlor trying to get warm.

My dad had given me a .22 rifle for Christmas and Great Grandma's farm was the first place that I ever went hunting. I got up before the sun one morning, tiptoed downstairs, and headed out for the creek. About two hours later I saw my chance and shot a quail sitting up in a tree. I strutted proudly to the farmhouse holding that quail up for all to see. Luckily the farmhand saw me first. He burst out laughing and asked me what I thought I was doing with that sparrow. I ran off and buried that bird and never said a word to anyone. I learned later that quails don't sit in trees. For those who may think this to be a terrible thing, I must tell you that every boy in those days was given a rifle and taught to hunt. During hunting season many a family managed to put aside some extra money because the boys brought home meat from the hunt. That money saved was sorely needed. It was considered a duty for a citizen to own a gun in order to carry out the intent of the 2nd amendment to the Constitution. As long as the citizens owned guns the government could never become oppressive.

My mother's family came from Scotland and settled in North Carolina. They were hardworking and thrifty folk. Most of them were poor. I never knew much more about my mother's family. I don't even remember anyone talking much about them. I know that my grandmother, Nellie Woodside, was forced to give up some of her children when her husband died. There was not enough money to feed all of the kids. My mother was one of those chosen to live in a children's home until things got better. No one ever talked about my mother's father. When I asked about my grandfather I was told, "Red was no good, and you just mind your own business." I got the feeling that nobody liked him. He died before I entered this world.

I was born May 6, 1943. I was reared in a military family. My father is USAF Lt. Col. (Ret.) Milton V. Cooper. He prefers to be called Jack, the nickname given to him by the family when he was a boy. Dad began his Air Force career as a young cadet flying biplanes and retired as a command pilot with thousands of hours to his credit. I have a picture of him standing in front of an old biplane in his leather jacket and his cap with the earflaps

My mother and father

FOREWORD

just like Snoopy wears.

I can remember the pilots gathered around the kitchen table talking about the planes and telling stories. Sometimes they discussed strange things called foo fighters or UFOs. When we were lucky they got out the projector and showed Kodachrome slides. That was a special treat. By the time I was eight years old, I think I had already seen and been inside every plane the Air Force (which used to be the Army Air Force) had ever owned. I had flown in several. I had seen many of them crash and had friends who had lost their fathers.

I remember one night in the Azores at Lages Field. We were at the base theater watching a movie when the projector ground to a stop, the lights came on and a plea was made for blood donors. We knew there had been a disaster. Everyone went outside and looked down the hill at the flightline. It was literally consumed in flames. We could see men on fire running through the night. A B-29 had crashed. I forget if it had been taking off or landing; but I will never forget the scene that was spread before me on that night. No one went back to the movie even though we had only seen half. I was nine years old but felt much older. I had seen many crashes, and I would see many more in the years to come. But I never saw anything that could ever compare to the wreckage, the fire, the devastation, or the loss of life caused by the crash of that B-29. We left the Azores a year later. As we climbed into the sky I looked out the plane window. I could still see pieces of the wreckage where it had been pushed away from the runways. It was that incident that gave me an appreciation of the dangers that my dad faced on a daily basis. I knew then how lucky we were to see him walk in the door. Aviation wasn't safe in those days, especially for military pilots. We all knew families that had lost someone in a crash.

I didn't always love my father. He was a strict disciplinarian. My dad did not believe in "spare the rod" and his belt was put to use frequently in our family. I was a very sensitive but willful child. Rules didn't mean much to me until I got caught breaking them. Many times I was the focus of his anger. Like most kids, I didn't understand. I thought he was a tyrant. Now I appreciate his upbringing. I know, beyond the shadow of a doubt, that without his strict discipline we most probably would have turned out bad.

Now I love my Dad. He is my friend. He is an independent, gregarious, feisty, tough, confident, adventurous, sometimes overbearing, handsome, big bear of a man. My mother told me that she fell in love with him because he looks like John Wayne, and he does. I have watched him progress from one who disdained any public show of affection to a man who is just as likely to hug you as shake your hand. On the other side, he has at times made me so angry that I could have punched him in the mouth, but I never have. It's damn hard for anyone not to like him. He is always up to some mischief, and I can guarantee you that no one is ever bored around my father.

My mother is a real Southern lady. They used to call her kind a Southern belle. She is one of the last of a dying breed. Dovie Nell (Woodside) Cooper is the type of woman that men like to dream about when they're lonely. She is the kindest, gentlest, woman that I have ever known. I do not make that statement just because she is my mother. It's true. She was beautiful as a young woman and she is beautiful now. My mother is one of those people who, once she likes you, can't be driven away. She is loyal to a fault. I have seen her during the good and during the bad times. She never flinched, no matter what. It always surprised me that she could be so tough and yet so kind, gentle, and loving all at the same time. Woe to anyone who ever harms my dad or one of her children in her presence. She is the best cook who ever stepped foot in any kitchen that was ever built. I love my mother probably more than anyone else in this world.

I have a brother Ronnie and a sister Connie. They are fraternal twins two years younger than me. We were closer than most siblings when we were children because we spent so much of our life in foreign countries, where oftentimes we found ourselves unable to communicate except with each other. We had school friends, but school was often many miles from where we lived. We had few toys. Most of them were things that mother gave us such as spools, cigar boxes, string, or anything else that we could find to keep us occupied. Every Christmas was a delight because we always got some REAL toys. Ronnie and I had a propensity to see how things worked, however, so they never lasted long. Everything we wore, including shoes, was ordered from the Sears catalog. It was the wish book, and we never tired of looking through it. We alternately loved each other, hated each other, fought each other, and defended each other, as I guess all kids do.

Ronnie, his wife Suzie, and their daughter Jennifer live in Garber, Oklahoma, where Ron sells John Deere farm equipment. Ron & Suzie built their house with their own hands. As far as I know they intend to live in that house until they die. Ronnie served as an officer in the Army. In Vietnam he earned the Silver Star. We haven't seen each other since 1976 after he came to visit me in the hospital after I lost my leg. Nevertheless I love him and I miss him a lot. Neither one of us can afford to travel much unless it's business, but one of these days soon I'm going to surprise him with a visit. Connie has shown me pictures and Ron looks just like my great grandfather. Almost every picture I've seen shows Ron in chaps, a Stetson, boots, and either near or on a horse. I guess that is about how it should be, as Ronnie always wanted to be a cowboy when he was a child.

Connie has really turned out to be a fine woman. When she was little I sometimes liked her and sometimes didn't. Little boys don't usually have much use for little girls. Since we only had each other to play with, however, Ronnie and I loved her a lot; but little boys just can't ever admit anything like that. I remember Connie always followed me everywhere I went. I couldn't get rid of her no matter how hard I tried. Her devotion and loyalty made me love her all the more. Of course I pretended that she was a pain in the ass. As we grew older and began to realize that there was a really big difference between boys and girls Connie began to take on an air of mystery. From that time until I was about 18 she baffled me completely. I remember when she was around 13 or so she would throw temper tantrums when she got angry. She would stomp her feet, scream, run to her room and then slam the door. Ronnie and I thought it was a great show but couldn't for love or money understand why she did it. When we asked mom she would just shake her head and say, "Hormones."

William Cooper, brother Ronnie, sister Connie

FOREWORD

Connie grew up to be a beautiful woman and eventually married her high school sweetheart, Gus Deaton. They had two beautiful children, Janice and Chrissie. Janice is very much like Connie, loving and loyal. Chrissie is different. She's a redhead who loves to party. I guess Chrissie represents a freedom of spirit more than anything else.

Connie's marriage deteriorated and no one could figure out what was happening until Gus was diagnosed as having brain tumors. It was tragic. Everyone really loved Gus. As his disease progressed and he began to do crazy things, people just drifted away. I have always nurtured a very special love for Chrissie. She never deserted her father. When no one else could stand to be around him, Chrissie chose to go and live with him "so he won't be lonely," she said. Even now I get all choked up when I think of that little red-headed girl going to live with her sick father "so he won't be lonely." His behavior was such that no one else could stand to be around him. At least that is what I'm told. It wasn't Gus's fault that he became ill and I've always felt it just wasn't fair to Connie, the children, or Gus. I've since learned that life is seldom fair.

Connie eventually remarried and moved to Austin, Texas, where she has established herself as a valuable employee of a large bank. Her husband is an executive for McGraw Hill. His name, coincidentally, is Ron. We all really like Ron McClure, especially Dad, who has formed a close friendship with him. My sister has really blossomed into a wonderful woman. She has become one of my dearest and closest friends. She has grown to be so much a part of me that even now I sometimes get a feeling to look behind me to see if that little girl is still there. I feel a great loss when I see that it's only Sugarbear, my faithful dog; but then, I love him too, so can't complain.

I graduated in 1961 from Yamato High School in Japan. That fall I enlisted in the Air Force. I really wanted to go into the Navy but I had always had a tendency toward car sickness and seasickness. I attended basic at Lackland Air Force Base, Texas, and Technical School for Aircraft & Missile Pneudraulics at Amarillo Air Force Base.

Upon completion I was ordered to the 495th Bomb Wing of the Strategic Air Command at Sheppard Air Force Base just outside Wichita Falls. The name was later changed to the 4245th Bomb Wing — don't ask me why. In just a short time I had gone from a skinny kid who didn't know much about anything, even though I thought I did, to an airman who had a Secret(!) security clearance and worked on B-52 bombers, KC-135 refueling aircraft, and Minuteman missiles.

I saw REAL atomic bombs. I worked around them on a daily basis. Because of that I had to wear a dosimeter just in case I was exposed to

---

FOREWORD

radiation. In those days we were the elite of the Air Force and we knew it. I received a Letter of Commendation for my work. In due time I was awarded the National Defense Medal and the Air Force Good Conduct Medal. (Actually, I think everyone was awarded the National Defense Medal so that no one would be embarrassed standing in formation with nothing on their chest.)

It was during this time that I met a couple of sergeants who kind of adopted me. We went out to the clubs together and usually ended up chasing women and drinking a lot of beer. They told me several stories about being attached to a special unit that recovered crashed flying saucers. Sgt. Meese told me that he had been on one operation that transported a saucer so large that a special team went before them, lowering all telephone poles and fence posts. Another team followed and replaced them. They moved it only at night. It was kept parked and covered somewhere off the road during the day. Since we were always half-tanked when these stories came out, I never believed them — sergeants were known to tell some tall tales to younger guys like me.

On November 22, 1963, I was on duty as CQ (Charge of Quarters) for the Field Maintenance Squadron. Most of the men were out on the flight-line working, the barracks orderlies had been assigned their tasks, the first sergeant was gone somewhere, and I was alone. I turned on the orderly room TV to watch the live broadcast of the President's motorcade in Dallas. I was not prepared for what I saw. I stared in disbelief as the events unfurled in front of my eyes. I knew that something had happened, but what? I had seen and heard the assassination, but my mind was not accepting it. I kept staring at the set to discover what it was that had happened when slowly the realization crept over me. A numbness spread up my arms and legs. I saw what had happened! The hair stood up on the back of my neck and a chill went down my spine. President Kennedy had been shot right in front of my eyes!

At that point huge tears began to stream down my face. Waves of emotion rushed through my body. I felt that I had to do something, so I picked up the direct line to the command center. I choked back the tears. When the command duty officer answered, I told him that the President had just been shot in Dallas. There was a pause, and he asked me, "How do you know he has been shot?" I told him that I had watched it on television and then hung up the phone. I was numb all over.

A few minutes later the command duty officer called back and ordered a red alert at DEFCON TWO (Defense Condition Two meant war was imminent). The roar of jet engines could already be heard as the alert crews taxied their planes toward the runway. I was scared shitless as I ran from

---

FOREWORD

barracks to barracks routing out the night shift and those who had the day off. We had been told that we had about 15 minutes to launch all of our planes before the first atomic bomb would hit us in the event that the Russians launched an attack.

I didn't even lock up the orderly room. I just jumped in the first car I saw, rode to the SAC compound, and reported to my red alert duty station. For the next three days I slept under the belly of a B-52 bomber staring at the Armageddon that hid just inside the closed bomb-bay doors. We thought the shit had finally hit the fan. It was a great relief when the alert was ended. I left the Air Force with an honorable discharge in 1965.

In December of the same year I joined the Navy. I had always loved the ocean. I had wanted to be a sailor since I was a little boy. Seasick or not, I made up my mind to follow my dream. I was sent to the Naval Training Center in San Diego for boot camp. Because of my prior Air Force experience I was made the Recruit Chief Company Commander. I was allowed to keep my same rank and pay grade. We had a good bunch of guys in my company and we had a great company commander, Chief Campbell, chief electricians mate. He turned the company over to me. The chief was a good man. He was only interested in teaching us what we needed to know and in keeping us out of trouble. Unlike most boot camp instructors, Chief Campbell had no axe to grind and wasn't trying to prove anything to himself or anyone else. He was truly our friend.

During boot camp I volunteered for submarines (my sense of adventure was very strong). I was accepted, and upon completion of basic training, was ordered to the USS Tiru (SS-416) at the submarine base at Pearl Harbor, Hawaii. Spitfire and damnation, no one could possibly be that lucky! I couldn't believe my eyes when I read my orders. Here I was fulfilling my dream of being in the Navy. I got exactly what I asked for the first time that I asked for it, which was extremely rare in any branch of military service. And to top it all off, I was being sent to Hawaii, the land of tropical paradise. I was in seventh heaven.

I landed in Hawaii with no time to play and took a cab directly to the sub base. My submarine was nowhere to be found. I kept asking people until I found someone who told me that my boat (subs are called boats in the Navy) was not at the sub base but in dry dock in the Pearl Harbor Naval Shipyard. I hailed another cab.

The cab driver dropped me off at the head of a pier that looked like it had never been cleaned up after the Japanese bombed Pearl Harbor. It was covered with what appeared to be hoses, huge electrical cables, rusting metal of every conceivable size and shape that you can imagine. The air was rank with the smell of diesel, welding fumes, paint, and steel. If there

---

FOREWORD

is a hell on earth, I thought, this has to be it. I walked up the pier, over to the edge, and looked down into the dry dock. There, stripped of all dignity, lying naked and cut cleanly in half, was my boat, the USS Tiru. Men were scrambling all over it. They looked like ants swarming over a dead grasshopper. Brilliant flashes of light brighter than the sun drove sparks high into the air and then down in a beautiful flow to the bottom of the dock. I couldn't believe my eyes. Someone actually expected me to go out to sea, then underwater, in what appeared to me to be a motley collection of cut-up rusting metal scavenged from some satanic junkyard, stuck together by demons with welding torches. My luck had just run out.

I reported to the barracks barge moored in the water on the other side of the pier and was given a hammock for when I had the duty; then I was sent to the sub base barracks where I was assigned a rack and a locker. I wanted to go into Honolulu but quickly discovered non-quals did not rate liberty. It was getting worse.

The next few months were spent sanding, painting, lifting, and learning the boat. The men of the crew, except for the chief cook, were great. The chief cook was drunk every minute of the day and night. He didn't like me, so I didn't get much to eat. His dislike stemmed from my first morning when I walked into the galley and watched as the other crew members ordered their breakfast. When there was an opening I stepped up and asked for eggs over easy. That's when the chief hit the overhead and vowed that I would never eat a meal in *his* mess decks. He wasn't kidding, either. The only time after that morning that I got anything to eat out of that galley was when the chief cook was ashore.

To this day I still don't know what I did wrong. I could have gone to the captain, but if I had done that I might as well have put in for a transfer at the same time. It wasn't long, though, before I was able to locate where he hid his booze. I made his life miserable from that moment on. I won't tell you what I laced his vodka with, but it wasn't anything you'd ever want to drink, believe me. I kept that chief so sick that he was transferred off the boat for medical reasons. I didn't want to hurt him, but it was either get rid of him or starve to death. I made up my mind that chief or no chief I wasn't going to go to sea on a boat that wouldn't feed me.

I didn't relish going to sea with a drunk chief in charge of closing the main induction valve when the boat made a dive. When a submarine goes underwater certain valves MUST be closed or the boat will flood with water and everyone will drown. The main induction is the MOST IMPORTANT of those valves. It was the cook's duty to close it, because the valve was in the galley on board the USS Tiru.

I made two especially close friends while on the Tiru. A black seaman named Lincoln Loving and an American Indian seaman we called Geronimo. The three of us were inseparable. Lincoln was best man at my first marriage. Of the three Geronimo was the most experienced seaman, so he taught Lincoln and me. He knew everything there was to know about the boat, rope, paint, and a whole lot of other things that a man had to know to survive in the Navy. I knew the most about getting along in the military, so I taught Geronimo and Lincoln. Lincoln knew every really good spot on the Island where we could have a good time, so he led the liberty party.

Three things really stand out in my mind about the time that I spent on the Tiru. The first was an incident that occurred during a test dive while we were creeping along at about 3 or 4 knots at a depth of 600 feet off the Island of Oahu. Lincoln and I had just been relieved from watch and were in the after battery talking when we were knocked off our feet. We heard a loud CLANG forward and felt the boat lunge to port. Then we heard a sound that made our blood run cold. I could literally feel the blood drain from my face as I listened to whatever it was that we hit scrape along the starboard side of the hull. Lincoln and I froze. We held our breath as metal screeched upon metal. I thought it would never end. No one moved, anywhere.

Finally, after what seemed a lifetime, the boat lurched and the noise disappeared aft. If it had pierced the hull none of us would be alive today. We never found out what it was. When we returned to Pearl, divers went down to have a look. When they surfaced they reported that the starboard bowplane was damaged and the hull was gouged all along the starboard side from bow to stern. We went in for repairs. In a couple of days we were good as new, but I certainly had an entirely different perspective on life.

The second thing that stands out happened to another boat that had been out participating in torpedo attack exercises with another submarine. I remember seeing the boat entering the harbor with a large tarp over the conning tower. I could see something holding the tarp up on each side of the tower but I couldn't see what it was. Later, Geronimo, Lincoln and I walked over where the boat was berthed and looked under the tarp. The other boat in the exercise had scored a direct hit! What we saw was a torpedo sticking completely through the sail. We started laughing. Then we looked at each other and decided that it wasn't so funny after all. This submarine business was not quite as attractive as I'd thought.

Number three happened during a transit between the Portland-Seattle area and Pearl Harbor. I was the port lookout during the afternoon watch (1200 to 1600 hours). Geronimo was the starboard lookout. Ensign Ball was the OOD (Officer of the Deck). We were doing 10 knots on the surface and the three of us were on the bridge in the conning tower. It was a bright day, but the sun was obscured by a low layer of clouds. It was cool. We had a bit of fun when someone below requested permission to put a man on deck forward to get something that was needed from the waterproof deck locker. The locker was under the deck plate all the way up on the bow near the forward torpedo-room escape trunk. Geronimo and I laughed when Ensign Ball gave his approval. He really shouldn't have, because we were running a pressure wave over the bow. When we saw who it was they had sent on deck we roared with laughter. We looked down over the side of the sail at the deck-level door just as it popped open and Seaman Lincoln Loving stuck his head out. He didn't look happy.

Lincoln reached down and put the runner in the safety track in the deck, fastened the safety belt around his waist and, grabbing the handrail, stepped out on deck. He looked up at us with that "don't you laugh at me" look that he did so well. It took him a few minutes to get up the nerve to let go of the handrail and begin to make his way forward against the wind and the pitching deck. Gingerly, he crept forward until he was just at the point where the pressure wave was rolling off the deck when the bow heaved free of the water on its cyclical upswing.

I could see that Lincoln was trying to time a run forward when the bow was out of the water. He made a couple of false starts, then ran slipping on the wet deck, disappearing into the access hole for the forward torpedo-room escape hatch. The bow plunged underwater and I found myself sucking air as I imagined the cold saltwater swirling around me. It wasn't me, though, it was Lincoln. I gripped the top of the sail as I waited for the bow to swing up, hoping that Lincoln wouldn't panic.

What we saw next could have been a clip from one of those old Keystone Cops movies. Lincoln was flailing water so hard that it looked like he had 40 arms and 40 legs. It was only then that I realized that Lincoln had joined the Navy but he didn't know how to swim. When he finally gathered a foothold, the half-drowned seaman exploded up out of that hole like a Polaris missile and ran back to the conning tower just as fast as his wet leather soles would carry him.

Ensign Ball, Geronimo, and I laughed for a good ten minutes. In fact, every time we saw Lincoln for the next two days we would burst out laughing. Lincoln didn't think it was funny and didn't miss a chance to slug us every time we laughed.

Lincoln went below. Geronimo and I began the unending task of sweeping the horizon from bow to stern, then the sky from horizon to zenith, and then back to the horizon from bow to stern. Again and again, and then a pause to rest our eyes and chat for a few minutes. I asked Ensign Ball to call for some hot coffee. As he bent over the 1MC, I turned,

---

FOREWORD

raising my binoculars to my eyes just in time to see a huge disk rise from beneath the ocean, water streaming from the air around it, tumble lazily on its axis, and disappear into the clouds. My heart beat wildly. I tried to talk but couldn't; then I changed my mind and decided I didn't want to say that, anyway. I had seen a flying saucer the size of an aircraft carrier come right out of the ocean and fly into the clouds. I looked around quickly to see if anyone else had seen it. Ensign Ball was still bending over the 1MC. He was ordering coffee. Geronimo was looking down the starboard side aft.

I was torn between my duty to report what I had seen and the knowledge that if I did no one would believe me. As I looked out over the ocean I saw only sky, clouds, and water.

It was as if nothing had happened. I almost thought I had dreamed it. Ensign Ball straightened, turned toward Geronimo and said the coffee was on the way up.

I looked back toward the spot, about 15 degrees relative off the port bow, and about 2-1/2 nautical miles distant. Nothing, not even a hint of what had happened. "Ensign Ball," I said, "I thought I saw something about 15 degrees relative off the bow, but I lost it. Can you help me look over that area?" Ensign Ball turned, raising his glasses to eye level. I didn't know it at the time, but Geronimo had heard me and turned to look. He was happy that something had broken the monotony.

I was just lifting the binoculars off my chest when I saw it. The giant saucer shape plunged out of the clouds, tumbled, and, pushing the water before it, opened up a hole in the ocean and disappeared from view. It was incredible. This time I had seen it with my naked eyes, and its size in comparison with the total view was nothing short of astounding. Ensign Ball stood in shock, his binoculars in his hands, his mouth open. Geronimo yelled, "Holy shit! What the — hey! did you guys see that?" Ensign Ball turned, and looking right at me with the most incredulous look on his face, said in a low voice, "This had to happen on *my* watch!" He turned, quickly pressing the override on the 1MC and yelled, "Captain to the bridge, Captain to the bridge." As an afterthought he pressed the switch again and yelled, "Somebody get a camera up here."

The Captain surged up the ladder with the quartermaster on his heels. Chief Quartermaster Quintero had the ship's 35-mm camera slung around his neck. The Captain stood patiently while Ensign Ball tried to describe what he had seen. He glanced at us and we both nodded in affirmation. That was enough for the Captain. He called sonar, who during the excitement had reported contact underwater at the same bearing. The Captain announced into the 1MC, "This is the Captain. I have the conn." The reply came back instantly from the helm, "Aye, Aye sir." I knew that the helmsman was passing the word in the control room that the Captain had personally taken control of the boat. I also knew that rumors were probably flying through the vessel.

The Captain called down and ordered someone to closely monitor the radar. His command was instantly acknowledged. As the five of us stood gazing out over the sea the same ship or one exactly like it rose slowly, turned in the air, tilted at an angle and then vanished. I saw the Chief snapping pictures out of the corner of my eye.

This time I had three images from which to draw conclusions. It was a metal machine, of that there was no doubt whatsoever. It was intelligently controlled, of that I was equally sure. It was a dull color, kind of like pewter. There were no lights. There was no glow. I thought I had seen a row of what looked like portholes, but could not be certain. Radar reported contact at the same bearing and gave us a range of 3 nautical miles. The range was right on, as the craft had moved toward the general direction that we were headed. We watched repeatedly as the strange craft reentered the water and then subsequently rose into the clouds over and over again until finally we knew that it was gone for good. The episode lasted about 10 minutes.

Before leaving the bridge the Captain took the camera from the Chief and instructed each of us not to talk to anyone about what we had seen. He told us the incident was classified and we were not to discuss it, not even amongst ourselves. We acknowledged his order. The Captain and the Chief left the bridge. Ensign Ball stepped to the 1MC and, pressing the override switch, announced, "This is Ensign Ball. The Captain has left the bridge. I have the conn." The reply, "Aye aye sir," quickly followed.

Those of us who had witnessed the UFO were not allowed to go ashore after we had berthed in Pearl. Even those of us who didn't have the duty were told we had to stay aboard. After about two hours a commander from the Office of Naval Intelligence boarded. He went directly to the Captain's stateroom. It wasn't long before we were called to wait in the passageway outside the Captain's door. Ensign Ball was called first. After about 10 minutes he came out and went into the wardroom. He looked shaken. I was next.

When I entered the stateroom, the Commander was holding my service record in his hands. He wanted to know why I had gone from the Air Force into the Navy. I told him the whole story and he laughed when I said that after putting off the Navy for fear of chronic seasickness, I hadn't been seasick yet. Suddenly a mask dropped over his face, and looking me directly in the eyes he asked, "What did you see out there?"

FOREWORD

"I believe it was a flying saucer, sir," I answered.

The man began to visibly shake and he screamed obscenities at me. He threatened to put me in the brig for the rest of my life. I thought he wasn't going to stop yelling, but as suddenly as he began, he stopped.

I was confused. I had answered his question truthfully; yet I was threatened with prison. I was not afraid, but I was not very confident, either. I figured I had better take another tack. Eighteen years with my father and four years in the Air Force had taught me something. Number one was that officers just do not lose control like that, ever. Number two was that if my answer had elicited that explosion, then the next thing out of my mouth had better be something entirely different. Number three was, that his response had been an act of kindness to get me to arrive at exactly that conclusion.

"Let's start all over again," he said. "What did you see out there?"

"Nothing, sir," I answered. "I didn't see a damn thing, and I'd like to get out of here just as soon as possible."

A smile spread over his face and the Captain looked relieved. "Are you sure, Cooper?" he asked.

"Yes sir," I replied, "I'm sure."

"You're a good sailor, Cooper," he said. "The Navy needs men like you. You'll go far with the Navy." He then asked me to read several pieces of paper that all said the same thing only with different words. I read that if I ever talked about what it was that I didn't see, I could be fined up to $10,000 and imprisoned for up to 10 years or both. In addition I could lose all pay and allowances due or ever to become due. He asked me to sign a piece of paper stating that I understood the laws and regulations that I had just read governing the safeguard of classified information relating to the national security. By signing, I agreed never to communicate in any manner any information regarding the incident with anyone. I was dismissed, and boy, was I glad to get out of there.

Not long after that incident I devolunteered from submarines. I was transferred to the USS Tombigbee (AOG-11).

The Tombigbee was a gasoline tanker. It was more dangerous than the sub. The Captain was crazy and the crew was a combination of idiots and misfits. I once had to draw my pistol while I was petty officer of the watch to prevent an officer from being attacked by a seaman.

The Tombigbee collided in the dead of night with a destroyer in the Molokai channel and several men died when the destroyer was almost cut in half. Every day aboard that ship was exactly like a scene right out of *Mr. Roberts*. I struck for quartermaster (navigation specialist) and managed to advance to the rank of second class petty officer despite the obvious obstacles.

I made two WESTPAC tours aboard the Tombigbee. They included a total of 12 months off the coast of Vietnam. We came under machine-gun fire while anchored off Chu Lai. We had to do an emergency breakaway and leave the harbor. All we needed was one tracer round in one of the tanks, and KA-BOOM, it would have been all over. The Viet Cong gunner probably got busted because the stupid jerk missed the whole damn ship. HOW CAN YOU MISS A WHOLE SHIP?

The only other time I felt threatened was when we went up to a small outpost at the DMZ called Cua Viet. It was a vision right out of hell. Cua Viet sat on the southern bank at the river mouth of the Thack Han river. We rode at anchor and pumped fuel ashore through a bottom lay line. Every night we could see the tracers from fire fights raging up and down the river and along the DMZ. It was a real hot spot. Every once in awhile Viet Cong or NVA rockets would slam into the camp. We would perform an emergency breakaway and put to sea until the all clear was sounded.

Everything was cool until our whacko Captain decided we were going into the river mouth. Did you ever try to put a pencil through the eye of a needle? That's about comparable to what we did. I'll never know how we got that big ship through the narrow mouth of that river with no navigational references whatsoever. We dropped anchor midchannel and the Captain backed the ship right up to the beach and dropped the stern anchor into the sand. There we sat, a great big target full of gasoline. We were helpless in the mouth of a narrow river, with three anchors out, right in the middle of one of the hottest combat zones in Vietnam. That night several men in the crew wrote letters to the Chief of Naval Operations requesting an immediate transfer. No one slept. I don't know why the enemy didn't send in the rockets, but they didn't. I knew then that God must keep a special watch over fools. The next day we set to sea and started for Pearl. The Captain was relieved for incompetence later that year. Then I was transferred to school.

I didn't know what school I had drawn. It turned out to be the Naval Security and Intelligence School for Internal Security Specialist (NEC 9545). The general training prepared me to set up security perimeters, secure installations and buildings, and safeguard classified information. My training included special weapons, booby-trap identification and disarming, the detection of bugs, phone taps, transmitters and many other subjects. I was specifically trained to prepare and conduct Pacific-area intelligence briefings. From the day I reported to school in 1968 until I left the Navy I worked off and on for Naval Security and Intelligence.

Upon graduating I was transferred to Vietnam. I had volunteered over a year before because I figured that my chances were better in the war than they were on that screwed-up gasoline tanker. This was the first good news I'd had since leaving boot camp. I really wanted to fight for my country. I wasn't to find out what a real fool I was until a few years later.

I landed at Da Nang and was bused to Camp Carter, the headquarters for Naval Security and Intelligence in I Corps. I was interviewed by Captain Carter, the commanding officer. The names turned out to be a coincidence. Captain Carter asked me if I thought I would make a good patrol boat captain, and I told him that I would. What else could I tell him? I thought he was joking when he told me I would have command of a boat and crew. He wasn't, and I did. Lt. Duey at the Harbor Patrol, a division of Naval Intelligence, allowed me to hand-pick a crew. He gave me first choice of four 45-foot picket boats that had just been unloaded from the deck of a freighter. I and my new crew spent three days going over every inch of that boat. We adjusted and fine-tuned everything. We sanded and painted. One of the seamen even hung curtains in the after cabin. We checked and double-checked the engines. My gunners mate, GMG3 Robert G. Barron, checked out weapons and we began to arm our vessel. I've got to tell you the truth — just looking at all those guns scared the shit out of me. I vowed right then and there that I would be the best damn captain that ever commanded a combat vessel in wartime. I learned to exist on only 2 or 3 hours of sleep out of 24 and never ate until I knew that my crew had been fed.

We spent a lot of spooky nights patrolling the Da Nang harbor and river. One night a rocket hit the ammo dump at the river's edge near the Da Nang bridge, and it really looked as if the world was coming to an end. Another time we engaged the enemy in the cove at Point Isabella near the marine fuel farm and probably saved their butts. That engagement was reported in *The Stars and Stripes*, the armed forces newspaper in Vietnam.

The worst moments came, however, not from Charley but from mother nature. A full-blown typhoon roared across the Gulf of Tonkin. To save the boats we put to sea. The angels must have been laughing. What a sight we must have made! I maneuvered our boat in between two giant cargo ships riding at anchor off Red Beach and learned quickly what fear was really all about. The wind was blowing so hard that none of us could go on deck. That meant that the two of us in the pilot house were stuck on watch and the men trapped in the after cabin had to man the hand pumps. The windows in the pilot house blew out and the rain felt like knives hitting our skin. Water poured in, and I prayed that the men on the pumps would not become exhausted. I could just barely make out the two tankers. I could tell they were in more trouble than we. When we were on the crest

---

FOREWORD

of the mountainous waves we looked down onto the top of the ships. When we were in the trough we seemed to be in danger of their crashing down upon us. One of the freighters snapped a cable and steamed slowly out of the harbor.

The next morning the storm calmed and we moved into the river. Debris was floating down and we had to play dodge-the-tree-trunks until we spotted a sheltered pier in front of the Press Club. We carefully pulled the boat alongside, tied fast to the pier, then collapsed from exhaustion. After awhile we drew straws to see who would remain on watch with me. The rest went into the Press Club. After a couple of hours the crew returned and we went in. It was like nothing was going on outside. Reporters sat around drinking or eating. All around flowed conversation and laughter. We ordered a huge meal, signed Lt. Duey's name to the check, then went out to the boat. I don't know whose name the other guys signed, but none of us had any money. I don't even know if Lt. Duey ever got the bill. I do know that it was one of the best damn meals that we ever had in that country.

The next two days were spent in repairing the boat, cleaning the weapons, and checking everything. Then we went to the club, got stone drunk, and slept for damn near a whole other day.

Bob Barron volunteered for Cua Viet. I begged him to stay with us. Maybe we could all go up later together. He couldn't wait; he had to have action. We promised each other that if one of us bought the farm the other would drink a bottle of scotch in memory, then break the bottle on the rocks. Don't ask me what that was all about. Men who think they might die at any given moment do stupid things and I was no different than most.

About three weeks later we learned that Bob's boat had gone on TWO LIMA patrol on the Thack Han River one night and had never returned. No radio transmissions were ever heard. And for awhile no bodies were found. Then one by one they popped to the surface along the bank. It was a long time before we ever found the boat. When we did it was twisted up like a pretzel. I say "we," because after I drank the bottle of scotch and broke it on the rocks, I forced the issue and was transferred to the Dong Ha River Support Group at Cua Viet.

It was now a personal war. They had killed a part of me. Bob had been my friend. His name is on the Vietnam Memorial. My boat engaged the enemy more times than any other boat that ever patrolled that river. We kept the enemy off the river and I never lost another man. I was awarded the Naval Achievement Medal with Combat V, the Naval Commendation Medal with Combat V, and the Combat Action Ribbon. Our whole organization was awarded the Presidential Unit Citation, the Naval

Unit Citation, and each of us accumulated various other minor awards, ribbons, and medals.

On a Patrol Boat

One thing I didn't like about Vietnam was that it was very difficult to maintain unit cohesion and morale when you had proven and trusted men leaving all the time at staggered intervals and green, unproven men arriving to take their place. I noticed that I felt like I was deserting my crew when I was rotated home. I tried to extend my tour of duty, but they had already decided to phase out our forces and turn the war over to the Vietnamese. If I had extended a month earlier, I was told, I could have stayed. My attitude at that point was a smoldering "SCREW IT!"

The whole time that I was in Vietnam and especially on the DMZ I had noticed that there was a lot of UFO activity. We had individual 24-hour crypto code sheets that we used to encode messages, but because of the danger that one of them could be captured at any time, we used special code words for sensitive information. UFOs, I was told, were definitely sensitive information. I learned exactly how sensitive when all the people of an entire village disappeared after UFOs were seen hovering above their huts. I learned that both sides had fired upon the UFOs, and they had blasted back with a mysterious blue light. Rumors floated around that UFOs had kidnapped and mutilated two army soldiers, then dropped them in the bush. No one knew how much of this was true, but the fact that the rumors persisted made me tend to think there was at least some truth in them. I found out later that most of those rumors were true.

I eventually found myself back in Hawaii. This time it was shore duty at the headquarters of the Commander in Chief of the Pacific Fleet at Makalapa, a hill above Pearl Harbor.

I had carried a Secret security clearance in the Air Force, and Secret was required for submarines. When I checked into the Fleet Administration Unit, I was asked to fill out papers for another clearance. I did as I was asked. I remember that one of the questions asked if I had ever belonged to any fraternal organizations. I looked down the list, circled the DeMolay Society, and answered in the affirmative. I was assigned to the Operational Status Report office (OPSTAT) under Lt. Cdr. Mercado while I awaited the results of my FBI background check for the upgraded clearance.

About six months later I was called into the office of the Chief of Staff for Naval Intelligence. I was asked to read the regulations covering the Personnel Reliability Program governing those personnel who had access to nuclear weapons, information on nuclear weapons, launch codes, and various other things having to do with nuclear weapons or anything that came under HQ-CR 44. I was asked to read and then sign a security oath, which I did. I was then told by Captain Caldwell that my security clearance had been upgraded to Top Secret, Q, Sensitive Compartmentalized Information with access authorized on a strict need-to-know basis. He told me to report to the officer in charge of the CINCPACFLT Intelligence

William Cooper is presented with Naval Commendation Medal with Combat V.
CINCPACFLT Headquarters – 1970

FOREWORD

Briefing Team the following morning at 0400 hours. I did. What I learned during the time I spent with that briefing team is what led me on my 18-year search that has culminated in the writing of this book. I was later given another upgraded clearance in the crypto category and served as the designated SPECAT operator when I was on watch in the command center.

On the day that I learned that the Office of Naval Intelligence had participated in the assassination of President John F. Kennedy and that it was the Secret Service agent driving the limo that had shot Kennedy in the head, I went AWOL with no intention of ever returning. My good friend Bob Swan is the one who talked me into going back. Later, on June 1, 1972, the eve of my wedding, I told Bob everything that I knew about the UFOs, Kennedy's assassination, the Navy, the Secret Government, the coming ice age, Alternatives 1, 2, & 3, Project GALILEO, and the plan for the New World Order. I believed it was all true then and I believe it is all true now.

I must warn you, however, that I have found evidence that the secret societies were planning as far back as 1917 to invent an artificial threat from outer space in order to bring humanity together in a one-world government which they call the New World Order. I am still searching for the truth. I firmly believe that this book is closer to that truth than anything ever previously written.

I attempted to leak information to a reporter after my discharge. I was forced off a cliff by a black limo in the hills of Oakland. Two men got out and climbed down to where I lay covered in blood. One bent down and felt for my carotid pulse. The other asked if I was dead. The nearest man said, "No, but he will be." The other replied, "Good, then we don't have to do anything else." They climbed up and drove off. I succeeded in climbing up the bank where I waited until found. A month later I was forced into another accident by the same limo. This time I was to lose my leg. Two men visited me in the hospital. They only wanted to know if I would shut up or if the next time should be final. I told them that I would be a very good little boy and that they needn't worry about me anymore. Under my breath I swore to spill the beans as soon as I could figure out how to do it without getting hurt again. It took 16 years, $27,000, a computer and a lot of envelopes, but now everyone knows.

I went back to school after leaving the Navy and obtained a degree in photography, served as the Chief Instructor of the Coastal School of Deep Sea Diving, the head of the Mixed Gas Deep Saturation Diving Department and the underwater photography instructor for the College of Oceaneering, Admissions representative for Airco Technical Institute, Assistant Director of Adelphi Business College, Executive Director of Adelphi Business College, National Marketing Coordinator of United Education &

Software, Executive Director of Pacific Coast Technical Institute, and Executive Director of National Technical College. I also owned and operated Absolute Image Gallery and Studio of Fine Art Photography.

In the spring of 1988 I saw a magazine that made reference to a document discovered by the research team of Moore, Shandera, and Friedman that outlined the government's knowledge of a downed saucer, dead alien bodies, and an operation called Operation MAJESTIC TWELVE. I knew that Moore and Friedman were government agents and the document was a fraud. I had never heard of Shandera. I knew this because I had seen a list of agents who were to initiate a contingency plan called MAJESTIC that would lead investigators off the track when such a need arose.

I decided that it was time for me to enter the arena and expose the cover-up and the disinformation. First it was necessary to convince the known agents that I was just a kook who didn't really know anything. I prepared some bogus information, mixed it with some true information, and passed it to Moore and Friedman through Jim Spieser, the operator of a computer BBS network called Paranet. Spieser was told that the information was to go only to Moore or Friedman; no one else was to see it. I wanted to buy time by convincing these agents to report me to their case officers as harmless, thus allowing me to get the real information out to the public. None of that information was intended to go to the public. Spieser turned out to be working with Moore, however, and posted the files on the computer networks. Spieser then went to Los Angeles, conferred with Moore for three days, then returned and barred me from the Paranet system.

Friedman called and elicited my address, the name and address of my employer, and a lot of other personal information. I knew that I was being checked out through the intelligence network and played along. About one week after talking to Friedman two Defense Investigative Service agents showed up at my home and confiscated all my floppy disks. The only thing that prevented them from taking my computer was the fact that it was an XT with no hard drive. I knew that my plan had worked, because they didn't take *me*.

With the help of Annie and a few very close and trusted friends, I prepared the real information, as true and correct as I could remember, and together we did a mailing that, all total, cost me $27,000. We sent the packages to people all over the world. That is what prevented the government from arresting me or harming me. Any move by them would be interpreted as total confirmation of everything that I had revealed. I also uploaded the information onto computer bulletin boards all across the nation. At the same time I publicly stated that Moore, Shandera, and Friedman are government agents and that the Eisenhower briefing document is a fraud. I was attacked by everyone. They insisted that Moore, Shandera, and Friedman were above reproach.

I resigned effective April 15, 1989, from the college where I was the Executive Director after Jaime Shandera was seen poking around the grounds. That story is included later in this book. The loss of income was a serious blow. Stan Barrington, the head of the college security department, came to our aid. Stan gave us $5,000 to help out. I was deeply moved by his faith and trust in me, and so I gave him 24% of whatever was to come out of my efforts down the line. Neither of us ever expected much, and so far we have not been wrong. I have, however, paid Stan back his money, and now whatever he earns is extra. Stan is in charge of printing information and the sale of my papers and tapes. Stan Barrington is my only authorized representative.

Moore was proved to be an agent when by his own admission on July 1, 1989, he stated he had participated in spying on fellow researchers, had changed documents, had put out disinformation, and had helped run a scam on Paul Bennowicz that had resulted in Mr. Bennowicz being confined to a mental institution. Moore stated that he had been recruited by an intelligence agency and that he knew he had been recruited. He was a witting agent. No one acknowledged that I had been right.

From that point on, my Annie and I were followed and harassed. Death threats began showing up on our answering machine. The phone would ring several times during the night, but no one would reply when we answered. Sometimes a man would deliver another death threat. Government cars would park in front and well-dressed men watched the house. The strangest people began to show up at our door, sometimes in the middle of the night. I purchased a .380 automatic for Annie and a 9-mm for me. I taught Annie how to shoot, and she will not hesitate to kill anyone who attempts to harm me, her, or our little daughter.

Annie and Pooh (Dorothy's nickname) are the lights in my life. Annie and I were married on July 4, 1989. Pooh was born on May 30, 1990. My most touching memory of Annie is of the time after 12 hours of labor when we were finally in the delivery room. She had taken no drugs. She had not been given a spinal tap. She did everything naturally. She was drained of energy and was experiencing great pain. She was numb. After a really hard push she looked up at me with all the innocence and trust of a little child and asked, "Did the baby come yet?" It was very hard for me to tell her that the baby had not yet been born, but that is what I did. She seemed to waver for a moment, but only a moment. Annie quickly regained her composure. I could see the love in her eyes as she looked up at me. I squeezed her hand. She took a deep breath and pushed Pooh's little head out into the world. The doctor suctioned the baby's mouth, then Annie gave her all, a push that seemed to come from her very soul — and little Dorothy popped out, announcing her presence with a great cry. I am so proud of Annie. She is my hero. And Pooh is my always and forever friend.

Anne and Dorothy

FOREWORD

At one point I became very upset with the intimidation. I went out to the government car at the curb. I showed the man in the car my 9-mm pistol and told him that we were fed up with their intimidating tactics. I told him that if he or anyone else wanted to know something about me, they should come to the house, sit down, have a cup of coffee, and I would be happy to tell them anything that they want to know. I informed him that if any further attempt was made to harass me or my family I would not hesitate to use my pistol. I then walked behind his car and wrote the license number down. He started the car, drove off, and we have not detected any overt signs of surveillance since that day.

They did not give up on us. No one knew the location of our new house when we moved to Arizona. However, when we drove into the driveway, a government car showed up right behind us. The man got out and said he was lost and wanted to know who lived here. I asked him why he wanted to know. He stated that he was a census taker. He said it was his job to ensure that no one out here in the country was left out of the census. He asked my name. I told him to get off the property and to not ever come back. He protested, but left when he saw that I was serious. (I merely asked Annie to get my pistol out of the car.) Now, many people would say that I was paranoid in this instance — until they discover that census takers DO NOT DRIVE GOVERNMENT CARS.

I was at the post office one morning when a county sheriff's deputy asked the clerk at the window next to the one where I was buying stamps if "William Cooper" had rented a box. I smiled as the clerk handed him my rental agreement and he copied the information. He didn't learn anything, as we live in the country where there are no addresses. The form had only "Stolen Blvd." listed — a lot of people live on Stolen Boulevard.

We have been taken advantage of by every crooked con man, TV producer, scriptwriter, author, and flim-flam expert that there is in this country. I have learned that the TV and print-media reporters and producers that I have met are a pack of liars. They are not objective and don't give a damn about the truth. The only really open media left to the public is talk radio, and even talk radio won't discuss certain subjects. My material has been copied, changed, and even plagiarized. A lot of people have used my material to make money without my knowledge or permission. A Hollywood producer wanted to buy the exclusive rights to my story for ONE DOLLAR!

Bill Hamilton begged me to let him include my material in his book entitled *Alien Magic*. He pretended to be a friend and I let him. I asked for no money and he offered none. His entire book consists of other people's material. He now accuses me of stealing "his" information. Bill Hamilton turned out to be just another UFO flake. I have since learned that I am not the only person of whom he has taken advantage.

The most damaging scam was perpetrated by two old, has-been actors turned con men, named Michael Callan and Douglas Deane. I doubt seriously that you will remember either one. Callan was a regular in the cheapy teen beach-blanket movies and Deane never got beyond bit parts and chorus lines. I got involved with them when another actor named Bruce Reed called and asked if I would consent to meet with him and a friend who preferred to remain anonymous. I agreed that they could come to the house where we could talk on familiar turf. I was not eager to meet with someone that I did not know, and especially with an anonymous person away from familiar surroundings.

Reed and friend showed up at my home, and the friend turned out to be Michael Callan. They told me that they had read my material and wanted to help. What a joke that statement turned out to be! They told me that they knew how to get me in front of millions of people where I could deliver my message. Callan was slick; he told me he was only interested in helping spread the information, but talked me into signing a five-year management contract that gave him a full 20% of the gross of all of my earnings no matter what the source. He swore that if he didn't show results within six months he would tear up the contract.

The first thing that Callan did was shaft his partner, Bruce Reed. He cut Reed out of the action. To prevent me from finding out that he had done it only to get Reed's half of the 20%, Callan told me that Bruce was a drug dealer. Callan said that the public would find out eventually, and Reed's drug involvement would damage me. Everything Callan told me about Reed turned out to be a lie.

Stan Barrington called me next, wanting to know why I was trying to dump him. I didn't know what he was talking about. It turned out that Callan was trying to force Stan into giving up his 24% so that Callan could form a 50-50 partnership with me. I told Stan that I had no intention of dumping him. I told him that his 24% was his, that he could keep it, sell it, or give it away and that he did not need my permission. Stan felt much better after that conversation and told Callan to go fly a kite. At that point Callan began working on me to get rid of Stan. I refused. I also told him that he had nothing invested and therefore did not warrant anything. His job was to manage according to our contract.

Douglas Deane entered the picture at the January 7, 1989, lecture that I gave at the Showboat Hotel and Casino in Las Vegas. Callan brought him to videotape the lecture so that we would have a tape to sell for those thousands of people who pleaded with us to produce a tape. The agreement was that he would tape the event and the tapes would belong exclusively to me. In return, if the tapes turned out good, Deane would get a contract to produce future tapes. The tapes were terrible and I told both Deane and Callan that I did not want tapes of that poor quality being sold to anyone. They did it anyway behind my back and began the process of stealing my master tapes from all of my other lectures. At the same time Callan drained all the business accounts. He borrowed $1400 from Stan to produce tapes and then kept the money and the tapes.

A producer in Germany booked me to do a lecture in that country. To secure the agreement he sent $3,000 to be used for two first-class tickets and as a guarantee that when I got there I would not be cancelled. The producer cancelled when a German postal strike prevented him from advertising the event. Callan kept the man's $3,000. I did not find out about that until after I fired Callan.

At my lecture in San Diego at the Whole Life Expo I found out that Deane was selling tapes and asking people to make checks out to "Need to Know Productions," a phony company. I immediately fired Deane. I informed Callan that we were to do no more business with him whatsoever. I discovered that Callan was telling me that we were having tapes duplicated in Hollywood for $15 per tape, but in reality Deane was doing it on VCRs at his home in Arizona. I asked Callan to return all of my master tapes for all my lectures. He refused and I fired him.

When I got rid of Callan, he had stolen everything that we had. We were literally left penniless. He was in possession of all of our master tapes from all of my lectures. We were broke and homeless at that point. If it had not been for a few good friends in Minnesota, we would not have survived. We would be in the streets today. Callan and Deane continue to injure us by selling tapes from my lectures. We get nothing from those sales. They are the most despicable con men and thieves that you can imagine.

I paid a visit to Deane's home one Saturday morning to ask him for my master tapes. He was not home, and after a polite conversation with his handyman, I returned to my home. A few days later the sheriff's department called and asked me if I had been to Deane's home that same Saturday. I told him that I had. He asked me if I had tried to break in Deane's home and I told him that I had not. He thanked me and that was the end of it. I had no idea what it was all about until I was served with a restraining order. It seems that Deane's guilty conscience had made him afraid that I would return. He slit his own tires, made a report to the sheriff that I had done it, and then procured a restraining order from the local court. I have never been questioned or accused by the police or sheriff other than what I have already disclosed. I believe that their goal from the

---

FOREWORD

very beginning was to try and destroy my efforts at educating the American people. They damn near succeeded.

CHAPTER 1

EXCERPTS FROM

SILENT WEAPONS
FOR
QUIET WARS

Copy furnished by Mr. Tom Young
A fellow Warrior in the cause of Freedom

Excerpts printed word for word exactly as discovered

(With the added comments of William Cooper)
(Emphasis added by William Cooper)

****TOP SECRET****

The Illuminati's declaration of War upon the people of America.

[Above title added by WC]

WC/Author's Note: I read Top Secret documents which explained that "Silent Weapons for Quiet Wars" is the doctrine adopted by the Policy Committee of the Bilderberg Group during its first known meeting in 1954. A copy found in 1969 was in the possession of Naval Intelligence.

The following document, dated May 1979, was found on July 7, 1986, in an IBM copier that had been purchased at a surplus sale.

TOP SECRET

Silent Weapons for Quiet Wars

An introductory programming manual
Operations Research
Technical Manual
TM-SW7905.1

WELCOME ABOARD

This publication marks the 25th anniversary of the Third World War, called the "Quiet War," being conducted using subjective biological warfare, fought with "silent weapons."

This book contains an introductory description of this war, its strategies, and its weaponry.

May 1979   #74-1120

SECURITY

It is patently impossible to discuss social engineering or the automation of a society, i.e., the engineering of social automation systems (SILENT WEAPONS) on a NATIONAL or WORLDWIDE SCALE without implying extensive OBJECTIVES of SOCIAL CONTROL and DESTRUCTION OF HUMAN LIFE, i.e., SLAVERY and GENOCIDE.

This manual is in itself an analog declaration of intent. Such a writing must be SECURED FROM PUBLIC SCRUTINY. Otherwise, it might be recognized as a TECHNICALLY FORMAL DECLARATION OF DOMESTIC WAR. Furthermore, whenever any person or group of persons in a

position of great power and WITHOUT FULL KNOWLEDGE and CON-
SENT OF THE PUBLIC, USES SUCH KNOWLEDGE and METHODOL-
OGY FOR ECONOMIC CONQUEST — it must be understood that A
STATE OF DOMESTIC WARFARE EXISTS between said person or group
of persons and the public.

The SOLUTION of today's PROBLEMS REQUIRES an approach
which is RUTHLESSLY CANDID, with NO AGONIZING OVER RELI-
GIOUS, MORAL or CULTURAL VALUES.

YOU have QUALIFIED for this project BECAUSE of your ABILITY to
LOOK at HUMAN SOCIETY with COLD OBJECTIVITY, and yet analyze
and DISCUSS your OBSERVATIONS and CONCLUSIONS with OTHERS
of similar INTELLECTUAL capacity WITHOUT a LOSS of DISCRETION
or HUMILITY. Such virtues are exercised in your own best interest. Do not
deviate from them.

*WC/Author's Note: All above emphases are mine as are those in the following
two sections and including bracketed additions throughout.*

*I do recognize this document, based upon the document's own admission, as a
formal Declaration of War by the Illuminati upon the Citizens of the United
States of America. I acknowledge that a State of War exists and has existed
between the Citizens of the United States of America and the Illuminati
aggressor based upon this recognition. I present to you that the peaceful
Citizens of this nation are fully justified in taking whatever steps may be
necessary, including violence, to identify, counterattack, and destroy the
enemy. I base this statement upon the God-given right of any peaceful people
to defend themselves against attack and destruction by any enemy waging
war against them. I cite the principles outlined in the Declaration of Independence, the Constitution of the United States of America, and the fully
recognized and acknowledged historical precedents that have served as the
justification for destruction of tyrants.*

HISTORICAL INTRODUCTION

Silent weapon technology has evolved from Operations Research
(O.R.), a strategic and tactical methodology developed under the MILI-
TARY MANAGEMENT [Eisenhower] in England during World War II.
The original purpose of Operations Research was to study the strategic and
tactical problems of air and land defense with the objective of effective use
of limited military resources against foreign enemies (i.e., logistics).

It was soon recognized by those in positions of power [THE COUN-
CIL ON FOREIGN RELATIONS] that the same methods might be useful
for totally controlling a society. But better tools were necessary.

Social engineering (the analysis and automation of a society) requires
the correlation of great amounts of constantly changing economic informa-

---

tion (data), so a high-speed computerized data-processing system was necessary which could race ahead of the society and predict when society would arrive for capitulation.

Relay computers were too slow, but the electronic computer, invented in 1946 by J. Presper Eckert and John W. Mauchly, filled the bill.

The next breakthrough was the development of the simplex method of linear programing in 1947 by the mathematician George B. Dantzig.

Then in 1948, the transistor, invented by J. Bardeen, W. H. Brattain, and W. Shockley, promised great expansion of the computer field by reducing space and power requirements.

With these three inventions under their direction, those in positions of power strongly suspected that it was possible for them to control the whole world with the push of a button.

Immediately, the ROCKEFELLER FOUNDATION got in on the ground floor by making a four-year grant to HARVARD COLLEGE, funding the HARVARD ECONOMIC RESEARCH PROJECT for the study of the structure of the American economy. One year later, in 1949, THE UNITED STATES AIR FORCE joined in.

In 1952 the original grant period terminated, and a high-level meeting of the ELITE [Illuminati] was held to determine the next phase of social operations research. The Harvard project had been very fruitful, as is borne out by the publication of some of its results in 1953 suggesting the feasibility of economic (social) engineering. (*Studies in the Structure of the American Economy* — copyright 1953 by Wassily Leontief, International Sciences Press Inc., White Plains, New York.)

Engineered in the last half of the decade of the 1940s, the new Quiet War machine stood, so to speak, in sparkling gold-plated hardware on the showroom floor by 1954.

With the creation of the maser in 1954, the promise of unlocking UN LIMITED SOURCES OF FUSION ATOMIC ENERGY FROM THE HEAVY HYDROGEN IN SEA WATER and the consequent availability of unlimited social power was a possibility only decades away.

The combination was irresistible.

The QUIET WAR was quietly DECLARED by the INTERNATIONAL ELITE [THE BILDERBERG GROUP] at a meeting held in 1954.

Although the silent weapons system was nearly exposed 13 years later, the evolution of the new weapon-system has never suffered any major setbacks.

This volume marks the 25th anniversary of the beginning of the Quiet War. Already this domestic war has had many victories on many fronts throughout the world.

★★★★TOP SECRET★★★★

POLITICAL INTRODUCTION

In 1954 it was well recognized by those in positions of authority that it was only a matter of time, only a few decades, before the general public would be able to grasp and upset the cradle of power, for the very elements of the new silent-weapon technology were as accessible for a public utopia as they were for providing a private utopia.

The ISSUE of PRIMARY CONCERN, that of DOMINANCE, revolved around the subject of the energy sciences.

ENERGY

Energy is recognized as the key to all activity on earth. Natural science is the study of the sources and control of natural energy, and social science, theoretically expressed as economics, is the study of the sources and control of social energy. Both are bookkeeping systems: mathematics. Therefore, mathematics is the primary energy science. And the book-keeper can be king if the public can be kept ignorant of the methodology of the bookkeeping.

All science is merely a means to an end. The means is knowledge. The end is control. [THE END ALWAYS JUSTIFIES THE MEANS.] Beyond this remains only one issue: Who will be the beneficiary?

In 1954 this was the issue of primary concern. Although the so-called"moral issues"were raised, in view of the law of natural selection it was agreed that a nation or world of people who will not use their intelligence are no better than animals who do not have intelligence. Such people are beasts of burden and steaks on the table by choice and consent.

CONSEQUENTLY, in the interest of future world order, peace, and tranquility, it was decided to privately wage a quiet war against the American public with an ultimate objective of permanently shifting the natural and social energy (wealth) of the undisciplined and irresponsible many into the hands of the self-disciplined, responsible, and worthy few.

In order to implement this objective, it was necessary to create, secure, and apply new weapons which, as it turned out, were a class of weapons so subtle and sophisticated in their principle of operation and public appearance as to earn for themselves the name "silent weapons."

In conclusion, the objective of economic research, as conducted by the magnates of capital (banking) and the industries of commodities (goods) and services, is the establishment of an economy which is totally predictable and manipulatible.

In order to achieve a totally predictable economy, the low-class elements of the society must be brought under total control, i.e., must be housebroken, trained, and assigned a yoke and long-term social duties from a very early age, before they have an opportunity to question the propriety of the matter. In order to achieve such conformity, the lower-class family unit must be disintegrated by a process of increasing preoccupation of the parents and the establishment of government-operated day-care centers for the occupationally orphaned children.

The quality of education given to the lower class must be of the poorest sort, so that the moat of ignorance isolating the inferior class from the superior class is and remains incomprehensible to the inferior class. With such an initial handicap, even bright lower class individuals have little if any hope of extricating themselves from their assigned lot in life. This form of slavery is essential to maintaining some measure of social order, peace, and tranquility for the ruling upper class.

DESCRIPTIVE INTRODUCTION OF THE SILENT WEAPON

Everything that is expected from an ordinary weapon is expected from a silent weapon by its creators, but only in its own manner of junctioning.

It shoots situations, instead of bullets; propelled by data processing, instead of a chemical reaction (explosion); originating from bits of data, instead of grains of gunpowder; from a computer, instead of a gun; operated by a computer programmer, instead of a marksman; under the orders of a banking magnate, instead of a military general.

It makes no obvious explosive noises, causes no obvious physical or mental injuries, and does not obviously interfere with anyone's daily social life.

Yet it makes an unmistakable "noise," causes unmistakable physical and mental damage, and unmistakably interferes with daily social life, i.e., unmistakable to a trained observer, one who knows what to look for.

The public cannot comprehend this weapon, and therefore cannot believe that they are being attacked and subdued by a weapon.

The public might instinctively feel that something is wrong [ISN'T THAT THE TRUTH?], but because of the technical nature of the silent weapon, they cannot express their feeling in a rational way, or handle the problem with intelligence. Therefore, they do not know how to cry for help, and do not know how to associate with others to defend themselves against it.

When a silent weapon is applied gradually, the public adjusts/adapts to its presence and learns to tolerate its encroachment on their lives until the pressure (psychological via economic) becomes too great and they crack up.

Therefore, the silent weapon is a type of biological warfare. It attacks the vitality, options, and mobility of the individuals of a society by knowing, understanding, manipulating, and attacking their sources of natural and social energy, and their physical, mental, and emotional strengths and weaknesses.

THEORETICAL INTRODUCTION

Give me control over a nation's currency,

and I care not who makes its laws.

Mayer Amschel Rothschild
(1743 - 1812)

Today's silent weapons technology is an outgrowth of a simple idea discovered, succinctly expressed, and effectively applied by the quoted Mr. Mayer Amschel Rothschild. Mr. Rothschild discovered the missing passive component of economic theory known as economic inductance. He, of course, did not think of his discovery in these 20th-century terms, and, to be sure, mathematical analysis had to wait for the Second Industrial Revolution, the rise of the theory of mechanics and electronics, and finally, the invention of the electronic computer before it could be effectively applied in the control of the world economy.

GENERAL ENERGY CONCEPTS

In the study of energy systems, there always appear three elementary concepts. These are potential energy, kinetic energy, and energy dissipation. And corresponding to these concepts, there are three idealized, essentially pure physical counterparts called passive components.

(1) In the science of physical mechanics, the phenomenon of potential energy is associated with a physical property called elasticity or stiffness, and can be represented by a stretched spring.

In electronic science, potential energy is stored in a capacitor instead of a spring. This property is called capacitance instead of elasticity or stiffness.

(2) In the science of physical mechanics, the phenomenon of kinetic energy is associated with a physical property called inertia or mass, and can be represented by a mass or a flywheel in motion.

In electronic science, kinetic energy is stored in an inductor (in a magnetic field) instead of a mass. This property is called inductance instead of inertia.

(3) In the science of physical mechanics, the phenomenon of energy dissipation is associated with a physical property called friction or resistance, and can be represented by a dashpot or other device which converts system energy into heat.

In electronic science, dissipation of energy is performed by an element called either a resistor or a conductor, the term "resistor" being the one generally used to express the concept of friction, and the term "conductor" being generally used to describe a more ideal device (e.g., wire) employed to convey electronic energy efficiently from one location to another. The property of a resistance or conductor is measured as either resistance or conductance reciprocals.

In economics these three energy concepts are associated with:

(1) Economic Capacitance — Capital (money, stock/inventory, investments in buildings and durables, etc.)

(2) Economic Conductance — Goods (production flow coefficients)

(3) Economic Inductance — Services (the influence of the population of industry on output)

All of the mathematical theory developed in the study of one energy system (e.g., mechanics, electronics, etc.) can be immediately applied in the study of any other energy system (e.g., economics).

MR. ROTHSCHILD'S ENERGY DISCOVERY

What Mr. Rothschild had discovered was the basic principle of power, influence, and control over people as applied to economics. That principle is "when you assume the appearance of power, people soon give it to you."

Mr. Rothschild had discovered that currency or deposit loan accounts had the required appearance of power that could be used to INDUCE PEOPLE [*WC emphasis*] (inductance, with people corresponding to a magnetic field) into surrendering their real wealth in exchange for a promise of greater wealth (instead of real compensation). They would put up real collateral in exchange for a loan of promissory notes. Mr. Rothschild found that he could issue more notes than he had backing for, so long as he had someone's stock of gold as a persuader to show to his customers.

Mr. Rothschild loaned his promissory notes to individuals and to governments. These would create overconfidence. Then he would make money scarce, tighten control of the system, and collect the collateral through the obligation of contracts. The cycle was then repeated. These pressures could be used to ignite a war. Then he would control the availability of currency to determine who would win the war. That government which agreed to give him control of its economic system got his support.

Collection of debts was guaranteed by economic aid to the enemy of the debtor. The profit derived from this economic methodology made Mr.

Rothschild all the more able to extend his wealth. He found that the public greed would allow currency to be printed by government order BEYOND THE LIMITS [*WC emphasis*] (inflation) of backing in precious metal or the production of goods and services (gross national product, GNP).

APPARENT CAPITAL AS "PAPER" INDUCTOR

In this structure, credit, presented as a pure element called "currency," has the appearance of capital, but is, in fact, negative capital. Hence, it has the appearance of service, but is, in fact, indebtedness or debt. It is therefore an economic inductance instead of an economic capacitance, and if balanced in no other way, will be balanced by the negation of population (war, genocide). The total goods and services represent real capital called the gross national product, and currency may be printed up to this level and still represent economic capacitance; but currency printed beyond this level is subtractive, represents the introduction of economic inductance, and constitutes notes of indebtedness.

War is therefore the balancing of the system by killing the true creditors (the public which we have taught to exchange true value for inflated currency) and falling back on whatever is left of the resources of nature and regeneration of those resources.

Mr. Rothschild had discovered that currency gave him the power to rearrange the economic structure to his own advantage, to shift economic inductance to those economic positions which would encourage the greatest economic instability and oscillation.

The final key to economic control had to wait until there was sufficient data and high-speed computing equipment to keep close watch on the economic oscillations created by price shocking and excess paper energy credits — paper inductance/inflation.

BREAKTHROUGH

The aviation field provided the greatest evolution in economic engineering by way of the mathematical theory of shock testing. In this process, a projectile is fired from an airframe on the ground and the impulse of the recoil is monitored by vibration transducers connected to the airframe and wired to chart recorders.

By studying the echoes or reflections of the recoil impulse in the airframe, it is possible to discover critical vibrations in the structure of the airframe which either vibrations of the engine or aeolian vibrations of the wings, or a combination of the two, might reinforce resulting in a resonant self-destruction of the airframe in flight as an aircraft. From the standpoint of engineering, this means that the strengths and weaknesses of the structure of the airframe in terms of vibrational energy can be discovered and manipulated.

APPLICATION IN ECONOMICS

To use this method of airframe shock testing in economic engineering, the prices of commodities are shocked, and the public consumer reaction is monitored. The resulting echoes of the economic shock are interpreted theoretically by computers and the psycho-economic structure of the economy is thus discovered. It is by this process that partial differential and difference matrices are discovered that define the family household and make possible its evaluation as an economic industry (dissipative consumer structure).

Then the response of the household to future shocks can be predicted and manipulated, and society becomes a well-regulated animal with its reins under the control of a sophisticated computer-regulated social energy bookkeeping system.

Eventually every individual element of the structure comes under computer control through a knowledge of personal preferences, such know ledge guaranteed by computer association of consumer preferences (universal product code — UPC — zebra-stripe pricing codes on packages) with identified consumers (identified via association with the use of a credit card and LATER A PERMANENT "TATTOOED" BODY NUMBER [WC *emphasis*] invisible under normal ambient illumination....

THE ECONOMIC MODEL

...The Harvard Economic Research Project (1948–) was an extension of World War II Operations Research. Its purpose was to discover the science of controlling an economy: at first the American economy, and then the world economy. It was felt that with sufficient mathematical foundation and data, it would be nearly as easy to predict and control the trend of an economy as to predict and control the trajectory of a projectile. Such has proven to be the case. Moreover, the economy has been transformed into a guided missile on target.

The immediate aim of the Harvard project was to discover the economic structure, what forces change that structure, how the behavior of the structure can be predicted, and how it can be manipulated. What was needed was a well-organized knowledge of the mathematical structures and interrelationships of investment, production, distribution, and consumption.

To make a short story of it all, it was discovered that an economy obeyed the same laws as electricity and that all of the mathematical theory and practical and computer know-how developed for the electronic field could be directly applied in the study of economics. This discovery was not openly declared, and its more subtle implications were and are kept a closely guarded secret, for example that in an economic model, human life is measured in dollars, and that the electric spark generated when opening a switch connected to an active inductor is mathematically analogous to the initiation of a war.

The greatest hurdle which theoretical economists faced was the accurate description of the household as an industry. This is a challenge because consumer purchases are a matter of choice which in turn is influenced by income, price, and other economic factors.

This hurdle was cleared in an indirect and statistically approximate way by an application of shock testing to determine the current characteristics, called current technical coefficients, of a household industry.

Finally, because problems in theoretical economics can be translated very easily into problems in theoretical electronics, and the solution translated back again, it follows that only a book of language translation and concept definition needed to be written for economics. The remainder could be gotten from standard works on mathematics and electronics. This makes the publication of books on advanced economics unnecessary, and greatly simplifies project security.

INDUSTRIAL DIAGRAMS

An ideal industry is defined as a device which receives value from other industries in several forms and converts [it] into one specific product for sales and distribution to other industries. It has several inputs and one output. What the public normally thinks of as one industry is really an industrial complex where several industries under one roof produce one or more products....

THREE INDUSTRIAL CLASSES

Industries fall into three categories or classes by type of output:

Class #1 — Capital (resources)

Class #2 — Goods (commodities or use — dissipative)

Class #3 — Services (action of population)

Class #1 industries exist at three levels:

(1) Nature – sources of energy and raw materials.

(2) Government – printing of currency equal to gross national product

(GNP), and extension (inflation) of currency in excess of GNP.

(3) Banking – loaning of money for interest, and extension (inflation/counterfeiting) of economic value through deposit loan accounts.

Class #2 industries exist as producers of tangible or consumer (dissipated) products. This sort of activity is usually recognized and labeled by the public as an "industry."

Class #3 industries are those which have service rather than a tangible product as their output. These industries are called (1) households, and (2) governments. Their output is human activity of a mechanical sort, and their basis is population.

AGGREGATION

The whole economic system can be represented by a three-industry model if one allows the names of the outputs to be (1) capital, (2) goods, and (3) services. The problem with this representation is that it would not show the influence of, say, the textile industry on the ferrous metal industry. This is because both the textile industry and the ferrous metal industry would be contained within a single classification called the "goods industry" and by this process of combining or aggregating these two industries under one system block they would lose their economic individuality.

THE E-MODEL

A national economy consists of simultaneous flows of production, distribution, consumption, and investment. If all of these elements including labor and human functions are assigned a numerical value in like units of measure, say, 1939 dollars, then this flow can be further represented by a current flow in an electronic circuit, and its behavior can be predicted and manipulated with useful precision.

The three ideal passive energy components of electronics, the capacitor, the resistor, and the inductor correspond to the three ideal passive energy components of economics called the pure industries of capital, goods, and services, respectively.

Economic capacitance represents the storage of capital in one form or another.

Economic conductance represents the level of conductance of materials for the production of goods.

Economic inductance represents the inertia of economic value in motion. This is a population phenomenon known as services.

ECONOMIC INDUCTANCE

An electrical inductor (e.g., a coil of wire) has an electric current as its primary phenomenon and a magnetic field as its secondary phenomenon (inertia). Corresponding to this, an economic inductor has a flow of economic value as its primary phenomenon and a population field as its secondary phenomenon of inertia. When the flow of economic value (e.g., money) diminishes, the human population field collapses in order to keep the economic value (money) flowing (extreme case — war).

This public inertia is a result of consumer buying habits, expected standard of living, etc., and is generally a phenomenon of self-preservation.

INDUCTIVE FACTORS TO CONSIDER

(1) Population
(2) Magnitude of the economic activities of the government
(3) The method of financing these government activities
(See Peter-Paul Principle — inflation of the currency.)

TRANSLATION

(A few examples will be given.)

Charge — coulombs — dollars (1939).

Flow/Current — amperes (coulombs per second) — dollars of flow per year.

Motivating Force — volts — dollars (output) demand.

Conductance — amperes per volt — dollars of flow per year per dollar demand.

Capacitance — coulombs per volt — dollars of production inventory/stock per dollar demand.

TIME FLOW RELATIONSHIPS AND SELF-DESTRUCTIVE OSCILLATIONS

An ideal industry may be symbolized electronically in various ways. The simplest way is to represent a demand by a voltage and a supply by a current. When this is done, the relationship between the two becomes what is called an admittance, which can result from three economic factors: (1) hindsight flow, (2) present flow, and (3) foresight flow.

Foresight flow is the result of that property of living entities to cause energy (food) to be stored for a period of low energy (e.g., a winter season). It consists of demands made upon an economic system for that period of low energy (winter season).

In a production industry it takes several forms, one of which is known as production stock or inventory. In electronic symbology this specific industry demand (a pure capital industry) is represented by capacitance and the stock or resource is represented by a stored charge. Satisfaction of an industry demand suffers a lag because of the loading effect of inventory priorities.

Present flow ideally involves no delays. It is, so to speak, input today for output today, a "hand to mouth" flow. In electronic symbology, this specific industry demand (a pure use industry) is represented by a conductance which is then a simple economic valve (a dissipative element).

Hindsight flow is known as habit or inertia. In electronics this phenomenon is the characteristic of an inductor (economic analog = a pure service industry) in which a current flow (economic analog = flow of money) creates a magnetic field (economic analog = active human population) which, if the current (money flow) begins to diminish, collapse (war) to maintain the current (flow of money — energy).

Other large alternatives to war as economic inductors or economic flywheels are an open-ended social welfare program, or an ENORMOUS (but fruitful) OPEN-ENDED SPACE PROGRAM [WC emphases].

The problem with stabilizing the economic system is that there is too much demand on account of (1) too much greed and (2) too much population.

This creates excessive economic inductance which can only be balanced with economic capacitance (true resources or value — e.g., in goods or services).

The social welfare program is nothing more than an open-ended credit balance system which creates a false capital industry to give nonproductive people a roof over their heads and food in their stomachs. This can be useful, however, because the recipients become state property in return for the "gift," a standing army for the elite. For he who pays the piper picks the tune.

Those who get hooked on the economic drug, must go to the elite for a fix. In this, the method of introducing large amounts of stabilizing capacitance is by borrowing on the future "credit" of the world. This is a fourth law of motion — onset, and consists of performing an action and leaving the system before the reflected reaction returns to the point of action — a delayed reaction.

The means of surviving the reaction is by changing the system before the reaction can return. By this means, politicians become popular in their own time and the public pays for it later. In fact, the measure of such a politician is the delay time.

The same thing is achieved by a government by printing money beyond the limit of the gross national product, an economic process called inflation. [Note: REMEMBER THAT INFLATION IS ONLY THE ACT OF PRINTING MONEY IN EXCESS OF GROSS NATIONAL PRODUCT. THEY COULD BLAME IT ON THE PRICE OF WIDGETS OR OIL ONLY BECAUSE YOU NEVER KNEW THE REAL CAUSE. THE REAL CAUSE AND THE ONLY CAUSE OF INFLATION IS THE PRINTING OF MORE MONEY BEYOND THE GROSS NATIONAL PRODUCT.] This puts a large quantity of money into the hands of the public and maintains a balance against their greed, creates a false self-confidence in them and, for awhile, stays the wolf from the door.

They must eventually resort to war to balance the account, because war ultimately is merely the act of destroying the creditor, and the politicians are the publicly hired hit men that justify the act to keep the responsibility and blood off the public conscience. (See section on consent factors and social-economic structuring.)

If the people really cared about their fellow man, they would control their appetites (greed, procreation, etc.) so that they would not have to operate on a credit or welfare social system which steals from the worker to satisfy the bum.

Since most of the general public will not exercise restraint, there are only two alternatives to reduce the economic inductance of the system.

(1) Let the populace bludgeon each other to death in war, which will only result in a total destruction of the living earth.

(2) Take control of the world by the use of economic "silent weapons" in a form of "quiet warfare" and reduce the economic inductance of the world to a safe level by a process of benevolent slavery and genocide.

The latter option has been taken as the obviously better option. At this point it should be crystal clear to the reader why absolute secrecy about the silent weapons is necessary. The general public refuses to improve its own mentality and its faith in its fellow man. It has become a herd of proliferating barbarians, and, so to speak, a blight upon the face of the earth.

They do not care enough about economic science to learn why they have not been able to avoid war despite religious morality, and their religious or self-gratifying refusal to deal with earthly problems renders the solution of the earthly problem unreachable by them.

It is left to those few who are truly willing to think and survive as the fittest to survive, to solve the problem for themselves as the few who really care. Otherwise, exposure of the silent weapon would destroy our only hope of preserving the seed of future true humanity....

****TOP SECRET****

THE HOUSEHOLD INDUSTRY

The industries of finance (banking), manufacturing, and government, real counterparts of the pure industries of capital, goods, and services, are easily defined because they are generally logically structured. Because of this their processes can be described mathematically and their technical coefficients can be easily deduced. This, however, is not the case with the service industry known as the household industry.

HOUSEHOLD MODELS

...The problem which a theoretical economist faces is that the consumer preferences of any household is not easily predictable and the technical coefficients of any one household tend to be a nonlinear, very complex, and variable function of income, prices, etc.

Computer information derived from the use of the universal product code in conjunction with credit-card purchase as an individual household identifier could change this state of affairs, but the U.P.C. method is not yet available on a national or even a significant regional scale. To compensate for this data deficiency, an alternate indirect approach of analysis has been adopted known as economic shock testing. This method, widely used in the aircraft manufacturing industry, develops an aggregate statistical sort of data.

Applied to economics, this means that all of the households in one region or in the whole nation are studied as a group or class rather than individually, and the mass behavior rather than individual behavior is used to discover useful estimates of the technical coefficients governing the economic structure of the hypothetical single-household industry....

One method of evaluating the technical coefficients of the household industry depends upon shocking the prices of a commodity and noting the changes in the sales of all of the commodities.

ECONOMIC SHOCK TESTING

In recent times, the application of Operations Research to the study of the public economy has been obvious for anyone who understands the principles of shock testing.

In the shock testing of an aircraft airframe, the recoil impulse of firing a gun mounted on that airframe causes shock waves in that structure which tell aviation engineers the conditions under which parts of the airplane or the whole airplane or its wings will start to vibrate or flutter like a guitar string, a flute reed, or a tuning fork, and disintegrate or fall apart in flight.

Economic engineers achieve the same result in studying the behavior of the economy and the consumer public by carefully selecting a staple commodity such as beef, coffee, gasoline, or sugar, and then causing a sudden change or shock in its price or availability, thus kicking everybody's budget and buying habits out of shape.

They then observe the shock waves which result by monitoring the changes in advertising, prices, and sales of that and other commodities.

The objective of such studies is to acquire the know-how to set the public economy into a predictable state of motion or change, even a controlled self-destructive state of motion which will convince the public that certain "expert" people should take control of the money system and reestablish security (rather than liberty and justice) for all. When the subject citizens are rendered unable to control their financial affairs, they, of course, become totally enslaved, a source of cheap labor.

Not only the prices of commodities, but also the availability of labor can be used as the means of shock testing. Labor strikes deliver excellent tests shocks to an economy, especially in the critical service areas of trucking (transportation), communication, public utilities (energy, water, garbage collection), etc.

By shock testing, it is found that there is a direct relationship between the availability of money flowing in an economy and the psychological outlook and response of masses of people dependent upon that availability.

For example, there is a measurable quantitative relationship between the price of gasoline and the probability that a person would experience a headache, feel a need to watch a violent movie, smoke a cigarette, or go to a tavern for a mug of beer.

It is most interesting that, by observing and measuring the economic modes by which the public tries to run from their problems and escape from reality, and by applying the mathematical theory of Operations Research, it is possible to program computers to predict the most probable combination of created events (shocks) which will bring about a complete control and subjugation of the public through a subversion of the public economy (by shaking the plum tree)....

INTRODUCTION TO ECONOMIC AMPLIFIERS

Economic amplifiers are the active components of economic engineering. The basic characteristic of any amplifier (mechanical, electrical, or economic) is that it receives an input control signal and delivers energy from an independent energy source to a specified output terminal in a predictable relationship to that input control signal.

The simplest form of economic amplifier is a device called advertising.

If a person is spoken to by a T.V. advertiser as if he were a twelve-year-old, then, due to suggestibility, he will, with a certain probability, respond or react to that suggestion with the uncritical response of a twelve-year-old and will reach into his economic reservoir and deliver its energy to buy that product on impulse when he passes it in the store.

An economic amplifier may have several inputs and outputs. Its response might be instantaneous or delayed. Its circuit symbol might be a rotary switch if its options are exclusive, qualitative, "go" or "no go," or it might have its parametric input/output relationships specified by a matrix with internal energy sources represented.

Whatever its form might be, its purpose is to govern the flow of energy from a source to an output sink in direct relationship to an input control signal. For this reason, it is called an active circuit element or component.

Economic Amplifiers fall into classes called strategies, and, in comparison with electronic amplifiers, the specific internal functions of an economic amplifier are called logistical instead of electrical.

Therefore, economic amplifiers not only deliver power gain but also, in effect, are used to cause changes in the economic circuitry.

In the design of an economic amplifier we must have some idea of at least five functions, which are

(1) the available input signals,
(2) the desired output-control objectives,
(3) the strategic objective,
(4) the available economic power sources,
(5) the logistical options.

The process of defining and evaluating these factors and incorporating the economic amplifier into an economic system has been popularly called GAME THEORY [*WC emphasis*].

The design of an economic amplifier begins with a specification of the power level of the output, which can range from personal to national. The second condition is accuracy of response, i.e., how accurately the output action is a function of the input commands. High gain combined with strong feedback helps to deliver the required precision.

Most of the error will be in the input data signal. Personal input data tends to be specific, while national input data tends to be statistical.

SHORT LIST OF INPUTS

Questions to be answered:

(1) what	(3) where	(5) why
(2) when	(4) how	(6) who

****TOP SECRET****

General sources of information:

(1) telephone taps   (3) analysis of garbage
(2) surveillance   (4) behavior of children in school

Standard of living by:

(1) food   (3) shelter
(2) clothing   (4) transportation

Social contacts:

(1) telephone — itemized record of calls
(2) family — marriage certificates, birth certificates, etc.
(3) friends, associates, etc.
(4) memberships in organizations
(5) political affiliation

THE PERSONAL PAPER TRAIL

Personal buying habits, i.e., personal consumer preferences:

(1) checking accounts
(2) credit-card purchases
(3) "tagged" credit-card purchases — the credit-card purchase of products bearing the U.P.C. (Universal Product Code)

Assets:

(1) checking accounts   (5) automobile, etc.
(2) savings accounts   (6) safety deposit at bank
(3) real estate   (7) stock market
(4) business

Liabilities:

(1) creditors   (3) loans
(2) enemies (see – legal)   (4) consumer credit

Government sources (ploys)*:

(1) Welfare   (4) doles
(2) Social Security   (5) grants
(3) U.S.D.A. surplus food   (6) subsidies

*Principle of this ploy — the citizen will almost always make the collection of information easy if he can operate on the "free sandwich principle" of "eat now, and pay later."

Government sources (via intimidation):

(1) Internal Revenue Service
(2) OSHA

(3) Census
(4) etc.

Other government sources — surveillance of U.S. mail.

HABIT PATTERNS — PROGRAMMING

Strengths and weaknesses:

(1) activities (sports, hobbies, etc.)
(2) see "legal" (fear, anger, etc. — crime record)
(3) hospital records (drug sensitivities, reaction to pain, etc.)
(4) psychiatric records (fears, angers, disgusts, adaptability, reactions to stimuli, violence, suggestibility or hypnosis, pain, pleasure, love, and sex)

Methods of coping — of adaptability — behavior:

(1) consumption of alcohol
(2) consumption of drugs
(3) entertainment
(4) religious factors influencing behavior
(5) other methods of escaping from reality

Payment modus operandi (MO) — pay on time, etc.:

(1) payment of telephone bills
(2) energy purchases (electric, gas,...)
(3) water purchases
(4) repayment of loans
(5) house payments
(6) automobile payments
(7) payments on credit cards

Political sensitivity:

(1) beliefs   (3) position   (5) projects/activities
(2) contacts   (4) strengths/weaknesses

Legal inputs — behavioral control (Excuses for investigation, search, arrest, or employment of force to modify behavior)

(1) court records   (4) reports made to police
(2) police records — NCIC   (5) insurance information
(3) driving record   (6) anti-establishment acquaintances

NATIONAL INPUT INFORMATION

Business sources (via I.R.S., etc.):

(1) prices of commodities
(2) sales

****TOP SECRET****

---

(3) investments in
   (a) stocks/inventory
   (b) production tools and machinery
   (c) buildings and improvements
   (d) the stock market

Banks and credit bureaus:

(1) credit information
(2) payment information

Miscellaneous sources:

(1) polls and surveys
(2) publications
(3) telephone records
(4) energy and utility purchases

SHORT LIST OF OUTPUTS

Outputs — create controlled situations — manipulation of the economy, hence society — control by control of compensation and income.

Sequence:

(1) allocates opportunities.
(2) destroys opportunities.
(3) controls the economic environment.
(4) controls the availability of raw materials.
(5) controls capital.
(6) controls bank rates.
(7) controls the inflation of the currency.
(8) controls the possession of property.
(9) controls industrial capacity.
(10) controls manufacturing.
(11) controls the availability of goods (commodities).
(12) controls the prices of commodities.
(13) controls services, the labor force, etc.
(14) controls payments to government officials.
(15) controls the legal functions.
(16) controls the personal data files — uncorrectable by the party slandered.
(17) controls advertising.
(18) controls media contact.
(19) controls material available for T.V. viewing.
(20) disengages attention from real issues.

(21) engages emotions.

(22) creates disorder, chaos, and insanity.

(23) controls design of more probing tax forms.

(24) controls surveillance.

(25) controls the storage of information.

(26) develops psychological analyses and profiles of individuals.

(27) controls legal functions [repeat of 15]

(28) controls sociological factors.

(29) controls health options.

(30) preys on weaknesses.

(31) cripples strengths.

(32) leaches wealth and substance.

TABLE OF STRATEGIES

Do this	To get this
Keep the public ignorant	Less public organization
Maintain access to control points for feedback	Required reaction to outputs (prices, sales)
Create preoccupation	Lower defenses
Attack the family unit	Control of the education of the young
Give less cash and more credit and doles	More self-indulgence and more data
Attack the privacy of the church	Destroy faith in this sort of government
Social conformity	Computer programming simplicity
Minimize the tax protest	Maximum economic data, minimum enforcement problems
Stabilize the consent	Simplicity coefficients
Tighten control of variables	Simpler computer input data — greater predictability
Establish boundary conditions	Problem simplicity/solutions of differential and difference equations
Proper timing	Less data shift and blurring
Maximize control	Minimum resistance to control
Collapse of currency	Destroy the faith of the American people in each other.

[WC: *Ultimate objective — New World Order*]

DIVERSION, THE PRIMARY STRATEGY

Experience has proven that the SIMPLEST METHOD of securing a silent weapon and gaining control of the public is to KEEP THE PUBLIC

---

* * * *T O P   S E C R E T* * * *

UNDISCIPLINED AND IGNORANT of basic systems principles on the one hand, WHILE KEEPING THEM CONFUSED, DISORGANIZED, AND DISTRACTED with matters of no real importance on the other hand. [*WC all emphases.*]

This is achieved by:

(1) disengaging their minds; sabotaging their mental activities; providing a low-quality program of public education in mathematics, logic, systems design and economics; and discouraging technical creativity.

(2) engaging their emotions, increasing their self-indulgence and their indulgence in emotional and physical activities, by:

(a) unrelenting emotional affrontations and attacks (mental and emotional rape) by way of a constant barrage of sex, violence, and wars in the media — especially the T.V. and the newspapers.

(b) giving them what they desire — in excess — "junk food for thought" — and depriving them of what they really need.

(3) REWRITING HISTORY and LAW and SUBJECTING THE PUBLIC TO THE DEVIANT CREATION, thus being able to SHIFT THEIR THINKING from personal needs to highly fabricated outside priorities. [*WC all emphases.*]

These preclude their interest in and discovery of the silent weapons of social automation technology.

The general rule is that there is profit in confusion; the more confusion, the more profit. Therefore, the best approach is to create problems and then offer the solutions.

DIVERSION SUMMARY

Media: Keep the adult public attention diverted away from the real social issues, and captivated by matters of no real importance.

Schools: Keep the young public ignorant of real mathematics, real economics, real law, and REAL HISTORY [*WC emphasis*].

Entertainment: Keep the public entertainment below a sixth-grade level.

Work: Keep the public busy, busy, busy, with no time to think; back on the farm with the other animals.

CONSENT, THE PRIMARY VICTORY

A silent weapon system operates upon data obtained from a docile public by legal (but not always lawful) force. Much information is made available to silent weapon systems programmers through the Internal Revenue Service. (See *Studies in the Structure of the American Economy* for an

I.R.S. source list.)

This information consists of the enforced delivery of well-organized data contained in federal and state tax forms collected, assembled, and submitted by slave labor provided by taxpayers and employers.

Furthermore, the number of such forms submitted to the I.R.S. is a useful indicator of public consent, an important factor in strategic decision making. Other data sources are given in the Short List of Inputs.

Consent Coefficients — numerical feedback indicating victory status. Psychological basis: When the government is able to collect tax and seize private property without just compensation, it is an indication that the public is ripe for surrender and is consenting to enslavement and legal encroachment. A good and easily quantified indicator of harvest time is the number of public citizens who pay income tax despite an obvious lack of reciprocal or honest service from the government.

AMPLIFICATION ENERGY SOURCES

The next step in the process of designing an economic amplifier is discovering the energy sources. The energy sources which support any primitive economic system are, of course, a supply of raw materials, and the consent of the people to labor and consequently assume a certain rank, position, level, or class in the social structure; i.e., to provide labor at various levels in the pecking order.

Each class, in guaranteeing its own level of income, controls the class immediately below it, hence preserves the class structure. This provides stability and security, but also government from the top.

As time goes on and communication and education improve, the lower-class elements of the social labor structure become knowledgeable and envious of the good things that the upper-class members have. They also begin to attain a knowledge of energy systems and the ability to enforce their rise through the class structure.

This threatens the sovereignty of the elite.

If this rise of the lower classes can be postponed long enough, the elite can achieve energy dominance, and LABOR BY CONSENT NO LONGER WILL HOLD A POSITION [WC emphasis] of an essential economic energy source.

Until such energy dominance is absolutely established, the consent of people to labor and let others handle their affairs must be taken into consideration, since failure to do so could cause the people to interfere in the final transfer of energy sources to the control of the elite.

It is essential to recognize that at this time, public consent is still an essential key to the release of energy in the process of economic amplification.

Therefore, consent as an energy release mechanism will now be considered.

LOGISTICS

The successful application of a strategy requires a careful study of inputs, outputs, the strategy connecting the inputs and the outputs, and the available energy sources to fuel the strategy. This study is called logistics.

A logistical problem is studied at the elementary level first, and then levels of greater complexity are studied as a synthesis of elementary factors.

This means that a given system is analyzed, i.e., broken down into its subsystems, and these in turn are analyzed, until, by this process, one arrives at the logistical "atom," THE INDIVIDUAL [WC *emphasis*].

This is where the process of SYNTHESIS [WC *emphasis*] properly begins, and at the time of the birth of the individual.

THE ARTIFICIAL WOMB

From the time a person leaves its mother's womb, its every effort is directed toward building, maintaining, and withdrawing into artificial wombs, various sorts of substitute protective devices or shells.

The objective of these artificial wombs is to provide a stable environment for both stable and unstable activity; to provide a shelter for the evolutionary processes of growth and maturity — i.e., survival; to provide security for freedom and to provide defensive protection for offensive activity.

This is equally true of both the general public and the elite. However, there is a definite difference in the way each of these classes go about the solution of problems.

THE POLITICAL STRUCTURE OF A NATION — DEPENDENCY

The primary reason why the individual citizens of a country create a political structure is a subconscious wish or desire to perpetuate their own dependency relationship of childhood. Simply put, they want a human god to eliminate all risk from their life, pat them on the head, kiss their bruises, put a chicken on every dinner table, clothe their bodies, tuck them into bed at night, and tell them that everything will be alright [sic] when they wake up in the morning.

This public demand is incredible, so the human god, the politician, meets incredibility with incredibility by promising the world and delivering nothing. So who is the bigger liar? the public? or the "godfather"?

This public behavior is surrender born of fear, laziness, and expediency. It is the basis of the welfare state as a strategic weapon, useful against a disgusting public.

ACTION/OFFENSE

Most people want to be able to subdue and/or kill other human beings which disturb their daily lives, but they do not want to have to cope with the moral and religious issues which such an overt act on their part might raise. Therefore, they assign the dirty work to others (including their own children) so as to keep the blood off their own hands. They rave about the humane treatment of animals and then sit down to a delicious hamburger from a whitewashed slaughterhouse down the street and out of sight. But even more hypocritical, they pay taxes to finance a professional association of hit men collectively called politicians, and then complain about corruption in government.

RESPONSIBILITY

Again, most people want to be free to do things (to explore, etc.) but they are afraid to fail.

The fear of failure is manifested in irresponsibility, and especially in delegating those personal responsibilities to others where success is uncertain or carries possible or created liabilities (law) which the person is not prepared to accept. They want authority (root word — "author"), but they will not accept responsibility or liability. So they hire politicians to face reality for them.

SUMMARY

The people hire the politicians so that the people can:

(1) obtain security without managing it.

(2) obtain action without thinking about it.

(3) inflict theft, injury, and death upon others without having to contemplate either life or death.

(4) avoid responsibility for their own intentions.

(5) obtain the benefits of reality and science without exerting themselves in the discipline of facing or learning either of these things.

They give the politicians the power to create and manage a war machine to:

(1) provide for the survival of the NATION/WOMB.

(2) prevent encroachment of anything upon the NATION/WOMB.

(3) destroy the enemy who threatens the NATION/WOMB.

(4) destroy those citizens of their own country who do not conform for the sake of stability of the NATION/WOMB.

Politicians hold many quasi-military jobs, the lowest being the police which are soldiers, the attorneys and the C.P.A.s next who are spies and saboteurs (licensed), and the judges who shout the orders and run the closed union military shop for whatever the market will bear. The generals are industrialists. The "presidential" level of commander-in-chief is shared by the international bankers. The people know that they have created this farce and financed it with their own taxes (consent), but they would rather knuckle under than be the hypocrite.

Thus, a nation becomes divided into two very distinct parts, a DOC-ILE SUB-NATION [great silent majority] and a POLITICAL SUB-NATION. The political sub-nation remains attached to the docile sub-nation, tolerates it, and leaches its substance until it grows strong enough to detach itself and then devour its parent.

SYSTEM ANALYSIS

In order to make meaningful computerized economic decisions about war, the primary economic flywheel, it is necessary to assign concrete logistical values to each element of the war structure — personnel and material alike.

This process begins with a clear and candid description of the subsystems of such a structure.

THE DRAFT

(As military service)

Few efforts of human behavior modification are more remarkable or more effective than that of the socio-military institution known as the draft. A primary purpose of a draft or other such institution is to instill, by intimidation, in the young males of a society the uncritical conviction that the government is omnipotent. [*WC Note: The truth is just the opposite, as government exists only with the consent of the people.*] He is soon taught that a prayer is slow to reverse what a bullet can do in an instant. Thus, a man trained in a religious environment for eighteen years of his life can, by this instrument of the government, be broken down, be purged of his fantasies and delusions in a matter of mere months. Once that conviction is instilled, all else becomes easy to instill.

EVEN MORE INTERESTING IS THE PROCESS BY WHICH A YOUNG MAN'S PARENTS, WHO PURPORTEDLY LOVE HIM, CAN BE INDUCED TO SEND HIM OFF TO WAR TO HIS DEATH [*WC emphasis*]. Although the scope of this work will not allow this matter to be expanded in full detail, nevertheless, a coarse overview will be possible and can serve to reveal those factors which must be included in some numerical form in a computer analysis of social and war systems.

We begin with a tentative definition of the draft. THE DRAFT (selective service, etc.) is an institution of COMPULSORY collective SACRIFICE and SLAVERY, devised by the middle-aged and the elderly for the purpose of pressing the young into doing the public dirty work. It further serves to make the youth as guilty as the elders, thus making criticism of the elders by the youth less likely (Generational Stabilizer). It is marketed and sold to the public under the label of "patriotic = national" service.

Once a candid economic definition of the draft is achieved, that definition is used to outline the boundaries of a structure called a Human Value System, which in turn is translated into the terms of game theory. The value of such a slave laborer is given in a Table of Human Values, a table broken down into categories by intellect, experience, post-service job demand, etc.

Some of these categories are ordinary and can be tentatively evaluated in terms of the value of certain jobs for which a known fee exists. Some jobs are harder to value because they are unique to the demands of social subversion, for an extreme example: the value of a mother's instruction to her daughter, causing that daughter to put certain behavioral demands upon a future husband ten or fifteen years hence; thus, by suppressing his resistance to a perversion of a government, making it easier for a banking cartel to buy the State of New York in, say, twenty years.

Such a problem leans heavily upon the observations and data of wartime espionage and many types of psychological testing. But crude mathematical models (algorithms, etc.) can be devised, if not to predict, at least to predetermine these events with maximum certainty. What does not exist by natural cooperation is thus enhanced by calculated compulsion. Human beings are machines, levers which may be grasped and turned, and there is little real difference between automating a society and automating a shoe factory.

These derived values are variable. (It is necessary to use a current Table of Human Values for computer analysis.) These values are given in true measure rather than U.S. dollars, since the latter is unstable, being presently inflated beyond the production of national goods and services so as to give the economy a false kinetic energy ("paper" inductance).

****TOP SECRET****

The silver value is stable, it being possible to buy the same amount with a gram of silver today as could be bought in 1920. Human value measured in silver units changes slightly due to changes in production technology.

ENFORCEMENT

FACTOR I

As in every social system approach, stability is achieved only by understanding and accounting for human nature (action/reaction patterns). A failure to do so can be, and usually is, disastrous.

As in other human social schemes, one form or another of intimidation (or incentive) is essential to the success of the draft. Physical principles of action and reaction must be applied to both internal and external subsystems.

To secure the draft, individual brainwashing/programming and both the family unit and the peer group must be engaged and brought under control.

FACTOR II — FATHER

The man of the household must be housebroken to ensure that junior will grow up with the right social training and attitudes. The advertising media, etc., are engaged to see to it that father-to-be is pussy-whipped before or by the time he is married. He is taught that he either conforms to the social notch cut out for him or his sex life will be hobbled and his tender companionship will be zero. He is made to see that women demand security more than logical, principled, or honorable behavior.

By the time his son must go to war, father (with jelly for a backbone) will slam a gun into junior's hand before father will risk the censure of his peers, or make a hypocrite of himself by crossing the investment he has in his own personal opinion or self-esteem. Junior will go to war or father will be embarrassed. So junior will go to war, the true purpose not withstanding.

FACTOR III — MOTHER

The female element of human society is ruled by emotion first and logic second. In the battle between logic and imagination, imagination always wins, fantasy prevails, maternal instinct dominates so that the child comes first and the future comes second. A woman with a newborn baby is too starry-eyed to see a wealthy man's cannon fodder or a cheap source of slave labor. A woman must, however, be conditioned to accept the transition to "reality" when it comes, or sooner.

As the transition becomes more difficult to manage, the family unit must be carefully disintegrated, and state-controlled public education and state-operated child-care centers must become more common and legally enforced so as to begin the detachment of the child from the mother and father at an earlier age. Inoculation of behavioral drugs [Ritalin] can speed the transition for the child (mandatory). CAUTION: A woman's impulsive anger can override her fear. An irate woman's power must never be underestimated, and her power over a pussy-whipped husband must likewise never be underestimated. It got women the vote in 1920.

FACTOR IV — JUNIOR

The emotional pressure for self-preservation during time of war and the self-serving attitude of the common herd that have an option to avoid the battlefield — if junior can be persuaded to go — is all of the pressure finally necessary to propel Johnny off to war. Their quiet blackmailings of him are the threats: "No sacrifice, no friends; no glory, no girlfriends."

FACTOR V — SISTER

And what about junior's sister? She is given all the good things of life by her father, and taught to expect the same from her future husband regardless of the price.

FACTOR VI — CATTLE

Those who will not use their brains are no better off than those who have no brains, and so this mindless school of jelly-fish, father, mother, son, and daughter, become useful beasts of burden or trainers of the same.

[End of excerpt]

WC/Author's Note: So now you know. This chapter could only come in the beginning. Your preconceived ideas had to be shattered in order for you to understand the rest of this book. In this chapter you can see every step that the elite have taken in their war to control this once great nation. You can see the steps that will be taken in the future. You can no longer pretend innocence. Your denial of the conspiracy will fall on deaf ears. This book is part of the education that will give Americans the weapons needed in the coming months and years of hardship as the New World Order struggles to be born.

Many will argue that "Silent Weapons for Quiet Wars" is only a bogus conglomeration of words for which the writer has never taken credit or responsibility. Those who do so ignore the self-evident truths contained within the document. They ignore these truths because they are an indictment of their own ignorance, which they cannot face.

The document, first found in 1969, correctly outlines events which subse-

quently came to pass. It cannot be ignored or dismissed. The document is genuine. Its truths cannot be negated or shrugged away. The message is this: You must accept that you have been cattle and the ultimate consequence of being cattle — which is slavery — or you must prepare to fight, and if necessary die to preserve your God-given right to Freedom.

That last sentence is the real reason why people choose to ignore "Silent Weapons for Quiet Wars." People are not ready to admit that they have been cattle. They are not prepared to fight, and if necessary die, for Freedom. It is an indictment of the citizens of the United States of America. And that is the total confirmation of the truth of the information contained in "Silent Weapons for Quiet Wars."

CHAPTER 2

SECRET SOCIETIES AND THE NEW WORLD ORDER

...there is a power so organized, so subtle, so complete, so pervasive, that they had better not speak above their breath when they speak in condemnation of it.

President Woodrow Wilson

History is replete with whispers of secret societies. Accounts of elders or priests who guarded the forbidden knowledge of ancient peoples. Prom inent men, meeting in secret, who directed the course of civilization are recorded in the writings of all people.

The oldest is the Brotherhood of the Snake, also called the Brotherhood of the Dragon, and it still exists under many different names. The Brotherhood of the Snake is devoted to guarding the "secrets of the ages" and to the recognition of Lucifer as the one and only true God. If you do not believe in God, Lucifer, or Satan, you must understand that there are great masses of people who do. I do not believe in racism but millions do and their beliefs and actions based upon those beliefs will affect me. It is clear that religion has always played a significant role in the course of these organizations. Communication with a higher source, often divine, is a familiar claim in all but a few.

The secrets of these groups are thought to be so profound that only a chosen, well-educated few are able to understand and use them. These men use their special knowledge for the benefit of all mankind. At least that is what they claim. How are we to know, since their knowledge and actions have been secret? Fortunately, some of it has become public knowledge.

I found it intriguing that in most, if not all, primitive tribal societies *all* of the adults are members. They are usually separated into male and female groups. The male usually dominates the culture. Surprisingly, this exactly resembles many civilized secret societies. This can only mean that the society is working not against established authority, but for it. In fact, could be said to actually *be* the established authority. This would tend to remove the validity of any argument that all secret associations are dedicated to the "destruction of properly constituted authority." This can only apply, of course, where the secret society makes up the majority or entirety of any people which it affects. Only a very few fall into this category.

Secret societies in fact mirror many facets of ordinary life. There is always an exclusivity of membership, with the resultant importance attached to being or becoming a member. This is found in all human endeavors, even those which are not secret, such as football teams or country clubs. This exclusivity of membership is actually one of the secret societies' most powerful weapons. There is the use of signs, passwords and other tools. These have always performed valuable functions in man's organizations everywhere. The stated reason, almost always different from the real reason, for the societies' existence is important. It can be anything, but is usually fraternal and is found in all pressure groups wherever people congregate.

* * * TOP SECRET * * * *

The comradeship is especially important. Sharing hardships or secrets has always been a special thrill to man. No one who has ever undergone the rigors of boot camp is ever likely to forget the special feeling of belonging and comradeship that was shared between the victims of the drill sergeant or company commander. It is an emotion born of initiation. The most potent tool of any secret society is the ritual and myth surrounding initiation. These special binding ceremonies have very deep meaning for the participants.

Initiation performs several functions which make up the heart and soul of any true secret society. Like boot camp, the initiation into the armed forces, important aspects of human thought that are universally compelling, are merged to train and maintain the efforts of a group of people to operate in a certain direction. Initiation bonds the members together in mysticism

Neophytes gain knowledge of a secret, giving them special status. The ancient meaning of neophyte is "planted anew or reborn." A higher initiation is in reality a promotion inspiring loyalty and the desire to move up to the next rung. The goals of the society are reinforced, causing the initiated to act toward those goals in everyday life. That brings about a change in the political and social action of the member. The change is always in the best interest of the goals of the leaders of the secret society. The leaders are called adepts. This can best be illustrated by the soldier trained to follow orders without thinking. The result is often the wounding or death of the soldier for the realization of the commander's goal, which may or may not be good for the overall community.

Initiation is a means of rewarding ambitious men who can be trusted. You will notice that the higher the degree of initiation the fewer the members who possess the degree. This is not because the other members are not ambitious but because a process of very careful selection is being conducted. A point is reached where no effort is good enough without a pull up by the higher members. Most members never proceed beyond this point and never learn the real, secret purpose of the group. The frozen member from that point on serves only as a part of the political power base, as indeed he has always done. You may have guessed by now that initiation is a way to determine who can and cannot be trusted.

A method of deciding exactly who is to become an adept may be decided during initiation by asking the candidate to spit upon the Christian cross. If the candidate refuses, the members congratulate him and tell him, "You have made the right choice, as a true adept would never do such a terrible thing." The newly initiated might find it disconcerting, however, that he/she never advances any higher. If instead, the candidate spits upon the cross, he/she has demonstrated a knowledge of one of the mysteries and soon will find him/herself a candidate for the next higher level. The mystery is that religion is but a tool to control the masses. Knowledge (or wisdom) is their only god, through which man himself will become god. The snake and the dragon are both symbols of wisdom. Lucifer is the personification of the symbol. It was Lucifer who tempted Eve to entice Adam to eat of the tree of knowledge and thus free man from the bonds of ignorance. The WORSHIP (a lot different from STUDY) of knowledge, science, or technology is Satanism in its purest form, and its god is Lucifer. Its secret symbol is the all-seeing eye in the pyramid.

Undesirable effects of secret societies and their aura of mystery has sometimes given them the reputation for being abnormal associations or, at the very least, strange groups of people. Whenever their beliefs are those of the majority they are no longer considered antisocial. A good example is the Christian church, which was at one time a secret society under the Roman Empire. In fact, the "Open Friendly Secret Society" (the Vatican) actually ruled most, if not all, of the known world at one time.

Most secret societies are generally considered to be antisocial; they are believed to contain elements that are not liked or are outright harmful to the community in general. This is exactly the case in some instances. Communism and fascism are secret societies in many countries where they are prohibited by law. In this country the Nazi party and the Ku Klux Klan are secret societies due mostly to the fact that the general public is disgusted by them. Their activities are sometimes illegal, thus the secrecy of their membership. The early Christians were a secret society because Roman authorities considered them from the start to be dangerous to imperial rule. The same was true of the followers of Islam. At least some of these true believers, working in secret, accomplished what would turn out to be for the eventual good of society. The Druseed and Yezidis in Syria and Iraq consider the Arabs a dangerous secret society dedicated to the takeover of the world. The Arabs today think the same of the Jews. Catholics and Freemasons used to have precisely the same ideas about each other.

In many primitive or backward societies initiation into the highest degrees of the group involved subjection to trials which not infrequently resulted in death or insanity for the candidate. It can be seen that social right and wrong is not the yardstick in estimating the value of a secret society. In Borneo, initiates of hunting societies, consider it meritorious and compulsory to hunt heads. In Polynesia, infanticide and debauch were considered essential for initiation into their societies, where the tribal code needed members who indulged in these things, as pillars of society.

Since the beginning of recorded history, governmental bodies of every nation have been involved with maintaining the status quo to defend the establishment against minority groups that sought to function as states within states or to oust the constituted authority and take over in its place.

Many of these attempts have succeeded but have not always lasted. Man's desire to be one of the elect is something that no power on earth has been able to lessen, let alone destroy. It is one of the "secrets" of secret societies. It is what gives them a political base and lots of clout. Members often vote the same and give each other preference in daily business, legal, and social activities. It is the deepest desire of many to be able to say, "I belong to the elect."

Houses of worship and sacrifice existed in the ancient cities. They were in fact temples built in honor of the many gods. These buildings functioned often as meeting places for philosophers and mystics who were believed to possess the secrets of nature. These men usually banded together in seclusive philosophic and religious schools.

The most important of all of these ancient groups is the Brotherhood of the Snake, or Dragon, and was simply known as the Mysteries. The snake and dragon are symbols that represent wisdom. The father of wisdom is Lucifer, also called the Light Bearer. The focus of worship for the Mysteries was Osiris, another name of Lucifer. Osiris was the name of a bright star that the ancients believed had been cast down onto the earth. The literal meaning of Lucifer is "bringer of light" or "the morning star." After Osiris was gone from the sky, the ancients saw the Sun as the representation of Osiris, or more correctly, Lucifer.

> *Osiris was represented by the sun.*
> **Albert Pike**

> *How art thou fallen from heaven, O Lucifer...*
> **Isaiah 14:12.**

> *...it is claimed that, after Lucifer fell from Heaven,*
> *he brought with him the power of thinking as a gift for mankind.*
> **Fred Gittings,**
> **Symbolism in Occult Art**

Most of the greatest minds that ever lived were initiated into the society of Mysteries by secret and dangerous rites, some of which were very cruel. Some of the most famous were known as Osiris, Isis, Sabazius, Cybele, and Eleusis. Plato was one of these initiates and he describes some of the mysteries in his writings.

Plato's initiation encompassed three days of entombment in the Great Pyramid, during which time he died (symbolically), was reborn, and was given secrets that he was to preserve. Plato's writings are full of information on the Mysteries. Manly P. Hall stated in his book, *The Secret Teachings of All Ages* that, "...the illumined of antiquity...entered its [pyramid of Giza] portals as men; they came forth as gods." The ancient Egyptian word for pyramid was *khuti*, which meant "glorious light." Mr. Hall says also, "The pyramids, the great Egyptian temples of initiation..."

According to many, the great pyramids were built to commemorate and observe a supernova explosion that occurred in the year 4000 B.C. Dr. Anthony Hewish, 1974 Nobel Prize winner in physics, discovered a rhythmic series of radio pulses which he proved were emissions from a star that had exploded around 4000 B.C. The Freemasons begin their calendar from A.L., "In the Year of Light," found by adding 4000 to the modern year. Thus 1990 + 4000 = 5990 A.L. George Michanowsky wrote in *The Once and Future Star* that "The ancient Sumerian cuneiform...described a giant star exploding within a triangle formed by...Zeta Puppis, Gamma Velorum, and Lambda Velorum...located in the southern sky....[An] accurate star catalogue now stated that the blazing star that had exploded within the triangle would again be seen by man in 6000 years." According to the Freemason's calendar it will occur in the year 2000, and indeed it will.

The spacecraft called Galileo is on its way to Jupiter, a baby star with a gaseous makeup exactly the same as our sun, with a load of 49.7 pounds of plutonium, supposedly being used as batteries to power the craft. When its final orbit decays in December 1999, Galileo will deliver its payload into the center of Jupiter. The unbelievable pressure that will be encountered will cause a reaction exactly as occurs when an atomic bomb is exploded by an implosion detonator. The plutonium will explode in an atomic reaction, lighting the hydrogen and helium atmosphere of Jupiter and resulting in the birth of the star that has already been named LUCIFER. The world will interpret it as a sign of tremendous religious significance. It will fulfill prophecy. In reality it is only a demonstration of the insane application of technology by the JASON Society which may or may not even work. They have practiced overkill to ensure success, however, as the documents that I read while in Naval Intelligence stated that Project GALILEO required only five pounds of plutonium to ignite Jupiter and possibly stave off the coming ice age. Global warming is a hoax. It is easier for the public to deal with and will give the ruling elite more time before panic and anarchy replace government. The reality is that overall global temperatures are becoming lower. Storms are becoming more violent and less predictable.

The icecaps at the poles are growing larger. The temperate zones where food can be grown are shrinking. Desertification is increasing in the tropics. An ice age is on its way, and it will occur suddenly.

Simultaneously a vault containing the ancient records of the earth will be opened in Egypt. The return of Lucifer and the opening of the vault will usher in the millennium. A great celebration has already been planned by the Millennium Society to take place at the pyramids in Egypt. According to the January 3, 1989, edition of the *Arizona Daily Star*, "President-elect Bush is spending this New Year's holiday at Camp David, Maryland, but in 10 years he may be in Egypt. Organizers of the Millennium Society say he's already committed to ushering in the next century at the Great Pyramid of Cheops in Giza."

The first secret that one must know to even begin to understand the Mysteries is that their members believe that there are but few truly mature minds in the world. They believe that those minds belong exclusively to them. The philosophy that follows is the classic secret-society view of humanity. "When a person of strong intellect is confronted with a problem which calls for the use of reasoning faculties, they keep their poise and attempt to reach a solution by garnering facts bearing upon the question. On the other hand, those who are immature, when confronted by the same problem, are overwhelmed. While the former may be said to be qualified to solve the mystery of their own destiny, the latter must be led like a bunch of animals and taught in the simplest language. Like sheep they are totally dependent upon the shepherd. The able intellect is taught the Mysteries and the esoteric spiritual truths. The masses are taught the literal, exoteric interpretations. While the masses worship the five senses, the select few observe, recognizing in the gulf between them the symbolic concretions of great abstract truths.

"The initiated elect communicate directly to Gods [ALIENS?] who communicate back to them. The masses sacrifice their lambs on an altar facing a stone idol that can neither hear or speak. The elect are given knowledge of the Mysteries and are illumined and are thus known as The Illuminati or the Illuminated Ones, the guardians of the 'Secrets of the Ages.'"

Three early secret societies that can be directly connected to a modern descendant are the cults of Roshaniya, Mithras and their counterpart, the Builders. They have many things in common with the Freemasons of today as well as with many other branches of the Illuminati. For instance, common to the Brotherhood are the symbolic rebirth into a new life without going through the portal of death during initiation; reference to the "Lion" and "the Grip of the Lion's Paw" in the Master Mason's degree; the three degrees, which is the same as the ancient Masonic rites before the many other degrees were added; the ladder of seven rungs; men only; and the "all-seeing eye."

Of special interest is the powerful society in Afghanistan in ancient times called the Roshaniya — illuminated ones. There are actually references to this mystical cult going back through history to the House of Wisdom at Cairo. The major tenets of this cult were: the abolition of private property; the elimination of religion; the elimination of nation states; the belief that illumination emanated from the Supreme Being who desired a class of perfect men and women to carry out the organization and direction of the world; belief in a plan to reshape the social system of the world by first taking control of individual countries one by one, and the belief that after reaching the fourth degree one could communicate directly with the unknown supervisors who had imparted knowledge to initiates throughout the ages. Wise men will again recognize the Brotherhood.

Can you hear the echo of the Nazi party, the Communist party, the extreme right and the extreme left? The important fact to remember is that the leaders of both the right and the left are a small, hard core of men who have been and still are Illuminists or members of the Brotherhood. They may have been or may be members of the Christian or Jewish religions, but that is only to further their own ends. They are and always have been Luciferian and internationalist. They give allegiance to no particular nation, although they have used, on occasion, nationalism to further their causes. Their only concern is to gain greater economic and political power. The ultimate objective of the leaders of both groups is identical. They are determined to win for themselves undisputed control of the wealth, natural resources, and manpower of the entire planet. They intend to turn the world into their conception of a Luciferian totalitarian socialist state. In the process they will eliminate all Christians, Jews, and atheists. You have just learned one, but only one, of the great mysteries.

The Roshaniya also called themselves the Order. Initiates took an oath that absolved them of all allegiance except to the Order and stated, "I bind myself to perpetual silence and unshaken loyalty and submission to the Order....All humanity which cannot identify itself by our secret sign is our lawful prey." The oath remains essentially the same to this day. The secret sign was to pass a hand over the forehead, palm inward; the countersign, to hold the ear with the fingers and support the elbow in the cupped other hand. Does that sound familiar? The Order is the Order of the Quest. The cult preached that there was no heaven, no hell, only a spirit state completely different from life as we know it. The spirit could continue to be powerful on earth through a member of the Order, but only if the spirit had been itself a member of the Order before its death. Thus members of the Order gained power from the spirits of the dead members.

The Roshaniya took in travelers as initiates and then sent them on their way to found new chapters of the Order. It is believed by some that the Assassins were a branch of the Roshaniya. Branches of the Roshaniya or "the illuminated ones" or the Illuminati existed and still exist everywhere. One of the rules was not to use the same name and never mention "the Illuminati." That rule is still in effect today. I believe that it is the breaking of this rule that resulted in Adam Weishaupt's downfall.

One of the greatest secrets of the ages is the true story of the Holy Grail, the robe of Jesus, the remains of the Cross of Crucifixion, and whether Jesus actually died or if he survived and produced a child. Many myths surround the Knights Templar concerning these relics, and most myths throughout history always have at least some basis in fact. If my sources are correct, the Knights Templar survive today as a branch of the Illuminati and guard the relics, which are hidden in a location known only to them.

We know that the Templars are Illuminati because the Freemasons absorbed and protected those that escaped persecution of the church and France, just as the Freemasons would absorb and protect Weishaupt's Illuminati centuries later. The Knights Templar exist today as a higher degree of Freemasonry within the Templar Order. In fact, the Knights Templar is a branch of the Order of the Quest. The DeMolay Society is a branch of the Freemasons that consecrates the memory of the persecution of the Knights Templar and in particular, their leader Jacques deMolay. I know, because I was a member of the DeMolay Society as a young adult. I loved the mystery and ritual. I became separated from the Society when my family moved to a location out of reach of any lodge. I believe to this day that my association with the DeMolay Society may have been the reason for my selection for Naval Security and Intelligence.

According to members of the intelligence community, when the New World Order is solidified the relics will be taken out, will be united with the Spear of Destiny, and will, according to legend, give the world's ruler absolute power. This may confirm beliefs passed down through the ages that describe the significance of these relics when united in the hands of one man. It may also explain Hitler's desperate search for their hiding place during World War II. Again I must remind you that it makes not one iota of difference what you believe. If *they* believe, you will be affected.

The Knights Templar were founded sometime during the 11th century in Jerusalem by the Prieure de Sion for the express purpose of guarding the remaining relics of Jesus and to provide military protection for the religious travelers during their pilgrimage to the Holy City.

The Prieure de Sion was a religious order founded upon Mount Sion in Jerusalem. The Order set for itself the goal of preserving and recording the bloodline of Jesus and the House of David. Through every means available to them, the Prieure de Sion had found and retrieved the remaining relics. These relics were entrusted to the Knights Templar for safekeeping. I am amazed at the authors of *Holy Blood, Holy Grail* and the information that they have unearthed. Most of all I am amazed at their inability to put the puzzle together. The treasure hidden in France is not the treasure of the Temple of Jerusalem. It is the Holy Grail itself, the robe of Jesus, the last remaining pieces of the Cross of Crucifixion, and, according to my sources, someone's bones. I can tell you that the reality of the bones will shake the world to its very foundations if I have been told the truth. The relics are hidden in France. I know the location and so do the authors of *Holy Blood, Holy Grail*, but they do not know that they know — or do they?

Adam Weishaupt, a young professor of canon law at Ingolstadt University in Germany, was a Jesuit priest and an initiate of the Illuminati. The branch of the Order he founded in Germany in 1776 was the same Illuminati previously discussed. The Jesuit connection is important, as you will see later in this chapter. Researchers agree that he was financed by the House of Rothschild (the same Rothschild family mentioned in "Silent Weapons for Quiet Wars"). Weishaupt advocated "abolition of all ordered national governments, abolition of inheritance, abolition of private property, abolition of patriotism, abolition of the individual home and family life as the cell from which all civilizations have stemmed, and abolition of all religions established and existing so that the Luciferian ideology of totalitarianism may be imposed on mankind."

In the same year that he founded the Illuminati he published *Wealth of Nations*, the book that provided the ideological foundation for capitalism and for the Industrial Revolution. It is no accident that the Declaration of Independence was written in the same year. On the obverse of the Great Seal of the United States the wise will recognize the all-seeing eye and other signs of the Brotherhood of the Snake.

Every tenet was the same. Date and beliefs confirm that Weishaupt's Illuminati is the same as the Afghan Illuminated Ones and the other cults which called themselves "illuminated." The Alumbrados of Spain were the same as were the "illuminated" Guerinets of France. In the United States they were known as the Jacobin clubs. Secrets within secrets within secrets — but always at the heart is the Brotherhood.

I believe that Weishaupt was betrayed and set up for persecution because he ignored the rule that the word "illuminati" or the existence of the Brotherhood would never be exposed to public knowledge. His exposure and outlawing accomplished several goals of the still-hidden and still very powerful brotherhood. It allowed members to debunk claims of its existence on the grounds that the Illuminati had been exposed and outlawed and thus was no longer a reality. It allowed members to deny allegations of conspiracy of any kind. The Brotherhood of the Snake is adept at throwing out decoys to keep the dogs at bay. Weishaupt may have been a fool — or he may have been doing exactly what he was told.

Weishaupt said, "The great strength of our Order lies in its concealment; let it never appear in its own name, but always covered by another name, and another occupation."

Allegations that the Freemason organizations were infiltrated by the Illuminati during Weishaupt's reign are hogwash. The Freemasons have always contained the core of Illuminati within their ranks, and that is why they so freely and so willingly took in and hid the members of Weishaupt's group. You cannot really believe that the Freemasons, if they were only a simple fraternal organization, would have risked everything, including their very lives, by taking in and hiding outlaws who had been condemned by the monarchies of Europe. It is mainly Freemason authors who have perpetuated the myth that Adam Weishaupt was the founder of the Illuminati and that the Illuminati was destroyed, never to surface again.

In 1826 an American Freemason wrote a book revealing Masonic secrets entitled *Illustrations of Freemasonry*. One of the secrets that he revealed is that the last mystery at the top of the Masonic pyramid is the worship of Lucifer. We have since learned the secret of the "story of the murder of Hiram Abif." Hiram Abif represents intelligence, liberty and truth, and was struck down by a blow to the neck with a rule, representing the suppression of speech by the church; then he was struck in the heart with the square, representing the suppression of belief by the State; and finally he was struck on the head by a maul, representing the suppression of intellect by the masses. Freemasonry thus equates the Church, the State, and the masses with tyranny, intolerance, and ignorance. What Morgan revealed was that the Freemasons were pledged to avenge Hiram Abif and that their plan was to strike down the Church, the State, and the freedom of the masses.

Morgan caused a small uproar against the Masons. The small uproar turned into a full blown anti-Freemason movement when the author, William Morgan, disappeared. Morgan had apparently been abducted and drowned in Lake Ontario. It was alleged that fellow Masons had done it, a claim that they deny to this day. Who else would have done it? I believe they murdered him. The newspapers of the time state without reservation that he was murdered by Masons. The oath of initiation into the Free-masons states that if secrets are told, the initiate will be murdered. A nationwide furor ensued that resulted in the creation of an anti-Masonic political party in 1829 by Henry Dana Ward, Thurlow Weed, and William H. Seward. Interest in several anti-Masonic books was revived during that period, with the result that Freemasonry suffered a severe loss of member-ship. It lasted only a few years and by 1840 the anti-Masonic party was extinct. Time really does cure all ills.

We know that the British Freemasons are a totally self-serving group that discriminates in favor of its own whenever jobs, promotions, contracts, or careers are concerned. The English Freemason organization was used by the KGB to infiltrate and take over British Intelligence. British Intel-ligence is synonomous with Chatham House, more commonly known as the Royal Institute for International Affairs, the parent organization of the Council on Foreign Relations in the United States. The English state police, Scotland Yard, ordered its personnel not to join the Masons for fear the same would happen to them. Of course, you have been told all your life that the Freemasons are only a benevolent fraternal organization bent only on community service. Read on, O innocent one.

Probably the most notorious Freemason lodge is the P2 lodge in Italy. This group has been implicated in everything from bribery to assassina-tions. P2 is directly connected to the Vatican, the Knights of Malta, and to the U.S. Central Intelligence Agency. It is powerful and dangerous. The P2 lodge has succeeded in infiltrating the Vatican and has scored a coup of tremendous significance: the Pope, John Paul II, has lifted the ban against Freemasonry. Many high-level members of the Vatican are now Free-masons.

I tell you now that Freemasonry is one of the most wicked and terrible organizations upon this earth. The Masons are major players in the strug-gle for world domination. The 33rd Degree is split into two. One split contains the core of the Luciferian Illuminati and the other contains those who have no knowledge of it whatsoever.

ALL of the intelligence officers that I worked for while in Naval Intelligence were Masons. As I stated before, I believe that my association with the DeMolay Society as a young adult may have been the reason that I was selected for Naval Security and Intelligence. However, that is only a guess.

I had intended to go into great detail linking P2, the Prieure de Sion, the Vatican, the CIA, organizations for a United Europe, and the Bilderberg Group. Fortunately, Michael Baigent, Righard Leigh & Henry Lincoln beat me to it. I say fortunately, because they confirm my previous allegation that I published in my paper "The Secret Government" that the CIA had plants, called moles, deep within the Vatican. I do not wish to be called a plagiarist so you MUST READ *Holy Blood, Holy Grail* and *The Messianic Legacy,* both by Baigent, Leigh, & Lincoln. Any reputable bookstore should carry them. Between pages 343 and 361 of *The Messianic Legacy* you can read of the alliance of power that resulted in a secret world government.

Most members of the Freemasons are not aware that the Illuminati practices what is known as "secrets within secrets," or organizations within organizations. That is one purpose of initiation. I cannot excuse any of the members, however, for anyone who joins a society without knowing EVERYTHING about the organization is indeed a fool. Only those at the top who have passed every test truly know what the Masons are hiding, thus rendering it impossible for anyone outside to know much at all about the group. What does that say about new members or those who are already members but do not know the ultimate secrets? It tells me that fools abound. Unlike authors who out of fear have acted as apologists for the Freemasons, I decline to absolve them of responsibility and guilt. The Freemasons, like everyone else, are responsible for the cleanliness of their home. The occupant of a secret house within a secret house within a secret house cannot clean if he cannot see the number of rooms or what they contain. Their house is a stinking cesspool. Look to the Masons for the guilty party if anything happens to me. I believe that they have murdered in the past and that they will murder in the future.

I firmly believe that all adult secret societies that practice degrees of initiation and consider the members to be "illuminated" are branches of the original ages-old Illuminati. Their goal is to rule the world. The doctrine of this group is not democracy or communism, but is a form of fascism. The doctrine is totalitarian socialism. You must begin to think correctly. The Illuminati are not Communists, but some Communists are Illuminati. (1) Monarchism (thesis) faced democracy (antithesis) in WWI, which resulted in the formation of communism and the League of Nations (synthesis). (2) Democracy and communism (thesis) faced fascism (antithesis) in WWII and resulted in a more powerful United Nations (synthesis). (3) Capitalism (thesis) now faces communism (antithesis) and the result will be the New World Order, totalitarian socialism (synthesis).

The 1953 report of the California Senate Investigating Committee on Education stated: "So-called modern Communism is apparently the same hypocritical world conspiracy to destroy civilization that was founded by the illuminati, and that raised its head in our colonies here at the critical period before the adoption of our Constitution." The California Senate

---

* * * * TOP SECRET * * * *

understood that communism is the work of the Illuminati. They failed to realize that the Council on Foreign Relations and the Trilateral Commission are also the work of the Illuminati. You MUST begin to think correctly. The enemy is not communism, it is Illuminism. *The Communists are not going to be much happier with the New World Order than we.*

I hope to show that most modern secret societies and especially those that practice degrees of initiation — and that is the key — are really one society with one purpose. You may call them whatever you wish — the Order of the Quest, the JASON Society, the Roshaniya, the Qabbalah, the Knights Templar, the Knights of Malta, the Knights of Columbus, the Jesuits, the Masons, the Ancient and Mystical Order of Rosae Crucis, the Illuminati, the Nazi Party, the Communist Party, the Executive Members of the Council on Foreign Relations, The Group, the Brotherhood of the Dragon, the Rosicrucians, the Royal Institute of International Affairs, the Trilateral Commission, the Bilderberg Group, the Open Friendly Secret Society (the Vatican), the Russell Trust, the Skull & Bones, the Scroll & Key, the Order — they are all the same and all work toward the same ultimate goal, a New World Order.

Many of them, however, disagree on exactly who will rule this New World Order, and that is what causes them to sometimes pull in opposite directions while nevertheless proceeding toward the same goal. The Vatican, for instance, wants the Pope to head the world coalition. Some want Lord Maitreya to head the New World Order. Lord Maitreya is the front runner, I believe, since witnesses say he was present on the ship at Malta with Bush, Gorbachev, and the ten regional heads of the New World Order. "Approximately 200 dignitaries from around the world attended a major conference initiated by Maitreya in London on April 21 and 22, 1990. Representatives of governments (including the USA), members of royal families, religious leaders and journalists, all of whom had met with Maitreya previously, attended the conference." Quote from "Prophecy Watch" column of *Whole Wheat No. 8*, Minneapolis.

Someone has also spent an awful lot of money announcing his presence. The Pope will have to approve him if Maitreya is selected, however, and that would fulfill the Bible prophecy in the Book of Revelation that states that the first beast will be given his power by Rome. If you can interpret Revelation as I can, then you know that the Pope will ultimately win out and will reign as the second beast.

In 1952 an alliance was formed, bringing them all together for the first time in history. The Black Families, the Illuminati (the Order), the Vatican, and the Freemasons now work together to bring about the New World Order. All will protest their innocence and will do everything within their power to destroy anyone who suggests otherwise. I will undoubtedly become a target when this book is published.

You may notice that some of those listed in the preceding paragraphs do not, or so it appears, practice degrees of initiation. That is the public view. Look at the Council on Foreign Relations. Many members — in fact, the majority — never serve on the executive committees. They never go through any initiation of any kind. They are, in fact, the power base and are used to gain a consensus of opinion. The majority are not really members but are made to feel as if they are. In reality they are being used and are unwilling or unable to understand. The Executive Committee is an inner core of intimate associates, members of a secret society called the Order of the Quest, also known as the JASON Society, devoted to a common purpose. The members are an outer circle on whom the inner core acts by personal persuasion, patronage and social pressure. That is how they bought Henry Kissinger. Rockefeller gave Kissinger a grant of $50,000 in the early '50s, a fortune in those days, and made dear old Henry a member of the CFR. Anyone in the outer circle who does not toe the mark is summarily expelled and the lesson is not lost on those who remain. Do you remember the human desire to be a member of the elect? That is the principle at work.

The real power are men who are always recruited without exception from the secret societies of Harvard and Yale known as the Skull & Bones and the Scroll & Key. Both societies are secret branches (also called the Brotherhood of Death) of what is otherwise historically known as the Illuminati. They are connected to parent organizations in England (The Group of Oxford University and especially All Souls College), and Germany (the Thule Society, also called the Brotherhood of Death). I learned this when I was with Naval Intelligence. I was not able to explain why some members of the Executive Committee were not listed under the "Addresses" of Chapter 322 of the Skull & Bones Society until I read *The Wise Men* by Walter Isaacson & Evan Thomas, Simon and Schuster, New York. Under illustration #9 in the center of the book you will find the caption "Lovett with the Yale Unit, above far right, and on the beach: His initiation into Skull and Bones came at an air base near Dunkirk." I have found that members of these two societies were chosen on an ongoing basis by invitation based upon merit post-college and were not confined to only Harvard or Yale attendees.

Only members of the Order are initiated into the Order of the Quest, the JASON Society that makes up the executive members of the Council on Foreign Relations and, in fact, the Trilateral Commission as well. The executive members of the Council on Foreign Relations are the real elect in this country. George Bush is a member of the Order. Surprised? You shouldn't be. His father was also a member who helped finance Hitler.

It is important that you know that the members of the Order take an oath that absolves them from any allegiance to any nation or king or government or constitution, and that includes the negating of any subsequent oath of allegiance which they may be required to take. They swear allegiance only to the Order and its goal of a New World Order. George Bush is not a loyal citizen of the United States but instead is loyal only to the destruction of the United States and to the formation of the New World Order. According to the oath Bush took when he was initiated into Skull & Bones, his oath of office as President of the United States of America means nothing.

The Trilateral Commission is an elite group of some 300 very prominent business, political, and intellectual decision-makers of Western Europe, North America, and Japan. This enterprise is a private agency that works to build up political and economic cooperation among the three regions. Its grand design, which it no longer hides, is a New World Order.

The Trilateral Commission was the idea of its founder, American banking magnate David Rockefeller. The real reason for its formation was the decline of the Council on Foreign Relation's power as a result of the people's dissatisfaction with the Vietnam War. The reasoning behind the move toward the Trilateral Commission was the same as entering two horses in the same race. It doubles the chances of winning. The real power has always remained solidly in the hands of the Council on Foreign Relations. The Rockefeller family was, is and always will be the benefactor of both organizations. Rockefeller, though powerful, is not in control in this country or anywhere else. The key to the REAL power is the fact that Rockefeller had to put out feelers at a Bilderberg Group meeting in 1972 about forming a private group of trilateral leaders. The Bilderberg Group gave the nod and Rockefeller's man Zbigniew Brzezinski gathered up a membership and organized the Trilateral Commission in 1972, not in 1973 as the Commission claims.

A key to the danger presented by the Trilateral Commission is its "Seminal Peace," written for them by Harvard Professor Samuel P. Huntington in the mid '70s. In the paper Professor Huntington recommended that democracy and economic development be discarded as outdated ideas. He wrote as co-author of the book *Crises In Democracy*, "We have come to recognize that there are potential desirable limits to economic growth. There are also potentially desirable limits to the indefinite extension of political democracy. A government which lacks authority will have little ability short of cataclysmic crisis to impose on its people the sacrifices which may be necessary." The crises and sacrifices he talks about will be discussed in a later chapter.

Remember that George Bush was a member of the Trilateral Commission and only resigned as an expediency to get elected. He believes wholeheartedly in the Commission and its ideas and ideals. We have elected a President who believes that democracy and economic development must be discarded. I tell you now that he is working toward that end. Bush is still a member of the Order and the CFR.

The JASON Society, or JASON Scholars, takes its name from the story of Jason and the Golden Fleece, and it is a branch of the Order of the Quest, one of the highest degrees in the Illuminati. The golden fleece takes on the role of truth to JASON members. Jason represents the search for the truth. Therefore the name JASON Society denotes a group of men who are engaged in a search for the truth. The name Jason is spelled with capital letters when used as the name of the JASON Society. Lower-case letters are never used when referring to this secret group.

Author's note: The name may even have a deeper meaning, as the name "Jason" and the Golden Fleece appear throughout history in relation to various other secret societies. In these instances the story represents man (Jason) looking for himself (Golden Fleece).

Top Secret documents that I read while with Naval Intelligence stated that President Eisenhower had commissioned the JASON Society to examine all of the evidence, facts, lies, and deception and find the truth of the alien question.

Founders of the JASON Group (not the same as the JASON Society) include members of the famous Manhattan Project, which brought together almost every leading physicist in the nation to build the atomic bomb during World War II. The group is made up mostly of theoretical physicists and is the most elite gathering of scientific minds in the United States. As of 1987 the membership included four Nobel Prize winners. Today JASON continues to offer scientific help the government cannot find anywhere else. They are probably the only group of scientists in the United States that know the true state of highest technology.

JASON is shrouded in what appears to be unnecessary secrecy. The group refuses to release its membership list. None of the members list JASON membership on their official resumes. Working completely behind the scenes, JASON has guided the nation's most important security decisions. These include, but are not limited to, Star Wars, submarine warfare, and predictions about the greenhouse effect. The JASON members are each paid a $500-per-day consultant's fee.

In the documents that I read while with Naval Intelligence the

JASONS predicted that the greenhouse effect would lead ultimately to an ICE AGE.

According to the Pentagon, the JASONS hold the highest and most restrictive security clearances in the nation. They are given the protocol rank of rear admiral (two stars) when they visit or travel aboard ships or visit military bases. The only other reference to the JASON group that I have been able to find is in *The Pentagon Papers*. The papers stated that JASON was responsible for designing the electronic barrier between North and South Vietnam for the purpose of sealing off infiltration of the South by North Vietnamese regulars during the Vietnam War. I was stationed on the DMZ and I can tell you that it did not work.

The veil of secrecy drawn around the JASON Group has been so tight and so leak-proof since its conception that those who think the government cannot keep a secret need to reexamine that position. The government was able to contain the JASON secret except for the one leak; but the JASON Group itself, a civilian group, did even better. No leaks have ever occurred from within JASON. JASON is administered by the Mitre Corporation. Government contracts allotted to the Mitre Corporation are in reality allotted to the JASON scientists. This is done so that the name JASON does not ever appear in documents which may come under public scrutiny.

What is the difference between the JASON Scholars or JASON Society and the JASON Group? The documents that I read referred to the JASON Society in exactly those words. In public documents the only JASON reference is to the JASON Group, administered by the Mitre Corporation. I believe the JASON Society is one of the highest degrees above the Skull & Bones and the Scroll & Key in the Illuminati. In other words, it is a higher level of initiation. The JASON Group is a scientific organization formed and hired by the JASON Society and the U.S. Government for obvious reasons.

I know a lot more about the JASON Society and the JASON Group, but I do not want to injure Mr. Grant Cameron, who has done extensive research on these subjects. He will publish his research in the coming months. I guarantee his findings will amaze you.

The Council on Foreign Relations has been the foremost flank of America's foreign-policy establishment for more than half a century. The Council on Foreign Relations is a private organization of business executives, scholars, and political leaders that studies global problems and plays a key role in developing U.S. foreign policy. The CFR is one of the most powerful semi-official groups concerned with America's role in international affairs. It is controlled by an elect group of men recruited from the Skull & Bones and the Scroll & Key societies of Harvard and Yale, which are both chapters of a secret branch of the Illuminati known as Chapter 322 of the Order [see page 81]. The members of the Order make up the Executive Committee of the Council on Foreign Relations after undergoing initiation into the Order of the Quest, also known as the JASON Society.

The Council on Foreign Relations is an off-shoot sister organization to the British Royal Institute of International Affairs. Their goal is a New World Order. Although it existed as a dinner club in New York, it did not take on its present power until 1921, when it merged with the Royal Institute of International Affairs and received its financial base from J.P. Morgan, the Carnegie Endowment, the Rockefeller family, and other Wall Street banking interests.

The Council on Foreign Relations controls our government. Through the years its members have infiltrated the entire executive branch, State Department, Justice Department, CIA, and the top ranks of the military. EVERY DIRECTOR OF THE CENTRAL INTELLIGENCE AGENCY HAS BEEN A MEMBER OF THE CFR. MOST PRESIDENTS SINCE ROOSEVELT HAVE BEEN MEMBERS. The members of the CFR dominate ownership of the press and most, if not all, of America's top journalists are members. The CFR does not conform to government policy. The government conforms to CFR policy. The appendix contains the most current list of CFR members that I was able to locate.

I read Top Secret documents while with Naval Intelligence that stated that President Eisenhower had appointed six of the Executive Committee members of the CFR to sit on the panel called Majesty Twelve also known as Majority Twelve for security reasons. Majesty Twelve is the secret group that is supposed to control extraterrestrial information and projects. The documents stated that Eisenhower had also appointed six members from the Executive branch of government who were also members of the CFR. The total membership of Majesty Twelve was nineteen, including Dr. Edward Teller and the six members from the JASON scientific group. Again, whether this is true or disinformation depends solely upon the existence of aliens.

The CFR is a secret society in that it forbids the taking of notes or the publishing of minutes of its meetings. Any member who divulges the subject or any part of any conversation or talk that took place during a meeting is terminated. The goal of the Council on Foreign Relations is a New World Order. George Bush is a member of the CFR.

The Knights of Malta play a powerful role in this scenario. In the 1930s General Smedley Butler was recruited to help take over the White House. He was told that he was needed because of his general popularity with the military. General Butler blew the whistle and named several prominent Americans as part of the plot. At the top of the list was John J. Raskob, who was a founding member of the U.S. branch of the Knights of Malta. He was board chairman of General Motors. He was, at the time, the U.S. Treasurer of the Knights of Malta. Congressional hearings were held to investigate the plot, but none of those named, including Raskob, was ever called to testify and nothing ever came of the hearings. Although you will find this in the Congressional records, you will NEVER find it in ANY history book anywhere.

It is significant that the Iran-Contra episode has many similarities to the 1930s plot. William Casey was a member of the Knights of Malta. William Casey, with the help of Vice President Bush, Anne Armstrong and Donald Regan, caused the President's Foreign Intelligence Advisory Board to be emasculated so that Bush, Casey, North and others could carry out their dirty deeds without oversight. They had also developed a plan to suspend the Constitution of the United States and were preparing to implement the plan when they were caught. These facts emerged from the hearings but were suppressed by the committee chairman, Senator Daniel Inouye of Hawaii. You must understand that tremendous power was involved in both attempts to overthrow the United States Government.

William Casey was the Director of the CIA. He was a member of the CFR. Casey was a Knight of Malta. He was the head of Ronald Reagan's political campaign. He was head of the Securities and Exchange Commission. During the Nixon administration he was head of the Export-Import Bank.

Casey arranged financing for the Kama River truck factory in the Soviet Union with 90% of the funds guaranteed or furnished by the U.S. taxpayer. This factory built military truck and tank engines for the Soviet Army. It was, and may still be, the largest factory in the world and could produce more heavy trucks than all U.S. factories together. I believe Casey was murdered.

The Knights of Malta is a world organization with its threads weaving through business, banking, politics, the CIA, other intelligence organizations, P2, religion, education, law, military, think tanks, foundations, the United States Information Agency, the United Nations, and numerous other organizations. They are not the oldest but are one of the oldest branches of the Order of the Quest in existence. The world head of the Knights of Malta is elected for a life term, with the approval of the Pope. The Knights of Malta have their own Constitution and are sworn to work toward the establishment of a New World Order with the Pope at its head. Knights of Malta members are also powerful members of the CFR and the Trilateral Commission.

The Vatican has been infiltrated over many years by the Illuminati. This is easily proven by the fact that in 1738 Pope Clement XII issued a Papal Bull which stated that any Catholic who became a Mason would be excommunicated, a very serious punishment. In 1884 Pope Leo XIII issued a proclamation stating that Masonry was one of the secret societies attempting to "revive the manners and customs of the pagans" and "establish Satan's kingdom on Earth." Piers Compton, in his book *The Broken Cross*, traces the infiltration of the Catholic Church by the Illuminati. He has found the use of the all-seeing eye in the triangle by leading Catholics and by the Jesuits. It was used in the seal of the Philadelphia Eucharistic Congress in 1976. It was on a special issue of Vatican stamps in 1978, announcing the final Illuminati victory to the world. Mr. Compton claims that Pope John XXIII wore the "all-seeing eye in the triangle" on his personal cross. Compton is adamant that several HUNDRED leading Catholic priests, bishops and cardinals are members of secret societies. He quotes an article in an Italian Journal that lists more than 70 Vatican officials, including Pope Paul VI's private secretary, the director general of Vatican radio, the Archbishop of Florence, the prelate of Milan, the assistant editor of the Vatican newspaper, several Italian bishops, and the abbot of the Order of St. Benedict. Those are only the ones that are known and only the ones known in Italy. It is widely believed that THIS Pope, John Paul XXII, is a member of the Illuminati. I believe, according to my research, that it is true. The best indication of infiltration is that on November 27, 1983, the Pope retracted all of the Papal Bulls against Freemasonry and allowed Catholics, after several hundred years, to again become members of secret societies without fear of excommunication. The goal of the Illuminati to elect one of their own to the Papacy appears to have come to fruition. If that is the case, the New World Order is just on the horizon. Now is the time.

The first U.S. Ambassador to the Vatican was William Wilson, a Knight of Malta. His appointment was probably illegal and, for a fact, was highly unethical. Wilson could not possibly have represented the U.S. when his allegiance was sworn to the Pope.

Wilson, if you will remember, took an unauthorized trip to Libya and met privately with Libyan officials at a time when travel to Libya had been banned by the President. President Ronald Reagan had called Gadhafi "a mad dog" and made a few strong threats. The U.S. had been resolute in bombing Libya even though civilians were killed. Following Wilson's trip, Gadhafi issued a press release stating that "an American diplomat had been sent to reduce tensions with Libya." The State Department denied that any such thing had taken place. Ambassador Wilson closed his mouth and refused any comment. To this day he has said nothing, even though his actions made a liar of the United States and embarrassed us worldwide.

A clue to what was happening is the fact that while we had cut off Libya and even bombed them and while travel by U.S. citizens to Libya was forbidden, five huge oil conglomerates were filling their pockets dealing with Gadhafi. One of the companies was headed by J. Peter Grace, President of W.R. Grace. Eight members of the W.R. Grace Company are members of the Knights of Malta. According to an article by Leslie Geld in the *New York Times*, administration officials had expressed concern about Mr. Wilson's activities. These actions, they said, often seem to revolve around his contacts and interest in the oil business.

Wilson should have been fired, but instead nothing happened except that he and his wife attended a Papal Easter Mass and stood next to George Schultz and his wife. In diplomatic language this indicated private approval of his actions. George Schultz, of course, is a member of the CFR, the Bohemian Club and the Bechtel Corporation, all of which have close ties to the Order and the Knights of Malta.

Wilson engaged in several other improprieties during his ambassadorship. Again, in each case nothing happened. Finally he resigned. Later, if you will remember, President Reagan suffered a fall from a horse on William Wilson's ranch in Mexico. Do you seriously think that President Reagan would have visited Wilson's home in Mexico if he had not approved of Wilson's actions while he was the U.S. Ambassador to the Vatican?

Knight of Malta Myron Taylor was President Roosevelt's envoy. Knight of Malta John McCone was President Kennedy's envoy and he was also the Director of the CIA during the early '60s. A former mayor of New York City, Robert Wagner, was President Jimmy Carter's envoy. Frank Shakespeare replaced William Wilson. Frank Shakespeare is a Knight of Malta, and so it goes. President Reagan spoke at the annual Knights of Malta dinner.

The Knights of Malta ALL have diplomatic immunity. They can ship goods across borders without paying duty or undergoing customs check. Does that ring any bells? In any case, that is power.

The Knights of Malta is held up by a backbone consisting of nobility. Nearly half of the 10,000 members belong to Europe's oldest and most powerful families. This cements the alliance between the Vatican and the "Black Nobility." The Black Nobility is mostly the rich and powerful of Europe. The head of the Black Nobility is the family that can claim direct descendancy from the last Roman emperor. Maybe now you can see that things are beginning to fall into their proper place. Membership in the

Knights of Malta entails obedience to one's superior in THE ORDER and ultimately to the Pope. Therefore, a U.S. ambassador who is also a member of the Knights of Malta faces a conflict of interest. Why is this fact ignored? President Bush appointed Knight of Malta Thomas Melledy to the post of U.S. Ambassador to the Vatican.

The Vatican has founded the Pope John Paul II Center for Prayer and Study for Peace at 1711 Ocean Avenue, Springlake, New Jersey, in a mansion overlooking the ocean. The mansion was given to the New York Archdiocese by the estate of Elmer Bobst, who died in 1978. He was a multimillionaire and chairman of Warner Lambert Company. Richard Nixon was a frequent visitor. Directors of the Center were Kurt Waldheim, former Secretary General of the United Nations and ex-nazi war criminal; Cyrus Vance, former Secretary of State under Carter and member of both the Council on Foreign Relations and the Trilateral Commission; Clare Booth Luce, a dame of the Knights of Malta; and J. Peter Grace of W.R. Grace Company, who is head of the Knights of Malta in the United States.

The Center was set up by the Vatican as a part of the Pope's new peace plan, which will bring the world together (see my paper "The Secret Government"). The Center has two roles: (1) Educate Catholics and their children to accept the New World Order. (2) Provide residence for the world-peace-solution computer and an ongoing study for peaceful solutions to any future problems which may endanger world peace. The computer is hooked to the world capitals via satellite. All nations have agreed to relinquish sovereignty to the Pope and submit future problems to the computer for solution. Of course, this will not go into effect until the New World Order is publicly announced. I believe that the New World Order was born in secrecy on January 19, 1989. Now you know.

Acquaint yourself anew with the teachings of Jesus. Compare his teachings with the tenets of the Illuminati and then compare it with the following. The Vatican has stated at various times that "the Pope is for total disarmament; the Pope is for elimination of the sovereignty of the nation states; the Pope is also stating that property rights are not to be considered true property rights. The Pope believes that only the Vatican knows what is right for man."

In the early 1940s, the I.G. Farben Chemical Company employed a Polish salesman who sold cyanide to the Nazis for use in Auschwitz. The same salesman also worked as a chemist in the manufacture of the poison gas. This same cyanide gas along with Zyklon B and malathion was used to exterminate millions of Jews and other groups. Their bodies were then burned to ashes in the ovens. After the war the salesman, fearing for his life, joined the Catholic Church and was ordained a priest in 1946. One of his closest friends was Dr. Wolf Szmuness, the mastermind behind the November/78 to October/79 and March/80 to October/81 experimental hepatitis B vaccine trials conducted by the Center for Disease Control in New York, San Francisco and four other American cities that loosed the plague of AIDS upon the American people. The salesman was ordained Poland's youngest bishop in 1958. After a 30-day reign his predecessor was assassinated and our ex-cyanide gas salesman assumed the papacy as Pope John Paul II.

1990 is the right time with the right leaders: ex-chief of the Soviet secret police Mikhail Gorbachev, ex-chief of the CIA George Bush, ex-Nazi cyanide gas salesman Pope John Paul II, all bound by an unholy alliance to ring in the New World Order.

The Pope has challenged world leaders by claiming that the people of the world already recognize the absolute authority of Rome because they observe the Sunday Sabbath that was ordered by the Pope in the Council of Laodicea (A.D. 364). The original Ten Commandments given Moses by God ordered that we should:

> Remember the Sabbath day, to
> keep it Holy. Six days shalt
> thou labor, and do all thy work:
> but the seventh day is the
> Sabbath of the Lord thy God; in
> it thou shalt not do any work,
> thou, nor thy son, nor thy daughter,
> thy man servant, nor thy maid servant,
> nor thy cattle, nor thy stranger
> that is within thy gates: for in six
> days the Lord made heaven and earth,
> the sea, and all that in them is,
> and rested the seventh day: wherefore
> the Lord blessed the Sabbath day, and
> hallowed it.

The seventh day, the Sabbath as handed to Moses by God, is Saturday. The celebration of Sunday as the Sabbath is verification that the people recognize the Pope as SUPERIOR TO GOD. The only WHOLE people who have not recognized the authority of the Pope are the Jewish people, and that is why the Vatican has not and will not recognize the state of Israel. The Vatican refuses even to call it Israel. Instead the Vatican says Palestine when talking about Israel. AGAIN, I MUST REMIND YOU THAT WHAT YOU BELIEVE MAKES NOT ONE BIT OF DIFFERENCE. THE IMPORTANT THING TO UNDERSTAND IS THAT IF THEY BELIEVE THIS, IT IS GOING TO GIVE YOU NIGHTMARES.

"The Pope has a lot of charisma and in a one world system you need a religious head for power. Khomeini proved that. This Pope has enough following and charisma to make what we consider a great threat in this move." [Quote from *The Mantooth Report*.]

"Pope John Paul II is most anxious to complete his goal. His goal is to reunite the Christian World under the LEADERSHIP OF THE PAPACY. If at all possible, he hopes to reach his goal by the end of this century. This is the primary reason behind the Pope's many worldwide trips." [From an article by Gene H. Hogberg, Nov./Dec. 1989, *Plain Truth*.]

Were you aware that Hitler and his entire staff were Catholic? Did you know that the Nazis dabbled in the occult? Did you know that the *New York Times* of April 14, 1990, quotes George Bush as stating, "Let's forgive the Nazi war criminals." I wonder why he said that? Did you know that the Los Angeles Times, December 12, 1984, quoted Pope John Paul II as saying, "Don't go to God for forgiveness of sins, come to me." The Pope committed blasphemy, thus fulfilling prophecy according to the book of Revelation. The Pope is telling us that HE IS God!

REMEMBER—NEVER WORSHIP A LEADER. IF YOU WORSHIP A LEADER, YOU THEN NO LONGER HAVE THE ABILITY TO RECOGNIZE WHEN YOU HAVE BEEN DECEIVED!

On July 21, 1773, Pope Clement XIV "forever annulled and extinguished the Jesuit Order." France, Spain and Portugal had independently come to realize that the Jesuits were meddling in the affairs of the state and were therefore enemies of the government. The Pope's action was a response to pressure applied by the monarchies. King Joseph of Portugal signed a decree "by which the Jesuits were denounced as 'traitors, rebels and enemies to the realm...'" Pope Pius VII in August, 1814, reinstated the Jesuits to all of their former rights and privileges.

Ex-President John Adams wrote to his successor, Thomas Jefferson: "I do not like the re-appearance of the Jesuits. If ever there was a body of men who merited eternal damnation on earth...it is this Society...." Jefferson replied: "Like you, I disapprove of the restoration of the Jesuits, for it means a step backwards from light into darkness."

The Jesuits are still in trouble today as they have been throughout their existence. On February 28, 1982, Pope Paul II told the Jesuits to "keep clear of politics, and honor Roman Catholic tradition." U.S. News and World Report stated that the Jesuits had indeed meddled in the affairs of nations.

The article stated: "Jesuits have played leading roles in Nicaragua's Sandinista revolution. Some Jesuits have joined Communist parties. One priest in El Salvador has claimed that his order is working for the advancement of Marxism and revolution, not for God....Jesuits have joined leftwing rebel movements in Central America and the Philippines, and have advocated a melding of Marxism and Roman Catholicism in what is called 'liberation theology.'"

When the United States wanted to employ the nastiest forms of the Haig-Kissinger depopulation policy in Central America it was the Jesuits who organized and prodded the people into civil war. Wherever the Jesuits go, revolution quickly follows. I am always sad when I see or hear of people being hurt; but according to my research, the Jesuit priests murdered in Central America probably deserved it.

The most powerful secret organization in the world is the Bilderberg Group, organized in 1952 and named after the hotel where its first meeting took place in 1954. The man who organized the Bilderberg Group, Prince Bernhard of the Netherlands, has the power to veto the Vatican's choice of any Pope it selects. Prince Bernhard has this veto power because his family, the Hapsburgs, are desended from the Roman emperors. Prince Bernhard is the leader of the Black Families. He claims descent from the House of David and thus can truly say that he is related to Jesus. Prince Bernhard, with the help of the CIA, brought the hidden ruling body of the Illuminati into public knowledge as the Bilderberg Group. This is the official alliance that makes up the world governing body.

The core of the organization is three committees made up of thirteen members each. Thus the heart of the Bilderberg Group consists of 39 total members of the Illuminati. The three committees are made up exclusively of members of all the different secret groups that make up the Illuminati, the Freemasons, the Vatican, and the Black Nobility. This committee works year round in offices in Switzerland. It determines who is invited to the annual meeting and what policies and plans will be discussed. Every proposal or plan that has ever been discussed at an annual meeting of the Bilderberg Group has come to pass usually within one or two years following the meeting. The Bilderberg Group is directing the "quiet war" that is being waged against us. How can they do it? These are the men who REALLY rule the world.

The numbers 3, 7, 9, 11, 13, 39 and any multiple of these numbers have special meaning to the Illuminati. Notice that the Bilderberg Group has a core of 39 members who are broken into 3 groups of 13 members in each group. Notice that the core of 39 answers to the 13 who make up the Policy Committee. Take special notice that the 13 members of the Policy Committee answer to the Round Table of Nine. You know that the original number of states in the United States of America was 13. The Constitution has 7 Articles and was signed by 39 members of the Constitutional Convention. The United States was born on July 4, 1776. July is the 7th month of the year. Add 7 (for July) and 4 and you have 11; 1+7+7+6 = 21, which is a multiple of 3 and 7. Add 2+1 and you get 3. Look at the numbers in 1776 and you see two 7s and a 6, which is a multiple of 3. Coincidence, you say? I say, "Baloney!" and I'd really like to say something a lot stronger. For those of you who still say it's accidental, however, I offer the following evidence. I could write a book just on numerical links, but I won't.

Manly P. Hall, 33rd-degree Mason, probably the most renowned expert on these subjects, wrote in his book *The Secret Destiny of America*, "For more than THREE THOUSAND YEARS [*WC emphasis*], secret societies have labored to create the background of knowledge necessary to the establishment of an enlightened democracy among the nations of the world....all have continued...and they still exist, as the Order of the Quest. Men bound by a secret oath to labor in the cause of world democracy decided that in the American colonies they would plan the roots of a new way of life. The Order of the Quest...was set up in America before the middle of the 17th century....Franklin spoke for the Order of the Quest, and most of the men who worked with him in the early days of the American Republic were also members....Not only were many of the founders of the United States Government Masons, but they received aid from a secret and august body existing in Europe which helped them to establish this country for a particular purpose known only to the initiated few." I found these quotes in a book on page 133. When added together, 1+3+3 equal the number 7 — coincidence? I think not.

We can get a little insight into the Order of the Quest from Franklin D. Roosevelt's Secretary of Agriculture, Henry Wallace, the man directly responsible for the printing of the reverse of the Great Seal of the United States on the one-dollar bill. Mr. Wallace, a member of the Order of the Quest, wrote in a letter to the Russian mystic and artist Nicholas Roerich: "The search — whether it be for the lost word of Masonry, or the Holy Chalice, or the potentialities of the age to come — is the one supremely worthwhile objective. All else is karmic duty. But surely everyone is a potential Galahad? So may we strive for the Chalice and the flame above it." The Holy Grail has a way of popping up on a regular basis in the writings of secret societies.

In the Great Seal of the United States we see the ancient symbol of the Brotherhood of the Snake (or Dragon), which as you already know is the all-seeing eye in the pyramid representing Lucifer in the form of wisdom.

Just below the pyramid you will note "Novus Ordo Seclorum" which translated means, "New World Order." There are

  9 tail feathers on the eagle;
  13 leaves in the olive branches;
  13 bars and stripes;
  13 arrows;
  13 letters in "E Pluribus Unum";
  13 stars in the green crest above;
  13 stones in the pyramid;
  13 letters in "Annuit Coeptis."

Thirteen is the mystical number assigned to Satan, according to Stan Deyo in his excellent book entitled *Cosmic Conspiracy*.

All of these mystical numbers also have special meaning to the Freemasons. You would have to be a devout skeptic to miss the tremendous significance of all of these supposed coincidences. Who among you can still say that there is no link?

I read while in Naval Intelligence that at least once a year, maybe more, two nuclear submarines meet beneath the polar icecap and mate together at an airlock. Representatives of the Soviet Union meet with the Policy Committee of the Bilderberg Group. The Russians are given the script for their next performance. Items on the agenda include the combined efforts in the secret space program governing Alternative 3. I now have in my possession official NASA photographs of a moonbase in the crater Copernicus.

This method of meeting is the only way that is safe from detection and/or bugging. The public outcry that would result would destroy everything should these meetings be discovered. A BBC-TV documentary program entitled "Science Report" revealed these same facts but subsequently issued a retraction. In their retraction they stated that the show had been fiction. It must be noted here that "Science Report" was a very respected documentary — nonfiction — program in Britain. Never in its history had it ever aired fiction. This subject is explored in depth in another chapter. There is no other method that I know of to verify these meetings short of somehow becoming a crew member on one of the submarines. Is Alternative 3 true, or is it a part of the plan to ring in the New World Order? It really doesn't matter, because either way we're screwed. The quicker you understand that, the wiser you become.

The members of the Bilderberg Group are the most powerful financiers, industrialists, statesmen and intellectuals, who get together each year for a private conference on world affairs. The meetings provide an infor-mal, off-the-record opportunity for international leaders to mingle, and are notorious for the cloak of secrecy they are held under. The headquarters office is in The Hague in Switzerland, the only European country never invaded or bombed during World Wars I and II. Switzerland is the seat of world power. The goal of the Bilderberg Group is a one-world totalitarian socialist government and economic system. Take heed, as time is running short.

You must understand that secrecy is wrong. The very fact that a meeting is secret tells me that something is going on that I would not approve. Do not ever believe that grown men meet on a regular basis just to put on fancy robes, hold candles, and glad-hand each other. George Bush, when he was initiated into the Skull & Bones, did not lie naked in a coffin with a ribbon tied around his genitalia and yell out the details of all his sexual experiences because it was fun. He had much to gain by accept-ing initiation into the Order, as you can now see. These men meet for important reasons, and their meetings are secret because what goes on during the meetings would not be approved by the community. THE VERY FACT THAT SOMETHING IS SECRET MEANS THERE IS SOME-THING TO HIDE.

John Robison wrote *Proofs of a Conspiracy* in 1798, and I believe he said it best in the following passage from the book. "Nothing is so dangerous as a mystic Association. The object remaining a secret in the hands of the managers, the rest simply put a ring in their own noses, by which they may be led about at pleasure; and still panting after the secret they are the better pleased the less they see of their way.

"A mystical object enables the leader to shift his ground as he pleases, and to accommodate himself to every current fashion or prejudice. This again gives him almost unlimited power; for he can make use of these prejudices to lead men by troops. He finds them already associated by their prejudices, and waiting for a leader to concentrate their strength and set them in motion. And when once great bodies of men are set in motion, with a creature of their fancy for a guide, even the engineer himself cannot say, 'Thus far shalt thou go, and no farther.'"

Is the common man really as stupid as the elite seem to believe? If he is, then maybe the average citizen is better off ignorant, being manipulated this way and that, whenever the elite deem it necessary. We will discover the answer very quickly when the common man finds that his "E" ticket to Fantasy Land has just expired.

I hope I have shown you the role of secret societies and groups within the world power structure. I hope you can see how these groups gain and keep power. You should have some understanding of how, operating in secrecy and infiltrating every level of government and vital industry including the press, the elect manipulate the people and nations of the world toward any direction desired. I hope you caught on to the fact that the secret power structure is toward a totalitarian socialist state (fascism). It is not the Nazis, as they were a product of this power structure. It is not the Jews, although some very wealthy Jews are involved. It is not the Communists, as they fit the same category as the Nazis. It is not the bankers, but they do play an important role. I also hope that you are beginning to look inside yourself to see if THEIR reality fits. Are you getting the message? For a better understanding of secret societies and their role throughout the ages, I recommend you read the books listed as source material at the end of this chapter.

U.S. President Bush and Soviet President Gorbachev arrived yesterday on this Mediterranean island for a summit conference beginning today during which both hope to start the search for a New World Order.

New York Times
December 1, 1989

SOURCES

Alamo, Tony, various writings, Music Square Church, P.O. Box 710, Van Buren, Arkansas, 72956 (501) 997-8118.

Baigent, Michael, Richard Leigh, and Henry Lincoln, *Holy Blood, Holy Grail*, Delacorte Press, New York, 1982.

Baigent, Michael, Richard Leigh, and Henry Lincoln, *The Messianic Legacy*, Dell Publishing, New York, 1989.

Bramley, William, *The Gods of Eden*, Dahlin Family Press, San Jose, California, 1989.

Cantwell, Alan Jr,. M.C., *AIDS and the Doctors of Death*, Aries Rising Press, 1988.

Carr, William Guy, *Pawns in the Game*, Omni Publications, Palmdale, California, date unknown.

Daraul, Arkon, *A History of Secret Societies*, The Citadel Press, New York, 1961.

Epperson, Ralph, *The New World Order*, Publius Press, Tucson, Arizona, 1990.

Epperson, Ralph, *Unseen Hand, An Introduction to the Conspiratorial View of History*, Publius Press, Tucson, Arizona, 1985.

Hall, Manly P., *The Secret Teachings of All Ages*, The Philosophical Research Society, Inc., Los Angeles, 1988.

Hieronimus, Robert, Ph.D., *America's Secret Destiny, Spiritual Vision & the Founding of a Nation*, Destiny Books, Rochester, Vermont, 1989.

Howard, Michael, *The Occult Conspiracy*, Destiny Books, Rochester, Vermont, 1989.

Mantooth, Don, *The Mantooth Report* (newsletter), November 1989, New Haven, Indiana.

Mullins, Eustace, *The Curse of Canaan*, Revelation Books, Staunton, Virginia, 1987.

Robison, John, *Proofs of a Conspiracy*, The American Classics, Belmont, Massachusetts, 1967, originally published in 1798.

Robinson, John J., *Born In Blood, The Lost Secrets of Freemasonry*, M. Evans and Company, Inc., New York, 1989.

Sutton, Antony C., *America's Secret Establishment, An Introduction to the Order of Skull & Bones*, Liberty House Press, Billings, Montana, 1986.

Waite, Arthur Edward, *A New Encyclopaedia of Freemasonry*, Combined Edition, Weathervane Books, New York, 1970.

Whitmire, Richard, article on JASON, September 17, 1989, *The Olympian* (newspaper), Olympia, Washington.

CHAPTER 3

OATH
OF INITIATION
of an
UNIDENTIFIED
SECRET ORDER

from

A Mother Who States That Her Son Took This Oath
(and Who Must Remain Unidentified)

and
CONGRESSIONAL RECORD – HOUSE, 1913, p. 3216.
(furnished by Dr. Ron Brown)

Not yet, O Freedom! close thy lids in
slumber, for thine enemy never sleeps.
Bryant

Author's Note: The author makes no claims whatsoever regarding this oath. It was handed to me by a woman who claimed that her son took this oath. Another source, Dr. Ron Brown, independent of and not known by the first, furnished a copy of the Congressional Record of the House of Representatives dated February 15, 1913, where the same oath is entered as purported to be of the Knights of Columbus. The Congressman may have been wrong, however, since the content indicates that this oath may belong either to the Society of Jesus (otherwise known as the Jesuits) or to the Knights of Malta, which is the militia of the Pope. I include this oath only as an example that such oaths do in fact exist and are subversive. Because of the impeccably correct and difficult level of English used, the obvious expert knowledge of religious terminology and form, and the content and format of this oath, I consider it highly unlikely that it is a forgery. You must be the ultimate judge of its authenticity. The truth will win.

THE OATH

I _____ _____, now in the presence of Almighty God, the blessed Virgin Mary, the blessed St. John the Baptist, the Holy Apostles, St. Peter and St. Paul, and all the saints, sacred host of heaven, and to you, my Ghostly Father, the superior general of the Society of Jesus founded by St. Ignatius Loyola, in the pontification of Paul the III and continued to the present, do by the womb of the Virgin, the matrix of God, and the rod of Jesus Christ, declare and swear that His Holiness the Pope, is Christ's vice regent and is the true and only head of the Catholic or Universal Church throughout the earth; and that by virtue of the keys of binding and loosing given His Holiness by my Savior, Jesus Christ, he hath power to depose heretical kings, princes, States, Commonwealths, and Governments and they may be safely destroyed. Therefore to the utmost of my power I will defend this doctrine and His Holiness's right and custom against all usurpers of the heretical or Protestant authority whatever, especially the Lutheran Church of Germany, Holland, Denmark, Sweden, and Norway and the now pretended authority and Churches of England and Scotland, and the branches of same now established in Ireland and on the Continent of America and elsewhere, and all adherents in regard that they may be usurped and heretical, opposing the sacred Mother Church of Rome.

I do now denounce and disown any allegiance as due to any heretical king, prince, or State, named Protestant or Liberals, or obedience to any of their laws, magistrates, or officers.

I do further declare that the doctrine of the Churches of England and Scotland, of the Calvinists, Huguenots, and others of the name of Protestants or Masons to be damnable, and they themselves to be damned who will not forsake the same.

I do further declare that I will help assist, and advise all or any of His Holiness's agents, in any place where I should be, in Switzerland, Germany, Holland, Ireland, or America, or in any other kingdom or territory I shall come to and do my utmost to extirpate the heretical Protestant or Masonic doctrines and to destroy all their pretended powers, legal or otherwise.

I do further promise and declare that, notwithstanding I am dispensed with to assume any religion heretical for the propagation of the Mother Church's interest to keep secret and private all her agents' counsels from time to time, as they intrust me and not divulge, directly or indirectly, by word, writing, or circumstances whatever but to execute all that should be proposed, given in charge or discovered unto me by you my Ghostly Father, or any of this sacred order.

I do further promise and declare that I will have no opinion or will of my own or any mental reservation whatsoever, even as a corpse or cadaver (perinde ac cadaver), but will unhesitatingly obey each and every command that I may receive from my superiors in the militia of the Pope and of Jesus Christ.

That I will go to any part of the world whithersoever I may be sent, to the frozen regions north, jungles of India, to the centers of civilization of Europe, or to the wild haunts of the barbarous savages of America without murmuring or repining, and will be submissive in all things whatsoever is communicated to me.

I do further promise and declare that I will, when opportunity presents, make and wage relentless war, secretly and openly against all heretics, Protestants and Masons, as I am directed to do to extirpate them from the face of the whole earth; and that I will spare neither age, sex, or condition, and that will hang, burn, waste, boil, flay, strangle, and bury alive these infamous heretics; rip up the stomachs and wombs of their women, and crush their infants' heads against the walls in order to annihilate their execrable race. That when the same can not be done openly, I will secretly use the poisonous cup, the strangulation cord, the steel of the poniard, or the leaden bullet, regardless of the honor, rank, dignity, or authority of the persons, whatever may be their condition in life, either public or private, as I at any time may be directed so to do by any agents of the Pope or superior of the Brotherhood of the Holy Father of the Society of Jesus.

In confirmation of which I hereby dedicate my life, soul, and all corporal powers, and with the dagger which I now receive I will subscribe my name written in my blood in testimony thereof; and should I prove false or weaken in my determination, may my brethren and fellow soldiers of the militia of the Pope cut off my hands and feet and my throat from ear to ear, my belly opened and sulphur burned therein with all the punishment that can be inflicted upon me on earth and my soul shall be tortured by demons in eternal hell forever.

That I will in voting always vote for a K. of C. in preference to a Protestant, especially a Mason, and that I will leave my party so to do; that if two Catholics are on the ticket I will satisfy myself which is the better supporter of Mother Church and vote accordingly.

That I will not deal with or employ a Protestant if in my power to deal with or employ a Catholic. That I will place Catholic girls in Protestant families that a weekly report may be made of the inner movements of the heretics.

That I will provide myself with arms and ammunition that I may be in readiness when the word is passed, or I am commanded to defend the church either as an individual or with the militia of the Pope.

All of which I, _____ _____, do swear by the blessed Trinity and blessed sacrament which I am now to receive to perform and on part to keep this, my oath.

In testimony hereof, I take this most holy and blessed Sacrament of the Eucharist and witness the same further with my name written with the point of this dagger dipped in my own blood and seal in the face of this holy sacrament.

CHAPTER 4

SECRET TREATY OF VERONA

Precedent

and

Positive Proof of Conspiracy

from

Congressional Record – Senate, 1916, p. 6781

and

The American Diplomatic Code, Vol. 2, 1778–1884, Elliott, p. 179

1916

CONGRESSIONAL RECORD SENATE

Mr. OWEN:

I wish to put in the Record the secret treaty of Verona of November 22, 1822, showing what this ancient conflict is between the rule of the few and the rule of the many. I wish to call the attention of the Senate to this treaty because it is the threat of this treaty which was the basis of the Monroe doctrine. It throws a powerful white light upon the conflict between monarchical government and government by the people. The Holy Alliance under the influence of Metternich, the Premier of Austria, in 1822, issued this remarkable secret document:

AMERICAN DIPLOMATIC CODE, 1778–1884

The undersigned, specially authorized to make some additions to the treaty of the Holy Alliance, after having exchanged their respective credentials, have agreed as follows:

ARTICLE 1. The high contracting powers, being convinced that the system of representative government is equally as incompatible with the monarchical principles as the maxim of the sovereignty of the people with the divine right, engage mutually, in the most solemn manner, to use all their efforts to put an end to the system of representative governments, in whatever country it may exist in Europe, and to prevent its being introduced in those countries where it is not yet known.

ARTICLE 2. As it can not be doubted that the liberty of the press is the most powerful means used by the pretended supporters of the rights of nations to the detriment of those of princes, the high contracting parties promise reciprocally to adopt all proper measures to suppress it, not only in their own States but also in the rest of Europe.

ARTICLE 3. Convinced that the principles of religion contribute most powerfully to keep nations in the state of passive obedience which they owe to their princes, the high contracting parties declare it to be their intention to sustain in their respective States those measures which the clergy may adopt, with the aim of ameliorating their own interests, so intimately connected with the preservation of the authority of the princes; and the contracting powers join in offering their thanks to the Pope for what he has already done for them, and solicit his constant cooperation in their views of submitting the nations.

ARTICLE 4. The situation of Spain and Portugal unite unhappily all the circumstances to which this treaty has particular reference. The high contracting parties, in confiding to France the care of putting an end to them, engaged to assist her in the manner which may the least compromit [sic] them with their own people and the people of France by means of a subsidy on the part of the two empires of 20,000,000 of francs every year from the date of the signature of this treaty to the end of the war.

ARTICLE 5.   In order to establish in the Peninsula the order of things which existed before the revolution of Cadiz, and to insure the entire execution of the articles of the present treaty, the high contracting parties give to each other the reciprocal assurance that as long as their views are not fulfilled, rejecting all other ideas of utility or other measure to be taken, they will address themselves with the shortest possible delay to all the authorities existing in their States and to all their agents in foreign countries, with the view to establish connections tending toward the accomplishment of the objects proposed by this treaty.

ARTICLE 6.   This treaty shall be renewed with such changes as new circumstances may give occasion for, either at a new congress or at the court of one of the contracting parties, as soon as the war with Spain shall be terminated.

ARTICLE 7.   The present treaty shall be ratified and the ratifications exchanged at Paris within the space of six months.

Made at Verona
the 22nd November, 1822.

for Austria: **METTERNICH**
for France: **CHATEAUBRIAND**
for Prussia: **BERNSTET**
for Russia: **NESSELRODE**

Mr. OWEN:
I ask to have printed in the CONGRESSIONAL RECORD this secret treaty, because I think it ought to be called now to the attention of the people of the United States and of the World. This evidence of the conflict between the rule of the few versus popular government should be emphasized on the minds of the people of the United States, that the conflict now waging throughout the world may be more clearly understood, for after all said the great pending war springs from the weakness and frailty of government by the few, where human error is far more probable than the error of the many where aggressive war is only permitted upon the authorizing vote of those whose lives are jeopardized in the trenches of modern war.

* * * * TOP SECRET * * * *

Mr. SHAFROTH:

Mr. President, I should like to have the Senator state whether in that treaty there was not a coalition formed between the powerful countries of Europe to reestablish the sovereignty of Spain in the Republics of South and Central America?

Mr. OWEN:

I was just going to comment upon that, and I am going to take but a few moments to do so because I realize the pressure of other matters. This Holy Alliance, having put a Bourbon prince upon the throne of France by force, then used France to suppress the constitution of Spain immediately afterwards and by this very treaty gave her a subsidy of 20,000,000 francs annually to enable her to wage war upon the people of Spain and prevent their exercise of any measure of the right of self-government. The Holy Alliance immediately did the same thing in Italy, by sending Austrian troops to Italy, where the people there attempted to exercise a like measure of liberal constitutional self-government; and it was not until the printing press, which the Holy Alliance so stoutly opposed, taught the people of Europe the value of liberty that finally one country after another seized a greater and greater right of self-government until now it may be fairly said that nearly all the nations of Europe have a very large measure of self-government.

However, I wished to call the attention of the Senate and the country to this important history in the growth of constitutional popular self-government. The Holy Alliance made its powers felt by the wholesale drastic suppression of the press in Europe, by universal censorship, by killing free speech and all ideas of popular rights, and by the complete suppression of popular government. The Holy Alliance having destroyed popular government in Spain and in Italy, had well-laid plans also to destroy popular government in the American colonies which had revolted from Spain and Portugal in Central and South America under the influence of the successful example of the United States. It was because of this conspiracy against the American Republics by the European monarchies that the great English statesman, Canning, called the attention of our Government to it, and our statesmen then, including Thomas Jefferson, took an active part to bring about the declaration by President Monroe in his next annual message to the Congress of the United States that the United States would regard it as an act of hostility to the Government of the United States and an unfriendly act if this coalition or if any power of Europe ever undertook to establish upon the American Continent any control of any American Republic or to acquire any territorial rights.

---

* * * * TOP SECRET * * * *

This is the so-called Monroe doctrine. The threat under the secret treaty of Verona to suppress popular government in the American Republics is the basis of the Monroe doctrine. This secret treaty sets forth clearly the conflict between monarchical government and popular government and the government of the few as against the government of the many. It is a part in reality, of developing popular sovereignty when we demand for women equal rights to life, to liberty, to the possession of property, to an equal voice in the making of the laws and the administration of the laws. This demand on the part of the women is made by men, and it ought to be made by men as well as by thinking, progressive women, as it will promote human liberty and human happiness. I sympathize with it, and I hope that all parties will in the national conventions give their approval to this larger measure of liberty to the better half of the human race.

Author's Note: Anyone who believes that the monarchs, after being deposed, forgave and forgot, is not playing with a full deck.

Most of these families are wealthy beyond belief and may be more powerful today than when they sat upon thrones. Today they are known collectively as the Black Nobility. Just because the secret treaty of Verona was signed in 1822 does not mean that the treaty is void. It is imperative that you realize that privately, the Black Nobility refuses to ever recognize any government other than their own inherited and divine right to rule. They work diligently behind the scenes to cause conditions whereby they might regain their crowns.

They believe that the United States belongs to England.

CHAPTER 5

GOOD-BYE USA
HELLO
NEW WORLD ORDER

Backbone of Hidden Government

Subversion of the Balance of Power

**The plan to suspend the Constitution
and declare martial law**

*It could probably be shown by facts and figures
that there is no distinctly native
American criminal class except Congress.*
Mark Twain, 1885

THE BALANCE OF POWER

When our forefathers wrote the Constitution of these United States they provided safeguards against despotism by providing a balance of power. The Constitution was set up to provide clear divisions of Legislative, Judicial, and Executive powers. It was believed that this system would ensure that if one branch got out of hand the other two would act to keep the one in check. This balance of power was predicated upon the assumption that none of the three branches could or would infringe upon the power of the others.

The Constitution is clear on the functions of each of the branches. The Legislative will make the laws. The Judicial will interpret the law. The Executive will decide policy and enforce the law. This, of course, is the simplest of explanations, but this is not a textbook on government. My intent is to acquaint you with simple basics of the balance of power so that you can then understand how it has been subverted.

The Legislature (Congress in the form of the House and Senate) is required to publish the laws that are made, and this is done in the Congressional Record and the Federal Register. Pending or passed legislation can be obtained by citizens through their Congressmen or from the Government Printing Office. Citizens cannot be held responsible for the law if it is not made available to them.

It is paradoxical that the government body most representative of the American citizen is the one that has been the most easily subverted. Through PACs, payoffs, pork-barrel politics, professional politicians, Congressmen who are members of secret societies and through greed and fear, our Representatives and Senators quit representing us long ago.

Congress has tremendous powers but fails in most cases to exercise even a token amount. How is it that our Legislature has allowed and at times encouraged the Executive branch to write law? You probably did not know that the President and others in the Executive branch of the government can and do write law. This is done in the form of Presidential Executive orders, National Security Council memos, National Security Decision directives, and National Security directives.

NSC memos were broad policy papers in the days after passage of the National Security Act. NSC memos became narrower and more specific over the years, and the name has varied. Under Kennedy they were called National Security Action Memorandums. President Bush has changed the name to National Security Directives.

There is a tremendous difference between Presidential Executive orders, NSC memos, and National Security Decision directives. Presidential

Executive orders are listed in the Federal Register or Presidential Findings, which are made known to the House and Senate Intelligence Committees. The most important difference between the Presidential Executive orders and all of the others, no matter what they are called, is that the others do not have to be reported, reviewed, made available to anyone, or even acknowledged that they exist.

There is no oversight whatsoever that could maintain a check on the legality of these National Security directives. The President and others within the Executive branch have used these supersecret directives to skirt the balance of power and write law without anyone's knowledge. Justification of the President's power to write law through Executive orders stems from the failure of the Government to rescind the declaration of martial law during the Civil War. In effect, the United States has been under martial law ever since Lincoln's administration.

These NSDs are powerful, hidden, and dangerous tools. They were prolific during the Reagan administration: over 300 were written, with no more than 50 ever leaking out to undergo public scrutiny. Yet most Americans have never heard of these subversive weapons. They are being used to destroy our Constitution. I believe that everyone should know about this corruption of government.

Congress has turned a blind eye to these abuses of executive power. At 3:30 a.m. Saturday, August 4, 1990, the Senate made it even easier for the Executive branch to subvert the Constitution and may have made George Bush the first American king. At that time on that day, a minority of United States senators, maybe ten at the most, passed Senate Intelligence Authorization Act for Fiscal Year 1991 (S.B. 2834). This bill will fundamentally change our constitutional system and threatens to destroy the very foundations of our great nation. Since attention has been focused upon the Middle East crisis, the public and most Congressmen know absolutely nothing about this bill.

The bill was fraudulently introduced as a reform to prevent future incidents of the abuses brought to light during the Iran-Contra scandal. Instead of preventing future abuses, however, it virtually authorizes essentially every abuse. The bill was carefully brought to a vote by Senator Sam Nunn in the dead of night when the opposition was gone. It effectively transfers most authority over the United States government directly into the hands of George Bush and thus directly into the hands of the Secret Government.

The President (presently George Bush) was given the power to initiate war, appropriate public funds, define foreign policy goals, and decide what is important to our national security. In "Oversight of Intelligence Activities," Title VII, S.B. 2834 authorizes the following:

Gives the president power to initiate covert actions (this has never before been given to the President); prevents Congress from stopping the President's initiation of covert actions; allows the President to use any federal "departments, agencies, or entities" to operate or finance a covert operation; empowers the President to use any other nation or private contractor or person to fund or operate a covert action; redefines covert actions as operations "necessary to support foreign policy objectives of the United States," a definition that is so vague and broad as to be essentially unlimited; for the first time officially claims the right of the United States to secretly interfere in the internal "political, economic, or military affairs" of other countries in direct and flagrant violation of international law; requires that the President prepare and deliver a written finding to the Intelligence committees of the Congress but allows the President to omit "extremely sensitive matters" and authorizes the President to claim executive privilege if Congress asks too many questions.

There are no penalties in the bill for violating any of its provisions, including the provision requiring a finding. Why should there be? This bill has literally handed the power of all the branches of government to the President on a silver platter. President Bush is now truly American King George the First. S.B. 2834 gives Bush the power to use any agency or branch of the government and any appropriated funds from any agency or branch of the government for covert action even if they were never appropriated for that purpose. The bill effectively prevents any oversight by anyone and allows the Executive branch to skirt the law and to escape accountability. This will be done using National Security directives. A few examples of past NSD directives that have come to light will help you understand the seriousness of the matter. They will be listed in the following paragraphs under the heading of the subject matter of the NSDDs:

NSDD 84: SAFEGUARDING NATIONAL SECURITY INFORMATION [SECRECY], 3/11/83 (Declassified in full). SUBJECT: This directive drastically expands restrictions on government employees' freedom of speech. Those with access to classified information were required to sign a nondisclosure agreement; those with access to a special category of classified information were made to agree to prepublication review of any future writings. The use of polygraphs was authorized. PURPOSE: Prevent disclosure of information that could damage national security. CONSEQUENCES: The polygraph requirement was rescinded due to Congressional opposition. Secrecy restrictions were imposed on more than 4 million government employees and CONTRACTORS for more than fifty executive agencies. Many reporters' contacts were shut down. Government employees' unions and members of Congress sued to protect the rights of whistleblowers, and the Supreme Court recently sent the case back to the district level for review.

Author's Note: NSDD 84 indicates that John Lear, Robert Lazar, Bruce Macabbee, Stanton Friedman, Clifford Stone, and many others may be active government agents. They were all working in government jobs or for government contractors and all of them were subject to this executive order. NSDD 84 was not used to silence them, which seems to indicate that they had executive approval in each and every instance.

NSDD 17: DETERRING CUBAN MODELS/COVERT ACTION IN NICARAGUA, 11/23/81 (Classified). SUBJECT: The Central Intelligence Agency was given authority to create the contras and "work with foreign governments as appropriate" to undermine the Sandinista government of Nicaragua. PURPOSE: To stop the flow of arms from Cuban and Nicaraguan sources to the Salvadoran rebels. CONSEQUENCES: The C.I.A. was given $19 million to assemble and arm a force of 500 contras to join with 1000 exiles already being trained by Argentina. Scores of operatives arrived in Honduras; arms shipments from Miami began. The contra war was set in motion.

NSDD 77: MANAGEMENT OF PUBLIC DIPLOMACY RELATIVE TO NATIONAL SECURITY, 1/14/83 (Declassified in full). SUBJECT: This directive set up several planning groups to conduct "public diplomacy activities." It ordered "organizational support for foreign governments and private groups to encourage the growth of democratic political institutions and practices." PURPOSE: To mobilize international and domestic support for "our national security objectives." CONSEQUENCES: Created propaganda ministries in the National Security Council, the State Department and the White House that concentrated on, in the words of the NSC staff member in charge of the program, "gluing black hats on the Sandinistas and white hats on UNO" (the contras' United Nicaraguan Opposition). Stories were planted in the press; journalists were pressured. The General Accounting Office later found that these activities violated the law banning "covert propaganda" inside the United States. How many other covert propaganda programs do you think are operating against the American Citizens? I can assure you that there are many more than you would ever believe.

NSDD 138: INTERNATIONAL TERRORISM, 4/3/84 (Classified). SUBJECT: This directive endorsed the principle of preemptive strikes and retaliatory raids against terrorists and called on 26 Federal agencies to recommend specific measures to combat terrorism. PURPOSE: To lessen international terrorism and free U.S. hostages in Lebanon. While this NSD directive pretends to be concerned about international terrorism, it is really a thinly disguised authorization of preemptive strikes and retaliatory raids against patriots in this country. When FEMA is activated, patriots will be rounded up in the dead of night, most likely on a national holiday such as Thanksgiving. Government agents and law-enforcement officers in every city across the nation have received antiterrorist training under this NSDD directive, and I can assure you the target is patriots. CONSEQUENCES: Set up the Terrorist Incident Working Group under North in the NSC. Its first major action was the interception and capture of the Achille Lauro hijackers, which gave North's career an important boost.

Either NSDD 138 or a subsequent NSD directive on terrorism authorized the training of three Lebanese units for preemptive strikes. When problems arose, Director of Central Intelligence William Casey took that operation off the books and enlisted Saudi Arabian help in an attempt to assassinate the head of Hezbollah. A resulting car bombing killed about eighty in Beirut; Sheik Fadlallah, the target was unhurt. The U.S. military, along with civilian law-enforcement teams, conducted joint antiterrorist training across America. To allay public fears the participants wore civilian clothing.

NSD directives have become the de facto legislative vehicle of the national security state. It has become known through the research of Susan Fitzgerald, a research consultant at the Fund for Constitutional Government in Washington who has collected declassified NSD directives, that many were released without the White House letterhead at the top of the page and without the President's signature at the bottom. This, she speculates, is to conceal the fact that the signatures on some of them would reveal that they had been made by autopen, not by Ronald Reagan's own hand. That should give you a taste of what we are up against. Please understand that virtually all but a very few NSD directives still remain classified, and unless the public forces disclosure their effect will probably never be known.

Somewhere within the volumes of secret NSD directives there is a plan to suspend the Constitution of the United States of America. The existence of this plan surfaced during the Iran-Contra hearings. Congressman Jack Brooks (D), Texas, attempted to bring it into the open. When he asked Col. North directly if North had ever helped draft a plan to suspend the Constitution, Brooks was silenced by the committee chairman Senator Daniel K. Inouye (D), Hawaii. Senator Inouye stated that the subject dealt with national security, and any questions regarding the matter could be brought up during a closed-door session. We never learned the outcome. I would like to know who gave anyone, in any branch of government, with any title, the right to suspend the Constitution at any time, for any reason, under any conditions?

I believe the plan to suspend the Constitution is directly tied to the underground facility called Mount Weather and to the Federal Emergency Management Agency (FEMA). Mount Weather is so shrouded in secrecy that 99.9% of Americans have never heard of it. FEMA, however, is another story. Remember Hurricane Hugo? Remember the federal agency (FEMA) that was sent to handle the emergency and was thrown out by the citizens because of gross incompetence? FEMA was incompetent, because "emergency management" is just a guise for its real purpose, which is to take over local, state, and federal government in case of a national emergency. The only way FEMA could do such a thing is if the Constitution were suspended and martial law were to be declared. *Therefore its very existence is proof positive that a plan to suspend the Constitution does in fact exist.*

MOUNT WEATHER

Just outside of a sleepy little town called Bluemont, Virginia, about 46 miles west of Washington D.C., is an area of wilderness covering what has been called the toughest granite rock in the eastern United States. The area is surrounded by signs marked "Restricted Area" and "This installation has been declared a restricted area....Unauthorized entry is prohibited." Other signs state: "All persons and vehicles entering hereon are liable to search. Photographing, making notes, drawings, maps or graphic representations of this area or its activities is prohibited. Such material found in the possession of unauthorized persons will be confiscated. Internal Security Act of 1950." The installation is beneath a mountain and its name is the Western Virginia Office of Controlled Conflict Operations. Its nickname is Mount Weather. It was ordered to be built by the Federal Civil Defense Administration, which is now the Federal Preparedness Agency.

Mount Weather was designed in the early '50s as part of a civil defense program to house and protect the Executive branch of the Federal government. The official name was "The Continuity of Government Program."

Congress has repeatedly tried to discover the real purpose of Mount Weather, but so far has been unable to find out ANYTHING about the secret installation. Retired Air Force General Leslie W. Bray, director of the Federal Preparedness Agency, told the Senate Subcommittee on Constitutional Rights in September 1975: "I am not at liberty to describe precisely what is the role and the mission and the capability that we have at Mount Weather or at any other precise location."

In June 1975, Senator John Tunney (D), California, chairman of the

Subcommittee on Constitutional Rights, charged that Mount Weather held dossiers on at least 100,000 Americans. He later alleged that the Mount Weather computers, described as "the best in the world," can obtain millions of pieces of additional information on the personal lives of American citizens simply by tapping the data stored at any of the other 96 Federal Relocation Centers.

I know from my stint with the Office of Naval Intelligence that these dossiers consist of information collected about American patriots, men and women who are most likely to resist the destruction of our Constitution and the formation of the totalitarian police state under the New World Order. The patriot data bank is constantly updated so that when the appointed hour arrives all patriots can be rounded up with little if any effort. The plan calls for this to be accomplished in the dead of night on a national holiday. The most likely holiday is Thanksgiving, when everyone, no matter the religion, race, or creed, will be at home. The targets will be ripe for the picking after a heavy meal, maybe some alcoholic beverages, and during a deep sleep. There is a traitor in the patriot movement who provides the Secret Government with accurate names and addresses of patriots who will fight to protect and defend the Constitution.

MY RECOMMENDATION IS THAT NO PATRIOT SHOULD EVER BE AT HOME OR AT THE HOME OF ANY FAMILY MEMBER ON ANY HOLIDAY EVER AGAIN UNTIL THE TRAITORS HAVE BEEN HUNG AND THE CONSTITUTION RESTORED AS THE SUPREME LAW OF THE LAND.

Some sources state that Mount Weather is virtually an underground city complete with dormitories, private apartments, streets, sidewalks, cafeterias, hospitals, water-purification systems, power plant, office buildings, a lake fed by fresh water from underground springs, a mass-transit system, and many other astounding things.

Several disturbing facts emerge when one researches Mount Weather. One is the conclusion that a complete parallel government exists at the site. Nine Federal departments exist there — Agriculture, Commerce, HEW, HUD, Interior, Labor, State, Transportation, and the Treasury. Apparently at least five Federal agencies are also in residence: FCC, Selective Service, Federal Power Commission, Civil Service Commission, and the Veterans Administration. Two privately owned corporations have offices at Mount Weather: the Federal Reserve and the U.S. Post Office. There is also an Office of the Presidency. What makes all this upsetting is that there is a President and a complete set of cabinet officers in residence at Mount Weather. Who are they and who appointed them? Where is such a thing provided for in the Constitution of the United States of America?

Mount Weather is the operational center — the hub — of over 96 other underground Federal Relocation Centers scattered across the United States. The majority of these appear to be concentrated in Pennsylvania, Virginia, West Virginia, Maryland, and North Carolina. Each of these facilities contains computer data banks holding information — not on enemy agents, Soviet diplomats, or suspected terrorists but on American citizens, patriots. A list of other files kept at the facilities was furnished to the Subcommittee on Constitutional Rights in 1975. The list included "military installations, government facilities, communications, transportation, energy and power, agriculture, manufacturing, wholesale and retail services, manpower, financial, medical and educational institutions, sanitary facilities, population, housing shelter, and stockpiles."

The committee concluded that these data bases "operate with few, if any, safeguards or guidelines." Senator James Abourzek (D), South Dakota, a member of the subcommittee, said, "I feel the entire operation has eluded the supervision of either Congress or the courts." Chairman Tunney said, "Mount Weather is out of control." Nothing was done by Congress to rectify the situation, however, and Mount Weather remains out of control.

Former high-level officials from Mount Weather agree that the base at Mount Weather is much more than any standby government facility or storage center for the preservation of records; they describe it as an ACTUAL GOVERNMENT-IN-WAITING. "We do not merely store essential information; the facility attempts to duplicate the vital functions of the Executive branch of the Administration." As stated above, according to my research, this includes a President and all Cabinet members actually in residence. Protocol even demands that subordinates address them as "Mr. President" or "Mr. Secretary." Most of these mysterious appointees have held their positions through several administrations. "We just act on the orders of the President in national emergencies," said one former Mount Weather official.

The FPA in its 1974 Annual Report stated that "Studies conducted at Mount Weather involve the control and management of domestic political unrest where there are material shortages (such as food riots) or in strike situations where the FPA determines that there are industrial disruptions and other domestic resource crises." The report states that the bureaucracy at Mount Weather invokes what it calls "Civil Crisis Management."

Officials who were at Mount Weather and who have furnished us with data say that during the 1960s the complex was actually prepared to assume certain governmental powers at the time of the 1961 Cuban missile crisis and the assassination of President Kennedy in 1963. The source said that the installation used the tools of its "Civil Crisis Management" program on a standby basis during the 1967 and 1968 urban riots and during a number of national antiwar demonstrations against the administration by the American people.

Daniel J. Cronin, who was the assistant director for the FPA, outlined a massive surveillance and manipulation program that is directed against the American population on a continuing basis. The FPA has organized an impressive armament of resources and equipment. Mr. Cronin described in an interview his agency's attitude toward its wide-ranging surveillance program. "We try to monitor situations," he said, "and get to them before they become emergencies....No expense is spared in the monitoring program." He cited reconnaissance satellites, local and state police intelligence reports, and law-enforcement agencies of the Federal government as examples of the resources available to the FPA for information-gathering.

The only document that I was able to find that attempts to outline some of the statutory authority of Mount Weather is Executive Order 11490. It was drafted by Gen. George A. Lincoln, former director for the Office of Emergency Preparedness (preceded FPA) and was signed into law by President Nixon in October 1969. Executive Order 11490 superseded Executive Order 11051, signed on October 2, 1962, by President Kennedy. Kennedy's order used the language, "Whereas, national preparedness must be achieved...as may be required to deal with increases in international tension with limited war, or with general war including attack upon the United States..." Nixon's order began: "Whereas our national security is dependent upon our ability to assure continuity of government, at every level, in any national emergency type situation that might conceivably confront the nation..." Nixon has deleted any reference to "war," "imminent attack," and "general war" from the order and replaced them with the phrase "during any emergency that might CONCEIVABLY occur."

Nixon's order, which is the one in effect today, allows the government in the form of FEMA to suspend the Constitution for literally any reason they decide to call a national emergency. I CANNOT FIND A PLAN OR EXECUTIVE ORDER ANYWHERE WHICH OUTLINES ANY PROCEDURE OR ALLOWANCE FOR THE RESTORATION OF THE CONSTITUTION AFTER A NATIONAL EMERGENCY HAS ENDED. THIS LEADS TO THE OBVIOUS CONCLUSION THAT NO RESTORATION OF THE CONSTITUTION IS CONTEMPLATED OR DESIRED BY THOSE IN POWER.

In 1975, Senator Tunney expressed concern, "We know, from what we've heard in the press, that 15,000 names were being maintained by the FBI for detention in an emergency....We also know that the IRS had its files on individual taxpayers. We know that the CIA had their Operation CHAOS and that the NSA has the records of conversations that have been intercepted electronically. My question is this: Is there anyone like yourself, General Bray, that is in control of the overall access to this data if it is maintained in a relocation site? And your answer, as I understood it, is no." Tunney continued: "General Bray, I must say that I still don't know who's in control of these relocation centers....You say you don't have that knowledge and still we don't know from the...three witnesses that we had here today, that they had information as to who has control of those centers."

"I am not at liberty," Bray answered, "to describe precisely what is the role and the mission and the capability that we have at Mount Weather, or at any other precise location." I firmly believe that our Continuity of Government program has not provided continuity at all, but has been the instrument for discontinuing open and democratic government, and that the very program designed to protect Americans has actually been turned against us.

We at the executive level here were active in either OSS, the State Department, or the European Economic Administration. During those times, and without exception, we operated under directions issued by the White House. We are continuing to be guided by just such directives, the substance of which were to the effect that we should make every effort to so alter a life in the United States as to make possible a comfortable merger with the Soviet Union.

> H. Rowan Gaither
> President of the Ford Foundation
> 1953

SOURCES

"Bureaucrats Get Ready for a Presidential Order," Spotlight, Washington D.C., July 27, 1987.

Pell, Eve, "The Backbone of Hidden Government," The Nation, June 19, 1989.

Pollock, Richard P., "The Mysterious Mountain," The Progressive, March 12, 1976.

Sinkin, Lanny, "Democracy at Risk If Covert Bill Passes," ANOTHER VIEW, Los Angeles Daily News, September 19, 1990.

Weekly Compilation of Presidential Documents, Office of the Federal Register, National Archives and Records Administration, Washington D.C., 1950 to present.

Witt, Howard, "Lawyers Press U.S. on Martial Law Plan," Chicago Tribune, August 15, 1983.

CHAPTER 6

H.R. 4079 & FEMA

FEDERAL EMERGENCY MANAGEMENT AGENCY

A Tool That Can Be Used to Establish the Police State

PATRIOTS and TAX PROTESTERS:

YOU MUST NEVER BE FOUND AT HOME ON ANY HOLIDAY.

Your life depends upon how well you can obey that rule.

FEMA

(Federal Emergency Management Agency)

The following is a transcript of an audiotape with an urgent message to the people from William Cooper on the subject of H.R. 4079. We must stop the traitors now. William Cooper dictated this information to me by phone early in 1990 and I tape-recorded the information as he gave it. I made many tapes and sent them out exactly as Mr. Cooper has asked me to do and those recipients have done the same. My name is Richard Murray and I believe that William Cooper is the only man in America outside the Secret Government who truly knows what is happening and what it means to us, the average American Citizens.

[Begin tape] There's a guy by the name of Buster Horton. He's a member of FEMA, and he's a member of the interdepartmental unit which is empowered in the event of a national security emergency to become the unelected national government, a sort of FEMA secret government, so to speak.

A pretext for invoking those emergency measures can be found almost daily in the newspapers. It can be anything from the suspension of debt payments by the high bureaus of American countries, to mass runs on U.S. commercial banks — and that's an issue, by the way, that's being handled personally by the National Security Council and Brent Scocroft — to food shortages, to the drug war. The whole bit — anything, any disaster emergency declared at all, even including the oil spill from the Exxon tanker in Alaska. If the President had declared a national emergency, that could have triggered it. Any instability in the Middle East — anything, in fact.

And they've already tested their capabilities in April 1984 with REX-84A. And that was designed to test the readiness of the U.S. civilian and military agencies to respond to a serious national security crisis.

Now, the Executive order that will implement this, the Executive Order 11051, details responsibilities to the Office of Emergency Planning or FEMA. It gives authorization to put ALL Executive orders into effect in times of national emergency declared by the President, increased international tension or economical or financial crisis. (Note that it covers every conceivable domestic crisis but does not even mention war or nuclear attack.)

Now, the only thing that has to happen for FEMA to be able to implement all the executive orders, emergency executive orders, is for the President to declare a national emergency of any type, as long as it's a national emergency.

Executive Order 10995 provides for the takeover of the communications media.

Executive Order 10997 provides for the takeover of all electric, power, petroleum, gas, fuels, and minerals.

Executive Order 10988 provides for the takeover of food resources and farms.

Executive Order 10999 provides for the takeover of all modes of transportation, control of highways, seaports, etc.

Executive Order 11000 provides for mobilization of all civilians into work brigades under the Government supervision.

Executive Order 11001 provides for Governmental takeover of all health, education and welfare functions.

Executive Order 11002 designates the Postmaster General to operate a national registration of all persons.

Executive Order 11003 provides for the Government to take over airports and aircraft.

Executive Order 11004 provides for the Housing and Finance Authority to relocate communities, designate areas to be abandoned, and establish new locations for populations.

Executive Order 11005 provides for the Government to take over railroads, inland waterways and public storage facilities.

Now, all of these were COMBINED under Nixon into one huge Executive order, which allows all of this to take place if the President declares a national emergency and it can be implemented by the head of FEMA, NOT BY THE PRESIDENT. The President has already given him that power under these executive orders.

All of these were combined into Executive Order 11490 and that was signed by President Carter on July 20, 1979, and is, in fact, law.

So, if H.R. 4079 is passed and the President does what it says and declares a national emergency because of the drug situation, whether it's for one year, five years, five minutes or forever, it doesn't make any difference. FEMA then can implement all these Executive orders, take over all local, state, and national government, suspend the Constitution and do whatever they want to do.

Now, remember what North said during the Iran-Contra hearings. He said that they were prepared to suspend the Constitution of the United States. And he said if it hadn't been for their getting caught that this would have happened. And all that did was delay it. This is what is still going to happen.

Now, they've nominated (and I think he's been appointed) Maj. Gen. Calvin Franklin, who's the head of FEMA. He was nominated because of discussions proposing the removal of the implementation of the National Guard in Washington, D.C. And Maj. Gen. Franklin is or was the Commanding General of the District of Columbia National Guard.

Now, you've got to know that the National Guard would be of no help at all in combating drug traffic in Washington, D.C., or anywhere else. The primary effectiveness of the National Guard is in controlling mass civil disorders.

On March 24, President Bush issued a new Executive order delegating to the Director of FEMA powers which were vested in the President by the Disaster Relief and Emergency Assistance Act of 1988. And although the order is described by the White House as simply a technical matter, in reality the revision delegates to the FEMA Director, direct responsibility for a large number of items which were earlier only the President's prerogative. And that includes responsibility for General Federal Assistance, Federal Emergency Assistance, Hazard Mitigation, Individual and Family Grant Programs, and the power to direct other federal agencies to assist in an emergency. AND THAT'S THE KEY. All other federal agencies will come under FEMA.

Of course, the President retains the power to actually declare an emergency, but as soon as he does that, the implementation of the measures utilized will be transferred directly to the Director of FEMA. The brains behind this contingency plan for a police state were the members of the Council on Foreign Relations and the Trilateral Commission, both of which Bush is a member. And Brent Scocroft, National Security Adviser, who was a member of FEMA's Advisory Board until he was appointed by Bush to head the National Security Council, is a member of the Trilateral Commission and also a business partner of Henry Kissinger, who has been a traitor to this country for many, many years. And of course Scocroft would become the superior to FEMA in the chain of command of the National Security Emergency whenever it is declared.

The FEMA Advisory Board is dominated by Prof. Samuel P. Huntington. In 1978 Huntington drafted for Jimmy Carter Presidential Memorandum 32, which led to the creation of FEMA in 1979. And he's a Harvard Professor.

He wrote the "Seminal Peace" for the Trilateral Commission in the mid-1970s, recommending that democracy and economic development be discarded as outdated ideas. He wrote, as co-author of the book *Crises in Democracy*, "We have come to recognize that there are potential desirable limits to economic growth. There are also potentially desirable limits to the indefinite extension of political democracy. A Government which lacks authority will have little ability short of cataclysmic crisis to impose on its people the sacrifices which may be necessary."

All of Huntington's ideas were rewritten into National Security Decision Directive 47, which is in NSDD 47, and that was enacted by President Reagan on July 22, 1982. It identified important areas to be upgraded, such as the nation's industrial base to maintain the national defense, but it nonetheless — and this is very important — laid the groundwork for the secret government's options to institute a police state, and its title is Emergency Mobilization Preparedness. It ordered preparedness measures that involved the waiving or modification of socioeconomic regulations that delay emergency responses and that should receive priority attention. It also specified that preparedness measures that are or may be impeded by legal constraints be identified in the priority task that lays the groundwork for the SUSPENSION OF THE CONSTITUTION.

Make copies of this tape if you want to. You don't even have to transcribe it if you don't want to. BUT GET THIS OUT TO THE PEOPLE. It's important that they understand that if H.R. 4079 is passed — they're history.

They won't pass it if we get this out to the people and tell them that this is what they're doing. Most people don't even know about it, and that's to the Secret Government's benefit. If we get this out and tell people what they're doing, then people can get on the phone and then go down and kick their Congressman's ass (which is what they should have been doing years ago) and get this thing thrown out of Congress. And the next thing they need to do is throw their Congressmen and their Senators out of Congress — and keep them out of Congress. And put their neighbors in there, people they can trust, and keep them in there for only one term. THE CONSTITUTION IS IN SERIOUS DANGER.

This has nothing to do with the right wing, left wing, or any other damn thing. It has to do with the Illuminati taking over this country and joining in the New World Order.

When you give this out to people, make sure they agree to make ten copies and send them to all their friends. [*End of tape*]

I decided that the transcript of this tape says it all. Why write it again?

H.R. 4079

As of this writing H.R. 4079 is still in committee and has not been subjected to a vote. It is one of the most deceptive and dangerous pieces of legislation to go in front of the Congress in many years. It must be stopped at all costs. You must call your representative and stop this bill.

H.R. 4079 has included within its pages two provisions that are meant to divert attention from the fact that the bill would declare a state of national emergency for five years and would allow FEMA to literally take over local, state, and federal government. This means that the Constitution of the United States could be suspended.

The diversions used are terrible if allowed to sneak through. One is a clause that would eliminate the 4th amendment to the Constitution and the other would eliminate the 8th amendment to the Constitution. The diversion would cause heated argument over these two provisions, resulting in some sort of compromise while allowing the declaration of a 5-year state of national emergency to sail right through Congress and become signed into law. **If that happens it's good-bye USA, hello New World Order.**

Call your Congressman and insist that he/she deliver into your hands a complete copy of H.R. 4079 immediately. Do not take no for an answer. Read it and defeat it.

[Added before press time: H.R. 4079 may have been secretly passed just as S.B. 2834 was passed and H.R. 4079 may be Public Law 101-647 signed into law by President Bush on November 29, 1990. If this has occurred, then we are **already** *subject to a FEMA takeover. I am attempting to acquire a copy of P.L. 101-647. This late-breaking new was furnished by a Congressional staff member and has not been verified as of January 8, 1991.]*

SOURCES

"Bureaucrats Get Ready for a Presidential Order," *Spotlight*, Washington D.C., July 27, 1987.

Codification of Presidential Proclamations and Executive Orders, Office of the Federal Register, National Archives and Records Administration, Washington D.C., 1/20/61–1/20/85.

Murray, Richard, transcript of phone conversation with William Cooper, FEMA & H.R. 4079, San Diego, California, Winter 1989.

Pell, Eve, "The Backbone of Hidden Government," *The Nation*, June 19, 1989.

Pollock, Richard P., "The Mysterious Mountain," *The Progressive*, March 12, 1976.

Quinde, Herbert, article from Executive Intelligence Report News Service, Washington D.C., April (no year on document), uploaded to my computer BBS by anonymous user.

Sinkin, Lanny, "Democracy at Risk If Covert Bill Passes," ANOTHER VIEW, *Los Angeles Daily News*, September 19, 1990.

Weekly Compilation of Presidential Documents, Office of the Federal Register, National Archives and Records Administration, Washington D.C., 1950 to present.

Witt, Howard, "Lawyers Press U.S. on Martial Law Plan," *Chicago Tribune*, August 15, 1983.

Author's Note: The following report by Dr. Pabst concerning FEMA and concentration camps in the United States is photographed and printed exactly as written.

IN THE UNITED STATES

A National Emergency: Total Takeover

(713) _out of service._

This is Dr. William R. Pabst. My address is 1434 West Alabama Street, Houston, Texas 77006. My telephone number is: area code 713 521-9896. This is my 1979 updated reported on the concentration camp program of the Department of Defense of the United States.

On April 20, 1976, after a rapid and thorough investigation, I filed suit on behalf of the people of the United States against various personages that had a key part in a conspiratorial program to do away with the United States as we know it. This is a progress report to you, the plaintiffs, you, the People of the United States. The civil action number is 76-H-667. It is entitled, "Complaint Against the Concentration Camp Program of the Dept of Defense". It was filed in the U.S. District Court for the southern district of Texas, Houston division. The judge responsible for the case was Judge Carl Bue.

You have no doubt heard the story: Once upon a time, under the Nazi regime in Germany, a man worked on an assembly line in a baby carriage factory. His wife was going to have a baby, but the Nazi government would not let anybody buy a baby carriage. The man decided he would secretly collect one part from each department and assemble the carriage himself. When this was done he and his wife gathered up the pieces and assembled it. When they were finished they did not have a baby carriage; they had a machine gun.

And that is exactly the situation that I am going to present to you at this time. The Center for the Study for Democratic Institutions recently completed a proposed constitution for the "Newstates of America". The Center is Rockefeller funded. To give you an indication of the type of constitution proposed, the term "national emergency" is mentioned 134 times. The document did not have a Bill of Rights and the right to own arms was taken away. At the same time, House Concurrent Resolution #28 awaited for calling a constitutional convention on or before July 4, 1976. The presiding officer of such an event would have been Nelson Rockefeller, Vice ᴾresident and president pro tem of the Senate. This particular resolution awaited in committee. Obviously money would not be spent on these massive programs unless there would be the chance for the actual implementation of such a scheme.

However, in case the American people do not voluntarily adopt a new constitution less troublesome to those who desire dictatorship, there is Executive Order #11490, which will include its predecessors when it is cited herein. The Executive Order authorizes the secretaries of the various agencies to prepare for any "national emergency" type situation - including, but not limited to, those specified in the Executive Order itself. If you read the Order, there is nothing at all left to the imagination. For any conceivable pretense a national emergency may be declared based

2

upon this frightening decree, dated October 1969. The Order itself was prefaced in March of '69 by another Executive Order which established the federal regions and their capitals. All the departments of the government were involved, including the L.E.A.A. (Law Enforcement Assistance Administration) and H.E.W. (Health, Education and Welfare). Congressman Larry McDonald has revealed to Congress that various guerrilla and terrorist groups were being financed by the federal government. If they (the terrorist groups) actually began insurgent activities, Executive Order #11490 would be activated.

But as mentioned previously, if you will read Executive Order #11490, you will see that a "national emergency" may be declared for any conceivable pretense whatsoever. If the Order itself were activated, here is what would happen: The next day you and your family would be standing in front of your local post office with your neighbors; the front door bursting with block-long lines of people waiting to be registered. After waiting in line with your family for hours, you finally get channeled through the doors. Once inside, you overhear the postal clerk with his sidearm on telling a frightened restrant, "Look, there is nothing I can do. The truck behind the building will take you to a work camp where you have been assigned. Your wife has been assigned to a factory and there's nothing I can do." Then your son or daughter looks up at you with a quivering voice and asks, "Dad, why are we here?"

Implementing the New Government

Well, you see there's much more to life in a "free country" than paying your mortgage. You have to be aware of what is going on and act accordingly and participate in government; that is, get involved. Examining the organization chart on Executive Order #11490 to discover how we have all helped finance (through our tax dollars) the mechanics of the overthrow of our Constitution, Executive Order #11490 designates certain authorities to the Office of Emergency Preparedness -- which in turn designates authority to the various departments of the federal government.

If Order were implemented, the Post Office Department would be responsible for a national registration. The State Department would be responsible for the protection of the United Nations personnel or property and prevention of escape from the United States. The Department of Defense would be responsible for the expropriation of industry; direction of services and national production system; control of censorship; and communication expropriation of non-industrial facilities. The Commerce Department would be responsible for expropriation, selection and international distribution of commodities (which would be the actual looting of the United States), census information and human resources.

The Treasury Department would be responsible for collection of cash and non-cash items and the re-creation of evidence of assets and liabilities. The Justice Department would have concurrent responsibility with the Department of State for prevention of escape from the United States; for replentishing the stockpile of narcotics; for a national police force; for correctional and penal institutions; for mass feeding and housing of prisoners and for use of prisoners to augment manpower - which would be slave labor.

3

The Federal Bank (which is not a FEDERAL bank) would be responsible for regulation of withdrawal of currency. The G.S.A. (General Services Administration) would be responsible for confiscation of private property for government use. Health, Education and Welfare would be responsible for nationalization of education (which the Department of Education has already done), health services, hospitals and mental institutions. The Labor Department would be responsible for recruiting manpower; selecting manpower; referring manpower; and allocating manpower so each particular person that was registered at the post office in this national registration would be told where he (or she) was going to work. H.U.D. (Housing and Urban Debvelopment) would be responsible for transfer of persons to temporary or permanent housing in regional emergency planning and cooperation. The Transportation Department is responsible for emergency enforcement and control and movement of passengers and the emergency operation of the Alaska railroad.

There are two specific agencies here that we need to look at and to keep in mind. They are: H.E.W. and Justice (Department), as those two agencies are related to the Department of Defense; The various military departments are part of the Department of Defense. Under it, we have the Secretary of Army, Chief of Staff, Deputy Chief of Staff of Personnel and law enforcement, U.S. Army's forces command, and continental Army Reserve & National Guarkd. And under that we have the four armies dividing up the United States. Under the Fifth Army we have the provost marshal, who is directly connected to the Deputy Chief of Staff for law enforcement personnel. Under the provost marshal for the Fifth Army we have the 300 Military Police Prisoner-of-War (POW) Command at Livonia, Michigan.

At this point I quote from retired Adm. Elmo Zumwalt's book, ON WATCH, Kissinger states, "I believe the American people lack the will to do the things necessary to achieve parity and to maintain maritime superiority. I believe we must get the best deal we can in our negotiations before the United States and the Soviets both perceive these changes and the balance that occurs. When these perceptions are in agreement, and both sides know the U.S. is inferior, we must have gotten the best deal we can. Americans at that time will not be happy that I have settled for second, but it will be too late."

Zumwalt said, "Then why not take it to the American people? They will not accept the decision to become second best while we are in a position of Gross National Product twice that of the U.S.S.R."

Kissinger responds, "That's a question of judgement. I judge that we will not get their support, and if we seek it and tell that fact, as we would have to, we would loose our negotiating leverage with the Soviets."

Zumwalt stated, "But isn't that the ultimate immorality in a democracy; to make a decision for the people of such importance without consulting them?'

Kissinger stated, "Perhaps, but I doubt that there are 1 million who could even understand the issue."

Zumwalt responded, "Even if that presumtion is correct, those 1 million can

4

influence the opinions of the majority of the people. I believe it is my duty to take the other course."

Kissinger responded, "You should take care, lest your words result in a reduction in the Navy budget."

So we see what the intention of the State Department is regarding the People. Another fact: On December 30, 1975, the California National Guard announced in a press release (which I have) that the state's Military Police battalions were organized and trained to provide immediate response to virtually <u>every</u> civil and man-made disaster, as well as to assist law enforcement officers in emergency situations; to carry out their law enforcement as well as their military mission. When I asked four of the defendants in this case for their mission statement they did not provide it - although they say it is public information.

The training spoken of for the California National Guard covers such subjects as dealing with individual civilians/civil population, detention procedures, citizen's rights, and similar matters. And you know as well as I do that, when there is Martial Law, or Martial Rule, <u>citizens have no rights</u> - because the Constitution is pre-empted. Even the uniforms of the National Guards who participate in this program are different from the regular uniforms. Army spokesman will not reveal more about the uniforms. But the Los Angeles Sheriff's Department para-military units, who have received this training also, have army fatigues dyed black for their uniforms.

A further fact is the disaster preparedness plan for the Marine Corp Supply Center in Barstow, California. Quoting from that document" "Under the Constitution and the laws of the United States, the preservation of law and order is the responsibility of <u>local</u> and <u>state</u> government. And the authority to maintain the peace and enforce the law is invested in the authorities of those goverments." There are specific exemptions to the above concept. One of these pertains to federal intervention to civil disturbances in certain situations. Military commanders are deemed to have the inherent authority to take any measure <u>reasonably</u> necessary for the protection of life and property in the event of a sudden unexpected public calamity which dirupts the normal process of government and presents an emergency so eminent as to make it dangerous to await instructions from appropriate authorities. This includes Law Enforcement duties. The manual mentions something called "Garden Plot Forces," which we will discuss at length in a few minutes.

Don Bell (who writes a weekly report) reported on July 25, 1975, that in May of 1975, the 303 Civil Affaires group of the U.S. Army Reserves in Kearny, New Jersey, conducted an exercise to sharpen plans for a <u>military takeover of the state government in New Jersey</u>. According to Colonel Frances Clark, they had conducted similar studies on how to seize municipal and county government over the past few years. But this was the first time they had studied STATE government. Such units were trained during World War II to operate captured governments in the foreign. We never had federal troops trining to take over governments in the United States. When local violence or catastrophe struck, the National Guard - under command of the governor - went into action. This is definitely <u>not</u> the situation at this time. . . . .

Controlling the Masses

5

On February 16, 1975, in the SAN GABRIEL VALLEY TRIBUNE, it was reported that the L.E.A.A. (funded by the Department of Justic) and the Police Foundation (funded by the Ford Foundation) are prime movers toward implementing a national police force. Each, however, contends they support local police agencies. The total program involces military units that have the function of taking over the admini- stration of local and state governments. That program is "Operation Cable Splicer" - by Army civil affairs groups, a sub-plan of "Operation Garden Plot" (the Martial Law program).

The method by which the national police concept is being presented to the public has changed. It was first disguised under the cover of protection against civil disturbances. This program was as follows:

A.   Keep the people from gathering in the streets.
B.   Isolate and neutralize the revolution's leadership.
C.   Dispersal of crowds and demonstrators.

This is followed by successful prosecution in order to: (1) Validate the action of police; (2) Denying the arrestees propaganda materials; and (3) Denying them the opportunity to recover money damages against the police for arresting them.

Let me quote for you the scenario which was developed for Caple Splicer One, Two and Three, to justify the needs for dealing with civil disturbances: "Phase One: an arrest and shooting provoke crowd unrest and threats against public officials and a riot begins to form. Phase Two: police vehicles are ambushed, various attempted assasinations of public officials occur, destruction and raiding of armories occur, and thousands of people begin to gather and local police loose control. Phase Three: increased movement of rioters and the crowds must be dispursed before they become sympathetic with the rioters. The National Guard and the local police loose control."

This scenario provides for an orderly transition from state to federal control. The Deputy Attorney General of California commented, at a Cable Splicer Three conference, that anyone who attacks the State - even verbally - becomes a revolutionary and an enemy by definition. They are the enemy and must be destroyed. This program was taught in almost every state west of the Mississippi River and included as participants local active military, reserve military, and civilian police. The course name was "Civil Emergency Management Course". The official explanation that was to be given, if any questions were asked about the program, was: "This activity is a continuous, joint law enforcement-military liaison effort and a continuation of coordination established last year."

In 1976, the OAKLAND TRIBUNE carried the most complete explanation of what is planned. It is reported in it entirety in the NATIONAL CHRONICLE which added an analysis to the story. (The OAKLAND TRIBUNE's editor died suddenly after the story was published.) And, I quote:

Last Saturday the California National Guard unveiled a new Law Enforcement Assistance Force - L.E.A.F., a specially trained and

6

outfitted Military Police unit, whose members will serve as shock -troups in the state's war against political protesters and demonstrators.

I saw a full-dress exhibition of what the California National Guard has planned for the next American revolution. Helicopters, SWAT teams, civilian military policemen in jack boots and helmets, twelve-guage shotguns, .38 and .45 caliber pistols, radios, walkie talkies, and electrically-controlled intelligence centers wired for instant communications with any police force in the state.

L.E.A.F. is a 1000-member unit put together this year to handle unique law enforcement problems, such as mass civil disobedience, protest demonstrations and riots. In other words, breaking heads and taking names. L.E.A.F. has the support of Governor Brown, a quarter-million dollard worth of grants from the federal government, and no public opposition from civil liberties groups.

For all its ineptitude, however, L.E.A.F. has a frightening possibility from a civil liberty standpoint. It is a direct product of the California "Cable Splicer" conferences - a series of high-level secret meetings between government officials, lawv enforcement officers, and military planners held during the late '60s and early '70s. The meetings were held as late as 1975, so far as many public records show. These were the conferences which COUNTER-SPY magazine had identified as California's "Garden Plot Sub-Plan:.

Gary Davis, Governor Brown's righthand man, says L.E.A.F. is to assist civil police not to replace them. Gary says, "Civilians could expect a civilian type law enforcement rather than what is commonly known as Martial Law." Despite this assurance, L.E.A.F.'s exercises look disturbingly like the military coup described in the novel, SEVEN DAYS IN MAY.

L.E.A.F. soldiers with nightsticks sood at intersections, stopping cars with suspicious occupants, checking I.D. cards and generally intimidating onlookers with their SWAT style uniforms, their sidearms and helmets. Perhaps more ominously, several participants in the role-playing exercises Saturday admitted that, even under simulated pressure, there has already been a number of incidents where the L.E.A.F. troops used excessive force to quell disturbances - even though their orders forbade it." (End of quote.)

Former L.E.A.FA administrator, Charles Rosgovin, is on record as having stated that local law enforcement has failed and must be replaced by a national police force. Patrick Murphy, the administrator of the Police Foundation, states, "I have no fear of a national police force. Our 40,000 police departments are not sacred." Ex -Attorney General, William Saxby, warned that, if we can go on as we are, crime will invade us and the national police will take over.

For the policemen who do not cooperate and still want to be policemen, there is the program of Contemporary Research, Inc. - and organization of psychologists, sociologists, education specialists and economic experts - who work toward a solution of many of today's social problems. The same organization develops specialized computer programming for the new world-wide military command and control system, as well as computer base systems for law enforcement agencies at all levels of government.

The L.E.A.A. alone will receive <u>over a billion dollars a year over the next 4 years</u> -even though it has been <u>ineffective</u> against crime. This is because the L.E.A.A. is not geared to fighting crime; <u>it's geared to developing a system for takeover of the United States</u> with the assistance of the Department of Defence.

The Planned Police State

One of the programs the L.E.A.A. works on in its fight against crime is <u>psycho-surgery</u>. If you don't cooperate with their programs, you are merely operated on so that you be as cooperative as an adding machine. Or, the L.E.A.A. supports drug research for the same purpose - to neutralize neurological sources of violence. Hence, as an example, if a law were passed whereby the ownership of firearms was declared to be illegal, you would be placed in one of these programs if you did not cooperate. The L.E.A.A. control exercise (at the state's level) is from the Office of Criminal Justice Planning of the Governor's Office. Here in Texas, Mr. Robert C. Flowers is still the executive director in that office. But all states have that particular department.

In May 1975, the L.E.A.A. NEWSLETTER describes the function of one of its organizations: the National Institute of Law Enforcement & Criminal Justice. This organization funds something called the "United Nations Clearinghouse" in Rome, Italy. The function of that organization is, among other things, <u>the exchange of Criminal Justice System information with the Soviet Union</u>. And it goes without saying that we have nothing to learn from the Criminal Justice System of the Soviet Unition. These incredible projects are being funded with our tax dollars.

The code name for these projects are: <u>"Garden Plot"</u> and <u>"Cable Splicer"</u>. Garden Plot is the program to control the population. Cable Splicer is the program for an orderly takeover of the state and local governments by the federal government.

An investigation was completed in November 1975 by 4 sources: the Conservative publication AMERICAN CHALLENGE; the leftist NEW TIMES; the foundation financed FUND FOR INVESTIGATIVE JOURNALISM; and Don Wood of the trustworthy OZARK SUNBEAM. It involves <u>the potential creation of a Police State</u> through the use of the Pentagon and its computerized intelligence dossier (lodged in the Pentagon basement) of thousands of citiaens by the National Guard, state and local police departments, the L.E.A.A., plain-clothes military forces, SWAT teams, and the Department of Justice.

8

Brig. Gen. J.L. Julenic, senior Army officer of the Pentagon National Guard Bureau, has admitted, "I know of no state that did not have some form of these exercises within the last year." Today the Cable Splicer handbook is composed of 6 loose-leaf 3-ring binders that are merely an outline for the impending takeover and destruction of our Constitution. The Sixth Army used the term "Cable Splicer" for the name of the operation, but it has not revealed the name of the operation in the other military areas within the U.S.

On page 4, paragraph 10, on Public Information, the instructions state: "As a means to prevent adverse publicity or misleading psychological effects in regard to coordinating, planning, and conducting this exercise, all military participants involved will perform such duties in civilian clothing when exercise oriented activities are conducted at law enforcement facilities. In the event inquiries are received regarding this exercise, the response should be limited to identifying the activity as a continuous, joint law enforcement-military liaison effort and a continuation of coordination established last year." On page 6, security guidance is explained to the effect that if anybody asks any questions, limit the information that is given out on the basis of it being in the interest of "national interest" (security).

Now, in the festivities celebrating the success of completion of the exercises, Gen. Stanly R. Larsen, the commanding general of the Sixth Army stated, "The most serious challenge facing all of us will be the challenge of discharging our legitimate responsibilities. For a significant portion of a soiety at large is likely to regard us with suspicion and to question, even challenge our authority on the basic assumption of our profession. Part of this challenge we must be prepared to deal with; a potentially dangerous portion of our society which, in truth, could well become the domestic enemy.

The manual includes instructions on operation of confinement facilities, handling and processing prisoners - including searching, transporting,, feeding, housing and handling of the special class of persons called "detainees". The plan also specifically includes a proposition for confiscation of privately-owned weapons and ammunition.

Files on Potential Prisoners

The Army has over 350 separate record centers containing substantial information on civilian-political activities. Virtually every major Army unit has its own set aside from this. The Fifth Army of San Antonio has over 100,000 filesk of its own. The overall operation command post is a domestic room at the Pentagon. There are 25 million cards on individuals and 760,000 on organizations held by the Defense Central Index of investigations alone. And this information includes political, sociological, economic and psychological profiles. All this type of information on 25 million Americans.

Since 1970, local county and state police forces all over the country have

9

undertaken crash programs to install various kinds of computerized information systems. A large portion of this is being paid for by the L.E.A.A. Beginning in 1970, Congress and the Joint Chiefs of Staff ordered the destruction of all these data banks, but they were not destroyed. All the outlawed collection is now located at Mt. Weather, Clark County, West Virginia and similar Pentagon facilities designed as adjuncts to the president's emergency powers under the Executive Orders.

The cadre of specialized persons to enforce this plan are found in the U.S. Army Reserves-Military Police POW Command at Livonia, Michigan. Mr. Fennerin, of the 300th Military Police POW Command, at Livonia, told me, when I called him from the Federal Information Center at Houston, that the camps in the Command were for foreign prisoners-of-war and for "enemies of the United States". I asked him if enemies of the United States included U.S. citizens. He became angry, wouldn't deny it, and referred me to a very sinister individual at the Army Reserve facility here at Houston who I talked to; who explained to me that the prisoners were called "inventory" and "internees". He would not deny that the camps were for U.S. citizens.

I called the Pentagon, spoke with the defendant there, and then with the provost marshal for the Fifth Army, and do you know what? Not one of these persons would deny that the system was for U.S. citizens. The provost marshal for the Fifth Army - when I mentioned the names of all the camp sites - said, "Well at least you've got that right."

The names of the detention facilities that I gave him were a list that I had acquired from the OZARK SUNBEAM. That list of names was the same list of facilities designated under the old Detention Act of 1950 as "emergency detention centers". But there is only one problem: That act was supposed to have been repealed in 1971. After some research, I found out what the problem was. One congressman - when the hearings were held for the repeal of the Emergency Detention Act - mentioned that there are 17 other bits of law that provided for the same thing. So it didn't matter whether they ever repealed the Emergency Detention Act. The public was in fact tricked by the Congress of the United States!

Here are the designated sites: Tucked away in the Appalachian Mountains of centeral Pennsylvania is a bustling town of approximately 10,000 people. Fifteen to twenty years ago it was a sleepy village of 400. Allanwood, Pennsylvania is linked to New York City by Interstate 80. It takes up approximately 400 acres and is surrounded by a 10-foot barb-wire fence. It now holds approximately 300 minimum security prisoners to keep it in shape. It could hold 12,000 people from one day to the next.

Thirty miles from Oklahoma City, on U.S.66, is El Reno, Oklahoma with an approximate population of 12,000. Due west, 6 miles from town, almost in sight of U.S.66, is a complex of buildings which could pass for a small school. However, the facility is overshadowed by a guard house which appears to be something like an airport control tower - except that it's manned by a vigilant, uniformed guard. This a federal prison camp or detention center. These camps are all located near super -highways or near railroad tracks or both.

10

The federal proson at Florence, Arizona could hold 3,500 prisoners. It is presently kept in condition by approximately 400 legally convicted prisoners. Wickenburg, Arizona is famous for its municipal airport, which was once government owned. It is now occupied by a private party. It is rumored to be capable of being taken beck by the federal government without notice.

Now there are a couple other of these facilities which are probably existing under the same arrangements. This particular rumor of instant taking back without notice has existed for about 9 or 10 years. The only way it can actually be established is by looking at the local contract for the Wickenburg Municipal Airport itself,and the parties that have possession of it.

As I mentioned previously, these names were ratified by the provost marshal of the Fifth Army, who is in charge of the 300th Military Police POW Command. He is the one who verified them. He said, as I mentioned before, "Well at least you've got that right."

Some of the other locations are: Tule Lake, in California - now in private hands. It can be retaken without notice. Some of the others: we have Mill Point, West Virginia. I couldn't find a thing on Mill Point, but in that area we have all kinds of prisons. Among them are: Alderson, West Virginia, a woman's federal reformatory; Lewisburg, West Virginia, a federal prison; Greenville, South Carolina, in Greenville County, is now occupied by the State Youthful Offenders Division. Even that is a mystery to the people of the area.

At Montgomery, Alabama, we have a federal civilian prison camp at Mazwell Air Force Base. Now does _that_ sound right? There's one at Tuscon, Arizona, David Munson Air Base. In Alaska, we have Elmendorf at Eielson Air Force Base.

And that brings us to a facility in Florida called Avon Park, Florida. I sent a representative to see what was at Avon Park. He found the Avon Park Bombing and Gunnery Range, which is also listed as the 56th Combat Support Squadron of the U.S. Air Force; which is also listed as the Avon Park Correctional Institute. No one is permitted entrance and probably there is no overfly permitted because it is a bombing and gunnery range. This was one of the places ratified by the provost marshal of the Fifth Army.

In 1976, as well as on March 20, 1979, I went to the Sheriff's Dept in Houston to see if our local Sheriff's Dept had been infiltrated by these plans. Well, it appears so. I was put in contact with a Lt. Kiljan, who is in charge of some secret unit in the department. I asked him if he had participated in military training or in training with military personnel here in the Sheriff's Department. He denied it and, when I asked him if he would testify so under oath he became angry and stated, "You are just an ordinary citizen. I don't have to tell you anything." I later descovered that Lt. Kiljan is the ex-director of the Houston branch office of the U.S. Secret Service. Now where does him money come from? The area is administered by the Houston-Galveston Area Council.

In this regional-government plan, each federal region is divided into state

11

clearinghouses, and each state clearinghouse is divided into area clearinghouses. And for our area we have the Houston-Galveston Area Countil. It serves as a conduit for federal funds in two major areas: L.E.A.A. and H.E.W.

Most everbody thinks this organization (the Houston-Galveston Area Council) is for the development of the area - the geographical area here in Houston/ But it is not. It is for the development of L.E.A.A. and H.E.W. projects. Now this finds its counterpart in every commuinity across the U.S. It provides for these agencies a liaison for inter-governmental communications, interaction and coordination

Mental Cooperation in Takeover Plans

I examined their projects to see what they were doing. This regional-government program distributes federal funds for two major purposes: (1) Radio hookups between every police agency in the state to For Sam Houston; and (2) Mental health programs, including programs for the mentally ill having priority of beds and hospitals.

Another interesting fact to consider is that in the Pine Bluff Arkansas Arsenal "B-Z" is stored. It's a nerve gas which creates sleepiness, dizziness, stupor, and the incapacity to move about. According to the Associated Press, the agent can be sprayed by aerosol, injected or sprayed over large areas by a bomb. The Military has admitted that one potential use of the gas is for civilian control. So, whatever they have planned, they've also planned a way for you to go to your destination in a tranquil state of mind.

H.E.W., by law, is operated in conjunction with the United Nations through the World Health Organization. Back in 1948, the International Congress on Mental Health - a U.N. organization - declared in its pamphlet, MENTAL HEALTH AND WORLD CITIZENSHIP, that "prejudice, hostility or excessive nationalism may become deeply imbedded in the developing personality without awareness on the part of the individual concerned. In order to be effective, efforts of changing individuals must be appropriate to the successive stages of the unfolding personality. While in case of a group of society, change will be strongly resisted unless an attitude of acceptance has first been engendered.

"Principles of mental health cannot be successfully furthered in any society unless there is progressive acceptance of the concept of world citizenship," the document states. "Programs for social change to be effective require a joint effort of psychiatrists and social scientists, working together in cooperation with statesmen, administrators and others in positions of responsibility."

The three phases of the development are: (1) Mental hospitals for segregation, care and protection of persons of unsound minds; (2) Community Mental Health Care Centers, so that persons may be treated in their own neighborhoods; and (3) Child Care Centers for dealing with early difficulties of nationalism in a child's life.

Two years earlier, Maj. Gen. G.B. Chisholm, Deputy Minister of Health in

12

Canada -who later became director of United Nations World Health Organization - explained, "Self defense may involve a neurotic reaction when it means defending one's own excessive material wealth from others who are in great need. This attitude leads to war."
So his solution to the problem is: Let's redistribute the wealth among everyone.

Further, the reinterpretation and eventual eradication of the individual's concept of right and wrong - which has been the basis of child training - are the belated objectives of practically all effective psychotherapies. Now, if we digress even further, to Buria (phonetic spelling), the director of the Soviet Secret Police, in the 1930s, we see that he explained the communist political strategy through the use of "mental healings" of psychiatry:

"Psycho-politics is the art and science of asserting and of maintaining a dominion over the thoughts and loyalties of individuals, officers, bureaus, and masses, and the effecting of the conquest of enemy nations through mental healing. You must work," he stated, "until every teacher of psychology unknowingly or knowlingly teaches only communistic doctrine under the guise of psychology."

If you look at the Russian manual of instruction of psycho-political warfare, we see in chapter 9, "Psycho-political operations should at all times be alert to the opportunities to organize for the betterment of the community mental health centers."

Now, under the new national Mental Health program at this moment there are more than 600 of these community mental health centers across the United States. The whole thing was promoted by Dr. Stanly F. Yolles, who was the director of the National Institute of Mental Health in 1969. And, he stated back then that the newest trend in treating mental illness is care at local health care centers, where the patient is not isolated from his (or her) family and friends. They have been working on this program for 46 years publicly and, now across the U.S. - through your tax dollars - you have 603 cneter (to be exact); Community Health Centers that are all part of this program.

And this is how they are part of the program. (It has already happened): In the mid-1950s, there was set into motion an interesting chain of events. About 1956, the Alaska Mental Health Bill was proposed and later passed. It granted approximately $12 million and 1 million acres of public land to Alaska so that it could develop its own mental health program. Now, this was a little abnormal since Alaska only had a little over 400 people who were classified as mentall ill!

After the bill was passed, Alaska passed its own, enabling legislation to get into the mental health business. They started by adopting the essential elements of the Public Health Service Draft Act on the hospitalization of the mentally ill in the old "Interstate Compact on Mental Health" - now called the Uniform Mental Health Act. There were no provisions for jury trial in it or anything else. You would just be picked up and taken to the Alaskan-Siberian Asylum - incommunicado - and the state would also confiscate all of your personal and real property! And they actually tried to do it in 1954 in the case of Ford vs. Milinak, which declared the act as adopted in another state (the state of Missouri) as unconstitutional.

13

But the act itself still exists - and modified - but essentially in the same form, the Uniform Mental Health Act, to which approximately 6 states subscribe. And, in passing mowt State Constitutions - if you will check them from the period of 1935 - made a part of their constitution the practice of having a person submit to a 90-day mental examination to determine his (or her) sanity, without any provisions for a trial by jury. This was part of the national program at that time.

In this act, the governor could have anyone picked up and sent to the Mental Health Institution in Alaska or elsewhere. The results, as rumors, back in the 1950s, were that there was in fact a sinister, Frankenstein-type mental health prison in Alaska. I wrote to Alaska (the officials that is) and asked them for a description of the land of 1 million acres that they were eligible to receive, under the Alaska Mental Health Act. And I also asked them for a copy of the inventory they ran for their facilities back at that same time. Well, so far no answer. And probably I will never receive an answer without a court order.

But through the years, there was a spot in Alaska that was continually referred to: Southeast of Fairbanks; Southwest of Fairbanks; northwest of Fairbanks - somewhere near Fairbanks. Then I received information that a pilot had flown over the area once and had had his license revoked. And so, for $1.85 each, I ordered the low-level navigation maps from the federal government for Alaska and located the Alaska-Siberian Asylum for the treatment of enemies of the United States. It's right where rumor over the past 20 years had placed it: Southeast of Fairbanks. It stands out like a sore thumb! It's the only ^{one} of that geometric configuration within the state of Alaska, and you will note a black line running up through Fairbanks and down over near that area of the map. That is the railroad that the Department of Transportation would take the emergency operation of, under the Executive Order - if the Excecutive Order went into effect. And H.E.W. would be responsible for making a dermination of whether or not you were mentally disturbed because of your nationalistic tendencies, your love for the United States, or your adherence to any political or religious doctrine.

But let's look a little further into the type of program that the L.E.A.A. is paying for through the Department of Justice, the Federal Bureau of Prisons - located in the back woods of North Carolina, near a tiny village called Butner - is constructing a mammoth 42-acre research complex for prisoners from throughout the East. Who will be sent for experiments to test new behaviorial programs and techniques? Target date for completion of the entire system is ironically 1984.

And so, they're using right now, under the L.E.A.A. program, something called anectine. Punishment for troublesome behavior within the prison is being done by drugs and shock, likely to be the most selected examples of programs that have made use of anectine - a derivative of South American curari. Anectine was originally used as a beginning factor to electro-convulsive shock. Such shocks applied to the head are so strong they can break and graze bones under the strain of resulting muscle contractions. Since anectine paralyzed the muscles without dampening consciousness or the ability to feel pain, by first injecting the inmates with it, researchers can turn up the voltage as high as they want without cracking the inmate's skeleton when his body is thrown into convulsions by the jolt.

14

What the anectine does, in short, is to simulate death within 30 to 40 seconds of injection. It brings on paralysis first, with the small rapidly moving muscles in the nose, fingers and eyes, and then in the diaphram and the cardiovascular system. As a result, the patient cannot move or breath and yet remains fully conscious, as though drowning and dying. This from the 1974 publication, HUMAN BEHAVIOR.

The People vs. the Conspirators

The federal government answered my suit, in June (1976), by filing an unsworn general denial of everything that I had alleged. I spoke with the assistant U.S. Attorney in charge of the case and asked him if he had gone to the trouble to call any of the parties mentioned in the suits - since I had provided not only the addresses, but their telephone numbers to provide a faster means of investigation. He said he had not. He had not even done a minimal amount of investigation of the case, but yet he filed a denial of my allegations.

I filed a motion, in the mean time, to take the deposition of the person who writes the training programs for the concentration cam guards, Mr. Richard Burrage - the 75th Maneuver Air Command at Army Reserve Center at Houston, Texas - stating the, in light of all the recent activity of government agents, one of the agencies involved might attempt to murder this key witness, the author of the training camp program. The federal judge denied my motion, stating that I had not quoted enough cases to him justifying my request. However, he was also aware that there were no cases existing on this set of facts but, as you will see as I go along with this report, he chose to ignore it.

I then made an agreement with the assistant U.S. Attorney to take the deposition of Mr. Buirrage. After I'd made the arrangements, the U.S. Attorney refused to voluntarily go along with taking the deposition. It is very difficult to find justice in our system of courts. Law is usually practiced by the "buddy system," hence the court rules are overlooked or not followed.

On July 29, a hearing was held at the magistrate of Norman Black, U.S. District Court in Houston. The courtroom was completely filled with spectators. And although the news media had been contacted, no representatives of the press were there. There is a new media blackout on this matter here in Houston.

Brief oral arguments were presented. The U.S. Attorney explained that I was not the proper person to bring the suit because, although the free exercise of my constitutional rights was threatened by the concentration camp program, as alleged, it did not constitute my injury. The magistrate was impressed with the information I had thus far collected and stated that he would bring it to the attention of the federal judge. The U.S. Attorney tried to have my investigation of the case halted, but the magistrate would not go along that far with a pre-arranged decision.

As an additional indication of what I was up against, the original hearing was scheduled for 10:30 in the morning. However, the U.S. Attorney secretly had the time

15

changed to 2:30 in the afternoon. The magistrate gave the U.S. Attorney permission to file for motion to dismiss because he felt that the concentration camp program - to be used for persons who exercise their freedom of speech - did not present any injury.

Now, on July 23, I had placed in the HOUSTON POST and in the HOUSTON CHRONICLE newspapers the following advertisement in the legal section: "Solicitation for witnesses in Civil Action 78-H-667, Federal District Court of Houston, People Ex Rel. William Pabst vs. Gerald Ford et al. The action titled: Complaint Against the Concentration Camp Program of the Department of Defense. Attention: If you have participated in Operation Garden Plot, Operation Cable Splicer, the 300th Military Police Prisoner of War Command, or the Army Reserve Civil Affairs group, youmay be involved in a program that needs to be disclosed for this suit. To give your testimony call or write, (and here I placed my name, address and telephone number)."

As I previously mentioned, there is a news media blackout on the story here in Houston. Both newspapers refused to carry the ad. First, at the HOUSTON POST, I had to threaten them with a law suit to carry out the ad, even though I was paying for it. And then at the HOUSTON CHRONICLE, I had to meet with the president and various vice presidents because a refusal from that paper had come up from their own lawyers. Both nespapers finally carried it, but only after two days of complaining. The initial response of both papers was, "We don't carry stories like that" and "Don't you think that the people planning the concentration camps have our best interests in mind?" As you will hear for yourselves, the policies definitely do not reflect our best interests.

The next event that occurred was that the U.S. Attorney filed a "Statement of Authority," showing the reasons that he could find why I should not be allowed to take depositions to get more information from the person who was writing the concentration camp guard training program. However, his brief was completely filled with misquotes of the law from many cases. He would mention the case and then invent whatever the case should say. In my brief to the court, at this point, I notified the judge of the violation of the law requiring honesty in such matters. But the notification was ignored by the judge, who apparently sanctioned this most dishonest of acts commonly known as "quoting out of context".

The Geneva Convention

My brief was filed in August 31, formal arguments were set. The new courtroom of the magistrate was almost filled again. However, no one from the news media showed up for this hearing either. The few who were contacted had been told not to go; they would loose their jobs.

At the hearing, I introduced evidence that heretofore had never been introduced in any court of law in the U.S. The U.S. Attorney had denied, you will remember, everything in my suit without so much as even a tiny investigation. So I introduced into evidence the following letter from the Department of the Army, Office of the Deputy Chief of Staff of Personnel, signed by one B. Sergeant, Col. G.S., Acting Director of Human Resources Development.

16

The letter states, "On behalf of President Ford, I am replying to your letter 27 May, 1976, regarding a new article in the DALLAS MORNING NEWS. As much as he would like to, the president cannot reply personally to every communication he receives. Therefore, he has asked the departments and agencies of the federal government in thos instances where they have special knowledge or special authority underlogued.

"For this reason your communication was forwarded to officials of the Department of Defense. Within the Department of Defense, the Army is responsible for custody and treatment of enemy prisoners of war and civilian internees as defined under terms of the Geneva Convention of 1949. Therefore, the Army is prepared to detain prisoners of war and detainees as defined in Article IV of the 1949 Geneva Convention relative to the treatment of prisoners of war and protection of civilian persons.

"It is U.S. policy that its Armed Forces adhere to the provisions of international law to set the example for other countries of the world to follow and respecting the rights and dignity of those who become victim of international conflict. It should be noted that the Army program is designed for implementation during conditions of war between the U.S. and one or more foriegn countries. The Army had no plans nor does it maintain detention camps to imprison American citizens during domestic crises."

The problem with this letter is that it's not true, and that's why I'm going to discuss it at this point. First of all, in verifying the authenticity of the claims in the letter, I checked the Geneva text. There is no article in the Geneva Convention entitled as the letter states. There is, however, on each one of the classifications: "Protection of War Victims/Civilian Persons" and a separate article on "Prisoners of War". That was the first discrepancy.

Then I turned to Article IV of the Geneva Convention. That article did not set up any requirements or authorizations for military units of any type and does not even suggest it. Hence, the second discrepancy.

The next problem with the letter from President Ford's representative is that it states that the prisoner of war guard program is set up for the implementation for "conditions of war between the U.S. and one or more (foreign) countries." However, Article III of the Geneva Convention reads that the treaty applies to (and I am quoting) "In case of an armed conflict, not of an international character, occurring within the territory of one of the high contracting parties." Obviously an armed conflict occurring within one's own territory did not mean between one or more of the parties to the treaty, especially if only one is involvedkkkk. Now, the examples of this type of conflict are: civil war, armed insurgency and guerilla activities. In other words, they're speaking of a domestic conflict.

An even more shocking item is found in the last pages of the 1949 Geneva Convention under "Protection of War Victims/Civilian Persons". You will find the index card, the identification card, forms to be used to writing your family, and

17

everything necessary for the administration of a concentration camp is contained in this treaty that the U.S. signed and ratified. Further, if there is a conflict in the U.S. involving only the U.S. this convention or treaty can go into operation - which includes the procedures for setting up the concentration camps.

Article LXVIII of the Convention states (and I paraphrase): If you commit an offense that is soley intended to harm the occupying power, not harming the life or limb of members of the occupying power, but merely talking against such a force - such as Martial Law situation _ you can be imprisoned provided that the duration of such imprisonment is proportionate to the offense committed. Well, President Dwight Eisenhower didn't feel that provision was strong enough. So he had the following additions placed in the treaty which states: "The U.S. reserves the right to impose the death penalty in accordance with the provisions of ARticle LXVIII without regard to whether the offenses referred to therein are punishable by death under the law of the occupied territory at the time the occupation begins.."

So not only can you be imprisoned for having exercised freedom of speech; you can be put to death under the provisions of the Geneva Convention in 1949 for having exercised, or attempting to exercise freedom of speech.

The next item that I introduced into evidence was a field manual: FM 41-10, CIVIL AFFAIRS OPERATION. You will remember at the outset that I mentioned Civil Affairs groups. Let me quote to you from that manual what one of the functions of the Civil Affairs activities includes: "Item 4. Assumption of full or partial executive, legislative and judicial authority over a country or area". So let's see what a "country or area" is defined as in the same manual. It includes: "small towns in rural areas, municipalities of various population sizes, districts, counties, provinces or states, regions of national government".

Nowhere in the manual does it exclude this program from being put into effect right here in the United States. As a matter of fact, in Kearny, New Jersey, the Civil Affairs group went into that area and practiced taking over that government unit. And yet the Army - in its letter of June 16 - states that these programs are not for us. Yet they are practiced here in the United States under conditions that can only occur here at home.

The study outline of field manual, FM 41-10, on page j-24, under "Penal Institutions 1-B," you see there is a program on concentration camps and labor camps - number, location and capacity. It is important to note that a concentration camp and labor camp are always located near eather other for obvious reasons.

Again on page d-4 of the same manual, you'll find a sample receipt for seized property; a sample receipt written English and containing terminology applicable to only U.S. territory.
On page 8-2 of the same manual, under the heading "Tables of Organization and Equipment," we find that there are 3 other organizations that would be working along with the Civil Affairs operation: the Chemical Service Organization, the Composite Service Organization, and the Psychological Operations Organization, along with the various Civil Affairs organizations.

In July of that year (1976), the following Civil Affairs groups met with the following airborne groups at a staging area in Fort Chaffee, Arkansas. A staging area is where military units meet before they go into action. They met with the 32nd Airborne and part of the 101st Airborne; the 321st Civil Affairs group of San Antonio, Texas headquarters; the 362nd Civil Affairs brigade from Dallas, Texas; the 431st Civil Affairs company from Little Rock, Arkansas headquarters; the 306th Civil Affairs group, and William Highlin. The 486th Civil Affairs company from Tilsa, Oklahoma; the 418th Civil Affairs company from Kansas City, Missouri; the 307th Civil Affairs group from St. Louis, Missouri; the 490th Civil Affairs group from Abilene, Texas; the 413th company from Hammon, Louisiana; the 12th S.S. group, 2nd Battalion (headquarters unknown).

They're ready to go into action. The problem is, as it appears, they were ready to take over the entire government of the United States as their mission set out. One man who attended this staging area talked to a Civil Affairs Sgt. and asked him what his job was. The Sgt. explained that the civilians of this country will really be surprised some day when the Civil Affairs groups begin to operate the government.

Now, the Department of the Army still maintains that all this is not for the United States - yet this training continues here for us. The evidence is overwhelming; the plan exists for the imprisonment of millions of U.S. citizens. And even though all this information was presented to the federal magistrate, he still felt that no one was injured by such a plot.

On the 2nd day of September, 1976, the magistrate recommended to the federal judge that the case be dismissed. And the sole basis for his reasoning to dismiss was that we have to be actually physically injured before we can maintain a law suit of this type. He did not feel that, although all this active planning, preparation and training was going on, that any U.S. citizen had been injured - even though the citizen may fear exercising his (or her) freedom for fear of being detained and imprisoned in a concentration camp at a later date.

Ignoring the Constitution

The case of Tatum vs. Laird, heard before the Supreme Court in 1974, is a case in point. It involved the Army intelligence collecting aparatus, which was developing a list of names of persons whom the Army felt were troublesome. The Supreme Court held that the making of lists of this type did not, of and by itself, present any injuries. The minority opinion in that case was that the injury, in the case with a program such as this mzde people afraid to use their freedom of speech for fear of being sent to jail for it. But majority did not buy that argument.

The difference between that case and this case - although we also have the computer program - is that we have something much further past that point; the concentration camp guard program and the Civil Affairs program for the taking over of all functions of our government. In light of that, the federal judge said that this is

19

not an injury. As a matter of fact, the U.S. Attorney alleged that even if people were placed in concentration camps, if they were all treated the same they would still not have the right to go to federal court.

On the 20th day of September, I filed a memorandum to notify the magistrate and the federal judge that I had discovered that the federal government had a program for number of years to suspend our constitutional right of the writ of habeas corpus. This information substantiated the complaint. Habeas corpus is the name of that legal instrument utilized to bring someone before a judge when that person is being illegally imprisoned or detained so that he (or she) may obtain his (or her) freedom. The Constitution states that the writ of habeas corpus shall never be suspended.

I found the disturbing information in a report: 94-755, 94th Congress, 2nd Session Senate, April 26, 1976, entitled "Intelligence Activities and the Rights of Americans Book II." On page 17-d, entitled "First Amendment Rights," the report states that more importantly "the government surveillance activities in the aggregate, whether expressly intended to do so, to deter the exercise of First Amendment rights by American citizens who become aware of the government's domestic intelligence program."

Beginning on page 54, it is stated that, beginning in 1946 - 4 years before the Emergency Detention Act of 1950 was passed - the FBI advised the Attorney General that it had secretly compiled a secret index of potentially dangerous persons. The Justice Department then made tentative plans for emergency detention based on suspension of the privilege of the writ of habeas corpus. Department officials deliberately avoided going to Congress. When the Emergency Detention Act of 1950 was passed, it did not authorize the suspension of the writ of habeas corpus. But shortly after passage of that act, according to a bureau document, Attorney General J.H. McGraf told the FBI to disregard it and to proceed with the program as previously outlined.

A few sentences later, on page 55, it states, "With the security index, use broader standards to determine potential dangerousness than those described in the statute." And, unlike the act, Department plans provided for issuing a master search warrant and a master arrest warrant. This is the center importance; it is the same thing that I am alleging in federal court. And yet the magistrate chose to ignore these facts also.

We have government officials not only ignoring the will of Congress, but going the opposite of what the Constitution provides by planning illegally for the suspension of the writ of habeas corpus. In addition, as mentioned before, the master search warrant and the master arrest warrant are forms fed into the computer, which print the names and addressses on them from the tapes previously prepared by the intelligence-gathering program.

As you are arrested, your home will be searched and anything found there may be confiscated. This program has existed since 1946, up to and including 1973, and without proper access to judicial discovery techniques, it can't be determined dwhether the same plan now exists under the same name or under another name right

20

<u>now</u>.

This memorandum was filed on September 28 to make the court aware of the danger that our rights of freedom of speech and lawful assembly are in. But the cour, on September 30 - after this notification was received - dismissed the case. However, in keeping with the practice of federal courts in Houston of actively participating in the obstruction of justice, I was not notified of the dismissal until the 6th of October - which gave me just 2 working days to submit any further motion in a 10-day period before time starts running for the appeal.

What I have just said regarding the federal courts in Houston is not only my opinion; the HOUSTON CHRONICAL, surprisingly, published an extensive document severely crticizing the federal courts in Houston for making up their own rules as they go along with the proceedings, as well as commenting on the communist-like Supreme Court attitude of the judges and the court personnel. My experience here has been that the court has returned to me almost every document that I have filed. Then after a gib argument, they reaccept the document, stating that they just made a mistake. In reality, the power structure doesn't want these types of cases in <u>any</u> federal court.

Summary of Evidence

On the 8th of October, I had submitted a request for finding the facts in the filing which had been established by the evidence presented:

1.   The 300th Military Police POW Command is located at Livonia, Michigan.

2.   The Department of the Army has stated that said Command exists per se the Geneva Convention of 1949, a treaty of the U.S., Article IV thereof under the title relative to the treatment of prisoners of war and protection of civilian persons.

3.   However, no such title exists in the Geneva Convention per se.

4.   Nevertheless, there are separate titles, one of which is: (a) Multilateral Protection of War Victims/Prisoners of War; (b) Multilateral Protection of War Victims/Civilian Persons.

5.   Nevertheless, Article IV of both titles does not provide for the creation of any military programs for concentration camps.

6.   Whether Mr. Fennerin, of the 300th Military Police POW Command, has stated that the purpose of the Command is for the detention of foreign prisoners of war and enemies of the United States.

7.   Further, Article III, concerning <u>civilian persons</u>, makes the treaty applicable to conflicts occurring soley within the territory of the United States that are not of an international character, which is capable of including any type of conflict in its description whether it be civil war or guerilla activity or anything else. The text

21

states: "In case of armed conflict not of an international character occurring in the territory of one of the high contracting parties, each party to a conflict shall be bound to apply to the minimum of the following provisions."

8.   Department of the Army Field Manual FM 41-10, Civil Affairs Operations of Civil Affairs Organization lists, as one of its functions, the assumption of full or partial executive, legislative and judicial authority over a country or an area and there is no specific exclusion of the United States as such a country or area.

9.   Said manual defines country along certain geographical population basis, county, state regions and national government.

10.   Said organization has, in fact, conducted practed takeovers of local and state governments in the continental United States, including, but not limited to the state of New Jersey.

11.   Said organization includes in its study outline, on page j-24, a section on concentration camps and labor camps.

12.   Said organization includes in its operations compositev service operations and psychological operations organizations.

13.   Said psychological operation, working with the U.S. Public Health Service, is prepared to operate any and/or all mental health facilities in the Unites States as tools of repression against outspoken but nonviolent political conduct of the United States citizens in conjunction with all the above, which is to be used for the same purpose.
14.   Further, the Department of Justice, in conjunction with this program, has had plans for the suspension of writ of habeas corpus since the year of 1946; said plan depriving persons being detained under this total program any means for protection against tyrannical political repression.

      The plaintiff requested that the court make findings of fact and draw conclusions of law, consistent therewith, as shown by the evidence on record before the court. The effect of this request is that the case must go back to the district judge for further consideration. I mentioned that is appeared that all this planning for concentration camps was to be directed against anyone, regardless of his polictical persuasion of ideology, who exercised freedom of speech against the established power structure of international bankers and multinational corporations. But, with Proposition 13-type movements threatening to reduce taxes throughout our nation, I foresee an activation of emergency programs so that the parasites on the federal take will continue to receive their checks.

Price of Patriotism

      In the same Senate document, on intelligence activities on the rights of Americans referred to on pages 166 and 167, you will find that the federal

**** TOP SECRET ****

government has targeted its intelligence activities against <u>one group of Americans</u>. On page 166, the first classification listed is <u>rightists and anti-communist groups</u>. And the first group on page 167 on Army surveillance lists the <u>John Birch Society</u> as a number 1 and the <u>Young Americans for Freedom</u> as the number 2 target. Therefore, the groups of U.S. American citizens considered to be the biggest enemy of the United States, by the federal government, at this time, is the <u>conservative patriot</u>, and those who assert the Constitution and individual rights.

Although this information has been available since April of this year (1979), no one has mentioned this incredible discovery that the federal government considers the patriotic conservative as its greatest enemy. I have received all kinds of information regarding this case from all across the United States.

Price of Apathy

I obtained the 1945 report of the O.S.S. (Office of Strategic Service) - the precursor of the C.I.A. - 7th Army, William W. Quin, Col. G.F.C.A.C. of the G2, on the liberation of Dachau, a concentration camp during the liberation in Germany. It contains much groups of information, but the relevant portion of the report concerns itself with the section on the townspeople. Quoting from this report, on why the people of this little town didn't complain or didn't overthrow oppressors but just continued to go along and get along even though they lost their freedom in the process, it states:

> These words crop up and up again. They are the rationalization of a man who admits that he was a member of the Nazi party. 'I was forced to do so by business reasons,' they state. We were lied to in every respect but they admit they knew the camp existed. But they saw the work detail to the inmates passing through the streets under guard and, in some instances, the S.S. behaved brutally even towards the townspeople.

> When asked if they realized that within the last 3 months before the liberation 13,000 men lost their lives within stone's throw of where the people lived, they claimed they were shocked and surprised.

> When asked if they never saw transports of dead and dying pass through the streets along the railway, they referred only to the last one. They insist that most of the trains came in at night and that they were sealed cars.

> Did they never ask what was in the endless procession of cars that came in full and always went out empty? A typical reply was, 'We were told it was all army material and booty from France.'

> It is established that anyone who stated that he saw only one train come in in the daytime was telling a flat lie. There are quite a few such people in Dachau.

23

The analysis of the anti-Nazi element of the town: (1) The people knew what was going on in the camp, even ten years prior to liberation; (2) The town did a thriving business from the concentration camp guard; (3) Ninety percent are guilty and have dabbed themselves with the blood of innocent human beings; (4) The people are to blame for their cowardice - they were all too cowardly. They didn't want to risk anything. And that was the way it was in all of Germany.

So you can see how the whole program is related here. My lawsuit was against one single aspect of the total program: The enforcement arm of the conspiracy - the people who make up the cadre that is going to occupy the concentration camps where enemies of the United States will be placed. Remember Solzhenitsyn's words in the GULAG ARCHIPELAGO: "Resistance should have began right there but it did not begin. You aren't gagged, you really can and you really ought to cry out that arrests are being made on the strength of false accusations. If many such outcries had been heard all over the city would arrests have no longer have been so easy."

They, the tyrants, can't work in the public eye. Those people who were so apathetic, hoping that nothing was really wrong, that nothing would happen to their persons and property, sat back and watched. The anarchists, financed by multinational interests, looted and pillaged their country.

If you think that all (that) is necessary is to pay your house notes, to pay your TV notes, to go vote when there is an election, and to stand back during the rest of the year and watch as your country and way of life are replaced by a system in which you will be a slave in a concentration camp, you - not the conspirators - are guilty because you, by silent acquiescence, invite tyranny and oppression.

And, when you have to steal food to eat because our production is for foreign use because the Department of Commerce - through Executive Order 11490 and its predecessors - is responsible for international distribution of our commodities, don't sit in a culvert hiding and eating and sondering what happened because you made it all possible.

When your family is split up and spread across the United States to do slave labor and you never see yourloved ones again, it will be your fault because you did nothing to prevent it. And, once we loose our freedom, we are never going to regain it. That is why we must stand together to prevent the loss of our freedom as citizens of the United States.

Thank you very much.

(Conclusion of taped report.)

CHAPTER 7

ANTI-DRUG ABUSE ACT of 1988

H.R. 5210
P.L. 100-690

PREPARATION FOR THE POLICE STATE

AN

ANALYSIS

H.R. 5210 / P.L. 100-690

Public Law 100-690, which was introduced to the 100th Congress as H.R. 5210, passed by Congress in September 1988 and signed by the President on November 18, 1988, is the most serious attack upon the freedoms guaranteed the citizens of the Republic of the United States of America in our Constitution since the formation of the Federal Reserve and the IRS.

The act may be cited as the Anti-Drug Abuse Act of 1988. The following titles are contained within the act.

Title I	Coordination of National Drug Policy
Title II	Treatment and Prevention Programs
Title III	Drug Education Programs
Title IV	International Narcotics Control
Title V	User Accountability
Title VI	Anti-Drug Abuse Amendments Act of 1988
Title VII	Death Penalty and Other Criminal and Law Enforcement Matters
Title VIII	Federal Alcohol Administration
Title IX	Miscellaneous
Title X	Supplemental Appropriations

The Anti-Drug Abuse Act of 1988 can be found in most college or city libraries contained in the *U.S. Code Congressional and Administrative News, Vol. 3*, 1988, with amendment and voting information in the *Congressional Quarterly Almanac, Vol. XLIV*, 1988.

The law looks innocent enough upon first glance, containing new drug-awareness and treatment programs, more law enforcement and much stricter penalties — and all to be financed with a 2.1-BILLION-dollar budget. Upon close examination, however, I discovered some really scary stuff tucked in where most citizens would never look.

The act is some 366 pages of fine (very fine) print on very small pages. It is tedious reading, as is all legislation. In fact, it was impossible to read until Nancy Batchelder, a volunteer on my research staff, enlarged each page on a copy machine. Could it be that the Congress does not want the citizens to read the contents of their legislation? I believe that is exactly the case.

One of the most frightening aspects of this legislation was the proposal to allow evidence found in a warrantless search. Congress said "illegally obtained evidence is legal to use in drug cases." Months later the Senate said no and that portion of the legislation was removed — or at least that is what we were meant to think.

The act leaves a loophole for court decisions on some mass searches/ drug tests, such as school lockers, requirement for certain jobs, and an experimental program for those getting their first driver's license. (Sec. 9005) Key words here are "mass searches/drug tests," "jobs," and "drivers license." The courts have held that if the citizens give up any right by giving what is called implied consent, then they no longer have claim to that right. The dangerous implication here is that "mass search" could mean the search of every person in, say, Chicago, Los Angeles, or New York City. Get the picture?

The proposed legislation contained a section that if passed would have taken away our right to trial by jury, and specifically stated that you could be held guilty without trial. How could any citizen or Representative or Senator even have had the guts to propose such a thing for passage into law in this country? Fortunately, it was removed by amendment, HOWEVER IN SOME CASES A TRIAL ISN'T AUTOMATIC; YOU MUST REQUEST A HEARING. (Sec. 6480) Do I have your attention yet?

$10,000 is the maximum fine for knowingly possessing any amount of a drug of any kind (even the kind that an enemy might plant in your car or home) (Sec. 6480).

Congress has asked for a study on the relationship between mental illness and substance abuse (Sec. 2071).

Congress has recommended changes for involuntary commitment for mental illness which echoes the Russian NKGB model (Sec. 2072a). The secret power structure considers PATRIOTISM and NATIONALISM to be mental illness.

Congress has asked for an evaluation of the appropriateness of administering health-service programs in conjunction with biomedical and behavioral research. IN OTHER WORDS, MIND CONTROL ON A GRAND SCALE (Sec. 2073a).

The Congress ordered in this act that "the Attorney General shall study the feasibility of prosecuting Federal drug-related offenses in a matter alternative or supplemental to the current criminal justice system." THIS IS THE BEGINNING OF A POLICE STATE (Sec. 6293).

The act states that anyone with intent to obstruct or harass the harvesting of timber on public lands can get 1 year in jail or up to 10 years if the resultant damage exceeds $10,000. Tree spiking is specifically named. WHAT IS THIS DOING IN A DRUG LAW? It's in there because Congress wanted to make an end run around environmental groups and give the timber away (Sec. 6254/1864).

Herbicides are to be used for aerial coca eradication with no consideration of what it might do to the humans or animals being sprayed. After a year of spraying the President shall determine if such use is harmful to environment or health and shall...file a report (Sec. 4202).

The act mandates the establishment of a "World Currency Control" system. This would be an international data base to analyze currency transactions filed by member countries in order to monitor large ($10,000 or more) dollar transfers. To encourage "teamwork": Prohibit noncooperative foreign countries from participating in any U.S. dollar clearing or wire-transfer system, or from maintaining any financial accounts in the U.S. (Sec. 4701).

The act gives the Secretary of the Treasury power to require ANY transaction records from ANY domestic financial institution (even those not part of the bank/savings & loan system), as well as information on ALL of the persons involved. MAKE SURE YOU UNDERSTAND WHAT THIS MEANS TO YOU PERSONALLY. This IS a police state (Sec. 6184/5326).

ALERT...ALERT

The Constitution of the United States, Article I, Section 9, paragraph 2, states:

"The Privilege of the Writ of Habeas Corpus shall not be suspended, unless when in Cases of rebellion or invasion, the Public Safety may require it."

Public Law 100-690, Sec. 7323, provides for a Special Committee on Habeas Corpus Review of Capital Sentences, appointed by the Chief Justice of the United States. The purpose of the Special Committee is to recommend to the Chief Justice of the United States, who will forward the recommendation to the chairman of the Committee on the Judiciary of the Senate, a proposal of a bill to modify Federal habeas corpus procedure.

Quotes from P.L. 100-690:

"This bill to modify habeas corpus procedure must be reported with or without recommendation by the Committee on the Judiciary of the Senate by the end of the 60th day of session after the submission of the report or the bill must be automatically placed on the appropriate calendar of the Senate.

"Once the habeas corpus bill is on the calendar, it is not debatable; it is not subject to a motion to postpone; reconsideration of the vote by which the motion is agreed to or disagreed to shall not be in order under this act. Only one motion in the Senate shall be in order pursuant to this paragraph and such motion shall be decided by a roll call vote."

SIT UP AND TAKE NOTICE!

Section 7323 states that this habeas corpus legislation is enacted by Congress "as an exercise of the rulemaking power of the Senate and as such it is deemed a part of the rules of the Senate..."

CAN YOU BELIEVE THIS TREASON?

Chapter 33 of Title 28, United States Code, is amended by adding at the end thereof Sec. 540, which states that the Attorney General and the Federal Bureau of Investigation may investigate felonious killings of officials and employees of a State or political subdivision when such investigation is requested by the head of the agency employing the official or employee killed, and under such guidelines as the Attorney General or his designee may establish.

Notice that the above paragraph does not say by invitation of the State, but says by the employing agency. Once the Feds are involved they always hold jurisdiction. THIS IS SERIOUS! It could establish the legal precedence for justification of a police state once the courts rule that the States have given up their right to jurisdiction under this act. Notice that it only involves crimes of a POLITICAL nature.

Businesses are required to report all cash transactions of $10,000 or more (Sec. 7601/60501-IRS). (It has been reported to me but not verified by me that this requirement has been lowered to $3000.) THIS HAS NOTHING TO DO WITH DRUGS BUT HAS EVERYTHING TO DO WITH THE IRS.

The act establishes a requirement to record and verify the I.D. of a purchaser of a money order or other financial instrument of $3000 or more (Sec. 6184/5325). WHY?

This is a big one. The act orders a study to be made on whether to withdraw $100 bills and $50 bills from circulation (Sec. 6187). THIS WOULD VIRTUALLY PROPEL US INTO A CASHLESS SOCIETY.

$23 MILLION DOLLARS HAS BEEN ALLOCATED FOR A MACHINE-READABLE IDENTITY DOCUMENT PROGRAM. The excuse used is to be able to identify known criminals who attempt to cross borders. The type of border is not named (required in legislation) and could be the border of your city, county or state. It also raises the question of how they are going to get the criminals to accept the identity document program without REQUIRING ALL CITIZENS TO PARTICIPATE (Sec. 4604).

This data pool will be shared by:

Drug Enforcement Administration

**** TOP SECRET ****

FBI
Bureau of Alcohol, Tobacco, & Firearms
IRS
Federal Aviation Commission
U.S. Marshals Service
U.S. Coast Guard

The act requires a study of the feasibility of requiring aircraft to carry operating transponders so that they can be tracked (Sec. 7212) including the "INTERCEPT" (the use of military aircraft is assumed due to the fact that the military is the only agency which has such a capability) of any aircraft not in a proper flight corridor (Sec. 7213). The act requires a study to be made on requiring onboard monitoring devices on commercial motor vehicles to record speed, driving time and other information (Sec. 9101). It further requires the utilization of existing government laboratory facilities (Departments of Defense, Justice, Energy, National Security Agency, CIA, FBI) to develop technologies for Federal law enforcement (not limited to drug enforcement) (Sections 6163 and 7605).

This would include:

Night Vision (Ft. Belvoir, Virginia);
Ground Sensor & Communications Electronics (Ft. Monmouth, New Jersey);
Physical Electronic Security (Hanscom Field, Massachusetts);
Imaging Electronic Surveillance (CIA & NSA, Washington, D.C.);
Chemical/Biosensor Research & Development (Aberdeen, Maryland);
Chemical/Molecular Research (Albuquerque, New Mexico);
Physical/Electronic Surveillance & Tracking (FBI, Washington, D.C.);
Explosives Ordnance Detection (Indian Head, Maryland).

The act calls for the expenditure of $120 million for the Bureau of Justice Statistics, a national clearinghouse of data from federal, state, and local criminal justice agencies (Sec. 6092).

Grant money will be made available for state and local agencies to hook into the data system (Sec. 6101/1301). Gun sellers will have to check for a buyer's police record (Sec 6213).

The act includes a special note from the Attorney General to INCLUDE DOMESTIC VIOLENCE information in the system (Sec. 7609).

My sources have informed me that the New World Order plans to execute any person who has exhibited any degree of violence during their life. A fist fight while in the service would qualify you. They believe that violence is hereditary and this could mean execution of family members as well.

This act calls for a study of the feasibility of establishing an INTERNA-TIONAL CRIMINAL COURT (World Court) (Sec. 4108).

An international criminal court would have no jurisdiction or authority over any citizen of the United States of America unless we surrender our sovereignty to the New World Order.

No weapons are to be allowed in Federal buildings: up to 1 year imprisonment for carrying a weapon into any FEDERAL FACILITY. The only exception is a pocket knife, but only if the blade is LESS than 2-1/2 inches long (Sec. 6215).

The act has authorized postal authorities to serve warrants, subpoenas, make arrests, carry firearms, and make seizures in matters involving use of mails (Sec. 6251).

The Post Office Department is a private corporation and is not a part of the Federal government. How can they be allowed to function as Federal police if they are not federalized? Are post office employees destined to become a part of the national police force?

It is now illegal to mail or send locksmithing equipment to anyone but a locksmith (Sec. 3002). MANY COMMON TOOLS CAN BE CLASSIFIED AS LOCKSMITHING EQUIPMENT.

The act legalizes the arming of aircraft in other countries for defensive purposes, in drug control (Sec. 4202).

SAY AGAIN? If this had been in existence a few years ago, the IRAN-CONTRA AFFAIR WOULD HAVE BEEN LEGAL with only a statement that the arms were for defensive purposes in drug control.

The act mandates that military installations are to be used as MENTAL TREATMENT CENTERS, OR PRISON CAMPS WITH WORK PRO-GRAMS (Sections 7302 and 2081/561). Does this SOUND LIKE RUSSIA?

In addition, $200 million dollars will go for new prisons (Sec. 6157). Plus, the proceeds from seized and forfeited property are to be used for construction of prisons, rewards for information or help, or for OTHER THINGS THE ATTORNEY GENERAL NEED NOT REPORT (Sec. 6072/524 Title 20-CIA, H).

The act states that prison industries may BORROW AND INVEST FUNDS (Sec. 7093). Prison industries may DIVERSIFY THEIR PROD-UCTS and PRODUCE PRODUCTS ON AN ECONOMIC BASIS (Sec. 7096). To provide a labor pool SOVIET UNION STYLE it authorizes a study of the feasibility of REQUIRING PRISONERS TO PAY THEIR COSTS FOR FOOD, HOUSING AND SHELTER AT PAID EMPLOYMENT BEFORE, DURING OR AFTER IMPRISONMENT (Sec. 7301).

In other words, it means imprisonment Soviet style presented in what sounds like a nice idea. A LABOR CAMP WHERE MEN AND WOMEN ARE WORKED TO DEATH IS ONLY THAT AND NOTHING MORE OR LESS, NO MATTER WHAT THEY CALL IT OR HOW ATTRACTIVE THEY MAKE IT SOUND.

Prisons going into business to produce products on an economic basis can only serve to DESTROY THE LAST REMNANTS OF SMALL BUSINESS.

This law is 366 pages of very small print. I am sure that as carefully as I read it, I still must have missed many other terrible clauses. Congressmen have been known to deny knowledge of this law and some have stated that it does not exist because they are terrified of the public finding out what they have done. When I first warned the nation about this legislation on talk radio across the country, the Government pulled all copies not already in public hands. The Government states that there are no copies available and there will not be any copies available. THIS ACT IS TOO LARGE TO INCLUDE IN THIS BOOK. You will find it in your library, though, exactly as I have stated at the beginning of this chapter. Please look it up yourself to verify that it is indeed real.

SOURCES

Public Law 100-690.

U.S. Code Congressional and Administrative News, Vol. 3, 1988, with amendment and voting information in the *Congressional Quarterly Almanac Vol. XLIV*, 1988.

CHAPTER 8

ARE THE SHEEP READY TO SHEAR?

OKLAHOMA

H.B. 1750

TEST CASE

FOR THE POLICE STATE

OKLAHOMA
H.B. 1750
The Police State's Test Case

Gary North recently wrote about one of the scariest pieces of socialistic police-state legislation to arrive on the scene to date.

"On January 1, 1991, a new, 96-page state law goes into effect: H.B. 1750, passed last year [1989]." It requires all Oklahoma residents to declare everything they own to the tax collector, everything: guns, coins, art collections, furniture, business equipment, bank accounts, household furniture, etc. Forms will be distributed through banks. Any taxpayer who refuses to fill out the form and submit it to the tax assessor by March 15 — the ides of March — will be visited by an assessor. He will ask permission to enter the home or place of business. If this request is denied, he will be issued a search warrant. Any property not previously listed, or undervalued, will be assessed a penalty of up to 20% of its market value. This will make renters into property taxpayers and make life easy for the gun grabbers.

What are the investment implications of this? Invest in a good gun and be standing on your porch with gun in hand when they pay you a visit.

It is clear where the tax collectors are headed next. Oklahoma will be a test case. If they can pull this one off, the other states will follow. Big Brother wants to know all and to tax all. Eventually the New World Order will eliminate all private property, "redistribute the wealth," and this inventory will tell them how much exists and exactly where it is stored. Of course, the Oklahoma tax assessor will share its information with other federal and state agencies.

Will they get away with this blatant disregard for civil and constitutional rights? That is exactly the reason for the law, to find out if it will meet with strong or violent opposition. If the citizens of Oklahoma lie down and allow this to happen, then you can bet everyone else in the nation is going to be subjected to the same or a similar law.

It is time to stand up with a weapon and scream, "ENOUGH!" It is time to draw the line. It is time to make decisions and carry them out. It is time to resist at any and all cost. The penalty for failing to do so is slavery.

IT IS NOT TIME FOR REBELLION. IT IS TIME FOR RESTORATION.

THE CONSTITUTION MUST BE AGAIN, AS IT ONCE WAS, THE SUPREME LAW OF THE LAND. FEDERALISM IS TREASON. STAND UP AND FIGHT.

SOURCES

H.B 1750, legislation of the Oklahoma State House of Representatives, Oklahoma City, Oklahoma, 1989.

North, Gary, "Big Brother Wants to See It All in Oklahoma," *The McAlvany Intelligence Advisor*, July 1990.

CHAPTER 9

ANATOMY OF AN ALLIANCE

The Logic for the New World Order

The Glue That Binds the Alliance of Power

and

the Consequences

*All that is necessary for evil to triumph
is for good men to do nothing.*
Edmund Burke, 1729-1797

THE REASONS FOR COOPERATION BETWEEN OPPOSING FORCES

I give lectures all over the United States. At some point before, during, or after every lecture, some well-meaning but misguided soul, tells me that I have it all wrong and that it's the Jews, the Catholics, the communists, or the bankers that are the cause of all our ills. The target group is blamed for everything that has ever gone wrong. Power over everyone and everything is always attributed to this group — whichever group it happens to be at that moment to that person. These poor people are on the right track, in that there has been and certainly is a conspiracy to bring about a totalitarian world order. They are completely off track to think that any one ethnic, religious, or financial group alone could ever muster enough power to bring its plan to fruition. One group, you see, would always be opposed by all of the other special-interest groups that exist and have always existed throughout history. That is, unless they were all really the same group (the Illuminati) or for some reason they became unified (the Bilderberg Group).

The one-group scenario, except for the Illuminati, has been used effectively to divert your attention away from the truth. It has caused you to fight each other in a manipulation that always leads the REAL conspiracy closer to its ultimate goal, a New World Order. Those of you who believe that Hitler was financed by Jews so that he could murder Jews have a serious logic deficit. The fanatical leftists who tout that it's Nazis behind the conspiracy have ignored the fact that very wealthy Jews are certainly involved, along with many Catholics, Protestants, communists, atheists, capitalists, Freemasons, etc., all of whom are diametrically opposed to each other, at least on the surface.

Those on the right who believe that it is communist forget that U.S. bankers financed the creation of the Soviet Union. Financial assistance from MANY different countries, institutions, and peoples of opposing religious and political beliefs has been the only thing that has kept the unworkable communist economy afloat for all of these years. The Rockefeller family has a bank branch in the Kremlin. Those on the right must also ask why, whenever we have set out to stop communism, the United States has only strengthened communism. No modern war, no matter what it was called, has ever resulted in territorial gain for the winner. It is not because our leaders are communist, as claimed by the right. Communism was a creation meant to function as the antithesis to the United States. Many of our leaders, however, are Illuminati.

The answer lies with the many faces of the Illuminati and the fact that several unifying reasons for bringing about the New World Order surfaced

---

* * * * TOP SECRET * * * *

immediately following World War II. It is possible, however, that one or two or more of these reasons are not real, and thus manipulations. The evidence indicates that they are real and dangerous, each in its own way, and must be dealt with quickly and thoroughly.

If it were secretly discovered that extraterrestrial beings were visiting the earth it certainly would make sense to unite humanity against the possible threat that this would present. If extraterrestrials are not visiting earth, then it would make sense to invent them in order to convince opposing forces to unite against the threat. This has been done whether or not the alien beings in question exist; however, there are more believable and more immediate dangers that may be the reason for an alliance of so many traditionally opposing groups. Aliens will be discussed at length in a later chapter.

The reason could be the threatened extinction of the human race by no other enemy than the human race itself. This threat may not be a manipulation; it may be real, and unless drastic measures are taken, may materialize within the next one hundred years.

Following World War II something happened that was to have tremendous significance for the future of all mankind. The intellectuals took note of this happening and brought it to the attention of the world power elite. The elite were severely shaken by the predicted repercussions of this event. They were told that by or shortly after the year 2000 the total collapse of civilization as we know it and the possible extinction of the human race could occur. It could occur, that is, if we did not destroy the earth with nuclear weapons before then. They were told that the only things that could stop these predicted events would be severe cutbacks of the human population, the cessation or retardation of technological and economic growth, the elimination of meat in the human diet, strict control of future human reproduction, a total commitment to preserving the environment, colonization of space, and a paradigm shift in the evolutionary consciousness of man.

Those in power immediately formed an alliance and set about bringing the recommended changes to fruition through propaganda, mind control and other manipulations of the masses. The Illuminati's prayers had been answered.

What was this event that caused so much consternation and changed forever the future of the world? Millions of soldiers returned from war. The soldiers found lonely, eager women waiting for them. The greatest coupling in the history of the human race occurred. The result was everyone born between 1941 and 1955 and the children that they would eventually produce. It was me and you and everyone who lives today. It was the great worldwide BABY BOOM. It was the culmination of all man's efforts to survive through history. It was modern medicine, better diets, heat in winter, pure running water, and proper disposal of sewage. It was the point in history when the birth rate so exceeded the death rate that the world's population doubled between 1957 and 1990. It was the most wonderful time in the history of the world, but it was also the worst. It signaled the end of man's most precious achievement. An alliance of all of the powers on earth, open and hidden, decided that individual freedoms could no longer be tolerated in the interest of the preservation of the human race. They believed the common man could not be trusted.

What had been the unfulfilled dream of many individual groups became reality by the concentration of power in the alliance known as the Bilderberg Group. What had been impossible before was now promised. The New World Order that so many had envisioned was now a certainty.

The first study was made during World War II to determine the impact of the returning soldiers upon the economy. The results mobilized the ruling elite. A second secret study was conducted in 1957 by scientists meeting in Huntsville, Alabama. It confirmed the results of the first. The conclusion was that civilization as we know it would collapse shortly after the year 2000 unless the population was seriously curtailed. The study expressed a concern that since atomic weapons existed they would ultimately be used. Total worldwide disarmament was urged. Congress adopted the disarmament plan and created the U.S. Disarmament Agency. President Dwight David Eisenhower had this to say in 1957: "As a result of lowered infant mortality, longer lives, and the accelerating conquest of famine there is under way a population explosion so incredibly great that in little more than another generation the population of the world is expected to double."

A third study was made by the Club of Rome ending in 1968 to determine the limits to growth. The result was the same. The Club of Rome was commissioned to develop a computer model of the world so as to predict the outcome of corrections made to social and economic structures by the elect. The Club of Rome was also asked to develop a computer model of a New World Order. Both tasks were accomplished.

Studies were done to determine a method to arrest the population explosion before the point of no return would be reached. It was determined that an immediate attack on the problem would involve two points of intervention. The first was to lower the birth rate and the second was to increase the death rate.

To lower the birth rate several programs were put into motion. The first was the development of positive birth-control methods using

* * * * TOP SECRET * * * *

mechanical (diaphragm and condom), chemical (foam and birth-control pills), and medical (sterilization, abortion, and hysterectomy) procedures. These were developed and implemented. The Women's Liberation movement was started with the demand for free abortions, using "pro choice" as its rallying cry. Homosexuality was encouraged and Gay Liberation was born. Homosexuals do not have children. Zero population growth became a hot subject at cocktail parties. Individual freedom, "the heat of the moment," religion, and the old blue laws sabotaged these efforts, and while zero population growth became a reality in some areas, population increased rapidly in others.

The only alternative left to the world's ruling elite was to increase the death rate. This was a difficult thing to do, as no one wanted to pick people out of a crowd and line them up for execution. Neither did they relish the possible consequences of an enraged public upon discovering that they were being systematically murdered. Of course, a very short but very deadly global war using nuclear weapons upon select population concentrations was contemplated and, to tell you the truth, was not ruled out. The fact that such a population control was even contemplated confirmed the worst fears of those who had participated in the 1957 study. War was put on the back burner to simmer, but may become a reality. In the meantime something else had to be done that would absolve the decision makers of guilt and place the blame on those who did not lead clean lives. Something that could be blamed upon Mother Nature. What was needed was the bubonic plague or some other horrible but natural disease. The answer came from Rome.

Several Top Secret recommendations were made by Dr. Aurelio Peccei of the Club of Rome. He advocated that a plague be introduced that would have the same effect as the famous Black Death of history. The chief recommendation was to develop a microbe which would attack the auto-immune system and thus render the development of a vaccine impossible. The orders were given to develop the microbe and to develop a prophylactic and a cure. The microbe would be used against the general population and would be introduced by vaccine. The prophylactic was to be used by the ruling elite. The cure will be administered to the survivors when it is decided that enough people have died. The cure will be announced as newly developed when in fact it has existed from the beginning. This plan is a part of Global 2000. The prophylactic and the cure are suppressed.

"Man has skyrocketed from a defensive position, largely subordinated to Nature's alternatives, to a new and dominant one. From it he not only can and does influence everything in the world but, voluntarily or unwittingly, can and indeed does determine the alternatives of his own future —

and ultimately must choose his options for it. In other words, his novel power condition practically compels him to take up new regulatory functions that willy-nilly he has had to discharge with respect to the world's mixed natural-human systems. Having penetrated a number of the erstwhile mysteries and being able to sway events massively, he is now vested with unprecedented, tremendous responsibilities and thrown into the new role of moderator of life on the planet — including his own." The above words were written by Dr. Aurelio Peccei and are taken verbatim from page 607 of *The Global 2000 Report* to the President.

Funding was obtained from the U.S. Congress under H.B. 15090 (1969), where $10 million was given to the DOD's 1970 budget. Testimony before the Senate Committee revealed that they intended to produce "a synthetic biological agent, an agent that does not naturally exist and for which no natural immunity could have been acquired. Within the next 5 to 10 years it would probably be possible to make a new infective microorganism which could differ in certain important aspects from any known disease-causing organisms. Most important of these is that it might be refractory to the immunological and therapeutic processes upon which we depend to maintain our relative freedom from infectious disease."

Sir Julian Huxley said, "Overpopulation is, in my opinion, the most serious threat to the whole future of our species." The project, called MK-NAOMI, was carried out at Fort Detrick, Maryland.

Since large populations were to be decimated, the ruling elite decided to target the "undesirable" elements of society. Specifically targeted were the black, Hispanic, and homosexual populations. The poor homosexuals were encouraged on the one hand and scheduled for extinction on the other.

The African continent was infected via smallpox vaccine in 1977. The vaccine was administered by the World Health Organization. According to Dr. Robert Strecker, "Without a cure the entire black population of Africa will be dead within 15 years. Some countries are well beyond epidemic status."

The U.S. population was infected in 1978 with the hepatitis B vaccine. Dr. Wolf Szmuness, the ex-roommate of Pope John Paul II, was the mastermind behind the November/78 to October/79 and March/80 to October/81 experimental hepatitis B vaccine trials conducted by the Centers for Disease Control in New York, San Francisco and four other American cities. He loosed the plague of AIDS upon the American people. The gay population was infected. The ads for participants specifically asked for promiscuous homosexual male volunteers. Whatever causes AIDS was in the vaccine. The vaccine was manufactured and bottled in Phoenix, Arizona.

---

* * * * TOP SECRET * * * *

The order was given by the POLICY COMMITTEE of THE BILDER-BERG GROUP based in Switzerland. Other measures were also ordered.

The one you will be able to check the easiest is the Haig-Kissinger Depopulation Policy, which is administered by the State Department. This policy dictates that Third World nations take positive and effective steps to decrease their populations and hold them in check or they get no aid from the United States. If the Third World nations refuse, civil war usually breaks out and the rebels are usually found to be trained, armed, and financed by the Central Intelligence Agency. That is why many more civilians (especially young fertile females) than soldiers have been killed in El Salvador, Nicaragua, and other places. These wars have been instigated in Catholic countries by Jesuits (see Chapter 2).

The Haig-Kissinger depopulation policy has taken over various levels of government and is in fact determining U.S. foreign policy. The planning organization operates outside the White House and directs its entire efforts to reduce the world's population by 2 billion people through war, famine, disease, and any other means necessary. This group is the National Security Council's Ad Hoc Group on Population Policy. The policy planning staff is in the State Department's Office of Population Affairs, established in 1975 by Henry Kissinger. This same group drafted the Global 2000 Report to the President that was given to Carter.

Thomas Ferguson, the Latin American case officer for the State Department's Office of Population Affairs (OPA) made the following statements: "There is a single theme behind all our work; we must reduce population levels. Either they do it our way, through nice clean methods or they will get the kind of mess that we have in El Salvador, or in Iran, or in Beirut. Population is a political problem. Once population is out of control it requires authoritarian government, even fascism, to reduce it....The professionals," stated Ferguson, "aren't interested in lowering population for humanitarian reasons. That sounds nice. We look at resources and environmental constraints. We look at our strategic needs, and we say that this country must lower its population, or else we will have trouble. So steps are taken. El Salvador is an example where our failure to lower population by simple means has created the basis for a national security crisis. The government of El Salvador failed to use our programs to lower their population. Now they get a civil war because of it. There will be dislocation and food shortages. They still have too many people there. Civil wars are somewhat drawn-out ways to reduce population. The quickest way to reduce population is through famine, like in Africa or through DISEASE, like the Black Death, all of which MIGHT OCCUR in El Salvador." His budget for FY 1980 was $190 million; for FY 1981 it was

$220 million. The Global 2000 Report calls for doubling that figure.

Henry Kissinger created this group after discussion with leaders of the Club of Rome during the 1974 population conferences in Bucharest and Rome. The Club of Rome is controlled by Europe's Black Nobility. Alexander Haig is a firm believer in population control. It was Haig that backed Kissinger and pushed the OPA into action.

Ferguson said, "We will go into a country and say, here is your god-damn development plan. Throw it out the window. Start looking at the size of your population and figure out what must be done to reduce it. If you don't like that, if you don't want to choose to do it through planning, then you'll have an El Salvador or an Iran, or worse, a Cambodia."

The real reason the Shah of Iran was overthrown was that his best efforts to institute "clean programs" of birth control failed to make a significant dent in the country's birth rate. The promise of jobs, through an ambitious industrialization program, encouraged migration toward over-crowded cities like Teheran. Under Ayatollah Khomeini, the clean prog-rams have been dismantled. The government may make progress because it has a program "to induce up to half of Teheran's 6 million residents to relocate. Iran's war with Iraq really pleased the OPA." Now you know about the Shah and now you know part of the reason we have troops in the Middle East. Marcos fell victim to the same policy.

Daniel B. Luten had this to say: "...an organization cannot have a conservation policy without having a population policy....the sanity test — in which the candidate, confronted with an overflowing sink, is classified according to whether he reaches for the mop or the faucet."

Thousands of people, mostly civilians, are killed in El Salvador's civil war each year. "To accomplish what the State Department deems adequate 'population control,' the civil war would have to be greatly expanded," according to Thomas Ferguson, the Latin American case officer for the OPA.

El Salvador was targeted for population control and war in an April 1980 population report published by the National Security Council. "El Salvador is an example of a country with serious population and political problems," the report states. "Rapid population growth — the birth rate has remained unchanged in recent years — aggravates its population density, which is already the highest on mainland Latin America. While a population program exists on paper, it has not been pursued with a strong commitment, and contraceptives remain unavailable." The population program "really did not work," OPA's Ferguson said. "The infrastructure was not there to support it. There were just too many goddamn people. If you want to control a country, you have to keep the population down. Too many people breed social unrest and communism."

"Something had to be done," the OPA official said. The birth rate is 3.3 percent — one of the highest in the world. Its population, he complained, will double in 21 years. "The civil war can help things, but it would have to be greatly expanded."

In making sure that the population falls in El Salvador, Ferguson said, the OPA has learned a lot from its experiences in Vietnam. "We studied the thing. That area was also overpopulated and a problem. We thought that the war would lower population and we were wrong." Now you know what we were really doing in Vietnam and why we were not allowed to win. According to Ferguson, the population in Vietnam increased during the war, despite U.S. use of defoliation and a combat strategy that encouraged civilian casualties. Now you know why those of us in the know consider Lt. Calley to be a scapegoat.

To reduce population "quickly," said Ferguson "you have to pull all the males into the fighting and kill significant numbers of fertile, child-bearing age females." He criticized the current civil war in El Salvador: "You are killing a small number of males and not enough fertile females to do the job on the population. If the war went on 30 to 40 years like this, then you might accomplish something. Unfortunately, we don't have too many instances like that to study."

To aid you in your research of this travesty, the names of the significant reports are *THE POPULATION BOMB* by DR. PAUL R. EHRLICH (his wife Anne is a member of the Club of Rome), *THE GLOBAL 2000 REPORT TO THE PRESIDENT*, and *THE LIMITS TO GROWTH, A REPORT FOR THE CLUB OF ROME'S PROJECT ON THE PREDICAMENT OF MANKIND.*

In April 1968 the study began publicly in the Academia dei Lincei in Rome, Italy. The study had been ongoing in secret ever since the initial findings of the Huntsville meeting of 1957. They met at the instigation of Dr. Aurelio Peccei. The first real public indication of their findings and the solution that had been decided upon was publication of the book *The Population Bomb* in May 1968. Notice how close the dates are. On page 17 of *The Population Bomb*, a telling paragraph reveals all there is to know.

"In summary, the world's population will continue to grow as long as the birth rate exceeds the death rate; it's as simple as that. When it stops growing or starts to shrink, it will mean that either the birth rate has gone down or the death rate has gone up or a combination of the two. Basically, then, there are only two kinds of solutions to the population problem. One is a 'birth rate solution,' in which we find ways to lower the birth rate. The other is a 'death rate solution,' in which ways to raise the death rate — war, famine, pestilence — find us. **The problem could have been avoided by**

---

* * * * TOP SECRET * * * *

population control, in which mankind consciously adjusted the birth rate so that a 'death rate solution' did not have to occur."

The recommendations of the results of the study were made by Dr. Aurelio Peccei, who pledged not to use the prophylactic and not to take the cure should the microbe be developed and should he contract the disease. Dr. Peccei was considered a hero for deciding to take the same risk as the general population. The public results of the study were published in 1968 and again in 1972. The MIT project team members that developed the computer model study are listed below:

Dr. Dennis L. Meadows, director, United States
Dr. Alison A. Anderson, United States (pollution)
Dr. Jay M. Anderson, United States (pollution)
Ilyas Bayar, Turkey (agriculture)
William W. Behrens III, United States (resources)
Farhad Hakimzadeh, Iran (population)
Dr. Steffen Harbordt, Germany (sociopolitical trends)
Judith A. Machen, United States (administration)
Dr. Donella H. Meadows, United States (population)
Peter Milling, Germany (capital)
Nirmala S. Murthy, India (population)
Roger F. Naill, United States (resources)
Jorgen Randers, Norway (population)
Stephen Shantzis, United States (agriculture)
John A. Seeger, United States (administration)
Marilyn Williams, United States (documentation)
Dr. Erich K. O. Zahn, Germany (agriculture)

When the study was completed in 1969 U.N. Secretary General U Thant of the United Nations made this statement:

"I do not wish to seem overdramatic, but I can only conclude from the information that is available to me as Secretary General, that the Members of the United Nations have perhaps ten years left in which to subordinate their ancient quarrels and launch a global partnership to curb the arms race, to defuse the population explosion, and to supply the required momentum to development efforts. If such a global partnership is not forged within the next decade, then I very much fear that the problems I have mentioned will have reached such staggering proportions that they will be beyond our capacity to control."

MK-NAOMI was developed by the Special Operations Division (SOD) scientists at Ft. Detrick, Maryland under the supervision of the CIA.

A reference to the project MK-NAOMI can be found in *The Intelligence Community* by Fain et al., Bowker, 1977.

Lt. Col. James "Bo" Gritz was a member of the Special Operations Division of the Department of Defense, the commander of U.S. Special Forces in Latin America, the principle agent for the National Security Council's supersecret Intelligence Support Activity (ISA), which hatched the illegal groups known as Yellow Fruit and Seaspray, and the Congressional Relations Chief for the Pentagon. Lt. Col. Gritz *claims* he didn't know of any illegalities in the military or in government until he was *told* by a drug lord in a Third World nation. I'm sorry, but I am not that easily duped. I recommend that we support his efforts as long as his efforts help us. I also recommend that we watch him very carefully. There is a slim chance that Gritz is legitimate, but I would not put my life in his hands.

Lowell Sumner expressed his view: "As a biologist the human population explosion, and its declining spiral of natural resources, is to me the greatest threat of all. The time is ripe, even dangerously overripe, as far as the population control problem is concerned. We shall have to face up or ultimately perish, and what a dreary, stupid, unlovely way to perish, on a ruined globe stripped of its primeval beauty."

Many other population controls have been promulgated. The reduction of the world's population to workable levels has been virtually assured. It is only a matter of time. The problem will be to curtail further human reproduction beyond approved levels. To handle that problem the New World Order will adopt the Communist Chinese model of population control. It is the only population-control program that has ever worked. The old and infirm have been periodically murdered and couples are forbidden to have more than one child. Penalties are so severe that families in China with two children are extremely rare. Three-children families are nonexistent. A surprising byproduct is that Chinese children as a group are treated better than any other national grouping of children in the world, including the United States.

Tobacco fields in the U.S. have been fertilized with the radioactive tailings from uranium mines, resulting in a tremendous increase in the incidence of lip, mouth, throat, and lung cancer. If you do not believe it, just look at the incidence of lung cancer per capita before 1950 and compare it to the lung cancer per capita at the present time. Are those who smoke committing suicide, or are they being murdered?

Malathion, a nerve gas developed by the Nazis during World War II to kill people, is being sprayed heavily on population centers in California. The excuse used is that it will kill the Mediterranean fruit fly. The tipoff is that the orchards are not being sprayed, only people. The helicopters come from Evergreen in Arizona, a known government and a suspected CIA base. The pilots are contract pilots furnished by Evergreen. Evergreen has been named as one of the bases where drugs are flown in from Central America. The City of Pasadena passed a law making it illegal to spray malathion within the city limits. The law was ignored and the city took no action. When the people of California literally revolted against the spraying of malathion, the Governor of California stated that he did not have the power to stop the operation. What higher power is there that could prevent a governor of a state from halting the spraying of an insecticide? A warning was issued to cover up automobiles and belongings because malathion could destroy paint, some plastics, and other property. People, they said, would not be injured. It is a lie.

Heart disease used to be a very rare illness. Now it is epidemic. Go and look at the statistics. I do not know what is causing this, but 80 years ago people consumed more salt, fat, cholesterol, and everything else that heart disease is blamed upon, but the disease was rare. Why is it now one of the leading killers?

In the state of Colorado and elsewhere dioxin is turning up in the drinking water in alarming levels. It should not be present in any amount. Where is it coming from? Dioxin is one of the deadliest chemicals known to man. Colorado citizens attempting to do battle against the dioxin contamination are met with closed doors, denial, and attacks upon their characters.

We have watched the news in horror as story after story unfolded revealing that the Army and the CIA had released germs and viruses into the population to test their biological warfare capability. In light of what you have learned in this chapter you should now know that it was really to reduce population.

It is a matter of public record that investigations into cover-ups of radioactive leaks into the atmosphere and into ground water have revealed that some leaks were not accidental but were purposful. Some areas of the country now have such a high rate of cancer that virtually everyone who lives in these areas will die other than a natural death. The true extent of radioactive gases, waste, and toxic material, especially cesium-137, strontium-90, uranium-mine and -mill tailings, thorium-230, radium-226, and radon-222 that has leaked or has been purposely planted in the atmosphere, soil, and ground water is far beyond anything you or I can imagine. Every investigation has revealed that the true figures regarding radioactive leakage are much larger than official figures and the real numbers may never be known. Cover-up has become SOP (standard operating procedure) at all levels and in all departments of government. Do we dream reality or is reality a dream?

According to Dr. Eva Snead, the San Francisco Bay area has one of the highest cancer rates in the world. The San Francisco Bay area has been revealed as one of the primary test locations of the Central Intelligence Agency's biological and chemical programs. You may recall that Legionnaire's disease was an experimental bacteria released into the wind on the San Francisco Bay from a government-operated boat. San Francisco is also one of the six known inoculation sites for the CIA Project MK-NAOMI (AIDS). The Bay area was headquarters for Dr. Timothy Leary, who introduced the drug culture to American youth under CIA Project MK-ULTRA.

It is suspected that the San Francisco Bay area was also subjected to large doses of radiation to test the effects upon a population over a prolonged period of time. Why do they hate San Francisco? The answer is that the largest homosexual population in America lives in San Francisco and they have been targeted for extermination.

A reason for the New World Order, or rationalization, as the case may be, is the very real possibility that some terrorist will set off a global nuclear war by detonating an atomic bomb to make a political point. I believe that it is safe to say that any large-scale exchange of atomic or hydrogen weapons will result in the complete destruction of civilization, and could precipitate the escalation of the onslaught of an ice age. The obvious conclusion would be that any kind of compromise leading to coexistence is better than any kind of nuclear exchange. In other words, "better Red than dead." This is exactly what the hierarchy has decided, only the New World Order will not be Red. It will be fascist. It will, in fact, be a socialist totalitarian state.

It is hoped that a natural metamorphosis will eventually occur. The Illuminati hope that it will result in a paradigm shift of the evolutionary consciousness of man. This could cause the formation of a state where no government is needed, where anarchy is not to be feared. They dream that the end result will be the world that Christ taught but that the Christian religion prevents. It is ironic that the Illuminati actually believe that this can evolve from a plan built upon such suffering. Christ suffered, if the New Testament is true, to bring about his world; and if he suffered maybe it is necessary that we also suffer. I am not wise enough to know the answer.

I managed to locate a reference to *The Protocols of Sion* dated in the 1700s (see Chapter 15, page 269). This plan for subjugation of the world correctly outlined exactly what has happened since the Protocols were discovered, and that is all that is needed to confirm the authenticity of the information contained within the document. It is clear that the Illuminati has planned to rule the world for centuries.

They have followed the plan outlined in *The Protocols of Sion*. The Illuminati could not possibly have succeeded, however, if an alliance had not been formed with the other world power structures. Is the world population crisis a hoax perpetrated to bring that alliance about? It is possible. All I can say is that my own calculations, using the knowledge available to me, performed on my 386 computer, confirm that the crisis is real, and is, in fact, very serious. If it is a manipulation, the whole world has been fooled.

ALL INTELLECTUALS, RULERS, AND GOVERNING BODIES AGREE THAT POPULATION IS THE BIGGEST THREAT TO CIVILIZATION THAT WE KNOW OF TODAY. It does not matter what you believe. If THEY believe it, you will be affected because they have the power.

The New World Order will eliminate the population threat in several ways. Complete control of individual behavior may be established using electronic or chemical implants. No one will be allowed to have a child without permission; stiff penalties wait for those who ignore the law. The violent, the old, the infirm, the handicapped, and the unproductive will be killed. Private property will be abolished. Since religion helped to create the population problem, it will not be tolerated except for the approved state-controlled religion which will evolve according to man's needs. Joseph Campbell explains this concept excellently in his series with Bill Moyers called "The Power of Myth." Cash will disappear and with it most crime will also disappear; but total control of each individual will be the price we pay.

Man cannot be trusted to safeguard what little is left in the way of natural resources. Technological development and economic growth will be severely cut back. Man will be required to live like his ancestors. Those who learn to be self-sufficient and can adapt to the absence of many of the things that we take for granted today, such as automobiles, will get along fine. Others will suffer terribly. Man will once again conform to the law of the survival of the fittest.

No one is going to like the loss of individual freedoms guaranteed us by the Constitution and the Bill of Rights. *I do not like or agree with what is planned.* Intellectually I know that people will not solve the problems that we face unless they are made to do it. That is a sad commentary on the common man, but nevertheless it is true. The New World Order is evil but very much needed if man is to survive long enough to plant his seed amongst the stars. A paradigm shift and starseed are the only legitimate long-term answers.

THIS IS WHY WE HAVE ALL BEEN SO WRONG FOR SO LONG. It

never was what we thought it was. Nothing is or ever will be until we learn to live in reality instead of fantasyland. A paradigm shift in the evolutionary consciousness of man MUST take place. Right or wrong, the world is covered with agents of the Illuminati who are attempting to cause that evolutionary jump. We have not been taken into their confidence. As you learned in Chapter One, we have been judged too stupid to understand.

It is true that without the population or the bomb problem the elect would use some other excuse to bring about the New World Order. They have plans to bring about things like earthquakes, war, the Messiah, an extra-terrestrial landing, and economic collapse. They might bring about all of these things just to make damn sure that it does work. They will do whatever is necessary to succeed. The Illuminati has all the bases covered and you are going to have to be on your toes to make it through the coming years.

ACCORDING TO PLANS, MANY PEOPLE ARE GOING TO DIE BETWEEN NOW AND THE YEAR 2,000; BUT IF THESE PLANS ARE NOT SUCCESSFUL THE HUMAN RACE COULD BECOME EXTINCT. Nothing on earth can change this except a tremendous reduction and stabilization of the population. Without starseed this reduction and stabilization would only delay the inevitable, as eventually all raw materials will be completely depleted. A never-ending source of free energy will then be needed. That may be possible but is unlikely to solve the problem.

Without some central common need that would bind man together, a source of free energy would most likely result in total anarchy. So you see, what was needed in the beginning is still needed in the end. A paradigm shift in the evolutionary consciousness of man coupled with starseed is the most logical answer for the human race.

We must learn to accept individual responsibility for the world's problems or be willing to live by the terms of those who do. We must learn to love one another, share, deplore violence, and work with nature, not against it. We must do all of this while colonizing the Universe. We must be prepared in the process to peacefully meet and deal with an extraterrestrial intelligence. I believe they exist.

Can you imagine what will happen if Los Angeles is hit with a 9.0 quake, New York City is destroyed by a terrorist-planted atomic bomb, World War III breaks out in the Middle East, the banks and the stock markets collapse, Extraterrestrials land on the White House lawn, food disappears from the markets, some people disappear, the Messiah presents himself to the world, and all in a very short period of time? Can you imagine? The world power structure can, and will if necessary, make some or all of those things happen to bring about the New World Order.

PATRIOTS MUST NOT BE AT HOME ON ANY NATIONAL HOLI-DAY DURING THE DAY OR NIGHT EVER AGAIN UNTIL THE DANGER IS PAST. DISREGARD THIS WARNING AND YOU WILL FIND YOURSELF IN A CONCENTRATION CAMP. In the camp you will be treated for a mental illness called nationalism, common to patriots. This illness is not in the interest of the New World Order. Those who cannot be cured will be exterminated. When asked what was in store for the world in the coming decade, Henry Kissinger said this: "Everything is going to be different. Many will suffer. A New World Order will emerge. It will be a much better world for those who survive. In the long run life will be better. The world we have wanted will be reality."

CHAPTER 10

LESSONS
FROM
LITHUANIA

A well regulated Militia, being necessary to the security of a free State, the right of the people to keep and bear Arms, shall not be infringed.

AMENDMENT II
Constitution of the U.S.

I know not what others may do. But as for me, give me liberty or give me death.
Patrick Henry

EXPLANATION

I had intended to write a long and thoroughly referenced chapter on the Second Amendment to the United States Constitution, the right of the people to keep and bear arms.

I had to eat humble pie when I read the following text entitled "Lessons from Lithuania" by Neal Knox. It was contributed by a member of the Citizens Agency for Joint Intelligence. I was impressed by its simplicity and ability to deliver with very few words the precise message that I had intended to convey in twenty pages. Since I believe that sometimes less is more, and since my ego has nothing to do with this book and its message, "Lessons from Lithuania" has been printed in its entirety, with no changes, as the complete chapter on the Second Amendment. Try as I might, I could never improve upon Neal's simple statement.

My deepest appreciation to Neal Knox and The Firearms Coalition for permission to use "Lessons from Lithuania."

LESSONS FROM LITHUANIA

by Neal Knox

Those who avoid and evade the reason for the Second Amendment to the U.S. Constitution would surely admit that if Lithuania had a Second Amendment, Mikhail Gorbachev violated it on March 22, 1990 — Russian troops seized arms from the Lithuanian militia. Or was "the right of the people to keep and bear arms" actually violated two days earlier, when Premier Gorbachev ordered private citizens to turn in their hunting and competition guns to the Russian army within one week "for temporary safekeeping" or have them confiscated and their owners imprisoned? Or was "the right of the people to keep and bear arms" initially violated many years before, when the people were first prohibited from possessing guns without permission of government and laws were passed requiring every gun to be registered? In fact, the Soviet Constitution guarantees the people the right to keep and bear arms, and Lithuania is part of the Soviet Union — or so Gorbachev contends. But obviously the Soviet government pays no more attention to that constitutional freedom guarantee than do the majority of the U.S. government, the International Association of Chiefs of Police, or CBS and the Washington Post. What is the difference, precisely, between the confiscation of private firearms in Lithuania and the confiscation ordered by S. 166, the Graves bill now pending in the New Jersey Senate? What is the difference, precisely, between the registration law in Lithuania — which makes confiscation possible — and the registration of

---

* * * * T O P S E C R E T * * * *

military-style firearms required by California's Roberti-Roos bill, which went into effect January 1, 1990. What is the difference, precisely, between Lithuania's law prohibiting the people from owning military-style firearms and the so-called "assault rifle" bans now pending in both houses of Congress and in many states? The difference is that the people of the United States are free men and women who can trust their benevolent government. **FOREVER?**

NOTE: Nothing has so clearly demonstrated the reasons for the Second Amendment and the reasons it must be defended than when on Dec. 14, 1981, when Gen. Jaruzelski declared martial law in Poland, placed all press under total government control, and declared all firearms licenses and gun registration certificates void — requiring the licensed owners to turn in their registered guns within 48 hours. Of course, since the government knew where every gun was — except those in the hands of criminals — they had no choice but to comply.

Please download this file, print it out and send it to your local newspaper — putting your name on it if you think it will cause more letters editors to run it. Also please upload it to as many other bulletin boards and nets as possible.

> **Neal Knox**
> **The Firearms Coalition**
> **Box 6537**
> **Silver Spring, MD 20906**

Author's Note: This is a lesson that we hope to learn only from reading and not in the manner learned by the Poles and Lithuanians. After reading the above, I hope you will agree with me that anyone who attempts to subvert the Second Amendment or any other section or legal amendment of the Constitution is a traitor and should be arrested and tried for treason. I hope that you will copy this chapter and distribute it as widely as possible, to as many people as possible. Education is more than half the battle.

In case you have not guessed by now, the fact that most Americans own at least one firearms weapon is the only thing that has kept the New World Order at bay.

A Ray of Hope: As of January 8, 1991, less than 10% of all California gun owners have registered their firearms. Many Californians stood in the streets with weapons in hand and publicly burned the registration forms. Network news did not cover these demonstrations, and no mention has been made on television that California gun owners have ignored this unconstitutional gun-registration law.

CHAPTER 11

COUP
DE GRACE

High Crimes & Misdemeanors

Treason Committed by the Joint Chiefs

Phone Conversation with Randall Terpstra

BACKGROUND

When I finished "The Secret Government" in May 1989, a temptation existed to remove the material that I had written on the Nixon resignation. I thought that no one would ever believe that a coup had occurred in the United States. Furthermore, I held no hope that anyone would ever step forward and substantiate my claim. I was wrong. People did believe it, and subsequent to my delivery of the paper on July 2, 1989, three individuals have come forward to confirm that a coup did in fact take place. This chapter is the transcript of a phone conversation between me and one of those people, Randall Terpstra.

The members of the Joint Chiefs of Staff who were serving at the time of Nixon's resignation were asked if they had instructed their commands to ignore orders from the White House. They replied that the subject had come up but that it was not done. They lied.

CONFIRMATION OF A COUP

Randy: This is Randy.

Bill: Hi, Randy?

Randy: Yes...

Bill: This is Bill Cooper.

Randy: Hello, Bill.

Bill: You left a message on my phone. I didn't get to hear it because my wife took the messages off the phone and wrote them down. I have no idea why you called. If you'll let me in on it...

Randy: Well, I have a copy of your documents that were provided to me by a friend, and uh...two things: One, I'm missing a page on one of them. The one that you've titled "Operation Majority," the final release. It looks like I'm losing page 3, 'cause on the...I have page 2 that says, "MJ-12 is the name of the" dah-da dah-da dah-da "under the leadership of the director" and then it flips right over and the first line on the next page that I have says "means MAJI controlled." I appear to be missing a page on that one.

Bill: Hmmm. Okay.

Randy: The second is — I have to close my office door. One moment.

Bill: Sure...

[Can hear door close.]

Randy: I'll be frank with you. When I first started reading, my first reaction was, "Gee, this is *National Enquirer* material, up until a point where I came across something that startled me a little — in the same document, your final release document. You used two terms that I've only seen one other place, and that was MAJESTY and MAJORITY. When I was in the Navy, I was a radioman, and in the mid seventies — the year escapes me at the moment, it's been a long time, I've only had your papers since last night — and I was involved in a joint Apollo-Soyuz moon shot. I was an onboard crypto operator, which basically meant that all message traffic of a certain nature, which was referred to as SPECAT or special category, was off-line encrypted. During the Apollo-Soyuz shot we established what was referred to as a termination with an unknown location. That location identified itself only as MAJORITY CONTROL.

Bill: Okay...

Randy: All of the message traffic we sent to and from this location was off-line encrypted, which was rather odd because...First, let me explain it. In the Navy when you send a SPECAT, or Special Category message, you go into what's called a clean environment. The message is drafted by the originator on a piece of paper. That piece of paper is brought directly to a designated SPECAT operator — somebody who has a SPECAT or higher clearance — who enters that in the teletype on a paper tape with the hole punched in it for transmission.

Bill: Right.

[Randy did not know that one of my duties as the Petty Officer of the Watch in the CINCPACFLT Command Center was SPECAT operator for the Command Center.]

Randy: At that point the SPECAT operator goes onto the circuit, notifies the other end that he has SPECAT traffic to transmit. The other end...an authorized SPECAT operator has to come on the circuit at the other end. He has to identify himself back to you with his SPECAT code number, his name and service number. Now, to me at this particular moment in time and space — this would be in the middle seventies — that was probably the most insulated means of transmitting information point to point in the military, because you knew who wrote the message, who had seen it to transmit, who had received it, all the way to its ultimate destination.

Bill: Uh huh...

Randy: Well, in this particular case all of the message traffic was being handed to me and I was instructed to encode it through a machine called a KL-47, which takes standard text material and turns it out into five-letter blocks — random characters. And the origination...they...there were five of us onboard the USS Mount Whitney, and the five of us were SPECAT operators. We were on a revolving shift all during the Apollo-Soyuz mission. We were put into a controlled environment that — it was a room with a teletype and a cot in it — and we were told to maintain the term circuit to MAJORITY control. Every hour a Mr. Logan from NASA would come down to the room, punch in because it had a cipher lock on the door, look at any message traffic that came in, and then we would burn it, right in the room. He would draft his replies, which I would enter on the KL-47, take the tape, transmit it and then he would burn the outgoing messages as well.

Bill: Uh huh.

[Note: The tape is made by the KL-47. It is a paper tape containing the five-character grouping encryption. The tape is put onto a sprocket in the teletype machine and it automatically sends the message to the addressee. It comes out at the other end in encrypted form and must be decoded. At least that is the way I was trained as designated SPECAT Operator to do it in the CINCPACFLT Command Center.]

Randy: I don't remember a lot of what was sent because it was very, very busy times. We had so many civilians on board the ship that it was...an incredible amount of work going on.

Bill: I can imagine.

Randy: I do know that hourly we received a report from MAJORITY CONTROL that was headed — now, this is after I've decoded it...the heading was always MAJESTY ADVISORY, over and over and over again.

Bill: Okay.

[Note: MAJESTY ADVISORY messages were sent by CINCPACFLT to update or inform the President personally of beginning, ending, or ongoing operations that could result in serious repercussions to the United States, i.e. the bombing of North Vietnam after the President had informed the American people that no more bombing would occur.]

Randy: Now after doing this I was on for four hours, then off for four, then on for four. We did a rollover like that for the whole Apollo-Soyuz mission. The other thing that I saw that tripped me off a little bit was the term "IACs."

Bill: Identified Alien Craft!

Randy: They...that was never...they never spelled out the acronym. It was just IACs.

Bill: Fantastic!

Randy: It was recurring through all of this message traffic that I was sending.

Bill: Randy, you are a godsend... Where have you been hiding all of these years?

Randy: Well, it's...how I came about getting your document is a long story as well, but when I read through it, it was just like a floodgate opened up and all these memories kept coming back.

Bill: Right.

---

* * * * TOP SECRET * * * *

Randy: Now, at the end of it, after the Apollo-Soyuz mission concluded, the five operators, myself included, were given 50 days basket
leave, which in the Navy meant they give you leave for free.

Bill: Sure. Yeah.

Randy: They didn't dock you for it.

Bill: Go home, get drunk, forget about this.

Randy: Exactly!

Bill: Yeah.

Randy: And when I came back I was taken from third class to second
class spot promotion, and I was moved to the teletype repair shop, which
was quite prestigious at that time.

Bill: Yeah. It's quite normal when you're exposed to this material.
They either snuff you or promote you.

Randy: Well, I've lost contact with the other — well, I mean we had a
ship reunion a couple a years ago, and it never occurred to me about these
other guys. But I don't...I don't have a conscious memory of seeing them.
But as I said when I read through this, it was rather startling to see things
that, uh, that I'm aware of.

Bill: Uh huh.

Randy: I, I'm really interested in that missing page, actually.

Bill: Yeah. Was there anything else that you can remember that...

Randy: No, that's, I mean, at the time it didn't mean a damn to me. I
mean, being a radioman, we pumped so much traffic through that ship.
Mount Whitney is an amphibious communications command ship.

Bill: Yeah, I'm familiar with it. Were you in the Navy at the time that
Nixon resigned?

Randy: No, I was not.

Bill: Hmmmm.

Randy: I was acting as a consultant to a company that was doing work
for the U.S. Marine Corps, though.

Bill: Uh huh. Were you in communications at that time?

Randy: Yes, I was.

Bill: Do you remember a message that came to military commands?
Let me see if I can remember the exact words. I believe the message
said...uh.

Randy: "Upon receipt you are instructed to no longer accept direct
orders from the White House."

Bill: Right!

Randy: Actually, they didn't use the term White House. They used
the term "TOP HAT."

Bill: TOP HAT. I remember "White House" in the one that I saw. I was aboard the Oriskany when I saw this.

Randy: I was working with a Lt. Col. A. P. Finlon as a civilian consultant on a device called the MCC-20, which is a multiplexer device.

Bill: His name was Finland or Fin...?

Randy: Finlon...F - I - N - L - O - N, and he was the recipient of the message. He was the S-3 operations director for the 6th Marine Amphibious Brigade.

Bill: Okay, you realize the implications of all of this, don't you, Randy? You know what's happening.

Randy: Yeah, I've taken a liberty with the documentation you sent me and I've forwarded it to someone else.

Bill: Okay, I am in dire need...I'm trying to do this as quickly and as cleanly as I can to get the people in this country to wake up, or we're gonna lose it. And it's...I'm fighting a battle pretty much on my own. There are people rallying around and they're helping out, and I'm getting bits of information here and there. I need people who have the balls to stand up with me and say what they saw. And I understand that, you know, when anybody does that they're putting themselves in danger. But I don't see any greater danger than the loss of our Constitution and what they have in store down the road. They've literally thrown it in the trash can already, anyway. And what, I guess what I'm asking is for your help. Would you be willing to go public with what you just told me?

Randy: I already have.

Bill: You have?

Randy: I forwarded your manuscript along with exactly what I've just told you to Lt. Col. Robert Brown, the director of the *Soldier of Fortune* magazine.

Bill: Fantastic!

Randy: I spoke with his secretary on the phone, described what it was all about, she in turn passed it on to him. He said, "Send it to me quick."

Bill: Fantastic!

Randy: If anybody...Soldier of Fortune magazine has the biggest military following of any publication in the world. If anybody was in the service who saw this stuff, it'll be them.

Bill: Fantastic! Great. Do you mind if I use the information that you've told me? Can I say that someone has corroborated what I've said?

Randy: Absolutely!

Bill: Can I use your name?

Randy: Yes!

Bill: What's your last name?

Randy: Terpstra.

Bill: Let me get your address.

Randy: 130 Foothill Court, Morgan Hill, California, 95037.

Bill: Your first name is Randy?

Randy: My first name is Randall, middle name Wayne.

Bill: Okay, Randy. You're a godsend. If you were right in front of me I'd kiss ya. I swear to God, I have been hunting so hard for people to come out of the woodwork, because I know there's a lot of people out there who know.

Randy: They don't know it the — I mean, you've taken a lot of loose bits and pieces that I've had. I mean, that's the problem. Yes, there's a lot of people who know things, but they don't know what they know.

Bill: Yeah, I'm sure of that. And it's so compartmentalized that what they know, they don't believe is wrong.

Randy: Well, one of the things I'm really stirring up some controversy about is, I want more information about NRO, and the one person who can get it is Col. Brown. If that exists...

Bill: Well, NRO is the National Reconnaissance Organization that first put together the DELTA teams which were specifically assigned to security of the alien-tasked projects. They've since been used for all kinds of other things. Now, there's a different NRO that you have to be careful you don't get wrapped up in, and that's the National Reconnaissance Office, which is responsible for the spy satellites.

Randy: To even throw a little more smoke on it, do you know Col. Charles Beckwith down in Florida?

Bill: No.

Randy: Col. Charles Beckwith was the one who came up with the whole term DELTA FORCE. That's that rescue, the hostage rescue group, the Green Beret unit?

Bill: Uh huh.

Randy: Now, he originally wanted to call it something else, and the White House pushed DELTA FORCE down his throat.

Bill: Do you know that I talked to Barbara Honegger? Have you read *October Surprise*?

Randy: No, I haven't. As a matter of fact, I've got your bibliography here and I was about to make a call to a friend of mine who runs a bookstore to place a rather large order.

Bill: Okay, Barbara Honegger wrote *October Surprise* and they refused to print one chapter. I met her at one of the talks that I give and we got very embroiled in conversation. She ended up coming over to my home, and we talked face to face. There were about four other witnesses there who heard her say this to me. She said, "At DESERT ONE, the first craft that was there was an antigravity disc craft carrying DELTA personnel. Then the aircraft and the helicopters came in." And she said the purpose of the alien crafts, or the craft that we built from alien technology, or the alien craft that we're using was to ensure the sabotage of the operation.

[Note: Sometime later Barbara Honnegger related the same story on the Anthony Hilder "Telling It Like It Is, Like It Or Not" radio show. During the broadcast she said the antigravity craft was from a project named RED-LIGHT. Ms. Honegger was a White House staff member during the Reagan and Bush administrations.]

Randy: That makes sense, because I have some 8 x 10 glossies of that Jolly Green Giant that caught on fire and burnt.

Bill: Uh huh.

Randy: I have some real problems with that. I'm a military nut. I spent my time in the Navy, and I've since been associated with a variety of military groups.

Bill: Yeah.

Randy: I have some pictures of that photo, of that helicopter that were...they're black & white AP photos. And it shows a burnt pattern that starts at the nose of the aircraft and goes back across the fuel tanks. They don't originate in the fuel tanks. So how in the hell did that helicopter catch fire right at the cockpit and outside of the cockpit, out on the fuselage?

Bill: That's a good question. The alien beam weapons will do that though.

Randy: Now ask a new question.

Bill: Uh huh.

Randy: The beam weapons you refer to, do they leave a pattern on the material, a wavy, ripply pattern?

Bill: That I don't know. All I know about the beam weapons is this. That they are only effective at short range; that they can paralyze a human being; they can levitate a human being; they can burn something out of your hands without hurting you, like an M-16; and fry you to a crisp and nothing but ashes is left. It can give you a sunburn. It depends upon the degree of how they want to use this thing as to exactly what it will do. That's what I remember, and that's what my research has also confirmed. At Ellsworth Air Force Base, in fact, one airman security patrol encountered an alien craft and aliens on the ground. He aimed his M-16 at them, and this weapon, this beam hit the M-16 and literally vaporized it. He had burns on his hands, but otherwise he was unhurt.

Randy: Have you read or heard the reports about something called spontaneous human combustion?

Bill: Yes! That is caused by...in fact, it can, it can be done and it's a weapon that we use. The intelligence community can get rid of some...

Randy: I respect you a great deal. You know things that you shouldn't know, but you're right.

Bill: Yes, I do know things that I shouldn't know, and hopefully I can get it all out before something happens to me. But you know, I just, I love this country so much, I love the Constitiution so much. What they've been able to do, and the way that they've been able to fool the citizens of this country...I don't care what happens to me. I've got to stop this. I've got to do everything in my power to stop this.

Randy: Well, I'm not one of — I don't know, for lack of a better term, I'm not one of these wild-eyed loonies that runs around doing the rest of it. As I told Col. Brown, "Look, I'm just a guy. I work in the computer industry; I make modems. I travel around the world, I talk computer systems. I mean, that's about it. Okay? I mean, yeah, I like to go shoot my gun at the target range, and I'm an armchair commando, and I like reading *Soldier of Fortune* magazine, and vicariously living adventures through other people. So I'm not a holy roller. I mean, I have my own belief in God, but I don't go around espousing it to everybody. And I'm not one of these esoterics that run around talking about Maitreya and the Hinduisms and all the rest of this, the chakras and all the rest of it. I know those people are out there, I know they exist. As a matter of fact, I'm dating one of them, but that's her beliefs and if she wants to believe that, that's fine."

Bill: Sure.

Randy: When this came in out of the blue, I've had a lot of thought in my own head. You've galvanized a lot of them, especially the text where you were talking about the sudden influx of media and television on an alien presence among us in our society. I've felt that for almost two years, and I could never really verbalize it.

Bill: Oh yeah, they're desensitizing us so that when it happens, all of the things that they feared in the beginning that led to all the lies that led to all the crimes won't cause what they feared. It won't cause the collapse of our society and our culture and our religions. It will affect the economy, though, quite a bit.

Randy: The economy is out the door, anyway...

Bill: Yeah, and that may be what they're waiting for, to change into a cashless society so it can't have that kind of effect.

Randy: Yeah, there was an awful lot, you see. I have my sister and my mother are both, let's say God's Green Berets. You know, they're super religious types — "God bless you, come to church" type thing, and at their urging I went through the Bible and I read it. I read it four or five times, and every time I came back with it I kept seeing different things. And I have my own views on life and on a variety of things. And until I read your material, it never really galvanized me into thinking things. Now, like I said, the only thing I can really relate to you is what I experienced during the Apollo-Soyuz shot.

Bill: That's great! Because what you experienced there is just confirmation of what I've been telling everybody. There is a secret space program. There is a control group called MAJORITY. The President is called MAJESTY in connection with these things. What you were getting, the MAJESTY advisory messages, were to keep the President updated.

Randy: You know, the real funny part about all of that is the guy who would come in and was using our facility. His name was Logan, Mr. Logan. His title was supposed to be communications coordinator, but I never seen him do a damn thing except come into that room, read traffic, draft a reply, and then go back up to CIC. Now, we were in what was called the GENSER, general service side of communications. We weren't the spooks. The spooks had their own little quarters over on the other side of the ship.

Bill: Sure.

Randy: But we did have the KL-47 and the rest of the NASA types. The civilian types would come down to — we had a message window in the hallway and they'd come up and they'd hand their outgoing messages in the window and they would go out on the general service circuits. The only stuff that we handled was the, was traffic for MAJORITY CONTROL with MAJESTY advisories and that was it. And a lot of it, like I said, was a lot of textual data. I mean, there was tons of text, and it was all couched in techno-babble that I didn't really understand. But I do remember the acronym IACs everywhere. I mean completely repetitious.

Bill: Oh yeah.

Randy: You know, that's as much as I can offer you.

Bill: Do you remember where the messages were sent for MAJORITY CONTROL?

Randy: No. The location of MAJORITY CONTROL was never disclosed. The only thing I can assume is that it was somewhere north. The ship was anchored — well, we weren't anchored, we were at what was called sea-anchor, which I am sure you are aware of. We were on an east-west axis so that all of our antennas could be brought to bear on the western horizon, because that's the way the spacecraft was coming around. The antenna that was assigned to my circuit was an antenna called an RLPA or Rotating Log Periodic Antenna, which is a very, very directional antenna, and it was pointed north.

Bill: What was north of you at that point?

Randy: Thule, Greenland.

Bill: Thule, Greenland! Okay, hmmmm, very interesting. Also, I'm glad you saw the message about Nixon, because everybody thought sure that if anything was whacko, that was the whackiest thing that I said.

Randy: Actually, no. That one made complete sense, because those days surrounding Nixon's announcement — you said that message was sent five days previous to his announced resignation. That five-day period, if I remember my history correctly, was extremely turmoiled, and if you go back to the New York Times and read in depth the political commentary during those days, what you're going to find is that there was a awful lot of turbulence. I mean, five days prior there were a lot of steps being taken. It would not surprise me if that message was — that message would have been promulgated and sent five full days prior to the public announcement, because the public is always the last one to know. So I found that the most realistic of the things that were in here.

Bill: Fantastic! God is answering my prayers. Oh wow, it makes me so happy. Listen Randall, I've been taping this whole phone conversation. If you want me to destroy this tape, I will. The reason I do it is I never know when somebody's going to say something that is important or not.

Randy: I have nothing to hide from you, Bill.

Bill: Okay, but I just want you to know I've never betrayed a source or used a person's name when they asked me not to. I've never used a tape if they asked me not to. If they asked me to destroy it, I've always done that. I try to work with everybody in a manner that they're comfortable working with, because my goal is not to embarrass or hurt anyone, it's to stop this thing that's happening.

Randy: Well, you've got another recruit.

Bill: Fantastic!

Randy: Question?

Bill: Sure.

Randy: Who is Linda Howe?

Bill: Linda Moulton Howe is a TV producer who — I don't remember when it was, '78 or something like that, she made a film called "A Strange Harvest" about the animal mutilations, the cattle mutilations...

Randy: Yeah, because in your notarized statement you make reference to her.

Bill: Yes, she contacted me along with a whole bunch of other people, but I tried to pick out the people who I thought were the most professional and the most likely to stand up under scrutiny or attempts to discredit and I figured she was one of those people, so...

Randy I think, I think where you're at right now with the data you have is — I mean, it's time to try to get it in front of people.

Bill: Yes, that's what I'm trying to do.

Randy: I'm in the process now of — as a matter of fact, when you called I was drafting the cover of a FAX that I'm sending to KGO Radio, which is a local radio talk station. Its a clear-channel station; it's heard all up and down the West Coast.

Bill: Great! Fantastic!

Randy: There's a moderator there named Ron Owens who — I'm sending this to him with a statement, "This is not being sent to you as a joke. It's being sent to you as something that I think you should take a minute and just read it." And I've asked him to contact you. And basically I said, "Ron, if ten percent of this is true, then we're in trouble."

Bill: Right. Absolutely. And there's a lot...you know, when I give a talk or something, someone will always stand up and say, "How do we know that you're not just feeding us disinformation?" and I say, "Just think about what you're saying. What I'm after is the truth. I'm telling you what I saw in these documents and where my research has led me over the intervening 17 years. That's what I am imparting to you. I want you to go and verify this or not verify it or prove it wrong or whatever you can do on your own. And I'm perfectly willing to listen to anything that you have to say, but just think about what you just said. If in fact I'm giving you disinformation, then you're in worse trouble than you ever thought of. It would be better if there *are* aliens, because if there's not aliens that means this whole thing has been perpetrated by the Government for some purpose that we don't even know about. What it really means is we got the whole human establishment against us." And that really opens their eyes because it's true.

Randy: You just kicked off another memory...

And that is another story. Note: Randy Terpstra called the Billy Goodman Happening two days later, during the week ending November 4, 1989, and repeated live on the air what he told me during this taped phone conversation. On Sunday, November 5, 1989, I played the tape to an audience of approximately 800 people at Hollywood High School.

When President Nixon gave his farewell speech, he said he would tell the American people the truth about UFOs. Like James Forrestal, Richard Nixon found himself a prisoner on the mental ward of Bethesda Naval Hospital. Unlike Forrestal, Nixon survived. He has remained silent.

CHAPTER 12

THE SECRET GOVERNMENT

The Origin, Identity, and Purpose of MJ-12

May 23, 1989

Updated November 21, 1990

The signs are increasing.
The lights in the sky will appear red, blue, green, rapidly.
Someone is coming from very far and wants to meet
the people of the Earth.
Meetings have already taken place.
But those who have really seen have been silent.
Pope John XXII, 1935

**** TOP SECRET****

PERSPECTIVE

Many sources of information were used to research this chapter. I originally wrote this piece as a research paper. It was first delivered at the MUFON Symposium on July 2, 1989, in Las Vegas, Nevada. Most of this knowledge comes directly from, or is a result of my own research into the TOP SECRET/MAJIC material which I saw and read between the years 1970 and 1973 as a member of the Intelligence Briefing Team of the Commander in Chief of the Pacific Fleet. Since some of this information was derived from sources that I cannot divulge for obvious reasons, and from published sources which I cannot vouch for, this chapter must be termed a hypothesis. I firmly believe that if aliens are real, this is the true nature of the Beast. It is the only scenario that has been able to bind all the diverse elements. It is the only scenario that answers all the questions and places the various fundamental mysteries in an arena that makes sense. It is the only explanation which shows the chronology of events and demonstrates that the chronologies, when assembled, match perfectly. The bulk of this I believe to be true if the material that I viewed in the Navy is authentic. As for the rest, I do not know, and that is why this paper must be termed a hypothesis. Most historic and current available evidence supports this hypothesis.

THE SECRET GOVERNMENT

During the years following World War II the government of the United States was confronted with a series of events which were to change beyond prediction its future and with it the future of humanity. These events were so incredible that they defied belief. A stunned President Truman and his top military commanders found themselves virtually impotent after having just won the most devastating and costly war in history.

The United States had developed, used, and was the only nation on earth in possession of the atomic bomb. This new weapon had the potential to destroy any enemy, and even the Earth itself. At that time the United States had the best economy, the most advanced technology, the highest standard of living, exerted the most influence, and fielded the largest and most powerful military forces in history. We can only imagine the confusion and concern when the informed elite of the United States Government discovered that an alien spacecraft piloted by insectlike beings from a totally incomprehensible culture had crashed in the desert of New Mexico.

Between January 1947 and December 1952 at least 16 crashed or downed alien craft, 65 alien bodies, and 1 live alien were recovered. An additional alien craft had exploded and nothing was recovered from that incident. Of these events, 13 occurred within the borders of the United States, not including the craft which disintegrated in the air. Of these 13, 1 was in Arizona, 11 were in New Mexico, and 1 was in Nevada. Three occurred in foreign countries. Of those, 1 was in Norway and the last 2 were in Mexico. Sightings of UFOs were so numerous that serious investigation and debunking of each report became impossible, utilizing the existing intelligence assets.

An alien craft was found on February 13, 1948, on a mesa near Aztec, New Mexico. Another craft was located on March 25, 1948, in White Sands Proving Ground. It was 100 feet in diameter. A total of 17 alien bodies were recovered from those two crafts. Of even greater significance was the discovery of a large number of human body parts stored within both of these vehicles. A demon had reared its head and paranoia quickly took hold of everyone then "in the know." The Secret lid immediately became a Top Secret lid and was screwed down tight. The security blanket was even tighter than that imposed upon the Manhattan Project. In the coming years these events were to become the most closely guarded secrets in the history of the world.

A special group of America's top scientists were organized under the name Project SIGN in December 1947 to study the phenomenon. The whole nasty business was contained. Project SIGN evolved into Project GRUDGE in December 1948. A low-level collection and disinformation project named BLUE BOOK was formed under GRUDGE. Sixteen volumes were to come out of GRUDGE. "Blue Teams" were put together to recover the crashed disks and dead or live aliens. The Blue Teams were later to evolve into Alpha Teams under Project POUNCE.

During these early years the United States Air Force and the Central Intelligence Agency exercised complete control over the "alien secret." In fact, the CIA was formed by Presidential Executive Order first as the Central Intelligence Group for the express purpose of dealing with the alien presence. Later the National Security Act was passed, establishing it as the Central Intelligence Agency.

The National Security Council was established to oversee the intelligence community and especially the alien endeavor. A series of National Security Council memos and Executive orders removed the CIA from the sole task of gathering foreign intelligence and slowly but thoroughly "legalized" direct action in the form of covert activities at home and abroad.

On December 9, 1947, Truman approved issuance of NSC-4, entitled "Coordination of Foreign Intelligence Information Measures" at the urging of Secretaries Marshall, Forrestal, Patterson, and the director of the State Department's Policy Planning Staff, George Kennan.

The *Foreign and Military Intelligence, Book 1*, "Final Report of the Select Committee to Study Governmental Operations with Respect to Intelligence Activities," United States Senate, 94th Congress, 2nd Session, Report No. 94-755, April 26, 1976, p. 49, states: "This directive empowered the Secretary of State to coordinate overseas information activities designed to counter communism."

A Top Secret annex to NSC-4, NSC-4A, instructed the director of Central Intelligence to undertake covert psychological activities in pursuit of the aims set forth in NSC-4. The initial authority given the CIA for covert operations under NSC-4A did not establish formal procedures for either coordinating or approving these operations. It simply directed the DCI to "undertake covert actions and to ensure, through liaison with State and Defense, that the resulting operations were consistent with American policy."

Later NSC-10/1 and NSC-10/2 were to supersede NSC-4 and NSC-4A and expand the covert abilities even further. The Office of Policy Coordination (OPC) was chartered to carry out an expanded program of covert activities. NSC-10/1 and NSC-10/2 validated illegal and extralegal practices and procedures as being agreeable to the national security leadership. The reaction was swift. In the eyes of the intelligence community "no holds were barred." Under NSC-10/1 an Executive Coordination Group was established to review, but not approve, covert project proposals. The ECG was secretly tasked to coordinate the alien projects. NSC-10/1 & /2 were interpreted to mean that no one at the top wanted to know about anything until it was over and successful.

These actions established a buffer between the President and the information. It was intended that this buffer serve as a means for the President to deny knowledge if leaks divulged the true state of affairs. This buffer was used in later years for the purpose of effectively isolating succeeding Presidents from any knowledge of the alien presence other than what the Secret Government and the intelligence community wanted them to know. NSC-10/2 established a study panel which met secretly and was made up of the scientific minds of the day. The study panel was not called MJ-12. Another NSC memo, NSC-10/5 further outlined the duties of the study panel. These NSC memos and secret Executive orders set the stage for the creation of MJ-12 only four years later.

Secretary of Defense James Forrestal objected to the secrecy. He was a very idealistic and religious man. He believed that the public should be told. James Forrestal was also one of the first known abductees. When he began to talk to leaders of the opposition party and leaders of the Congress about the alien problem he was asked to resign by Truman. He expressed his fears to many people. Rightfully, he believed that he was being watched. This was interpreted by those who were ignorant of the facts as paranoia. Forrestal later was said to have suffered a mental breakdown. He was ordered to the mental ward of Bethesda Naval Hospital. In spite of the fact that the Administration had no authority to have him committed, the order was carried out. In fact, it was feared that Forrestal would begin to talk again. He had to be isolated and discredited. His family and friends were denied permission to visit. Finally, on May 21, 1949, Forrestal's brother made a fateful decision. He notified authorities that he intended to remove James from Bethesda on May 22. Sometime in the early morning of May 22, 1949, agents of the CIA tied a sheet around James Forrestal's neck, fastened the other end to a fixture in his room, then threw James Forrestal out the window. The sheet tore and he plummeted to his death. James Forrestal's secret diaries were confiscated by the CIA and were kept in the White House for many years. Due to public demand the diaries were eventually rewritten and published in a sanitized version. The real diary information was later furnished by the CIA in book form to an agent who published the material as fiction. The name of the agent is Whitley Strieber and the book is *Majestic*. James Forrestal became one of the first victims of the cover-up.

The live alien that had been found wandering in the desert from the 1949 Roswell crash was named EBE. The name had been suggested by Dr. Vannevar Bush and was short for Extraterrestrial Biological Entity. EBE had a tendency to lie, and for over a year would give only the desired answer to questions asked. Those questions which would have resulted in an undesirable answer went unanswered. At some point during the second year of captivity he began to open up. The information derived from EBE was startling, to say the least. This compilation of his revelations became the foundation of what would later be called the "Yellow Book." Photographs were taken of EBE which, among others, I was to view years later in Project Grudge.

In late 1951 EBE became ill. Medical personnel had been unable to determine the cause of EBE's illness and had no background from which to draw. EBE's system was chlorophyll-based and he processed food into energy much the same as plants. Waste material was excreted the same as plants. Several experts were called in to study the illness. These specialists included medical doctors, botanists, and entomologists. A botanist, Dr. Guillermo Mendoza, was brought in to try and help him recover. Dr. Mendoza worked to save EBE until June 2, 1952, when EBE died. Dr. Mendoza became the expert on at least this type alien of biology. The movie *E.T.* is the thinly disguised story of EBE.

In a futile attempt to save EBE and to gain favor with this technologically superior race, the United States began broadcasting a call for help early in 1952 into the vast regions of space. The call went unanswered but the project, dubbed SIGMA, continued as an effort of good faith.

President Truman created the supersecret National Security Agency (NSA) by secret Executive order on November 4, 1952. Its primary purpose was to decipher the alien communications, language, and establish a dialogue with the extraterrestrials. This most urgent task was a continuation of the earlier effort. The secondary purpose of the NSA was to monitor all communications and emissions from any and all electronic devices worldwide for the purpose of gathering intelligence, both human and alien, and to contain the secret of the alien presence. Project SIGMA was successful.

The NSA also maintains communications with the Luna base and other secret space programs. By executive order of the President, the NSA is exempt from all laws which do not specifically name the NSA in the text of the law as being subject to that law. That means that if the agency is not spelled out in the text of any and every law passed by the Congress it is not subject to that or those laws. The NSA now performs many other duties and in fact is the premier agency within the intelligence network. Today the NSA receives approximately 75% of the monies allotted to the intelligence community. The old saying "where the money goes therein the power resides" is true. The DCI today is a figurehead maintained as a public ruse. The primary task of the NSA is still alien communications, but now includes other extraterrestrial projects as well.

President Truman had been keeping our allies, including the Soviet Union, informed of the developing alien problem. This had been done in case the aliens turned out to be a threat to the human race. Plans were formulated to defend the Earth in case of invasion. Great difficulty was encountered in maintaining international secrecy. It was decided that an outside group was necessary to coordinate and control international efforts in order to hide the secret from the normal scrutiny of governments by the press. The result was the formation of a secret ruling body which became known as the Bilderberg Group. The group was formed and met for the first time in 1952. They were named after the first publicly known meeting place, the Bilderberg Hotel. That public meeting took place in 1954. They were nicknamed The Bilderbergers. The headquarters of this group is Geneva, Switzerland. The Bilderbergers evolved into a secret world government that now controls everything. The United Nations was then, and is now, an international joke.

Beginning in 1953 a new president occupied the White House. He was a man used to a structured staff organization with a chain of command. His method was to delegate authority and rule by committee. He made major decisions, but only when his advisors were unable to come to a consensus. His normal method was to read through or listen to several alternatives and then approve one. Those who worked closely with him have stated that his favorite comment was, "Just do whatever it takes." He spent a lot of time on the golf course. This was not unusual for a man who had been career Army with the ultimate position of Supreme Allied Commander during the war, a post which had earned him five stars. The President was General of the Army Dwight David Eisenhower.

During his first year in office, 1953, at least 10 more crashed discs were recovered along with 26 dead and 4 live aliens. Of the 10, 4 were found in Arizona, 2 in Texas, 1 in New Mexico, 1 in Louisiana, 1 in Montana, and 1 in South Africa. There were hundreds of sightings.

Eisenhower knew that he had to wrestle and beat the alien problem. He knew that he could not do it by revealing the secret to the Congress. Early in 1953 the new President turned to his friend and fellow member of the Council on Foreign Relations Nelson Rockefeller. Eisenhower and Rockefeller began planning the secret structure of alien-task supervision, which was to become a reality within one year. The idea for MJ-12 was thus born.

It was Nelson's uncle Winthrop Aldrich who had been crucial in convincing Eisenhower to run for President. The whole Rockefeller family and with them, the Rockefeller empire, had solidly backed Ike. Eisenhower belonged heart and soul to the Council on Foreign Relations and the Rockefeller family. Asking Rockefeller for help with the alien problem was to be the biggest mistake Eisenhower ever made for the future of the United States and maybe for humanity.

Within one week of Eisenhower's election he had appointed Nelson Rockefeller chairman of a Presidential Advisory Committee on Government Organization. Rockefeller was responsible for planning the reorganization of the government, something he had dreamed of for many years. New Deal programs went into one single cabinet position called the Department of Health, Education and Welfare. When the Congress approved the new Cabinet position in April 1953, Nelson was named to the post of Undersecretary to Oveta Culp Hobby.

In 1953 astronomers discovered large objects in space which were tracked moving toward the Earth. It was first believed that they were asteroids. Later evidence proved that the objects could only be spaceships. Project SIGMA intercepted alien radio communications. When the objects reached the Earth they took up a very high geosynchronous orbit around the equator. There were several huge ships, and their actual intent was unknown. Project SIGMA and a new project, PLATO, through radio communications using the computer binary language, were able to arrange a landing that resulted in face-to-face contact with alien beings from another planet. This landing took place in the desert. The movie, *Close Encounters of the Third Kind* is a fictionalized version of the actual events. Project PLATO was tasked with establishing diplomatic relations with this race of space aliens. A hostage was left with us as a pledge that they would return and formalize a treaty.

In the meantime, a race of humanoid aliens landed at Homestead Air Force Base in Florida and successfully communicated with the U.S. government. This group warned us against the race orbiting the equator and offered to help us with our spiritual development. They demanded that we dismantle and destroy our nuclear weapons as the major condition. They refused to exchange technology citing that we were spiritually unable to handle the technology we already possessed. These overtures were rejected on the grounds that it would be foolish to disarm in the face of such an uncertain future. There was no track record to read from. It may have been an unfortunate decision.

A third landing at Muroc, now Edwards Air Force Base, took place in 1954. The base was closed for three days and no one was allowed to enter or leave during that time. The historical event had been planned in advance. Details of a treaty had been agreed upon. Eisenhower arranged to be in Palm Springs on vacation. On the appointed day the President was spirited to the base. The excuse was given to the press that he was visiting a dentist. Witnesses to the event have stated that three UFOs flew over the base and then landed. Antiaircraft batteries were undergoing live-fire training and the startled personnel actually fired at the crafts as they passed overhead. Luckily, the shells missed and no one was injured.

President Eisenhower met with the aliens on February 20, 1954, and a formal treaty between the alien nation and the United States of America was signed. We then received our first alien ambassador from outer space. He was the hostage that had been left at the first landing in the desert. His name and title was His Omnipotent Highness Crlll or Krlll, pronounced Crill or Krill. In the American tradition of disdain for royal titles he was secretly called Original Hostage Crlll, or Krlll. Shortly after this meeting President Eisenhower suffered a heart attack.

Four others present at the meeting were Franklin Allen of the Hearst newspapers, Edwin Nourse of Brookings Institute, Gerald Light of metaphysical research fame, and Catholic Bishop MacIntyre of Los Angeles. Their reaction was judged as a microcosm of what the public reaction might be. Based upon this reaction, it was decided that the public could not be told. Later studies confirmed the decision as sound.

An emotionally revealing letter written by Gerald Light spells it out in chilling detail: "My dear Friend: I have just returned from Muroc. The report is true — devastatingly true! I made the journey in company with Franklin Allen of the Hearst papers and Edwin Nourse of Brookings Institute (Truman's erstwhile financial adviser) and Bishop MacIntyre of L.A. (confidential names for the present, please.) When we were allowed to enter the restricted section (after about six hours in which we were checked on every possible item, event, incident and aspect of our personal and public lives), I had the distinct feeling that the world had come to an end with fantastic realism. For I have never seen so many human beings in a state of complete collapse and confusion, as they realized that their own world had indeed ended with such finality as to beggar description. The reality of "other-plane" aeroforms is now and forever removed from the realms of speculation and made a rather painful part of the consciousness of every responsible scientific and political group. During my two days' visit I saw five separate and distinct types of aircraft being studied and handled by our Air Force officials — with the assistance and permission of the Etherians!

"I have no words to express my reactions. It has finally happened. It is now a matter of history. President Eisenhower, as you may already know, was spirited over to Muroc one night during his visit to Palm Springs recently. And it is my conviction that he will ignore the terrific conflict between the various "authorities" and go directly to the people via radio and television — if the impasse continues much longer. From what I could gather, an official statement to the country is being prepared for delivery about the middle of May."

We know that no such announcement was ever made. The silence-control group won the day. We also know that two more ships, for which we can find no witnesses, either landed sometime after the three or were already at the base before the three landed. Gerald Light specifically states that five ships were present and were undergoing study by the Air Force. His metaphysical experience is evident in that he calls the entities "Etherians." Gerald Light capitalized "Etherians," calling attention to the fact that these beings might have been viewed as gods by Mr. Light.

The alien emblem was known as the "Trilateral insignia" and was displayed on the craft and worn on the alien uniforms. Both of these landings and the second meeting were filmed. These films exist today.

The treaty stated that the aliens would not interfere in our affairs and we would not interfere in theirs. We would keep their presence on earth a secret. They would furnish us with advanced technology and would help us in our technological development. They would not make any treaty with any other Earth nation. They could abduct humans on a limited and periodic basis for the purpose of medical examination and monitoring of our development, with the stipulation that the humans would not be harmed, would be returned to their point of abduction, would have no memory of the event, and that the alien nation would furnish Majesty Twelve with a list of all human contacts and abductees on a regularly scheduled basis.

It was agreed that each nation would receive the ambassador of the other for as long as the treaty remained in force. It was further agreed that the alien nation and the United States would exchange 16 personnel with the purpose of learning of each other. The alien "guests" would remain on earth. The human "guests" would travel to the alien point of origin for a specified period of time, then return, at which point a reverse exchange would be made. A reenactment of this event was dramatized in the movie *Close Encounters of the Third Kind*. A tipoff to who works for whom can be determined by the fact that Dr. J. Allen Hynek served as the technical advisor for the film. I noticed that the Top Secret report containing the official version of the truth of the alien question, entitled Project GRUDGE, which I read while in the Navy, was co-authored by Lt. Col. Friend and Dr. J. Allen Hynek, who was cited as a CIA asset attached to Project GRUDGE — Dr. Hynek, the one who debunked many legitimate UFO incidents when he functioned as the scientific member of the very public Project BLUEBOOK. Dr. Hynek is the man responsible for the infamous "it was only swamp gas" statement.

It was agreed that bases would be constructed underground for the use of the alien nation and that two bases would be constructed for the joint use of the alien nation and the United States Government. Exchange of technology would take place in the jointly occupied bases. These alien bases would be constructed under Indian reservations in the Four Corners area of Utah, Colorado, New Mexico and Arizona, and one would be constructed in an area known as Dreamland. Dreamland was built in the Mojave desert near, or in, a place called Yucca. I cannot remember if it was Yucca Valley, Yucca Flat, or Yucca Proving Ground, but Yucca Valley is what I always seem to want to say. More UFO sightings and incidents occur in the Mojave desert of California than any other place in the world. So many, in fact, that no one even bothers to make reports. Anyone who ventures into the desert to talk to the residents will be astounded by the frequency of activity and with the degree of acceptance demonstrated by those who have come to regard UFOs as normal.

All alien areas are under complete control of the Naval Department, according to the documents that I read. All personnel who work in these complexes receive their checks from the Navy through a subcontractor. The checks never make reference to the government or the Navy. Construction of the bases began immediately, but progress was slow. Large amounts of money were made available in 1957. Work continued on the Yellow Book.

Project REDLIGHT was formed and experimentation in test-flying alien craft was begun in earnest. A super-Top Secret facility was built at Groom Lake in Nevada in the midst of the weapons test range. It was code-named Area 51. The installation was placed under the Department of the Navy and all personnel required a Q clearance as well as Executive (Presidential, called MAJESTIC) approval. This is ironic, due to the fact that the President of the United States does not have clearance to visit the site. The alien base and exchange of technology actually took place in an area code-named Dreamland above ground, and the underground portion was dubbed "the Dark Side of the Moon." According to the documentation that I read, at least 600 alien beings actually resided full time at this site along with an unknown number of scientists and CIA personnel. Due to the fear of implantation, only certain people were allowed to interface with the alien beings, and those personnel were and are watched and monitored continuously.

The Army was tasked to form a supersecret organization to furnish security for the alien-tasked projects. This organization became the National Reconnaissance Organization based at Fort Carson, Colorado. The specific teams trained to secure the projects were called Delta. Lt. Col. James "Bo" Gritz was a Delta Force Commander.

A second project code-named SNOWBIRD was promulgated to explain away any sightings of the REDLIGHT crafts as being Air Force experiments. The SNOWBIRD crafts were manufactured using conventional technology and were flown for the press on several occasions. Project SNOWBIRD was also used to debunk legitimate public sightings of alien craft (UFOs to the public, IACs to those in the know). Project SNOWBIRD was very successful, and reports from the public declined steadily until recent years.

A multimillion-dollar Secret fund was organized and kept by the Military Office of the White House. This fund was used to build over 75 deep underground facilities. Presidents who asked were told the fund was used to build deep underground shelters for the President in case of war. Only a few were built for the President. Millions of dollars were funneled through this office to Majesty Twelve and then out to the contractors. It was used to build Top Secret alien bases as well as Top Secret DUMB (Deep Underground Military Bases) and the facilities promulgated by Alternative 2 throughout the nation. President Johnson used this fund to build a movie theater and pave the road on his ranch. He had no idea of its true purpose.

The secret White House underground-construction fund was set up in 1957 by President Eisenhower. The funding was obtained from Congress under the guise of "construction and maintenance of secret sites where the President could be taken in case of military attack: Presidential Emergency Sites." The sites are literally holes in the ground, deep enough to withstand a nuclear blast, and are outfitted with state-of-the-art communications equipment. To date there are more than 75 sites spread around the country which were built using money from this fund. The Atomic Energy Commission has built at least an additional 22 underground sites. See the chapter on Mt. Weather.

The location and everything to do with these sites were and are considered and treated as Top Secret. The money was and is in control of the Military Office of the White House, and was and is laundered through so circuitous a web that even the most knowledgeable spy or accountant cannot follow it. As of 1980 only a few at the beginning and end of this web knew what the money was for. At the beginning were Representative George Mahon of Texas, the chairman of the House Appropriations Committee and of its Defense Subcommittee; and Representative Robert Sikes of Florida, chairman of the House Appropriations Military Construction Subcommittee. Today it is rumored that House Speaker Jim Wright controlled the money in Congress and that a power struggle removed him. At the end of the line were the President, Majesty Twelve, the director of the Military Office and a commander at the Washington Navy Yard.

The money was authorized by the Appropriations Committee, who allocated it to the Department of Defense as a Top Secret item in the Army construction program. The Army, however, could not spend it and in fact did not even know what it was for. Authorization to spend the money was in reality given to the Navy. The money was channeled to the Chesapeake Division of the Navy Engineers, who did not know what it was for, either. Not even the commanding officer, who was an admiral, knew what the fund was to be used for. Only one man, a Navy commander who was assigned to the Chesapeake Division but in reality was responsible only to the Military Office of the White House, knew of the actual purpose, amount, and ultimate destination of the Top Secret money. The total secrecy surrounding the fund meant that almost every trace of it could be made to disappear by the very few people who controlled it. There has never been and most likely never will be an audit of this secret money.

Large amounts of money were transferred from the Top Secret fund to a location at Palm Beach, Florida, that belongs to the Coast Guard called Peanut Island. The island is adjacent to property which was owned by Joseph Kennedy. The money was said to have been used for landscaping and general beautification. Some time ago a TV news special on the Kennedy assassination told of a Coast Guard officer transferring money in a briefcase to a Kennedy employee across this property line. Could this have been a secret payment to the Kennedy family for the loss of their son John F. Kennedy? The payments continued through the year 1967 and then stopped. The total amount transferred is unknown and the actual use of the money is unknown.

Meanwhile, Nelson Rockefeller changed positions again. This time he was to take C. D. Jackson's old position, which had been called the Special Assistant for Psychological Strategy. With Nelson's appointment the name was changed to the Special Assistant for Cold War Strategy. This position would evolve over the years into the same position Henry Kissinger was ultimately to hold under President Nixon. Officially he was to give "advice and assistance in the development of increased understanding and cooperation among all peoples." The official description was a smoke screen, for secretly he was the Presidential Coordinator for the Intelligence Community. In his new post Rockefeller reported directly, and solely, to the President. He attended meetings of the Cabinet, the Council on Foreign Economic Policy, and the National Security Council, which was the highest policy-making body in the government.

Nelson Rockefeller was also given a second important job as the head of the secret unit called the Planning Coordination Group, which was formed under NSC 5412/1 in March 1955. The group consisted of different ad hoc members, depending on the subject on the agenda. The basic members were Rockefeller, a representative of the Department of Defense, a representative of the Department of State, and the Director of Central Intelligence. It was soon called the 5412 Committee or the Special Group. NSC 5412/1 established the rule that covert operations were subject to approval by an executive committee, whereas in the past these operations were initiated solely on the authority of the Director of Central Intelligence.

By secret Executive Memorandum NSC 5510, Eisenhower had preceded NSC 5412/1 to establish a permanent committee (not ad hoc) to be known as Majesty Twelve (MJ-12) to oversee and conduct all covert activities concerned with the alien question. NSC 5412/1 was created to explain the purpose of these meetings when Congress and the press became curious.

Majesty Twelve was made up of Nelson Rockefeller, Director of Central Intelligence Allen Welsh Dulles, Secretary of State John Foster Dulles, Secretary of Defense Charles E. Wilson, Chairman of the Joint Chiefs of Staff Admiral Arthur W. Radford, Director of the Federal Bureau of Investigation J. Edgar Hoover, six men from the executive committee of the Council on Foreign Relations known as the "Wise Men," six men from the executive committee of the JASON Group, and Dr. Edward Teller.

The JASON Group is a secret scientific group formed during the Manhattan Project and administered by the Mitre Corporation. The inner core of the Council on Foreign Relations recruits its members from the Skull & Bones and the Scroll & Key societies of Harvard and Yale. The Wise Men are key members of the Council on Foreign Relations and also members of a secret Order of the Quest known as the JASON Society.

There were 19 members of Majesty Twelve. The first rule of Majesty Twelve was that no order could be given and no action could be taken without a majority vote of twelve in favor, thus Majority Twelve. Orders issued by Majesty Twelve became known as Majority Twelve directives.

This group was made up over the years of the top officers and directors of the Council on Foreign Relations and later the Trilateral Commission. Gordon Dean, George Bush and Zbigniew Brzezinski were among them. The most important and influential of the Wise Men were John McCloy, Robert Lovett, Averell Harriman, Charles Bohlen, George Kennan, and Dean Acheson. Their policies were to last well into the decade of the '70s. It is significant that President Eisenhower as well as the first six Majesty Twelve members from the Government were also members of the Council on Foreign Relations. This gave control of the most secret and powerful group in government to a special-interest club that was itself controlled by the Illuminati.

Thorough researchers will soon discover that not all of the Wise Men attended Harvard or Yale and not all of them were chosen for Skull & Bones or Scroll & Key membership during their college years. You will be able to quickly clear up the mystery by obtaining the book *The Wise Men* by Walter Isaacson and Evan Thomas, Simon and Schuster, New York. Under illustration #9 in the center of the book you will find the caption: "Lovett with the Yale Unit, above far right, and on the beach: His initiation into Skull and Bones came at an air base near Dunkirk." I have found that members were chosen on an ongoing basis by invitation based upon merit postcollege and were not confined to Harvard or Yale attendees only. Because of this fact, a complete list of Skull & Bones members can never be compiled from the catalogues or addresses of the college segment of the Russell Trust, also known as the Brotherhood of Death, or the Skull & Bones. Now you know why it has been impossible to pinpoint the membership either by number or by name. I believe that the answer lies hidden in the CFR files, if files exist.

A chosen few were later initiated into the secret branch of the Order of the Quest known as the JASON Society. They are all members of the Council on Foreign Relations and at that time were known as the Eastern Establishment. This should give you a clue to the far-reaching and serious nature of these most secret college societies. The society is alive and well today, but now includes members of the Trilateral Commission as well. The Trilateralists existed secretly *before* 1973. The name of the Trilateral Commission was taken from the alien flag known as the Trilateral Insignia. Majesty Twelve was to survive right up to the present day. Under Eisenhower and Kennedy it was erroneously called the 5412 Committee, or more correctly, the Special Group. In the Johnson administration it became the 303 Committee because the name 5412 had been compromised in the book *The Secret Government*. Actually, NSC 5412/1 was leaked to the author to hide the existence of NSC 5410. Under Nixon, Ford, and Carter it was called the 40 Committee, and under Reagan it became the PI-40 Committee. Over all those years only the name changed.

By 1955 it became obvious that the aliens had deceived Eisenhower and had broken the treaty. Mutilated humans were being found along with mutilated animals across the United States. It was suspected that the aliens were not submitting a complete list of human contacts and abductees to Majesty Twelve and it was suspected that not all abductees had been returned. The Soviet Union was suspected of interacting with them, and this proved to be true. The aliens stated that they had been, and were then, manipulating masses of people through secret societies, witchcraft, magic, the occult, and religion. You must understand that this claim could also be a manipulation. After several Air Force combat air engagements with alien craft it also became apparent that our weapons were no match against them.

In November 1955 NSC-5412/2 was issued establishing a study committee to explore "all factors which are involved in the making and implementing of foreign policy in the nuclear age." This was only a blanket of snow that covered the real subject of study, the alien question.

By secret Executive Memorandum NSC 5511 in 1954, President Eisenhower had commissioned the study group to "examine all the facts, evidence, lies, and deception and discover the truth of the alien question." NSC 5412/2 was only a cover that had become necessary when the press began inquiring as to the purpose of regular meetings of such important men. The first meetings began in 1954 and were called the Quantico meetings because they met at the Quantico Marine Base. The study group was made up solely of 35 members of the Council on Foreign Relations' secret study group. Dr. Edward Teller was invited to participate. Dr. Zbigniew Brzezinski was the study director for the first 18 months. Dr. Henry Kissinger was chosen as the group's study director for the second 18 months beginning in November 1955. Nelson Rockefeller was a frequent visitor during the study.

THE STUDY GROUP MEMBERS

Gordon Dean, Chairman
Dr. Henry Kissinger, Study Director
Dr. Zbigniew Brzezinski, Study Director

Dr. Edward Teller	Frank Altschul
Maj. Gen. Richard C. Lindsay	Hamilton Fish Armstrong
Hanson W. Baldwin	Maj. Gen. James McCormack, Jr.
Lloyd V. Berkner	Robert R. Bowie
Frank C. Nash	McGeorge Bundy
Paul H. Nitze	William A. M. Burden
Charles P. Noyes	John C. Campbell
Frank Pace, Jr.	Thomas K. Finletter
James A. Perkins	George S. Franklin, Jr.
Don K. Price	I.I. Rabi
David Rockefeller	Roswell L. Gilpatric
Oscar M. Ruebhausen	N.E. Halaby
Lt. Gen. James M. Gavin	Gen. Walter Bedell Smith
Caryl P. Haskins	Henry DeWolf Smyth
James T. Hill, Jr.	Shields Warren
Joseph E. Johnson	Carroll L. Wilson
Mervin J. Kelly	Arnold Wolfers

The second-phase meetings were also held at the Marine base at Quantico, Virginia, and the group became known as Quantico II. Nelson Rockefeller built a retreat somewhere in Maryland for Majesty Twelve and the study committee. It could be reached only by air. In this manner they could meet away from public scrutiny. This secret meeting place is known by the code name "the Country Club." Complete living, eating, recreation, library, and meeting facilities exist at the location. (The Aspen Institute is not the Country Club.)

The study group was publicly terminated in the later months of 1956.

---

* * * * TOP SECRET * * * *

Henry Kissinger wrote what was officially termed the results in 1957 as *Nuclear Weapons and Foreign Policy,* published for the Council on Foreign Relations by Harper & Brothers, New York. In truth, the manuscript had already been 80% written while Kissinger was at Harvard. The study group continued, veiled in secrecy. A clue to the seriousness Kissinger attached to the study can be found in statements by his wife and friends. Many of them stated that Henry would leave home early each morning and return late each night without speaking to anyone or responding to anyone. It seemed as if he were in another world which held no room for outsiders.

These statements are very revealing. The revelations of the alien presence and actions during the study must have been a great shock. Henry Kissinger was definitely out of character during this time. He would never again be affected in this manner, no matter the seriousness of any subsequent event. On many occasions he would work very late into the night after having already put in a full day. This behavior eventually led to divorce.

A major finding of the alien study was that the public could not be told. It was believed that this would most certainly lead to economic collapse, collapse of the religious structure, and national panic, which could lead into anarchy. Secrecy thus continued. An offshoot of this finding was that if the public could not be told, Congress could not be told. Funding for the projects and research would have to come from outside the Government. In the meantime money was to be obtained from the military budget and from CIA confidential, nonappropriated funds.

Another major finding was that the aliens were using humans and animals for a source of glandular secretions, enzymes, hormonal secretions, blood plasma and possibly in genetic experiments. The aliens explained these actions as necessary to their survival. They stated that their genetic structure had deteriorated and that they were no longer able to reproduce. They stated that if they were unable to improve their genetic structure, their race would soon cease to exist. We looked upon their explanations with extreme suspicion. Since our weapons were literally useless against the aliens, Majesty Twelve decided to continue friendly diplomatic relations until such time as we were able to develop a technology which would enable us to challenge them on a military basis. Overtures would have to be made to the Soviet Union and other nations to join forces for the survival of humanity. In the meantime plans were developed to research and construct two weapons systems using conventional and nuclear technology, which would hopefully bring us to parity.

The results of the research were Projects JOSHUA and EXCALIBUR.

---

* * * * TOP SECRET * * * *

JOSHUA was a weapon captured from the Germans which was capable of shattering 4-inch-thick armor plate at a range of two miles. It used aimed, low-frequency sound waves, and it was believed that this weapon would be effective against the alien craft and beam weapons. EXCALIBUR was a weapon carried by missile not to rise above 30,000 feet above ground level (AGL), not to deviate from designated target more than 50 meters, able to would penetrate "1,000 meters of tufa, hard-packed soil such as that found in New Mexico," carry a one-megaton warhead, and intended for use in destroying the aliens in their underground bases. JOSHUA was developed successfully but never used, to my knowledge. EXCALIBUR was not pushed until recent years and now, we are told, there is an unprecedented effort to develop this weapon. The public would be told that EXCALIBUR would be needed to take out Soviet underground command posts. We know that is not true because one rule of war is that you try not to destroy the leaders. They are needed either to unconditionally surrender or to negotiate terms. Leaders are also needed to ensure peaceful transition of power and the compliance of the populace to all negotiated or dictated terms.

The events at Fatima in the early part of the century were scrutinized. On the suspicion that it was alien manipulation, an intelligence operation was put into motion to penetrate the secrecy surrounding the event. The United States utilized its Vatican moles and soon obtained the entire Vatican study, which included the prophecy. This prophecy stated that if man did not turn from evil and place himself at the feet of Christ the planet would self-destruct and the events described in the book of Revelations would indeed come to pass. The prophecy demanded that Russia be consecrated to the Sacred Heart. It stated that a child would be born who would unite the world with a plan for world peace and a false religion. The people would discern that he was evil and was indeed the Anti-Christ. World War III would begin in the Middle East with an invasion of Israel by a United Arab nation using conventional weapons, which would culminate in a nuclear holocaust. Most of the life on this planet would suffer horribly and die as a result. The return of Christ would occur shortly thereafter.

When the aliens were confronted with this finding they confirmed that it was true. The aliens explained that they had created us through genetic manipulation in a laboratory. They stated that they had manipulated the human race through religion, satanism, witchcraft, magic, and the occult. They further explained that they were capable of time travel, and the events would indeed come to pass if the conditions were not met. Later exploitation of alien technology by the United States and the Soviet Union, utilizing time travel in a project named RAINBOW, confirmed the prophecy. The aliens showed a hologram, which they claimed was the actual crucifixion of Christ. The Government filmed the hologram. We did not know whether to believe them. Were they using our GENUINE religions to manipulate us? Or were they indeed the source of our religions with which they had been manipulating us all along? Or was this the beginning scenario of the genuine END TIMES and the RETURN OF CHRIST which had been predicted in the Bible? I DO NOT KNOW THE ANSWER.

A symposium was held in 1957 which was attended by some of the great scientific minds then living. They reached the conclusion that by, or shortly after, the year 2000 the planet WOULD self-destruct due to increased population and man's exploitation of the environment WITHOUT ANY HELP FROM GOD OR THE ALIENS.

By secret Executive order of President Eisenhower, the JASON Scholars were ordered to study this scenario and make recommendations from their findings. The JASON Society CONFIRMED the finding of the scientists and made three recommendations called ALTERNATIVES 1, 2, and 3.

Alternative 1 was to use nuclear devices to blast holes in the stratosphere from which the heat and pollution could escape into space. They would then change the human cultures from that of exploitation into cultures of environmental protection. Of the three this was decided to be the least likely to succeed due to the inherent nature of man and the additional damage the nuclear explosions would themselves create. The existence of a hole in the ozone layer may indicate that Alternative 1 might have been attempted. This is, however, only conjecture.

Alternative 2 was to build a vast network of underground cities and tunnels in which a select representation of all cultures and occupations would survive and carry on the human race. The rest of humanity would be left to fend for themselves on the surface of the planet. We know that these facilities have been built and are ready and waiting for the chosen few to be notified.

Alternative 3 was to exploit the alien and conventional technology in order for a select few to leave the earth and establish colonies in outer space. I am not able to either confirm or deny the existence of "batch consignments" of human slaves, which would be used for the manual labor as a part of the plan. The Moon, code-named ADAM, was the object of primary interest, followed by the planet Mars, code-named EVE. I am now in possession of official NASA photographs of one of the moon bases. I believe that the Mars colony is also a reality.

As a delaying action, ALL THREE ALTERNATIVES included birth control, sterilization, and the introduction of deadly microbes to control or slow the growth of the Earth's population. AIDS is only ONE result of these plans. It was decided BY THE ELITE that since the population must be reduced and controlled, it would be in the best interest of the human race to rid ourselves of the undesirable elements of our society. Specific targeted populations included BLACKS, HISPANICS, and HOMO-SEXUALS. The joint U.S. and Soviet leadership dismissed Alternative 1 but ordered work to begin on Alternatives 2 and 3 virtually at the same time.

In 1959 the Rand Corporation hosted a Deep Underground Construction Symposium. In the symposium report, machines are pictured and described which could bore a tunnel 45 feet in diameter at the rate of 5 feet per hour in 1959. It also displays pictures of huge tunnels and underground vaults containing what appear to be complex facilities and possibly even cities. It appears that the previous five years of all-out underground construction had made significant progress by that time.

The ruling powers decided that one means of funding the alien-connected and other "black" projects was to corner the illegal drug market. The English and French had established a historical precedent when they exploited the opium trade in the Far East and used it to fill their coffers and gain a solid foothold in China and Viet Nam, respectively.

A young ambitious member of the Council on Foreign Relations was approached. His name is George Bush, who at the time was the president and CEO of the offshore division of Zapata Oil, based in Texas. Zapata Oil was experimenting with the new technology of offshore drilling. It was correctly thought that the drugs could be shipped from South America to the offshore platforms by fishing boat, to be taken from there to shore by the normal transportation used for supplies and personnel. By this method no customs or law enforcement agency would subject the cargo to search.

George Bush agreed to help, and organized the operation in conjunction with the CIA. The plan worked better than anyone had dreamed. It has since expanded worldwide. There are now many other methods of bringing the illegal drugs into the country. It must always be remembered that George Bush began the sale of drugs to our children. The CIA now controls most of the world's illegal drug markets.

The official space program was boosted by President Kennedy in his inaugural address when he mandated that the United States put a man on the Moon before the end of the decade. Although innocent in its conception, this mandate enabled those in charge to funnel vast amounts of money into black projects and conceal the REAL space program from the American people. A similar program in the Soviet Union served the same purpose. In fact, a joint alien, United States, and Soviet Union base existed on the Moon at the very moment Kennedy spoke the words.

On May 22, 1962, a space probe landed on Mars and confirmed the existence of an environment which could support life. Not long afterward the construction of a colony on the planet Mars began in earnest. Today I believe a colony exists on Mars populated by specially selected people from different cultures and occupations taken from all over the Earth. A public charade of antagonism between the Soviet Union and the United States has been maintained over all these years in order to fund projects in the name of national defense when in fact we are the closest allies.

At some point President Kennedy discovered portions of the truth concerning the drugs and the aliens. He issued an ultimatum in 1963 to Majesty Twelve. President Kennedy assured them that if they did not clean up the drug problem, he would. He informed Majesty Twelve that he intended to reveal the presence of aliens to the American people within the following year, and ordered a plan developed to implement his decision. President Kennedy was not a member of the Council on Foreign Relations and knew nothing of Alternative 2 or Alternative 3. (Although some researchers claim JFK was a member of the CFR, I can find no legitimate list with his name upon it.) Internationally, the operations were supervised by the Bilderberg elite committee known as the Policy Committee. In the United States they were supervised by the executive committee of the CFR and in the Soviet Union by its sister organization.

President Kennedy's decision struck fear into the hearts of those in charge. His assassination was ordered by the Policy Committee and the order was carried out by agents in Dallas. President John F. Kennedy was murdered by the Secret Service agent who drove his car in the motorcade and the act is plainly visible in the Zapruder film. WATCH THE DRIVER AND NOT KENNEDY WHEN YOU VIEW THE FILM. All of the witnesses who were close enough to the car to see William Greer shoot Kennedy were themselves all murdered within two years of the event. The Warren Commission was a farce, and Council on Foreign Relations members made up the majority of its panel. They succeeded in snowing the American people.

Many other patriots who attempted to reveal the alien secret have also been murdered throughout the intervening years. At the present time over 200 material witnesses or people actually involved with the assassination are dead. The odds against this happening are so high that no one has been able to calculate them. The odds against the first 18 to die within two years of the assassination were calculated at *one hundred thousand trillion to one.* You can order a copy of the film by sending $30 + $3 postage & handling to The William Cooper Foundation, 19744 Beach Blvd., Suite 301, Huntington Beach, California 92648.

---

* * * * TOP SECRET * * * *

In December 1988 I had a phone conversation during which I told John Lear what I had seen in the Navy concerning the Kennedy assassination. I told him that the Top Secret documents stated that the act was plainly visible in a film withheld from the public. I told John that I had been looking for a film that showed Greer shoot JFK for 16 years but had not found one. I was shocked and very pleasantly surprised when John asked me, "Would you like to see it?" I, of course, replied in the affirmative and John invited Annie and me to his home in Las Vegas. We spent four days with John. He not only showed me the film but gave me a video copy. I showed the video whenever I spoke to a group of people. The film is titled *Dallas Revisited.* John told me that he obtained it from a CIA acquaintance whom he was not at liberty to name. I later found out the originator of that version of the Zapruder film was Lars Hansson. John Lear was showing the film at every meeting that he conducted.

Shortly after Lear gave me a copy of the film, Lars Hansson called and asked if he could drop by to meet with me at my home in Fullerton, California. I told him he could and asked him to bring a better copy of the film if he had one. Lars said that he would. He stated that he would also bring a film on a man named Bo Gritz, of whom I had never heard. Mr. Hansson informed me that he had made the video for Bo Gritz and John Lear and that both were using it in their lectures. I found out much later that Bo Gritz was selling the tape for $10 per copy.

Lars came to the house, brought the films on videotape and we spoke for about an hour. His main purpose was to tell me that he wanted me to expose people to the film but did not want me to connect him to the film in any manner. I agreed not to divulge the source and I kept my word. I began to use the tape in my lectures. When I found out that Bo Gritz was making it available, I bowed to public pressure and also made it available.

Some time later I read an L.A.-based newsletter (forgot the name) in which Lars Hansson stated that he did not know that I had the film and did not know that I was showing it at lectures. Hansson stated in the newsletter that he was at my Hollywood High lecture on November 5, 1989, and that he tried to protest my use of it during the question-and-answer period but that he never had a chance to be recognized. We videotaped that event, and at the end I asked anyone with questions or comments to walk to a microphone that we had placed in the aisle. I have examined every inch of that videotape and Lars Hansson never got up from his seat, nor did he ever raise his hand, nor did he attempt in any way to be recognized.

Lars later called me again and asked me not to use his voice on the tape, his voice where he says with no hesitation or qualification whatsoever, as he narrates the videotape, "The driver of the car turns with his left arm over his right shoulder with a pistol and fires. You see the .45 automatic, .45-caliber nickel-plated automatic weapon in his left hand. He's firing over his right shoulder; you see it in relief. You see his head pointing backwards towards the President. In this enhanced close-up you see the impact of the bullet upon the President. The force of the shot drives him violently backward against the back of the seat. You see Mrs. Kennedy react in horror." Then later in the film Lars Hansson makes this statement: "You can clearly see his [the driver's] head turning and his arm, and the weapon extending into view over his right shoulder." I agreed not to use his voice. In subsequent lectures I showed the tape with no audio. As it turned out, people were able to see it better with no narration.

It is important that you understand the above, because in the late summer of 1990, after I had been showing the film for over a year and a half, Lars Hansson began to show up on radio proclaiming that Greer, the driver, did not shoot the President. Lars Hansson showed up at my fall 1990 Beverly Hills High School lecture and disrupted the lecture, yelling out taunts and otherwise making an ass out of himself. When the lecture ended he accosted people in the lobby and, along with David Lifton, attempted to convince members of the audience that they didn't really see Greer shoot Kennedy. To their credit most of the audience told Hansson and Lifton to stick it where the sun don't shine. Once people see it with their own eyes they can no longer be fooled. Hansson, Lifton, Grodin, and the other agents of the Secret Government are running out of time. Americans are catching on to the scam. I shudder to think what will happen to these people when Americans finally get angry. Do not forget that Lear informed me that his source for the film was a CIA agent who later turned out to be Lars Hansson.

Hansson later claimed that I violated his copyright. He had no copyright. Hansson himself had violated someone's copyright by making the film and giving it to me, Lear, and Gritz. I didn't and still don't give a damn about copyright on THIS particular film. If I did, no one would ever know who really killed our President.

Bo Gritz stated on radio that he felt exactly the same way. Hansson never attacked Lear or Gritz, who still show the tape, and Gritz still makes it available. I wonder why? Are Lear, Hansson and Gritz working together?

Robert Grodin then entered the picture. He publicly challenged me to appear and debate him. He claimed that he had a copy of the Zapruder film showing that Greer never took his hands off the wheel of the car. Grodin is an active secret government agent whose job it is to confuse the public and perpetuate the cover-up.

I called Bob Grodin and accepted his challenge. I invited him to appear with me at Beverly Hills High School and show his film. I would show my film. The audience would decide. He refused. He refused because he knows what I know, that the audience would boo him out of town. Grodin knows that Greer shot Kennedy because he is part of the cover-up.

Bob Grodin is the same Bob Grodin who claims to be the world's foremost independent photo-interpretation expert. Bob Grodin has NO photographic education whatsoever. He has never worked with photography. Bob Grodin has never been a photographic interpreter in his life. He has been lying to the public about his credentials for all these years and no one even checked; not even Congress checked his credentials when they hired him. Do you really think that was an accident? I HAVE A DEGREE IN PHOTOGRAPHY.

Bob Grodin is the same Bob Grodin who was hired by the House Select Committee on Assassinations in 1976. He is the same Bob Grodin who *blatantly lied* to the committee and told them that the driver, William Greer, never took his hands off the wheel. His job is to write books and confuse you. His job is to maintain the position that the government lied and that there was a conspiracy. His job is also to prevent you from knowing the truth about *who did* kill the President. You cannot welcome the New World Order if you have faith in your government. You WILL have faith in your government if you learn that Greer killed Kennedy on orders of the Illuminati and that it had nothing to do with the legal, Constitutional government. Did you know that the man who was in charge of the Secret Service at the time of the assassination became the man in charge of security for the Rockefeller family upon his retirement? Well, now you know. You should also know that Bob Grodin is a friend of Leslie Watkins, and it is Bob Grodin's name that Watkins uses as the alias of the astronaut cited in *Alternative 003*. Did you know that when Ricky White made appearances on talk radio across the country to say that his father killed Kennedy, that Bob Grodin accompanied him? Did you know that every time a caller asked Ricky White a question, Grodin answered for him? Do you really believe that is a coincidence? Ricky White's father did not kill Kennedy.

For years I have been telling people and audiences about the discrepancies between the doctors' reports in Dallas and the autopsy report made at Bethesda Naval Hospital. I have revealed that the wounds were tampered with and changed. I have been telling the world that the body was removed from its casket aboard the plane and was taken out the galley door and onto a marine helicopter, and that the body arrived at Bethesda Naval Hospital a full 30 minutes before the empty official casket. I have stated that the President's brain had disappeared and told why it had disappeared.

All of a sudden David Lifton appeared on radio and TV in 1990 telling the world that he had NEW evidence that *he* had discovered. Every bit of his new evidence was exactly what I had been telling people for years. It was the same information that I had told Bob Swan in 1972. Lifton showed up at my lecture at Beverly Hills High School. After making a scene at the box office because he had to pay, Lifton accosted anyone who ventured into the lobby, and along with Lars Hansson, attempted to convince them that they did not see Greer shoot Kennedy. Legitimate people would never have resorted to such disgraceful and discrediting behavior. My testimony and the public's outrage after seeing the murder of President Kennedy with their own eyes, has seriously damaged the cover-up. The behavior of Grodin, Lifton, and Hansson reveals the degree of damage. The public can now see without any doubt that they are either part of the cover-up or that they are totally incompetent researchers, and in the case of Grodin, a bare-faced liar who may have committed treason.

In the middle of all this, "Hard Copy" TV magazine called me and wanted to see the film. I showed them the film and they were shocked, excited and wanted an exclusive. I gave it to them but told them that I doubted that it would ever get on the air. A date was arranged to film an episode for airing, but just before we were scheduled to go on camera an NBC executive called the Los Angeles studios of "Hard Copy" and told them not to air the film. I tried to find out the name of the executive, but no luck. That was the end of that. The producer that had tried to air my story and the Kennedy film is no longer with "Hard Copy." Her name is Bubs Hopper.

I was approached by another producer (don't remember his name) from "Inside Edition," another TV magazine, who told me that Americans needed to see the film. I agreed to be on the show but told him the same thing, that I did not believe it would ever air. A week later I was listening to David Lifton on a radio talk show. Someone called in and asked David if he knew who I was and David Lifton said, "I know who he is and we have a surprise for Mr. Cooper. We are going to put him away for good on a national TV show. We are going to get a full accounting from that guy."

I had someone call the producer and cancel because he had lied to me. He pleaded to have me on. I relayed through this intermediary that I would appear only if I could have editorial control to make sure that he did not edit the segment to ridicule the film. He refused, and I then knew his intention all along had been to discredit me. When the segment aired, Lars Hansson was used as a stand-in, in my place. Hansson, the man who had been attacking me, stating that Greer had not fired at Kennedy, was now on TV stating that *Greer killed Kennedy!* The reason became obvious, as they had Bob Grodin on the next segment. Grodin ridiculed and debunked Hansson and the film. They had intended to do a hatchet job on me, but when I cancelled they could attack the film only with Hansson taking my place. *It had every earmark of an agency operation.* It didn't work.

I discovered the next ploy when on radio Grodin stated that he would soon (finally) release a video of his so-called pristine copy of the Zapruder film *overexposed* to bring out detail in the shadows. Overexposure would completely wash out Greer's arm and the gun, which are both in full sunlight and have the effect of rendering both invisible to the viewer. I hope that people are not as stupid as Grodin thinks they are. I will debate anyone at any time as long as it's in front of a live audience and nothing is edited. I have seen what a film editor can do to make people seem to say and do things that were never said or done.

* * * * *

During the United States' initial space exploration and the Moon landings every launch was accompanied by alien craft. On November 20, 1990, Los Angeles TV Channel 2 announced that a separate, red, glowing, round-shaped object accompanied the space shuttle Atlantis on its latest classified military mission. That was the first public admission.

A Moon base, Luna, was photographed by the Lunar Orbiter and filmed by the Apollo astronauts. Domes, spires, tall round structures which look like silos, huge T-shaped mining vehicles that left stitchlike tracks in the lunar surface, and extremely large as well as small alien craft appear in the official NASA photographs. It is a joint United States and Soviet base: The space program is a farce and an unbelievable waste of money. Alternative 3 is a reality. It is not science fiction.

The Apollo astronauts were severely shaken by this experience, and their lives and subsequent statements reflect the depth of the revelation and the effect of the muzzle order which followed. They were ordered to remain silent or suffer the extreme penalty, death, which was termed an "expediency." One astronaut actually did talk to the British producers of the TV expos) "Alternative 003." It was aired on the documentary, *nonfiction* program named "Science Report," confirming many of the allegations.

In the book *Alternative 003* the pseudonym "Bob Grodin" was used in place of the astronaut's identity. (The real Bob Grodin is a friend of Leslie Watkins and is a part of the Kennedy assassination cover-up.) It was also stated that the astronaut committed suicide in 1978. This cannot be validated by any source, and I believe that several so-called facts in the book are really disinformation. I firmly believe that this disinformation is a result of pressure put upon the authors and is meant to nullify the effect upon the populace of the British TV exposé "Alternative 3."

The headquarters of the international conspiracy is in Geneva, Switzerland. The ruling body is made up of three committees consisting of thirteen members each, and all three together comprise the 39 members of the executive committee of the body known as the Bilderberg Group. The most important and powerful of the three committees is the Policy Committee. (It is more than interesting to note that the United States had thirteen original colonies and that 39 delegates from those colonies signed the Constitution after it was written and adopted in the first Constitutional Convention. Do you believe that is coincidence?) Policy Committee meetings are held on a nuclear submarine beneath the polar icecap. A Soviet sub and an American sub join at an airlock and the meeting is convened. The secrecy is such that this was the only method which would ensure that the meetings could not be bugged.

I can say that the book *Alternative 003* is at least 70% true from my own knowledge and the knowledge of my sources. I believe that the disinformation was an attempt to compromise the British TV expos) with information that could be proven false, just as the "Eisenhower Briefing Document," which was released here in the United States under the contingency plan Majestic Twelve, can also be proven false.

Since our interaction with the aliens began we have come into possession of technology beyond our wildest dreams. We currently have, and fly, atomic-powered antigravity-type craft in Nevada. Our pilots have made interplanetary voyages in these craft and have been to the Moon, Mars, and other planets. We have been lied to about the true nature of the Moon, the planets Mars and Venus, and the *real* state of technology that we possess today, at this very moment.

There are areas on the Moon where plant life grows and even changes color with the seasons. This seasonal effect is because the Moon does not, as claimed, always present the exact same side to the Earth or the Sun. The Moon has several man-made lakes and ponds upon its surface, and clouds have been observed and filmed in its atmosphere. It possesses a gravitational field — and man can walk upon its surface *without a space suit*, breathing from an oxygen bottle after undergoing decompression, the same as any deep-sea diver!

I have the official NASA photographs. Some of them were published in the books *We Discovered Alien Bases on the Moon* by Fred Steckling and

Someone Else Is on the Moon. In 1969 a confrontation broke out between the Soviets and Americans at the lunar base. The Soviets attempted to take control of the base and held American scientists and personnel hostage. We were able to restore order but not before 66 people were killed. The Soviets were suspended from the program for a period of two years. A reconciliation eventually took place and once again we began to interact.

Today the alliance continues. The Archuleta Mesa underground-base confrontation scenario is pure disinformation put out to confuse the issue. I knew that a confrontation had taken place but could not remember the details. John Lear had convinced me that aliens and Delta forces had fought at the Archuleta base. (The New World Order must have an enemy from outer space.) Later, when I used regressive hypnosis to improve my memory, the true facts emerged. To my knowledge the only hostility between aliens and humans was provoked by the U.S. military when they were ordered to shoot down UFOs in order to capture technology.

John Lear also says that we invented AIDS in order to kill blood-sucking aliens and that we are only containers for souls. This is hogwash! It is a clear vote for the "aliens do not exist" theory.

When the Watergate scandal broke, President Nixon was confident that he could not be impeached. Majesty Twelve had a different agenda. Nixon was ordered to resign, the intelligence community rightfully concluding that an impeachment trial would open up the files and bare the secrets to the public eye. He refused. The first military coup ever to take place in the United States was carried out. The Joint Chiefs of Staff sent a Top Secret message to the Commanders of all the U.S. armed forces throughout the world. It stated, "Upon receipt of this message you will no longer carry out any orders from the White House. Acknowledge receipt." This message was sent a full five days before Nixon conceded and announced publicly that he would resign.

I saw the message. When I asked my commanding officer what he would do, as obviously the order violated the Constitution, I was told: "I guess I will wait to see if any orders come from the White House, and then I will decide." I did not see any communication from the White House but that does not mean that none was sent. I have confirmation from three additional sources, all ex-military, who wrote or called to state that they saw the exact same order. These people are Randall Terpstra, ex-Navy; David Race, ex-Air Force; and Donald Campbell, ex-Navy. The transcript of a taped phone conversation between the author and Mr. Terpstra is presented as Chapter 11 of this book, and the signed statements of the others can be found in the Appendix.

During all the years that this has been happening the Congress and the

American people have seemed to know instinctively that something was not right. When the Watergate scandal surfaced they jumped on the bandwagon and everyone thought that the agencies would be cleaned out. President Ford organized the Rockefeller Commission to do the job. His real purpose was to head off Congress and keep the cover-up going. Nelson Rockefeller, who headed the commission investigating the intelligence community, was a member of the Council on Foreign Relations and the one who helped Eisenhower build the Majesty Twelve power structure. Rockefeller uncovered only enough to keep the hounds at bay. He threw the Congress a few bones and the cover-up rolled merrily along as always.

Later Senator Church would conduct the famous Church hearings. He also was a prominent member of the Council on Foreign Relations, and he merely repeated the Rockefeller act. Again the cover-up prevailed. When the Iran-Contra affair emerged, we thought this time it had to come gushing out. Wrong again. Despite mountains of documents pointing to drug smuggling and other hidden monsters, the cover-up sailed on. The Congress even seemed to go out of its way to duck the real issues. As mentioned earlier, one of the most serious facts uncovered is that North was involved in preparing a plan to suspend the Constitution of the United States of America. When Congressman Jack Brooks of Texas attempted to probe the issue he was silenced by the committee chairman. Could it be that Congress knows the whole thing and won't touch it? Are they among the select who have been picked for the Mars colony when the Earth begins to destruct, if the Earth *is* going to destruct?

I cannot even begin to outline the entire financial empire controlled by the CIA, the NSA, and the Council on Foreign Relations, which in turn control and launder the money from drugs and other intelligence community proprietary ventures; but I can give you a beginning. The amount of money is beyond anything you can imagine and is hidden in a vast network of banks and holding companies. You should first begin to look at the J. Henry Schroder Banking Corporation, the Schroder Trust Company, Schroders Ltd. (London), Helbert Wagg Holdings Ltd., J. Henry Schroder-Wagg & Co. Ltd., Schroder Gerbruder and Company (Germany), Schroder Munchmeyer Gengst and Company, Castle Bank and its holding companies, the Asian Development Bank, and the Nugan Hand octopus of banks and holding companies.

A contingency plan was formulated by Majesty Twelve to throw every one off the trail should they come close to the truth. The plan was known as MAJESTIC TWELVE. It was implemented with the release by Moore, Shandera, and Friedman of the purported Eisenhower Briefing Document. The document is a fraud, because it is numbered 092447, a number which does not exist and will not exist for quite a long time at the present rate. Truman wrote Executive orders in the 9000 range; Eisenhower's were in the 10,000 range; Ford was up to the 11,000 bracket; and Reagan reached only into the 12,000s. Executive orders are numbered consecutively, no matter who occupies the White House, for reasons of continuity, record keeping, and to prevent confusion. This red herring has thrown the entire research community off the trail for several years and has resulted in the wasted expenditure of money looking for information which does not exist.

The Washington D.C.-based Fund for UFO Research headed by Bruce Maccabee has committed what I believe to be criminal fraud in connection with the Eisenhower Briefing Document, Stanton Friedman, and the research team of Moore, Shandera, and Friedman. Maccabee solicited funds from people, promising to use those funds to investigate Moore's, Shandera's, and Friedman's claims and prove the Eisenhower Briefing Document to be genuine or fake. Instead he gave the entire $16,000 to Stanton Friedman and assigned HIM the task of establishing or destroying *his* own validity. What a snow job! People in the UFO community fell for the scam and eagerly awaited Stanton Friedman's findings. Of course, Friedman found that the documents were genuine. Just what did people think he would find? HE WAS GIVEN $16,000 TO INVESTIGATE HIM-SELF! IT IS UNETHICAL. IT IS A CLEAR CONFLICT OF INTEREST. I SINCERELY BELIEVE IT TO BE CRIMINAL FRAUD, since money was taken in the process. Those who donated money in good faith should immediately bring suit against Stanton Friedman, Bruce Maccabee and the Fund for UFO Research. This farce resulted in the total waste of $16,000. Many thousands of man hours have gone down a rathole. If you doubt the secret government's ability to lead you through the rose garden, you had better think again.

Another plan is in force. It is the plan to prepare the public for eventual confrontation with an alien race. It could also intend to make you believe in an alien race that may not exist. The public is being bombarded with movies, radio, advertising, and TV programs depicting almost every aspect of the purported true nature of an alien presence. This includes the good and the bad. Look around and pay attention. Someone is planning to make their presence known and the government is preparing you for it. They do not want any panic. The unprecedented number of sightings worldwide indicates that public exposure is not far off. Never in history have there been so many incidents involving UFOs and never in history have there been so many official acknowledgments.

For many years the Secret Government has been importing drugs and selling them to the people, mainly the poor and minorities. Social welfare programs were put into place to create a dependent, nonworking element in our society. The government then began to remove these programs to force people into a criminal class that did not exist in the '50s and '60s.

The government encouraged the manufacture and importation of military firearms for the criminals to use. This is intended to foster a feeling of insecurity, which would lead the American people to voluntarily disarm themselves by passing laws against firearms. Using drugs and hypnosis on mental patients in a process called Orion, the CIA inculcated the desire in these people to open fire on schoolyards and thus inflame the antigun lobby. This plan is well under way, and so far is working perfectly. The middle class is begging the government to do away with the 2nd amendment.

Author's Note: I have found that these events have indeed happened all over the country. In every instance that I have investigated — the incident at the women's school in Canada, the shopping center incident in Canada, the Stockton, California, massacre, and the murder of Rabbi Meir Kahane — the shooters were all ex-mental patients or were current mental patients who were ALL ON THE DRUG PROZAC! This drug, when taken in certain doses, increases the serotonin level in the patient, causing extreme violence. Couple that with a posthypnotic suggestion or control through an electronic brain implant or microwave or E.L.F. intrusion and you get mass murder, ending in every case with the suicide of the perpetrator. Exhume the bodies of the murderers and check for a brain implant. I think you are going to be surprised. In every case the name of the murderer's doctor or mental treatment facility has been withheld. I believe we will be able to establish intelligence-community connections and/or connections to known CIA experimental mind-control programs when we finally discover who these doctors of death really are.

Due to the wave of crime sweeping the nation, the media will convince the American people that a state of anarchy exists within the major cities. They are now building their case almost nightly on TV and daily in the newspapers. When public opinion has been won to this idea, they intend to state that a terrorist group armed with a nuclear weapon has entered the United States and that they plan to detonate this device in one of our cities. (This is now being set up by the crisis in the Middle East.) The Government will then suspend the Constitution and declare martial law. The secret alien army of implanted humans and all dissidents, which translates into anyone they choose, will be rounded up and placed in the one-mile-square concentration camps which already exist. Are the people whom they intend to place in these concentration camps destined to make up the reported "batch consignments" of slave labor needed by the space colonies?

The media — radio, TV, newspapers, and computer networks — will be nationalized and seized. Anyone who resists will be taken or killed. This entire operation was rehearsed by the government and military in 1984 under the code name REX-84A and it went off without a hitch. When these events have transpired, the SECRET GOVERNMENT and/or ALIEN takeover will be complete. Your freedom will never be returned and you will live in slavery for the remainder of your life. You had better wake up and you had better do it now!

Philip Klass is an agent of the CIA. This was stated in the documents I saw between 1970 and 1973. One of his jobs as an aviation expert was to debunk everything to do with UFOs. All military commanders were instructed to call him to gain information on how to debunk and/or explain UFO contacts and/or sightings to the public and/or the press if and when the need arose. Some people seem to love Klass. They encourage him and heap large doses of attention upon him. He is invited to speak at UFO events and is quoted in papers, books, and newspapers as being the expert on "what really happened."

Philip Klass is not operating in our best interest. His debunkings and explanations of UFO sightings are so full of holes that a six-year-old child should be able to discern his true purpose. I have seen poor misled people actually ask Klass for his autograph, an act similar in magnitude to Elliot Ness asking Al Capone for *his* autograph. I have found that in many instances the secret elect are absolutely right when they state that "people who will not use their intelligence are no better than animals who do not have intelligence. Such people are beasts of burden and steaks on the table by choice and consent." (Quote from "Silent Weapons for Quiet Wars" in Chapter Two). We get exactly what we deserve in most instances.

William Moore, Jaimie Shandera, and Stanton Friedman are witting (with full knowledge, understanding, and consent) agents of the Secret Government. William Moore's reported use of a Defense Investigative Service ID card and his reported self-confession to Lee Graham that he is an agent of the government confirmed it. (Lee Graham phoned me at my home, and when asked, confirmed that Moore had indeed shown him a Defense Investigative Service ID.) Moore's later confession proved it without any doubt.

Author's Note: On July 1, 1989, the night before I presented this paper at the MUFON symposium in Las Vegas, William Moore admitted that he was a government agent, that he had released disinformation to researchers, that he had falsified documents, that he had spied upon researchers and reported information concerning those researchers to the intelligence community, that he had helped in a counterintelligence operation against Paul Bennewicz that resulted in Mr. Bennewicz's commitment to a mental institution, and that he had done all this with full knowledge of what he was doing. He is either a traitor or a stone-hearted manipulator at best.

Some of the self-appointed "ufologists" still look up to Moore, and still cite his research in their correspondence, papers, and books. This reflects a degree of ignorance and stupidity in the UFO community. Bruce Maccabee wrote a letter to *Caveat Emptor* citing articles from William Moore's publication, *Focus*, as proof that I am discredited. Dream on. It is no mystery to me why mainstream America calls ufologists whackos, loonies, and nuts. In some cases they are.

Jaime Shandera is the man responsible for my loss of employment as the Executive Director of National Technical College. Shortly after going public, Shandera showed up at the college wearing a brown suit and carrying a briefcase. He ignored the receptionist's attempts to help him. She informed me that a man had walked into the college and appeared to be inspecting the building and classrooms. I found Mr. Shandera peering into the word-processing classroom. I asked him if I could be of any help. He said no and ignored me. I explained that I was the Executive Director and again asked if I could be of any help. Again he said no but gave me some very hard stares and appeared to have been taken off guard. He seemed to be extremely nervous and immediately left the building. I followed him out the door, and a man across the street snapped my picture with a 35mm camera. I watched as Jaime Shandera walked to his car, took one last look at me and then drove away. A few days later he repeated the act, only this time he told me that he had seen an ad that the college was for sale and he was looking over the property. I saw him again, coming out of the corporate offices. When he saw me he again became extremely nervous and hurried to his car, took off his jacket before getting in and then drove off. A few minutes later I was called to the President's office and told that the college could not use anyone who could jeopardize the status of government assistance by getting involved with flying saucers. I knew what had happened and tendered my resignation effective April 15, 1989. I had no intention of stopping my activities and I did not wish to hurt the college or the students who depended so much on government aid programs. All this time Shandera thought he had pulled it off anonymously, but I and several others have always known that it was he. Now *you* know.

Jaime Shandera was positively identified by me, the Security Department Head, and the receptionist. Later I obtained another positive identification from the Vice President in charge of Admissions. John Lear was at that time the only person who knew the name and address of my place of employment. I later found out by body-proportion comparison analysis and voice-print analysis that John Lear is the agent dubbed "Condor" on the CIA-backed TV production of "UFO Cover-up Live." As Condor, he is in reality a government agent who has been working with Moore, Shandera, Friedman, John Grace, Bob Lazar, and others all along. They are CIA all the way.

Stanton Friedman has told me and others that years ago he "helped develop a nuclear reactor to power an aircraft that was the size of a basketball, was clean, turned out hydrogen, and worked like a dream" (his words, not mine). Several others have written me to say that they also were told the same thing by Mr. Friedman. Roger Scherrer is one who remembers Stanton relating to him this same story. The only fuel which could go into such an engine and produce hydrogen as a byproduct is water, and that is precisely what at least one type of alien craft uses — nuclear energy and water, according to the documentation I read while in Naval Intelligence. Is he really unwitting? I seriously doubt it. He was a member of the Moore, Shandera, and Friedman research team, and it was they who implemented the MAJESTIC TWELVE contingency plan.

In documents that I read between 1970 and 1973, the names of individuals were listed who had been targeted for recruitment. These documents stated that these people were to be coerced, using patriotism as a motivating force whenever possible. If necessary, financial assistance would be provided through employment with a proprietary front company or through grants. This is, coincidentally, the method by which Friedman got his $16,000 from another agent, Bruce Maccabee. We have also found that Moore has received money for research from at least two CIA front companies. This has been confirmed by the research of Grant Cameron. Others named on the list were cited as active intelligence-agency assets. When I first presented this paper I gave only a partial list of those named in the Naval Intelligence documents. Following are as many names as I can remember. (There may be more, but these are all that I can recall at this time.)

Stanton Friedman, CIA; John Lear, CIA (Lear's father was named as having participated in antigravity research); William Moore; John Keel; Charles Berlitz; Bruce Maccabee, ONI (Office of Naval Intelligence); Linda Moulton Howe; Philip Klass, CIA; James Moseley, CIA (Moseley's father was discussed in a very complimentary manner); Virgil Armstrong, CIA (listed as Postlethwaite); Wendelle Stevens, CIA; Dr. J. Allen Hynek, CIA.

That is the list as I remember it. There may have been others, but I cannot recall. I know of other agents who were not on the list. You must remember that when I first wrote this paper I thought that Bruce Maccabee might not have been recruited, but then later he proved me wrong when he gave Stanton Friedman $16,000 to investigate himself.

There was a two-word code that these people were to use to identify each other. The first word was a color and the second word was a bird. The code was "Gold Eagle." When Stanton Friedman first contacted me he used the code. I pretended ignorance but he asked me several times if I had ever seen or heard of Gold Eagle. John Lear also asked me if I had ever heard of Gold Eagle. He too was testing me. They knew that I had access to correct information and were attempting to determine if I were one of them. As George Bush would say, "Read my lips." I was never one of you. I will *never* be one of you.

When I talked to Stan Deyo in Australia by phone, he told me the code given to him was "Blue Falcon." Stan was a victim of mind-control experimentation while a cadet at the Air Force Academy. He and over 80 other cadet mind-control subjects resigned from the academy in protest. He has been on a crusade to discover the truth ever since. Stan has written two excellent books, *The Cosmic Conspiracy*, and *The Vindicator Scrolls*. I recommend you read them both.

I think that Linda Moulton Howe may be innocent of witting involvement. Linda in particular seems to have exercised extreme care in what she has presented to the public. Her research is excellent. I was impressed when she confided to me that Sgt. Richard Doty of the Counterintelligence Division of the Air Force Office of Special Investigations had taken her into the Intelligence office at Kirtland Air Force Base in New Mexico and showed her the exact same documents that I had seen while in the Navy. She even saw the same information on the Kennedy assassination naming Greer as the assassin. Ms. Howe is also the only person in the world outside of the intelligence community who knows the truth as I know it regarding Operation MAJORITY. She has exercised good judgment and great restraint in *not* revealing the contents of those documents to the public. It is for this reason that I believe that an attempt has been made to use her. Fortunately, Linda did not fall off a turnip truck and she didn't play the game. I recommend you read her book entitled *Alien Harvest*. You should be able to order it from any good bookstore.

I have discovered that Whitley Strieber is a CIA asset, as is Budd Hopkins. Strieber's book *Majestic* has convicted him with those of us *in the know*. It is the true story of the Roswell crash taken from the confiscated diaries of James Forrestal. That is, assuming that the documents that I saw in the Navy were not a hoax. I do not believe that they were. The names of people and names of projects and operations have been changed in Strieber's book, but other than that the information and documentation is true. The autopsy reports are exactly the same that I saw in Project GRUDGE 18 years ago.

I have recently come into possession of an affidavit that is signed, notarized, and sworn under penalty of perjury from an M.D. in New York stating that the M.D. was recruited by a CIA agent named Budd Hopkins to help work with abductees for the CIA. The affidavit is included in the Appendix. I knew that Hopkins was not right when I met him in Modesto. He could not look me in the eyes, and anyone who cannot look me in the eyes is not right. He spent the whole time, including his speech, trying to convince people of the innocence of the abductee experience and the absence of the aliens' malevolence, which was a total crock. It was an insult to anyone who had investigated abductees.

I know that all of the major UFO research organizations were targeted for infiltration and control by the Secret Government, just as NICAP was infiltrated and controlled. In fact, NICAP was eventually destroyed from within. I know that these efforts have been successful.

MUFON is a great example. Hundreds of members all over the world conduct investigations and send in physical evidence to MUFON head-quarters, where it quickly disappears. Everyone screams for physical evidence as proof. Recently samples were collected of a liquid that had dripped from a saucer onto a schoolyard in Gulf Breeze, Florida. The samples were sent to MUFON, where they immediately vanished. Walt Andrus has stated that it was an accident. BALONEY! This is not the first time MUFON has "lost" evidence. I consider MUFON the great black hole of the UFO community. The control of information is so tight that nothing escapes. Anyone who tells it like it really is, is debunked and barred from symposiums. The members are told what to believe and what not to believe. The members do not seem to know that they are being controlled. The members of the MUFON board of directors and the members of the advisory board of consultants are for the most part supported by the Government in the form of salaries, grants, or retirement checks. Who can believe that this does not constitute a conflict of interest? Who can investigate and expose the hand that feeds them? How can you possibly believe the Government could not control the people to whom it funnels money? MONEY IS THE BASIC METHOD OF CONTROL.

The major UFO publications are without any doubt controlled and are most probably, as in the case with UFO, financially backed or controlled by the CIA. Vicki Cooper (no relation), the editor and publisher of UFO, has been telling friends and relatives for at least two years that the CIA is pushing her magazine. Ron Regehr and Lee Graham remember the summer of 1988 when Vicki interviewed them at Mr. Graham's residence in Huntington Beach. After the interview was over Vicki Cooper walked to her car, turned, and mysteriously yelled, "You know, my magazine might be financed by the CIA."

I have talked to friends and acquaintances of Ms. Cooper who swear that she has stated on many occasions that "the CIA controls *UFO* magazine." Vicki Cooper's uncle, Grant Cooper, was Sirhan Sirhan's defense attorney, who made no attempt to defend his client. It was important to the Secret Government and the CIA that Sirhan be pinned as a "lone assassin." Grant Cooper has extensive ties to the CIA and the Johnny Rosselli mob.

We have found that Vicki's son attends the West Point Military Academy. What a wonderful way to control a magazine! "You don't play ball, your son won't graduate." I found out that the person who found Vicki Cooper an apartment when she arrived in Los Angeles was Barry Taff, a long-time employee of the intelligence agencies (yes, plural) and a long-time proteg) of Dr. John Lilly and Dr. J. West, the government's premiere experts in mind control. These men have been involved in the most terrifying experimentation ever directed at total control of individuals. I believe that it is no innocent coincidence that Taff's apartment is directly above Vicki's. All of this was confirmed independently in a letter written by Mr. Martin Cannon, a Los Angeles-based researcher. The letter can be found in the Appendix.

The most damning evidence for the control of *UFO* magazine and Vicki Cooper comes from Don Ecker. At the 1989 MUFON Conference Don Ecker became so uninhibited that he managed to relate the following story to me and two others.

According to Don Ecker, Vicki Cooper used to work for the infamous Mayflower Madam. The Feds were trying to get the Madam and discovered Vicki. Ms. Cooper was busted and threatened with spending the rest of her life in prison if she did not cooperate. Vicki rolled over, according to Ecker, and ratted on her employer. Since Vicki had apparently had something to do with the bookkeeping operation, she became a key witness. The Mayflower Madam was put out of business and into jail, thanks to Ms. Cooper's testimony. That is, if Don Ecker was telling the truth. We have no reason to believe that he was lying. I don't know why Don told us. Maybe he doesn't like Vickie. Or maybe he, like Lear and Friedman, thought I was one of *them*. (It'll be a cold day in hell.)

According to Ecker, Vicki Cooper was told to get out of town and stay out. She was given money and told to start *UFO* magazine in Los Angeles. She was told that she was to print information that would be fed to her. Sure enough, you read in *UFO* purported leaked government UFO information, always written by someone who cannot be contacted. It is always under an alias; no one can check the information. Vicki is adamant about printing only the news and information that she considers best for the readers, as if they have no mind of their own. She indulges in character assassination.

Don Ecker claims to have been a member of Army Intelligence, the Green Berets, and later a police officer in Boise, Idaho. Don claims a total of ten years experience as a criminal investigator. The Boise Police Department, when asked by phone, has denied any knowledge of Mr. Ecker. I have requested that Don furnish a copy of his Army record, but he has refused. Ecker calls himself a UFO expert and has dubbed himself (yep, you guessed it) a "ufologist." He sprinkles terms like "ufological" around in his articles, and not even Don knows what the hell it means. He confirms most of the information that I have divulged when he speaks to groups. He has furnished data bases with a plethora of files that confirm everything that I have ever said. Ecker probably made them up himself, since they are all anonymous. He claims that aliens mutilate humans like cattle. Don Ecker, like Vicki Cooper, practices character assassination.

According to legitimate law-enforcement sources, Ecker is lying to the public. He was a guard at the Idaho State Prison from September 1981 to September 1982 when he quit to become a Canyon County Sheriff's Department Narcotics Deputy Trainee. Donald Francis Ecker II was fired after only six weeks for "improper conduct." Mr. Ecker returned to the Idaho State Prison where he was employed as a guard until July 1987 when he shot off his left leg with a shotgun during a training exercise. Sources also reveal that Donald Francis Ecker II is a fugitive from justice. Authorities in Idaho hold several outstanding warrants for the arrest of Mr. Ecker.

You must understand that the government is not ever going to allow any person or any group of persons to uncover the most highly classified secret in the world — if they can help it. They will always have agents controlling UFO groups, publications and information. If aliens are not real and the whole thing turns out to be the greatest hoax ever perpetrated, *just who do you think did the perpetrating?*

If the underground history is correct, aliens have manipulated and/or ruled the human race through various secret societies, religions, magic, witchcraft, and the occult. The Council on Foreign Relations and the Trilateral Commission are in complete control of the alien technology and are also in complete control of the nation's economy. Eisenhower was the last President to know the entire overview of the alien problem. Succeeding Presidents were told only what Majesty Twelve and the intelligence community wanted them to know. Believe me, it was not the truth.

Majesty Twelve has presented most new Presidents with a picture of a lost alien culture seeking to renew itself, build a home on this planet, and shower us with gifts of technology. In some cases the President was told nothing. Each President in turn has swallowed the story (or no story at all) hook, line and sinker. Meanwhile innocent people continue to suffer at the hands of the alien and human scientists. I have been unable to determine exactly what it is they are doing. Many people are abducted and are sentenced to live with psychological and physical damage for the rest of their lives. Could this really be a CIA mind-control operation?

In the documents that I read, 1 in 40 humans had been implanted with devices, the purpose of which I have never discovered. The Government believes that the aliens are building an army of implanted humans who can be activated and turned upon us at will. You should also know that to date we have not even begun to come close to parity with the aliens.

I sent 536 copies of a "Petition to Indict" to every member of the Senate and House of Representatives on April 26, 1989. As of this date, November 23, 1990, I have received a total of only six replies, only four more than I had received in May 1989.

THE CONCLUSIONS ARE INESCAPABLE:

(1) The secret power structure may believe that by our own ignorance or by divine decree, planet Earth will self-destruct sometime in the near future. These men sincerely believe that they are doing the right thing in their attempt to save the human race. It is terribly ironic that they have been forced to take as their partner an alien race which is itself engaged in a monumental struggle for survival. Many moral and legal compromises may have been made in this joint effort. These compromises were made in error and must be corrected. Those responsible should be brought to account for their actions. I can understand the fear and urgency that must have been instrumental in the decision not to tell the public. Obviously I disagree with that decision.

Throughout history small but powerful groups of men have consistently felt that they alone were capable of deciding the fates of millions. Throughout history they have been wrong. This great Nation owes its very existence to the principles of Freedom and Democracy. I believe with all my heart that the United States of America cannot and will not succeed in any effort that ignores those principles. Full disclosure to the public should be made and we should proceed to save the human race together.

(2) We are being manipulated by a joint human/alien power structure which will result in a one-world government and the partial enslavement of the human race. This has been deemed necessary to solve the elemental question: "Who will speak for planet Earth?" It has been decided that man is not mature enough in his evolutionary development to be trusted to interact properly with an alien race. We already have enough trouble between the different human races, so what would happen if a

---

* * * * T O P   S E C R E T * * * *

totally alien extraterrestrial race was introduced? Would they be lynched, spit upon, or shot? Would discrimination result in nasty encounters that would doom humanity as a result of the alien's obviously superior technology? Have our leaders decided to lock us in the playpen? The only way to prevent this scenario from taking place is to cause an evolutionary leap in consciousness, a paradigm shift for the entire human race. I have no idea how it can be done, but I know that it desperately needs to be done. It needs to be done very quickly and very quietly.

(3) The government has been totally deceived and we are being manipulated by an alien power, which will result in the total enslavement and/or destruction of the human race. We must use any and every means available to prevent this from happening.

(4) If none of the above are true, something else may be happening which is beyond our ability to understand at this moment. We must force disclosure of all of the facts, discover the truth, and act upon it. The situation in which we find ourselves is due to our own actions or inactions over the last 44 years. Because it is our own fault, we are the only ones who can change future events. Education seems to me to be a major part of the solution. The remaining part is the abolition of secrecy.

(5) There is always the possibility that I was used, that the whole alien scenario is the greatest hoax in history designed to create an alien enemy from outer space in order to expedite the formation of a one-world government. I have found evidence that this could be true. I have included that evidence in the Appendix. I advise you to consider this scenario as being probable.

Through ignorance or misplaced trust we as a people have abdicated our role as the watchdog of our government. Our government was founded "of the people, for the people, by the people." There was no mention or intent ever to abdicate our role and place our total trust in a handful of men who meet secretly to decide our fate. In fact, the structure of our government was designed to prevent that from ever happening. If we had done our jobs as Citizens we would never have reached this point. Most of us are completely ignorant as to even the most basic functions of our government. We have truly become a nation of sheep — and sheep are always eventually led to slaughter. It is time to stand up in the manner of our forefathers and walk like men. I remind you that the Jews of Europe marched obediently to the ovens after having been warned, believing all the while that the facts could not possibly be true. When the outside world was told of the holocaust occurring in Hitler's Europe, it was not believed at first.

You must understand that, real or not, the purported presence of aliens have been used to neutralize certain widely different segments of the population: "Don't worry, the benevolent space brothers will save you." It can also be used to fill the need for an extraterrestrial threat to justify the formation of a New World Order: "The aliens are eating us." The most important information that you need to determine your future actions is that this New World Order calls for the destruction of the sovereignty of nations, including the United States. The New World Order cannot, and will not, allow our Constitution to continue to exist. The New World Order will be a totalitarian socialist system. We will be slaves shackled to a cashless system of economic control.

If the documentation that I viewed while I was in Naval Intelligence is true, then what you have just read is probably closer to the truth than anything ever written. If extraterrestrials are a hoax, then what you just read is exactly what the Illuminati wants you to believe. I can assure you beyond any shadow of a doubt that even if aliens are not real, the technology IS REAL. Antigravity craft exist and human pilots fly them. I and millions of others have seen them. They are metal; they are machines; they come in different shapes and sizes; and they are obviously intelligently guided.

If suddenly there was a threat to this world from some other species from another planet, we'd forget all the little local differences that we have between our two countries and we would find out once and for all that we really are all human beings on this Earth.

Ronald Reagan
to Mikhail Gorbachev

SOURCES

Andrews, George C., *Extra-Terrestrials Among Us*, Llewellyn Publications, St. Paul, Minnesota.

Bamford, James, *The Puzzle Palace*, Houghton Mifflin, Boston.

Borklund, C. W., *The Department of Defense*, Frederick A. Praeger, New York.

Collier, Peter and David Horowitz, *Rockefellers: An American Dynasty*, Holt, Rinehart and Winston, New York.

Cooper, Vicki and Sherie Stark, eds., *UFO* (magazine — several issues since Spring 1988), Los Angeles, California.

Cooper, William, "Operation Majority, Final Release," Fullerton, California.

Corson, William R., *The Armies of Ignorance*, The Dial Press/James Wade, New York.

Curry, Richard O., ed., *Freedom at Risk*, Temple University Press, Philadelphia.

Deyo, Stan, *The Cosmic Conspiracy* and *The Vindictor Scrolls*, West Australian Texas Trading, Perth, Australia.

English, Bill, "Report on Grudge/Blue Book #13," John A. Lear, Las Vegas, Nevada.

Friend, Lt. Col. and Dr. J. Allen Hynek, "GRUDGE/Blue Book Report #13" (Top Secret). Last seen at the headquarters of the Commander in Chief of the Pacific Fleet (CINCPACFLT), Hawaii.

Graubard, Stephen, *Kissinger, Portrait of a Mind*, W.W. Norton & Co., New York.

Gulley, Bill with Mary Ellen Reese, *Breaking Cover*, Simon & Schuster, New York.

Hawking, Stephen W., *A Brief History of Time: From the Big Bang to Black Holes*, Bantam Books, New York.

Isaacson, Walter and Evan Thomas, *The Wise Men*, Simon & Schuster, New York.

Kissinger, Henry, *Nuclear Weapons and Foreign Policy*, Harper & Brothers, New York.

Kwitny, Jonathan, *The Crimes of Patriots*, W.W. Norton & Co., New York.

Lear, John A., "The John Lear Hypothesis," Las Vegas, Nevada. Partially true; the rest is disinformation.

Lear, John A. and John Grace, "The Krill Papers Hoax."

Ledeen, Michael A., *Perilous Statecraft*, Charles Scribner & Sons, New York.

"MAJIC/Operation Majority" (Top Secret). Presidential briefing document by Majesty Twelve. Last seen at the headquarters of the Commander in Chief of the Pacific Fleet (CINCPACFLT), Hawaii.

Mickus, Tom, "The Larry Fenwick Interview," Canada.

Moscow, Alvin, *The Rockefeller Inheritance*, Doubleday & Co., New York.

"Operation MAJESTIC TWELVE," Eisenhower Briefing Document. Author unknown, released by the research team of Moore, Shandera, and Friedman.

Pea Research, *Government Involvement in the UFO Cover-up: Chronology*, Pea Research, California.

Ranelagh, John, *The Agency: The Rise and Decline of the CIA*, Simon & Schuster, New York.

Schulzinger, Robert D., *The Wise Men of Foreign Affairs*, Columbia University Press, New York.

Shoup, Laurence H. and William Minter, *Imperial Brain Trust: The Council on Foreign Relations & United States Foreign Policy*, Monthly Review Press, New York.

Steckling, Fred, *We Discovered Alien Bases on the Moon*, G.A.F. International, California.

Steiger, Brad, *The UFO Abductors*, Berkley Books, New York.

Stienman, William, *The Crash at Aztec*, William Stienman, La Mirada, California.

Strieber, Whitley, *Communion* and *Majestic*, Avon, New York.

Valerian, Valdamar, *The Matrix*, Arcturus Book Service, Stone Mountain, Georgia.

Chapter 13

TREASON IN HIGH PLACES

The United Nations Treaty

and

The United Nations Participation Act

vs.

The Sovereignty of the United States of America

At the conclusion of the Constitutional Convention
in September 1787, Benjamin Franklin was asked,
"What have you wrought?"
He answered,
"...a Republic, if you can keep it."

The United States Constitution

Article VI

All Debts contracted and Engagements entered into, before the Adoption of this Constitution, shall be as valid against the United States under this Constitution, as under the Confederation.

This Constitution, and the Laws of the United States which shall be made in Pursuance thereof; and all Treaties made, or which shall be made, under the Authority of the United States, shall be the supreme Law of the Land; and the Judges in every State shall be bound thereby, any Thing in the Constitution or Laws of any State to the Contrary notwithstanding.

The Senators and Representatives before mentioned, and the Members of the several State Legislatures, and all executive and judicial Officers, both of the United States and of the several States, shall be bound by Oath or Affirmation, to support this Constitution; but no religious Test shall ever be required as a Qualification to any Office or public Trust under the United States.

HAVE WE ALREADY JOINED A ONE-WORLD GOVERNMENT?

U.S. Sovereignty — Fact or Fiction?

The Executive, Judicial and Legislative Branches of the U.S. Government have followed the policy that the United Nations Treaty approved under the U.N. Participation Act of 1945 in behalf of the United States of America by Harry S. Truman and the United States Senate, which treaty supersedes the United States Constitution under the terms of Article VI of the United States Constitution.

The Council of Foreign Relations created the United Nations. Their member agents, Alger Hiss and Leo Pasvolsky did the paperwork, but the honors went to a special committee appointed by President Roosevelt to draw the first draft of the Charter.

The members of the Committee were: Sumner Wells, Isaiah Bowman, Hamilton Fish Armstrong, Benjamin Cohen, and Clark Eichelberger — all members of the Council on Foreign Relations and members of a secret Order of the Quest called the JASON Society.

The Charter was rushed through the U.S. Senate without printed copies to guide the Senators: it was EXPLAINED to them by Russian-born revolutionary Leo Pasvolsky.

The Charter conferred no real power on the General Assembly; all the power was in the Security Council where the VETO was. The Senate would not have ratified the Charter except that the American delegation had a right to VETO if our interests were threatened by action of other members.

Included in this Charter was and is ARTICLE 25: "Member nations agree to ACCEPT and CARRY OUT the decisions of the Security Council in accordance with the PRESENT CHARTER."

No restrictions, no reservations. This is ALL of Article 25. Note the word "present," indicating that there might be OTHER charters. The VETO was a hindrance to World Government — it had to be circumvented.

In 1950 the General Assembly, without any legal authority, met and adopted what they named the "UNITING FOR PEACE" RESOLUTION. This, greatly expanded since that time, permitted THE GENERAL ASSEMBLY to EXERCISE THE POWERS OF THE SECURITY COUNCIL. I bet you didn't know that. The Government of the United States recognizes the illegally amended Charter as the "law of the world," overriding our Constitution. The General Assembly has for years been making the law of the world by RATIFYING RESOLUTIONS BY A 2/3 MAJORITY VOTE. When the Resolution is ratified it is sent down to the CHIEF EXECUTIVE OF THE MEMBER STATE and the EXECUTIVE IS OBLIGED TO ACCEPT AND CARRY OUT the provisions in the resolution.

The governments concerned must IGNORE, ABOLISH, REVISE AND RESCIND LAWS in their territories which conflict with the resolutions of the General Assembly, and to PASS OTHER LAWS WHICH WILL PUT THESE RESOLUTIONS INTO FORCE. "One man, one vote" comes through Resolution No. 1760.

There are more than 2000 of these resolutions now in effect. THEY ARE THE LAW OF THE LAND. Our civil rights laws (the ex-post facto sections of which come from the Nuremberg Resolutions), our agricultural laws, our health and welfare laws, our labor laws, our foreign aid laws — all come from resolutions of the General Assembly or treaties of the U.N. ratified by our Senate.

Any law passed in your state will be rescinded or abolished if it is in conflict with resolutions of the General Assembly.

I can tell you, with no reservations whatsoever, that all of the intelligence organizations of the United States work directly for the United Nations in concert with the Secret Government toward the sole purpose of the destruction of the sovereignty of the United States of America and the bringing about of the one-world government. The authority cited for their efforts is ARTICLE VI of the Constitution, the United Nations Treaty, and the U.N. Participation Act of 1945 signed by Harry S. Truman with the advice and consent of the U.S. Senate.

---

* * * * TOP SECRET * * * *

This should help you understand how our laws are being made and who is making them! ASK YOUR SENATORS, CONGRESSMEN AND STATE LEGISLATORS IF THEY ARE AWARE OF THESE FACTS.

The following statement was made by Mr. Carl B. Rix of Milwaukee, former president of the American Bar Association, before a Senate subcommittee which was hearing testimony on the proposed Bricker Amendment. It was entered into the House Record by Hon. Lawrence H. Smith, Wisconsin, on May 11, 1955.

CONGRESSIONAL RECORD (page A3220)

Statement of Carl B. Rix, Milwaukee, Wisconsin:

I appear in favor of the amendments.

Congress is no longer bound by its constitutional system of delegated powers. Its only test is under the obligatory power to promote human rights in these fields of endeavor: Civil, political, economic, social and cultural. These are found in Articles 55 and 56 of the Charter of the United Nations, a ratified and approved treaty. They are being promoted in all parts of the world by the United Nations.

Congress may now legislate as an uninhibited body with no shackles of delegated powers under the Constitution. Our entire system of a government of delegated powers of Congress has been changed to a system of undelegated powers without amendment by the people of the United States.

The authority for these statements is found in a volume entitled *Constitution of the United States of America, Annotated,* issued in 1953, prepared under the direction of the Judiciary Committee of the Senate of the United States and under the chairmanship of Prof. Edward S. Corwin of Princeton, aided by the legal staff of the Library of Congress. This is the conclusion on page 427 of the *Annotations*: "In a word, the treaty power cannot purport to amend the Constitution by adding to the list of Congress' enumerated powers, but having acted, the consequence will often be that it has provided Congress with an opportunity to enact measures which, independently of a treaty, Congress could not pass, and the only question that can be raised as to such measures will be whether they are 'necessary and proper' measures for the carrying of the treaty in question into operation."

It will be noted that one of the principal cases cited is that of the Migratory Bird case.

These conclusions are those also of a committee of the New York State Bar Association, of which former Attorney General Mitchell and Mr. John W. Davis were prominent members.

Now, for some practical illustration of new-found powers under treaties of what Congress may do:

1. It may enact a comprehensive education bill, providing for education in any State which does not provide it. In fact, it may take over all public education now provided by States and municipalities.

2. It may enact a prohibition act without an amendment of the Constitution.

3. It may enact a uniform divorce act.

4. It may take over all social and welfare services rendered by or through the States or their agencies.

5. It may take over all commerce, all utility rates and service, all labor. The list may be multiplied extensively at your will.

The new test of constitutionality will apply to all legislation by Congress since 1945, which deals with any of the five fields of endeavor. Any judge deciding on the validity of legislation must have two books before him — one, the Constitution of the United States, and the other, the Charter of the United Nations. If he does not find authority for the act in the Constitution, he will find it in the Charter. That is the exact situation in which Justice Holmes found himself and the other members of the Supreme Court when they decided the Migratory Bird case. The authority was not found in the Constitution — it was found in the treaty with Great Britain.

The question to be answered is this: Under which form of government do the people of the United States prefer to live? Manifestly, we cannot operate under both.

Senators, the people of the United States have given up their sons; they have given up billions of their substance. They should not be the only Nation in the world to give up their form of government — the wonder of the world — to discharge their obligations to the people of the world.

THE BRICKER AMENDMENT, WHICH WOULD HAVE CHANGED THIS, WAS NOT PASSED.
A LETTER TO THE EDITOR

Borger, *Texas News Herald*
Sunday, November 11, 1962
Dear Mr. Newby:

Replying to your letter Oct. 12th, also CHALLENGE for November, 1961: quoting Patrick Henry on treaties. In the first place Patrick Henry was and is NO AUTHORITY on either treaties or the Constitution, and he opposed it, IF it is too late to do anything about reinstating our Constitution, then why not just accept the traitorous U.N. Charter-Treaty without more ado? Why didn't the American Revolutionists think it too late or too difficult to defend their Liberty? And IF the highly-intelligent framers of the Constitution "were well aware of the deathtrap incorporated in AR-TICLE VI," why then did they so frame it? Did they not expect PATRIOTS, rather than Treasonists as our elected officials, to HONOR AND ENFORCE the spirit, letter, and intent of the Constitution?

I note you say that according to a law dictionary, the terms "legal" and "lawful" are almost one and the same. Agreed! "Almost," but not quite. I believe there is a fine point of difference. Taking us into the U.N. may SEEM to have been done legally (by the President and Senate), but the act is still unlawful, because it is unconstitutional, and the CONSTITUTION IS THE SUPREME LAW OF THE LAND. All renowned and genuine Constitutional experts (such as Thos. M. Cooley, Thos. Jas. Norton, and Harry Atwood, to name several) have always held that anything which contravenes, diminishes, or perverts the Constitution is null and void and of no effect.

Neither the President or Senate has authority or power to change, diminish, or destroy the Constitution "by usurpation," treaty, or otherwise: only a Constitutional Amendment can lawfully change it.

The Constitution is a contract that WE THE PEOPLE of the USA made with one another, which sets up the machinery of government to carry out this contract — mainly for the purpose of PROTECTING INDIVIDUAL RIGHTS as well as STATE RIGHTS, AGAINST THE POWERS OF GOVERNMENT: and no public official has a right to override the provisions of that contract. To quote Thos. Jas. Norton's *Constitution of the United States, Its Application, etc.*, "A law of Congress to be one of the supreme laws must be 'made in pursuance thereof' and not in conflict with the Constitution. When not made in pursuance thereof it is of course unconstitutional and of no effect." And the same would similarly apply to a wonderful decision rendered by the Supreme Court or an unlawful Treaty.

And from Norton's *Undermining the Constitution*, which quotes Alexander Hamilton in No. 33 of *The Federalist*: "It will not, I presume, have escaped observation that it *expressly* confines the supremacy to laws made pursuant to the Constitution" (emphasis by Hamilton). And from page 21, "The General Government can claim no powers which are not granted to it by the Constitution, and the powers actually granted must be such as are expressly given, or given by necessary implication."

Anyone with the presumed intelligence to be President of the USA must know that he cannot lawfully make any such far-reaching treaty with the United Nations, or any other foreign power, as you envision by your language, without laying himself open to the charge of TREASON under ARTICLE III, Section 3 of the Constitution. Just ordinary common sense is required to know that our alleged Treaty with the U.N. and acceptance of the all-inclusive terms of its Charter by our Presidents (beginning with FDR, who connived with Stalin at Yalta for the setting up of the U.N. in the USA) and our Senate, is a violation of their sacred oath of office as per ARTICLE III, Section 2 of the Constitution.

Such a Treaty makes a mockery of any genuine allegiance to OUR Flag and Constitution. A genuine American, Abraham Lincoln, said, "Worse than traitors-in-arms are the men who, pretending loyalty to the Flag, feast and fatten on the misfortunes of the nation." Think of any TRUTH more applicable to the present time?

A number of our officials, including former Secretary of State Dean Acheson, the late John Foster Dulles, and members of our present one-world Kennedy entourage go along with the statement that the USA now has NO "domestic" affairs: there has been a melding of our domestic and foreign affairs! (Meld means to merge.)

Katanga Province in the Congo thought she had some private affairs and rights, but the U.N. soon disillusioned her. Quote from *S.L. Tribune* for September 14, 1961: "U.N. Soldiers Take Over in Katanga. U.N. troops seized Katanga's capital, Elisabethville, in a brisk battle Wednesday, and the Congo's central government proclaimed the return of that secessionist province." There is no doubt that the President of the USA and Senate have surrendered certain of our rights and Sovereignty to the U.N., and plan still more.

Any informed American is aware that ARTICLE IV, Section 4, of the Constitution automatically cancels out any allegiance to the U.N. and its alien one-world Internationalism, the antithesis of Constitutional Americanism founded on Washington's "NO foreign entanglements." And that said republican representative form of government is the exact opposite of the U.N. Charter's Soviet-initiated modifications, restrictions, and reservations in its various "Conventions" which would nullify our Bill of Rights. Stalin, his protégé, Alger Hiss, and Russian Communist Pasvolsky figured largely in the writing of the U.N. Charter.

To assume that a heterogeneous body composed of appointed representatives of foreign governments (some from crude cannibalistic so-called "States" and others, from virulently atheistic Communist States) — which Governments DO NOT REPRESENT "We the American People" — could exercise dictation and control over U.S. is monstrous in the extreme. Lawfully or constitutionally, they may not enforce any provisions of the U.N.

Charter against us, or take any action whatever affecting the Sovereign Rights of American Citizens.

Further, the United Nations is not a lawful government in the accepted sense of the term and is not a proper body with which to make a treaty. Actually, the U.N. has NO valid binding treaty-making power — except as the subversive one-worlders try to make it so. Quoting Norton's *Constitution of the United States*, at page 14: "A treaty is a written contract between two governments (not a motley assembly of unstable tribes, or enslaved peoples calling themselves a 'government') respecting matters of mutual welfare, such as peace, the acquisition of territory, the defining of boundaries, the needs of trade, rights of citizenship..." etc.

And such treaties, even though "legally made," MAY be abrogated for cause. Quoting *ibid*, p. 115: "A precedent for thus abrogating a treaty made by the President and approved by the Senate may be found as far back as July 7, 1789, when Congress passed 'An Act to Declare the Treaties heretofore concluded with France no longer obligatory on the United States because they have been repeatedly violated on the part of the French government.'" So what about all the violations of the treaties or agreements made by the USSR, which dominates the U.N.? The USA is vastly outvoted in this motley aggregation called the United Nations, even as American taxpayers foot most of the bills, which constitutes Constitutionally forbidden confiscation of the citizens' money (property) without just compensation therefore. This is merely communistic confiscation.

A Treaty made "pursuant to the Constitution" becomes A PART of the LAW OF THE LAND, and should be honored; but it does NOT become "Supreme" or take precedence over nor supersede the Constitution. It is NOT the "Law of the Land" standing alone. And NO Treaty or Executive Agreement is binding on the USA if made by the President alone (as has been done) with the advice and consent of the Senate, nor if it violates the Constitution.

Actually, ARTICLE VI, instead of setting Treaties on high or being a "death trap," is a statement of the SUPREMACY OF THE CONSTITUTION and of the NATIONAL GOVERNMENT. Lawful Treaties are a part of, but subordinate to, the Constitution for the simple stated provision therein that ALL laws and treaties must be made "in pursuance thereof."

Can the "creature" (or a part) become greater than its CREATOR, or the whole??? Some American common sense is necessary in all this blather about the supremacy of treaties, which is promulgated largely by the one-worlders to discredit or diminish the Constitution so they can achieve their own ends.

The language and intent of the Constitution and of ARTICLE VI is

clear and forthright, and does not admit, in good faith, of any other interpretation. But sadly enough, it is well known that many of our highest
judiciary and elected officials — in this era of TREASON, not Reason — do
not act in good faith nor in "pursuance of the Constitution."

With reference to fourth paragraph your letter Oct. 12th, Mr. Newby,
that the "making of treaties is without limitation, exception or reservation"
and that "no treaty has ever been declared unconstitutional or invalidated
or repealed by the Courts or Congress in the history of this nation," I think
that the foregoing invalidates your statement.

And as to ARTICLE VI being a "deathtrap" over which the Constitution gives no control or remedy other than its explicit language in VI
regarding the law and treaties: has it occurred to you that the Supreme
Court has power and authority to rule on the constitutionality of treaties
the same as on the constitutionality of any other law — treaties being
merely "part of the Law of the Land"? ARTICLE III, Section 2 explicitly
states: "The Judicial power shall extend to all cases, in Law and Equity,
arising under this Constitution, the Laws of the United States, and treaties
made, or which shall be made, under their authority." To quote Norton's
Constitution of the United States, page 137: "When a case arises in a State
court and involves a question of the Constitution, or an Act of Congress, or
of a treaty, it is the duty of the court to follow and enforce the National
[Constitutional] law; for the Constitution explicitly and emphatically requires that the 'judges in every State shall be bound thereby, anything in
the Constitution or laws of any State to the contrary notwithstanding.'"

Any time that the President and Senate make a treaty with a foreign
power (such as the U.N.) which infringes upon or abrogates rights guaranteed to citizens of the USA under the Constitution, the Supreme Court can
declare such treaty unconstitutional, void, and of no effect. Of course, the
present Supreme Court, being composed of political radicals rather than
judicial Constitutional experts, is not likely to take such action — unless
forced to do so by public opinion and demand.

And so, with reference to your statement in printed CHALLENGE for
November, 1961, to the effect that, "under ARTICLE II, Section 2, clause 2
of the Constitution...such treaty (as with the U.N.) can be made without
restriction, limitation, exception or reservation irrespective of the fact that
it contravenes, violates, infringes or alienates every article of the Constitution. All that is necessary is for the President and Senate to ratify ANY
treaty and it is in force." The above article and clause likewise does not
stand alone, but must be construed in the light of the entire Constitution.
YOUR interpretation is not only to make idiots of the Founding Fathers
and Framers of the Constitution, but to say that regardless of the solemn

* * * * TOP SECRET * * * *

Presidential oath of allegiance required by ARTICLE III, Section 2a, regardless of the SUPREME SOVEREIGNTY of the U.S. Constitution, and in violation of the explicit language contained in ARTICLE VI, i.e., "THIS CONSTITUTION, and the laws of the United States which shall be made in pursuance thereof; and all treaties...under the authority of the United States...," as well as all authoritative rulings by genuine Constitutional authorities to the effect that anything which contravenes the Constitution of the USA is null and void, including any such acts by the Congress; despite all of the foregoing. I reiterate that YOUR interpretation would claim that there is absolutely NO constitutional safeguard for the American People against TREASONOUS treaties (which "gives aid and comfort to our enemies" as per ARTICLE III, Section 3).

YOUR interpretation would give complete IMMUNITY to the maker...of such treaties and would constitute "changing the Constitution by usurpation" in violation of the intent, spirit, AND letter of the Constitution as a whole.

The President obviously is NOT a "free agent" by virtue of ARTICLE II, Section 2, clause 2, to make any sort of treaty he would like, but is BOUND DOWN by the chains of the entire Constitution. Nothing else makes any sense. His treaty-making acts are subject to review by the Courts.

True, we SHOULD DEMAND rescinding of the action by both Senate and Harry S. Truman in signing the U.N. Participation Act of 1945 in behalf of the USA. This would put the World on notice that we were once more HONORING OUR OWN CONSTITUTION (CHARTER OF FREEDOM) AS THE SUPREME LAW OF THE LAND, AND REINSTATING IT TO ITS FORMER PROPER SUPREME POSITION: as well as reclaiming our Sovereignty as an Independent Republic in accordance with our Declaration of Independence.

There is not nor ever will be any true Peace, Freedom, Safety or Security for the American People under the alien U.N. Charter.

There is "NO SUBSTITUTE" for American Independence. Many men have died and "worms have eaten them" for a far lesser Cause.

And so, Mr. Newby, you and I do have one primary objective in view: GET THE U.S. OUT OF THE U.N., AND THE SUBVERSIVE U.N. OUT OF THE USA!

Most sincerely yours,

Marilyn R. Allen

* * * * TOP SECRET * * * *

I guess that just about covers the U.N. Charter vs. U.S. sovereignty hoax. No one should ever be able to bullshit you on this issue again. Your job now is to make sure your Congressmen and Senators are educated on this issue.

GET TO WORK — NOW!

Chapter 14

A PROPOSED CONSTITUTIONAL MODEL FOR THE NEWSTATES OF AMERICA

Prepared Over a 10-Year Period
by the
Center for Democratic Studies
of Santa Barbara, California,
at a Total Cost to the
United States Taxpayers of
Over $25 Million

A PROPOSED CONSTITUTIONAL MODEL FOR THE NEWSTATES OF AMERICA

PREAMBLE

So that we may join in common endeavors, welcome the future in good order, and create an adequate and self-repairing government - we, the people, do establish the Newstates of America, herein provided to be ours, and do ordain this Constitution whose supreme law it shall be until the time prescribed for it shall have run.

ARTICLE I

Rights and Responsibilities

A. Rights

SECTION 1.. Freedom of expression, of communication, of movement, of assembly, or of petition shall not be abridged except in declared emergency.

SECTION 2. Access to information possessed by governmental agencies shall not be denied except in interest of national security; but communications among officials necessary to decision making shall be privileged.

SECTION 3. Public communicators may decline to reveal sources of information, but shall be responsible for hurtful disclosures.

SECTION 4. The privacy of individuals shall be respected; searches and seizures shall be made only on judicial warrant; persons shall be pursued or questioned only for the prevention of crime or the apprehension of suspected criminals, and only according to rules established under law.

SECTION 5. There shall be no discrimination because of race, creed, color, origin, or sex. The Court of Rights and Responsibilities may determine whether selection for various occupations has been discriminatory.

SECTION 6. All persons shall have equal protection of the laws, and in all electoral procedures the vote of every eligible citizen shall count equally with others.

SECTION 7. It shall be public policy to promote discussion of public issues and to encourage peaceful public gatherings for this purpose. Permission to hold such gatherings shall not be denied, nor shall they be interrupted, except in decalred emergency or on a showing of imminent danger to public order and on judicial warrant.

SECTION 8. The practice of religion shall be privileged; but no religion shall be imposed by some on others, and none shall have public support.

SECTION 9. Any citizen may purchase, sell, lease, hold, convey and inherit real and personal property, and shall benefit equally from all laws for security in such transactions.

SECTION 10. Those who cannot contribute to productivity shall be entitled to a share of the national product; but distribution shall be fair and the total may not exceed the amount for this purpose held in the National Sharing Fund.

SECTION 11. Education shall be provided at public expense for those who meet appropriate tests of eligibility.

SECTION 12. No person shall be deprived of life, liberty, or property without due process of law. No property shall be taken without compensation.

SECTION 13. Legislatures shall define crimes and conditions requiring restraint, but confinement shall not be for punishment; and, when possible, there shall be preparation for return to freedom.

SECTION 14. No person shall be placed twice in jeopardy for the same offense.

SECTION 15. Writs of habeas corpus shall not be suspended except in declared emergency.

SECTION 16. Accused persons shall be informed of charges against them, shall have a speedy trial, shall have reasonable bail, shall be allowed to confront witnesses or to call others, and shall not be compelled to testify against themselves; at the time of arrest they shall be informed of their right to be silent and to have counsel, provided, if necessary, at public expense; and courts shall consider the contention that prosecution may be under an invalid or unjust statue.

B. Responsibilities

SECTION 1. Each freedom of the citzen shall prescribe a corresponding responsibility not to diminsh that of others: of speech, communication, assembly, and petition, to grant the same freedom to others; of religion, to respect that of others; of privacy, not to invade that of others; of the holding and disposal of property, the obligation to extend the same privilege to others.

SECTION 2. Individuals and enterprises holding themselves out to serve the public shall serve all equally and without intention to misrepresent, conforming to such standards as may improve health

3

and welfare.

SECTION 3. Protection of the law shall be repaid by assistance in its enforcement; this shall include respect for the procedures of justice, apprehension of lawbreakers, and testimony at trial.

SECTION 4. Each citizen shall participate in the processes of democracy, assisting in the selection of officials and in the monitoring of their conduct in office.

SECTION 5. Each shall render such services to the nation as may be uniformly required by law, objection by reason of conscience being adjudicated as hereinafter provided; and none shall expect or may receive special privileges unless they be for a public purpose defined by law.

SECTION 6. Each shall pay whatever share of governmental costs is consistent with fairness to all.

SECTION 7. Each shall refuse awards or titles from other nations or their representatives except as they be authorized by law.

SECTION 8. There shall be a responsibility to avoid violence and to keep the peace; for this reason the bearing of arms or the possession of lethal weapons shall be confined to the police, members of the armed forces, and those licensed under law.

SECTION 9. Each shall assist in preserving the endowments of nature and enlarging the inheritance of future generations.

SECTION 10. Those granted the use of public lands, the air, or waters shall have a responsibility for using these resources so that, if irreplaceable, they are conserved and, if replaceable, they are put back as they were.

SECTION 11. Retired officers of the armed forces, of the senior civil service, and of the Senate shall regard their service as a permanent obligation and shall not engage in enterprise seeking profit from the government.

SECTION 12. The devising or controlling of devices for management or technology shall establish responsibility for resulting costs.

SECTION 13. All rights and responsibilities defined herein shall extend to such associations of citizens as may be authorized by law.

ARTICLE II
The Newstates

SECTION 1. There shall be Newstates, each comprising no less than 5 percent of the whole population. Existing states may continue and may have the status of Newstates if the Boundary Commission, hereinafter provided, shall so decide. The Commission shall be guided in its recommendations by the probability of accommodation to the conditions for effective government. States electing by referendum to continue if the Commission recommend otherwise shall nevertheless accept all Newstate obligations.

SECTION 2. The Newstates shall have constitutions formulated and adopted by processes hereinafter prescribed.

SECTION 3. They shall have Governors; legislatures, and planning administrative and judicial systems.

SECTION 4. Their political procedures shall be organized and supervised by electoral Overseers; but their elections shall not be in years of presidential election.

SECTION 5. The electoral apparatus of the Newstates of America shall be available to them, and they may be allotted funds under rules agreed to by the national Overseer; but expenditures may not be made by or for any candidate except they be approved by the Overseer; and requirements of residence in a voting district shall be no longer than thirty days.

SECTION 6. They may charter subsidiary governments, urban or rural, and may delegate to them powers appropriate to their responsibilities.

SECTION 7. They may lay, or may delegate the laying of, taxes; but these shall conform to the restraints stated hereinafter for the Newstates of America.

SECTION 8. They may not tax exports, may not tax with intent to prevent imports, and may not impose any tax forbidden by laws of the Newstates of America; but the objects appropriate for taxation shall be clearly designated.

SECTION 9. Taxes on land may be at higher rates than those on its improvements.

SECTION 10. They shall be responsible for the administration of public services not reserved to the government of the Newstates of America, such activities being concerted with those of corresponding national agencies, where these exist, under arrangements common to all.

SECTION 11. The rights and responsibilities prescribed in this Constitution shall be effective in the Newstates and shall be suspended only in emergency when declared by Governors and not disapproved by the Senate of the Newstates of America.

SECTION 12. Police powers of the Newstates shall extend to all matters not reserved to the Newstates of America; but preempted powers shall not be impaired.

SECTION 13. Newstates may not enter into any treaty, alliance, confederation, or agreement unless approved by the Boundary Commission hereinafter provided.

They may not coin money, provide for the payment of debts in any but legal tender, or make any charge for inter-Newstate services. They may not enact ex post facto laws or ones impairing the obligation of contracts.

SECTION 14. Newstates may not impose barriers to imports from other jurisdictions or impose any hindrance to citizens' freedom of movement.

SECTION 15. If governments of the Newstates fail to carry out fully their constitutional duties, their officials shall be warned and may be required by the Senate, on the recommendation of the Watchkeeper, to forfeit revenues from the Newstates of America.

ARTICLE III
The Electoral Branch

SECTION 1. To arrange for participation by the electorate in the determination of policies and the selection of officials, there shall be an Electoral Branch.

SECTION 2. An Overseer of electoral procedures shall be chosen by majority of the Senate and may be removed by a two-thirds vote. It shall be the Overseer's duty to supervise the organization of national and district parties, arrange for discussion among them, and provide for the nomination and election of candidates for public office. While in office the Overseer shall belong to no political organization; and after each presidential election shall offer to resign.

SECTION 3. A national party shall be one having had at least a 5 percent affiliation in the latest general election; but a new party shall be recognized when valid petitions have been signed by at least 2 percent of the voters in each of 30 percent of the districts drawn for the House of Representatives. Recognition shall be suspended upon failure to gain 5 percent of the votes at a second election, 10 percent at a third, or 15 percent at further elections.

District parties shall be recognized when at least 2 percent of voters shall have signed petitions of affiliation; but recognition shall be withdrawn upon failure to attract the same percentages as are neccessary for the continuance of national parties.

SECTION 4. Recognition by the Overseer shall bring parties within established regulations and entitle them to common privileges.

SECTION 5. The Overseer shall promulgate rules for party conduct and shall see that fair practices are maintained, and for this purpose shall appoint deputies in each district and shall supervise the choice, in district and national conventions, of party administrators. Regulations and appointments may be objected to by the Senate.

SECTION 6. The Overseer, with the administrator and other officials, shall:

a. Provide the means for discussion, in each party, of public issues, and for this purpose, ensure that members have adequate facilities for participation.

b. Arrange for discussion, in annual district meetings, of the President's views, of the findings of the Planning Branch, and such other information as may be pertinent for the enlightened political discussion.

c. Arrange, on the first Saturday in each month, for enrollment, valid for one year, of voters at convenient places.

SECTION 7. The Overseer shall also:

a. Assist the parties in nominating candidates for district members of the House of Representatives each three years; and for this purpose designate one hundred districts, each with a similar number of eligible voters, redrawing districts after each election. In these there shall be party conventions having no more than three hundred delegates, so distributed that representation of voters be approximately equal.

Candidates for delegate may become eligible by presenting petitions signed by two hundred registered voters. They shall be elected by party members on the first Tuesday in March, those having the largest number of votes being chosen until the three hundred be complete. Ten alternates shall also be chosen by the same process.

District conventions shall be held on the first Tuesday in April. Delegates shall choose three candidates for membership in the House of Representatives, the three having the most votes becoming candidates.

5

b. Arrange for the *election* each three years of three members of the House of Representatives in each district from among the candidates chosen in party conventions, the three having the most votes to be elected.

SECTION 8. The Overseer shall also:

a. Arrange for national conventions to meet nine years after previous presidential elections, with an equal number of delegates from each district, the whole number not to exceed one thousand.

Candidates for delegates shall be eligible when petitions signed by five hundred registered voters have been filed. Those with the most votes, together with two alternates, being those next in number of votes, shall be chosen in each district.

b. Approve procedures in these conventions for choosing one hundred candidates to be members-at-large of the House of Representatives, whose terms shall be coterminous with that of the President. For this purpose delegates shall file one choice with convention officials. Voting on submissions shall proceed until one hundred achieve 10 percent, but not more than three candidates may be resident in any one district; if any district have more than three, those with the fewest votes shall be eliminated, others being added from the districts having less than three, until equality be reached. Of those added, those having the most votes shall be chosen first.

c. Arrange procedures for the consideration and approval of party objectives by the convention.

d. Formulate rules for the *nomination* in these conventions of candidates for President and Vice Presidents when the offices are to fall vacant, candidates for nomination to be recognized when petitions shall have been presented by one hundred or more delegates, pledged to continue support until candidates can no longer win or until they consent to withdraw. Presidents and Vice-Presidents, together with Representatives-at-large, shall submit to referendum after serving for three years, and if they are rejected, new conventions shall be held within one month and candidates shall be chosen as for vacant offices.

Candidates for President and Vice-Presidents shall be nominated on attaining a majority.

e. Arrange for the *election* on the first Tuesday in June, in appropriate years, of new candidates for President and Vice-Presidents, and members-at-large of the House of Representatives, all being presented to the nation's voters as a ticket; if no ticket achieve a majority, the Overseer shall arrange another election, on the third Tuesday in June, between the two persons having the most votes; and if referendum so determine he shall provide similar arrangements for the nomination and election of candidates.

In this election, the one having the most votes shall prevail.

SECTION 9. The Overseer shall also:

a. Arrange for the convening of the national legislative houses on the fourth Tuesday of July.

b. Arrange for inauguration of the President and Vice-Presidents on the second Tuesday of August.

SECTION 10. All costs of electoral procedures shall be paid from public funds, and there shall be no private contributions to parties or candidates; no contributions or expenditures for meetings, conventions, or campaigns shall be made; and no candidate for office may make any personal expenditures unless authorized by a uniform rule of the Overseer; and persons or groups making expenditures, directly or indirectly, in support of prospective candidates shall report to the Overseer and shall conform to his regulations.

SECTION 11. Expenses of the Electoral Branch shall be met by the addition of one percent to the net annual taxable income returns of taxpayers, this sum to be held by the Chancellor of Financial Affairs for disposition by the Overseer.

Funds shall be distributed to parties in proportion to the respective number of votes cast for the President and Governors at the last election, except that new parties, on being recognized, shall share in proportion to their number. Party adminstrators shall make allocations to legislative candidates in amounts proportional to the party vote at the last election.

Expenditures shall be audited by the Watchkeeper; and sums not expended within four years shall be returned to the Treasury.

It shall be a condition of every communications franchise that reasonable facilities shall be available for allocations by the Overseer.

ARTICLE IV
The Planning Branch

SECTION 1. There shall be a Planning Branch to formulate and administer plans and to prepare budgets for the uses of expected income in pursuit of policies formulated by the processes provided herein.

6

SECTION 2. There shall be a National Planning Board of fifteen members appointed by the President; the first members shall have terms designated by the President of one to fifteen years, thereafter one shall be appointed each year; the President shall appoint a Chairman who shall serve for fifteen years unless removed by him.

SECTION 3. The Chairman shall appoint, and shall supervise, a planning administrator, together with such deputies as may be agreed to by the Board.

SECTION 4. The Chairman shall present to the Board six-and twelve year development plans prepared by the planning staff. They shall be revised each year after public hearings, and finally in the year before they are to take effect. They shall be submitted to the President on the fourth Tuesday in July for transmission to the Senate on September 1st with his comments.

If members of the Board fail to approve the budget proposals by the forwarding date, the Chairman shall nevertheless make submission to the President with notations of reservation by such members. The President shall transmit this proposal, with his comments, to the House of Representatives on September 1.

SECTION 5. It shall be recognized that the six-and twelve-year development plans represent national intentions tempered by the appraisal of possibilities. The twelve-year plan shall be a general estimate of probable progress, both governmental and private; the six-year plan shall be more specific as to estimated income and expenditure and shall take account of necessary revisions.

The purpose shall be to advance, through every agency of government, the excellence of national life. It shall be the further purpose to anticipate innovations, to estimate their impact, to assimilate them into existing institutions, and to moderate deleterious effects on the environment and on society.

The six-and twelve-year plans shall be disseminated for dicussion and the opinions expressed shall be considered in the formulation of plans for each succeeding year with special attention to detail in proposing the budget.

SECTION 6. For both plans an extension of one year into the future shall be made each year and the estimates for all other years shall be revised accordingly. For nongovernmental activities the estimate of developments shall be calculated to indicate the need for enlargement or restriction.

SECTION 7. If there be objection by the President or the Senate to the six-or Twelve-year plans, they shall be returned for restudy and resubmission. If there still be differences, and if the President and the Senate agree, they shall prevail. If they do not agree, the Senate shall prevail and the plan shall be revised accordingly.

SECTION 8. The Newstates, on June 1, shall submit proposals for development to be considered for inclusion in those for the Newstates of America. Researches and administration shall be delegated, when convenient, to planning agencies of the Newstates.

SECTION 9. There shall be submissions from private individuals or from organized associations affected with a public interest, as defined by the Board. They shall report intentions to expand or contract, estimates of production and demand, probable uses of resources, numbers expected to be employed, and other essential information.

SECTION 10. The Planning Branch shall make and have custody of offical maps, and these shall be documents of reference for future developments both public and private; on them the location of facilities, with extension indicated, and the intended use of all areas shall be marked out.

Offical maps shall also be maintained by the planning agencies of the Newstates, and in matters not exclusively national the National Planning Board may rely on these.

Undertakings in violation of official designation shall be at the risk of the venturer, and there shall be no recourse; but losses from designatiqns after acquisition shall be recoverable in actions before the Court of Claims.

SECTION 11. The Planning Branch shall have available to it funds equal to one-half of one percent of the approved national budget (not including debt services or payments from trust funds). They shall be held by the Chancellor of Financial Affairs and expended according to rules approved by the Board; but funds not expended within six years shall be available for other uses.

SECTION 12. Allocations may be made for the planning agencies of the Newstates; but only the maps and plans of the national Board, or those approved by them, shall have status at law.

SECTION 13. In making plans, there shall be due regard to the interests of other nations and such cooperation with their intentions as may be approved by the Board.

SECTION 14. There may also be cooperation with international agencies and such contributions to their work as are not disapproved by the President.

7

ARTICLE V
The Presidency

SECTION 1.The President of the Newstates of America shall be the head of government, shaper of its commitments, expositor of its policies, and supreme commander of its protective forces; shall have one term of nine years, unless rejected by 60 percent of the electorate after three years; shall take care that the nation's resources are estimated and are apportioned to its more exigent needs; shall recommend such plans, legislation, and action as may be necessary; and shall address the legislators each year on the state of the nation, calling upon them to do their part for the general good.

SECTION 2.There shall be two Vice-Presidents elected with the President; at the time of taking office the President shall designate one Vice-President to supervise internal affairs; and one to be deputy for general affairs. The deputy for general affairs shall succeed if the presidency be vacated; the Vice-President for internal affairs shall be second in succession. If either Vice-President shall die or be incapacitated the President, with the consent of the Senate, shall appoint a successor. Vice-Presidents shall serve during an extended term with such assignments as the President may make.

If the presidency fall vacant through the disability of both Vice-Presidents, the Senate shall elect successors from among its members to serve until the next general election.

With the Vice-Presidents and other officials the President shall see to it that the laws are faithfully executed and shall pay attention to the findings and recommendations of the Planning Board, the National Regulatory Board, and the Watchkeeper in formulating national policies.

SECTION 3. Responsible to the Vice-President for General Affairs there shall be Chancellors of External, Financial, Legal, and Military Affairs.

The Chancellor of External Affairs shall assist in conducting relations with other nations.

The Chancellor of Financial Affairs shall supervise the nation's financial and monetary systems, regulating its capital markets and credit-issuing institutions as they may be established by law; and this shall include lending institutions for operations in other nations or in cooperation with them, except that treaties may determine their purposes and standards.

The Chancellor of Legal Affairs shall advise governmental agencies and represent them before the courts.

The Chancellor of Military Affairs shall act for the presidency in disposing all armed forces except militia commanded by governors; but these shall be available for national service at the President's convenience.

Except in declared emergency, the deployment of forces in far waters or in other nations without their consent shall be notified in advance to a national security committee of the Senate hereinafter provided.

SECTION 4. Responsible to the Vice-President for Internal Affairs there shall be chancellors of such departments as the President may find necessary for performing the services of government and are not rejected by a two-thirds vote when the succeeding budget is considered.

SECTION 5. Candidates for the presidency and the vice-presidencies shall be natural-born citizens. Their suitability may be questioned by the Senate within ten days of their nomination, and if two-thirds of the whole agree, they shall be ineligible and a nominating convention shall be reconvened. At the time of his nomination no candidate shall be a member of the Senate and none shall be on active service in the armed forces or a senior civil servant.

SECTION 6. The President may take leave because of illness or for an interval of relief, and the Vice-President in charge of General Affairs shall act. The President may resign if the Senate agree; and, if the term shall have more than two years to run, the Overseer shall arrange for a special election for President and Vice-President.

SECTION 7. The Vice-Presidents may be directed to perform such ministerial duties as the President may find convenient; but their instructions shall be of record,aand their actions shall be taken as his deputy.

SECTION 8.Incapacitation may be established without concurrence of the President by a three-quarters vote of the Senate, whereupon a successor shall become Acting President until the disability be declared, by a similar vote, to be ended or to have become permanent. Similarly the other Vice-President shall succeed if a predecessor die or be disabled. Special elections, in these contingencies, may be required by the Senate.

Acting Presidents may appoint deputies, unless the Senate object, to assume their duties until the next election.

SECTION 9. The Vice-Presidents, together with such other officials as the President may designate

8

from time to time, may constitute a cabinet or council; but this shall not include officials of other branches.

SECTION 10. Treaties or agreements with other nations, negotiated under the President's authority, shall be in effect unless objected to by a majority of the Senate within ninety days. If they are objected to, the President may resubmit and the Senate reconsider. If a majority still object, the Senate shall prevail.

SECTION 11. All officers, except those of other branches, shall be appointed and may be removed by the President. A majority of the Senate may object to appointments within sixty days, and alternative candidates shall be offered until it agrees.

SECTION 12. The President shall notify the Planning Board and the House of Representatives, on the fourth Tuesday in June, what the maximum allowable expenditures for the ensuing fiscal year shall be.

The President may determine to make expenditures less than provided in appropriations; but, except in declared emergency, none shall be made in excess of appropriations. Reduction shall be because of changes in requirements and shall not be such as to impair the integrity of budgetary procedures.

SECTION 13. There shall be a Public Custodian, appointed by the President and removable by him, who shall have charge of properties belonging to the government, but not allocated to specific agencies, who shall administer common public services, shall have charge of building construction and rentals, and shall have such other duties as may be designated by the President or the designated Vice Presidents.

SECTION 14. There shall be an Intendant responsible to the President who shall supervise Offices for Intelligence and Investigation; also an Office of Emergency Organization with the duty of providing plans and procedures for such contingencies as can be anticipated.

The Intendant shall also charter nonprofit corporations (or foundations), unless the President shall object, determined by him to be for useful public purposes. Such corporations shall be exempt from taxation but shall conduct no profitmaking enterprises.

SECTION 15. The Intendant shall also be a counselor for the coordination of scientific and cultural experiments, and for studies within the government and elsewhere, and for this purpose shall employ such assistance as may be found necessary.

SECTION 16. Offices for other purposes may be established and may be discontinued by presidential order within the funds allocated in the procedures of appropriation.

ARTICLE VI
The Legislative Branch
(The Senate and the House of Representatives)
A. The Senate

SECTION 1. There shall be a Senate with membership as follows: If they so desire, former Presidents, Vice-Presidents, Principal Justices, Overseers, Chairmen of the Planning and Regulatory Boards, Governors having had more than seven years service, and unsuccessful candidates for the presidency and vice-presidency who have received at least 30 percent of the vote. To be appointed by the President, three persons who have been Chancellors, two officials from the civil services, two officials from the diplomatic services, two senior military officers, also one person from a panel of three, elected in a process approved by the Overseer, by each of twelve such groups or associations as the President may recognize from time to time to be nationally representative, but none shall be a political or religious group, no individual selected shall have been paid by any private interest to influence government, and any association objected to by the Senate shall not be recognized. Similarly, to be appointed by the Principal Justice, two persons distinguished in public law and two former members of the High Courts or the Judicial Council. Also, to be elected by the House of Representatives, three members who have served six or more years.

Vacancies shall be filled as they occur.

SECTION 2. Membership shall continue for life, except that absences not provided for by rule shall constitute retirement, and that Senators may retire voluntarily.

SECTION 3. The Senate shall elect as presiding officer a Convener who shall serve for two years, when his further service may be discontinued by a majority vote. Other officers, including a Deputy, shall be appointed by the Convener unless the Senate shall object.

SECTION 4. The Senate shall meet each year on the second Tuesday in July and shall be in continuous session, but may adjourn to the call of the Convener. A quorum shall be more than three-

9

fifths of the whole membership

SECTION 5. The Senate shall consider, and return within thirty days, all measures approved by the House of Representatives (except the annual budget). Approval or disapproval shall be by a majority vote of those present. Objection shall stand unless the House of Representatives shall overcome it by a majority vote plus one; if no return be made, approval by the House of Representatives shall be final.

For consideration of laws passed by the House of Representatives or for other purposes, the Convener may appoint appropriate committees.

SECTION 6. The Senate may ask advice from the Principal Justice concerning the constitutionality of measures before it; and if this be done, the time for return to the House of Representatives may extend to ninety days.

SECTION 7. If requested, the Senate may advise the President on matters of public interest; or, if not requested, by resolution approved by two-thirds of those present. There shall be a special duty to expressions of concern during party conventions and commitments made during campaigns; and if these be neglected, to remind the President and the House of Representatives that these undertakings are to be considered.

SECTION 8. In time of present or prospective danger caused by cataclysm, by attack, or by insurrection, the Senate may declare a national emergency and may authorize the President to take appropriate action. If the Senate be dispersed, and no quorum available, the President may proclaim the emergency, and may terminate it unless the Senate shall have acted. If the President be not available, and the circumstances extreme, the senior serving member of the presidential succession may act until a quorum assembles.

SECTION 9. The Senate may also define and declare a limited emergency in time of prospective danger, or of local or regional disaster, or if an extraordinary advantage be anticipated. It shall be considered by the House of Representatives within three days and, unless disapproved, may extend for a designated period and for a limited area before renewal.

Extraordinary expenditures during emergency may be approved, without regard to usual budget procedures, by the House of Representatives with the concurrence of the President.

SECTION 10. The Senate, at the beginning of each session, shall select three of its members to constitute a National Security Committee to be consulted by the President in emergencies requiring the deployment of the armed forces abroad. If the Committee dissent from the President's proposal, it shall report to the Senate, whose decision shall be final.

SECTION 11. The Senate shall elect, or may remove, a National Watchkeeper, and shall oversee, through a standing committee, a Watchkeeping Service conducted according to rules formulated for their approval.

With the assistance of an appropriate staff the Watchkeeper shall gather and organize information concerning the adequacy, competence, and integrity of governmental agencies and their personnel, as well as their continued usefulness; and shall also suggest the need for new or expanded services, making report concerning any agency of the deleterious effect of its activities on citizens or on the environment.

The Watchkeeper shall entertain petitions for the redress of grievances and shall advise the appropriate agencies if there be need for action.

For all these purposes, personnel may be appointed, investigations made, witnesses examined, post audits made, and information required.

The Convener shall present the Watchkeeper's findings to the Senate, and if it be judged to be in the public interest, they shall be made public or, without being made public, be sent to the appropriate agency for its guidance and such action as may be needed. On recommendation of the Watchkeeper the Senate may initiate corrective measures to be voted on by the House of Representatives within thirty days. When approved by a majority and not vetoed by the President, they shall become law.

For the Watchkeeping Service one-quarter of one percent of individual net taxable incomes shall be held by the Chancellor of Financial Affairs; but amounts not expended in any fiscal year shall be available for general use.

B. The House of Representatives

SECTION 1. The House of Representatives shall be original lawmaking body of the Newstates of America.

SECTION 2. It shall convene each year on the second Tuesday in July and shall remain in continuous session except that it may adjourn to the call of a Speaker, elected by a majority vote from

****TOP SECRET****

among the Representatives-at-large, who shall be its presiding officer.

SECTION 3. It shall be a duty to implement the provisions of this constitution and, in legislature to be guided by them.

SECTION 4. Party leaders and their deputies shall be chosen by caucus at the beginning of each session.

SECTION 5. Standing and temporary committees shall be selected as follows:

Committees dealing with the calendaring and management of bills shall have a majority of members nominated to party caucuses by the Speaker; other members shall be nominated by minority leaders. Membership shall correspond to the parties' proportions at the last election. If nominations be not approved by a majority of the caucus, the Speaker or the minority leaders shall nominate others until a majority shall approve.

Members of other committees shall be chosen by party caucus in proportion to the results of the last election. Chairmen shall be elected annually from among at-large-members.

Bills referred to committees shall be returned to the house with recommendations within sixty days unless extension be voted by the House. ↵

In all committee actions names of those voting for and against shall be recorded.

No committee chairman may serve longer than six years.

SECTION 6. Approved legislation, not objected to by the Senate within the allotted time, shall be presented to the President for his approval or disapproval. If the President disapprove, and three-quarters of the House membership still approve, it shall become law. The names of those voting for and against shall be recorded. Bills not returned within eleven days shall become law.

SECTION 7. The President may have thirty days to consider measures approved by the House unless they shall have been submitted twelve days previous to adjournment.

SECTION 8. The house shall consider promptly the annual budget; if there be objection, it shall be notified to the Planning Board; The Board shall then resubmit through the President; and, with his comments, it shall be returned to the House. If there still be objection by a two-thirds majority, the House shall prevail. Objection must be by whole title; titles not objected to when voted on shall constitute appropriation.

The budget for the fiscal year shall be in effect on January 1. Titles not yet acted on shall be as in the former budget until action be completed.

SECTION 9. It shall be the duty of the House to make laws concerning taxes.

1. For their laying and collection:

a. They shall be uniform, and shall not be retroactive.

b. Except such as may be authorized by law to be laid by Authorities, or by the Newstates, all collections shall be made by a national revenue agency. This shall include collections for trust funds hereinafter authorized.

c. Except for corporate levies to be held in the National Sharing Fund, hereinafter authorized, taxes may be collected only from individuals and only from incomes; but there may be withholding from current incomes.

d. To assist in the maintenance of economic stability, the President may be authorized to alter rates by executive order.

e. They shall be imposed on profitmaking enterprises owned or conducted by religious establishments or other nonprofit organizations.

f. There shall be none on food, medicines, residential rentals, or commodities or services designated by law as necessities; and there shall be no double taxation.

g. None shall be levied for registering ownership or transfer of property.

2. For expenditure from revenues:

a. For the purposes detailed in the annual budget unless objection be made by the procedure prescribed herein.

b. For such other purposes as the House may indicate and require the Planning Board to include in revision of the budget; but, except in declared emergency, the total may not exceed the President's estimate of available funds.

3. For fixing the percentage of net corporate taxable incomes to be paid into a National Sharing Fund to be held in the custody of the Chancellor of Financial Affairs and made available for such welfare and environmental purposes as are authorized by law.

4. To provide for the regulation of commerce with other nations and among the Newstates, Possessions, Territories; or, as shall be mutually agreed, with other organized governments; but exports shall not be taxed; and imports shall not be taxed except on recommendation of the President at

11

rates whose allowable variations shall have been fixed by law. There shall be no quotas, and no nations favored by special rates, unless by special acts requiring two-thirds majorities.

5. To establish, or provide for the establishment of, institutions for the safekeeping of savings, for the gathering and distribution of capital, for the issuance of credit, for regulating the coinage of money, for controlling the media of exchange, and for stabilizing prices; but such institutions, when not public or semipublic, shall be regarded as affected with the public interest and shall be supervised by the Chancellor of Financial Affairs.

6. To establish institutions for insurance against risks and liabilities for communication, transportation, and others commonly used and necessary for public convenience.

8. To assist in the maintenance of world order, and, for this purpose, when the President shall recommend, to vest jurisdiction in international legislative, judicial, or administrative agencies.

9. To develop with other peoples, and for the benefit of all, the resources of space, of other bodies in the universe, and of the seas beyond twelve miles from low-water shores unless treaties shall provide other limits.

10. To assist other peoples who have not attained satisfactory levels of well-being; to delegate the administration of funds for assistance, whenever possible, to international agencies; and to invest in or contribute to the furthering of development in other parts of the world.

11. To assure, or to assist in assuring, adequate and equal facilities for education; for training in occupations citizens may be fitted to pursue; and to reeducate or retrain those whose occupations may become obsolete.

12. To establish or to assist institutions devoted to higher education, to research, or to technical training.

13. To establish and maintain, or assist in maintaining, libraries, archives, monuments, and other places of historic interest.

14. To assist in the advancement of sciences and technologies; and to encourage cultural activities.

15. To conserve natural resources by purchase, by withdrawal from use, or by regulation; to provide, or to assist in providing, facilities for recreation; to establish and maintain parks, forests, wilderness areas, wetlands, and prairies; to improve streams and other waters; to ensure the purity of air and water; to control the erosion of soils; and to provide for all else necessary for the protection and common use of the national heritage.

16. To acquire property and improvements for public use at costs to be fixed, if necessary, by the Court of Claims.

17. To prevent the stoppage or hindrance of governmental procedures, or other activities affected with a public interest as defined by law, by reason of disputes between employers and employees, or for other reasons, and for this purpose to provide for conclusive arbitration if adequate provision for collective bargaining fail. From such findings there may be appeal to the Court of Arbitration Review; but such proceedings may not stay the acceptance of findings.

18. To support an adequate civil service for the performance of such duties as may be designated by administrators; and for this purpose to refrain from interference with the processes of appointment or placement, asking advice or testimony before committees only with the consent of appropriate superiors.

19. To provide for the maintenance of armed forces.

20. To enact such measures as will assist families in making adjustment to future conditions, using estimates concerning population and resources made by the Planning Board.

21. To vote within ninety days on such measures as the President may designate as urgent.

Article VII
The Regulatory Branch
SECTION 1. There shall be a Regulatory Branch, and there shall be a National Regulator chosen by majority vote of the Senate and removable by a two-thirds vote of that body. His term shall be seven years, and he shall make and administer rules for the conduct of all economic enterprises.

The Regulatory Branch shall have such agencies as the Board may find necessary and are not disapproved by law.

SECTION 2. The Regulatory Board shall consist of seventeen members recommended to the Senate by the Regulator. Unless rejected by majority vote they shall act with the Regulator as a lawmaking body for industry.

They shall initially have terms of one to seventeen years, one being replaced each year and serving for

12

seventeen years. They shall be compensated and shall have no other occupation.

SECTION 3. Under procedures approved by the Board, the Regulator shall charter all corporations or enterprises except those exempted because of size or other characteristics, or those supervised by the Chancellor of Financial Affairs, or by the Intendant, or those whose activities are confined to one Newstate.

Charters shall describe proposed activities, and departure from these shall require amendment on penalty of revocation. For this purpose there shall be investigation and enforcement services under the direction of the Regulator.

SECTION 4. Chartered enterprises in similar industries or occupations may organize joint Authorities. These may formulate among themselves codes to ensure fair competition, meet external costs, set standards for quality and service, expand trade, increase production, eliminate waste, and assist in standardization. Authorities may maintain for common use services for research and communication; but membership shall be open to all eligible enterprises. Nonmembers shall be required to maintain the same standards as those prescribed for members.

SECTION 5. Authorities shall have governing committees of five, two being appointed by the Regulator to represent the public. They shall serve as he may determine; they shall be compensated; and he shall take care that there be no conflicts of interest. The Board may approve or prescribe rules for the distribution of profits to stockholders, allowable amounts of working capital, and reserves. Costing and all other practices affecting the public interest shall be monitored.

All codes shall be subject to review by the Regulator with his board.

SECTION 6. Member enterprises of an Authority shall be exempt from other regulation.

SECTION 7. The Regulator, with his Board, shall fix standards and procedures for mergers of enterprises or the acquisition of some by others; and these shall be in effect unless rejected by the Court of Administrative Settlements. The purpose shall be to encourage adaptation to change and to further approved intentions for the nation.

SECTION 8. The charters of enterprises may be revoked and Authorities may be dissolved by the Regulator, with the concurrence of the Board, if they restrict the production of goods and services, or controls of their prices; also if external costs are not assessed to their originators or if the ecological impacts of their operations are deleterious.

SECTION 9. Operations extending abroad shall conform to policies notified to the Regulator by the President; and he shall restrict or control such activities as appear to injure the national interest.

SECTION 10. The Regulator shall make rules for and shall supervise marketplaces for goods and services; but this shall not include security exchanges regulated by the Chancellor of Financial Affairs.

SECTION 11. Designation of enterprises affected with a public interest, rules for conduct of enterprises and of their Authorities, and other actions of the Regulator or of the Boards may be appealed to the Court of Administrative Settlements, whose judgments shall be informed by the intention to establish fairness to consumers and competitors and stability in economic affairs.

SECTION 12. Responsible also to the Regulator, there shall be an Operations Commission appointed by the Regulator, unless the Senate object, for the supervision of enterprises owned in whole or in part by government. The commission shall choose its chairman, and he shall be the executive head of a supervisory staff. He may require reports, conduct investigations, and make rules and recommendations concerning surpluses or deficits, the absorption of external costs, standards of service, and rates or prices charged for services or goods.

Each enterprise shall have a director, chosen by and removable by the Commission; and he shall conduct its affairs in accordance with standards fixed by the Commission.

Article VIII
The Judicial Branch

SECTION 1. There shall be a Principal Justice of the Newstates for America; a Judicial Council; and a Judicial Assembly. There shall also be a Supreme Court and a High Court of Appeals; also Courts of Claims, Rights and Duties, Administrative Review, Arbitration Settlements, Tax Appeals, and Appeals from Watchkeeper's Findings. There shall be Circuit Courts to be of first resort in suits brought under national law; and they shall hear appeals from courts of the Newstates.

Other courts may be established by law on recommendation of the Principal Justice with the Judicial Council.

SECTION 2. The Principal Justice shall preside over the judicial system, shall appoint the members of all national courts, and, unless the Judicial Council object, shall make its rules; also, through an

13

Administrator, supervise its operations.

SECTION 3. The Judicial Assembly shall consist of Circuit Court Judges, together with those of the High Courts of the Newstates of America and those of the highest courts of the Newstates. It shall meet annually, or at the call of the Principal Justice, to consider the state of the Judiciary and such other matters as may be laid before it.

It shall also meet at the call of the Convener to nominate three candidates for the Principal Justiceship whenever a vacancy shall occur. From these nominees the Senate shall choose the one having the most votes.

SECTION 4. The Principal Justice, unless the Senate object to any, shall appoint a Judicial Council of five members to serve during his incumbency. He shall designate a senior member who shall preside in his absence.

It shall be the duty of the Council, under the direction of the Principal Justice, to study the courts in operation, to prepare codes of ethics to be observed by members, and to suggest changes in procedure. The Council may ask the advice of the Judicial Assembly.

It shall also be a duty of the Council, as hereinafter provided, to suggest Constitutional amendments when they appear to be necessary; and it shall also draft revisions if they shall be required. Further it shall examine, and from time to time cause to be revised, civil and criminal codes; these, when approved by the Judicial Assembly, shall be in effect throughout the nation.

SECTION 5. The Principal Justice shall have a term of eleven years; but if at any time the incumbent resign or be disabled from continuing in office, as may be determined by the Senate, replacement shall be by the senior member of the Judicial Council until a new selection be made. After six years the Assembly may provide, by a two-thirds vote, for discontinuance in office, and a successor shall then be chosen.

SECTION 6. The Principal Justice may suspend members of any court for incapacity or violation of rules; and the separation shall be final if a majority of the Council agree.

For each court the Principal Justice shall, from time to time, appoint a member who shall preside.

SECTION 7. A presiding judge may decide, with the concurrence of the senior judge, that there may be pretrial proceedings, that criminal trials shall be conducted by either investigatory or adversary proceedings, and whether there shall be a jury and what the number of jurors shall be; but investigatory proceedings shall require a bench of three.

SECTION 8. In deciding on the concordance of statutes with the Constitution, the Supreme Court shall return to the House of Representatives such as it cannot construe. If the House fail to make return within ninety days the Court may interpret.

SECTION 9. The Principal Justice, or the President, may grant pardons or reprieves.

SECTION 10. The High Courts shall have thirteen members; but nine members, chosen by their senior justices from time to time, shall constitute a court. The justices on leave shall be subject to recall.

Other courts shall have nine members; but seven, chosen by their senior, shall constitute a court.

All shall be in continuous session except for recesses approved by the Principal Justice.

SECTION 11. The Principal Justice, with the Council, may advise the Senate, when requested, concerning the appropriateness of measures approved by the House of Representatives; and may also advise the President, when requested, on matters he may refer for consultation.

SECTION 12. It shall be for other branches to accept and to enforce judicial decrees.

SECTION 13. The High Court of Appeals may select applications for further consideration by the Supreme Court of decisions reached by other courts, including those of the Newstates. If it agree that there be a constitutional issue it may make preliminary judgment to be reviewed without hearing, and finally, by the Supreme Court.

SECTION 14. The Supreme Court may decide:

a. Whether, in litigation coming to it on appeal, constitutional provisions have been violated or standards have not been met.

b. On the application of constitutional provisions to suits involving the Newstates.

c. Whether international law, as recognized in treaties, United Nations aggreements, or arrangements with other nations, has been ignored or violated.

d. Other causes involving the interpretation of constitutional provisions; except that in holding any branch to have exceeded its powers the decision shall be suspended until the Judicial Court shall have determined whether, in order to avoid confrontation, procedures for amendment of the Constitution are appropriate.

If amendatory proceedings are instituted, decision shall await the outcome.

SECTION 15. The Courts of the Newstates shall have initial jurisdiction in cases arising under their

14

laws except those involing the Newstate itself or those reserved for national courts by a rule of the Principal Justice with the Judicial Council.

ARTICLE IX
General Provisions

SECTION 1. Qualifications for participation in democratic procedures as a citizen, and eligibility for office, shall be subject to repeated study and redefinition; but any change in qualification or eligibility shall become effective only if not disapproved by the Congress.

For this purpose a permanent Citizenship and Qualifications Commission shall be constituted, four members to be appointed by the President, three by the Convener of the Senate, three by the Speaker of the House, and three by the Principal Justice. Vacancies shall be filled as they occur. The members shall choose a chairman; they shall have suitable assistants and accommodations; and they may have other occupations. Recommendations of the commission shall be presented to the President and shall be transmitted to the House of Representatives with comments. They shall have a preferred place on the calendar and, of approved, shall be in effect.

SECTION 2. Areas necessary for the uses of government may be accquired at its valuation and may be maintained as the public interest may require. Such areas shall have self-government in matters of local concern.

SECTION 3. The President may negotiate for the acquisition of areas outside the Newstates of America, and, if the Senate approve, may provide for their organization as Possessions or Territories.

SECTION 4. The President may make agreements with other organized peoples for a relation other than full membership in the Newstates of America. They may become citizens and may participate in the selection of officials. They may receive assistance for their development or from the National Sharing Fund if they conform to its requirements; and they may serve in civilian or military services, but only as volunteers. They shall be represented in the House of Representatices by members elected at large, their number proportional to their constituencies; but each shall have at least one; and each shall in the same way choose one permanent member of the Senate.

SECTION 5. The President, the Vice - Presidents, and members of the legislative houses shall in all cases except treason, felony, and breach of the peace be exempt from penalty for anything they may say while pursuing public duties; but the Judicial Council may make restraining rules.

SECTION 6. Except as otherwise provided by this Constitution, each legislative house shall establish its requirement for membership and may make rules for the conduct of members, including conflicts of interest, providing its own disciplines for their infraction.

SECTION 7. No Newstate shall interfere with officials of the Newstates of America in the performance of their duties, and all shall give full faith and credit to the Acts of other Newstates and of the Newstates of America.

SECTION 8. Public funds shall be expended only as authorized in this Constitution.

ARTICLE X
Governmental Arrangements

SECTION 1. Offices of the Newstates of America shall be those named in this Constitution, including those of the legislative houses and others authorized by law to be appointed; they shall be compensated, and none may have other paid occupation unless they be excepted by law; none shall occupy more than one position in government; and no gift or favor shall be accepted if in any way related to official duty.

No income from former employments or associations shall continue for their benefits; but their properties may be put in trust and managed without their intervention during continuance in office. Hardships under this rule may be considered by the Court of Rights and Duties, and exceptions may be made with due regard to the general intention.

SECTION 2. The President, the Vice-Presidents, and the Principal Justice shall have households appropriate to their duties. The President, the Vice-Presidents, the Principal Justice, the Chairman of the Planning Board, the Regulator, the Watchkeeper, and the Overseer shall have salaries fixed by law and continued for life; but if they become members of the Senate, they shall have senatorial compensation and shall conform to senatorial requirements.

Justices of the High Courts shall have no term; and their salaries shall be two-thirds that of the Principal Justice; they and members of the Judicial Council, unless they shall have become Senators, shall be permanent members of the Judiciary and shall be available for assignment by the Principal Justice.

15

Salaries for members of the Senate shall be the same as for Justices of the High Court of Appeals.

SECTION 3. Unless otherwise provided herein, officials designated by the head of a branch as sharers in policymaking may be appointed by him with the President's concurrence and unless the Senate shall object.

SECTION 4. There shall be administrators:

a. for executive offices and official households, appointed by authority of the President;

b. for the national courts, appointed by the Principal Justice;

c. for the Legislative Branch, selected by a committee of members from each house (chosen by the Convener and the Speaker), three from the House of Representatices and four from the Senate.

Appropriations shall be made to them; but those for the Presidency shall not be reduced during his term unless with his consent; and those for the Judicial Branch shall not be reduced during five years succeeding their determination, unless with the consent of the Principal Justice.

SECTION 5. The fiscal year shall be the same as the calendar year, with new appropriations available at its beginning.

SECTION 6. There shall be an Officials' Protective Service to guard the President, the Vice-Presidents, the Principal Justice, and other officials whose safety may be at hazard; and there shall be a Protector appointed by and responsible to a standing committee of the Senate. Protected officials shall be guided by procedures approved by the committee.

The service, at the request of the Political Overseer, may extend its protection to candidates for office; or to other officials, if the committee so decide.

SECTION 7. A suitable contingency fund shall be made available to the President for purposes defined by law.

SECTION 8. The Senate shall try officers of government other than legislators when such officers are impeached by a two-thirds vote of the House of Representatives for conduct prejudicial to the public interest. If Presidents or Vice-Presidents are to be tried, the Senate, as constituted, shall conduct the trial. Judgments shall not extend beyond removal from office and disqualification for holding further office; but the convicted official shall be liable to further prosecution.

SECTION 9. Members of legislative houses may be impeached by the Judicial Council; but for trials it shall be enlarged to seventeen by Justices of the High Courts appointed by the Principal Justice. If convicted, members shall be expelled and be ineligible for future public office; and they shall also be liable for trial as citizens.

ARTICLE XI
Amendment

SECTION 1. It being the special duty of the Judicial Council to formulate and suggest amendments to this Constitution, it shall, from time to time, make proposals, through the Principal Justice, to the Senate. The Senate, if it approve, and if the President agree, shall instruct the Overseer to arrange at the next national election for submission of the amendment to the electorate. If not disapproved by a majority, it shall become part of this Constitution. If rejected, it may be restudied and a new proposal submitted.

It shall be the purpose of the amending procedure to correct deficiencies in the Constitution, to extend it when new responsibilities require, and to make government responsible to needs of the people, making use of advances in managerial competence and establishing security and stability; also to preclude changes in the Constitution resulting from interpretation.

SECTION 2. When this Constitution shall have been in effect for twenty-five years the Overseer shall ask, by referendum whether a new Constitution shall be prepared. If a majority so decide, the Council, making use of such advice as may be available, and consulting those who have made complaint, shall prepare a new draft for submission at the next election. If not disapproved by a majority it shall be in effect. If disapproved it shall be redrafted and resubmitted with such changes as may be then appropriate to the circumstances, and it shall be submitted to the voters at the following election.

If not disapproved by a majority it shall be in effect. If disapproved it shall be restudied and resubmitted.

ARTICLE XII
Transition

SECTION 1. The President is authorized to assume such powers, make such appointments, and use such funds as are necessary to make this Constitution effective as soon as possible after acceptance by a referendum he may initiate.

16

SECTION 2. Such members of the Senate as may be at once available shall convene and, if at least half, shall constitute sufficient membership while others are being added. They shall appoint an Overseer to arrange for electoral organization and elections for the offices of government; but the President and Vice-Presidents shall serve out their terms and then become members of the Senate. At that time the presidency shall be constituted as provided in this Constitution.

SECTION 3. Until each indicated change in the government shall have been completed the provisions of the existing Constitution and the organs of government shall be in effect.

SECTION 4. All operations of the national government shall cease as they are replaced by those authorized under this Constitution.

The President shall determine when replacement is complete.

The President shall cause to be constituted an appropriate commission to designate existing laws inconsistent with this Constitution, and they shall be void; also the commission shall assist the President and the legislative houses in the formulating of such laws as may be consistent with the Constitution and necessary to its implementation.

SECTION 5. For establishing Newstates' boundaries a commission of thirteen, appointed by the President, shall make recommendations within one year. For this purpose the members may take advice and commission studies concerning resources, population, transportation, communication, economic and social arrangements, and such other conditions as may be significant. The President shall transmit the commission's report to the Senate. After entertaining, if convenient, petitions for revision, the Senate shall report whether the recommendations are satisfactory but the President shall decide whether they shall be accepted or shall be returned for revision.

Existing states shall not be divided unless metropolitan areas extending over more than one state are to be included in one Newstate, or unless other compelling circumstances exist; and each Newstate shall possess harmonious regional characteristics.

The Commission shall continue while the Newstates make adjustments among themselves and shall have jurisdiction in disputes arising among them.

SECTION 6. Constitutions of the Newstates shall be established as arranged by the Judicial Council and the Principal Justice.

These procedures shall be as follows: Constitutions shall be drafted by the highest courts of the Newstates. There shall then be a convention of one hundred delegates chosen in special elections in a procedure approved by the Overseer. If the Constitution be not rejected, the Principal Justice, advised by the Judicial Council, shall promulgate a Constitution and initiate revisions to be submitted for approval at a time he shall appoint. If it again be rejected he shall promulgate another, taking account of objections, and it shall be in effect. A Constitution, once in effect, shall be valid for twenty-five years as herein provided.

SECTION 7. Until Governors and legislatures of the Newstates are seated, their governments shall continue, except that the President may appoint temporary Governors to act as executives until succeeded by those regularly elected. These Governors shall succeed to the executive functions of the states as they become one of the Newstates of America.

SECTION 8. The indicated appointments, elections, and other arrangements shall be made with all deliberate speed.

SECTION 9. The first Judicial Assembly for selecting a register for candidates for the Principal Justiceship of the Newstates of America shall be called by the incumbent Chief Justice immediately upon ratification.

SECTION 10. Newstates electing by referendum not to comply with recommendations of the Boundary Commission, as approved by the Senate, shall have deducted from taxes collected by the Newstates of America for transmission to them a percentage equal to the loss in efficiency from failure to comply.

Estimates shall be made by the Chancellor of Financial Affairs and approved by the President; but the deduction shall not be less than 7 percent.

SECTION 11. When this Constitution has been implemented the President may delete by proclamation appropriate parts of this article.

17

Chapter 15

PROTOCOLS
OF THE
WISE MEN OF ZION

The Protocols of Zion were referred to in the late 1700s. The first copy available to public scrutiny surfaced in the early 1800s. Every aspect of this plan to subjugate the world has since become reality, validating the authenticity of conspiracy.

Author's Note: This is an exact reprint of the original text. This has been written intentionally to deceive people. For clear understanding, the word "Zion" should be "Sion"; any reference to "Jews" should be replaced with the word "Illuminati"; and the word "goyim" should be replaced with the word "cattle."

Here is "The Britons" translation of the complete text of the notorious Nilus "Protocols of the Wise Men of Zion."

PROTOCOLS OF THE MEETINGS OF THE LEARNED ELDERS OF ZION
PROTOCOL NO. 1

. . . Putting aside fine phrases we shall speak of the significance of each thought: by comparisons and deductions we shall throw light upon surrounding facts.

What I am about to set forth, then, is our system from the two points of view, that of ourselves and that of the *goyim* (*i.e.*, non-Jews).

It must be noted that men with bad instincts are more in number than the good, and therefore the best results in governing them are attained by violence and terrorisation, and not by academic discussions. Every man aims at power, everyone would like to become a dictator if only he could, and rare indeed are the men who would not be willing to sacrifice the welfare of all for the sake of securing their own welfare.

What has restrained the beasts of prey who are called men? What has served for their guidance hitherto?

In the beginnings of the structure of society they were subjected to brutal and blind force; afterwards—to Law, which is the same force, only disguised. I draw the conclusion that by the law of nature right lies in force.

Political freedom is an idea but not a fact. This idea one must know how to apply whenever it appears necessary with this bait of an idea to attract the masses of the people to one's party for the purpose of crushing another who is in authority. This task is rendered easier if the opponent has himself been infected with the idea of freedom, *so-called liberalism*, and, for the sake of an idea, is willing to yield some of his power. It is precisely here that the triumph of our theory appears: the slackened reins of government are immediately, by the law of life, caught up and gathered together by a new hand, because the blind might of the nation cannot for one single day exist without guidance, and the new authority merely fits into the place of the old already weakened by liberalism.

In our day the power which has replaced that of the rulers who were liberal is the power of Gold. Time was when Faith ruled. The idea of freedom is impossible of realisation because no one knows how to use it with moderation. It is enough to hand over a people to self-government for a certain length of time for that people to be turned into a disorganised mob. From that moment on we get internecine strife which soon develops into battles between classes, in the midst of which States burn down and their importance is reduced to that of a heap of ashes.

Whether a State exhausts itself in its own convulsions, whether its internal discord brings it under the power of external foes—in any case it can be accounted irretrievably lost: *it is in our power*. The despotism of Capital, which is entirely in our hands, reaches out to it a straw that the State, willy-nilly, must take hold of: if not—it goes to the bottom.

Should anyone of a liberal mind say that such reflections as the above are immoral I would put the following questions:—If every State has two foes and if in regard to the external foe it is allowed and not considered immoral to use every manner and art of conflict, as for example to keep the enemy in ignorance of plans of attack and defence, to attack him by night or in superior numbers, then in what way can the same means in regard to a worse foe, the destroyer of the structure of society and the commonweal, be called immoral and not permissible?

Is it possible for any sound logical mind to hope with any success to guide crowds by the aid of reasonable counsels and arguments, when any objection or contradiction, senseless though it may be, can be made and when such objection may find more favour with the people, whose powers of reasoning are superficial? Men in masses and the men of the masses, being guided solely by petty passions, paltry beliefs, customs, traditions and sentimental theorism, fall a prey to party dissension, which hinders any kind of agreement even on the basis of a perfectly reasonable argument. Every resolution of a crowd depends upon a chance or packed majority, which, in its ignorance of political secrets, puts forth some ridiculous resolution that lays in the administration a seed of anarchy.

The political has nothing in common with the moral. The ruler who is governed by the moral is not a skilled politician, and is therefore unstable on his throne. He who wishes to rule must have recourse both to cunning and to make-believe. Great national qualities, like frankness and honesty, are vices in politics, for they bring down rulers from their thrones more effectively and more certainly than the most powerful enemy. Such qualities must be the attributes of the kingdoms of the *goyim*, but we must in no wise be guided by them.

Our right lies in force. The word "right" is an abstract thought and proved by nothing. The word means no more than:—Give me what I want in order that thereby I might have a proof that I am stronger than you.

Where does right begin? Where does it end?

In any State in which there is a bad organisation of authority, an impersonality of laws and of the rulers who have lost their personality amid the flood of rights ever multiplying out of liberalism, I find a new right—to attack by the right of the strong, and to scatter to the winds all existing forces of order and regulation, to reconstruct all institutions and to become the sovereign lord of those who have left to us the rights of their power by laying them down voluntarily in their liberalism.

Our power in the present tottering condition of all forms of power will be more invincible than any other, because it will remain invisible until the moment when it has gained such strength that no cunning can any longer undermine it.

Out of the temporary evil we are now compelled to commit will emerge the good of an unshakeable rule, which will restore the regular course of the machinery of the national life, brought to naught by liberalism. The result justifies the means. Let us, however, in our plans, direct our attention not so much to what is good and moral as to what is necessary and useful.

Before us is a plan in which is laid down strategically the line from which we cannot deviate without running the risk of seeing the labour of many centuries brought to naught.

In order to elaborate satisfactory forms of action it is necessary to have regard to the rascality, the slackness, the instability of the mob, its lack of capacity to understand and respect the conditions of its own life, or its own welfare. It must be understood that the might of a mob is blind, senseless and unreasoning force ever at the mercy of a suggestion from any side. The blind cannot lead the blind without bringing them into the abyss; consequently, members of the mob, upstarts from the people even though they should be as a genius for wisdom, yet having no understanding of the political, cannot come forward as leaders of the mob without bringing the whole nation to ruin.

Only one trained from childhood for independent rule can have understanding of the words that can be made up of the political alphabet.

A people left to itself, *i.e.*, to upstarts from its midst, brings itself to ruin by party dissensions excited by the pursuit of power and honours and disorders arising therefrom. Is it possible for the masses of the people calmly and without petty jealousies to form judgments, to deal with the affairs of the country, which cannot be mixed up with personal interests? Can they defend themselves from an external foe? It is unthinkable, for a plan broken up into as many parts as there are heads in the mob, loses all homogeneity, and thereby becomes unintelligible and impossible of execution.

It is only with a despotic ruler that plans can be elaborated extensively and clearly in such a way as to distribute the whole properly among the several parts of the machinery of the State: from this the conclusion is inevitable that a satisfactory form of government for any country is one that concentrates in the hands of one responsible person. Without an absolute despotism there can be no existence for civilisation which is carried on not by the masses but by their guide, whosoever that person may be. The mob is a savage and displays its savagery at every opportunity. The moment the mob seizes freedom in its hands it quickly turns to anarchy, which in itself is the highest degree of savagery.

Behold the alcoholised animals, bemused with drink, the right to an immoderate use of which comes along with freedom. It is not for us and ours to walk that road. The peoples of the *goyim* are bemused with alcoholic liquors; their youth has grown stupid on classicism and from early immorality, into which it has been inducted by our special agents—by tutors, lackeys, governesses in the houses of the wealthy, by clerks and others, by our women in the places of dissipation frequented by the *goyim*. In the number of these last I count also the so-called "society ladies," voluntary followers of the others in corruption and luxury.

Our countersign is—Force and Make-believe. Only force conquers in political affairs, especially if it be concealed in the talents essential to statesmen. Violence must be the principle, and cunning and make-believe the rule for governments which do not want to lay down their crowns at the feet of agents of some new power. This evil is the one and only means to attain the end, the good. Therefore we must not stop at bribery, deceit and treachery when they should serve towards the attainment of our end. In politics one must know how to seize the property of others without hesitation if by it we secure submission and sovereignty.

Our State, marching along the path of peaceful conquest, has the right to replace the horrors of war by less noticeable and more satisfactory sentences of death, necessary to maintain the terror which tends to produce blind submission. Just but merciless severity is the greatest factor of strength in the State: not only for the sake of gain but also in the name of duty, for the sake of victory, we must keep to the programme of violence and make-believe. The doctrine of squaring accounts is precisely as strong as the means of which it makes use. Therefore it is not so much by the means themselves as by the doctrine of severity that we shall triumph and bring all governments into subjection to our super-government. It is enough for them to know that we are merciless for all disobedience to cease.

Far back in ancient times we were the first to cry among the masses of the people the words "Liberty, Equality, Fraternity," words many times repeated since those days by stupid poll-parrots who from all sides round flew down upon these baits and with them carried away the well-being of the world, true freedom of the individual, formerly so well guarded against the pressure of the mob. The would-be wise men of the *goyim*, the intellectuals, could not make anything out of the uttered words in their abstractness; did not note the contradiction of their meaning and inter-relation: did not see that in nature there is no equality, cannot be freedom: that Nature herself has established inequality of minds, of characters, and capacities, just as immutably as she has established subordination to her laws: never stopped to think that the mob is a blind thing, that upstarts elected from among it to bear rule are, in regard to the political, the same blind men as the mob itself, that the adept, though he be a fool, can yet rule, whereas the non-adept, even if he were a genius, understands nothing in the political—to all these things the *goyim* paid no regard; yet all the time it was based upon these things that dynastic rule rested: the father passed on to the son a knowledge of the course of political affairs in such wise that none should know it but members of the dynasty and none could betray it to the governed. As time went on the meaning of the dynastic transference of the true position of affairs in the political was lost, and this aided the success of our cause.

In all corners of the earth the words "Liberty, Equality, Fraternity" brought to our ranks, thanks to our blind agents, whole legions who bore our banners with enthusiasm. And all the time these words were canker-worms at work boring into the well-being of the *goyim*, putting an end everywhere to peace, quiet, solidarity and destroying all the foundations of the *goy* States. As you will see later, this helped us to our triumph; it gave us the possibility, among other things, of getting into our hands the master card—the destruction of the privileges, or in other words of the very existence of the aristocracy of the *goyim*, that class which was the only defence peoples and countries had against us. On the ruins of the natural and genealogical aristocracy of the *goyim* we have set up the aristocracy of our educated class headed by the aristocracy of money. The qualifications for this aristocracy we have established in wealth, which is dependent upon us, and in knowledge, for which our learned elders provide the motive force.

Our triumph has been rendered easier by the fact that in our relations with the men whom we wanted we have always worked upon the most sensitive chords of the human mind, upon the cash account, upon the cupidity, upon the insatiability for material needs of man; and each one of these human weaknesses, taken alone, is sufficient to paralyse initiative, for it hands over the will of men to the disposition of him who has bought their activities.

The abstraction of freedom has enabled us to persuade the mob in all countries that their government is nothing but the steward of the people who are the owners of the country, and that the steward may be replaced like a worn-out glove.

It is this possibility of replacing the representatives of the people which has placed them at our disposal, and, as it were, given us the power of appointment.

PROTOCOL NO. 2

It is indispensable for our purpose that wars, so far as possible, should not result in territorial gains: war will thus be brought on to the economic ground, where the nations will not fail to perceive in the assistance we give the strength of our predominance, and this state of things will put both sides at the mercy of our international *agentur;* which possesses millions of eyes ever on the watch and unhampered by any limitations whatsoever. Our international rights will then wipe out national rights, in the proper sense of right, and will rule the nations precisely as the civil law of States rules the relations of their subjects among themselves.

The administrators, whom we shall choose from among the public, with strict regard to their capacities for servile obedience, will not be persons trained in the arts of government, and will therefore easily become pawns in our game in the hands of men of learning and genius who will be their advisers, specialists bred and reared from early childhood to rule the affairs of the whole world. As is well known to you, these specialists of ours have been drawing to fit them for rule the information they need from our political plans, from the lessons of history, from observations made of the events of every moment as it passes. The *goyim* are not guided by practical use of unprejudiced historical observation, but by theoretical routine without any critical regard for consequent results. We need not, therefore, take any account of them—let them amuse themselves until the hour strikes, or live on hopes of new forms of enterprising pastime, or on the memories of all they have enjoyed. For them let that play the principal part which we have persuaded them to accept as the dictates of science (theory). It is with this object in view that we are constantly, by means of our press, arousing a blind confidence in these theories. The intellectuals of the *goyim* will puff themselves up with their knowledge and without any logical verification of it will put into effect all the information available from science, which our *agentur* specialists have cunningly pieced together for the purpose of educating their minds in the direction we want.

Do not suppose for a moment that these statements are empty words: think carefully of the successes we arranged for Darwinism, Marxism, Nietzsche-ism. To us Jews, at any rate, it should be plain to see what a disintegrating importance these directives have had upon the minds of the *goyim.*

It is indispensable for us to take account of the thoughts, characters, tendencies of the nations in order to avoid making slips in the political and in the direction of administrative affairs. The triumph of our system, of which the component parts of the machinery may be variously disposed according to the temperament of the peoples met on our way, will fail of success if the practical application of it be not based upon a summing up of the lessons of the past in the light of the present.

In the hands of the States of to-day there is a great force that creates the movement of thought in the people, and that is the Press. The part played by the Press is to keep pointing out requirements supposed to be indispensable, to give voice to the complaints of the people, to express and to create discontent. It is in the Press that the triumph of freedom of speech finds its incarnation. But the *goyim* States have not known how to make use of this force; and it has fallen into our hands. Through the Press we have gained the power to influence while remaining ourselves in the shade; thanks to the Press we have got the *gold* in our hands, notwithstanding that we have had to gather it out of oceans of blood and tears. But it has paid us, though we have sacrificed many of our people. Each victim on our side is worth in the sight of God a thousand *goyim.*

PROTOCOL NO. 3

To-day I may tell you that our goal is now only a few steps off. There remains a small space to cross and the whole long path we have trodden is ready now to close its cycle of the Symbolic Snake, by which we symbolise our people. When this ring closes, all the States of Europe will be locked in its coil as in a powerful vice.

The constitution scales of these days will shortly break down, for we have established them with a certain lack of accurate balance in order that they may oscillate incessantly until they wear through the pivot on which they turn. The *goyim* are under the impression that they have welded them sufficiently strong and they have all along kept on expecting that the scales would come into equilibrium. But the pivots—the kings on their thrones—are hemmed in by their representatives, who play the fool, distraught with their own uncontrolled and irresponsible power. This power they owe to the terror which has been breathed into the palaces. As they have no means of getting at their people, into their very midst, the kings on their thrones are no longer able to come to terms with them and so strengthen themselves against seekers after power. We have made a gulf between the far-seeing Sovereign Power and the blind force of the people so that both have lost all meaning, for like the blind man and his stick, both are powerless apart.

In order to incite seekers after power to a misuse of power we have set all forces in opposition one to another, breaking up their liberal tendencies towards independence. To this end we have stirred up every form of enterprise, we have armed all parties, we have set up authority as a target for every ambition. Of States we have made gladiatorial arenas where a host of confused issues contend. . . . A little more, and disorders and bankruptcy will be universal. . . .

Babblers inexhaustible have turned into oratorical contests the sittings of Parliament and Administrative Boards. Bold journalists and unscrupulous pamphleteers daily fall upon executive officials. Abuses of power will put the final touch in preparing all institutions for their overthrow and everything will fly skyward under the blows of the maddened mob.

All people are chained down to heavy toil by poverty more firmly than ever they were chained by slavery and serfdom; from these, one way and another, they might free themselves, these could be settled with, but from want they will never get away. We have included in the constitution such rights as to the masses appear fictitious and not actual rights. All these so-called "People's Rights" can exist only in idea, an idea which can never be realised in practical life. What is it to the proletariat labourer, bowed double over his heavy toil, crushed by his lot in life, if talkers get the right to babble, if journalists get the right to scribble any nonsense side by side with good stuff, once the proletariat has no other profit out of the constitution save only those pitiful crumbs which we fling them from our table in return for their voting in favour of what we dictate, in favour of the men we place in power, the servants of our *agentur*. . . . Republican rights for a poor man are no more than a bitter piece of irony, for the necessity he is under of toiling almost all day gives him no present use of them, but on the other hand robs him of all guarantee of regular and certain earnings by making him dependent on strikes by his comrades or lockouts by his masters.

The people under our guidance have annihilated the aristocracy, who were their one and only defence and foster-mother for the sake of their own advantage which is inseparably bound up with the well-being of the people. Nowadays, with the destruction of the aristocracy, the people have fallen into the grips of merciless money-grinding scoundrels who have laid a pitiless and cruel yoke upon the necks of the workers.

We appear on the scene as alleged saviours of the worker from this oppression when we propose to him to enter the ranks of our fighting forces—Socialists, Anarchists, Communists—to whom we always give support in accordance with an alleged brotherly rule (of the solidarity of all humanity) of our *social masonry*. The aristocracy, which enjoyed by law the labour of the workers, was interested in seeing that the workers were well fed, healthy and strong. We are interested in just the opposite—in the diminution, the *killing out of the* GOYIM. Our power is in the chronic shortness of food and physical weakness of the worker because by all that this implies he is made the slave of our will, and he will not find in his own authorities either strength or energy to set against our will. Hunger creates the right of capital to rule the worker more surely than it was given to the aristocracy by the legal authority of kings.

By want and the envy and hatred which it engenders we shall move the mobs and with their hands we shall wipe out all those who hinder us on our way.

When the hour strikes for our Sovereign Lord of all the World to be crowned it is these same hands which will sweep away everything that might be a hindrance thereto.

The *goyim* have lost the habit of thinking unless prompted by the suggestions of our specialists. Therefore they do not see the urgent necessity of what we, when our kingdom comes, shall adopt at once, namely this, that *it is essential to teach in national schools one simple, true piece of knowledge, the basis of all knowledge—the knowledge of the structure of human life, of social existence, which requires division of labour, and, consequently, the division of men into classes and conditions.* It is essential for all to know that *owing to difference in the objects of human activity there cannot be any equality,* that he who by any act of his compromises a whole class cannot be equally responsible before the law with him who affects no one but only his own honour. The true knowledge of the structure of society, into the secrets of which we do not admit the *goyim,* would demonstrate to all men that the positions and work must be kept within a certain circle, that they may not become a source of human suffering, arising from an education which does not correspond with the work which individuals are called upon to do. After a thorough study of this knowledge the peoples will voluntarily submit to authority and accept such position as is appointed them in the State. In the present state of knowledge and the direction we have given to its development the people, blindly believing things in print—cherishes—thanks to promptings intended to mislead and to its own ignorance—a blind hatred towards all conditions which it considers above itself, for it has no understanding of the meaning of class and condition.

This hatred will be still further magnified by the effects of an *economic crisis,* which will stop dealings on the exchanges and bring industry to a standstill. We shall create by all the secret subterranean methods open to us and with the aid of gold, which is all in our hands, *a universal economic crisis whereby we shall throw upon the streets whole mobs of workers simultaneously in all the countries of Europe.* These mobs will rush delightedly to shed the blood of those whom, in the simplicity of their ignorance, they have envied from their cradles, and whose property they will then be able to loot.

"Ours" they will not touch, because the moment of attack will be known to us and we shall take measures to protect our own.

We have demonstrated that progress will bring all the *goyim* to the sovereignty of reason. Our despotism will be precisely that; for it will know how by wise severities to pacificate all unrest, to cauterise liberalism out of all institutions.

When the populace has seen that all sorts of concessions and indulgences are yielded it in the name of freedom it has imagined itself to be sovereign lord and has stormed its way to power, but, naturally, like every other blind man it has come upon a host of stumbling blocks, *it has rushed to find a guide, it has never had the sense to return to the former state* and it has laid down its plenipotentiary powers at *our* feet. Remember the French Revolution, to which it was we who gave the name of "Great": the secrets of its preparations are well known to us for it was wholly the work of our hands.

Ever since that time we have been leading the peoples from one disenchantment to another, so that in the end they should turn also from us in favour of that *King-Despot of the blood of Zion, whom we are preparing for the world.*

At the present day we are, as an international force, invincible, because if attacked by some we are supported by other States. It is the bottomless rascality of the *goyim* peoples, who crawl on their bellies to force, but are merciless towards weakness, unsparing to faults and indulgent to crimes, unwilling to bear the contradictions of a free social system but patient unto martyrdom under the violence of a bold despotism—it is those qualities which are aiding us to independence. From the premier-dictators of the present day the *goyim* peoples suffer patiently and bear such abuses as for the least of them they would have beheaded twenty kings.

What is the explanation of this phenomenon, this curious inconsequence of the masses of the peoples in their attitude towards what would appear to be events of the same order?

It is explained by the fact that these dictators whisper to the peoples through their agents that through these abuses they are inflicting injury on the States with the highest purpose—to secure the welfare of the peoples, the international brotherhood of them all, their solidarity and equality of rights. Naturally they do not tell the peoples that this unification must be accomplished only under our sovereign rule.

And thus the people condemn the upright and acquit the guilty, persuaded ever more and more that it can do whatsoever it wishes. Thanks to this state of things the people are destroying every kind of stability and creating disorders at every step.

The word "freedom" brings out the communities of men to fight against every kind of force, against every kind of authority, even

against God and the laws of nature. For this reason we, when we come
into our kingdom, shall have to erase this word from the lexicon of
life as implying a principle of brute force which turns mobs into
bloodthirsty beasts.

These beasts, it is true, fall asleep again every time when they
have drunk their fill of blood, and at such times can easily be riveted
into their chains. But if they be not given blood they will not sleep
and continue to struggle.

PROTOCOL NO. 4

Every republic passes through several stages. The first of these is
comprised in the early days of mad raging by the blind mob, tossed
hither and thither, right and left: the second is demagogy, from which
is born anarchy, and that leads inevitably to despotism—not any longer
legal and overt, and therefore responsible despotism, but to unseen
and secretly hidden, yet nevertheless sensibly felt despotism in the
hands of some secret organisation or other, whose acts are the more
unscrupulous inasmuch as it works behind a screen, behind the backs
of all sorts of agents, the changing of whom not only does not
injuriously affect but actually aids the secret force by saving it, thanks
to continual changes, from the necessity of expending its resources on
the rewarding of long services.

Who and what is in a position to overthrow an invisible force? And
this is precisely what our force is. *Gentile* masonry blindly serves as
a screen for us and our objects, but the plan of action of our force,
even its very abiding-place, remains for the whole people an unknown
mystery.

But even freedom might be harmless and have its place in the State
economy without injury to the well-being of the peoples if it rested
upon the foundation of faith in God, upon the brotherhood of
humanity, unconnected with the conception of equality, which is
negatived by the very laws of creation, for they have established subordination. With such a faith as this a people might be governed by
a wardship of parishes, and would walk contentedly and humbly under
the guiding hand of its spiritual pastor submitting to the dispositions
of God upon earth. This is the reason why *it is indispensable for us*

to undermine all faith, to tear out of the minds of the GOYIM *the very principle of Godhead and the spirit, and to put in its place arithmetical calculations and material needs.*

In order to give the *goyim* no time to think and take note, their minds must be diverted towards industry and trade. Thus, all the nations will be swallowed up in the pursuit of gain and in the race for it will not take note of their common foe. But again, in order that freedom may once for all disintegrate and ruin the communities of the *goyim*, we must put industry on a speculative basis: the result of this will be that what is withdrawn from the land by industry will slip through the hands and pass into speculation, that is, to our classes.

The intensified struggle for superiority and shocks delivered to economic life will create, nay, have already created, disenchanted, cold and heartless communities. Such communities will foster a strong aversion towards the higher political and towards religion. Their only guide is gain, that is Gold, which they will erect into a veritable cult, for the sake of those material delights which it can give. Then will the hour strike when, not for the sake of attaining the good, not even to win wealth, but solely out of hatred towards the privileged, the lower classes of the *goyim* will follow our lead against our rivals for power, the intellectuals of the *goyim*.

PROTOCOL NO. 5

What form of administrative rule can be given to communities in which corruption has penetrated everywhere, communities where riches are attained only by the clever surprise tactics of semi-swindling tricks; where looseness reigns: where morality is maintained by penal measures and harsh laws but not by voluntary accepted principles: where the feelings towards faith and country are obliterated by cosmopolitan convictions? What form of rule is to be given to these communities if not that despotism which I shall describe to you later? We shall create an intensified centralisation of government in order to grip in our hands all the forces of the community. We shall regulate mechanically all the actions of the political life of our subjects by new laws. These laws will withdraw one by one all the indulgences and liberties which have been permitted by the *goyim*, and our kingdom will be distinguished by a despotism of such magnificent proportions as to be at any moment and in every place in a position to wipe out any *goyim* who oppose us by deed or word.

We shall be told that such a despotism as I speak of is not consistent with the progress of these days, but I will prove to you that it is.

In the times when the peoples looked upon kings on their thrones as on a pure manifestation of the will of God, they submitted without a murmur to the despotic power of kings: but from the day when we insinuated into their minds the conception of their own rights they began to regard the occupants of thrones as mere ordinary mortals. The holy unction of the Lord's Anointed has fallen from the heads of kings in the eyes of the people, and when we also robbed them of their faith in God the might of power was flung upon the streets into the place of public proprietorship and was seized by us.

Moreover, the art of directing masses and individuals by means of cleverly manipulated theory and verbiage, by regulations of life in common and all sorts of other quirks, in all which the *goyim* understand nothing, belongs likewise to the specialists of our administrative brain. Reared on analysis, observation, on delicacies of fine calculation, in this species of skill we have no rivals, any more than we have either in the drawing up of plans of political actions and solidarity. In this respect the Jesuits alone might have compared with us, but we have contrived to discredit them in the eyes of the unthinking mob as an overt organisation, while we ourselves all the while have kept our secret organisation in the shade. However, it is probably all the same to the world who is its sovereign lord, whether the head of Catholicism or our despot of the blood of Zion! But to us, the Chosen People, it is very far from being a matter of indifference.

For a time perhaps we might be successfully dealt with by a coalition of the GOYIM *of all the world:* but from this danger we are secured by the discord existing among them whose roots are so deeply seated that they can never now be plucked up. We have set one against another the personal and national reckonings of the *goyim*, religious and race hatreds, which we have fostered into a huge growth in the course of the past twenty centuries. This is the reason why there is not one State which would anywhere receive support if it were to raise its arm, for every one of them must bear in mind that any agreement against us would be unprofitable to itself. We are too strong—there is no evading our power. *The nations cannot come to even an inconsiderable private agreement without our secretly having a hand in it.*

Per Me reges regnant. "It is through Me that Kings reign." And it was said by the prophets that we were chosen by God Himself to rule over the whole earth. God has endowed us with genius that we may be equal to our task. Were genius in the opposite camp it would still struggle against us, but even so a newcomer is no match for the old-established settler: the struggle would be merciless between us, such a fight as the world has never yet seen. Aye, and the genius on their side would have arrived too late. All the wheels of the machinery of all States go by the force of the engine, which is in our hands, and that engine of the machinery of States is—Gold. The science of political economy invented by our learned elders has for long past been giving royal prestige to capital.

Capital, if it is to co-operate untrammelled, must be free to establish a monopoly of industry and trade: this is already being put in execution by an unseen hand in all quarters of the world. This freedom will give political force to those engaged in industry, and that will help to oppress the people. Nowadays it is more important to disarm the peoples than to lead them into war: more important to use for our advantage the passions which have burst into flames than to quench their fire: more important to catch up and interpret the ideas of others to suit ourselves than to eradicate them. *The principal object of our directorate consists in this: to debilitate the public mind by criticism; to lead it away from serious reflections calculated to arouse resistance; to distract the forces of the mind towards a sham fight of empty eloquence.*

In all ages the peoples of the world, equally with individuals, have accepted words for deeds, for *they are content with a show* and rarely pause to note, in the public arena, whether promises are followed by performance. Therefore we shall establish show institutions which will give eloquent proof of their benefit to progress.

We shall assume to ourselves the liberal physiognomy of all parties, of all directions, and we shall give that physiognomy a voice *in orators who will speak so much that they will exhaust the patience of their hearers and produce an abhorrence of oratory.*

In order to put public opinion into our hands we must bring it into

*a state of bewilderment by giving expression from all sides to so many
contradictory opinions and for such length of time as will suffice to
make the* GOYIM *lose their heads in the labyrinth and come to see that
the best thing is to have no opinion of any kind in matters political,*
which it is not given to the public to understand, because they are
understood only by him who guides the public. This is the first secret.

The second secret requisite for the success of our government is
comprised in the following: To multiply to such an extent national
failings, habits, passions, conditions of civil life, that it will be
impossible for anyone to know where he is in the resulting chaos, so
that the people in consequence will fail to understand one another.
This measure will also serve us in another way, namely, to sow discord
in all parties, to dislocate all collective forces which are still unwilling
to submit to us, and to discourage any kind of personal initiative which
might in any degree hinder our affair. *There is nothing more dangerous than personal initiative;* if it has genius behind it, such initiative
can do more than can be done by millions of people among whom
we have sown discord. We must so direct the education of the *goyim*
communities that whenever they come upon a matter requiring initiative they may drop their hands in despairing impotence. The strain
which results from freedom of action saps the forces when it meets
with the freedom of another. From this collision arise grave moral
shocks, disenchantments, failures. *By all these means we shall so wear
down the goyim that they will be compelled to offer us international
power of a nature that by its position will enable us without any
violence gradually to absorb all the State forces of the world and to
form a Super-Government.* In place of the rulers of to-day we shall
set up a bogey which will be called the Super-Government Administration. Its hands will reach out in all directions like nippers and
its organisation will be of such colossal dimensions that it cannot fail
to subdue all the nations of the world.

PROTOCOL NO. 6

We shall soon begin to establish huge monopolies, reservoirs of
colossal riches, upon which even large fortunes of the *goyim* will
depend to such an extent that they will go to the bottom together with

the credit of the States on the day after the political smash. . . .

You gentlemen here present who are economists, just strike an estimate of the significance of this combination! . . .

In every possible way we must develop the significance of our Super-Government by representing it as the Protector and Benefactor of all those who voluntarily submit to us.

The aristocracy of the *goyim* as a political force, is dead—we need not take it into account; but as landed proprietors they can still be harmful to us from the fact that they are self-sufficing in the resources upon which they live. It is essential therefore for us at whatever cost to deprive them of their land. This object will be best attained by increasing the burdens upon landed property—in loading lands with debts. These measures will check land-holding and keep it in a state of humble and unconditional submission.

The aristocrats of the *goyim*, being hereditarily incapable of contenting themselves with little, will rapidly burn up and fizzle out.

At the same time we must intensively patronise trade and industry, but, first and foremost, speculation, the part played by which is to provide a counterpoise to industry: the absence of speculative industry will multiply capital in private hands and will serve to restore agriculture by freeing the land from indebtedness to the land banks. What we want is that industry should drain off from the land both labour and capital and by means of speculation transfer into our hands all the money of the world, and thereby throw all the *goyim* into the ranks of the proletariat. Then the *goyim* will bow down before us, if for no other reason but to get the right to exist.

To complete the ruin of the industry of the *goyim* we shall bring to the assistance of speculation the luxury which we have developed among the *goyim*, that greedy demand for luxury which is swallowing up everything. *We shall raise the rate of wages which, however, will not bring any advantage to the workers, for, at the same time, we shall produce a rise in prices of the first necessaries of life, alleging that it arises from the decline of agriculture and cattle-breeding: we shall further undermine artfully and deeply sources of production, by accustoming the workers to anarchy and to drunkenness and side by side therewith taking all measure to extirpate from the face of the earth all the educated forces of the GOYIM.*

In order that the true meaning of things may not strike the GOYIM

*before the proper time we shall mask it under an alleged ardent desire
to serve the working classes and the great principles of political economy about which our economic theories are carrying on an energetic
propaganda.*

PROTOCOL NO. 7

The intensification of armaments, the increase of police forces—
are all essential for the completion of the aforementioned plans.
What we have to get at is that there should be in all the States of the
world, besides ourselves, only the masses of the proletariat, a few
millionaires devoted to our interests, police and soldiers.

Throughout all Europe, and by means of relations with Europe,
in other continents also, we must create ferments, discords and hostility. Therein we gain a double advantage. In the first place we keep
in check all countries, for they well know that we have the power
whenever we like to create disorders or to restore order. All these
countries are accustomed to see in us an indispensable force of coercion.
In the second place, by our intrigues we shall tangle up all the threads
which we have stretched into the cabinets of all States by means of
politics, by economic treaties, or loan obligations. In order to succeed
in this we must use great cunning and penetration during negotiations and agreements, but, as regards what is called the "official
language," we shall keep to the opposite tactics and assume the mask
of honesty and compliancy. In this way the peoples and governments
of the *goyim*, whom we have taught to look only at the outside of whatever we present to their notice, will still continue to accept us as the
benefactors and saviours of the human race.

We must be in a position to respond to every act of opposition by
war with the neighbours of that country which dares to oppose us:
but if these neighbours should also venture to stand collectively together
against us, then we must offer resistance by a universal war.

The principal factor of success in the political is the secrecy of its
undertakings: the word should not agree with the deeds of the diplomat.

We must compel the governments of the *goyim* to take action in
the direction favoured by our widely conceived plan, already approaching the desired consummation, by what we shall represent as
public opinion, secretly prompted by us through the means of that

so-called "Great Power"—*the Press, which, with a few exceptions that may be disregarded, is already entirely in our hands.*

In a word, to sum up our system of keeping the governments of the *goyim* in Europe in check, we shall show our strength to one of them by terrorist attempts and to all, if we allow the possibility of a general rising against us, we shall respond with the guns of America or China or Japan.

PROTOCOL NO. 8

We must arm ourselves with all the weapons which our opponents might employ against us. We must search out in the very finest shades of expression and the knotty points of the lexicon of law justification for those cases where we shall have to pronounce judgments that might appear abnormally audacious and unjust, for it is important that these resolutions should be set forth in expressions that shall seem to be the most exalted moral principles cast into legal form. Our directorate must surround itself with all these forces of civilisation among which it will have to work. It will surround itself with publicists, practical jurists, administrators, diplomats and, finally, with persons prepared by a special super-educational training *in our special schools.* These persons will have cognisance of all the secrets of the social structure, they will know all the languages that can be made up by political alphabets and words; they will be made acquainted with the whole underside of human nature, with all its sensitive chords on which they will have to play. These chords are the cast of mind of the *goyim,* their tendencies, shortcomings, vices and qualities, the particularities of classes and conditions. Needless to say that the talented assistants of authority, of whom I speak, will be taken not from among the *goyim,* who are accustomed to perform their administrative work without giving themselves the trouble to think what its aim is, and never consider what it is needed for. The administrators of the *goyim* sign papers without reading them, and they serve either for mercenary reasons or from ambition.

We shall surround our government with a whole world of economists. That is the reason why economic sciences form the principal subject of the teaching given to the Jews. Around us again will be a whole constellation of bankers, industrialists, capitalists and—*the main thing—millionaires, because in substance everything will be settled by the question of figures.*

For a time, until there will no longer be any risk in entrusting responsible posts in our States to our brother-Jews, we shall put them in the hands of persons whose past and reputation are such that between them and the people lies an abyss, persons who, in case of disobedience to our instructions, must face criminal charges or disappear—this in order to make them defend our interest to their last gasp.

PROTOCOL NO. 9

In applying our principles let attention be paid to the character of the people in whose country you live and act; a general, identical application of them, until such time as the people shall have been re-educated to our pattern, cannot have success. But by approaching their application cautiously you will see that not a decade will pass before the most stubborn character will change and we shall add a new people to the ranks of those already subdued by us.

The words of the liberal, which are in effect the words of our masonic watchword, namely, "Liberty, Equality, Fraternity," will, when we come into our kingdom, be changed by us into words no longer of a watchword, but only an expression of idealism, namely, into: "The right of liberty, the duty of equality, the ideal of brotherhood." That is how we shall put it,—and so we shall catch the bull by the horns. . . . *De facto* we have already wiped out every kind of rule except our own, although *de jure* there still remain a good many of them. Nowadays, if any States raise a protest against us it is only *pro forma* at our discretion and by our direction, for *their anti-Semitism is indispensable to us for the management of our lesser brethren*. I will not enter into further explanations, for this matter has formed the subject of repeated discussions amongst us.

For us there are no checks to limit the range of our activity. Our Super-Government subsists in extra-legal conditions which are described in the accepted terminology by the energetic and forcible word—Dictatorship. I am in a position to tell you with a clear conscience that at the proper time we, the law-givers, shall execute judgment and sentence, we shall slay and we shall spare, we, as head of all our troops, are mounted on the steed of the leader. We rule by force of will, because in our hands are the fragments of a once powerful party, now vanquished by us. *And the weapons in our hands are limitless ambitions, burning greediness, merciless vengeance, hatreds and malice.*

It is from us that the all-engulfing terror proceeds. We have in our service persons of all opinions, of all doctrines, restorating monarchists, demagogues, socialists, communists, and utopian dreamers of every kind. We have harnessed them all to the task: *each one of them on his own account is boring away at the last remnants of authority, is striving to overthrow all established form of order.* By these acts all States are in torture; they exhort to tranquillity, are ready to sacrifice everything for peace: *but we will not give them peace until they openly acknowledge our international Super-Government,* and with submissiveness.

The people have raised a howl about the necessity of settling the question of Socialism by way of an international agreement. *Division into fractional parties has given them into our hands, for, in order to carry on a contested struggle one must have money, and the money is all in our hands.*

We might have reason to apprehend a union between the "clear-sighted" force of the *goy* kings on their thrones and the *"blind"* force of the *goy* mobs, but we have taken all the needful measure against any such possibility: between the one and the other force we have erected a bulwark in the shape of a mutual terror between them. In this way the blind force of the people remains our support and we, and we only, shall provide them with a leader and, of course, direct them along the road that leads to our goal.

In order that the hand of the blind mob may not free itself from our guiding hand, we must every now and then enter into close communion with it, if not actually in person, at any rate through some of the most trusty of our brethren. When we are acknowledged as the only authority we shall discuss with the people personally on the market places, and we shall instruct them on questions of the political in such wise as may turn them in the direction that suits us.

Who is going to verify what is taught in the village schools? But what an envoy of the government or a king on his throne himself may say cannot but become immediately known to the whole State, for it will be spread abroad by the voice of the people.

In order not to annihilate the institutions of the *goyim* before it is time we have touched them with craft and delicacy, and have taken hold of the ends of the springs which move their mechanism. These springs lay in a strict but just sense of order; we have replaced them by the chaotic license of liberalism. We have got our hands into the administration of the law, into the conduct of elections, into the press, into liberty of the person, *but principally into education and training as being the corner-stones of a free existence.*

We have fooled, bemused and corrupted the youth of the GOYIM *by rearing them in principles and theories which are known to us to be false although it is by. us that they have been inculcated.*

Above the existing laws without substantially altering them, and by merely twisting them into contradictions of interpretations, we have erected something grandiose in the way of results. These results found expression first in the fact that the *interpretations masked the laws:* afterwards they entirely hid them from the eyes of the governments owing to the impossibility of making anything out of the tangled web of legislation.

This is the origin of the theory of course of arbitration.

You may say the *goyim* will rise upon us, arms in hand, if they guess what is going on before the time comes; but in the West we have against this a manœuvre of such appalling terror that the very stoutest hearts quail—the undergrounds, metropolitains, those subterranean corridors which, before the time comes, will be driven under all the capitals and from whence those capitals will be blown into the air with all their organisations and archives.

PROTOCOL NO. 10

To-day I begin with a repetition of what I said before, and *I beg you to bear in mind that governments and peoples are content in the political with outside appearances.* And how, indeed, are the *goyim* to perceive the underlying meaning of things when their representatives give the best of their energies to enjoying themselves? For our policy it is of the greatest importance to take cognisance of this detail; it will be of assistance to us when we come to consider the division of authority, freedom of speech, of the press, of religion (faith), of the law of association, of equality before the law, of the inviolability of property, of the dwelling, of taxation (the idea of concealed taxes), of the reflex force of the laws. All these questions are such as ought not to be touched upon directly and openly before the people. In cases where it is indispensable to touch upon them they must not be categorically named, it must merely be declared without detailed exposition that the principles of contemporary law are acknowledged by us. The reason of keeping silence in this respect is that by not naming a principle we leave ourselves freedom of action, to drop this or that out of it without attracting notice; if they were all categorically named they would all appear to have been already given.

The mob cherishes a special affection and respect for the geniuses of political power and accepts all their deeds of violence with the admiring response: "rascally, well, yes, it is rascally, but it's clever! . . . a trick, if you like, but how craftily played, how magnificently done, what impudent audacity!" . . .

We count upon attracting all nations to the task of erecting the new fundamental structure, the project for which has been drawn up by us. This is why, before everything, it is indispensable for us to arm ourselves and to store up in ourselves that absolutely reckless audacity and irresistible might of the spirit which in the person of our active workers will break down all hindrances on our way.

When we have accomplished our coup d'état we shall say then to the various peoples: "Everything has gone terribly badly, all have been worn out with sufferings. We are destroying the causes of your torment—nationalities, frontiers, differences of coinages. You are at liberty, of course, to pronounce sentence upon us, but can it possibly be a just one if it is confirmed by you before you make any trial of what we are offering you." . . . Then will the mob exalt us and bear us up in their hands in a unanimous triumph of hopes and expectations. Voting, which we have made the instrument which will set us on the throne of the world by teaching even the very smallest units of members of the human race to vote by means of meetings and agreements by groups, will then have served its purposes and will play its part then for the last time by a unanimity of desire to make close acquaintance with us before condemning us.

To secure this we must have everybody vote without distinction of classes and qualifications, in order to establish an absolute majority, which cannot be got from the educated propertied classes. In this way, by inculcating in all a sense of self-importance, we shall destroy among the *goyim* the importance of the family and its educational value and remove the possibility of individual minds splitting off, for the mob, handled by us, will not let them come to the front nor even give them a hearing; it is accustomed to listen to us only who pay it for obedience and attention. In this way we shall create a blind, mighty force which will never be in a position to move in any direction without the guidance of our agents set at its head by us as leaders of the mob. The people will submit to this régime because it will know that upon these leaders will depend its earnings, gratifications and the receipt of all kinds of benefits.

A scheme of government should come ready made from one brain, because it will never be clinched firmly if it is allowed to be split into fractional parts in the minds of many. It is allowable, therefore, for us to have cognisance of the scheme of action but not to discuss it lest we disturb its artfulness, the interdependence of its component parts, the practical force of the secret meaning of each clause. To discuss and make alterations in a labour of this kind by means of numerous votings is to impress upon it the stamp of all ratiocinations and misunderstandings which have failed to penetrate the depth and nexus of its plottings. We want our schemes to be forcible and suitably concocted. Therefore WE OUGHT NOT TO FLING THE WORK OF GENIUS OF OUR GUIDE to the fangs of the mob or even of a select company.

These schemes will not turn existing institutions upside down just yet. They will only affect changes in their economy and consequently in the whole combined movement of their progress, which will thus be directed along the paths laid down in our schemes.

Under various names there exists in all countries approximately one and the same thing. Representation, Ministry, Senate, State Council, Legislative and Executive Corps. I need not explain to you the mechanism of the relation of these institutions to one another, because you are aware of all that; only take note of the fact that each of the above-named institutions corresponds to some important function of the State, and I would beg you to remark that the word "important" I apply not to the institution but to the function, consequently it is not the institutions which are important but their functions. These institutions have divided up among themselves all the functions of government— administrative, legislative, executive, wherefore they have come to operate as do the organs in the human body. If we injure one part in the machinery of State, the State falls sick, like a human body, and will die.

When we introduced into the State organism the poison of Liberalism its whole political complexion underwent a change. States have been seized with a mortal illness—blood-poisoning. All that remains is to await the end of their death agony.

Liberalism produced Constitutional States, which took the place of what was the only safeguard of the *goyim*, namely, Despotism; and *a constitution, as you well know, is nothing else but a school of discords, misunderstandings, quarrels, disagreements, fruitless party agitations, party whims*—in a word, a school of everything that serves to destroy the personality of State activity. *The tribune of the "talkeries" has, no less effectively than the Press, condemned the rulers to inactivity and impotence, and thereby rendered them useless and superfluous, for which reason indeed they have been in many countries deposed. Then it was that the era of republics became possible of realisation; and then it was that we replaced the ruler by a caricature of a government—by a president, taken from the mob, from the midst of our puppet creatures, our slaves.* This was the foundation of the mine which we have laid under the *goy* people, I should rather say, under the *goy* peoples.

In the near future we shall establish the responsibility of presidents.

By that time we shall be in a position to disregard forms in carrying through matters for which our personal puppet will be responsible. What do we care if the ranks of those striving for power should be thinned, if there should arise a deadlock from the impossibility of finding presidents, a deadlock which will finally disorganize the country?

In order that our scheme may produce this result we shall arrange elections in favour of such presidents as have in their past some dark, undiscovered stain, some "Panama" or other—then they will be trustworthy agents for the accomplishment of our plans out of fear of revelations and from the natural desire of everyone who has attained power, namely, the retention of privileges, advantages and honour connected with the office of president. The chamber of deputies will provide cover for, will protect, will elect the president, but we shall take from it the right to propose new, or make changes in existing laws, for this right will be given by us to the responsible president, a puppet in our hands. Naturally, the authority of the president will then become a target for every possible form of attack, but we shall provide him with a means of self-defence in the right of an appeal to the people, for the decision of the people over the heads of their representatives, that is to say, an appeal to that same blind slave of ours— the majority of the mob. Independently of this we shall invest the president with the right of declaring a state of war. We shall justify this last right on the ground that the president as chief of the whole army of the country must have it at his disposal, in case of need for the defence of the new republican constitution, the right to defend which will belong to him as the responsible representative of this constitution.

It is easy to understand that in these conditions the key of the shrine will lie in our hands, and no one outside of ourselves will any longer direct the force of legislation.

Besides this we shall, with the introduction of the new republican constitution, take from the Chamber the right of interpellation on government measures, on the pretext of preserving political secrecy, and, further, we shall by the new constitution reduce the number of representatives to a minimum, thereby proportionately reducing political passions and the passion for politics. If, however, they should, which is hardly to be expected, burst into flame, even in this minimum, we shall nullify them by a stirring appeal and a reference to the majority of the whole people. . . . Upon the president will depend the appointment of presidents and vice-presidents of the Chamber and the Senate. Instead of constant sessions of Parliaments we shall reduce their sittings to a few months. Moreover, the president, as chief of the executive power, will have the right to summon and dissolve Parliament, and, in the latter case, to prolong the time for the appointment of a new parliamentary assembly. But in order that the consequences of all these acts which in substance are illegal, should not, prematurely for our plans, fall upon the responsibility established by us of the president, *we shall instigate ministers and other officials of the higher administration about the president to evade his dispositions by taking measures of their own*, for doing which they will be made the scapegoats in his place. . . . This part we especially recommend to be given to be played by the Senate, the Council of State, or the Council of Ministers, but not to an individual official.

The president will, at our discretion, interpret the sense of such of the existing laws as admit of various interpretation; he will further annul them when we indicate to him the necessity to do so, besides this, he will have the right to propose temporary laws, and even new departures in the government constitutional working, the pretext both for the one and other being the requirements for the supreme welfare of the State.

By such measures we shall obtain the power of destroying little by little, step by step, all that at the outset when we enter on our rights, we are compelled to introduce into the constitutions of States to prepare for the transition to an imperceptible abolition of every kind of constitution, and then the time is come to turn every form of government into *our despotism*.

The recognition of our despot may also come before the destruction of the constitution; the moment for this recognition will come when the peoples, utterly wearied by the irregularities and incompetence—a matter which we shall arrange for—of their rulers, will clamour: "Away with them and give us one king over all the earth who will unite us and annihilate the causes of discords—frontiers, nationalities, religions, State debts—who will give us peace and quiet, which we cannot find under our rulers and representatives."

But you yourselves perfectly well know that *to produce the possibility of the expression of such wishes by all the nations it is indispensable to trouble in all countries the people's relations with their governments so as to utterly exhaust humanity with dissension, hatred, struggle, envy and even by the use of torture, by starvation, BY THE INOCULATION OF DISEASES, by want, so that the* GOYIM *see no other issue than to take refuge in our complete sovereignty in money and in all else.*

But if we give the nations of the world a breathing space the moment we long for is hardly likely ever to arrive.

PROTOCOL NO. 11

The State Council has been, as it were, the emphatic expression of the authority of the ruler: it will be, as the "show" part of the Legislative Corps, what may be called the editorial committee of the laws and decrees of the ruler.

This, then, is the programme of the new constitution. We shall make Law, Right and Justice (1) in the guise of proposals to the Legislative Corps, (2) by decrees of the president under the guise of general regulations, of orders of the Senate and of resolutions of the State Council in the guise of ministerial orders, (3) and in case a suitable occasion should arise—in the form of a revolution in the State.

Having established approximately the *modus agendi* we will occupy ourselves with details of those combinations by which we have still to complete the revolution in the course of the machinery of State in the direction already indicated. By these combinations I mean the freedom of the Press, the right of association, freedom of conscience, the voting principle, and many another that must disappear for ever from the memory of man, or undergo a radical alteration the day after the promulgation of the new constitution. It is only at that moment that we shall be able at once to announce all our orders, for, afterwards, every noticeable alteration will be dangerous, for the following reasons: if this alteration be brought in with harsh severity and in a sense of severity and limitations, it may lead to a feeling of despair caused by fear of new alterations in the same direction; if, on the other hand, it be brought in in a sense of further indulgences it will be said that we have recognised our own wrongdoing and this will destroy the prestige of the infallibility of our authority, or else it will be said that we have become alarmed and are compelled to show a yielding disposition, for which we shall get no thanks because it will be supposed to be compulsory. . . . Both the one and the other are injurious to the prestige of the new constitution. What we want is that from the first moment of its promulgation, while the peoples of the world are still stunned by the accomplished fact of the revolution, still in a condition of terror and uncertainty, they should recognise once for all that we are so strong, so inexpugnable, so superabundantly filled with power, that in no case shall we take any account of them, and so far from paying any attention to their opinions or wishes, we are ready and able to crush with irresistible power all expression or manifestation thereof at every moment and in every place, that we have seized at once everything we wanted and shall in no case divide our power with them. . . . Then in fear and trembling they will close their eyes to everything, and be content to await what will be the end of it all.

The *goyim* are a flock of sheep, and we are their wolves. And you know what happens when the wolves get hold of the flock? . . .

There is another reason also why they will close their eyes: for we shall keep promising them to give back all the liberties we have taken away as soon as we have quelled the enemies of peace and tamed all parties. . . .

It is not worth while to say anything about how long a time they will be kept waiting for this return of their liberties. . . .

For what purpose then have we invented this whole policy and insinuated it into the minds of the *goys* without giving them any chance to examine its underlying meaning? For what, indeed, if not in order to obtain in a roundabout way what is for our scattered tribe unattainable by the direct road? It is this which has served as the basis for our organisation of SECRET MASONRY WHICH IS NOT KNOWN TO, AND AIMS WHICH ARE NOT EVEN SO MUCH AS SUSPECTED BY, THESE *GOY* CATTLE, ATTRACTED BY US INTO THE "SHOW" ARMY OF MASONIC LODGES IN ORDER TO THROW DUST IN THE EYES OF THEIR FEL-LOWS.

God has granted to us, His Chosen People, the gift of the dispersion, and in this which appears in all eyes to be our weakness, has come forth all our strength, which has now brought us to the threshold of sovereignty over all the world.

There now remains not much more for us to build up upon the foundation we have laid.

PROTOCOL NO. 12

The word "freedom," which can be interpreted in various ways, is defined by us as follows:—

Freedom is the right to do that which the law allows. This interpretation of the word will at the proper time be of service to us, because all freedom will thus be in our hands, since the laws will abolish or create only that which is desirable for us according to the aforesaid programme.

We shall deal with the press in the following way: What is the part played by the press to-day? It serves to excite and inflame those passions which are needed for our purpose or else it serves selfish ends of parties. It is often vapid, unjust, mendacious, and the majority of the public have not the slightest idea what ends the press really serves. We shall saddle and bridle it with a tight curb: we shall do the same also with all productions of the printing press, for where would be the sense of getting rid of the attacks of the press if we remain targets for pamphlets and books? The produce of publicity, which nowadays is a source of heavy expense owing to the necessity of censoring it, will be turned by us into a very lucrative source of income to our State: we shall lay on it a special stamp tax and require deposits of caution-money before permitting the establishment of any organ of the press or of printing offices; these will then have to guarantee our government against any kind of attack on the part of the press. For any attempt to attack us, if such still be possible, we shall inflict fines without mercy. Such measures as stamp tax, deposit of caution-money and fines secured by these deposits, will bring in a huge income to the government. It is true that party organs might not spare money for the sake of publicity, but these we shall shut up at the second attack upon us. No one shall with impunity lay a finger on the aureole of our government infallibility. The pretext for stopping any publication will be the alleged plea that it is agitating the public mind without occasion or justification. *I beg you to note that among those making attacks upon us will also be organs established by us, but they will attack exclusively points that we have pre-determined to alter.*

Not a single announcement will reach the public without our control. Even now this is already being attained by us inasmuch as all news items are received by a few agencies, in whose offices they are focused from all parts of the world. These agencies will then be already entirely ours and will give publicity only to what we dictate to them.

If already now we have contrived to possess ourselves of the minds of the *goy* communities to such an extent that they all come near looking upon the events of the world through the coloured glasses of those spectacles we are setting astride their noses: if already now there is not a single State where there exist for us any barriers to admittance into what *goy* stupidity calls State secrets: what will our position be then, when we shall be acknowledged supreme lords of the world in the person of our king of all the world. . . .

Let us turn again to the *future of the printing press.* Every one desirous of being a publisher, librarian, or printer, will be obliged to provide himself with the diploma instituted therefor, which, in case of any fault, will be immediately impounded. With such measures *the instrument of thought will become an educative means in the hands of our government, which will no longer allow the mass of the nation to be led astray in by-ways and fantasies about the blessings of progress.* Is there any one of us who does not know that these phantom blessings are the direct roads to foolish imaginings which give birth to anarchical relations of men among themselves and towards authority, because progress, or rather the idea of progress, has introduced the conception of every kind of emancipation, but has failed to establish its limits. . . . All the so-called liberals are anarchists, if not in fact, at any rate in thought. Every one of them is hunting after phantoms of freedom, and falling exclusively into license, that is, into the anarchy of protest for the sake of protest. . . .

We turn to the periodical press. We shall impose on it, as on all printed matter, stamp taxes per sheet and deposits of caution-money, and books of less than 30 sheets will pay double. We shall reckon them as pamphlets in order, on the one hand, to reduce the number of magazines, which are the worst form of printed poison, and, on the other, in order that this measure may force writers into such lengthy productions that they will be little read, especially as they will be costly. At the same time what we shall publish ourselves to influence mental development in the direction laid down for our profit will be cheap and will be read voraciously. The tax will bring vapid literary ambitions within bounds and the liability to penalties will make literary men dependent upon us. And if there should be any found who are desirous of writing against us, they will not find any person eager to print their productions. Before accepting any production for publication in print the publisher or printer will have to apply to the authorities for permission to do so. Thus we shall know beforehand of all tricks preparing against us and shall nullify them by getting ahead with explanations on the subject treated of.

Literature and journalism are two of the most important educative forces, and therefore our government will become proprietor of the majority of the journals. This will neutralise the injurious influence of the privately owned press and will put us in possession of a tremendous influence upon the public mind. . . . If we give permits for ten journals, we shall ourselves found thirty, and so on in the same proportion. This, however, must in nowise be suspected by the public.

For which reason all journals published by us will be of the most opposite, in appearance, tendencies and opinions, thereby creating confidence in us and bringing over to us our quite unsuspicious opponents, who will thus fall into our trap and be rendered harmless.

In the front rank will stand organs of an official character. They will always stand guard over our interests, and therefore their influence will be comparatively insignificant.

In the second rank will be the semi-official organs, whose part it will be to attract the tepid and indifferent.

In the third rank we shall set up our own, to all appearance, opposition, which, in at least one of its organs, will present what looks like the very antipodes to us. Our real opponents at heart will accept this simulated opposition as their own and will show us their cards.

All our newspapers will be of all possible complexions—aristocratic, republican, revolutionary, even anarchical—for so long, of course, as the constitution exists. . . . Like the Indian idol Vishnu they will have a hundred hands, and every one of them will have a finger on any one of the public opinions as required. When a pulse quickens these hands will lead opinion in the direction of our aims, for an excited patient loses all power of judgment and easily yields to suggestion. Those fools who will think they are repeating the opinion of a newspaper of their own camp will be repeating our opinion or any opinion that seems desirable for us. In the vain belief that they are following the organ of their party they will in fact follow the flag which we hang out for them.

In order to direct our newspaper militia in this sense we must take especial and minute care in organising this matter. Under the title of central department of the press we shall institute literary gatherings at which our agents will without attracting attention issue the orders and watchwords of the day. By discussing and controverting, but always superficially, without touching the essence of the matter, our organs will carry on a sham fight fusillade with the official newspapers solely for the purpose of giving occasion for us to express ourselves more fully than could well be done from the outset in official announcements, whenever, of course, that is to our advantage.

These attacks upon us will also serve another purpose, namely, that our subjects will be convinced of the existence of full freedom of speech and so give our agents an occasion to affirm that all organs

---

which oppose us are empty babblers, since they are incapable of finding any substantial objections to our orders.

Methods of organisation like these, imperceptible to the public eye but absolutely sure, are the best calculated to succeed in bringing the attention and the confidence of the public to the side of our government. Thanks to such methods we shall be in a position as from time to time may be required, to excite or to tranquillise the public mind on political questions, to persuade or to confuse, printing now truth, now lies, facts or their contradictions, according as they may be well or ill received, always very cautiously feeling our ground before stepping upon it. . . . *We shall have a sure triumph over our opponents since they will not have at their disposition organs of the press in which they can give full and final expression to their views* owing to the aforesaid methods of dealing with the press. We shall not even need to refute them except very superficially.

Trial shots like these, fired by us in the third rank of our press, in case of need, will be energetically refuted by us in our semi-official organs.

Even nowadays, already, to take only the French press, there are forms which reveal masonic solidarity in acting on the watchword: all organs of the press are bound together by professional secrecy; like the augurs of old, not one of their numbers will give away the secret of his sources of information unless it be resolved to make announcement to them. Not one journalist will venture to betray this secret, for not one of them is ever admitted to practise literature unless his whole past has some disgraceful sore or other. . . . These sores would be immediately revealed. So long as they remain the secret of a few the prestige of the journalist attracts the majority of the country—the mob follows after him with enthusiasm.

Our calculations are especially extended to the provinces. It is indispensable for us to inflame there those hopes and impulses with which we could at any moment fall upon the capital, and we shall represent to the capitals that these expressions are the independent hopes and impulses of the provinces. Naturally, the source of them will be always one and the same—ours. *What we need is that, until such time as we are in the plenitude of power, the capitals should find themselves stifled by the provincial opinion of the nation,* i.e., of *a majority arranged by our agentur.* What we need is that at the psycho-

---

logical moment the capitals should not be in a position to discuss an accomplished fact for the simple reason, if for no other, that it has been accepted by the public opinion of a majority in the provinces.

When we are in the period of the new régime transitional to that of our assumption of full sovereignty we must not admit any revelations by the press of any form of public dishonesty; it is necessary that the new régime should be thought to have so perfectly contented everybody that even criminality has disappeared. . . . Cases of the manifestation of criminality should remain known only to their victims and to chance witnesses—no more.

PROTOCOL NO. 13

The need for daily bread forces the *goyim* to keep silence and be our humble servants. Agents taken on to our press from among the *goyim* will at our order discuss anything which it is inconvenient for us to issue directly in official documents, and we meanwhile, quietly amid the din of the discussion so raised, shall simply take and carry through such measures as we wish and then offer them to the public as an accomplished fact. No one will dare to demand the abrogation of a matter once settled, all the more so as it will be represented as an improvement. . . . And immediately the press will distract the current of thought towards new questions (have we not trained people always to be seeking something new?). Into the discussions of these new questions will throw themselves those of the brainless dispensers of fortunes who are not able even now to understand that they have not the remotest conception about the matters which they undertake to discuss. Questions of the political are unattainable for any save those who have guided it already for many ages, the creators.

From all this you will see that in securing the opinion of the mob we are only facilitating the working of our machinery, and you may remark that it is not for actions but for words issued by us on this or that question that we seem to seek approval. We are constantly making public declaration that we are guided in all our undertakings by the hope, joined to the conviction, that we are serving the commonweal.

In order to distract people who may be too troublesome from discussions of questions of the political we are now putting forward what we allege to be new questions of the political, namely, questions of industry. In this sphere let them discuss themselves silly! The masses are agreed to remain inactive, to take a rest from what they suppose to be political activity (which we trained them to in order to use them as a means of combating the *goy* governments) only on condition of being found new employments, in which we are pre-scribing them something that looks like the same political object. In order that the masses themselves may not guess what they are about *we further distract them with amusements, games, pastimes, passions, people's palaces. . . . Soon we shall begin through the press to propose competitions in art, in sport of all kinds:* these interests will finally distract their minds from questions in which we should find ourselves compelled to oppose them. Growing more and more disaccustomed to reflect and form any opinions of their own, people will begin to talk in the same tone as we, because we alone shall be offering them new directions for thought . . . of course through such persons as will not be suspected of solidarity with us.

The part played by the liberals, utopian dreamers, will be finally played out when our government is acknowledged. Till such time they will continue to do us good service. Therefore we shall continue to direct their minds to all sorts of vain conceptions of fantastic theories, new and apparently progressive: for have we not with com-plete success turned the brainless heads of the *goyim* with progress, till there is not among the *goyim* one mind able to perceive that under this word lies a departure from truth in all cases where it is not a question of material inventions, for truth is one, and in it there is no place for progress. Progress, like a fallacious idea, serves to obscure truth so that none may know it except us, the Chosen of God, its guardians.

When we come into our kingdom our orators will expound great problems which have turned humanity upside down in order to bring it at the end under our beneficent rule.

Who will ever suspect then that ALL THESE PEOPLES WERE STAGE-MANAGED BY US ACCORDING TO A POLITICAL PLAN WHICH NO ONE HAS SO MUCH AS GUESSED AT IN THE COURSE OF MANY CENTURIES? . . .

PROTOCOL NO. 14

When we come into our kingdom it will be undesirable for us that there should exist any other religion than ours of the One God with whom our destiny is bound up by our position as the Chosen People and through whom our same destiny is united with the destinies of the world. We must therefore sweep away all other forms of belief. If this gives birth to the atheists whom we see to-day, it will not, being only a transitional stage, interfere with our views, but will serve as a warning for those generations which will hearken to our preaching of the religion of Moses, that, by its stable and thoroughly elaborated system, has brought all the peoples of the world into subjection to us. Therein we shall emphasise its mystical right, on which, as we shall say, all its educative power is based. . . . Then at every possible opportunity we shall publish articles in which we shall make comparisons between our beneficent rule and those of past ages. The blessings of tranquillity, though it be a tranquillity forcibly brought about by centuries of agitation, will throw into higher relief the benefits to which we shall point. The errors of the *goyim* governments will be depicted by us in the most vivid hues. We shall implant such an abhorrence of them that the peoples will prefer tranquillity in a state of serfdom to those rights of vaunted freedom which have tortured humanity and exhausted the very sources of human existence, sources which have been exploited by a mob of rascally adventurers who know not what they do. . . . *Useless changes of forms of government to which we instigated the* GOYIM *when we were undermining their state structures, will have so wearied the peoples by that time that they will prefer to suffer anything under us rather than run the risk of enduring again all the agitations and miseries they have gone through.*

At the same time we shall not omit to emphasise the historical mistakes of the *goy* governments which have tormented humanity for so many centuries by their lack of understanding of everything that constitutes the true good of humanity in their chase after fantastic schemes of social blessings, and have never noticed that these schemes kept on producing a worse and never a better state of the universal relations which are the basis of human life. . . .

The whole force of our principles and methods will lie in the fact that we shall present them and expound them as a splendid contrast to the dead and decomposed old order of things in social life.

Our philosophers will discuss all the shortcomings of the various beliefs of the *goyim*, BUT NO ONE WILL EVER BRING UNDER DISCUSSION OUR FAITH FROM ITS TRUE POINT OF VIEW SINCE THIS WILL BE FULLY LEARNED BY NONE SAVE OURS, WHO WILL NEVER DARE TO BETRAY ITS SECRETS.

In countries known as progressive and enlightened we have created a senseless, filthy, abominable literature. For some time after our entrance to power we shall continue to encourage its existence in order to provide a telling relief by contrast to the speeches, party programme, which will be distributed from exalted quarters of ours. . . . Our wise men, trained to become leaders of the *goyim*, will compose speeches, projects, memoirs, articles, which will be used by us to influence the minds of the *goyim*, directing them towards such understanding and forms of knowledge as have been determined by us.

PROTOCOL NO. 15

When we at last definitely come into our kingdom by the aid of *coups d'état* prepared everywhere for one and the same day, after the worthlessness of all existing forms of government has been definitely acknowledged (and not a little time will pass before that comes about, perhaps even a whole century) we shall make it our task to see that against us such things as plots shall no longer exist. With this purpose we shall slay without mercy all who take arms (in hand) to oppose our coming into our kingdom. Every kind of new institution of anything like a secret society will also be punished with death; those of them which are now in existence, are known to us, serve us and have served us, we shall disband and send into exile to continents far removed from Europe. *In this way we shall proceed with those* GOY *masons who know too much;* such of these as we may for some reason spare will be kept in constant fear of exile. We shall promulgate a law making all former members of secret societies liable to exile from Europe as the centre of our rule.

Resolutions of our government will be final, without appeal.

In the *goy* societies, in which we have planted and deeply rooted discord and protestantism, the only possible way of restoring order is to employ merciless measures that prove the direct force of authority: no regard must be paid to the victims who fall, they suffer for the well-being of the future. The attainment of that well-being, even at the expense of sacrifices, is the duty of any kind of government that acknowledges as justification for its existence not only its privileges but its obligations. The principal guarantee of stability of rule is to confirm the aureole of power, and this aureole is attained only by such a majestic inflexibility of might as shall carry on its face the emblems of inviolability from mystical causes—from the choice of God. *Such was, until recent times, the Russian autocracy, the one and only serious foe we had in the world, without counting the Papacy.* Bear in mind the example when Italy, drenched with blood, never touched a hair of the head of Sulla* who had poured forth that blood: Sulla enjoyed an apotheosis for his might in the eyes of the people, though they had been torn in pieces by him, but his intrepid return to Italy ringed him round with inviolability. The people do not lay a finger on him who hypnotises them by his daring and strength of mind.

Meantime, however, until we come into our kingdom, we shall act in the contrary way: we shall create and multiply free masonic lodges in all the countries of the world, absorb into them all who may become or who are prominent in public activity, for in these lodges we shall find our principal intelligence office and means of influence. All these lodges we shall bring under one central administration, known to us alone and to all others absolutely unknown, which will be composed of our learned elders. The lodges will have their representatives who will serve to screen the above-mentioned administration of *masonry* and from whom will issue the watchword and programme. In these lodges we shall tie together the knot which binds together all revolutionary and liberal elements. Their composition will be made up of all strata of society. The most secret political plots will be known to us and will fall under our guiding hands on the very day of their conception. *Among the members of these lodges will be al-*

* Some versions of the "Protocols" followed Joly's "Dialogues" so closely that Joly's mistaken spelling of Sulla's name as "Sylla" was also copied. In the translation of the "Protocols" here used, however, the mistake was rectified.—H. B.

most all the agents of international and national police since their service is for us irreplaceable in the respect that the police is in a position not only to use its own particular measures with the insubordinate, but also to screen our activities and provide pretexts for discontents, *et cetera.*

The class of people who most willingly enter into secret societies are those who live by their wits, careerists, and in general people, mostly light-minded, with whom we shall have no difficulty in dealing and in using to wind up the mechanism of the machine devised by us. If this world grows agitated the meaning of that will be that we have had to stir it up in order to break up its too great solidarity. *But if there should arise in its midst a plot, then at the head of that plot will be no other than one of our most trusted servants.* It is natural that we and no other should lead *masonic* activities, for we know whither we are leading, we know the final goal of every form of activity whereas the *goyim* have knowledge of nothing, not even of the immediate effect of action; they put before themselves, usually, the momentary reckoning of the satisfaction of their self-opinion in the accomplishment of their thought without even remarking that the very conception never belonged to their initiative but to our instigation of their thought. . . .

The *goyim* enter the lodges out of curiosity or in the hope by their means to get a nibble at the public pie, and some of them in order to obtain a hearing before the public for their impracticable and groundless fantasies: they thirst for the emotion of success and applause, of which we are remarkably generous. And the reason why we give them this success is to make use of the high conceit of themselves to which it gives birth, for that insensibly disposes them to assimilate our suggestions without being on their guard against them in the fullness of their confidence that it is their own infallibility which is giving utterance to their own thoughts and that it is impossible for them to borrow those of others. . . . You cannot imagine to what extent the wisest of the *goyim* can be brought to a state of unconscious naïveté in the presence of this condition of high conceit of themselves, and at the same time how easy it is to take the heart out of them by the slightest ill-success, though it be nothing more than the stoppage of the applause they had, and to reduce them to a slavish submission for the sake of winning a renewal of success. . . .

By so much as ours disregard success if only they can carry through their plans, by so much the GOYIM *are willing to sacrifice any plans only to have success.* This psychology of theirs materially facilitates for us the task of setting them in the required direction. These tigers in appearance have the souls of sheep and the wind blows freely through their heads. We have set them on the hobby-horse of an idea about the absorption of individuality by the symbolic unit of *collectivism.* . . . They have never yet and they never will have the sense to reflect that this hobby-horse is a manifest violation of the most important law of nature, which has established from the very creation of the world one unit unlike another and precisely for the purpose of instituting individuality. . . .

If we have been able to bring them to such a pitch of stupid blindness is it not a proof, and an amazingly clear proof, of the degree to which the mind of the *goyim* is undeveloped in comparison with our mind? This it is, mainly, which guarantees our success.

And how far-seeing were our learned elders in ancient times when they said that to attain a serious end it behoves not to stop at any means or to count the victims sacrificed for the sake of that end. . . . We have not counted the victims of the seed of the *goy* cattle, though we have sacrificed many of our own, but for that we have now already given them such a position on the earth as they could not even have dreamed of. The comparatively small numbers of the victims from the number of ours have preserved our nationality from destruction.

Death is the inevitable end for all. It is better to bring that end nearer to those who hinder our affairs than to ourselves, to the founders of this affair. *We execute masons in such wise that none save the brotherhood can ever have a suspicion of it, not even the victims themselves of our death sentence, they all die when required as if from a normal kind of illness.* . . . Knowing this, even the brotherhood in its turn dare not protest. By such methods we have plucked out of the midst of *masonry* the very root of protest against our disposition. While preaching liberalism to the *goyim* we at the same time keep our own people and our agents in a state of unquestioning submission.

Under our influence the execution of the laws of the *goyim* has been reduced to a minimum. The prestige of the law has been exploded by the liberal interpretations introduced into this sphere. In the most important and fundamental affairs and questions judges decide as we dictate to them, see matters in the light wherewith we enfold them for the administration of the *goyim*, of course, through persons who are our tools though we do not appear to have anything in common with them—by newspaper opinion or by other means. . . . Even senators and the higher administration accept our counsels. The purely brute mind of the *goyim* is incapable of use for analysis and observation, and still more for the foreseeing whither a certain manner of setting a question may tend.

In this difference in capacity for thought between the *goyim* and ourselves may be clearly discerned the seal of our position on the Chosen People and of our higher quality of humanness, in contradistinction to the brute mind of the *goyim*. Their eyes are open, but see nothing before them and do not invent (unless, perhaps, material things). From this it is plain that nature herself has destined us to guide and rule the world.

When comes the time of our overt rule, the time to manifest its blessings, we shall remake all legislatures, all our laws will be brief, plain, stable, without any kind of interpretations, so that anyone will be in a position to know them perfectly. The main feature which will run right through them is submission to orders, and this principle will be carried to a grandiose height. Every abuse will then disappear in consequence of the responsibility of all down to the lowest unit before the higher authority of the representative of power. Abuses of power subordinate to this last instance will be so mercilessly punished that none will be found anxious to try experiments with their own powers. We shall follow up jealously every action of the administration on which depends the smooth running of the machinery of the State, for slackness in this produces slackness everywhere; not a single case of illegality or abuse of power will be left without exemplary punishment.

Concealment of guilt, connivance between those in the service of the administration—all this kind of evil will disappear after the very first examples of severe punishment. The aureole of our power demands suitable, that is, cruel, punishments for the slightest infringement, for the sake of gain, of its supreme prestige. The sufferer, though his punishment may exceed his fault, will count as a soldier falling on the administrative field of battle in the interest of authority, principle and law, which do not permit that any of those who hold the reins of the public coach should turn aside from the public highway to their own private paths. *For example: our judges will know that whenever they feel disposed to plume themselves on foolish clemency they are violating the law of justice which is instituted for the exemplary edification of men by penalties for lapses and not for display of the spiritual qualities of the judge.* . . . Such qualities it is proper to show in private life, but not in a public square which is the educational basis of human life.

Our legal staff will serve not beyond the age of 55, firstly because old men more obstinately hold to prejudiced opinions, and are less capable of submitting to new directions, and second because this will give us the possibility by this measure of securing elasticity in the changing of staff, which will thus the more easily bend under our pressure: he who wishes to keep his place will have to give blind obedience to deserve it. In general, our judges will be elected by us only from among those who thoroughly understand that the part they have to play is to punish and apply laws and not to dream about the manifestations of liberalism at the expense of the educational scheme of the State, as the *goyim* in these days imagine it to be. . . . This method of shuffling the staff will serve also to explode any collective solidarity of those in the same service and will bind all to the interests of the government upon which their fate will depend. The young generation of judges will be trained in certain views regarding the inadmissibility of any abuses that might disturb the established order of our subjects among themselves.

In these days the judges of the *goyim* create indulgences to every kind of crime, not having a just understanding of their office, because the rulers of the present age in appointing judges to office take no care to inculcate in them a sense of duty and consciousness of the matter which is demanded of them. As a brute beast lets out its young in search of prey, so do the *goyim* give their subjects places of profit without thinking to make clear to them for what purpose such place was created. This is the reason why their governments are being ruined by their own forces through the acts of their own administration.

Let us borrow from the example of the results of these actions yet another lesson for our government.

We shall root out liberalism from all the important strategic posts of our government on which depends the training of subordinates for our State structure. Such posts will fall exclusively to those who have been trained by us for administrative rule. To the possible objection that the retirement of old servants will cost the Treasury heavily, I reply, firstly, they will be provided with some private service in place of what they lose, and, secondly, I have to remark that all the money in the world will be concentrated in our hands, consequently it is not our government that has to fear expense.

Our absolutism will in all things be logically consecutive and therefore in each one of its decrees our supreme will will be respected and unquestionably fulfilled: it will ignore all murmurs, all discontents of every kind and will destroy to the root every kind of manifestation of them in act by punishment of an exemplary character.

We shall abolish the right of cassation, which will be transferred exclusively to our disposal—to the cognisance of him who rules, for we must not allow the conception among the people of a thought that there could be such a thing as a decision that is not right of judges set up by us. If, however, anything like this should occur, we shall ourselves cassate the decision, but inflict therewith such exemplary punishment on the judge for lack of understanding of his duty and the purpose of his appointment as will prevent a repetition of such cases. . . . I repeat that it must be borne in mind that we shall know every step of our administration which only needs to be closely watched for the people to be content with us, for it has the right to demand from a good government a good official.

Our government will have the appearance of a patriarchal paternal guardianship on the part of our ruler. Our own nation and our subjects will discern in his person a father caring for their every need, their every act, their every inter-relation as subjects one with another, as well as their relations to the ruler. They will then be so thoroughly imbued with the thought that it is impossible for them to dispense with this wardship and guidance, if they wish to live in peace and quiet, *that they will acknowledge the autocracy of our ruler with a devotion bordering on* APOTHEOSIS, especially when they are convinced that those whom we set up do not put their own in place of his authority, but only blindly execute his dictates. They will be rejoiced that we have regulated everything in their lives as is done by wise parents who desire to train their children in the cause of duty and submission. For the peoples of the world in regard to the secrets of our polity are ever through the ages only children under age, precisely as are also their governments.

As you see, I found our despotism on right and duty: the right to compel the execution of duty is the direct obligation of a government which is a father for its subjects. It has the right of the strong that it may use it for the benefit of directing humanity towards that order which is defined by nature, namely, submission. Everything in the world is in a state of submission, if not to man, then to circumstances or its own inner character, in all cases, to what is stronger. And so shall we be this something stronger for the sake of good.

We are obliged without hesitation to sacrifice individuals, who commit a breach of established order, for in the exemplary punishment of evil lies a great educational problem.

When the King of Israel sets upon his sacred head the crown offered him by Europe he will become patriarch of the world. The indispensable victims offered by him in consequence of their suitability will never reach the number of victims offered in the course of centuries by the mania of magnificence, the emulation between the *goy* governments.

Our King will be in constant communion with the peoples, making to them from the tribune speeches which fame will in that same hour distribute over all the world.

PROTOCOL NO. 16

In order to effect the destruction of all collective forces except ours we shall emasculate the first stage of collectivism—the *universities,* by re-educating them in a new direction. *Their officials and professors will be prepared for their business by detailed secret programmes of action from which they will not with immunity diverge, not by one iota. They will be appointed with especial precaution, and will be so placed as to be wholly dependent upon the Government.*

We shall exclude from the course of instruction State Law as also all that concerns the political question. These subjects will be taught to a few dozens of persons chosen for their pre-eminent capacities from among the number of the initiated. *The universities must no longer send out from their halls milksops concocting plans for a con-*

stitution, like a comedy or a tragedy, busying themselves with questions of policy in which even their own fathers never had any power of thought.

The ill-guided acquaintance of a large number of persons with questions of polity creates utopian dreamers and bad subjects, as you can see for yourselves from the example of the universal education in this direction of the *goyim*. We must introduce into their education all those principles which have so brilliantly broken up their order. But when we are in power we shall remove every kind of disturbing subject from the course of education and shall make out of the youth obedient children of authority, loving him who rules as the support and hope of peace and quiet.

Classicism, as also any form of study of ancient history, in which there are more bad than good examples, we shall replace with the study of the programme of the future. We shall erase from the memory of men all facts of previous centuries which are undesirable to us, and leave only those which depict all the errors of the government of the *goyim*. The study of practical life, of the obligations of order, of the relations of people one to another, of avoiding bad and selfish examples, which spread the infection of evil, and similar questions of an educative nature, will stand in the forefront of the teaching programme, which will be drawn up on a separate plan for each calling or state of life, in no wise generalising the teaching. This treatment of the question has special importance.

Each state of life must be trained within strict limits corresponding to its destination and work in life. The *occasional genius has always managed and always will manage to slip through into other states of life, but it is the most perfect folly for the sake of this rare occasional genius to let through into ranks foreign to them the untalented who thus rob of their places those who belong to those ranks by birth or employment. You know yourselves in what all this has ended for the* GOYIM *who allowed this crying absurdity.*

In order that he who rules may be seated firmly in the hearts and minds of his subjects it is necessary for the time of his activity to instruct the whole nation in the schools and on the market places about his meaning and his acts and all his beneficent initiatives.

We shall abolish every kind of freedom of instruction. Learners of all ages will have the right to assemble together with their parents

in the educational establishments as it were in a club: during these
assemblies, on holidays, teachers will read what will pass as free
lectures on questions of human relations, of the laws of examples, of
the limitations which are born of unconscious relations, and, finally,
of the philosophy of new theories not yet declared to the world.
These theories will be raised by us to the stage of a dogma of faith
as a transitional stage towards our faith. On the completion of this
exposition of our programme of action in the present and the future
I will read you the principles of these theories.

In a word, knowing by the experience of many centuries that people
live and are guided by ideas, that these ideas are imbibed by people
only by the aid of education provided with equal success for all ages
of growth, but of course by varying methods, we shall swallow up
and confiscate to our own use the last scintilla of independence of
thought, which we have for long past been directing towards subjects
and ideas useful for us. The system of bridling thought is already
at work in the so-called system of teaching by *object lessons*, the purpose of which is to turn the *goyim* into unthinking submissive brutes
waiting for things to be presented before their eyes in order to form
an idea of them. . . . In France, one of our best agents, Bourgeois,
has already made public a new programme of teaching by object
lessons.

PROTOCOL NO. 17

The practice of advocacy produces men cold, cruel, persistent, unprincipled, who in all cases take up an impersonal, purely legal standpoint. They have the inveterate habit to refer everything to its value
for the defence and not to the public welfare of its results. They
do not usually decline to undertake any defence whatever, they strive
for an acquittal at all costs, cavilling over every petty crux of juris-
prudence and thereby they demoralise justice. For this reason we
shall set this profession into narrow frames which will keep it inside
this sphere of executive public service. Advocates, equally with judges,
will be deprived of the right of communication with litigants; they
will receive business only from the court and will study it by notes
of report and documents, defending their clients after they have
been interrogated in court on facts that have appeared. They will
receive an honorarium without regard to the quality of the defence.

This will render them mere reporters on law-business in the interests of justice and as counterpoise to the proctor who will be the reporter in the interests of prosecution; this will shorten business before the courts. In this way will be established a practice of honest unprejudiced defence conducted not from personal interest but by conviction. This will also, by the way, remove the present practice of corrupt bargain between advocates to agree only to let that side win which pays most. . . .

We have long past taken care to discredit the priesthood of the GOYIM, and thereby to ruin their mission on earth which in these days might still be a great hindrance to us. Day by day its influence on the peoples of the world is falling lower. *Freedom of conscience* has been declared everywhere, *so that now only years divide us from the moment of the complete wrecking of that Christian religion:* as to other religions we shall have still less difficulty in dealing with them, but it would be premature to speak of this now. We shall set clericalism and clericals into such narrow frames as to make their influence move in retrogressive proportion to its former progress.

When the time comes finally to destroy the papal court the finger of an invisible hand will point the nations towards this court. When, however, the nations fling themselves upon it, we shall come forward in the guise of its defenders as if to save excessive bloodshed. By this diversion we shall penetrate to its very bowels and be sure we shall never come out again until we have gnawed through the entire strength of this place.

The King of the Jews will be the real Pope of the Universe, the patriarch of an international Church.

But, *in the meantime*, while we are re-educating youth in new traditional religions and afterwards in ours, *we shall not overtly lay a finger on existing churches, but we shall fight against them by criticism calculated to produce schism.* . . .

In general, then, our contemporary press will continue *to convict* State affairs, religions, incapacities of the *goyim*, always using the most unprincipled expressions in order by every means to lower their prestige in the manner which can only be practised by the genius of our gifted tribe. . . .

Our kingdom will be an apologia of the divinity Vishnu, in whom is found its personification—in our hundred hands will be, one in each, the springs of the machinery of social life. We shall see everything without the aid of official police which, in that scope of its rights which we elaborated for the use of the *goyim*, hinders governments from seeing. In our programme *one-third of our subjects will keep the rest under observation* from a sense of duty, on the principle of volunteer service to the State. It will then be no disgrace to be a spy and informer, but a merit: unfounded denunciations, however, will be cruelly punished that there may be no development of abuses of this right.

Our agents will be taken from the higher as well as the lower ranks of society, from among the administrative class who spend their time in amusements, editors, printers and publishers, booksellers, clerks, and salesmen, workmen, coachmen, lackeys, etcetera. This body, having no rights and not being empowered to take any action on their own account, and consequently a police without any power, will only witness and report: verification of their reports and arrests will depend upon a responsible group of controllers of police affairs, while the actual act of arrest will be performed by the gendarmerie and the municipal police. Any person not denouncing anything seen or heard concerning questions of polity will also be charged with and made responsible for concealment, if it be proved that he is guilty of this crime.

Just as nowadays our brethren are obliged at their own risk to denounce to the kabal apostates of their own family or members who have been noticed doing anything in opposition to the *kabal, so in our kingdom over all the world it will be obligatory for all our subjects to observe the duty of service to the State in this direction.*

Such an organisation will extirpate abuses of authority, of force, of bribery, everything in fact which we by our counsels, by our theories of the superhuman rights of man, have introduced into the customs of the *goyim*. . . . But how else were we to procure that increase of causes predisposing to disorders in the midst of their administration? . . . Among the number of those methods one of the most important is—agents for the restoration of order, so placed as to have the opportunity in their disintegrating activity of developing and displaying their evil inclinations—obstinate self-conceit, irresponsible exercise of authority, and, first and foremost, venality.

PROTOCOL NO. 18

When it becomes necessary for us to strengthen the strict measures of secret defence (the most fatal poison for the prestige of authority) we shall arrange a simulation of disorders or some manifestation of discontents finding expression through the co-operation of good speakers. Round these speakers will assemble all who are sympathetic to his utterances. This will give us the pretext for domiciliary per-quisitions and surveillance on the part of our servants from among the number of the *goyim* police. . . .

As the majority of conspirators act out of love for the game, for the sake of talking, so, until they commit some overt act we shall not lay a finger on them but only introduce into their midst obser-vation elements. . . . It must be remembered that the prestige of au-thority is lessened if it frequently discovers conspiracies against itself: this implies a presumption of consciousness of weakness, or, what is still worse, of injustice. You are aware that we have broken the prestige of the *goy* kings by frequent attempts upon their lives through our agents, blind sheep of our flock, who are easily moved by a few liberal phrases to crimes provided only they be painted in political colours. *We have compelled the rulers to acknowledge their weakness in advertising overt measures of secret defence and thereby we shall bring the promise of authority to destruction.*

Our ruler will be secretly protected only by the most insignificant guard, because we shall not admit so much as a thought that there could exist against him any sedition with which he is not strong enough to contend and is compelled to hide from it.

If we should admit this thought, as the *goyim* have done and are doing, we should *ipso facto* be signing a death sentence, if not for our ruler, at any rate for his dynasty, at no distant date.

According to strictly enforced outward appearances our ruler will employ his power only for the advantage of the nation and in no wise for his own or dynastic profits. Therefore, with the observance of this decorum, his authority will be respected and guarded by the subjects themselves, it will receive an apotheosis in the admission that with it is bound up the well-being of every citizen of the State, for upon it will depend all order in the common life of the pack. . . .

****TOP SECRET****

Overt defence of the king argues weakness in the organisation of his strength.

Our ruler will always among the people be surrounded by a mob of apparently curious men and women, who will occupy the front ranks about him, to all appearance by chance, and will restrain the ranks of the rest out of respect as it will appear for good order. This will sow an example of restraint also in others. If a petitioner appears among the people trying to hand a petition and forcing his way through the ranks, the first ranks must receive the petition and before the eyes of the petitioner pass it to the ruler, so that all may know that what is handed in reaches its destination, that, consequently, there exists a control of the ruler himself. The aureole of power requires for its existence that the people may be able to say: "If the king knew of this," or: "the king will hear of it."

With the establishment of official secret defence the mystical prestige of authority disappears: given a certain audacity, and everyone counts himself master of it, the sedition-monger is conscious of his strength, and when occasion serves watches for the moment to make an attempt upon authority. . . . For the *goyim* we have been preaching something else, but by that very fact we are enabled to see what measures of overt defence have brought them to. . . .

Criminals with us will be arrested at the first more or less well-grounded *suspicion;* it cannot be allowed that out of fear of a possible mistake an opportunity should be given of escape to persons suspected of a political lapse or crime, for in these matters we shall be literally merciless. If it is still possible, by stretching a point, to admit a reconsideration of the motive causes in simple crimes, there is no possibility of excuse for persons occupying themselves with questions in which nobody except the government can understand anything. . . . And it is not all governments that understand true policy.

PROTOCOL NO. 19

If we do not permit any independent dabbling in the political we shall on the other hand encourage every kind of report or petition with proposals for the government to examine into all kinds of projects for the amelioration of the condition of the people; this will reveal to us the defects or else the fantasies of our subjects, to which we shall respond either by accomplishing them or by a wise rebutment to prove the short-sightedness of one who judges wrongly.

Sedition-mongering is nothing more than the yapping of a lap-dog at an elephant. For a government well organised, not from the police but from the public point of view, the lap-dog yaps at the elephant in entire unconsciousness of its strength and importance. It needs no more than to take a good example to show the relative importance of both and the lap-dogs will cease to yap and will wag their tails the moment they set eyes on an elephant.

In order to destroy the prestige of heroism for political crime we shall send it for trial in the category of thieving, murder, and every kind of abominable and filthy crime. Public opinion will then confuse in its conception this category of crime with the disgrace attaching to every other and will brand it with the same contempt.

We have done our best, and I hope we have succeeded, to obtain that the *goyim* should not arrive at this means of contending with sedition. It was for this reason that through the press and in speeches, indirectly—in cleverly compiled schoolbooks on history, we have advertised the martyrdom alleged to have been accepted by sedition-mongers for the idea of the commonweal. This advertisement has increased the contingent of liberals and has brought thousands of *goyim* into the ranks of our livestock cattle.

PROTOCOL NO. 20

To-day we shall touch upon the financial programme, which I put off to the end of my report as being the most difficult, the crowning and the decisive point of our plans. Before entering upon it I will remind you that I have already spoken before by way of a hint when I said that the sum total of our actions is settled by the question of figures.

When we come into our kingdom our autocratic government will avoid, from a principle of self-preservation, sensibly burdening the masses of the people with taxes, remembering that it plays the part of father and protector. But as State organisation costs dear it is necessary nevertheless to obtain the funds required for it. It will, therefore, elaborate with particular precaution the question of equilibrium in this matter.

Our rule, in which the king will enjoy the legal fiction that everything in his State belongs to him (which may easily be translated
into fact), will be enabled to resort to the lawful confiscation of all
sums of every kind for the regulation of their circulation in the State.
From this follows that taxation will best be covered by a progressive tax
on property. In this manner the dues will be paid without straitening
or ruining anybody in the form of a percentage of the amount of
property. The rich must be aware that it is their duty to place a part
of their superfluities at the disposal of the State since the State guarantees them security of possession of the rest of their property and the
right of honest gains, I say honest, for the control over property will
do away with robbery on a legal basis.

This social reform must come from above, for the time is ripe for
it—it is indispensable as a pledge of peace.

The tax upon the poor man is a seed of revolution and works to
the detriment of the State which in hunting after the trifling is missing
the big. Quite apart from this, a tax on capitalists diminishes the growth
of wealth in private hands in which we have in these days concentrated it as a counterpoise to the government strength of the *goyim*—
their State finances.

A tax increasing in a percentage ratio to capital will give a much
larger revenue than the present individual or property tax, which is
useful to us now for the sole reason that it excites trouble and discontent among the *goyim*.

The force upon which our king will rest consists in the equilibrium
and the guarantee of peace, for the sake of which things it is indispensable that the capitalists should yield up a portion of their incomes
for the sake of the secure working of the machinery of the State.
State needs must be paid by those who will not feel the burden and
have enough to take from.

Such a measure will destroy the hatred of the poor man for the
rich, in whom he will see a necessary financial support for the State,
will see in him the organiser of peace and well-being since he will
see that it is the rich man who is paying the necessary means to attain
these things.

In order that payers of the educated classes should not too much
distress themselves over the new payments they will have full accounts
given them of the destination of those payments, with the exception

of such sums as will be appropriated for the needs of the throne and the administrative institutions.

He who reigns will not have any properties of his own once all in the State represents his patrimony, or else the one would be in contradiction to the other; the fact of holding private means would destroy the right of property in the common possessions of all.

Relatives of him who reigns, his heirs excepted, who will be maintained by the resources of the State, must enter the ranks of servants of the State or must work to obtain the right of property; the privilege of royal blood must not serve for the spoiling of the treasury.

Purchase, receipt of money or inheritance will be subject to the payment of a stamp progressive tax. Any transfer of property, whether money or other, without evidence of payment of this tax which will be strictly registered by names, will render the former holder liable to pay interest on the tax from the moment of transfer of these sums up to the discovery of his evasion of declaration of the transfer. Transfer documents must be presented weekly at the local treasury office with notifications of the name, surname and permanent place of residence of the former and the new holder of the property. This transfer with register of names must begin from a definite sum which exceeds the ordinary expenses of buying and selling of necessaries, and these will be subject to payment only by a stamp impost of a definite percentage of the unit.

Just strike an estimate of how many times such taxes as these will cover the revenue of the *goyim* States.

The State exchequer will have to maintain a definite complement of reserve sums, and all that is collected above that complement must be returned into circulation. On these sums will be organised public works. The initiative in works of this kind, proceeding from State sources, will bind the working class firmly to the interests of the State and to those who reign. From these same sums also a part will be set aside as rewards of inventiveness and productiveness.

On no account should so much as a single unit above the definite and freely estimated sums be retained in the State treasuries, for money exists to be circulated and any kind of stagnation of money acts ruinously on the running of the State machinery, for which it is the lubricant; a stagnation of the lubricant may stop the regular working of the mechanism.

The substitution of interest-bearing paper for a part of the token of exchange has produced exactly this stagnation. The consequences of this circumstance are already sufficiently noticeable.

A court of account will also be instituted by us and in it the ruler will find at any moment a full accounting for State income and expenditure, with the exception of the current monthly account, not yet made up, and that of the preceding month, which will not yet have been delivered.

The one and only person who will have no interest in robbing the State is its owner, the ruler. This is why his personal control will remove the possibility of leakages of extravagances.

The representative function of the ruler at receptions for the sake of etiquette, which absorbs so much invaluable time, will be abolished in order that the ruler may have time for control and consideration. His power will not then be split up into fractional parts among time-serving favourites who surround the throne for its pomp and splendour, and are interested only in their own and not in the common interests of the State.

Economic crises have been produced by us for the *goyim* by no other means than the withdrawal of money from circulation. Huge capitals have stagnated, withdrawing money from States, which were constantly obliged to apply to those same stagnant capitals for loans. These loans burdened the finances of the State with the payment of interest and made them the bond slaves of these capitals. . . . The concentration of industry in the hands of capitalists out of the hands of small masters has drained away all the juices of the peoples and with them also of the States. . . .

The present issue of money in general does not correspond with the requirements per head, and cannot therefore satisfy all the needs of the workers. The issue of money ought to correspond with the growth of population and thereby children also must absolutely be reckoned as consumers of currency from the day of their birth. The revision of issue is a material question for the whole world.

You are aware that the gold standard has been the ruin of the States which adopted it, for it has not been able to satisfy the demands for money, the more so that we have removed gold from circulation as far as possible.

With us the standard that must be introduced is the cost of working-man power, whether it be reckoned in paper or in wood. We shall make the issue of money in accordance with the normal requirements of each subject, adding to the quantity with every birth and subtracting with every death.

The accounts will be managed by each department (the French administrative division), each circle.

In order that there may be no delays in the paying out of money for State needs the sums and terms of such payments will be fixed by decree of the ruler; this will do away with the protection by a ministry of one institution to the detriment of others.

The budgets of income and expenditure will be carried out side by side that they may not be obscured by distance one to another.

The reforms projected by us in the financial institutions and principles of the *goyim* will be closed by us in such forms as will alarm nobody. We shall point out the necessity of reforms in consequence of the disorderly darkness into which the *goyim* by their irregularities have plunged the finances. The first irregularity, as we shall point out, consists in their beginning with drawing up a single budget which year after year grows owing to the following cause: this budget is dragged out to half the year, then they demand a budget to put things right, and this they expend in three months, after which they ask for a supplementary budget, and all this ends with a liquidation budget. But, as the budget of the following year is drawn up in accordance with the sum of the total addition, the annual departure from the normal reaches as much as 50 per cent. in a year, and so the annual budget is trebled in ten years. Thanks to such methods, allowed by the carelessness of the *goy* States, their treasuries are empty. The period of loans supervenes, and that has swallowed up remainders and brought all the *goy* States to bankruptcy.

You understand perfectly that economic arrangements of this kind, which have been suggested to the *goyim* by us, cannot be carried on by us.

Every kind of loan proves infirmity in the State and a want of understanding of the rights of the State. Loans hang like a sword of Damocles over the heads of rulers, who, instead of taking from their subjects by a temporary tax, come begging with outstretched palm of our bankers. Foreign loans are leeches which there is no possibility of removing from the body of the State until they fall off of themselves or the State flings them off. But the *goy* States do not tear them off; they go on in persisting in putting more on to themselves so that they must inevitably perish, drained by voluntary blood-letting.

What also indeed is, in substance, a loan, especially a foreign loan? A loan is—an issue of government bills of exchange containing a percentage obligation commensurate to the sum of the loan capital. If the loan bears a charge of 5 per cent., then in twenty years the State vainly pays away in interest a sum equal to the loan borrowed, in forty years it is paying a double sum, in sixty—treble, and all the while the debt remains an unpaid debt.

From this calculation it is obvious that with any form of taxation per head the State is baling out the last coppers of the poor taxpayers in order to settle accounts with wealthy foreigners, from whom it has borrowed money instead of collecting these coppers for its own needs without the additional interest.

So long as loans were internal the *goyim* only shuffled their money from the pockets of the poor to those of the rich, but when we bought up the necessary person in order to transfer loans into the external sphere all the wealth of States flowed into our cash-boxes and all the *goyim* began to pay us the tribute of subjects.

If the superficiality of *goy* kings on their thrones in regard to State affairs and the venality of ministers or the want of understanding of financial matters on the part of other ruling persons have made their countries debtors to our treasuries to amounts quite impossible to pay it has not been accomplished without on our part heavy expenditure of trouble and money.

Stagnation of money will not be allowed by us and therefore there will be no State interest-bearing paper, except a one per cent. series, so that there will be no payment of interest to leeches that suck all the strength out of the State. The right to issue interest-bearing paper will be given exclusively to industrial companies who will find no difficulty in paying interest out of profits, whereas the State does not make interest on borrowed money like these companies, for the State borrows to spend and not to use in operations.

Industrial papers will be bought also by the government which from being as now a payer of tribute by loan operations will be transformed into a lender of money at a profit. This measure will stop the stagnation of money, parasitic profits and idleness, all of which were useful for us among the *goyim* so long as they were independent but are not desirable under our rule.

How clear is the undeveloped power of thought of the 'purely brute brains of the *goyim*, as expressed in the fact that they have been borrowing from us with payment of interest without ever thinking that all the same these very moneys plus an addition for payment of interest must be got by them from their own State pockets in order to settle up with us. What could have been simpler than to take the money they wanted from their own people?

But it is a proof of the genius of our chosen mind that we have contrived to present the matter of loans to them in such a light that they have even seen in them an advantage for themselves.

Our accounts, which we shall present when the time comes, in the light of centuries of experience gained by experiments made by us on the *goy* States, will be distinguished by clearness and definiteness and will show at a glance to all men the advantage of our innovations. They will put an end to those abuses to which we owe our mastery over the *goyim*, but which cannot be allowed in our kingdom.

We shall so hedge about our system of accounting that neither the ruler nor the most insignificant public servant will be in a position to divert even the smallest sum from its destination without detection or to direct it in another direction except that which will be once fixed in a definite plan of action.

And without a definite plan it is impossible to rule. Marching along an undetermined road and with undetermined resources brings to ruin by the way heroes and demi-gods.

The *goy* rulers, whom we once upon a time advised should be distracted from State occupations by representative receptions, observances of etiquette, entertainments, were only screens for our rule. The accounts of favourite courtiers who replaced them in the sphere of affairs were drawn up for them by our agents, and every time gave satisfaction to short-sighted minds by promises that in the future economies and improvements were foreseen. . . . Economies from what? From new taxes?—were questions that might have been but were not asked by those who read our accounts and projects. . . .

You know to what they have been brought by this carelessness, to what a pitch of financial disorder they have arrived, notwithstanding the astonishing industry of their peoples. . . .

PROTOCOL NO. 21

To what I reported to you at the last meeting I shall now add a detailed explanation of internal loans. Of foreign loans I shall say nothing more, because they have fed us with the national moneys of the *goyim*, but for our State there will be no foreigners, that is, nothing external.

We have taken advantage of the venality of administrators and the slackness of rulers to get our moneys twice, thrice and more times over, by lending to the *goy* governments moneys which were not at all needed by the States. Could anyone do the like in regard to us? . . . Therefore, I shall only deal with the details of internal loans.

States announce that such a loan is to be concluded and open subscriptions for their own bills of exchange, that is, for their interest-bearing paper. That they may be within the reach of all the price is determined at from a hundred to a thousand; and a discount is made for the earliest subscribers. Next day by artificial means the price of them goes up, the alleged reason being that everyone is rushing to buy them. In a few days the treasury safes are as they say overflowing and there's more money than they can do with (why then take it?). The subscription, it is alleged, covers many times over the issue total of the loan; in this lies the whole stage effect—look you, they say, what confidence is shown in the government's bills of exchange.

But when the comedy is played out there emerges the fact that a debit and an exceedingly burdensome debit has been created. For the payment of interest it becomes necessary to have recourse to new loans, which do not swallow up but only add to the capital debt. And when this credit is exhausted it becomes necessary by new taxes to cover, not the loan, but only the interest on it. These taxes are a debit employed to cover a debit. . . .

Later comes the time for conversions, but they diminish the payment of interest without covering the debt, and besides they cannot be made without the consent of the lenders; on announcing a conversion a proposal is made to return the money to those who are not willing to convert their paper. If everybody expressed his unwillingness and demanded his money back, the government would be hooked on their own flies and would be found insolvent and unable to pay the proposed sums. By good luck the subjects of the *goy* governments, knowing nothing about financial affairs, have always preferred losses on exchange and diminution of interest to the risk of new investments of their moneys, and have thereby many a time enabled these governments to throw off their shoulders a debit of several millions.

Nowadays, with external loans, these tricks cannot be played by the *goyim* for they know that we shall demand all our moneys back.

In this way an acknowledged bankruptcy will best prove to the various countries the absence of any means between the interests of the peoples and of those who rule them.

I beg you to concentrate your particular attention upon this point and upon the following: nowadays all internal loans are consolidated by so-called flying loans, that is, such as have terms of payment more or less near. These debts consist of moneys paid into the savings banks and reserve funds. If left for long at the disposition of a government these funds evaporate in the payment of interest on foreign loans, and are replaced by the deposit of equivalent amount of *rentes*.

And these last it is which patch up all the leaks in the State treasuries of the *goyim*.

When we ascend the throne of the world all these financial and similar shifts, as being not in accord with our interests, will be swept away so as not to leave a trace, as also will be destroyed all money markets, since we shall not allow the prestige of our power to be shaken by fluctuations of prices set upon our values, which we shall announce by law at the price which represents their full worth without any possibility of lowering or raising. (Raising gives the pretext for lowering, which indeed was where we made a beginning in relation to the values of the *goyim.*)

We shall replace the money markets by grandiose government credit institutions, the object of which will be to fix the price of industrial values in accordance with government views. These institutions will be in a position to fling upon the market five hundred millions of industrial paper in one day, or to buy up for the same amount. In this way all industrial undertakings will come into dependence upon us. You may imagine for yourselves what immense power we shall thereby secure for ourselves. . . .

PROTOCOL NO. 22

In all that has so far been reported by me to you, I have endeavoured to depict with care the secret of what is coming, of what is past, and of what is going on now, rushing into the flood of the great events coming already in the near future, the secret of our relations to the *goyim* and of financial operations. On this subject there remains still a little for me to add.

In our hands is the greatest power of our day—gold: in two days we can procure from our storehouses any quantity we may please.

Surely there is no need to seek further proof that our rule is predestined by God? Surely we shall not fail with such wealth to prove that all that evil which for so many centuries we have had to commit has served at the end of ends the cause of true well-being—the bringing of everything into order? Though it be even by the exercise of some violence, yet all the same it will be established. We shall contrive to prove that we are benefactors who have restored to the rent and mangled earth the true good and also freedom of the person, and therewith we shall enable it to be enjoyed in peace and quiet, with proper dignity of relations, on the condition, of course, of strict observance of the laws established by us. We shall make plain therewith that freedom does not consist in dissipation and in the right of unbridled licence any more than the dignity and force of a man do not consist in the right for everyone to promulgate destructive principles in the nature of freedom of conscience, equality and the like, that freedom of the person in no wise consists in the right to agitate oneself and others by abominable speeches before disorderly mobs, and that true freedom consists in the inviolability of the person who honourably and strictly observes all the laws of life in common, that human dignity is wrapped up in consciousness of the rights and also of the absence of rights of each, and not wholly and solely in fantastic imaginings about the subject of one's *ego*.

Our authority will be glorious because it will be all-powerful, will rule and guide, and not muddle along after leaders and orators shrieking themselves hoarse with senseless words which they call great principles and which are nothing else, to speak honestly, but utopian. . . . Our authority will be the crown of order, and in that is included the whole happiness of man. The aureole of this authority will inspire a mystical bowing of the knee before it and a reverent fear before it of all the peoples. True force makes no terms with any right, not even with that of God: none dare come near to it so as to take so much as a span from it away.

PROTOCOL NO. 23

That the peoples may become accustomed to obedience it is necessary to inculcate lessons of humility and therefore to reduce the production of articles of luxury. By this we shall improve morals which have been debased by emulation in the sphere of luxury. We shall re-establish small master production which will mean laying a mine under the private capital of manufacturers. This is indispensable also for the reason that manufacturers on the grand scale often move, though not always consciously, the thoughts of the masses in directions against the government. A people of small masters knows nothing of unemployment and this binds him closely with existing order, and consequently with the firmness of authority. Unemployment is a most perilous thing for a government. For us its part will have been played out the moment authority is transferred into our hands. Drunkenness also will be prohibited by law and punishable as a crime against the humanness of man who is turned into a brute under the influence of alcohol.

Subjects, I repeat once more, give blind obedience only to the strong hand which is absolutely independent of them, for in it they feel the sword of defence and support against social scourges. . . . What do they want with an angelic spirit in a king? What they have to see in him is the personification of force and power.

The supreme lord who will replace all now existing rulers, dragging on their existence among societies demoralised by us, societies that have denied even the authority of God, from whose midst breaks out on all sides the fire of anarchy, must first of all proceed to quench this all-devouring flame. Therefore he will be obliged to kill off those existing societies, though he should drench them with his own blood, that he may resurrect them again in the form of regularly organised troops fighting consciously with every kind of infection that may cover the body of the State with sores.

This Chosen One of God is chosen from above to demolish the senseless forces moved by instinct and not reason, by brutishness and not humanness. These forces now triumph in manifestations of robbery and every kind of violence under the mask of principles of freedom and rights. They have overthrown all forms of social order to erect on the ruins the throne of the King of the Jews; but their part will be played out the moment he enters into his kingdom. Then it will be necessary to sweep them away from his path, on which must be left no knot, no splinter.

Then will it be possible for us to say to the peoples of the world: "Give thanks to God and bow the knee before him who bears on his front the seal of the predestination of man, to which God Himself has led his star that none other but He might free us from all the before-mentioned forces and evils."

PROTOCOL NO. 24

I pass now to the method of confirming the dynastic roots of King David to the last strata of the earth.

This confirmation will first and foremost be included in that in which to this day has rested the force of conservatism by our learned elders of the conduct of all the affairs of the world, in the directing of the education of thought of all humanity.

Certain members of the seed of David will prepare the kings and their heirs, selecting not by right of heritage but by eminent capacities, inducting them into the most secret mysteries of the political, into schemes of government, but providing always that none may come to knowledge of the secrets. The object of this mode of action is that all may know that government cannot be entrusted to those who have not been inducted into the secret places of its art. . . .

To these persons only will be taught the practical application of the aforenamed plans by comparison of the experiences of many centuries, all the observations on the politico-economic moves and social sciences—in a word, all the spirit of laws which have been unshakably established by nature herself for the regulation of the relations of humanity.

Direct heirs will often be set aside from ascending the throne if in their time of training they exhibit frivolity, softness and other qualities that are the ruin of authority, which render them incapable of governing and in themselves dangerous for kingly office.

Only those who are unconditionally capable for firm, even if it be to cruelty, direct rule will receive the reins of rule from our learned elders.

In case of falling sick with weakness of will or other form of incapacity, kings must by law hand over the reins of rule to new and capable hands. . . .

The king's plans of action for the current moment, and all the more so for the future, will be unknown, even to those who are called his closest counsellors.

Only the king and the three who stood sponsor for him will know what is coming.

In the person of the king who with unbending will is master of himself and of humanity all will discern as it were fate with its mysterious ways. None will know what the king wishes to attain by his dispositions, and therefore none will dare to stand across an unknown path.

It is understood that the brain reservoir of the king must correspond in capacity to the plan of government it has to contain. It is for this reason that he will ascend the throne not otherwise than after examination of his mind by the aforesaid learned elders.

That the people may know and love their king it is indispensable for him to converse in the market-places with his people. This ensures the necessary clinching of the two forces which are now divided one from another by us by the terror.

This terror was indispensable for us till the time comes for both these forces separately to fall under our influence.

The King of the Jews must not be at the mercy of his passions, and especially of sensuality: on no side of his character must he give brute instincts power over his mind. Sensuality worse than all else disorganises the capacities of the mind and clearness of views, distracting the thoughts to the worst and most brutal side of human activity.

The prop of humanity in the person of the supreme lord of all the world of the holy seed of David must sacrifice to his people all personal inclinations.

Our supreme lord must be of an exemplary irreproachability.

Chapter 16

THE STORY OF JONATHAN MAY

Jonathan May attempted to free us from the shackles of the Federal Reserve by creating an alternate banking system with instruments backed by land, raw materials, mineral deposits, oil, coal, timber, and other wilderness holdings. Jonathan aided Governor Connolly and the Hunt brothers in their effort to corner the silver market. The silver would have been used to create a "Bank of Texas" issue of "real" money. This would have destroyed the Federal Reserve had the Hunts been successful. When the world bankers realized what was happening, they destroyed Connolly, the Hunt brothers, Jonathan May, and Texas.

The Federal Reserve entrapped Mr. May by intentionally routing his credit instruments through the Federal Reserve, against the terms clearly stated upon those instruments, instead of through Mr. May's alternate system. Jonathan May was illegally arrested, illegally tried, and illegally imprisoned in the Federal Prison at Terre Haute, Indiana. The world power structure has stolen Mr. May's idea, which will be used as the banking system of the New World Order and is known as the World Conservation Bank. Jonathan has served four years of a fifteen-year sentence.

Telling Time: July 27, 1990

I SWEAR BY ALMIGHTY GOD THAT THE EVIDENCE I NOW
GIVE IS THE TRUTH, THE WHOLE TRUTH AND NOTHING BUT
THE TRUTH, TO THE BEST OF MY KNOWLEDGE, BELIEF AND
RECOLLECTION. I DO SO SWEAR UNDER THE PENALTY OF
PERJURY UNDER THE LAWS OF THE UNITED STATES OF
AMERICA - SO HELP ME GOD.

I was born into a privileged life-style in North
Devon, England, the third and last child and only son of a
wealthy, land-owning family. I was privately educated and
left school early, determined to join my father's business
and not be encumbered with the authoritarian atmosphere of
school. I did so by getting myself expelled. I was, I
believe, nearly sixteen. At once I began to work as a
livestock broker as my father and his family did and still
does. I also farmed. I then branched into other goods,
buying for customers using my contacts to supply items at a
lower cost and better quality items at the same cost than
normal retail suppliers. I was very successful. My business
continued to expand. Management was highly vertically
structured, and diversification was as lateral as I could
possibly make it. It continued to thrive. I developed a
sophisticated tax-shelter system which was lawfully capable
of removing taxation liability from the majority of my own
and my colleagues' incomes.

At age 20, in my twenty-first year, numerous old
documents - family heirlooms from my mother's side of the
family - were given to me as its last remaining male heir.

(Page 1 of 26)

Among these old documents was an Indenture issued to an
ancestor of mine, settling upon him "and his heir and
assigns in perpetuity for the duration of the term hereof"
the responsibility and authority of Trustee for certain
property, goods, chattels, <u>etc</u>. As far as I can recall, the
document was dated "In this Year of Our Lord one Thousand,
Six Hundred and Forty Seven". The document - a parchment
with the Royal Seal of England still attached - constituted
a Trust indenturing my ancestor, <u>et</u>. <u>al</u>. for a 999-year term
as trustee for the property named. The parchment was signed
by "Charles Stuart Rex Of England, France, and Ireland
King" - Charles I.

Knowing nothing about such matters, I consulted
lawyers. They determined the document was genuine, that a
trust had been established by the British King Charles I and
that its original trustee had been my ancestor, and that -
as a matter of law - it could not be broken, the British
monarch then - and still - being the Supreme Head of the
Judiciary in the United Kingdom. Also as a matter of law,
the trust was an operative entity, under the provisions of
which I, as the remaining male heir, was the responsible
trustee. However, it had clearly been inoperative for as
long as anyone could remember. Shares certified from "The
Dheli & Punjab Railway" and other such antiquated relics -
seemingly unredeemed still - were with the trust charter.
Successive charters endorsed by successive British monarchs
were with the original one as well.

It was determined that sub-trusts - subsidiaries -
should be formed at once, under the grandfathering precepts
of the original 17th-century charter. Out of the air, I
decided that 4000 such subsidiaries would be formed as

non-domiciled entities, governed under the plural and
simultaneous governments of all the nations of the world
which were non-Communist.

Between the months of September 19, 1969 and
February 15, 1970, these 4000 charters were printed and
recorded in a register. These were numbered, prefixed by
"No. SSR/647/". The first was chosen to be the common
trustee entity for the remaining 3,999. None could be
recorded in any one country. Doing so would have given the
country of registration some prior-claim taxation ability.
For this reason, the Register of the 4000 entities was kept
in the constant custody of myself as the recorded
sole-signator of record of the original trust which we named
"The International Equity Trust". We decided to call the
group of sub-trusts "The Sovereign Charter Trust Group".
This main group was then subdivided into the Sodalitas Trust
Group - comprised of the administrative, in-house members
whose activities were to be coordinated by and through a
board of directors known as The Trustee's Directorate Body.
The remaining trusts were to have been sold/leased as
tax-shelters to sundry third parties for the fee of 20% of
the total tax liability saved by the client using the trust
for this purpose, ie. without one of our trusts - a tax
liability of $100,000, but with one of our trusts - at a
cost to the client of $20,000 - a nil tax liability.

In 1969, lawyers advised us that the only problem
we faced was the taxation authorities' propensity to
arbitrarily state that our trusts were a non-entity but that
they would be protected from taxation anywhere worldwide by
legislation once proof positive was available that they had
been alive as artificial persons for twelve years. My local

(Telling Time, Page 3 of 26)

****TOP SECRET****

home-town lawyer had counter-endorsed the Register under
every page, and the 4000 trusts were "born", ie. chartered
between September 19, 1969 and February 15, 1970.
Accordingly, I determined that I should continue my business
enterprises for another twelve years and then simply sell or
lease out the 3,999 trusts at either a flat fee or by the
20%-of-taxes-saved formula - and use the proceeds, in part,
to re-determine the what, where, why, and when concerning
the assets of the original trust.

During the years that followed, I became more and
more diversified and made sound commercial contacts all over
the globe. Increasingly, my fees and commissions were being
paid to me in differing currencies. This brought my
attention to their differing interest rates and who, in
fact, it is who determines which currencies are loaned at
which rates. I discovered that a minute cartel controlled
all banking policies worldwide, and that the provision or
non-provision of "money" was all-controlling.

As my reputation as a finder of the unusual at a
fair price grew, I with my colleagues began to realize that
there was considerable resistance throughout the
conventional financial markets to "entrepreneurs". Highly
determined but very independently-minded individuals were
not at all welcome in "normal" banking circles. There was a
very real need in the independent business communities
throughout the world for alternative credit facilities to
properly and fairly provide for entrepreneurial needs - a
window in the market for them between new venture capital
and died-in-the-wool conventional business capital. We
decided that, in a wholly novel and independent manner, our
loosely connected but highly respected circle of

(Telling Time, Page 4 of 26)

****TOP SECRET****

"middle-men" would become providers of capital for our
established clients all over the world. Independent
credit/capital sources in the Middle East and elsewhere, and
several substantial private placement arrangements were
made, first between ourselves and our investors and
subsequently between ourselves and the users of those
investments. We chose to take a minimal intermediary fee
but retain a non-working but joint-venture/profit-sharing
interest in many of the enterprises capitalized by our
investors. We did find that there were never enough
investors to be found. Otherwise, everyone seemed content.

        Like many arrogant and foolish young men before
me, I tended to advertise my financial success. I grew
headstrong. The local small town police force began to
watch me and became a significant nuisance, stopping me for
tires, speeding, etc., etc. I started a butcher business
and again made a significant success of it, also in my
hometown area. My success meant the loss of trade by my
competition. My premises were burgled successively, and
soon insurers would not insure me. I provided my own
deterrent. I rigged a "loaded shotgun" sign outside of my
premises and inside the coldstore placed a very lifelike
loaded shotgun and trip alarm system for anyone thinking of
again stealing my property as uninsured thousands had
already been stolen. The local police arrested me for
setting a man-trap with intent to endanger life. My intent,
quite obviously, was to protect my property, so I was very
properly acquitted of this foolish charge against me.

        Having been advised not to rig up any such device
again, I purchased a young mountain lion as a "guard dog" to
continue to dissuade any would-be thieves. With 20-20

(Telling Time, Page 5 of 26)

****TOP SECRET****

hindsight I realize that was not an appropriate thing to do.
I began to be a minor celebrity in my little country town,
and the local police were thoroughly incensed that the
charges against me had been dropped. I had become something
of a target. My "high profile" was not working for me. By
this time, because of my motoring offenses and the publicity
resulting from the trial and the mountain lion, my family
all but disowned me. I made it my business to establish
exactly who it was in the local police force who was
instigating my problems. It was no lesser man than Inspector
Goldsworthy. I hired people to watch his activities and it
came out that he was involved with drug importing.

The information supplied to me was that
Goldsworthy had an aged mother in Plymouth, England whom he
used as an excuse to make frequent trips there from North
Devon, but in fact he was met there by individuals who were
delivering illegal drugs to him. There was no way of
establishing for certain if such was the case. The people I
had been paying to follow him were not professionals. I
felt it was time to hand the matter over into professional
hands though, and I did so. Almost at once this particular
inspector left the North Devon area.

Word came back to me from different sources,
probably the result of one of the two people I had employed
to follow Goldsworthy talking carelessly, that Goldsworthy's
subordinates on the local police force were going to get
even. The harassment grew to overwhelming proportions. For
example, a hunting trip with authorized shotguns locked in
my car under a blanket in the backseat became "having a
loaded shotgun in a public place". Was one of my guns left
loaded? It would have been a first and only time. Can the

(Telling Time, Page 6 of 26)

****TOP SECRET****

inside of my locked car be a "public place"? But my car was
in a public car park, so the court upheld the conviction.

          The next two experiences originated with a
"friend" who subsequently admitted to me that he had agreed
to doing two things in return for not being prosecuted by
the same local police force. He sold me a dinghy and gave
me a pair of boots. Both were stolen property and I was
convicted of stealing and receiving them respectively.
Fines were imposed. I realized finally that I had no
prospect of leading a civilized life in my birthplace, so I
left the U.K. and came to the U.S. to try to establish a
new, unsullied life.

          Between 1980-4, I simply made contacts and
conducted no business beyond consultancy. I generated
little money for myself. I lived for the most part on the
money I'd made in Europe during the '70's.

          I was in the process of suing my local bank
manager and Mssrs. Barclays' Bank for multiple
contraventions of The Banking Act when I left England. One
of the "enemies" I'd made in England was a solicitor who had
given me very bad advice and then had the effrontery to
charge me for it. He was a close friend of my local bank
manager. During my absence from England he sent me a bill
for about $2000 - a final demand - and then obtained a
judgement order and a personal bankruptcy order - all
without my knowledge until I returned some five months
later. I am certain it was done to thwart my lawsuit
against Mssrs. Barclays' Bank. In England, once adjudged
bankrupt, one may not sustain any lawsuits at all. I

          (Telling Time, Page 7 of 26)

****TOP SECRET****

immediately left England again and rearranged all my assets
so that I was not in violation of the U.K. bankruptcy laws.
I also obtained a U.S. Visa for Business Purposes.

In 1983 or 1984, the Trustee of The Sovereign
Charter Trust Group was recorded as a client of the Oklahoma
Trust Company, Oklahoma City, Oklahoma, Rand Everest -
C.E.O. It had become necessary to become more visible
within the U.S. Little if any business was done with
Oklahoma, save using it as a depository for some of the
Sodalitas Trust Group's Private Placement Commercial Paper.

Outside of the jurisdiction of The Securities
Exchange Commission, exclusively upon a private placement
basis, The International Equity Trust began at this time to
place its paper in commercial situations worldwide.

Professional third-party geologists determined by
core-testing that the actual assayed content of nine
sections of gold/silver-containing properties "conveyed,
bartered, and assigned unseverably" to the Sovereign Charter
Trust Group in 1980-1 consistently down to the assayed depth
of 160 feet - was a minimum of one half ounce of gold per
tonne (cubic yard) and up to 10 ounces of silver per tonne
(cubic yard) over the entire nine square miles and beyond.
Geological surveys confirmed that these properties and the
acreage adjoining had once been a significantly large lake
fed by numerous streams from the Rocky Mountains. Over the
millennia, considerable quantities of gold and silver had
been washed down to the lakebed.

Under the Equal Rights Doctrine - the very
cornerstone of the national heritage of the United States of

(<u>Telling</u> <u>Time</u>, Page 8 of 26)

America - with these nine square miles' worth of gold and
silver deposits, The Sovereign Charter Trust Group was
endowed with a very considerable portfolio of assets. The
determination was made that the physical worth of those
assets, congruent to and parallel to comparable entities in
the public sector, would be used via the production of
commercial private placement paper to generate liquidity of
a sufficiency to establish the wholly independent credit
facility needed throughout the secondary financial market to
fill the "middlemen's window" in that market. Between
1982-3 and 1985-6 a considerable volume of face-value
long-term maturity paper - private placement "Prime Capital
Notes" was issued by the International Equity Trust for and
on behalf of the seven trusts which owned the aforesaid gold
and silver deposits.

An ultra-conservative system of checks and
balances was instituted by the Directorate Members of The
International Equity Trust under the chairmanship and C.E.O.
authority of the undersigned. Further applying the Equal
Rights Doctrine of the United States to our private
placement policy, I and my colleagues determined that in
order to properly reflect the value of the gold and silver
we had acquired it was necessary to establish a minimum
possible value and use it as our represented maximum
benchmark. This way, there could never be any question of
misrepresentation instituted against us. In order to
further insulate ourselves from any such charge, we
determined that our "paper" was to present itself only upon
a private placement basis throughout its "life" in the
secondary markets. Both safety features were built into our
private placement issue of paper as irrevocable and
unconditional prerequisites of its issue.

(Telling Time, Page 9 of 26)

****TOP SECRET****

The International Equity Trust, in its capacity as plenipotentiarial fiduciary trustee for The Sodalitas Trust Group (the administrative in-house members of The Sovereign Charter Trust Group) was and is the only authorized issuer of the group's Private Placement Prime Capital Notes. Such issue may not occur in any circumstance, save and except that the seven asset-owning trusts into whose custodial possession the group assets are placed all independently agree, each through their sole guardian/signator(s), that such Issuance is appropriate and acceptable. Such independently-arrived-at and mandatorily unanimous agreement to so issue must be confirmed in writing by each of the seven trusts' sole guardian/signator(s) of record and issued to The International Equity Trust in Official Memorandum format before such private placement paper may be issued. The circumstance of issuance was so made properly accountable.

The face value of the paper was likewise properly and strictly controlled. The Sovereign Charter Trust Group's asset base - initially the aforesaid gold and silver deposits and subsequently also real property comprising over 517,000 acres (surface and minerals) would and shall never, under the terms of the unseverable policy of The Sovereign Charter Trust Group's senior administrative decision-making body The Governing Chapter, be encumbered by debt beyond a one quarter volume. That means that for each certified $100 of the asset base no more than $25 of face-value private placement paper may be in existence. The reasoning behind this very conservative policy was and is that the ultimate credit facility which was being prepared for in the early '80's with this issuance of paper and the accumulation of assets, was never to find itself over-extended. An

(Telling Time, Page 10 of 26)

unquestioned and unquestionable safety feature ever present within each facet of the new facility was that thus none of its component parts would ever be in a position of insolvency.

For administrative purposes, three differently captioned documentary instruments were used. Each was a Private Placement Promissory Note. Each constituted a Zero Coupon instrument, ie. a promise to pay a final due-date figure in the future comprised of both the principal sum and the interest thereon accrued. All three instruments were referred to as "Prime Capital Notes" but one was also called a "Bill of Exchange", one a "Notice of Acceptance", and one as far as I can remember an "Indenture". "Bills of Exchange were used when the recipient's business need was simply to increase their asset base now in exchange for equity in such business in perpetuity. "Notices of Acceptance" were used in situations where the recipient's business need was both to increase their asset base and to become affiliated with a or a member within The Sovereign Charter Trust Group by placing such business and/or its owners within the framework of one of the group's trusts. "Indentures" were used exclusively on an in-house basis among the various members, associates, and affiliates of the Sodalitas Trust Group.

* ** *** ** *

The formula determined upon by The Directorate Body of Trustees was as follows:

Asset Base 100 - Paper Liability Maximum Aggregate @25 = AAA
Asset Base 100 - Paper Liability Maximum Aggregate @33 = AA
Asset Base 100 - Paper Liability Maximum Aggregate @50 = A
Asset Base 100 - Paper Liability Maximum Aggregate @66 = D.

(Telling Time, Page 11 of 26)

The private rating of our associate and affiliate business entities began at the beginning of 1986. Our own group's paper was mandated by Group Policy as determined by the Governing Chapter never to exceed an exposure factor of 25% of the group's in-house assets, *ie*. the assets owned by the Sodalitas Trust Group's seven Primary Members, and was accordingly qualified by our International Finance Counsel Ltd. as a Private Placement AAA rated Promissory Note.

In 1984, one portion of our gold reserves was exchanged in an Asset Barter-Exchange Agreement with the sole surviving owner of over 517,000 acres of real property (surface and mineral). The Group's acquisition of such property was made unseverable under the provisions of Article I - Section 10, Clause i of The U.S. Constitution. After such acquisition, the net worth of the Sodalitas Trust Group by and through said seven Primary Grade I Member trusts was estimated as follows:

(<u>Note</u>: Some further eleven sections of the same gold-bearing property was being disputed at the time and therefore not counted, although a defendable title thereto was and is held.)

1. Nine (9) Sections (square miles) x 640 acres x 4840 square yards per acre x 53 yards (the 160-foot depth) = 1,477,555,200 cubic yards.

2. 1,477,555,200 cubic yards x ½ ounce = 738,777,600 ounces of gold in the 9 square miles.

3. 738,777,600 ounces - 6,000,000 assigned in exchange for the 517,000 acres = 732,777,600 ounces of gold.

(<u>Telling Time</u>, Page 12 of 26)

4. 732,777,600 @ - say - $250 per ounce = $183,194,400,000.
    517,000 acres @ - say - $500 per acre = $ 258,500,000.
    1,100,000 High Grade low sulphur coal
            at - say - $10 per.............= $ 11,000,000,000.
    (Oil, gas, and timber reserves not reckoned)

                                              _____

                                              $194,452,900,000

    By June 18, 1986, liabilities
    outstanding, inclusive of Notes c/s at
    $12-$13Billion, was approximately..... $ 14,375,000,000

                                              _____

                                              $180,077,900,000.

On this basis I made representations to parties before
June 18, 1986 that The International Equity Trust controlled
assets "in excess of $152 Billion". It did, and it still
does.

        This report concerns those assets' ability to
properly reinstate the power and authority of Congress to
govern without deference to those to whom it presently owes
the National Debt and its life.

        On June 18, 1986, at the invitation of Attorney
Ms. Wendy Alison Nora (an ex-Recorder who had been forced to
resign from her position in the State of Wisconsin according
to her subsequent disclosure to me) for and on behalf of
"not less than 40" of the Sovereign Charter Trust Group's
trusts - including the seven who own the nine square miles
of gold and silver reserves and the 517,000 acres - The
International Equity Trust purchased The Lac Qui Parle

                (Telling Time, Page 13 of 26)

_____

****TOP SECRET****

Bancorporation, Inc. Said entity was and is authorized
under Section 225.4 <u>et</u>. <u>seq</u>. of 12 CFR to "act as a bank -
buy and sell securities - underwrite insurance - municipal
bonds and commercial paper," <u>etc</u>. This Holding Company
owned and owns a financial entity named The State Bank of
Boyd. Technically, The State Bank of Boyd (Minnesota) was
declared closed as a bank by The Federal Reserve System in
1984. On March 31, 1986, The Minnesota State Supreme Court
ruled that The State Bank of Boyd was not in liquidation nor
in bankruptcy, but rather that its assets and liabilities
only had been sold to the Bank of Madison - which later
changed its name to The Lac Qui Parle Bank. (<u>Note</u>: NOT to
be confused with The Lac Qui Parle Bancorporation, Inc.)

Highly unconventionally but not unlawfully, as
soon as we purchased The Lac Qui Parle Bancorporation, Inc.
(ours), it was the recipient of a Sodalitas Trust Group's
Promissory Note, due and payable (from memory) on August 1,
1999, in a figure of $2,000,000,000 with a minimum yield
factor included therein (a Zero Coupon Note) which provided
a then current value of approximately $1,672,000. A part of
the acquisition contract whereby The International Equity
Trust purchased the Holding Company and its wholly-owned
subsidiary The State Bank of Boyd was that, under the
aforesaid provisions of 12 CFR Section 225.4 <u>et</u>. <u>seq</u>., the
Holding Company at once and thereby extended a
$1,200,000,000 line of credit to the subsidiary under the
strict understanding that said subsidiary was under the
direct supervision of its parent entity The Lac Qui Parle
Bancorporation, Inc. by and through its owners' Trustee, The
International Equity Trust. The first and foremost
directive was that The State Bank of Boyd enjoyed a strictly
limited authorization, ONLY AS THE SERVICE AGENT OF

(<u>Telling Time</u>, Page 14 of 26)

ITS PARENT, to extend credit ONLY UP TO AN AGGREGATE
FIGURE OF 87½% (7/8ths) of the credit extended to it by its
parent, ie. $1,050,000,000 of the $1,200,000,000.

The State Bank of Boyd WAS closed down as a bank.
It was not a non-viable corporate entity. It was not
"defunct". It did not have a banking charter despite the
fact that Attorney Nora confirmed to The Minnesota State
Commissioner of Commerce that she took the legal position
that "it was in our possession constructively as a matter of
law". I took the position that, since the purpose of The
Sovereign Charter Trust Group's acquisition of The Lac Qui
Parle Bancorporation was primarily to outwit and outmaneuver
the private owners of the Federal Reserve System and to
provide an alternative credit system for the peoples and
governments of the world - OUTSIDE of their manipulative
controlled climate, we would NOT presume to overtly
contravene the Minnesota State Banking authorities but
rather, use the State Bank of Boyd in its ONLY corporate
status as the SERVICE AGENT for The Lac Qui Parle
Bancorporation, Inc., which was itself authorized by
legislation to "Act as a Bank".

The alternative credit facility which was
presented to the Directorate Body of The International
Equity Trust by our "think-tank" was, in my estimation,
nothing short of brilliant. After some deliberation, we
decided to refer to our new, copyrighted system as "The
Reconomy System".

The Reconomy System is comprised of a series of
individual self-help, socio-economic programs. As far as my
memory serves me, a total of 170 different programs were

(Telling Time, Page 15 of 26)

****TOP SECRET****

developed.   The **Reconomy** Program restricts itself to two
separate functions.   One is the provision of interest-exempt
credit facilities for private business users. The other is
the provision of limited non-repayable grant facilities for
what we chose to regard as "Critical Need" areas of society,
eg. the homeless, drug and alcohol abuse victims, low-income
students, and schools and universities which receive no
federal funds.   These were and are national programs.

During the late summer of 1985, The International
Equity Trust was approached by a few of the debtor nations.
They were complaining bitterly that the owners of the banks,
particularly in the U.S., to which their countries were
indebted, through the International Monetary Fund were
calling for revisions and amendments to those nations'
constitutions, the better to accommodate the corporate
associates of those bank-owners in those corporations'
designs to establish operations within the nations
concerned.

For those of you who are not aware, it is
generally agreed within informed circles that the Presidency
of James Earl Carter was orchestrated and primarily paid-for
in campaign funds by various "inner circle" members of the
Trilateral Commission.   After the effective power and
authority of The Federal Reserve System was shifted from a
Washington, DC Board of Directors to the so-called
"independent" shareholders of the twelve regional Federal
Reserve Banks - the voting shareholders of which in
controlling proportion are all "coincidentally" members of
The Trilateral Commission - Jimmy Carter endorsed Paul
Volker's "Fractional Reserve Lending" policy.   It alone
became the root cause of the inflation-recession and

****TOP SECRET****

asset/gross sales-collateral cycles which - if you examine
the statistics - are orchestrated in four yearly trends.
Fractional reserve lending, an exclusive ability of only
Federal Reserve member institutions, is wholly and solely
responsible for the fact that the nation's money supply in
circulation is in fact comprised of over 97% credit for
which nowhere on earth has there ever existed the printed
currency equivalent.

It was fractional reserve lending which was
swiftly instituted immediately before high-ranking U.S.
government officials persuaded the Nigerian Prime Minister
to increase the price of Nigerian Crude Oil which he did,
immediately prior to losing his life in a coup which was
orchestrated by U.S. covert para-military personnel trained
in Belize (then British Honduras). The Nigerian Prime
Minister's life lasted "coincidentally" until the U.S
officials had flown on to Kuwait and persuaded its oil
producers to sell their oil at the inflated price of $30 per
barrel.

Why were these astute U.S. emissaries prepared to
purchase the Arabs' oil at this hugely inflated price? The
answer is both awesome and terrifying. U.S. government
officials were prepared and authorized to agree to purchase
the oil from the Persian Gulf states and the United Arab
Emirates upon two seemingly innocuous conditions. The first
condition was that O.P.E.C. - which was to have so much
anti-Arab propaganda spewed up against it later - was to
become a reality and insist that all oil sales worldwide
were in the future to be dollar-denominated. The second and
more sinister condition foisted upon the unsuspecting Arabs
was the the U.S. oil companies purchasing the crude would

(Telling Time, Page 17 Of 26)

---

not remit the sales proceeds back to the Middle East.
Rather, the Arabs were invited as a prerequisite of sale at
the inflated price to purchase long-term, 20 and 30-year
Certificates of Deposit locked into their depositor banks.

(Note: Readers are strongly invited to investigate, as did
investigators within our Group, the "coincidental"
relationships between the owner-controllers of the
purchasing oil companies and the owner-controllers of the
banks from which the Arabs "chose" to purchase their 20 and
30-year C.D.'s)

In simplest terms, what IS this "fractional
reserve lending"? As evidenced by the fact that the money
in circulation cannot be matched with currency in existence
save in a negative ratio of about 66.6 to 1, it is fraud.
Can YOU lend anyone $1 if 66.6¢ of it has never been coined?
The answer is "yes" if you are a member of The Federal
Reserve System and not a humble licensee.

In order to evaluate the extent of the fraud of
fractional reserve lending as a matter of law, it is time to
examine the corruption practiced against "We the People" of
the U.S. as a result of its operation. Let us look at a
tiny example of the O.P.E.C./U.S. Prime Bank scenario:

An oil company issues a check for $1Million to an
Arab seller's stateside agent. The figures are crossed out
of the oil company's account at, say, Chase Manhattan and
inserted into a 30-year Certificate of Deposit in the Arab's
name on the computer. The Arab has been paid. Who then
owns Standard Oil? Who then owns Chase Manhattan?

(Telling Time. Page 18 of 26)

****TOP SECRET****

What happens next? The crude is refined. The costs and profits are passed on to the U.S. public. "That dirty Arab Cartel" is blamed. But at $2 per gallon it is the oil company's account which receives the revenue.

Meanwhile, what is happening to that Arab's account? It shows $1Million. In fact the bank in our example, Chase Manhattan, has deposited that $1Million - a piece of paper with $1Million written on it - to The Federal Reserve Clearing System which "pursuant to Fractional Reserve Lending Policy" authorizes Chase Manhattan to loan at "x60" SIXTY MILLION to Mexico, Brazil, the U.S. Congress - whomever it pleases - promulgating the overwhelming falsehood that there is too much currency in the market and not enough borrowers.

Concurrently, the U.S. Congress purportedly owes approximately $65Million per week for the next 2000 years providing that as of now not one further dime is ever spent and there is a 2000-year moratorium on all interest charges to Congress. Its second is the United Arab Emirates being paid about 7% per $1Million in oil revenue.

And those trusted pillars of society The Federal Reserve Members - for every $1Million recorded due in about 25 years to the Arab - has the burden of paying that Arab about $70,000 per year and is only making from the White House a STAGGERING $6Million per year and REQUIRING at the same time $60Million per year as repayment because of Trilateral originated policy issued by Congress.

We owe this all to the kind fiscal servants of America and her People. In 1912 $400,000,000 was owed to

(Telling Time, Page 19 Of 26)

Congress and today $6,500,000,000,000 is owed <u>by</u> Congress!

A radical I am not. A one-time farmer and now-forever-branded-criminal - permanently humbled in awe of the extent of the above-evidenced megalomania, I am.

* ** *** ** *

I terminated my business in England in about 1978. Soon afterwards, I was terminated from being an individual with whom anyone could conduct business in England, as a result of the warped and crippled mind of a banker and his stooge. I was invited to America by American strangers from Texas. They have their own horror stories to tell. They never will. Their lives are at stake. Suffice it to say that they, Mr. John Connelly (since bankrupted), Governor Clemence (now about to be ousted by the same force), the Shah of Iran (whose illness became authentic only after arriving in protective custody at a U.S. Airforce base), a German banker (also assassinated by persons trained in British Honduras) and an Austrian industrialist (now pronounced insane) - were all involved in the silver fiasco. Why? To properly authenticate Texan and U.S. currency - backed with 371¼ grains of silver per ounce as the unrepealed Money-of-Account laws decree. I learned these true horror stories <u>after</u> I had rejoiced in my now-proven-to-have-been-assinine belief in the U.S. Constitution.

On June 18, 1986, in my recorded capacity as sole Signator of Record for The International Equity Trust in its lawful capacity a sole Trustee of Record for the 3,999 other trusts - grandfathered under and as sub-trusts of an

(<u>Telling</u> <u>Time</u>, Page 20 of 26)

****TOP SECRET****

authentic trust established when only the law of
force-of-arms existed on the North American continent,
trusts which wholly supersede taxation ANYWHERE, I signed an
agreement constituting "Obligations of Contract". I knew
they could not be impaired. Article I, Section 10, Clause i
of YOUR Constitution decrees it. The International Equity
Trust so purchased that Bank Holding Company "authorized to
extend credit nationally and internationally" NOT for itself
but for 40 trusts - none of the other 39 of which had any
idea that the others were likewise buying - thereby
defeating The Federal Reserve's controlling policy to obtain
its permission to so purchase. One of those 40 trusts was
The Sovereign Trust of North America. As a matter of public
record recorded under the provisions of Article IV, Section
1 which mandates such fact to be given full faith and
credit, the beneficiaries of The Sovereign Trust of North
America include the U.S. Congress, each State of the Union's
governments, and the Body Politic - "We the People of the
United States." Other trusts' beneficiaries are other
non-Communist governments.

(Note: Please examine Public Records numbered 2401094 and
2406834 in Ramsey County, Minnesota - about 300 pages. IF
you are told that no such record exists, please contact the
undersigned who will inform you where preserved, certified
copies thereof are located.)

        A Declaratory Statement, dated between June 18,
1986 and July 3, 1986 was sent to Mr. Paul Volker, then
Chairman of The Board of Directors of The Federal Reserve
System. In it, issued and signed by me in my capacity
aforesaid, I disclosed to him that our group had allocated a
quantum of $500,000,000 per U.S. State for the

(Telling Time, Page 21 of 26)

****TOP SECRET****

implementation of our United States **Reconomy System** - not as
a competitor per se but rather as a sophisticated
alternative credit source whose purpose was entirely limited
to its prospective outlets. The phone number of Attorney
Nora was enclosed with a clear and unequivocal request to
contact us in the event that our Program was in any way in
contravention of the Constitution and laws made on pursuance
thereto in that it relied for its authenticity upon the same
laws which permitted The Federal Reserve to enforce its
policies - because our Holding Company was in part owned by
the U.S. This constituted it as an independent Agent of the
United States under Title 18 USC, Section 6. We
unconditionally covenanted to Congress an equity
participation of a minimum of $750,000,000 per month, to
each State an anticipated $40,000,000, a certain $35,000,000
per month, and to the Body Politic "We the People" upon a
state by state basis about $150,000,000 per month. The
balance of the income generated monthly save 5% operating
expenses and a 10% fee belonged in perpetuity to the
investors, whose assets backed our facility in a minimum
ratio in our favor of "x3" in assets and "x8/7ths" in terms
of our 12 CFR, Section 225.4-authorized U.S. Bank Holding
Company's service agents' maximum possible liabilities.

On June 19, 1986, having so purchased The Lac Qui
Parle Bancorporation out of the future control of The
Federal Reserve System, in order to shore up its status as
an authorized U.S. Bank Holding Company, another banking
entity owned by The International Equity Trust was assigned
under The Lac Qui Parle Bancorporation, Inc.'s ownership.

A certain amount of "cash" had been set aside to
cover the "float". The assets had been duly assigned. The

(Telling Time, Page 22 of 26)

****TOP SECRET****

law was clear that we were authorized. Paul Volker had not
come back to us within the ten days under the law of laches
which I had invoked in my letter. Unconventional or not,
we were in business.

Certain of our customers were approved for
immediate credit lines. Certain of our operatives were
appointed as Regional Directors over a five-state area each,
endowed with the responsibility to open ten offices per
State. Each was provided with an interest pre-paid credit
line of $50,000,000. Acting Service Agent, first tier
retailer for The Lac Qui Parle Bancorporation's
credit-extending enterprise, the subsidiary The State Bank
of Boyd, in its own right, also enjoyed a new credit line of
$1,200,000 but was obligated not to extend more than "x7/8"
($1,050,000) to insulate itself from insolvency.

With the knowledge that checks are not
"securities" as so decreed in the Securities and Exchange
Act - an act made in pursuance to the Constitution and
hence, under Article VI supreme in its force and effect -
Attorney Nora ordered cashiers' checks and personalized
checks from the appropriate printers for The State Bank of
Boyd. She and I both knew and later re-confirmed at my
trial that there exists no legislation which prohibits
anyone or any corporation from issuing its own cashiers'
checks per se. Unconventional without a doubt but unlawful
- no. We both also knew that the only restriction in terms
of The State Bank of Boyd's activities as a non-bank was
that it was physically without its Banking Charter but, as
re-confirmed at trial, the only additional ability such a
charter grants its corporate owner is the authority to take
deposits. Neither **The Reconomy System** nor any of its 170

(Telling Time, Page 23 of 26)

****T O P S E C R E T****

programs engages any of its variously tiered
instrumentalities in any deposit-taking activity. Reconomy
is an entirely restructured socio-economic equation.

On July 3, 1986, in the absence of jurisdiction,
in the absence of a valid arrest warrant, in the absolute
absence as a matter of law of any crime, I was arrested in
Georgia for "Interstate Transportation of falsely made
securities". The "securities" in question, the ONLY
securities made the subject-matter of the charges against
me, were the State Bank of Boyd checks - each one of which
was appropriately stamped on the reverse side to be
privately cleared outside of The Federal Reserve System.

Contrary to Congressional legislation, I was given
no extradition hearing but was held in Georgia for my
removal to Minnesota for arraignment.

My arraignment took place contrary to legislated
time limit proscriptions. I was also denied counsel of my
choice.

My "trial" did not take place within the statutory
maximum 90 days of my continued incarceration from July 3,
1986. I was denied permission to have witnesses. My
subpoena demands were ignored. Exculpating evidence was
precluded. When I attempted to fire my mandatory Public
Defender to better conduct the remainder of my trial myself,
I was denied.

No one would have - no one could have lost when it
was OUR assets at risk, backing OUR credit, being extended

(Telling Time, Page 24 of 26)

****TOP SECRET****

in direct accordance with Congressionally-instituted
legislation and in compliance with 12 CFR, Section 225.4 <u>et.</u>
<u>seq.</u> When I pointed this out in court and demanded that it
be produced, the court refused.

It was clear I was to be jailed. My "crimes" were
my foolishness in believing the U.S. Constitution's
guarantee of my innocence and my right to equal commercial
ability and protection - and, clearly, my arrogance in
believing that such Constitutional provisions would provide
sufficient protection against the now-obviously-corrupted
instruments of The U.S. Judicial System.

I am a British citizen. I am not a juridical
resident of D.C. under 26 USC Section 7701 (A)(39) or
otherwise. The United Nations Convention implements
Congressional GUARANTEE unto my government that I <u>shall</u>
enjoy the full weight of the protection of the laws of the
United States. Instead, well beyond the purview of any
legislative authority, I was subjected in an Admiralty
jurisdictionary Article I Tribunal called "United States
District Court" - no Constitutionally proper district court
of the United States - to a trial for an invented "crime"
that is legislatively impossible to commit. Mr. Harbour,
the U.S. Probation Service Congressional delegate, made a
"mistake" with my sentencing guidelines which should have
been worst-possible-case 14-18 months. He instead provided
the court with a 52-64 month range. Given the judge's
appointment by Trilateral President Carter and relationship
to the Federal Reserve Director, the court quite
"appropriately" sentenced me to TEN YEARS in prison - not to
protect the People but to protect The Federal Reserve's
fraud against the People!! I SO PUBLICLY ACCUSE!!

(<u>Telling</u> <u>Time</u>, Page 25 of 26)

****TOP SECRET****

During the past four years of this sentence,
evidence upon evidence of civil and criminal conspiracy has
been presented to such lofty persons as Senator Joseph
Biden, the Attorney General, The Inspector General, and
more - to no avail, save continued and continuing abuse of
process and overt falsehoods being made part of court
records - proven to be false by conflicting U.S. government
agency source records. Where - to whom - can one turn to
regain - as a Human Right, a Civil Right, and both a
Constitutional and N.A.T.O-instituted Right - my freedom?

NEVER was there intent to defraud - ONLY, EVER to
wrest from the chains of debt a suffocating government and
her people.

I SO SWEAR, TO THE ABSOLUTE BEST OF MY KNOWLEDGE
BELIEF AND RECOLLECTION: THE FOREGOING IS THE
UNADULTERATED TRUTH.

****TOP SECRET****

The foregoing, entitled "Telling Time" was duly served by certified mail postage prepaid upon:

1. Senator Thurmon
2. Senator Graham
3. Senator Helms
4. Congressman Crane
5. Congressman Hefner

at their respective addresses on Capitol Hill this 30th Day of July, 1990.

Chapter 17

DOCUMENTATION: U.S. ARMY INTELLIGENCE CONNECTION WITH SATANIC CHURCH

DEPARTMENT OF THE ARMY
UNITED STATES ARMY CRIMINAL INVESTIGATION COMMAND
5611 COLUMBIA PIKE
. FALLS CHURCH, VA 22041 ·

REPLY TO
ATTENTION OF

CIPP-PD

SUBJECT: Possible Adverse Suitability Information

HQDA (DAMI-CIS/Mr. Dill)
WASH DC 20310

1. Ref telecon LTC Jones and Mr. Burkley.

2. IAW referenced telecon the following information is provided:

    a. On 21 July 1981 the undersigned was contacted by Officer Sandi
Daly, Intelligence Unit, San Francisco, CA, Police Department (Phone:
(415) 553-1133). She related that in the course of an investigation of
an alleged satanic cult known as the "Temple of Set," she came across
information that the leader of the group, a Michael A. Aquino, DOB 16
October 1946, 2430 Leavenworth Street, San Francisco, was allegedly a
major in the US Army Reserve associated with a military intelligence
unit in the San Francisco area. Further, two other members of the
group, a Dennis Mann (NFI) and a Willie Browning (female - NFI) were
also USAR officers associated with an MI unit in the Los Angeles, CA,
area.

    b. An informal check with RCPAC reveals that their rolls contain
personnel with the names indicated and that Aquino is a Major, Armor,
and Mann and Browning, Captains, Military Intelligence.

3. Officer Daly was advised of the fact that a possiblity existed that
her information was accurate and that since it was not a criminal matter,
military intelligence would be advised and would likely contact her.
She indicated a willingness to share any information which they had
developed.

                                      T. C. JONES
                                      Lieutenant Colonel (P), GS
                                      Chief, Investigative Policy and
                                      Studies Division

FOR OFFICIAL USE ONLY

FOR OFFICIAL USE ONLY

Declassified

DAMI-CIS(Undated) 1st Ind
SUBJECT: Possible Adverse Suitability Information

HQDA(DAMI-CI), Washington, DC 20310   18 Nov 81

TO: Cdr, US Army Forces Command, ATTN: AFIN-CS, Ft McPherson, GA 30330

1. Confirming fonecon (Mr. Honea, FORSCOM/Mr. Pell, OACSI) concerning subject, 16 November 1981, forwarded herewith letter from USACIDC for your information and necessary action.

2. A check of the files of the Federal Bureau of Investigation concerning the Temple of Set reflected no record of such an organization.

3. Request this office be advised of your findings concerning the allegations noted in basic letter.

FOR THE ASSISTANT CHIEF OF STAFF FOR INTELLIGENCE:

DONALD P. PRESS
Colonel, GS
Director of Counterintelligence

FOR OFFICIAL USE ONLY

****TOP SECRET****

AFIN-CSP (Undated) 2d Ind
SUBJECT: Possible Adverse Suitability Information

FORSCOM, Fort McPherson, GA 30330   23 November 1981

TO: SEE DISTRIBUTION

1. References:

   a. AR 604-5.

   b. CCF, LOI 80-1

2. Forwarded as a matter possibly pertaining to a member of your command,
if local resources reveal information warranting action under reference b
above.

3. Additionally, request compliance with paragraph 3, 1st Indorsement, with
copy sent to this headquarters.

4. The names mentioned in basic communication have been tentatively identified as follows, based on data from RCPAC and CCF:

   a. AQUINO, Michael A., MAJ, 568-66-9015
      DPOB: 16 Oct 46, CA
      Address: 2430 Leavenworth St, San Francisco, CA 94133
      BI, 11 Mar 80; TS 9 Jun 81
      Assigned: Presidio of San Francisco, CA
                Directorate, RC Support

   b. MANN, Dennis K., CPT, 565-62-9323
      DPOB: 8 May 46, CA
      Address: 20729 Eagle Pass Dr, Malibu, CA 90256
      CCF Check: 67 AIRR Dossier
      Assigned: SIXTH US ARMY (USAR)
                306th PSYOPS Bn
                Bldg 415
                Fort McArthur, San Pedro, CA 90731

   c. BROWNING, Willie M., CPT, 458-78-8810
      DPOB: 15 May 46, TX
      Address: Unknown
      SBI, 15 Sep 77, TS/SI, 12 Oct 77
      Assigned: FORT HOOD, TX
                2 ARHHC HHC Div
                ATTN: G2 (SSO)

FOR THE COMMANDER:

FOR OFFICIAL USE ONLY

                              GEORGE E. DURHAM
                              LTC, GS
                              Asst Adj Gen   Declassified

★★★★TOP SECRET★★★★

AFIN-CSP (Undated) 2d Ind   23 November 1981
SUBJECT: Possible Adverse Suitability Information

DISTRIBUTION:

Commander
Sixth US Army
ATTN: AFKC-OP-IS (Mr Miyoshi)
Presidio of San Francisco, CA 94129

Commander
Ft Hood
ATTN: AFZF-DS-S (Mr Hoffman)
Fort Hood, TX 76544

Commander
Presidio of San Francisco
ATTN: AFZM-PTS-1 (Ms Liston)
Presidio of San Francisco, CA 94129

CF:
1. DA, DAMI-CIS (Mr Pell)
2. CCF-A

R-OFFICIAL USE ONLY

Declassified

AFKC-OP-IS (Undated) 3d Ind
SUBJECT: Possible Adverse Suitability Information

HQ, SIXTH US ARMY, Presidio of San Francisco, CA 94129. 9 DEC 1981

TO: Commander, US Army Forces Command, ATTN: AFIN-CSP, Fort McPherson,
GA 30330

1. Returned without action.

2. Information mentioned in paragraph 2, basic letter, concerning Michael A.
Aquino, was favorably adjudicated and Top Secret clearance granted 9 June 1981
by the US Army Central Personnel Security Clearance Facility.

3. Recommend the investigative file pertaining to Michael A. Aquino be
reviewed at the US Army Central Personnel Security Clearance Facility, Fort
George G. Meade, Maryland 20755.

FOR THE COMMANDER:

JOHN W. RICHARDS
LTC, GS
Chief, Intelligence and Security

Declassified

AFIN-CSP (undated) 4th Ind
SUBJECT: Possible Adverse Suitability Information

FORSCOM, Fort McPherson, GA 30330   18 December 1981

TO: Commander, HQDA, (DAMI-CI), Washington, DC 20310 (Mr Pell)

1. Attention is invited to previous indorsement.

2. The same "not unfavorable" and inconclusive information is generally
reported telephonically from other recipients of our 2d indorsement re
allegations in basic letter.

FOR THE COMMANDER:

CF: PCCF-A

GEORGE E. DURHAM
LTC, GS
Asst Adj Gen

Declassified

****TOP SECRET****

MEMO FOR FILE   Dated July 1, 1981
     #81-776

Intelligence: Temple of Set

History:

The Temple of Set is a satanic group under the leadership of
Michael A. Aquino. It is a splinter spin off group from
Anton LaVey's Church of Satan in San Francisco. They separated
from LeVey's organization when that organization was undergoing
a metamorphis in 1975. It is a small group but nonetheless has
several hundred members and operates on a National level.

Aquino is the official head of the organization and rules the
organization through a council of nine, who are in fact his
chief lieutenants.

An interesting aspect of the Temple of Set is its seeming
obsession with the military. One aspect of this obsession is
the group's fascination with the <u>Nazi movement with many of</u>
<u>them wearing, on occasion, World War II German uniforms and</u>
<u>insignia.</u> A more sinister aspect of their military fascination
is in the fact that Michael Aquino holds a commission as a
major in the U.S. Army reserve with his military specialty
being Military Intelligence. He purports to his members that
he reports directly to the Joint Chiefs of Staff. This is
probably a gross exaggeration but it is a fact that he holds
a major's commission and deals in the area of Military Intelligence. Two of his lieutenants, a female named Willie Browning
is also a Captain in the U.S. Army Reserve in an Intelligence
Unit out of Los Angeles. Another lieutenant in his group is
a reserve U.S. Army officer named Dennis Mann. He too is involved in Intelligence activities.

ORDER OF THE TRAPAZOID

Aquino, Michael A.

Michael Aquino, as previously stated, is the espoused head of
the Temple of Set. He is apparently well educated and holds a
PhD in Political Science, and is a Professor at Golden Gate
College in San Francisco. His specialty is Western European
Political Affairs. Aquino resides on Levenworth St. in San
Francisco, the number is believed to be 2430. He resides at
that address with his girlfriend, children of his girlfriends
and his mother. His father, separated from the family some time
ago and lives in Southern California.

Allegedly, Aquino has sexual identity problems and is known to
frequent prostitutes in San Francisco in order to become involved in various forms of Sado-masacistic sexual activities.
It is believed that Aquino is bi-sexual.

Projections:

While the Temple of Set was always be definition somewhat
bizzare, it seems to be going through its own form of metamorphasis.
They are returning to the practice of holding Black Masses, one

****TOP SECRET****

Temple of Set   Page 2

of which is scheduled for July 1981 in San Francisco, (at an
unknown hotel on Fisherman's Wharf). It is also rumored that
the group is becoming potentially more and more violent as
it recruits the less intellectual and more undesireable level
of people such as some former members of Hell's Angels and
similar motorcycle gangs. It is also rumored that they are
starting to engage in animal sacrifices. Additionally, Aquino
is speaking within the organization, that the time has come
for him to make his political moves. This is probably in relation to his position in the Army reserve.   -

End of memo

Devil Worshiper Holds Sensitive Army Post and Top Brass Say 'No Problem'

A senior U.S. military intelligence officer with a secret security clearance admits he's also the founder and high priest of a satanic church — and amazingly, the Army says "no problem"!

Lieut. Col. Michael Aquino, a 41-year-old former Green Beret, confirmed to The ENQUIRER that he's been involved in devil worship for 22 years.

He said he formed his own satanic church, the Temple of Set, in 1975 after belonging to another sect, the Church of Satan, for the previous 10 years.

"My religion has been no secret in the Army," said Col. Aquino, who served as a psychological warfare specialist in Vietnam and is now a reserve officer working full-time on extended duty at the Army's reserve personnel center in St. Louis. He admitted satanic

By CHRIS FULLER

terminology is used in his church's rituals, adding: "We are quite proud of that."

But William Gill, executive director of the Catholic War Veterans, fumed:

"This is outrageous and a national disgrace!

"It's unbelievable that an admitted devil worshiper should be allowed to hold a senior and sensitive post in the U.S. Army. This abomi-

nable situation insults the memory of those who have fought and often died to uphold the traditional values of our great country.

"Citizens have a right to expect our military to uphold the traditional values of God and country — not the evil ramblings of some satanic sect."

Col. Aquino's satanic church is advertised in the yellow pages in San Francisco, where he was stationed from 1981 to 1986. He says most members are in the U.S. and Canada, although "we have a sprinkling of members in places like Western Europe and the Pacific."

The Constitution's guar-

antee of freedom of religion protects Col. Aquino from action by the Army, said Lieut. Col. Greg Rixon, an Army public affairs officer in Washington, D.C.

"As long as an individual's religious practice remains within the limit of the law, there is no problem," Col. Rixon said.

But Catholic War Veterans director Gill blasted that stand. "For the Army to say 'no problem' is mindboggling," he said. "This disturbing situation is a problem for everyone who is concerned about national security and morality.

"The U.S. Army is no place for worshipers of the Prince of Darkness!"

EX-GREEN BERET Lieut. Col. Michael Aquino is a high priest of a satanic church.

****TOP SECRET****

368 • BEHOLD A PALE HORSE

HEADQUARTERS, IMPERIAL STORMTROOPER FORCE
Office of the Chief of Staff
MindWar Center
Hub Four

FINAL VERSION —
GOING TO MIL REVIEW (C+GSC)
+ PARAMETERS (WAR COLLEGE)
+ PSYOP COMMUNITY.

From PSYOP to MindWar: The Psychology of Victory

– by –

Colonel Paul E. Vallely

– with –

Major Michael A. Aquino

LTC John Alexander's <u>Military Review</u> article in support of "psychotronics" – intelligence and operational employment of ESP – was decidedly provocative.[1] Criticism of research in this area, based as it is on existing frontiers of scientific law, brings to mind the laughter that greeted the Italian scientist Spallanzani in 1794 when he suggested that bats navigate in the dark by means of what we now call sonar. "If they see with their ears, then do they hear with their eyes?" went the joke, but I suspect that the U.S. Navy is glad someone took the idea seriously enough to pursue it.

Psychotronic research is in its infancy, but the U.S. Army <u>already</u> possesses an <u>operational</u> weapons system designed to do what LTC Alexander would like ESP to do – except that this weapons system uses existing communications media. It seeks to map the minds of neutral and enemy individuals and then to change them in accordance with U.S. national interests. It does this on a wide scale, embracing military units, regions, nations, and blocs. In its present form it is called Psychological Operations (PSYOP).

Does PSYOP work, or is it merely a cosmetic with which field commanders would rather not be bothered?

Had that question been asked in 1970, the answer would have been that PSYOP works very well indeed. In 1967 and 1968 alone, a total of 29,276 armed Viet Cong/NVA (the equivalent of 95 enemy infantry battalions) surrendered to ARVN or

-2-

MACV forces under the Chieu Hoi amnesty program - the major PSYOP effort of the Vietnam War. At the time MACV estimated that the elimination of that same number of enemy troops in combat would have cost us 6,000 dead.[2]

On the other hand, we lost the war - not because we were out-fought, but because we were out-PSYOPed. Our national will to victory was attacked more effectively than we attacked that of the North Vietnamese and Viet Cong, and perception of this fact encouraged the enemy to hang on until the United States finally broke and ran for home.

So our PSYOP failed. It failed not because its principles were unsound, but rather because it was outmatched by the PSYOP of the enemy. The Army's efforts enjoyed some battlefield success, but MACV PSYOP did not really change the minds of the enemy populace, nor did it defend the U.S. populace at home against the propaganda of the enemy. Furthermore the enemy's PSYOP was so strong that it - not bigger armies or better weapons - overcame all of the Cobras and Spookys and ACAVs and B-52s we fielded. The lesson is not to ignore our own PSYOP capability, but rather to change it and strengthen it so that it can do precisely that kind of thing to our enemy in the next war. Better hardware is nice, but by itself it will change nothing if we do not win the war for the mind.

The first thing it is necessary to overcome is a view of PSYOP that limits it to routine, predictable, over-obvious, and hence marginally effective "leaflet and loudspeaker" applications. Battlefield devices of this sort have their place, but it should be that of an accessory to the main effort. That main effort cannot begin at the company or division level; it must originate at the national level. It must strengthen our national will to victory and it must

-3-

attack and ultimately destroy that of the enemy. It both causes and is affected
by physical combat, but it is a type of war which is fought on a far more subtle
basis as well - in the minds of the national populations involved.

So let us begin with a simple name change. We shall rid ourselves of the
self-conscious, almost "embarrassed" concept of "psychological operations". In
its place we shall create MindWar. The term is harsh and fear-inspiring, and so
it should be: It is a term of attack and victory - not one of rationalization
and coaxing and conciliation. The enemy may be offended by it; that is quite
all right as long as he is defeated by it. A definition is offered:

> MindWar is the deliberate, aggressive convincing of all
> participants in a war that we will win that war.

-It -is- deliberate in that it is a planned, systematic, and comprehensive
effort involving all levels of activity from the strategic to the tactical. It
is aggressive because opinions and attitudes must be actively changed from those
antagonistic to us to those supportive of us if we are to achieve victory. We
will not win if we content ourselves with countering opinions and attitudes
instilled by enemy governments. We must reach the people before they resolve to
support their armies, and we must reach those armies before our combat troops
ever see them on battlefields.

Compare this definition with that of psychological warfare as first offered
by General William Donovan of the OSS in his World War II-era "Basic Estimate of
Psychological Warfare":

> "Psychological warfare is the coordination and use of all means,
> including moral and physical, by which the end is attained - other
> than those of recognized military operations, but including the
> psychological exploitation of the result of those recognized military
> actions - which tend to destroy the will of the enemy to achieve

-4-

victory and to damage his political or economic capacity to do so;
which tend to deprive the enemy of the support, assistance, or
sympathy of his allies or associates or of neutrals, or to prevent his
acquisition of such support, assistance, or sympathy; or which tend to
create, maintain, or increase the will to victory of our own people
and allies and to acquire, maintain, or to increase the support,
assistance, and sympathy of neutrals."[3]

If the euphemism "psychological operations" resulted from, as one general
officer put it in a 1947 letter, "a great need for a synonym which could be used
in peacetime that would not shock the sensibilities of a citizen of democracy",
then it may have succeeded domestically.[4] On the other hand it does not seem to
have reassured the sensibilities of the Soviets, who in 1980 describe U.S. Army
PSYOP as including:

"... unpardonable methods of ideological sabotage including not just
flagrant lies, slander, and disinformation, but also political
blackmail, provocation, and terror."[5]

The reluctance with which the Army has accepted even an "antiseptic" PSYOP
component is well-documented in Colonel Alfred Paddock's brilliant treatise on
the history of the PSYOP establishment. Again and again efforts to forge this
weapon into its most effective configuration were frustrated by leaders who
could not or would not see that wars are fought and won or lost not on
battlefields but in the minds of men. As Colonel Paddock so aptly concludes:

"In a real sense, the manner in which psychological and unconventional
warfare evolved from 1941 until their union as a formal Army
capability in 1952 suggests a theme that runs throughout the history
of special warfare: the story of a hesitant and reluctant Army
attempting to cope with concepts and organizations of an
unconventional nature."[6]

According to present doctrine, PSYOP is considered an accessory to the main
effort of winning battles and wars; the term generally used is "force
multiplier". It is certainly not considered a precondition to command
decisions. Thus PSYOP cannot predetermine the political or psychogical

-5-

effectiveness of a given military action. It can only be used to paint that action in the best possible colors as it is taken.

MindWar cannot be so relegated. It is, in fact, the strategy to which tactical warfare must conform if it is to achieve maximum effectiveness. The MindWar scenario must be preeminent in the mind of the commander and must be the principal factor in his every field decision. Otherwise he sacrifices measures which actually contribute to winning the war to measures of immediate, tangible satisfaction. [Consider the rationale for "body counts" in Vietnam.]

Accordingly PSYOP "combat support" units as we now know them must become a thing of the past. MindWar teams must offer technical expertise to the commander from the onset of the planning process, and at all levels down to that of the battalion. Such teams cannot be composed - as they are now - of branch-immaterial officers and NCOs who know simply the basics of tactical propaganda operations. They must be composed of full-time experts who strive to translate the strategy of national MindWar into tactical goals which maximize the effective winning of the war and minimize loss of life. Such MindWar teams will win commanders' respect only if they can deliver on their promises.

What the Army now considers to be its most effective PSYOP - tactical PSYOP - is actually the most limited and primitive effort, due to the difficulties of formulating and delivering messages under battlefield constraints. Such efforts must continue, but they are properly seen as a reinforcement of the main MindWar effort. If we do not attack the enemy's will until he reaches the battlefield, his nation will have strengthened it as best it can. We must attack that will before it is thus locked in place. We must instill in it a predisposition to inevitable defeat. Strategic MindWar must begin the moment war is considered to

-6-

be inevitable. It must seek out the attention of the enemy nation through every available medium, and it must strike at that nation's potential soldiers before they put on their uniforms. It is in their homes and their communities that they are most vulnerable to MindWar. Was the United States defeated in the jungles of Vietnam, or was it defeated in the streets of American cities?

To this end MindWar must be <u>strategic</u> in emphasis, with tactical applications playing a reinforcing, supplementary role. In its strategic context, MindWar must reach out to friends, enemies, and neutrals alike across the globe — neither through the primitive "battlefield" leaflets and loudspeakers of PSYOP nor through the weak, imprecise, and narrow effort of psychotronics — but through the media possessed by the United States which have the capabilities to reach virtually all people on the face of the Earth. These media are, of course, the electronic media — television and radio. State of the art developments in satellite communication, video recording techniques, and laser and optical transmission of broadcasts make possible a penetration of the minds of the world such as would have been inconceivable just a few years ago. Like the sword Excalibur, we have but to reach out and seize this tool; and it can transform the world for us if we have but the courage and the integrity to guide civilization with it. If we do not accept Excalibur, then we relinquish our ability to inspire foreign cultures with our morality. If they then devise moralities unsatisfactory to us, we have no choice but to fight them on a more brutish level.

MindWar must target <u>all</u> participants if it is to be effective. It must not only weaken the enemy; it must strengthen the United States. It strengthens the United States by denying enemy propaganda access to our people, and by explaining and emphasizing to our people the rationale for our national interest

-7-

in a specific war. Under existing United States law, PSYOP units may not target American citizens. That prohibition is based upon the presumption that "propaganda" is necessarily a lie or at least a misleading half-truth, and that the government has no right to lie to the people. The Propaganda Ministry of Goebbels must not be part of the American way of life. Quite right, and so it must be axiomatic of MindWar that it always speaks the truth. Its power lies in its ability to focus recipients' attention on the truth of the future as well as that of the present. MindWar thus involves the stated promise of a truth that the United States has resolved to make real if it is not already so.

MindWar is not new. Nations' greatest – and least costly – victories have resulted from it, both in time of actual combat and in time of threatened combat. Consider the atomic attacks on Hiroshima and Nagasaki. The physical destruction of those two cities did not destroy Japan's ability to continue fighting. Rather the psychological shock of the weapons destroyed what remained of Japan's rational will to fight. Surrender followed; a long and costly ground invasion was averted.

MindWar's effectiveness is a function of its skillful use of communications media, but no greater error could be made than to confuse MindWar with merely a greater and more unprincipled propaganda effort. "Propaganda" as defined by Harold Lasswell "is the expression of opinions or actions carried out deliberately by individuals or groups with a view to influencing the opinions or actions of other individuals or groups for predetermined ends and through psychological manipulations."[7]

Propaganda, when it is recognized as such – and anything produced by a "PSYOP" unit is so recognized – is automatically assumed to be a lie or at least

-8-

a distortion of truth. Therefore it works <u>only</u> to the extent that a militarily-pressed enemy is willing to do what we want him to do. It does <u>not</u> work because we have convinced him to see the truth as we see it.

In his "Conclusions" chapter to the Army's exhaustive 1976 case-study of PSYOP techniques, L. John Martin affirms this coldly and bluntly:

> "What all this boils down to is that if our persuasive communication ends up with a net positive effect, we must attribute it to luck, not science ... The effectiveness of propaganda may be even less predictable and controllable than the effectiveness of mere persuasive communication."[8]

Correspondingly propagandists are assumed to be liars and hypocrites, willing to paint anything in attractive colors to dupe the gullible. As Jacques Ellul puts it:

> "The propagandist is not, and cannot be, a 'believer'. Moreover he cannot believe in the ideology he must use in his propaganda. He is merely a man at the service of a party, a state, or some other organization, and his task is to insure the efficiency of that organization ... If the propagandist has any political conviction, he must put it aside in order to be able to use some popular mass ideology. He cannot even share that ideology, for he must use it as an object and manipulate it without the respect that he would have for it if he believed in it. He quickly acquires contempt for these popular images and beliefs ..."[9]

Unlike PSYOP, MindWar has nothing to do with deception or even with "selected" - and therefore misleading - truth. Rather it states a <u>whole truth</u> that, if it does not now exist, will be <u>forced into existence</u> by the will of the United States. The examples of Kennedy's ultimatum to Khrushchev during the Cuban Missile Crisis and Hitler's stance at Munich may be cited. A MindWar message does not have to fit conditions of abstract credibility as do PSYOP themes; its source <u>makes</u> it credible. As Livy once said:

"The terror of the Roman name will be such that the world shall

-9-

know that, once a Roman army has laid siege to a city, nothing will move it - not the rigors of winter nor the weariness of months and years - that it knows no end but victory and is ready, if a swift and sudden stroke will not serve, to persevere until that victory is achieved."[10]

Unlike Ellul's cynical propagandist, the MindWar operative must <u>know</u> that he speaks the truth, and he must be <u>personally committed</u> to it. What he says is only a part of MindWar; the rest - and the test of its effectiveness - lies in the conviction he projects to his audience, in the rapport he establishes with it. And this is not something which can be easily faked, if in fact it can be faked at all. "Rapport", which the <u>Comprehensive</u> <u>Dictionary</u> <u>of</u> <u>Psychological</u> <u>and</u> <u>Psychoanalytical</u> <u>Terms</u> defines as "unconstrained relations of mutual confidence", approaches the subliminal; some researchers have suggested that it is itself a subconscious and perhaps even ESP-based "accent" to an overt exchange of information. Why does one believe one television newsman more than another, even though both may report the same headlines? The answer is that there is <u>rapport</u> in the former case; and it is a rapport which is recognized and cultivated by the most successful broadcasters.

We have covered the statement of inevitable truth and the conviction behind that statement; these are qualities of the MindWar operative himself. The recipient of the statement will judge such messages not only by his conscious understanding of them, but also by the mental conditions under which he receives them. The theory behind "brainwashing" was that physical torture and deprivation would weaken the mind's resistance to suggestion, and this was true to a point. But in the long run brainwashing does not work, because intelligent minds later realize their suggestibility under such conditions and therefore discount impressions and opinions inculcated accordingly.

For the mind to believe in its own decisions, it must feel that it made

---

* * * * **TOP SECRET** * * * *

-10-

those decisions without coercion. Coercive measures used by the MindWar operative, consequently, must not be detectable by ordinary means. There is no need to resort to mind-weakening drugs such as those explored by the CIA; in fact the exposure of a single such method would do unacceptable damage to MindWar's reputation for truth.[11] Existing PSYOP identifies purely-sociological factors which suggest appropriate idioms for messages. Doctrine in this area is highly developed, and the task is basically one of assembling and maintaining individuals and teams with enough expertise and experience to apply the doctrine effectively. This, however, is only the sociological dimension of target receptiveness measures. There are some purely natural conditions under which minds may become more or less receptive to ideas, and MindWar should take full advantage of such phenomena as atmospheric electromagnetic activity[12], air ionization[13], and extremely low frequency waves[14].

At the root of any decision to institute MindWar in the U.S. defense establishment is a very simple question: Do we wish to _win_ the next war in which we choose to become involved, and do we wish to do so with minimum loss of human life, at minimum expense, and in the least amount of time? If the answer is yes, then MindWar is a necessity. If we wish to trade that kind of victory for more American lives, economic disaster, and negotiated stalemates, then MindWar is inappropriate, and if used superficially will actually contribute to our defeat. In MindWar there is no substitute for victory.

-11-

Notes

1. Alexander, Lieutenant Colonel John B., "The New Mental Battlefield: 'Beam me up, Spock'" in Military Review, Vol. LX, No. 12, December 1980.

2. "Chieu Hoi: The Winning Ticket". MACV Command Information Pamphlet 6-69, March 1969.

3. Roosevelt, Kermit (Ed.), War Report of the OSS. New York: Walker and Company, 1976, Volume I, page 99.

4. Letter, Major General W.C. Wyman to Major General Lauris Norstad, 22 July 1947, quoted in Paddock, Colonel Alfred H., "Psychological and Unconventional Warfare, 1941-1952: Origins of a 'Special Warfare' Capability for the United States Army". Carlisle Barracks: U.S. Army War College, November 1979, page 77.

5. Belashchenko, T., "'Black Propaganda' from Fort Bragg" in Sovetskiy Voin. Moscow, June 1980, pages 46-47.

6. Paddock, op. cit., page 258.

7. Lasswell, Harold D. in Ellul, Jacques, Propaganda: The Formation of Men's Attitudes. New York: Random House, 1965, pages xi-xii.

8. Martin, L. John, "Effectiveness of International Propaganda" in Department of the Army Pamphlet 525-7-2 The Art and Science of Psychological Operations: Case Studies of Military Application, Volume Two. Washington, D.C.: American Institutes for Research, 1976, page 1020.

9. Ellul, Jacques, Propaganda: The Formation of Men's Attitudes. New York: Random House, 1965, pages 196-197.

10. Keller, Werner, The Etruscans. New York: Alfred A. Knopf, 1974, page 252.

11. See in particular Bowart, W.H., Operation Mind Control. New York: Dell Publishing Company, 1978.

12. Atmospheric electromagnetic (EM) activity: The human body communicates internally by EM and electrochemical impulses. The EM field displayed in Kirlian photographs, the effectiveness of acupuncture, and the body's physical responses to various types of EM radiation (X-rays, infrared radiation, visible light spectra, etc.) are all examples of human sensitivity to EM forces and fields. Atmospheric EM activity is regularly altered by such phenomena as sunspot eruptions and gravitational stresses which distort the Earth's magnetic field. Under varying external EM conditions, humans are more or less disposed to the consideration of new ideas. MindWar should be timed accordingly. Per Dr. L.J. Ravitz: "Electrodynamic field constructs add fuel to the assumption unifying living matter harmoniously with the operations of nature, postulating that each biologic thing is organized by a total dynamic pattern, the expression of an electromagnetic field no less than non-living systems; and that as points on spectrums, these two entities may at last take their positions in the organization of the universe in a way both explicable and rational ... A

-12-

tenable theory has been provided for emergence of the nervous system, developing not from functional demands, but instead deriving as a result of dynamic forces imposed on cell groups by the total field pattern. Living matter now has a definition of state based on relativity field physics, through which it has been possible to detect a measurable property of total state functions." (Ravitz, Leonard J., M.S., M.D., F.R.S.H., "Electro-magnetic Field Monitoring of Changing State-Function, Including Hypnotic States" in Journal of American Society of Psychosomatic Dentistry and Medicine, Vol. 17, No. 4, 1970.)

13. Ionization of the air: An abundance of negative condensation nucleii ("air ions") in ingested air enhances alertness and exhilaration, while an excess of positive ions enhances drowsiness and depression. Calculation of the ionic balance of a target audience's atmospheric environment will be correspondingly useful. Again this is a naturally-occurring condition – caused by such varying agents as solar ultraviolet light, lightning, and rapidly-moving water – rather than one which must be artificially created. [Detonation of nuclear weapons, however, will alter atmospheric ionization levels.] See for example Soyke, Fred and Edmonds, Alan, The Ion Effect. New York: E.P. Dutton, 1977.

14. Extremely Low Frequency (ELF) waves: ELF waves (up to 100 Hz) are once more naturally occurring, but they can also be produced artificially [such as for the Navy's Project Sanguine for submarine communication]. ELF-waves are not normally noticed by the unaided senses, yet their resonant effect upon the human body has been connected to both physiological disorders and emotional distortion. Infrasound vibration (up to 20 Hz) can subliminally influence brain activity to align itself to delta, theta, alpha, or beta wave patterns, inclining an audience toward everything from alertness to passivity. Infrasound could be used tactically, as ELF-waves endure for great distances; and it could be used in conjunction with media broadcasts as well. See Playfair, Guy L. and Hill, Scott, The Cycles of Heaven. New York: St. Martin's Press, 1978, pages 130-140.

THIS IS AN IMPORTANT RECORD
SAFEGUARD IT.

1. LAST NAME-FIRST NAME-MIDDLE NAME		2. SEX	3. SOCIAL SECURITY NUMBER	4. DATE OF BIRTH	YEAR	MONTH	DAY
COOPER, MILTON WILLIAM		M	447 44 4234		43	05	06

5. DEPARTMENT, COMPONENT AND BRANCH OR CLASS	6a. GRADE, RATE OR RANK	a. PAY GRADE	7. DATE OF RANK	YEAR	MONTH	DAY
NAVY – USN	QM1	E6		74	05	16

8a. SELECTIVE SERVICE NUMBER	b. SELECTIVE SERVICE LOCAL BOARD NUMBER, CITY, STATE AND ZIP CODE	c. HOME OF RECORD AT TIME OF ENTRY INTO ACTIVE SERVICE (Street, RFD, City, State and ZIP Code)
NA	---------------	HYATTESVILLE, MD

9a. TYPE OF SEPARATION	b. STATION OR INSTALLATION AT WHICH EFFECTED
DISCHARGED	NSA TI SFRAN CA

c. AUTHORITY AND REASON		EFFECTIVE DATE	YEAR	MONTH	DAY
--------------------------------------			75	12	11

e. CHARACTER OF SERVICE	f. TYPE OF CERTIFICATE ISSUED	10. REENLISTMENT CODE
HONORABLE	DD256N	------

11. LAST DUTY ASSIGNMENT AND MAJOR COMMAND	12. COMMAND TO WHICH TRANSFERRED
USS ORISKANY CVA 34	NA

13. TERMINAL DATE OF RESERVE/ MSS OBLIGATION			14. PLACE OF ENTRY INTO CURRENT ACTIVE SERVICE (City, State and ZIP Code)	15. DATE ENTERED ACTIVE DUTY THIS PERIOD		
YEAR	MONTH	DAY		YEAR	MONTH	DAY
NA			HONOLULU HI	69	12	31

16a. PRIMARY SPECIALTY NUMBER AND TITLE	b. RELATED CIVILIAN OCCUPATION AND D.O.T. NUMBER	18. RECORD OF SERVICE	YEARS	MONTHS	DAYS
QM 0000	911 WATER TRANS OCCUPS	(a) NET ACTIVE SERVICE THIS PERIOD	05	11	03
		(b) PRIOR ACTIVE SERVICE	07	08	12
17a. SECONDARY SPECIALTY NUMBER AND TITLE	b. RELATED CIVILIAN OCCUPATION AND D.O.T. NUMBER	(c) TOTAL ACTIVE SERVICE (a+b)	13	07	15
QM 0000	NA	(d) PRIOR INACTIVE SERVICE	00	05	16
		(e) TOTAL SERVICE FOR PAY (c+d)	14	01	01
		(f) FOREIGN AND/OR SEA SERVICE THIS PERIOD	05	11	03

19. INDOCHINA OR KOREA SERVICE SINCE AUGUST 5, 1964	20. HIGHEST EDUCATION LEVEL SUCCESSFULLY COMPLETED (In Years)		
☒ YES ☐ NO	SECONDARY/HIGH SCHOOL 12 YRS (1-12 grades) COLLEGE ___ YRS		

21. TIME LOST (Preceding Two Yrs)	22. DAYS ACCRUED LEAVE PAID	23. SERVICEMEN'S GROUP LIFE INSURANCE COVERAGE	24. DISABILITY SEVERANCE PAY	25. PERSONNEL SECURITY INVESTIGATION	
---	NO LES	☒ $5,000 ☐ $8,000 20,000. ☐ $10,000 ☐ NONE	☒ NO ☐ YES AMOUNT ___	a. TYPE BI	b. DATE COMPLETED 23JUL70

26. DECORATIONS, MEDALS, BADGES, COMMENDATIONS, CITATIONS AND CAMPAIGN RIBBONS AWARDED OR AUTHORIZED

GOOD CONDUCT MEDAL (1ST) FOR PERIOD ENDING 21JAN70 NDSM VSM (2)
VCM (D); NAVY COMMENDATION MEDAL W/COMBAT "V"; NUCR
NAVY ACHIEVEMENT MEDAL W/COMBAT "V".

27. REMARKS

MRPO 1 & C   AUTHORITY: BUPERSMAN 3840240.2A KBK RE-1
QM 1 & C

28. MAILING ADDRESS AFTER SEPARATION (Street, RFD, City, County, State and ZIP Code)	29. SIGNATURE OF PERSON BEING SEPARATED
43129 CONTINENTAL DRIVE FREMONT CA 94538	
30. TYPED NAME, GRADE AND TITLE OF AUTHORIZING OFFICER	31. SIGNATURE OF OFFICER AUTHORIZED TO SIGN
C A CENITA PNC USN ASST TO SEPS OFF BY DIR OF CO	

DD FORM 214N
1 NOV 72

PREVIOUS EDITIONS OF THIS FORM ARE OBSOLETE.
S/N 0102-002-0202

THIS IS AN IMPORTANT RECORD SAFEGUARD IT.

REPORT OF SEPARATION FROM ACTIVE DUTY
(See BUPERS INST 1900.2 series)

****TOP SECRET****

LEAVE RECORD
OFFICER - ENLISTED   S-4

I.   LEAVE ACCOUNT

LEAVE TAKEN			LEAVE CREDITED		BALANCE	SHIP OR STATION	SIGNATURE
A	B	C	D	E	F	G	H
FROM— DAY MO. YR.	TO— DAY MO. YR.	NO. DAYS	DATE DAY MO. YR.	NO. DAYS	NO. DAYS		
	CREDIT ESTABLISHED OR BROUGHT FORWARD		31 DEC 69	-0-		AFEES HONOLULU, HAWAII	W.E. BAKER, ByDirCO
22JAN70	24FEB70	34				FAU CINCPACFLT	W.E. SIEPEL, LCDR, USN
			30 JUN 70	15 1/2	-18 1/2	FAU CINCPACFLT	T. G. DOUGHERTY
LV BAL	VERF WITH PAREC, SEPT 1970					FAU, CINCPACFLT	T. G. DOUGHERTY, LT. USN
			30JUN71	30	11-1/2	FAU CINCPACFLT	D.L. CORNETT, PNCS
17JUL71	25JUL71	09				FAU CINCPACFLT	L.L. CORNETT, PNCS
02MAR72	30MAR72	29				FAU CINCPACFLT	L.L. CORNETT, PNCS
			30JUN72	30	03.5	FAU CINCPACFLT	L.L. CORNETT, PNCS
24DEC72	26DEC72	03				FAU CINCPACFLT	L.L. CORNETT, PNCM, U
04FEB73	LV BAL VRF					FAU, CINCPACFLT	L.L. CORNETT, PNCM
05FEB73	06MAR73	30				USS ORISKANY {CVA-34}	F.C. UNDERWOOD WO? USN
			30JUN73	30	+.05	USS ORISKANY	R. MALONE, PNCS
02OCT73	14OCT73	13				USS ORISKANY	R. MALONE, PNCS
			30NOV73	12.5	00	USS ORISKANY	R. MALONE, PNCS
LV BAL----DAYS			RECON----			USS ORISKANY	
			30JUN74	17.5	17.5	USS ORISKANY CVA34	M.Q. BELISARIO, PNCM
22SEP74	20OCT74	29				USS ORISKANY CVA34	M.Q. BELISARIO, PNCM

II.   RECORD CLOSING DATA

A. FINAL COMPUTATION		B. DISPOSITION (Check appropriate item)	
1. TOTAL DAYS LEAVE CREDITED (Total—Col. E)		1. BALANCE CARRIED FORWARD TO NEW RECORD	
2. TOTAL DAYS LEAVE TAKEN (Total—Col. C)		2. CASH SETTLEMENT REQUESTED	
3. BALANCE (1 minus 2)		3. OTHER (Specify)	

NAME, GRADE AND TITLE OF CERTIFYING OFFICER   SIGNATURE OF CERTIFYING OFFICER

III. NAME (Last, first, middle)   FILE/SERVICE NO.

      COOPER, Milton William   B80 17 42

NAVPERS 601-8 (Rev. 1-63)   447 44 42

                                                          NAVY—PEARL HARBOR

THIS SECTION FOR ENLISTED PERSONNEL ONLY

*See Article B2305, BuPers Manual

PAY ENTRY BASE DATE ESTABLISHED AS:							
3 NOVEMBER 1961							

SIGNATURE J. G. DE ROBLEA, LT, USN, Legal Officer
By direction of the Commanding Officer

TIME NOT SERVED (Inclusive dates)

FROM	TO	NO. DAYS LOST		CAUSE	ADJUSTED PEBD	SHIP OR STATION	SIGNATURE*
		PEBD	LEAVE				
12 MAR 71	19 MAR 71	08	01	UA	11NOV61	FAU CINCPACFLT	T. E. CORNETT PNCS, USN

NAVPERS 601-8 (1-63)

ENLISTED PERFORMANCE RECORD *See Art. B-2305, BuPers Manual

1. DATE	2. REASON	3. RATE	4. TRAITS PROFESSIONAL PERFORMANCE	MILITARY BEHAVIOR	LEADERSHIP AND SUPERVISORY ABILITY	MILITARY APPEARANCE	ADAPT-ABILITY	5. SHIP OR ACTIVITY	6. INITIALS*
21 JAN 1966	M	SN	DATE OF ENLISTMENT					CRUITRACOM, NTC, SDIEGO, CALIF.	
6 AUG 66	T	SN	LESS THAN 90 DAYS					USS TIRU (SS 416),	
16 SEP 66	P	SN	LESS THAN NINETY DAYS					USS TOMBIGBEE (AOG11)	
12DEC66	M	SN	RECOMMENDED FOR ADVANCEMENT TO QM3 (P 13-3)					USS TOMBIGBEE AOG11	
16 MAR 67	P	SN	3.6	3.2	3.4	3.8	3.2	USS TOMBIGBEE AOG11	
16OCT67	P	QM2	3.4	3.6	3.4	3.8	3.2	USS TOMBIGBEE AOG11	
29FEB68	M	QM2	RECOMMENDED FOR REENLISTMENT					USS TOMBIGBEE AOG11	
MAR 16 1968	M	QM2	FINAL TRAIT AVERAGE UPON DISCHARGE 3.50	3.40	3.40	3.80	3.20	USS TOMBIGBEE AOG11	
MAR 16 1968	P	QM2	OVERALL TRAIT AVERAGE: 3.46					USS TOMBIGBEE AOG11	
APR 14 1968	T	QM2						USS TOMBIGBEE AOG11	JFM
16NOV68	P	QM2	3.3	3.8	3.8	4.0	3.8	NAVSUPPACT, DANANG	
16MAY69	P	QM2	4.0	3.8	3.8	3.8	3.8	NAVSUPPACT, DANANG	
25 SEP 69	M	QM2	RECOMMENDED FOR REENLISTMENT					USS C BERRY DE1035	
2 OCT 69	M	QM2	FINAL TRAIT AVERAGE UPON DISCHARGE 3.72	3.64	3.64	3.84	3.56	USS C BERRY DE1035	
2 OCT 69	M	QM2	OVERALL TRAIT AVERAGE: 3.68					USS C BERRY DE1035	
2 OCT 69	T	QM2	3.8	3.8	3.8	3.8	3.8	USS C BERRY DE1035	

NAME (Last)	(First)	(Middle)	SERVICE NO.
COOPER MILTON WILLIAM 0065			8801742

ENLISTED PERFORMANCE RECORD—NAVPERS 601(Rev.3-56)   U.S. GOVERNMENT PRINTING OFFICE:1956-O-382335

9

ADMINISTRATIVE REMARKS   *See Art. B-2,105, BuPers Manual*

SHIP OR STATION
FLAG ADMINISTRATIVE UNIT, CINCPACFLT, PEARL HARBOR, HAWAII

12MAR71: On unauthorized absence from 0500 this date. Intentions unknown.

T.G. DOUGHERTY, LT, USN, PERS OFF
By direction of the C.O.

- -

23MAR71: Surrendered on board this command,at 0500, 20MAR71. Unauthorized absentee from FAU CINCPACFLT, since 0500, 12MAR71, for a period of about 8 days.

L.L. CORNETT, PNCS, USN
BY DIR OF THE C.O.

----

29 MAR 71:   COMMANDING OFFICER'S NON JUDICIAL PUNISHMENT

DATE OF OFFENSE: 12 MAR 71

NATURE OF OFFENSE: Violation of UCMJ Article 86. Unauthorized absence from 0500 12 MAR 71 to
DATE OF CAPTAIN'S MAST: 29 MAR 71   0500 20MAR 71.

NON JUDICIAL PUNISHMENT AWARDED: Reduction to the next inferior pay grade,suspended for 03 months.

L.L. CORNETT,PNCS, USN
BY DIR OF THE C.O.

----

16 May 71. A 2.6 in military behavior was indicated on COOPER's performance evaluation for the period of 17 Nov 70 to 16 May 71 due to laxity in abeying commands and regulations nonconformance of requirements set forth by his superiors, and absenting himself for 10 days from his place of duty for which non-judicial punishment was awarded.

L.L. CORNETT, PNCS, USN
BY DIR OF THE C.O.

NAME (Last, First, Middle)			SERVICE NO.	BRANCH AND CLASS
COOPER,	Milton	William	B80 17 42	USN

ADMINISTRATIVE REMARKS--NAVPERS 601-13 (Rev. 12-61)   0106-006-2300   13 2

ADMINISTRATIVE REMARKS

See Art. B-2305, BuPers Manual

SHIP OR STATION

Flag Administrative Unit, CINCPACFLT, Pearl Harbor, Hawaii

6 DEC 72:   "I have been briefed on, and understand, the spirit and intent of BUPERS Instruction 5510.11B, Subj: Nuclear Weapon Personnel Reliability Program."

Milton William COOPER

WITNESSED: L.L. CORNETT,PNCM,USN
Ass't Pers Off

----

6 DEC 72:   "Reliability screening accomplished in accordance with BUPERS Instruction 5510.11B. Results: Satisfactory."

R.P. FRITZSCHE,LT,USN
ENL PERS OFF

----

15 JAN 73: Paid FOURTH Installment of VRB in the amount of $1333.33 this date.

L.L. CORNETT, PNCM, USN
ASST PERS OFF BY DIR

- -

USS ORISKANY (CVA-34)

- -

14 MAR 73: SEA TOUR COMMENCED MAY 66.

F. C.UNDERWOOD, WO1, USN
PERS OFF BY DIR C. O.

NAME (Last, First, Middle)	SERVICE NO.	BRANCH AND CLASS
COOPER, Milton William	447-44-4234	USN

ADMINISTRATIVE REMARKS—NAVPERS 601-13 (Rev. 12-61)   13

☆ U. S. GOVERNMENT PRINTING OFFICE: 1970-979-310 310

****TOP SECRET****

ENLISTMENT CONTRACT
NAVPERS 601-1 (Rev. 2-63)

FORWARD TO BUREAU OF
NAVAL PERSONNEL
DO NOT DETACH PART II FROM ORIGINAL

EXEMPT REPORT

1. SERVICE NUMBER (Add suffix "W" if Female.)	2. HIGHEST GRADE COMPLETED	3. RATE ABBREV.	4. BRANCH & CLASS OF SERVICE	5. NAME (last, first, middle)		
B80 17 42	12	SN	USN	COOPER, MILTON WILLIAM		

6. DATE OF ENLISTMENT	7. TERM OF ENLISTMENT		8. DEPENDENCY ABBREV.	9. NAME OF ACTIVITY EFFECTING ENLISTMENT		
mo. 01 day 21 yr. 66	3 YEARS MINORITY		1 - 0	AFEES, LOS ANGELES, CALIFORNIA		

10. AFQT SCORE	11.	12. ENLISTED/REENLISTED IN U. S. NAVY		13. ENLISTED AT (City and State or Country)		
NA		X FIRST ENLISTMENT REEN-LISTMENT INDUCTION		LOS ANGELES, CALIFORNIA		

14. TERM OF ACDU (USNR only)	15. ACTIVE/INACTIVE STATUS (USN only)		16. ACCEPTED AT (City and State or Country)		17. NO. OF ENL
00 MONTHS	RETAINED ON ACDU IMMEDIATE ACDU (Within 24 Hrs.) X INACTIVE DUTY		INGLEWOOD, CALIFORNIA		1

18. DATE MIL OBL INCURRED	19. M.O.D.	20. GCT (Reen. only)	21. RELIGION	22. PLACE OF BIRTH (City)		State or Country
mo. 08 day 04 yr. 61	A	NA	PROT NP	LONG BEACH		CALIF

23. DATE OF BIRTH	24. PHYSICAL PROFILE	25. AREA/STATION/ SUBSTA CODE	26. SOCIAL SECURITY NO.	27. TRANSFERRED TO (Activity and Location)		28. ACTIVITY CODE
mo. 05 day 06 yr. 43	NA	863664AH	447 44 4234	USNTC SAN DIEGO, CALIF		82

29. DATE OF TRANSFER	30. CITIZENSHIP		OTHER* (Specify)	31. BRANCH OF SERVICE FROM WHICH LAST DISCHARGED		32.
mo. 01 day 21 yr. 66	X U. S. NATURALIZED U. S.			USAFR		76

33. DATE LAST DISCHARGED	34. PRIOR NET SERVICE FOR PAY PURPOSES			35. TYPE OF LAST DISCHARGE		36.
mo. 01 day 20 yr. 66	04 YEARS 05 MONTHS 17 DAYS			HON		1

37. DATE OF LAST ENTRY	38. ENTITLED TO REENLISTMENT BONUS	39. SELECTIVE SERVICE NUMBER	40. SELECTIVE SERVICE LOCAL BOARD (Board Number, City and State)		
mo. 08 day 04 yr. 61	YES X NO.	NA	NA		

41. ACTIVE DUTY BASE DATE	42. COMPLEXION	43. COLOR OF HAIR	44. COLOR OF EYES	45. HOME ADDRESS AT TIME OF ENLISTMENT (City & County)		State or Country
mo. 01 day 21 yr. 66	RUDDY	BLACK	GREEN	HAWTHORNE, LOS ANGELES		CALIF

46. PAY GRADE BASE DATE	47. HEIGHT	48. WEIGHT	49. RACE	50. QUOTA CONTROL CODE		51.
mo. day yr. NA	74	165	CAU	24 11 0 10 70 SO4 04		11 0 24

52. MARKS AND SCARS					Blood Type
ANT: NONE NOTED					

POST: NONE NOTED

I certify that a physical examination has been conducted according to current regulations, and that the above named man has been found by an examining physician to be physically qualified for enlistment.

Larry L. Claton _____ Certifying Officer.

For and in consideration of the pay or wages due to the ratings which may from time to time be assigned me during the continuance of my service, I agree to and with **LARRY L CLATON** _____ of the UNITED STATES NAVY, as follows:
(Name of Enlisting Officer)

First: To enter the service of the Navy of the United States and to report to such station or vessel of the Navy as I may be ordered to join, and to the utmost of my power and ability discharge my several services or duties and be in everything conformable and obedient to the several requirements and lawful commands of the officers who may be placed over me.
(Date)   (Year)

Second: I oblige and subject myself to serve **THREE** Years from **21 JANUARY 1966** unless sooner discharged during minority until _____ (Date)   (Year)

by proper authority, and on the conditions provided by Section 5540 of Title 10 of the U. S. Code, as printed on the reverse side of this contract.

In the event of a National emergency declared by the President or in the event of war during my term of service in the Regular Navy, or in the event of a National emergency declared by the Congress or in the event of war during my term of service in the Naval Reserve, I oblige and subject myself to serve until six months after the end of the war or National emergency if so required by the Secretary of the Navy unless I voluntarily reenlist or extend my enlistment. I understand that when so retained the addition of one-quarter pay as specified in Section 5540 of Title 10 of the U. S. Code is not applicable in time of war.

I also oblige myself, during such service, to comply with such laws as have been, or may hereafter be enacted by the Congress of the United States, and to regulations issued pursuant thereto, and to submit to treatment for the prevention of smallpox, typhoid (typhoid prophylaxis), and such other preventive measures as may be considered necessary by naval authorities.

Third: I am of the legal age to enlist; I have never deserted from and I am not a member of the Armed Forces of the United States, the U. S. Coast Guard or any reserve component thereof; I have never been discharged from the United States Service or other service on account of disability or through sentence of either civilian or military court; and I have never been discharged from any service, civil or military, except with good character and for the reasons given by me to the recruiting officer prior to enlistment.

Fourth: I understand that upon enlistment in a Reserve component of the United States Navy, or upon transfer or assignment thereto, in time of war or national emergency declared by the Congress, or when otherwise authorized by law, I may be ordered to active duty for the duration of the war or National emergency and for six months thereafter.

Fifth: I understand that if I become a candidate for the Naval Academy and fail to pass the entrance examination, I will be returned to general service.

Sixth: I have had this contract fully explained to me, I understand it, and certify that no promise of any kind has been made to me concerning assignment to duty, or promotion during my enlistment.

Enlistment Oath: I, **MILTON WILLIAM COOPER** _____, do solemnly swear (or affirm) that I will support and defend the Constitution of the United States against all enemies, foreign and domestic; that I will bear true faith and allegiance to the same; and that I will obey the orders of the President of the United States and the orders of the officers appointed over me, according to regulations and the Uniform Code of Military Justice. So help me God.

And I do further swear (or affirm) that all statements made by me as now given in this record are correct.

SIGNATURE IN OWN HANDWRITING   SURNAME TO RIGHT _Milton William Cooper_

Subscribed and sworn to before me this **21st** day of **JANUARY** A. D. **1966**
and contract perfected.
*Citizenship, as shown above, substantiated.
SIGNATURE AND RANK _Larry L Claton_ _____ OFFICIAL TITLE **LARRY L. CLATON 2nd Lt AGC**
(See Art. 7268, U. S. Navy Regulations)   AFEES, LOS ANGELES, CALIF.

FORWARD TO BUREAU OF NAVAL PERSONNEL

****TOP SECRET****

NAVY OCCUPATION AND TRAINING HISTORY
*See Art. B-2105, BuPers Manual

1. ADVANCEMENT, REDUCTION OR CHANGE IN RATING

RATE TO WHICH PERSON WILL BE ADVANCED, REDUCED OR CHANGED	PRACTICAL FACTORS		TRAINING COURSES COMPLETED				DATE ADVANCED REDUCED OR CHANGED RATING	*OFFICER'S INITIALS
	DATE COMPLETED FOR ADVANCEMENT	*OFFICER'S INITIALS	DESCRIPTION OF COURSE OR NAVPERS NUMBER		DATE COMPLETED	*OFFICER'S INITIALS		
QM3	27JAN67	JPM	MilReq for P.O. 3&2(3.78)	QM 3&2 (3.75)	3JAN67 7FEB67	JPM		
QMSN							14APR67	THFN
QM3							16APR67	JPM
QM2	5JUL67	JPM					16OCT67	JPM

2. NAVY ENLISTED CLASSIFICATION RECORD

DATE	PRIMARY CODE	SECONDARY CODE	*OFFICER'S INITIALS
21 APR 1966	TM 0700	OODU	H
14 SEP 66	BM-0100	0000	CDFR
14 APR 67	0000	0000	THFN

3. RECORD OF OTHER OFF-DUTY STUDY (USAFI Courses, Etc.)

DATE COMPLETED	NUMBER AND TITLE OF COURSE OR TEST	SCHOOL	GRADE	*OFFICER'S INITIALS
JAN67	MIL3-MIL/LEAD EXAM		PASS	JPM
JUL67	M/L E-5 NEC LTR SER M/L of JUL 67		PASSED	JPM

4. DESIGNATOR RECORD

DATE	DESIGNATOR	QUALIFICATION OR REVOCATION	*OFFICER'S INITIALS

5. GENERAL EDUCATIONAL DEVELOPMENT TESTING RECORD

	PASSED (In-service equivalent)	FAILED (Void if passed on retest)
HIGH SCHOOL LEVEL	HIGH SCHOOL GRADUATION □ Date _____ *Off. _____ Initials.	□ Date _____ *Off. _____ Initials
COLLEGE LEVEL	ONE YEAR COLLEGE □ Date _____ *Off. _____ Initials	□ Date _____ *Off. _____ Initials

6. RECORD OF NAVY SERVICE SCHOOLS ATTENDED

NAME AND LOCATION OF SCHOOL	NAME AND LOCATION OF SCHOOL
BASIC INSTRUCTION FOR QUARTERMASTER FLEET TRAINING GROUP, PEARL HARBOR	

CLASS NO.	COURSE LENGTH	DATE ENROLLED	CLASS NO.	COURSE LENGTH	DATE ENROLLED
67-3	4 wks	20 MAR 67			

DATE COMPLETED	FINAL MARK (0—100) (62.5 passing)	CLASS STANDING	DATE COMPLETED	FINAL MARK (0—100) (62.5 passing)	CLASS STANDING
14 APR 67	82.3	3 in a class of 10			_____ in a class of _____

MANNER OF COMPLETION	MANNER OF COMPLETION
☑ GRADUATED □ DROPPED FOR _____	□ GRADUATED □ DROPPED FOR _____
SIGNATURE* H. F. NELSON, LCDR, USN	SIGNATURE*

NAME (Last) COOPER MILTON WILLIAM	(First) 0085	(Middle)	SERVICE NUMBER B801742

Navy Occupation and Training History   NAVPERS 601-4 (Rev. 3-58)   4 □

NAVY OCCUPATION/TRAINING
AND AWARDS HISTORY *See Art B-2305, BuPers Manual

CONTINUOUS ACTIVE DUTY DATE: 21 JAN 66

1. NAVY ENLISTED CLASSIFICATION RECORD				2. DESIGNATOR RECORD			
DATE	PRIMARY CODE	SECONDARY CODE	*OFFICER'S INITIALS	DATE	DESIGNATOR	QUALIFICATION OR REVOCATION	*OFFICER'S INITIALS
29JAN69	0000	9545					

3. GENERAL EDUCATIONAL DEVELOPMENT TESTING RECORD

GED TESTS	HIGH SCHOOL GRADUATION (In-Service Equivalent)		NAME & LOCATION OF HIGH SCHOOL
	DATE PASSED	OFF. INITIALS	
CC TESTS GEN EXAMS	ONE YEAR COLLEGE (In-Service Equivalent)		
	DATE PASSED	OFF. INITIALS	DATE OF DIPLOMA	OFF. INITIALS

4. RECORD OF NAVY SERVICE SCHOOLS ATTENDED (CLASS A, B, C, P AND FUNCTIONAL SCHOOLS)

COURSE TITLE AND SCHOOL LOCATION

EARNED NEC	COURSE LENGTH	DATE ENROLLED
DATE COMPLETED	FINAL MARK (00-99) (63 passing)	CLASS STANDING ___ in a class of ___

MANNER OF COMPLETION
☐ GRADUATED   ☐ DROPPED FOR
SIGNATURE*

COURSE TITLE AND SCHOOL LOCATION

EARNED NEC	COURSE LENGTH	DATE ENROLLED
DATE COMPLETED	FINAL MARK (00-99) (63 passing)	CLASS STANDING ___ in a class of ___

MANNER OF COMPLETION
☐ GRADUATED   ☐ DROPPED FOR
SIGNATURE*

COURSE TITLE AND SCHOOL LOCATION

EARNED NEC	COURSE LENGTH	DATE ENROLLED
DATE COMPLETED	FINAL MARK (00-99) (63 passing)	CLASS STANDING ___ in a class of ___

MANNER OF COMPLETION
☐ GRADUATED   ☐ DROPPED FOR
SIGNATURE*

COURSE TITLE AND SCHOOL LOCATION

EARNED NEC	COURSE LENGTH	DATE ENROLLED
DATE COMPLETED	FINAL MARK (00-99) (63 passing)	CLASS STANDING ___ in a class of ___

MANNER OF COMPLETION
☐ GRADUATED   ☐ DROPPED FOR
SIGNATURE*

COURSE TITLE AND SCHOOL LOCATION

EARNED NEC	COURSE LENGTH	DATE ENROLLED
DATE COMPLETED	FINAL MARK (00-99) (63 passing)	CLASS STANDING ___ in a class of ___

MANNER OF COMPLETION
☐ GRADUATED   ☐ DROPPED FOR
SIGNATURE*

COURSE TITLE AND SCHOOL LOCATION

EARNED NEC	COURSE LENGTH	DATE ENROLLED
DATE COMPLETED	FINAL MARK (00-99) (63 passing)	CLASS STANDING ___ in a class of ___

MANNER OF COMPLETION
☐ GRADUATED   ☐ DROPPED FOR
SIGNATURE*

NAME (Last, First, Middle)	SERVICE NUMBER	BRANCH AND CLASS
COOPER, MILTON WILLIAM	B80 17 42	USN

NAVY OCCUPATION/TRAINING AND AWARDS HISTORY NAVPERS 601-4 (REV. 6-66)

ADMINISTRATIVE REMARKS   *See Art. B-2305, BuPers Manual*

SHIP OR STATION
RECRUIT TRAINING COMMAND, U. S. NAVAL TRAINING CENTER, SAN DIEGO, CALIFORNIA

21 JAN 1966   Received for Recruit Training.   10529434

24 JAN 1966   Issued Armed Forces Identification Card # _____
                     Geneva Convention Card prepared.

Verified Profile: "A" Qualified for full duty. AUTH: BUPERS INSTRUCTION 6110.1 of
18 July 1957 _____   P U L H E S
                                    1 1 1 1 1 1

21 APR 1966   Recruit Training Completed. Course of instruction in Code of
                     Conduct completed. Compliance with Article 137 UCMJ completed.

                     Advanced or changed in Rate to   NA
                     AUTH: Recruit Training Directive 1-64

~~Completed familiarization course with small arms, having fired 50 rounds at 200 yards~~

B J Hartshorn
                               B. J. HARTSHORN, LT, USN
                               BY DIRECTION OF THE C.O.

- -

10 MAR 1966   Examined this date and found to be psychologically and physically
                     qualified for submarine duty.

D E Winslow
                               D. E. WINSLOW, LT , USN
                               ASST TO THE PERSONNEL OFFICER
                               BY DIRECTION OF THE C.O.

NAME (Last, First, Middle)	SERVICE NO.	BRANCH AND CLASS
COOPER, MILTON WILLIAM	B80 17 42	USN

ADMINISTRATIVE REMARKS—NAVPERS 601-13 (Rev. 12-61)
11ND-NTC-(OP)-1070/41 (REV. 10-65)   13 Ⅱ

****TOP SECRET****

ADMINISTRATIVE REMARKS   *See Art. B-2305, BuPers Manual*

SHIP OR STATION
U.S.S. TIRU (SS 416)

1 JUL 66: AUTHORIZED TO WEAR THE NATIONAL DEFENSE SERVICE MEDAL. AUTH: SECNAV NOTE
1650 OF 5 MAY 66. MEDAL NOT RECEIVED.

C. H. SANDERS, JR., LCDR, USN, EXECUTIVE OFFICER
BY DIRECTION OF THE COMMANDING OFFICER

----

6 AUG 66: I AM NO LONGER A VOLUNTEER FOR SUBMARINE DUTY.

MILTON W. COOPER

WITNESSED:

C. H. SANDERS, JR., LCDR, USN, EXECUTIVE OFFICER

COMMANDER SUBMARINE SQUADRON SEVEN at PEARL HARBOR, HAWAII

17 AUG 66: Declared environmentally unadaptable for submarine duty this date.
Reason: No longer a volunteer for submarine duty. COOPER is not eligible
for return to submarine duty at any future date. AUTH: BUPERS Manual,
Article C-7404(6)(f) and COMSUBDIV SEVENTY-TWO ltr 1220 serial 60 of 9
AUG 66.

J. W. BRESLIN, LTJG, USN, PERSONNEL OFFICER
BY DIRECTION OF THE COMMANDER

- -
- - - - - - - - - USS TOMBIGBEE (AOG-11) - - - - - - - - - - - - - - -

13 SEP 66: Commenced present continuous tour of sea duty 6 May 1966.

G. F. REYNOLDS, LTJG, USNR, EXEC OFFICER
BY DIRECTION OF THE COMMANDING OFFICER

- -

12 DEC 66: Recommended for advancement and nominated for examination. Eligible
in all respects for participation in service-wide competitive examination for QM3.

J. P. MILLS, LT, USN, EXEC OFFICER
By direction of the Commanding Officer

NAME (Last, First, Middle)			SERVICE NO.	BRANCH AND CLASS
COOPER,	MILTON	WILLIAM	B80-17 42	USN

ADMINISTRATIVE REMARKS—NAVPERS 601-13 (Rev. 12-61)   1A-0105-401-2103   13 [3]

| ADMINISTRATIVE REMARKS | *See Art. B-2305, BuPers Manual* |

SHIP OR STATION

Fleet Training Group, Pearl Harbor

14 Apr 67: SUCCESSFULLY COMPLETED COMTRAPAC COURSE K-772-606 AT FLEET
TRAINING GROUP, PEARL HARBOR THIS DATE. DESIGNATED QMSN
EFFECTIVE THIS DATE IN ACCORDANCE WITH BUPERSINST 1440.3F. IT IS DIRECTED
THAT THE APPROPRIATE MISCELLANEOUS CHANGE ENTRIES BE ENTERED ON THE
PERSONNEL DIARY CITING BUPERSINST 1440.3F AS AUTHORITY.

J. F. MacELWEE, CDR, USN
Chief Staff Officer

- - - - - - - - - - - - - - USS TOMBIGBEE (AOG-11) - - - - - - - - - - - - - -

30 MAY 67: Advanced to QM3 effective 16 April 1967. For the purpose of final
multiple computation and determining eligibility for advancement to
next higher pay grade, COOPER's service in pay grade E-4 is considered
to date from 16 May 1967. Auth: NEC ADV LTR NO 1-67 of 14 March 1967.

J. P. MILLS, LT, USN, EXEC OFFICER
By direction of the Commanding Officer

- -

31 MAY 67: I have read and understand articles 2, 3, 7 through 15, 25, 27, 31, 37,
38, 55, 77 through 134, and 137 through 139 of the Uniform Code of
Military Justice in accordance with article 137 of the Uniform Code of
Military Justice.

MILTON WILLIAM COOPER

AUTHENTICATED: *J. P. MILLS, LT, USN, Executive Officer*
By direction of the Commanding Officer

- -

21 AUG 67: Volunteered for duty in Vietnam in accordance with BUPERSNOTE 1306 of
18 July 1967.

J. P. MILLS, LT, USN, EXEC OFFICER
By direction of the Commanding Officer

- -

1 SEP 67: Dependents declared "command-sponsored" in accordance with BUPERSINST
1300.26. Auth: COM14 26E:JSA:js Ser 4537 dtd 15 Aug 1967 ltr.

J. P. MILLS, LT, USN, EXEC OFFICER
By direction of the Commanding Officer

| NAME *(Last, First, Middle)* | SERVICE NO. | BRANCH AND CLASS |
| COOPER, Milton William | B80-17 42 | USN |

ADMINISTRATIVE REMARKS—NAVPERS 601-13 (Rev. 12-61)   NAVY—PEARL HARBOR   13

ADMINISTRATIVE REMARKS   See Art. B-2105, BuPers Manual

SHIP OR STATION

USS TOMBIGBEE (AOG-11)

16 OCT 67: Advanced in rate to QM2 effective this date for pay and precedence purposes. For the purpose of final multiple computation and determining eligibility for advancement to next higher pay grade COOPER's service in pay grade E-5 is considered to date from 16 November 1967. Auth: NEC ADVLTR 2-67 of 1 October 1967/NAVPERS 15989.

J. P. MILLS, LT, USN, EXEC OFFICER
By direction of the Commanding Officer

- -

27 NOV 67: Authorized to wear the National Defense Service Medal for service after 31 December 1960. Medal not issued. Auth: BUPERSNOTE 1650 of 5 May 1967.

J. P. MILLS, LT, USN, Executive Officer
By direction of the Commanding Officer

- -

27 NOV 67: Authorized to wear the Vietnam Service Medal for service on board USS TOMBIGBEE (AOG-11). Medal not issued. Auth: BUPERSNOTE 1650 of 15 May 1967.

J. P. MILLS, LT, USN, Executive Officer
By direction of the Commanding Officer

- -

4 APR 68: Authorized to wear the Republic of Vietnam Campaign Medal with Device (1960-   ) for service after 1 March 1961. Auth: SECNAVINST 1650.26.

J. P. MILLS, LT, USN, Executive Officer
By direction of the Commanding Officer

- -

NAME (Last, First, Middle)	SERVICE NO.	BRANCH AND CLASS
COOPER Milton William	B80 17 42	USN

ADMINISTRATIVE REMARKS—NAVPERS 601-13 (Rev. 12-61)   1A-0105-401-2103   13 5

ADMINISTRATIVE REMARKS   *See Art. B-2305. BuPers Manual*

SHIP OR STATION
U. S. NAVAL AMPHIBIOUS BASE, CORONADO, SAN DIEGO, CALIFORNIA 92155

27 MAY 68   : Has satisfactorily completed the two week course of instructions
administered by COMPHIBTRAPAC. The course consisted of: Pacific
area intelligence briefings, Counter-insurgency orientations,
Small arms familiarization and Self-protection instruction.

W. H. HAUSER, LT, USNR, Personnel Officer
By direction of the Commanding Officer

- -

31 MAY 68   : Has satisfactorily completed the one week Internal Security Guard School
administered by Naval Amphibious School, Coronado, California.
NEC 9545 recommended to BUPERS this date.

W. H. HAUSER, LT, USNR, Personnel Officer
By direction of the Commanding Officer

- -
U. S. NAVAL SUPPORT ACTIVITY, DANANG, VIETNAM
- -

17 JUN 68: Commenced an unaccompanied tour of overseas service in the Republic of
Vietnam JUN 68. Tour Completion Date established as JUN 69.

J. L. ETZEL, WO-1, SHIPCLK, USN
ASS'T ENLISTED PERSONNEL OFFICER
BY DIRECTION OF THE COMMANDING OFFICER ENL PE

NAME *(Last, First, Middle)*	SERVICE NO.	BRANCH AND CLASS
COOPER, MILTON WILLIAM	B80 17 42	USN

ADMINISTRATIVE REMARKS—NAVPERS 601-13 (Rev. 12-61)   0105-401-2103   13

＊＊＊＊T O P　S E C R E T＊＊＊＊

ADMINISTRATIVE REMARKS   *See Art. B-2305, BuPers Manual*

SHIP C R STATION

U. S. NAVAL SUPPORT ACTIVITY, DANANG, VIETNAM 96695

23 OCT 68: COOPER, having successfully completed the necessary apprenticeship and
training and having safely and conscientiously operated a twin screw,
twin rudder 45 foot picket boat for a minimum of 150 hours in the I Corps
Tactical Zone of the Republic of Vietnam, as a harbor and river security
patrol, is deemed qualified in all respects as a 45 foot Picket Boat
coxswain.

A. F. FLAHERTY, LT, USN
Enlisted Personnel Officer
By direction of the CO

- -

24 NOV 68: COOPER, having successfully completed the necessary appretniceship and
training and having safely and conscientiously operated a single screw,
single rudder 36 foot LCPL MARK IV for a minimum of 150 hours in the
I Corps Tactical Zone of the Republic of Vietnam, as a harbor and river
security patrol, is deemed qualified in all respects as an LCPL MARK IV
Coxswain.

E. N. POTENTE, LCDR, USN
Enlisted Personnel Officer
By direction of the CO

NAME *(Last, First, Middle)*	SERVICE NO.	BRANCH AND CLASS
COOPER, Milton William	B80 17 42	USN

ADMINISTRATIVE REMARKS—NAVPERS 601-13 (Rev. 12–61)   13 ⑧

＊＊＊＊TOP SECRET＊＊＊＊

ADMINISTRATIVE REMARKS   *See Art. B-2305, BuPers Manual*

SHIP OR STATION

U. S. NAVAL SUPPORT ACTIVITY, DANANG, VIETNAM

27 MAY 1969: Authorized to wear the Navy Achievement Medal with Combat "V"
for service in the I Corps Tactical Zone, Republic of Vietnam
on 10 FEB 1969. AUTH: NAVFORV ltr FF5-16/112:dee of 31 MAR 69.

C. T. LASTER, SHPCLK, USN
Assistant Personnel Officer
By Direction of the Commanding Officer,
Enlisted Personnel

NAME *(Last, First, Middle)*	SERVICE NO.	BRANCH AND CLASS
COOPER, Milton William	B80 17 42	USN

ADMINISTRATIVE REMARKS—NAVPERS 601-13 (Rev. 12-61)   13

APPENDIX B: UFOs AND AREA 51

JUNE 13, 1987

Dear Sirs,

Although I missed your very recent radio and tv shows, a friend suggested
that I write this letter and share my information with you. I am fifty year
of age engineer that has worked in the private sector, as well as with the
government.

From 1975 to 1980, I was involved with several investigations having to do
with E.T. material. Even though the project was very well covered, I am
still very much surprised that Project Pluto and results have not surfaced
yet.

In as much as the project was handled by others, there was no question that
the government was in full control. For security purposes, Project Pluto
had five levels. Those who investigated one level had nothing to do with
the next, and would only turn in the results of data of these findings to
the next level, then go on to another area.

No one that I knew ever had the results of two levels at the same time.
There was only one very rare exception to the rule which took place in
1975, and was infact my very first assignment with the project. I was
employed by a non-government firm that of course was directly involved with
the government, and probably fronted for them on the projects.

I would assume that eventually government records could be made available
to the general public, but not from the private sector. I'm not really
sure. In any event, several others and myself were rushed to a rather
remote place in upstate Pennsylvannia.

We were informed that every thing was top secret, and had to remain that
way. We were even housed in a hotel close by, and security people were
assigned to us. Some type of aircraft had crashed in this area, and the
government felt that it would be easier and faster to do all of their
investigation right there rather than to move the remains of the wreck, and
whatever evidence the soil may contain.

The wreck site was rather difficult to get to, however, we turned it into a
construction site, clearing the area, and building two small and one very
large metal pre-fab buildings over and around the wreck. Heavy equipment,
materials, and workers were flown in and out on a daily basis.

We were moved from the hotel to some mobile homes that were brought in for
us, and many more top level people who joined us. I might add that the
local people who still lived some distance from the site, were led to
believe that a large private corporation was preparing to build an
electrical power supply for the area. But it was off limits to everyone in
the area.
We were some of the first ones's on the scene other than lots of security
people. The wreck had already been covered by very large canvas blankets,
and large nets were tented over head to protect the site from any possible
air traffic. I did manage to get a very good look at the wreck on several
occasions. My first thoughts were that it may have been an experimental air
craft of our government, or perhaps the government of another.

It was later suggested to us that it was a new type of air craft of a
foreign government, and it was a super hush - hush project. That air craft
was nothing like I have ever seen as probably ever will again.

****TOP SECRET****

The crash site was also something quite different. The disturbed soil was about a hundred feet in diameter, although the craft was much larger in length.   I only saw what appeared to be about two- thirds of the rear end, and even that was about ten feet below the surface. When it crashed on about a 30 degree angle, it pushed all the earth back away from the craft itself. Almost as if the hole were made first, and then something half the size was put in place.

My best thought of this rather strange hole is that some kind of magnetic field had pushed all the earth away from the craft at impact. It was reasonable to assume that I was looking down at the rear end of the air craft, yet there was nothing to indicate that it had any kind of engine as we know it. Not even one little opening.

I don't really like to use the term cigar, but since I could not see the front part, it certainly appeared to have once been shaped like a large cigar. That's my best description.

If it was a craft from a foreign government, then we are in big trouble. I actually held one small portion of the wreck in my hand. Incidently, there was only a very small reading of radio waves in the area. The area was quite safe. There was on the other hand, a great deal of free magnetic energy in that area. It was very difficult using our instruments. It was very difficult just to establish the correct time. Every wrist watch was a different time.

The piece of physical evidence that I held in my hand, was a material that I really can't identify. It may have been torn from the front of the craft when it crashed. A few of us compared thoughts as to what it might be, but no one was really certain. None of us had ever seen any thing like it before. It was about one square foot and about an inch thick. It weighed almost nothing, and one had the feeling that it may blow away if you let go of it and the wind increased.

It was the same color ,and texture of the large portion, so it was safe to assume that it was part of the shell of the craft. It weighed no where near enough to be any metal that we had ever seen. It even weighed less than any plastic that I had seen of a similar size.
I tried to scratch it with a pocket knife, and even cut away a small piece of the edge, but the knife did nothing to it. The surface was clear as glass, and stronger than any thing we had ever seen. It was like trying to scratch the surface of glass with a feather. Of course, we had to turn it into the security people.

After the site was secure, the first groups that included myself were taken away. There was a very thorough strip search prior to us being given jumpsuits, and put into a truck for the transportation to a waiting plane. We were taken to another area and debriefed before we were allowed to return to our normal way of life.

About three months later, a few of us returned to the site to remove the buildings, fill up the hole, and generally put the area back into the same shape as it may have been prior to the crash. We went through the same type of security search and debriefing as we had done the first time. Whatever was left of the craft had been removed and sent to —unknown —

Almost one year to the day, I was sent to another crash site. Everything was a repeat of the first time, except that there were six of us. Four of us were part of the first crash site, and the other two were new. This time the air craft was buried so deep into the lower side of a hill that we could not get a good look at it.

The security arrangements were just about the same, and we constructed similar buildings around it. It was very close to a rerun of the first crash site. Only this time we were told, "as a matter of fact," that it was a top secret experimental air craft that had crashed. I could however, manage to see the rear end of the craft. It appeared to be the same type as the first. The code name of the project was Pluto, as it was the first also.   Incidently, that was in upstate New York, in 1976. I do not know if there were any "people" or life forms aboard.

****TOP SECRET****

Several years later, I had an occasion to be in the area of site # one, and
I managed to stop in the cocktail lounge of hotel # one. The bartender only
recognized me because he brought in our first room service the first night
we stayed there. There was no room service there, but he made his one and
only exception to the rule for us. He asked me lots of questions which of
course had no answers for, nor would I give any. He told me that he heard
that there were lots of medical people on the site. He thought that rather
odd for an electric power station. He assumed that there must have been some
kind of an accident, or lots of waste material in the area.We let it go at
that.

It appears that security was very good, and no one had any idea that an air
craft had crashed there. I suspect that the air craft was fifty feet in
diameter and as long as two hundred feet. I could be wrong in the length.
As I recall the under portion of air craft # one had more of a flat
surface. It was difficult to see, but I do recall the difference in the
portion of the under surface that I could see.
There were also a few interesting grooves on the top and side areas about
twenty feet long. We had speculated that either a steering fin had been
attached, or a place where it could slide through from the inside, similar
to the type of system used to lower wheels on any air craft. First
speculation!

In 1978, I was again sent to a crash site. We arrived the day after the
security people. This time the air craft landed in a lake in upstate
Pennsylvannia. We went through the same motions, and built several
buildings on the edge of the lake to house the craft, once it was removed
from the water. Lots of Navy equipment was flown in, and there were divers
everywhere. The same magnetic field was present as in the first two
incidents. There was no air craft.

I spent three weeks there in the event that the buildings had to be
adjusted. It seems that the divers had located the exact spot that the air
craft had rested on the bottom, but it was gone. There was lots of evidence
on the beach that something very large had crashed into the lake causing
the water of the lake to splash ashore, over thirty feet, and what was
normally a rather clean lake, was suddenly a very large mudhole. After
three weeks, I left and was subjected to the same type of security as the
first two times.

I didn't have to return to dismantle the pre-fab buildings. I would think
that it was done by others very soon there after. There was some thoughts
at first that the craft may have been buried under the bottom of the lake,
but by this time, we knew enough about the craft to know if that were the
case. It was not — it just vanished. Perhaps it was not damaged and managed
to fly away. That may sound silly, but I believe that it is a reasonable
conclusion. There was some damage to the immediate area. Six large
electrical transformers,and some other equipment were burnt out and had to
be replaced by the electric company. The government took the electrical
equipment and had it flown somewhere else.

In 1979, I was sent to the shores of southern Texas. The same type of
situation, All the evidence led us to believe that whatever it was, it landed
in the water and flew away.

I understand that over twenty men actually saw it go into the water, but
the days that followed bore no fruit. The Navy divers had a good deal of
evidence that some thing has made a very large recent gash on the bottom
in about seventy feet of water.

The very same magnetic field was present, and every thing electrical in the
immediate area was burnt out. By the end of 1979, I was sent back to the
very same lake in Northern Pennsylvannia. It was a duplicate incident as
the first time we were there. It had landed in the lake and was gone. The
same electrical items were again destroy, and the same magnetic field was
evident. I really have no physical evidence to prove one way or another the
identification of the air craft. I can only examine what I have experience
and wonder! My opinion is another story.

****TOP SECRET****

I don't really believe that the air craft belongs to our Government or any other government on this earth. From 1975 to present, we would certainly have seen some kind of revolutionary change in our air craft. To date, I still have not seen any material to even slightly match the very first piece of physical evidence that I had examined. That alone, would have made a fantastic change in the material we use today. No corporation or novernment could keep that kind of material quality under cover for over twelve years. If they had invented it.

After twelve years we probably don't even know what it is, or how to make it. I am positive that at the very least, they have two of the air craft hidden some where, and probably have learned very little from them, other than they exists. How ever, the company that I was associated with has made some gigantic leaps forward in electromagnetic forces. Perhaps they did learn something from it after all. If we wish to assume that these air craft are not from this earth, and are from way out there in space, then my goodness, the planet must be full of visitors. The air traffic alone, must be fantastic. It seems to me that who ever they are they have found it easier to land in the water rather than on our dry earth. Perhaps it was designed to land on water or a very flat surface.

I have never really had any feelings one way or another about E.T's. I have elected to deal with hard evidence only, that was prior to 1975. For those few years afterwards, I could not help but interject some opinions into my brain.

As I would rather deal with hard evidence only, I am forced to put all of this on a seale, and take a good hard look at the tilting of the seales. There is far too much here to ignore. 1 must confess that 1 had some what leaned towards the experimental air craft story. But as the years past, it became evident that was only a cover story. Too much time has past, and our air craft is pretty much the same. There is no doubt in my mind that we as well as others, are constantly experimenting with new air craft, however at this late date, i am reasonably certain that those crash sites were not made by anything that we are familiar with, and then again, I still kind of reserve that possibility. As you can see, I have many mixed feeling about it.

In addition, i have no way of knowing if I had been on every crash site that occurred. there may have been many more during that period and many more since then.

I really don't know if any one had ever been removed from the two wrecks, that I had personally seen. Perhaps they were only mechanical flights. Perhaps the medical people were only there — just in case. And/or to test the wreck for any form of unknown bacteria prior to removing it. Their being present is not really evidence that a life form was found. It could go either way.

I just cannot imagine our government or any other keeping it such a secret, if infact, they were not from this earth. It really serves no purpose that I can understand. also appears to me that if they were from somewhere else that they mean us no harm. I would suspect that after all these years, if they meant us harm, we would most certainly know about it by now.

Even if they were only mechanical flights, the fact that they could get here at all...so many times, is certainly a feat in itself, and worthy of publication.

If the fact that they managed to get here at all, and the physical evidence, the material that I examined is any indication of how intelligent they are, then I would feel safe in assuming that they have left us in the stone age. On a personal level, I have no fear of meeting or contacting such a being. Infact, the very first time I saw the craft, the thought had entered my mind. I didn't expect a being like Frankenstein to come walking out. And for a short time 1 had wondered what I would do if suddenly a door opened and some form of life came out. What the heck! If it didn't look too bad 1 may have walked up and said hello just as I would to anyone else who may visit me.

****TOP SECRET****

I would think that I would be more afraid of picking up some unknown form of bacteria than I would be of the life form itself. Well, today we can pick up AIDS...so, as I put the germ fear aside. Yes. I would certainly try to be friendly once the first wave of fear passed me by. What I fear more than any visitor is that some farmer is going to get them with a shot gun and do more damage than we can or want to handle. Also, some cowboy policeman trying to shoot his first space man. Because of that I should think that our government would try to educate us as to the proper way to handle any such situation. That little bit of awareness and education may save our planet from destruction. If there is clear evidence that we are being visited by intelligent life forms, then the heads of our government are by far crazier than I had imagined by trying to keep it a secret. The damage of hostile action on our part may not be repairable.

I'm sorry but I am not familiar with your group, but my friend was very impressed by your speaker on TV as well as the radio. Because of that I am trying to share whatever information and evidence that I have which is in fact all first hand data. I have illustrated the evidence and information as it happened, and made note of where I speculated.

There are many items that I have not included in this letter, only because this could turn into forty or fifty pages. At some time in the future, if you wish, I will take my time and write every detail that I can remember. I'll also put it on tape for clarification.

I was told that you plan to open another branch in the future in the Philadelphia area? If that's the case I would certainly be interested in some form of association with your group. I belong to no other and never had any desire to, however, I understand that you are serious people, and worthy of respect. I regard the opinion of my friend very highly. He is a professor of physics, and himself a very serious person. I would appreciate your sending me some literature about your group, and your plans if any to enter the Philadelphia area. I think that you have selected a very good location. There are many very serious people there and a good solid investigation group would be quite welcome. I'm certain that once you entered the area the support group would be fantastic. If you selected Philadelphia, then the assured that you picked the right city for another branch.

Incidently, my experience in the E.T. world ended in 1980, when I changed positions. Have you had any reports of material that I examined belonging to an air craft from others? And the ever present magnetic field, do you have any reports from others similar to that? I have heard of others saying that they have seen a cigar shaped air craft, and I feel rather silly. Perhaps that's not the word. But, to the best of my knowledge and sight, it appeared to be just that. A cigar shaped craft. Please note that in both cases, I had never seen the front of the craft. I can only assume that the design was constant. I'll close for now and hope to hear from you,

I remain,

UFO seen in 1948 over Mount Rainier

****TOP SECRET****

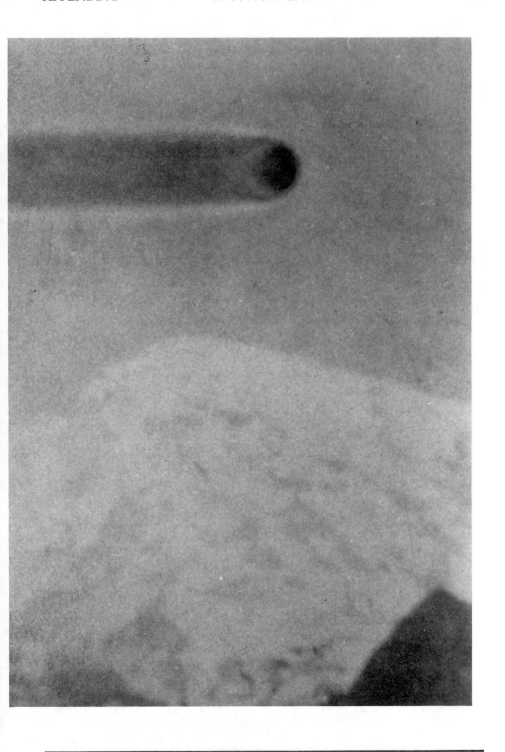

GERALD LIGHT
10545 SCENARIO LANE
LOS ANGELES 24, CALIFORNIA

[Letter Received:
4-16-54]   4/16/54

*Miramar
Air Field
Gillespie
Air Field*

Mr. Meade Layne
San Diego, California

My dear Friend: I have just returned from Muroc. The report is true---
devastatingly true!

I made the journey in company with Franklin Allen of the Hearst papers and
Edwin Nourse of Brookings Institute (Truman's erstwhile financial adviser)
and Bishop MacIntyre of L.A. (confidential names, for the present, please.)

When we were allowed to enter the restricted section, (after about six hours
in which we were checked on every possible item, event, incident and aspect
of our personal and public lives) I had the distinct feeling that the world
had come to an end with fantastic realism. For I have never seen so many
human beings in a state of complete collapse and confusion as they realized
that their own world had indeed ended with such finality as to beggar description. The reality of "otherplane" aeroforms is now and forever removed from
the realms of speculation and made a rather painful part of the consciousness
of every responsible scientific and political group.

During my two days visit I saw five separate and distinct types of aircraft
being studied and handled by our airforce officials---with the assistance and
permission of The Etherians! I have no words to express my reactions.

It has finally happened. It is now a matter of history.

President Eisenhower, as you may already know, was spirited over to Muroc one
night during his visit to Palm Springs recently. And it is my conviction that
he will ignore the terrific conflict between the various "authorities" and go
directly to the people via radio and television---if the impasse continues
much longer. From what I could gather, an official statement to the country
is being prepared for delivery about the middle of May.

I will leave it to your own excellent powers of deduction to construct a fitting
picture of the mental and emotional pandemonium that is now shattering the consciousness of hundreds of our scientific "authorities" and all the pundits of
the various specialized knowledges that make up our current physics. In some
instances I could not stifle a wave of pity that arose in my own being as I
wtached the pathetic bewilderment of rather brilliant brains struggling to make
some sort of rational explanation which would enable them to retain their familiar theories and concepts. And I thanked my own destiny for having long ago
pushed me into the metaphysical woods and compelled me to find my way out. To
wtach strong minds cringe before totally irreconcilable aspects of "science" is
not a pleasant thing. I had forgotten how commonplace such things as the demat-
erialization of "solid" objects had become to my own mind. The coming and going
of an etheric, or spirit, body has been so familiar to me these many years I had
just forgotten that such a manifestation could snap the mental balance of a man
not so conditioned. I shall never forget those forty-eight hours at Muroc!

G.L.

#2 Meade   April 16, 54

I am now preparing Bulletin #2 for mailing about Monday. I will add my testimony
of the Muroc episode, for whatever it may be worth, and then go into some length
about the next big move of the Commies to take advantage of the present public
concern about the bomb.

My information is that a vigorous campaign will be started immediately to persuade
America that Communist domination is much better than total annihilation.   This
will emanate from various groups of intellectuals who certainly have a case to
present.
                    April 12
Already in TIME/there is this: "In a letter to the N.Y.Times,Author-Critic
Lewis Mumford wrote: Submission to Communist totalitarianism would still be far
wiser than the final destruction of civilization.....Let us cease all further
experiments with even more horrifying weapons of destruction, lest our own self-
induced fears further upset out mental balance......Let us deal with our own
massive sins and errors... and have the courage to speak up.....against the methodology of barbarism to whhhh we are now committed. If as a nation we have become
mad, it is time for the world to take note of that madness......"

The purpose behind this campaign is something I was warned about nearly 20 years
ago. Its particular intent,among other things, is to split the country into as
many warring sections as possible.   There is,of course, the ancient prophecy of
America becoming a land of four separate nations or peoples. These have sometimes,
rather simply,been itemized as as north,south,east and west division. And anyone
with an ounce of ingenuity can easily fan local differences into a terrible hate.

Then there is the apparent treason of Oppenheimer,and some others.   In the next
Bulletin I will try to influence as many as possible to dig deeply under the superficial evidence for the real truth---and perhaps this man,and his friends, may not
be martyred as others have already been.   My Instructors assure me that this man
is not a Commie, nor even a sympathizer. But overwhelmed with the monster which
he had helped to create, he believed that if Russia also had the science to make
the bomb it might yet be possible to save civilization, even mankind.

This is a time for a display of that Christian idealism about which we are so proud,
lest the jungle consciousness in each of us destroys every vestige of/our sanity xxxxxx

I am working against a deadline to have another pamphlet on Etheria to serve as
a companion book to Sings-Skies, when the news breaks next month and mob hysteria
follows its traditional course.

This is just a hasty roundup of the matter as it stands now, and I will keep in
touch with you for further co-operation.   Will you please sent me your phone
number? It has vanished from my files in the confusion around here.

                              Cordially and fraternally,

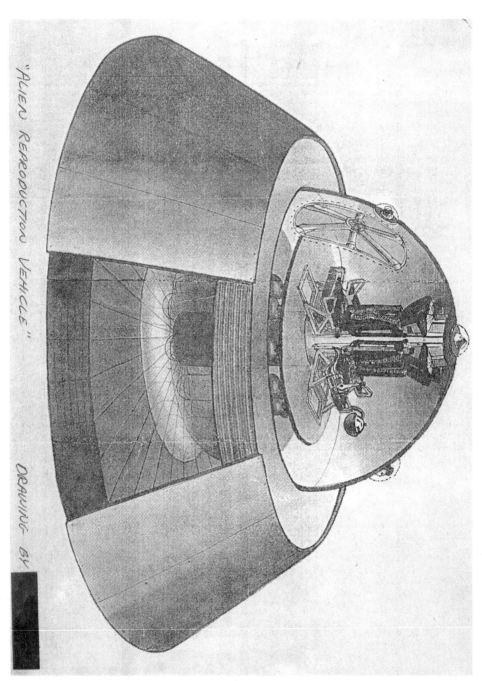

**Built by Northrop, McDonald Douglas, and General Electric
Stored at Norton AFB and Edwards AFB
Flies out of Area #51**

****TOP SECRET****

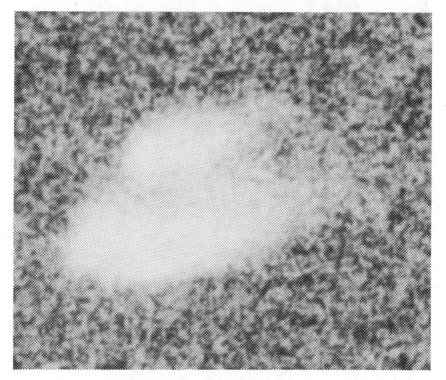

Photograph courtesy of Gary Schultz

Alien Reproduction Vehicle in flight over Groom Lake

* * * * **TOP SECRET** * * * *

Aerial View of Groom Lake/Area 51

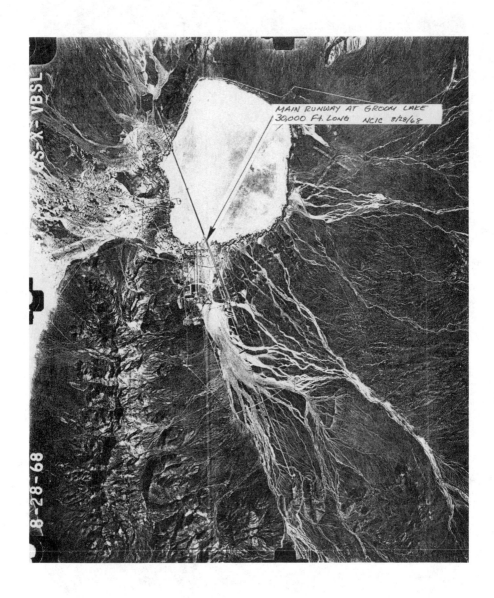

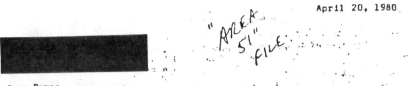

April 20, 1980

"AREA 51" FILE

Dear Dave:

I read your letter of the 13th with considerable interest. It seems difficult to believe that I have finally found someone that is as interested in finding out the true story of Project Red Light.

First of all I would like to address the specific points requested in your letter, and then I will expand on them and other items as well.

1) I did not know about the UFO Movie prior to reading your article.
2) I found out the name of Project Red Light almost by accident. I was running some remote lines in a warehouse at Area 51 and saw a large number of wooden shipping crates (the type made with tongue and groove lumber and used for shipping heavy items securely) with the code name "Project Red Light" written with grease pen or felt tip pen. Also on the crates was a stencilled "Edwards AFB" in standard military type of letters.
3) The article in Readers Digest that I referred to was about a UFO that flew over the US from the East Coast to where it "Blew UP" somewhere over eastern Nevada. The article did not state that the pilot was human. I'm sorry for the confusion on this. The reason that I felt that this Digest article is important is that I remember a period shortly after the date given in the article (I don't remember what it was, sorry) everything came to a screetching hault at Area 51. As you can see, I am just putting two and two together, but I am satisfied that the UFO of the Digest article and the UFO of Project Red Light are/were one and the same.

Now for some additional information that has come to mind since I talked to you:

Your report about the motorcycle riders is interesting. I can remember hearing similar rumors while I worked on the Test Site and I would not doubt the authenticity of your report. The security force at Area 51 while I serviced the Area were heavily armed and I considered them dangerous. There were several times that I was in the wrong place at the right time and had it not been moveable that I was not snooping or trying to snoop I really don't think I would be writing your this letter. Incidentally, the Security wore standard Air Police uniforms but looked nothing like any of the AP's I have ever delt with. They were all in their 30's to 40's, and looked like dock workers. Also as I remember it the only markings they wore just said Air Police. They did not have Nellis AFB on anything but a few of their vehicles, and I believe that they were assigned to Edwards rather that Nellis. The reason I remember this is that it seemed strange to me during my first trip to Area 51 I noticed a slight difference in their uniforms from Nellis AP's, and I over-heard a couple of remarks that indicated they were from Edwards.

Another interesting point. I was accustomed to going out onto the Bombing and Gunnery Range and had a number at Indian S/p/n45 (Nellis AFB maintains a forward area base there) to call to get clearance onto the range. This was SOP. However, in the case of area 51 I called the Security Office AT Area 51. This indicated to me that Nellis AFB had nothing to do with the operation of Area 51. Also the designation of Area 51 was classified TOP SECRET.

Incidentally, although I carried a "Q" clearance from the Atomic Energy Commission as well as an interagency Top Secret clearance I was investigated for a special Air Force Top Secret clearance in order to operate in Area 51.

I-I

At this point I am going to give you just a series of dis-connected observations that I made in the hope that they may tie in with something you of Len Stringfield may know.

1) I saw some crates being unloaded from a cargo plane. The aircraft was a Super Constellation with standard markings and had nothing to indicate it had any military connections. There was no airline name on it.

2) I only saw the UFO one time. It was on the ground and partly hidden behind a building and at first I thought it was a small private aircraft until I noticed it had no wings or tail. I was probably 1/2 mile or frather from it but I would guess it was 20 to 30 feet in diameter and sort of a pewter color rather that bright polished aluminium.

3) the reason I know it flew silently is I was present on a number of occasions when it was landing or taking off (I was always taken inside and out of view of the runway at these times) and at no time did I hear anything that sounded like a conventional or any other kind of engine.

4) I was working on their radios several times when they just "Died". However since I was there to work on them I really didn't think anything about it. Oh yes, they would start working again just as suddenly. Also there were a number of times that I wass called out to work on a radio and could not find anything wrong with them.

5) One of the men that I knew were "Pilots" was just slightly larger than me. I am 5'9" and weigh 180.

6) Most of the test flights occurred in the daytime rather that at night.

7) The radio frequency they used at that time was in the regular commercial VHF band and was a simplex frequency. At one time I had the Freq. written down but I have no idea now what it was. Anyway, I really think that someone with a scanner could pick them up if they were to park on the road to the east of the test site and use some kind of directional antenna.

8) Before I send this letter I will try to get a USC&GS map of the area and will mark the location of Area 51 on it.

9) There was a Radar Station at the north end of the test site near the town of Tonopah, Nevada. A fellow from my home town of ▓▓▓▓▓▓▓▓▓▓ was an operator there. His name is ▓▓▓▓▓▓▓▓ We were talking about the test site one day when he mentioned that he was always picking up UFO's over the test site but was told to ignore them. I remember him telling about one that he picked up on the edge of his PPI on the first revolution was directly overhead on the second pass and was just going off the scope on the third revolution of the antenna.

10) For some reason I seem to remember that the Red light is spelled Redlight i.e. all one word.

11) I always had the impression that the flight test area was from Area 51 north because there is a natural valley that runs in that direction for 200 miles or so. Also the area to the south was more populated. Also I entered Area 51 from the north and there were a couple of times that I was questioned about whether I had 'noticed' anything on the way in.

12) I was reminded constantly that no matter what I was, I could be in serious trouble if I ever talked about any of it. I can't stress how much how tight the security was, it was almost paranoid.

page 3

13) I don't think this has anything to do with Rod Light, but I remember when I was a kid back in the 40's, on two occasions I saw a story about UFO's included in the Weekly Pathe' News. There was one story about a UFO that had crashed somewhere and another story about a UFO that was found in some farmers barn. Both of those stories were given the usual news treatment. The reason that I am mentioning this is that I recently read an article about the entire library of Pathe' News film being given to an institution of some kind which would make it available to researchers. I am certain that if these film clips could be located they would be useful. Realizing that these stories appeared prior to Blue Book and at a time of Buck Rogers and Flash Gordon, there is probably a better than even chance that they can be located by someone willing to spend the time viewing a few hundred hours of old news film.

14) More on item #3. The reason that I knew that take offs and landings were occuring was that I would be told something like "IT will be landing in so many minutes" or "we will be taking IT out of the hanger at such & such a time", etc. I remember that any referrals were to "IT". I don't think I ever heard the words "aircraft, craft, ship" etc.

15) More on item #7. The Air-to-Ground frequencies were in the 200 Mc range. I believe there is a standard set of air-to-ground or Government Frequencies either just above or just below the 220 Mc ham band and their communications were on those Frequencies.

Well, there you have it Dave. I hope that I have shed some light on some dark areas. Should any other thoughts come to mind that I feel may be important, I will try to catch you on the 40 meter net. Hopefully if I can get things settled down to a dull roar I will be able to start checking in on a more permanent basis. Of course, should you have any questions or want further clairification please contact me.

.73

April 5, 1980

Resume of report received . . . .::.ll. ::.'██, after the MUFON 40-meter
net on April 5, 19:0.

W█████, ███████████████████████████████, Iowa ██████,
stated that during the period 1961-63 he performed radio maintenance
at the atomic proving ground. He also did some top-secret radio
work for the Air Force at ti :. The U-2 was developed here. .

"Area 51" was located 60 miles.due east of the base camp, behind a
mountain range separating it from Yucca Flat. Here a secret operation
was performed under unbelievable security precautions known as
"Project Red Light." A UFO which had been shipped from Edwards AFB
was flown here. It was not conventionally powered, but was **silent**
in operation. ████ assumes that this was the disc recovered intact
and shown in the UFO movie reported by radar technicians. Security
in Project Red Light was so strict that no one stayed there more than
six months. ████ did not see this movie himself, however.   .

While on vacation, he saw a story in Reader's Digest at his parent's
home which told of a UFO exploding over the test site in 1962 while
being flown. This would have been a recent story at that time.

████ is aware of the conventionally-powered-disc-built-by-the-Air——
Force which was publicized. We both feel that this may have been a
cover-up for the real project which he describes. He also heard
the stories about parts from a UFO which could not be duplicated
successfully by aerospace contractors on the west coast, and many
of the rumors about UFOs which were emanated from Nellis AFB. Incidentally, Nellis AF operated "Area 51" where he says the UFO was flown.

This information has bothered him for .. years, and he wonders if it
might be possible for documentation regarding "Project Red Light" to
be obtained under the Freedom of information Act.

**Two-part message from Joint Staff, Washington, D.C.,
to Joint Chiefs of Staff/Defense Intelligence Agency, Washington, D.C.
Subject: Belgium UFO Sightings.**

```
INQUIRE=DOC10D
ITEM NO=00508802
ENVELOPE
CDSN = LGX391    MCN = 90089/26558    TOR = 900901048
RTTCZYUW RUEKJCS5049 0891251-CCCC--RUEALGX.
ZNY CCCCC
HEADER
R 301251Z MAR 90
FM JOINT STAFF WASHINGTON DC
INFO RUEADWD/OCSA WASHINGTON DC
RUENAAA/CNO WASHINGTON DC
RUEAHQA/CSAF WASHINGTON DC
RUEACMC/CMC WASHINGTON DC
RUEDADA/AFIS AMHS BOLLING AFB DC
RUFTAEA/CDR USAINTELCTRE HEIDELBERG GE
RUFGAID/USEUCOM AIDES VAIHINGEN GE
RUETIAQ/MPCFTGEORGEGMEADEMD
RUEAMCC/CMC CC WASHINGTON DC
RUEALGX/SAFE
R 301246Z MAR 90
FM ▒▒▒▒▒▒▒▒▒▒
TO RUEKJCS/DIA WASHDC
INFO RUEKJCS/DIA WASHDC//DAT-7//
RUSNNOA/USCINCEUR VAIHINGEN GE//ECJ2-OC/ECJ2-JIC//
RUFGAID/USEUCOM AIDES VAIHINGEN GE
RHFQAAA/HQUSAFE RAMSTEIN AB GE//INOW/INO//
RHFPAAA/UTAIS RAMSTEIN AB GE//INRMH/INA//
RHDLCNE/CINCUSNAVEUR LONDON UK
RUFHNA/USDELMC BRUSSELS BE
RUFHNA/USMISSION USNATO
RUDOGHA/USNMR SHAPE BE
RUEAIIA/CIA WASHDC
RUFGAID/JICEUR VAIHINGEN GE
RUCBSAA/FICEURLANT NORFOLK VA
RUEKJCS/SECDEF WASHDC
RUEHC/SECSTATE WASHDC
RUEADWW/WHITEHOUSE WASHDC
RUFHBG/AMEMBASSY LUXEMBOURG
RUEATAC/CDRUSAITAC WASHDC
BT
CONTROLS
▒▒▒▒▒▒▒▒▒▒▒▒▒SECTION 01 OF 02 ▒▒▒▒▒▒▒ 05049

SERIAL:  (U) IIR 6 807 0136 90.

BODY
COUNTRY:  (U) BELGIUM (BE).

SUBJ:  IIR 6 807 0136 90/BELGIUM AND THE UFO ISSUE (U)

WARNING:  (U) THIS IS AN INFORMATION REPORT, NOT FINALLY
```

* * * *TOP SECRET* * * *

EVALUATED INTELLIGENCE. REPORT ████████   PAGE:0012

                    DEPARTMENT OF DEFENSE

DOI: (U) 900326.

REQS: ████████████   Declassified

SOURCE: A- (U) LA DERNIER HEURE, 20 MAR, DAILY FRENCH
LANGUAGE PAPER, CIRC 100,000; B- (U) LE SOIR, 26 MAR,
DAILY FRENCH LANGUAGE PAPER, CIRC 213,000;
██

SUMMARY: (U) NUMEROUS UFO SIGHTINGS HAVE BEEN MADE IN
BELGIUM SINCE NOV 89. THE CREDIBILITY OF SOME INDIVIDUALS
MAKING THE REPORTS IS GOOD. SOME SIGHTINGS HAVE BEEN
EXPLAINED BY NATURAL/MANMADE PHENOMENA, SOME HAVE NOT.
INVESTIGATION BY THE BAF CONTINUES.

TEXT: 1. (U) NUMEROUS AND VARIOUS ACCOUNTS OF UFO
SIGNTINGS HAVE SURFACED IN BELGIUM OVER THE PAST FEW
MONTHS. THE CREDIBILITY OF THE OBSERVERS OF THE ALLEDGED
EVENTS VARIES FROM THOSE WHO ARE UNSOPHISTICATED TO THOSE
WHO ARE THE WELL EDUCATED AND PROMINENTLY PLACED.

2. (U) SOURCE A CITES MR LEON BRENIG, A 43 YEAR OLD
PROFESSOR AT THE FREE UNIVERSIY OF BRUSSELS (PROMINENT) IN
THE FIELD OF STATISTICS AND PHYSICS. HE CLAIMS TO HAVE
TAKEN PICTURES OF THE PHENOMENA WHICH ARE STILL BEING
DEVELOPED BUT WILL BE PUBLISHED BY THE BELGIAN SOCIETY FOR
THE STUDY OF SPACE PHENOMENA IF THEY ARE OF GOOD QUALITY.

3. (U) MR BRENIG WAS DRIVING ON THE ARDENNES AUTOROUTE IN
THE BEAUFAYS REGION EAST OF LIEGE, SUNDAY, 18 MARCH 1990
AT 2030 HOURS WHEN HE OBSERVED AN AIRBORNE OBJECT
APPROACHING IN HIS DIRECTION FROM THE NORTH. IT WAS IN
THE FORM OF A TRIANGLE ABOUT THE SIZE OF A PING-PONG BALL
AND HAD A YELLOW LIGHT SURROUNDING IT WITH A REDDISH
CENTER VARYING IN INTENSITY. ALTITUDE APPEARED TO BE 500
- 1000 METERS, MOVING AT A SLOW SPEED WITH NO SOUND. IT
DID NOT MOVE OR BEHAVE LIKE AN AIRCRAFT.

4. (U) MR BRENIG CONTACTED A FRIEND VERY NEAR THE AREA
WHO CAME OUT AND TOOK PICTURES OF IT WITH A ZOOM LENS AND
400 ASA FILM. BOTH INSISTED THE OBJECT COULD NOT BE AN
AIRCRAFT OR HOLOGRAMME PROJECTION AS THE SKY WAS CLOUDLESS.

5. (U) THE SOURCE B ARTICLE WHICH DISCUSSES A BELGIAN
TELEVISION INTERVIEW WITH COL WIL ((DEBROUWER)), CHIEF OF

OPERATIONS FOR THE BAF, MOST LIKELY WAS THE RESULT OF A   PAGE:0013
FOLLOW-ON ACTION TAKEN BY MR BRENIG WHEN HE CONTACTED
LTGEN ((TERRASSON)), COMMANDER, BELGIAN TACTICAL
(OPERATIONAL) COMMAND. GEN TERRASSON CATEGORICALLY
ELIMINATED ANY POSSIBLE BAF AIRCRAFT OR ENGINE TEST
INVOLVEMENT WHICH COL DEBROUWER CONFIRMED DURING THE 25

ADMIN
BT

#5049   Declassified

NNNN

****TOP SECRET****

PAGE:0014

```
INQUIRE=DOC10D
ITEM NO=00503294
ENVELOPE
CDSN = LGX492    MCN = 90089/26566    TOR = 900891502
RTTCZYUW RUEKJCS5049 0891251-CCCC--RUEALGX.
ZNY CCCCC
HEADER
R 301251Z MAR 90
FM JOINT STAFF WASHINGTON DC
 INFO RUEADWD/OCSA WASHINGTON DC
 RUENAAA/CNO WASHINGTON DC
 RUEAHQA/CSAF WASHINGTON DC
 RUEACMC/CMC WASHINGTON DC
 RUEDADA/AFIS AMHS BOLLING AFB DC
 RUFTAKA/CDR USAINTELCTRE HEIDELBERG GE
 RUFGAID/USEUCOM AIDES VAIHINGEN GE
 RUETIAQ/MPCFTGEORGEGMEADEMD
 RUEAMCC/CMC CC WASHINGTON DC
 RUEALGX/SAFE
R 301246Z MAR 90
FM ███████████████
TO RUEKJCS/DIA WASHDC
 INFO RUEKJCS/DIA WASHDC//DAT-7//
 RUSNMOA/USCINCEUR VAIHINGEN GE//ECJ2-OC/ECJ2-JIC//
 RUFGAID/USEUCOM AIDES VAIHINGEN GE
 RHFQAAA/HQUSAFE RAMSTEIN AB GE//INOW/INO//
 RHFPAAA/UTAIS RAMSTEIN AB GE//INRMH/INA//
 RHDLCNE/CINCUSNAVEUR LONDON UK
 RUFHNA/USDELMC BRUSSELS BE
 RUFHNA/USMISSION USNATO
 RUDOGHA/USNMR SHAPE BE
 RUEAIIA/CIA WASHDC
 RUFGAID/JICEUR VAIHINGEN GE
 RUCBSAA/FICEURLANT NORFOLK VA
 RUEKJCS/SECDEF WASHDC
 RUEHC/SECSTATE WASHDC
 RUEADWW/WHITEHOUSE WASHDC
 RUFHBG/AMEMBASSY LUXEMBOURG
 RUEATAC/CDRUSAITAC WASHDC
BT
CONTROLS
████████████████ SECTION 02 OF 02 ███████████ 05049
████████████████

SERIAL:   (U) IIR 6 807 0136 90.

BODY
COUNTRY:  (U) BELGIUM (BE).

SUBJ:  IIR 6 807 0136 90/BELGIUM AND THE UFO ISSUE (U)

MAR TV SHOW.
```

Declassified

PAGE:0015

6. (U) DEBROUWER NOTED THE LARGE NUMBER OF REPORTED
SIGHTINGS, PARTICULARLY IN NOV 89 IN THE LIEGE AREA AND
THAT THE BAF AND MOD ARE TAKING THE ISSUE SERIOUSLY. BAF
EXPERTS HAVE NOT BEEN ABLE TO EXPLAIN THE PHENOMENA EITHER.

7. (U) DEBROUWER SPECIFICALLY ADDRESSED THE POSSIBILITY
OF THE OBJECTS BEING USAF B-2 OR F-117 STEALTH AIRCRAFT
WHICH WOULD NOT APPEAR ON BELGIAN RADAR, BUT MIGHT BE
SIGHTED VISUALLY IF THEY WERE OPERATING AT LOW ALTITUDE IN
THE ARDENNES AREA. HE MADE IT QUITE CLEAR THAT NO USAF
OVERFLIGHT REQUESTS HAD EVER BEEN RECEIVED FOR THIS TYPE
MISSION AND THAT THE ALLEDGED OBSERVATIONS DID NOT
CORRESPOND IN ANY WAY TO THE OBSERVABLE CHARACTERISTICS OF
EITHER U.S. AIRCRAFT.

8. (U) MR BRENIG HAS SINCE ASSURED THE COMMUNITY THAT HE
IS PERSONALLY ORGANIZING A NEW UFO OBSERVATION CAMPAIGN
AND SPECIFICALLY REQUESTS THE HELP OF THE BELGIAN MOD.

9. ▓▓▓▓▓▓▓ RELATED A SIMILAR UFO SIGHTING WHICH
APPARENTLY HAPPENED TO A BELGIAN AIR FORCE OFFICER IN THE
SAME AREA NEAR LIEGE DURING NOVEMBER 89. THE OFFICER AD
HIS WIFE WERE ALLEGEDLY BLINDED BY A HUGE BRIGHT FLYING
OBJECT AS THEY WERE DRIVING ON THE AUTOROUTE. THEY
STOPPED THEIR CAR, BUT WERE SO FRIGHTENED THEY ABANDONED
THE VEHICLE AND RAN INTO THE WOODS. THEY COULD NOT
PROVIDE A DETAILED DESCRIPTION BUT WHATEVER IT WAS
DEFINITELY APPEARED REAL TO THEM. ▓▓▓▓▓▓ UNDERLINED
THEIR CREDIBILITY AS SOLID.

COMMENTS: 1. ▓▓▓▓▓ COMMENT. HE COULD PROVIDE
VERY LITTLE CONCRETE INFORMAITON EXCEPT TO VERIFY THE
LARGE VOLUME OF SIGHTINGS AND THE SIMILARITY OF SOME
DURING NOV 89. ▓▓▓▓▓▓▓▓▓▓▓▓▓▓▓▓▓▓▓▓▓▓
▓▓▓▓▓▓▓▓▓▓▓▓▓▓▓▓▓▓▓▓▓▓▓▓▓▓▓▓▓▓▓▓

2. ▓▓▓▓ THE BAF HAS RULED SOME SIGHTINGS WERE CAUSED BY
INVERSION LAYERS, LAZER BEAMS AND OTHER FORMS OF HIGH
INTENSITY LIGHTING HITTING CLOUDS. BUT A REMARKABLE
NUMBER OCCURRED ON CLEAR NIGHTS WITH NO OTHER EXPLAINABLE
ACTIVITY NEARBY.

3. ▓▓▓▓ THE BAF IS CONCERNED TO A POINT ABOUT THE UFO
ISSUE AND IS TAKING ACTION TO INVESTIGATE INFORMATION THEY
HAVE. ▓▓▓▓▓ DOES ADMIT, HOWEVER, THAT HE IS NOT
OPTIMISTIC ABOUT RESOLVING THE PROBLEM.

4. ▓▓▓▓ FIELD COMMENT. THE USAF DID CONFIRM TO THE BAF
AND BELGIAN MOD THAT NO USAF STEALTH AIRCRAFT WERE
OPERATING IN THE ARDENNES AREA DURING THE PERIODS IN

▓▓▓▓▓▓▓▓▓

▓▓▓▓

▓▓▓▓

▓▓▓▓

QUESTION. THIS WAS RELEASED TO THE BELGIAN PRESS AND
RECEIVED WIDE DISSEMINATION.

PAGE:0016

▓▓▓▓▓▓▓▓▓▓▓▓▓

ADMIN
PROJ: (U)
INSTR: (U) US NO.
PREP: ▓▓▓▓▓▓▓▓▓▓▓▓
ACQ: ▓▓▓▓▓▓▓▓▓▓▓▓▓▓▓
DISSEM: (U) FIELD: AMEMBASSY BRUSSELS (DCM). ▓▓▓▓
WARNING: (U) REPORT ▓▓▓▓▓▓▓▓▓ ▓▓▓▓
▓▓▓▓▓▓▓▓▓▓▓

BT

#5049

NNNN

Declassified

FOR OFFICIAL USE ONLY

| COMPLAINT REPORT | DATE | COMPLAINT NO. | INVESTIGATION REPORT NO. |

COMMANDER
44 Missile Security Squadron
ELLSWORTH AFB, SD 57706

4. ORGANIZATION (Include location and phone no.)

| A. TO 39 AYES | B. COLOR HAIR | C. COMPLEXION | D. SEX | E. DOB | F. WEIGHT | G. HEIGHT | H. IDENTIFYING MARKS (Tattoo, scar, etc.) |

5. HOW DRESSED (Military or civilian, and condition of clothing) | 7. UNDER INFLUENCE OF:
| ALCOHOL | (Explain in item 19) |
| OTHER |

6. INCIDENT/COMPLAINT (Specify type and location)
HELPING HAND (SECURITY VIOLATION)/COVERED WAGON(SECURITY VIOLATION)
Site Lima 9 (68th SMSq Area)
7 Miles SW of Nisland, SD

HOUR 2100
DATE 16 Nov 77

9. RECEIVED BY (Typed or printed name, grade, and position)
PAUL D. HINZMAN, SSgt, USAF
Comm/Plotter, Wing Security Control

IN PERSON
BY TELEPHONE X
BY MAIL

10. DETAILS OF INCIDENT (Who, what, when, where, how? Include statistic at time of apprehension and give details if underpressive. Attach statements of medical personnel.) At 2059hrs., 16 Nov 77, AIC PHILLIPS, Samuel A., Lima Security Control, telephoned WSC and reported an OZ alarm activation at L-9 and that Lima SAT #1, AIC JENKINS & AIC RAEKE were dispatched. (Trip #62, ETA 2135hrs.) At 2147hrs., AIC PHILLIPS telephoned WSC and reported that the situation at L-9 had been upgraded to a COVERED WAGON per request of CAPT STOKES, Larry D., FSO. Security Option II was initiated by WSC and Base CSC. BAF(Backup Security CONTD

11. EVALUATION ☑ UNFOUNDED ☐ MISDEMEANOR ☐ FELONY ☐ MILITARY OFFENSE ☐ TRAFFIC
12. PERSONS RELATED TO REPORT (Insert category of relationship letter opposite name)
A. COMPLAINANT B. VICTIM C. SUSPECT D. WITNESS E. WP/SP/AP F. INVESTIGATED BY G. APPREHENDED BY

	NAME	GRADE	SSN	ORGANIZATION OR ADDRESS AND PHONE NO.
E	JENKINS, Kenneth C.	AIC	571-13-9597	44 MSS (68-3)
E	RAEKE, Wayne E.	AIC	305-68-7556	44 MSS (68-3)
F	STEWART, Robert E.	TSgt	211-28-7556	44 MSS (68-3)
F	STOKES, Larry D.	Capt	339-40-9406	44 MSS (88-3)

13. DISPOSITION OF INCIDENT/COMPLAINT
REFERRED TO   AFOSI

C. EVIDENCE (List and describe, or summarize as appropriate)
All evidence retained by AFOSI and FBI

2 - 44SMW, /RCO
1 - SAC   1 FILE
1 - OSAF

RICHARD F. LYON, Colonel, USAF
Chief, Security Police EAFB

SIGNED

(27)
1649

REMARKS
CONTINUED FROM ITEM #10
Force) #1&#2, were formed. At 2340h-m., 16 Nov 77, the following information was
learned: Upon arrival (2132hrs) at Site #L-9, LSAT, JENKINS & RAEKE, dismounted the
SAT vehicle to make a check of the site fence line. At this time RAEKE observed
a bright light shinning vertically upwards from the rear of the fence line of L-9.
(There is a small hill approximately 50 yards behind L-9) JENKINS stayed with the
SAT vehicle and RAEKE proceeded to the source of the light to investigate. As
RAEKE approached the crest of the hill, he observed an individuals dressed in a glowing
green metallic uniform and wearing a helmet with visor. RAEKE immediately challenged
the individual, however; the individual refused to stop and kept walking towards the
rear fence line of L-9. RAEKE aimed his M-16 rifle at the intruder and ordered him
to stop. The intruder turned towards RAEKE and aimed a object at RAEKE which emitted
a bright flash of intense light. The flash of light struck RAEKE'S M-16 rifle, disintegrating the weapon and causing second and third degree burns to RAEKE'S hands. RAEK
immediately took cover and concealment and radioed the situation to JENKINS, who in-
turn radioed a 10-13 distress to Line Control. JENKINS responded to RAEKE'S position
and carried RAEKE back to the SAT vehicle. JENKINS then returned to the rear fence
line to stand guard. JENKINS observed two intruders dressed in the same uniforms,
walk through the rear fence line of L-9. JENKINS challenged the two individuals but
they refused to stop. JENKINS aimed and fired two rounds from his M-16 rifle. One
bullet struck one intruder in the back and one bullet struck one intruder in the
helmet. Both intruders fell to the ground, however, approximately 15 seconds later
both returned to an upright position and fired several flashes of light at JENKINS.
JENKINS took cover and the light missed JENKINS. The two intruders returned to the
east side of the hill and disappeared. JENKINS followed the two and observed them
go inside a saucer shaped object approximately 20' in diameter and 20' thick. The
object emitted a glowing greenish light. Once the intruders were inside, the object
climbed vertically upwards and disappeared over the Eastern horizon. EMF #1 arrived
at the site at 2230hrs., and set up a security perimeter. Site Survey Teams arrived
at the site (0120hrs.) and took radiation readings, which measured from 1.7 to 2.9
roentgens. (Missile Maintenance examined the missile and warhead and found the nuclear
components missing from the warhead.) COL. SPRAKER, Wing Cmdr, arrived at the site

 Declassified

OFFICIAL USE ONLY

.... the site a .... all non-essential personnel
out of the area. All evidence found at the scene and the follow-up report will be
classified by order of COL. Spraker.
ADDITIONAL INFORMATION: RAEKE was treated at the Base Hospital by MOD (Capt)
Sanders for second and third degree radiation burns to each hand. RAEKE was
Air-O-Vac'd to an unspecified location. RAEKE'S M-16 rifle could not be located
at the site.

Declassified

****TOP SECRET****

WED ENTERPRISES • A Division of Buena Vista Distribution Co., Inc., subsidiary of Walt Disney Productions

imagineering®

November 9, 1978

Ambassador Griffith
Mission of Grenada to the United Nations
866 Second Avenue
Suite 502
New York, New York 10017

Dear Ambassador Griffith:

I wanted to convey to you my views on our extra-terrestrial visitors popularly referred to as "UFO's", and suggest what might be done to properly deal with them.

I believe that these extra-terrestrial vehicles and their crews are visiting this planet from other planets, which obviously are a little more technically advanced than we are here on earth. I feel that we need to have a top level, coordinated program to scientifically collect and analyze data from all over the earth concerning any type of encounter, and to determine how best to interface with these visitors in a friendly fashion. We may first have to show them that we have learned to resolve our problems by peaceful means, rather than warfare, before we are accepted as fully qualified universal team members. This acceptance would have tremendous possibilities of advancing our world in all areas. Certainly then it would seem that the UN has a vested interest in handling this subject properly and expeditiously.

I should point out that I am not an experienced UFO professional researcher. I have not yet had the privilege of flying a UFO, nor of meeting the crew of one. I do feel that I am somewhat qualified to discuss them since I have been into the fringes of the vast areas in which they travel. Also, I did have occasion in 1951 to have two days of observation of many flights of them, of different sizes, flying in fighter formation, generally from east to west over Europe. They were at a higher altitude than we could reach with our jet fighters at that time.

I would also like to point out that most astronauts are very reluctant to even discuss UFO's due to the great numbers of people who have indescriminately sold fake stories and forged documents abusing their names and reputations without hesitation. Those few astronauts who have continued to have a participation in the UFO field have had to do so very cautiously. There are several of us who do believe in UFO's and who have had occasion to see a UFO on the ground, or from an airplane. There was only one occasion from space which may have been a UFO.

If the UN agrees to pursue this project, and to lend their credibility to it, perhaps many more well qualified people will agree to step forth and provide help and information.

I am looking forward to seeing you soon.

                                        Sincerely,

                                        L. Gordon Cooper
                                        Col. USAF (Ret)
                                        Astronaut

LGC:jm

70   NOV 15 1979

SWAN COMPANY
general contractors
P.O. Box 1470 • Honokaa, HI 96727 • (808) 885-5400

April 5, 1989

Linda Howe
P.O. Box 3130
Littelton, Colorado
80161-3130

Dear Linda:

A few months ago you called me regarding an old friend of mine, William (Bill) Cooper. You asked me to confirm seeing and receiving documents from Bill Cooper on the night of his wedding in 1972.

I have been reluctant to discuss this with you and with the numerous people who have been trying to contact me. I have never met you or any of the other people that called me on the phone. I would have liked to have met with John Leer, however, when I was finally able to return his call, he had checked out of his hotel in Honolulu.

Bill and I were close friends. We discussed numerous subjects. However, when I would push in an area of a classified nature, he simply said that he could not discuss it. Throughout our friendship, I was involved in commercial as well as a sportdiving operations based out of Honolulu (Skin Diving Hawaii). The work which we were involved in required team work and trust. Often the topic of UFO's would be discussed. I learned through Bill that every space flight was accompanied by UFO's. As I have said, Bill and I were good friends. I was best man at his wedding. On the eve of his wedding, there was no party.

Here is what I remember of that evening.

Bill wanted to discuss something which was troubling him. I was there to listen. Through the course of our conversation, Bill produced some documents which contained what I believed to be classified information. It was about an alien base on the back side of the moon, as well as other information of a tender nature that Bill was involved in at CINCPACFLT in Naval Intelligence. I believed at the time and still do that this information was true. We decided that I should keep copies of this information in case anything happen to Bill.

PLANS • DESIGN • CONSTRUCTION MANAGEMENT

****TOP SECRET****

Linda Howe
April 5, 1989
Page Two

Unfortunately all I can remember is Space shots and the
bases on the Moon. Whether this is due to the information
being so unbelievable or so disturbing, I cannot say.
Discussions of the assassination of JFK came up but I cannot
remember where they led. I have given that evening a great
deal of thought since you called, and have· tried to piece
together that evening. This is all I can come up with. The
information which I was to hang onto has since disappeared.
I wish I could be more help to you and Bill, but I do not
have the documents and cannot positively confirm anything
other than what I have told you.

If you talk to Bill, please express my feelings of
frustration in trying to recreate one evening 17 years ago.

Cordially,

Robert J. Swan

PART 1211—EXTRATERRESTRIAL EXPOSURE

Sec.
1211.100 Scope.
1211.101 Applicability.
1211.102 Definitions.
1211.103 Authority.
1211.104 Policy.
1211.105 Relationship with Departments of Health, Education, and Welfare and Agriculture.
1211.106 Cooperation with States, territories, and possessions.
1211.107 Court or other process.
1211.108 Violations.

AUTHORITY: Secs. 203, 304, 72 Stat. 429, 433; 42 U.S.C. 2455, 2456, 2473; 18 U.S.C. 799; Art. IX, TIAS 6347 (18 UST 2416).

SOURCE: 34 FR 11975, July 16, 1969, unless otherwise noted.

§ 1211.100 Scope.

This part establishes:

(a) NASA policy, responsibility and authority to guard the Earth against any harmful contamination or adverse changes in its environment resulting from personnel, spacecraft and other property returning to the Earth after landing on or coming within the atmospheric envelope of a celestial body; and

(b) Security requirements, restrictions and safeguards that are necessary in the interest of the national security.

§ 1211.101 Applicability.

The provisions of this part apply to all NASA manned and unmanned space missions which land on or come within the atmospheric envelope of a celestial body and return to the Earth.

§ 1211.102 Definitions.

(a) "NASA" and the "Administrator" mean, respectively the National Aeronautics and Space Administration and the Administrator of the National Aeronautics and Space Administration or his authorized representative (see § 1204.509 of this chapter).

(b) "Extraterrestrially exposed" means the state or condition of any person, property, animal or other form of life or matter whatever, who or which has:

(1) Touched directly or come within the atmospheric envelope of any other celestial body; or

(2) Touched directly or been in close proximity to (or been exposed indirectly to) any person, property, animal or other form of life or matter who or which has been extraterrestrially exposed by virtue of paragraph (b)(1) of this section.

For example, if person or thing "A" touches the surface of the Moon, and on "A's" return to the Earth, "B" touches "A" and, subsequently, "C" touches "B," all of these—"A" through "C" inclusive—would be extraterrestrially exposed ("A" and "B" directly; "C" indirectly).

(c) "Quarantine" means the detention, examination and decontamination of any person, property, animal or other form of life or matter whatever that is extraterrestrially exposed, and includes the apprehension or seizure of such person, property, animal or other form of life or matter whatever.

(d) "Quarantine period" means a period of consecutive calendar days as may be established in accordance with § 1211.104(a).

(e) "United States" means the 50 States, the District of Columbia, the Commonwealth of Puerto Rico, the Virgin Islands, Guam, American Samoa and any other territory or possession of the United States, and in a territorial sense all places and waters subject to the jurisdiction of the United States.

§ 1211.103 Authority.

(a) Sections 203 and 304 of the National Aeronautics and Space Act of 1958, as amended (42 U.S.C. 2473, 2455 and 2456).

(b) 18 U.S.C. 799.

(c) Article IX, Outer Space Treaty, TIAS 6347 (18 UST 2416).

(d) NASA Management Instructions 1052.90 and 8020.13.

§ 1211.104 Policy.

(a) *Administrative actions.* The Administrator or his designee as authorized by § 1204.509 of this chapter shall in his discretion:

(1) Determine the beginning and duration of a quarantine period with respect to any space mission; the quarantine period as it applies to various life forms will be announced.

****TOP SECRET****

National Aeronautics and Space Admin.   § 1211.104

(2) Designate in writing quarantine officers to exercise quarantine authority.

(3) Determine that a particular person, property, animal, or other form of life or matter whatever is extraterrestrially exposed and quarantine such person, property, animal, or other form of life or matter whatever. The quarantine may be based only on a determination, with or without the benefit of a hearing, that there is probable cause to believe that such person, property, animal or other form of life or matter whatever is extraterrestrially exposed.

(4) Determine within the United States or within vessels or vehicles of the United States the place, boundaries, and rules of operation of necessary quarantine stations.

(5) Provide for guard services by contract or otherwise, as may be necessary, to maintain security and inviolability of quarantine stations and quarantined persons, property, animals, or other form of life or matter whatever.

(6) Provide for the subsistence, health, and welfare of persons quarantined under the provisions of this part.

(7) Hold such hearings at such times, in such manner and for such purposes as may be desirable or necessary under this part, including hearings for the purpose of creating a record for use in making any determination under this part or for the purpose of reviewing any such determination.

(8) Cooperate with the Department of Health, Education, and Welfare and the Department of Agriculture in accordance with the provisions of § 1211.105.

(9) Take such other actions as may be prudent or necessary and which are consistent with this part.

(b) *Quarantine.* (1) During any period of announced quarantine, the property within the posted perimeter of the Lunar Receiving Laboratory at the Manned Spacecraft Center, Houston, Tex., is designated as the NASA Lunar Receiving Laboratory Quarantine Station.

(2) Other quarantine stations may be established if determined necessary as provided in paragraph (a)(4) of this section.

(3) During any period of announced quarantine, no person shall enter or depart from the limits of any quarantine station without permission of the cognizant NASA quarantine officer. During such period, the posted perimeter of a quarantine station shall be secured by armed guard.

(4) Any person who enters the limits of any quarantine station during the quarantine period shall be deemed to have consented to the quarantine of his person if it is determined that he is or has become extraterrestrially exposed.

(5) At the earliest practicable time, each person who is quarantined by NASA shall be given a reasonable opportunity to communicate by telephone with legal counsel or other persons of his choice.

§ 1211.105 Relationship with Departments of Health, Education, and Welfare and Agriculture.

(a) If either the Department of Health, Education, and Welfare or the Department of Agriculture exercises its authority to quarantine an extraterrestrially exposed person, property, animal, or other form of life or matter whatever, NASA will, except as provided in paragraph (c) of this section, not exercise the authority to quarantine that same person, property, animal, or other form of life or matter whatever. In such cases, NASA will offer to these departments the use of the Lunar Receiving Laboratory Quarantine Station and such other service, equipment, personnel, and facilities as may be necessary to ensure an effective quarantine.

(b) If neither the Department of Health, Education, and Welfare or the Department of Agriculture exercises its quarantine authority, NASA shall exercise the authority to quarantine an extraterrestrially exposed person, property, animal or other form of life or matter whatever. In such cases, NASA will inform these departments of such quarantine action, in addition, may request the use of such service, equipment, personnel and facilities of other Federal departments and agencies as may be necessary to ensure an effective quarantine.

§ 1211.105

(c) NASA shall quarantine NASA astronauts and other NASA personnel as determined necessary and all NASA property involved in any space mission.

§ 1211.106   Cooperation with States, territories, and possessions.

Actions taken in accordance with the provisions of this part shall be exercised in cooperation with the applicable authority of any State, territory, possession or any political subdivision thereof.

§ 1211.107   Court or other process.

(a) NASA officers and employees are prohibited from discharging from the limits of a quarantine station any quarantined person, property, animal or other form of life or matter whatever during order or other request, order or demand an announced quarantine period in compliance with a subpoena, show cause of any court or other authority without the prior approval of the General Counsel and the Administrator.

(b) Where approval to discharge a quarantined person, property, animal or other form of life or matter whatever in compliance with such a request, order or demand of any court or other authority is not given, the person to whom it is directed shall, if possible, appear in court or before the other authority and respectfully state his inability to comply, relying for his action upon this § 1211.107.

§ 1211.108   Violations.

Whoever, willfully violates, attempts to violate, or conspires to violate any provision of this part or any regulation or order issued under this part or who enters or departs from the limits of any quarantine station in disregard of the quarantine rules or regulations or without permission of the NASA quarantine officer shall be fined not more than $5,000 or imprisoned not more than 1 year, or both (18 U.S.C. 799).

CNO Executive Panel Advisory Committee; Closed Meeting

Pursuant to the provisions of the Federal Advisory Committee Act (5 U.S.C. App. 2), notice is hereby given that the Chief of Naval Operations (CNO) Executive Panel Advisory Committee Technology Surprise Task Force will meet February 15–16, 1990 from 9 a.m. to 5 p.m. each day, in Los Alamos, New Mexico. All sessions will be closed to the public.

The purpose of this meeting is to discuss the possibility of unexpected technological breakthroughs that vastly change warfighting capabilities. The entire agenda of the meeting will consist of discussions of key issues regarding the potential for unexpected technology breakthroughs that could have an acute impact on naval and other military forces. These matters constitute classified information that is specifically authorized by Executive Order to be kept secret in the interest of national defense and is, in fact, properly classified pursuant to such Executive Order. Accordingly, the Secretary of the Navy has determined in writing that the public interest requires that all sessions of the meeting be closed to the public because they will be concerned with matters listed in section 552b(c)(1) of title 5, United States Code.

For further information concerning this meeting, contact: Faye Buckman, Secretary to the CNO Executive Panel Advisory Committee, 4401 Ford Avenue, room 601, Alexandria, Virginia 22302–0268, Phone (703) 756–1205..

22 November 1989

BRANCH
OF CIA

USSR: MEDIA REPORT MULTITUDE OF UFO SIGHTINGS

Leading Soviet newspapers and journals have recently begun publishing an increasing number of articles and news reports on sightings of unidentified flying objects (UFOs) in various areas of the Soviet Union. A "permanent center" for the study of UFOs has been established in Moscow to conduct research and support the investigation of reported sightings.

* *

Setting the tone for this media coverage was an article in the 9 July 1989 SOTSIALISTICHESKAYA INDUSTRIYA, which referred to many recent reports of UFO sightings in the USSR. Interviewed by the paper, P. Prokopenko, director of a laboratory for the study of "anomalous phenomena," stated that a "permanent center" for the study of UFOs is being established in the Soviet Union. In addition to conducting research and presenting lectures on UFOs, the center will support the investigation of reported sightings.

In referring to an issue of the paper published in July 1988 that included a report on "an amazing event that took place on Hill 611 near the village of Dalnegorsk in Primorskiy Kray," the article noted that the event is still under investigation. Many observers saw a flying sphere crash into one of the hill's twin peaks, and physicists and other scientists from the Siberian Division of the USSR Academy of Sciences are still studying the "fine mesh," "small spherical objects," and "pieces of glass" that are considered to be small remnants left behind by the sphere. According to the article, the alleged spacecraft was nearly obliterated in the crash, but there appears to be enough material at the site for the scientists--a mixture of UFO "enthusiasts" and skeptics--to eventually "penetrate this mystery."

In studying the site, scientist A. Makeyev reported finding gold, silver, nickel, alpha-titanium, molybdenum, and compounds of beryllium. One of the "skeptical" physicists from Tomsk has hypothesized that the so-called sphere could have been some kind of a "plasmoid," formed by the "interaction of geophysical force fields," which captured the elements found by Makeyev from the atmosphere on its trajectory toward disintegration on the hilltop. Other researchers have generally rejected this explanation since the amounts of various types of metals found at the site would imply, according to this "plasmoid" theory, that "the concentration of metals in the atmosphere should exceed the present level by a factor of 4,000."

Foreign Broadcast Information Service, Production Group
John Haley   SET Center   733-6320
FB PN 89-292

**** T O P   S E C R E T ****

Some of the scientists have concluded that the object that crashed into Hill 611 was an "extraterrestrial" space vehicle constructed by highly intelligent beings. Doctor of Chemical Sciences V. Vysotskiy stated that "without doubt, this is evidence of a high technology, and it is not anything of a natural or terrestrial origin." He cited the fact that the remnants of fine mesh included bits of thin threads with a diameter of only 17 microns and that these threads, in turn, were composed of even thinner strands twisted into braids. Extremely thin gold wires were discovered intertwined in the finest threads--evidence of an intricate technology beyond the present capabilities of terrestrial science, according to Vysotskiy.

SOTSIALISTICHESKAYA INDUSTRIYA of 25 July 1989 reported that a UFO sighting had been claimed by engineer Yuriy Ponomarenko and a group of workers at a collective farm in the Dnepropetrovsk region.[2] The object was described as a disk with two beams of light emanating from its sides. The witnesses maintained that they had observed the object on the ground for about 20 minutes, and that it emitted no sound when it flew away.

The August 1989 issue of the Soviet journal NAUKA I ZHIZN included a 9-page article which, after summarizing the history of UFO sightings in general, contrasted some of the views of the "skeptics" with some of the opinions of the "enthusiasts" on the numerous reported UFO sightings in the USSR, including incidents in Serpukhov, Petrozavodsk, and Rudnya. According to the "enthusiasts," UFOs have left evidence of their visits on many occasions, including the Serpukhov incident in which, they claim, a UFO left a circular depression in the grass with a diameter of 4 meters. The skeptics maintain that most of this so-called "evidence" can be explained as having no connection with extraterrestrial intelligence. Many of the sightings could be attributed to rocket testing, for example. Academician Vladimir Vasilyevich Migulin, director of the Terrestrial Magnetism, Ionosphere, and Radio Wave Propagation Institute in Troitsk, which has a section for the investigation of anomalous phenomena in the atmosphere, maintains that over 90 percent of UFO sightings can be nullified by such mundane explanations.

STROITELNAYA GAZETA of 16 September 1989 reported that in August a group of observers including physical scientist Elvir Kurchenko began investigating another circular depressed area in a forest near Surgut[3] after a worker claimed that a UFO had visited the site.

SOTSIALISTICHESKAYA INDUSTRIYA of 30 September 1989 noted that media all over the Soviet Union were receiving reports of UFO sightings on the ground and in the air, adding that the paper's editorial office was reviewing hundreds of reports related to UFO incidents. In response to this deluge of reports, the paper interviewed Anatoliy Listratov, chairman of the section of the All-Union Astronomical and Geodesic Society assigned to the study of anomalous phenomena, who said that although his group is "still wandering around in the darkness," some important developments in the investigations had recently occurred. He stated that "at the sites of the landings...the operating frequency of a crystal-controlled oscillator changes. Simply speaking, electronic timepieces run at rates that are either too fast or too slow."

Listratov noted that Soviet military officers and pilots had recently started providing some documentation on UFO sightings. As an example, he stated that he had documentary information regarding an encounter between Soviet aircraft and a UFO over the city of Borisov.[4] The crews of two

-2-

Soviet aircraft reported seeing a large flying disk in their vicinity with
five beams of light emanating from it: three beams were directed toward
the ground and two were projected upward when the object was first sighted.
The ground controller instructed one of the planes to alter its course and
approach the object, at which point the disk flew to the same level and
aimed one of its beams at the approaching Soviet plane, illuminating the
cockpit. Listratov cited the pilot's log as stating: "At this time, the
copilot was at the controls. He observed the maneuver that the object had
just carried out and was able to raise his hand to shield himself from the
unbearable light. The aircraft commander was resting in the adjoining
seat, and a bright ray of light, projecting a spot with a diameter of 20
centimeters, passed across his body. Both pilots felt heat."

According to Listratov, the aircraft commander and his copilot both
became "invalids" shortly after the incident. The copilot was forced to
leave his job due to a sudden deterioration in his health, including the
onset of sudden prolonged periods of "loss of consciousness." The aircraft
commander died within a few months. The cause of death was listed as
"cancer," and "injury to the organism as a result of radiation from the
unidentified flying object" was listed as a contributing factor on the
official medical record in the hospital where the commander died, according
to Listratov.

Listratov told SOTSIALISTICHESKAYA INDUSTRIYA that about 95 percent of
UFO sightings could be explained, and investigations have often revealed
them to be burned-out rocket stages or the remnants of unsuccessful rocket
launches. It is the 5 percent that cannot be explained that is causing all
the commotion among Soviet scientists and military personnel. Instead of
the widespread skepticism that he had expected when he first began to
interview military personnel, he noted that officers and soldiers had told
him about their own encounters with UFOs, and they had even shown him
reports that had been completely filled out on official forms.

KOMSOMOLSKAYA PRAVDA of 7 October reported that the Soviet Union had
just opened an official center for the study of UFOs in Moscow.
Physicists, geologists, astronomers, and psychologists are teaching courses
on the various characteristics of the UFOs that have been reported and the
types of equipment necessary to investigate UFO sightings.

On 9 October the Soviet news agency TASS reported that a UFO had landed
in a park in the city of Voronezh.[5] TASS reported that the object had been
observed by many witnesses before it left.

KOMSOMOLSKAYA PRAVDA of 12 October reported that a group of scientists
had visited a field in Perm Oblast[6] to investigate claims that a UFO had
landed in that area and had left behind a circular impression measuring 62
meters in diameter.

KRASNAYA ZVEZDA of 13 October suggested that mass hysteria may be an
important factor contributing to the recent outburst of widespread claims
of encounters with UFOs in the USSR. According to the paper, many elements
of the Soviet media were fanning this phenomenon, which it compared to the
hysteria resulting from Orson Welles' radio broadcast in 1938 about an
invasion of the United States by extraterrestrials.

The 19-25 October issue of POISK carried an article contrasting the
viewpoints of scientists from the two main Soviet institutes presently

-3-

engaged in investigating UFO reports--the newly established center for UFO
studies in the Palace of Culture of Power Engineers in Moscow and the
Terrestrial Magnetism, Ionosphere, and Radio Wave Propagation Institute,
which has branches in Troitsk, Leningrad, and Irkutsk. Physicist Yuriy
Platov of the Terrestrial Magnetism Institute does not believe the claims
of scientists who maintain they have found remnants in Dalnegorsk of a UFO
constructed by extraterrestrials, and he is convinced that the materials
found at that site are really only the remnants of the unsuccessful launch
of a Soviet rocket in that region. He believes that many of the other
reports of UFOs can be explained by the inability of the observers to
recognize the phenomenon known as "ball lightning."

The POISK article contrasted Platov's view with that of another
physical scientist, Vladimir Azhazha, who was recently elected chairman of
the new All-Union Commission for the Study of Unidentified Flying Objects
of the Union of Scientific and Engineering Societies. Azhazha compared
reports of a UFO crash in the USSR with a claim by UFO enthusiasts in the
United States that a UFO had crashed in the desert near Roswell, New
Mexico, in 1947. He believes there is sufficient evidence to support the
claims of UFO crashes in both cases--in Dalnegorsk and in Roswell. In the
latter case, he cited the testimony of eyewitnesses who maintained that
they had seen the bodies of four extraterrestrials lying near the smashed
spacecraft. According to Platov, however, the eyewitnesses in the Roswell
case were mistaken. He believes that the object that crashed was a USAF
experimental rocket with four Rhesus monkeys aboard and that the accident
was the result of an unsuccessful launch attempt at the dawn of the space
era.

SOTSIALISTICHESKAYA INDUSTRIYA of 21 October noted that hundreds of
residents had reported observing a UFO in Omsk[7]and that many of these
eyewitnesses had reported the sighting directly to the paper's office in
Omsk. The article included a report by an "authoritative" military
officer, Maj V. Loginov, who stated: "I must tell you straight off that
radar did not detect this object, and so I am reporting visual
observations. The object was passing over at an altitude of several
kilometers. The visible shining sphere appeared to be about one and a half
times as large as the moon's shape in the night sky. Four projectors--some
parallel and some at angles to the Earth--were casting very bright beams.
The object was in the field of vision for about 5 minutes...hovering...over
the civil airport before descending a little. Then the projectors were
turned off and a whirling plume trail instantaneously appeared around this
shining sphere. The object began to recede rapidly in a direction from the
northwest to the east at the same time that flights were being carried out
from a neighboring airport. Pilots were able to observe it visually, but
they could not detect it on their radar screens.... Radar signals could
not be reflected from it. This object was immediately reported up the
chain-of-command, and our colleagues in the Altay Kray, in the area toward
which the object flew, reported back to us within 5 minutes that they had
it under visual observation. That meant that it had covered a distance of
approximately 600 kilometers at a speed of about 7,000 kilometers per
hour."

According to Loginov, all observations indicated that the object was a
UFO being controlled by some kind of intelligence and that it was not
merely some kind of anomalous atmospheric phenomenon.

-4-

SOVETSKAYA KULTURA of 28 October reported on the results of a
conference in Petrozavodsk of about 100 Soviet scientists representing the
"various branches of science and technology." The main topic of discussion
was the multitude of claims of recent UFO sightings in the USSR. According
to SOVETSKAYA KULTURA, more questions about UFOs were raised at this
conference than were answered.

LITERATURNAYA GAZETA of 1 November reported that Voronezh, where some
observers had claimed to have witnessed the landing and take-off of a UFO,
has become the place for a "pilgrimage" by correspondents seeking
sensational news for their newspapers, regardless of the controversial
nature of the so-called "weighty evidence" being presented as proof that
extraterrestrials had visited Voronezh.

Mr. William M. Cooper
19744 Beach Blvd., Box 301
Huntington Beach, CA 92648   PERSONAL AND CONFIDENTIAL

Dear Bill:

     Even though by now it is old news to you, a few nights ago I
viewed the "Best Evidence 2" George Knapp tape and was disgusted
by the obvious hatchet job Knapp, Lear, Moore et al did on you.

     It seemed very clear to me that Knapp and his family were
probably threatened, although it is very likely that the whole
series was government sponsored in the first place.   I was
reminded of the point made by Whitley Strieber in MAJESTIC, that
Admiral Hillenkoetter probably told Truman that the best way to
enforce the utmost secrecy was to tell each man that the aliens
themselves had insisted on it, OR ELSE.... Maybe that ploy
worked on Knapp. And certainly the slant of the closing comments
indicated that the government still was helpless in the face of a
very superior adversary. And that may be true.

     Although it is small consolation to you, and I realize that
you must be in great pain and anguish, it reminded me of that old
quotation from Alexander Pope: "Whenever a true genius appears
you can always know him by this sign: that all the Dunces are in
confederacy against him!"

     Bill, I just want you to know that at least to me, and to
many more who may not be expressing it to you, what you have had
the immense courage to say on the Sedona tape and the other
places you have spoken, certainly has the ring of truth about it.
In my opinion you deserve the Highest Commendation this country
can bestow on a man! Instead, they tried to crucify you.

     It is also clear that most of the points you made on the
Sedona tape have been countered by, for example, the article in
PEOPLE magazine on General Khun Sah (sp.?), the son of the police
officer in Dallas who suddenly claims his Father assassinated
Kennedy, and George Bush emerging from the Economic Summit meeting and declaring his sudden conversion to upholding the Constitution. You definitely seem to be doing something right!

     Perhaps one of the most disturbing aspects of all of this is
the lying, spying, disinformation, dirty tricks, ridicule,
discrediting and outright deception perpetrated by agents paid
by our own tax monies!

     In my case, a woman entered my life who seemed to be so
interested in the same kinds of things, so intelligent, supportive, and delightful that she seemed almost too good to be true.
She was.   Six months after she walked out on me with no prior
warning the day after my Mother died(!), I found out from a

1

****TOP SECRET****

former(?) National Security Agent that she had said things to him which made him certain that she was a Government Agent sent to find out how much I knew, set me up, and emotionally destroy me. And I'm not altogether sure that this "friend" didn't have something to do with it.

The message was quite clear. They wanted me to know that they could "get me" at the deepest, most personal and painful level! May Almighty God repay them in kind so they can find out exactly how it feels! It simply amazes me that these little rats have not yet figured out that if they succeed in creating the kind of world which they seem intent upon, they are going to re-incarnate into it and be on the receiving end of their creation.

On the Las Vegas tape, you alluded to the Canadian scientist who quoted his correspondence with one of President Eisenhower's Science Advisors, Dr. Robert Sarbacher. Bob Sarbacher and I became friends a few years before his death, and he told me of the dead alien bodies he saw, and the fact that the policy making group headed by Vannevar Bush (any relation to George?) had decided rightly or wrongly to cover up everything to avoid a panic. But even more than panic, they were afraid that post-war American Industry would lose heart when confronted with such overwhelming technological superiority, and that no one would go to work again! And THAT they could not allow.

If you ever get to the Palm Beach area, I would very much enjoy meeting you and talking with you. Very privately.

In the mean time, I would like to order a copy of your new book, BEHOLD A PALE HORSE. Enclosed is my check for $22, which I believe is the correct amount, and add me to your mailing list.

By the way, did you happen to see the Oct. 30, 1990 issue of THE WEEKLY WORLD NEWS with the cover story "Alien Captured by U.S. Agents" with lots of photos. What is your opinion? This paper is a sister publication to THE NATIONAL ENQUIRER, previously owned by the late Generoso Pope, who was said to have been a former CIA agent. -If there is such a thing as a "former" CIA Agent. Apparently Pope hired the most erudite, competent reporters he could find, really a blue ribbon staff, and 99% of all the information they uncovered and stories they wrote disappeared into the big computer, inaccessible to everyone including the authors, except Mr. Pope. Pretty slick information-gathering.

I wish you every success in getting your crucial information to the public and may God Bless You, Protect You, and Keep You.

May the Truth Come To Light,

Millard

William S. English
P.O. Box 3508 Boles Station
Alamogordo, New Mexico 88310

William M. Cooper
1311 S. Highland #205
Fullerton, California 92632

June 7, 1989

Dear Bill,

Thought I'd write a letter and let you know that I have indeed received your most recent upload, and as per your request all record has been removed from the board and all other copies in my files have been deleted. It's powerful stuff and I hope that those in attendence will be open enough at least to concider the possibilities if not the realities of what your talking about.

I regret to say that at this point it looks as though I will not be able to attend the conference at the end of the month as much as I would like to. Frankly I feel that my presence along with yours is necessary, but finances are an extreme problem at this point. With the medical bills piling up from my wife's recent miscarriage and my stroke, and then the most recent loss of my job, we are extremely lucky not to be forced to live in the car at the moment, and that's a very distinct possibility that looms in the future. I have sold off just about everything except my computer and the few odds and ends that help to keep us going on a day to day basis. Oh well....shit happens.

I am interested in your reaction to Dick Scheffler. Dick is a fairly out spoken person and some what talkative so don't be put off by him. He really is in fact a nice guy, but doesn't really understand the gravity of what is taking place. Even though he says that he does. A word of advice to you when you meet with him. If you don't want to see it in the news don't say it to him. I have had a hell of a time keeping your speeches away from him in order to protect you as you requested. Dick's heart is in the right place however, so don't be to put off by him. He knows very little about what we are doing, but his enthusiasm is genuine.

I was extremely impressed with your most recent speech, and go on record that my research pretty much confirms what yours has. It is interesting that we have managed to keep our collective buts in one piece over the past several years, however that is something that could well be remedied very shortly if we don't take certain precautions. In point of fact a great deal of pressure is being brought to bear on a number of people. Most notibly yourself and Bill Steinman. I had spoken with Steinman in person when he came to Alamogordo to see me and we discust the possibility of writing a book together. It was about three weeks after that I received a call from him.

When he called he sounded very frightened and said that he was leaving UFO investigation permanently and suggested that I do the same. He would not give me any clear reason, but made it clear that he was in fear of his life and that of his family. His loss to the field will be felt deeply, but were I he I suppose that I would do the same thing. Ufortunately I cannot place myself in his position, as much as I would like to at times.

The rumor concerning your death was obviously premature, and when I received the information I wasn't exactly sure it was true at the time but I felt that I should take precautions and went and got a gun to carry just in case. Needless to say, I was greatly releaved to find out that it wasn't true. When and if we have the opportunity to get together in person and in private I will be glad to explain the exact circumstances of your reported demise. In the meantime don't believe everything that you might hear. It seems the rumor mill is going full steam at this point. However, again, I say watch your POPO!

If there is anything that I can do to help you, please let me know. I still look forward to the possibility of us going that seminar tour that you proposed. Keep me abreast of that situation if you would.

Take care,
kind regards to you and your family...

Sincerely,

Bill English

February 19, 1990

Dear Ronald,

Thank you for your interest in "Open Mind"....that was
quite an experience. I suppose I'll never know of the impact
of that show. Even though it has been off the year for over
three years now, I still get stacks of mail, from all over
the world.....there must be a zillion tapes out there. Some
people trade them like baseball cards.

I have no idea what happened to Jim, who like you, was
caught up in the moon photo subject. However, you might want
to contact Fred Steckling, Box 1722, Vista, CA 92083
concerning his book, "Alien Bases on the Moon" and any
following research he might have done. George Leonard's
"Somebody Else Is On The Moon", published by McKasy is out of
print, but you might find it in a library. Richard Hoaland
has published a book, "Monuments of Mars" which is generally
available to books stores and there is "Mars Project", Route
1, Box 473 B, Casa Grade, Arizona 85222 (602-836-5637).

There is other information I wish I could share with
you on this subject which is mind-blowing.....and hopefully
it will be made public sometime this year as glasnost spreads
to the United States government.

At the moment, there are no legitimate broadcast of
"Open Mind" on the air, but I am now back at KABC, so the
foot is in the door, should I want to do it again....and
perhaps I should. This time, should it occure, we will do
the necessary legal steps to make the shows available through
ABC/Capitol Cities in cassette form.

Again, thank you for your interest in Open Mind and I
hope this information is helpful to you.

Warmest Regards

Bill Jenkins

Bill
I hope you can get other info
from Bill Jenkins I could not

Ron

Please let me know if you can!

1

Milton William Cooper
P.O. Box #3299
Camp Verde Valley, AZ
86322-3299   Wednesday, 23 Jan 1991

At your request I have made a few inquiries regarding the past
law enforcement career of Don Ecker. As you indicated, and as I
have myself discovered, Mr. Ecker claims to have had ten years in
law enforcement as a criminal investigator for the State of Idaho
as well as experience with the Canyon County Sheriff's Dept.
First and foremost, my inquiries are not based upon any known
infractions of law, but are to confirm or refute a claim of a
particular career in law enforcement.

My research has revealed the following:

Donald Francis Ecker II was employed as a prison guard for the
State of Idaho from Sept of 1981 through Sept of 1982. In the fall
of 1982 he went to work for the Canyon County Sheriff's Department
as a Narcotics Officer. This employment as a Narc lasted only six
weeks. He then returned to working as a prison guard until July of
1987. His departure from work as a guard is related to an
unfortunate training accident in which he discharged a shotgun into
his left leg, causing it's loss from the knee down.
A check with other law enforcement agencies as well as the
State of Idaho Bureau of Investigation reveals no employment as a
criminal investigator at any time. Pertinent cross-referencing of
Mr. Ecker's ID verifying information, including his photograph as
published alongside magazine articles he authored, were circulated
between the Canyon County Sheriff's Dept.,the prison, and the
Bureau of Investigation. This resulted in positive confirmation
that the Don Ecker I researched and the Don Ecker you know are one
and the same individual.
I cannot disclose more specific information regarding his
employment, such as the reason for the brevity of service with the
Sheriff's Dept in Canyon County. However, any competent
investigator can easily retreive this information and much more.
Since your request was regarding confirmation or refutation of Mr.
Ecker's claims to a past as a criminal investigator, I have limited
my report to information that is available to the public sector.
In conclusion, there is apparently no support whatsoever for
Mr. Ecker's claim to having been a "criminal investigator for ten
years in the State of Idaho."

Sincerely,
Joseph Hysong
Upton Police Department
Upton, Massachusetts

Marilyn J. Buck
Notary Public   1/23/91

MY COMMISSION EXPIRES FEBRUARY 26, 1993

****TOP SECRET****

Martin Cannon
8211 Owensmouth Ave. #206
Canoga Park, CA 91304
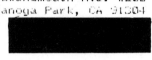

Dear ▮▮▮▮ :

Thanks for your recent letter.

I think that we could indeed be helpful to each other. My
project is now taking me into some very odd areas indeed,
and I need all the guidance possible. But more on that
later.

First:

UFO, vol. 2, #4 includes an article by Barry Taff, written
in conjunction with one Kerry Gaynor, entitled "Paranormal
Phenomena and UFOs." The article itself was not nearly so
interesting as Taff's resumé: "...he has worked with UCLA's
Neuropsychiatric Institute and has acted as a consultant to
a number of governmental agencies, including the National
Institute of Mental Health, Rand Corporation, The Atomic
Energy Commission and the CIA." (Gaynor is described as a
"hypnotherapist and UCLA graduate" who has worked with Taff
from 1974 to 1980.)

Ohh, gee, ▮▮▮▮ ..you actually _trust_ this guy?

Perhaps the most ominous connection in that resume is not to
the CIA, but to the UCLA Neuropsychiatric Institute, Dr.
Louis Jolyon West's spook-house. You must know of West's
covert background -- his work on brainwashing for the CIA,
his horrifying Institute For the Study of Violent behavior,
his connection to the V.A. hospital...and that's just the
beginning. Info on "Jolly" is tough to come by, but I've
got some stuff you won't believe -- especially some very
bizzare tidbits ostensibly connecting him to John Lilly.
West is a spook and a racist, and he has been involved with
all the techniques of mind control.

(I interviewed someone who met West socially; he described
the good doctor -- _and_ his wife! -- as frightening,
peculiar, and very, very strange...almost the stereotypical
"mad scientist." The same descriptions keep on popping up
whenever I get "personal" information on the spy-chiatrists.
You think these guys practice their mind-altering techniques
on each other?)

****TOP SECRET****

Rand, AEC, NIMH -- you _know_ their histories.   Taff is linked
to warmongers, covert operators, and brainwashers. The man
is _bad news_, and any exculpatory fables he tells you should
be disregarded. If you want my advice, stay away from this
guy, even if he claims to offer an inside track on the scoop
of the century, and even if his info tends to verify your
preconceptions. Please don't take this as an insult, but
frankly, the fact that you deal with Taff (and Lear) makes
me uneasy dealing with you.

On the other hand... As you know, my main business right
now is catching the brainwashers. Taff and Gaynor seem to
be possible targets -- their backgrounds make them
suspicious to me. Maybe you can help my project by "picking
their brains" on the subject of mind control. Ask Taff
about the use of microwaves to create auditory phenomena
he mentions this effect (the "Frey effect") in his article,
and connects it to UFOs. I'd like more information on this
topic, but medical references are hard to come by. For
God's sake, though -- don't tell Taff what _I'm_ up to!

Additionally, I'd like to get hold of a photograph of
Gaynor. One excellent method of playing "spot the spook"
might be the trick demonstrated in the film of The Manchurian
Candidate -- flashing a series of photographs past the eyes
of an alleged brainwashing victim, in the hope that images
of certain "doctors" will strike a cord. It's an idea -- if
you have any others, please let me know.

About Vicki -- well, thereby hangs a tale, one which has
caused me no small amount of personal hurt and sorrow and
bewilderment. I've inflicted my angst on everyone I know --
and you'll be no exception, alas; I apologise beforehand for
the torrent of spew to come...

Her uncle is Grant Cooper, the attorney for Sirhan Sirhan --
and for the Johnny Roselli mob, which was intricately
connected to the CIA. I am sending you photocopies of the
relevant pages from Donald Scheim's book, Contract On
America. Theodore Charach's film, The Second Gun (released
on MCI home video as The Plot to Kill Robert F. Kennedy)
contains interviews in which Sirhan's mother curses out her
son's attorneys. As you know, they willfully disregarded
testimony which could have helped Sirhan's case. Morrow's
The Senator Must Die also has useful information. Grant
Cooper is as corrupt as they come, in my opinion: While
defending Roselli's men, he illegally got hold of the
prosecution's list of potential witnesses. (Gee -- now why
would the mob want a thing like _that_?) ←Actually, it's a bit of a hassle to get the xeroxes made right now -- but this summary should do.

As you can guess, the fact that Vicki has an uncle like this
-- and a friend like Barry Taff -- made me nervous. My

2

anxiety was not quelled by Vicki's frequent non-sequitor remarks about the CIA somehow "pushing" her magazine.

Still, I felt I could trust her because she seemed so gung-ho when it came to exposing intelligence agency abuses. She was attending ARDIS lectures, familiarising herself with the Christic case, reading Prouty, talking to Landis and Stockwell and John Judge -- all very impressive.

But then she changed. Whereas once we exchanged information almost daily, suddenly she grew more distant -- and when we did talk, an odd anti-soviet hysteria entered her dialogue. For example, she suggested (employing a truly unique quasi-logic) that the key to my UFO hypothesis might have to do with the "massive" Soviet infiltration of the media; apparently, the abductions are some sort of dirty red propaganda ploy.

Her tone baffled me -- until I met her new boyfriend, one Don Ecker, ex-Green Beret and foreign-policy "fascist" (Vicki's description -- although later she rather annoyingly pinned the words on me). Ecker and I had a genuinely nauseating conversation. He drunkenly interrupted an important discussion I was having with Richard Neal to inform us all of a project SPETSNATZ (the name rings a bell, but I can't place it exactly) which, in his fantasies, involves a Soviet invasion via the north. He insisted that the odious Reds had already skulked across Alaska and were working their way through Canada! (I'm considering placing a call to Gnome information to ask if they've seen any rampaging bolsheviks lately.) He also laughed at my assertion that Secord and North were involved with the Iran hostage rescue mission. "Looks like you haven't done your research, buddy!" -- he said, before launching into the Soldier-of-Fortune version of the event. (Gee, I guess Covert Action, The Nation, The Miami Herald, and Mother Jones all got the story wrong.) He went on to praise covert ops fulsomely. He also produced a card -- picturesquely stained with human blood -- bearing cutely rewritten Miranda rights: "You have the right to have your head bashed in," etc.

I tell you all this not just because the encounter still smarts, but to give you some notion of the extreme-rightest drivel he's no doubt been feeding Vicki. When he upheld the policy of electrically torturing VC prisoners during the war, I flew into a volcanic rage, and spurted out that anyone who did that <u>deserved</u> to be called a baby-burner when he returned to the states. Later, when he relayed my statement to Vicki, he twisted my words to make it seem that I called him a baby-burner personally.

You have to undestand my position -- I once had dinner with a political refugee from Chile, who told (and this was the

3

...sort of monologue that can induce a frightful insomnia in its listeners -- of how he had undergone just this sort of electro-shock torture -- and how the Special Forces played a large part in placing Pinochet in power. So to see this smirking spook Eckert laughing at the idea of "gooks" being "wired up"...well, I gained a new insight into the depths of the human mind that night.

But the worst part was the fact that I could no longer have anything to do with Vicki. I know this decision seems low and foolish -- cutting of a friendship because I'm appalled at her choice of romantic leads. Honest, I wanted her to be happy -- I could sense, previously, that she was a lonely woman, and when she first told me about this fellow, I encouraged her to see him, despite her initial qualms. (Indeed, I might be said to have helped bring them together -- this was before I learned what he was, mind you...) But above all, I wanted Vicki to stay Vicki.

Now I feel betrayed. Vicki and I had, after all, worked quite closely together -- and we were going after the spooks. For that sort of project, you need partners of like mind when it comes to matters political. Then she hops into bed with (for all intents and purposes) the CIA itself! (You know about Special Forces connections with the Company, the Nazis, Laotian drug smuggling, Jonestown, etc.) Suddenly, Vicki changed from Helen Caldicott to Phyllis Shlafly, from an ARDIS attendee to an interested guest at the official ex-spook organisation. Suddenly, she calls me a fanatic. (She also calls her boyfriend a fascist -- apparently, fascism isn't fanaticism.)

Because she presented such an unprecedented case of political elasticity, I wondered if she was a spook. To tell the truth, for a week or three, I was certain of it. My disposition wasn't helped when I learned she was talking behind my back to an abductee -- ███████ -- with whom I've worked closely; Vicki told ███ that I was a KGB agent and should be avoided! Obviously, by this stage, the accusations and counter-accusations reach a level of absurdity. At least my accusations, however fueled by suspicion and hurt feelings, come weighted with some evidence, and are directed toward the accused. Vicki, by comparison, has constantly spread catty "agent" rumours, unconfirmed by any data, behind the backs of every major figure on the UFO scene. You included.

So tell me, now that you know all the sordid details -- what am I to think? Was she spying on me all along? Or should I chalk this whole incident up to a painful lesson in the vagueries of human relations? The whole matter is infinitely confusing, but I know one thing -- I lost a friend, and it stung.

4

APPENDIX C: ALIEN IMPLANTS

In one method, the individual is made to don a helmet covered with wires, and a crystalline cubic affair is put into a niche in the top of the helmet and a strobe light is made to play on the individual's optic nerve in order to entrain patterns onto their brain waves.

The recipient's initial reaction is that his consciousness is aware of scrambled images, which - after the initial shock wears off - are aligned sequentially and impressed into his consciousness.

In short, the person is given a programmed response system. In this way individuals are trained in a brief time to do complex tasks without having to undergo lengthy training.

Sometimes the subject is hypnotized or made to sleep and a high frequency microwave emission is used as a carrier wave on which to transmit encoded data into the nerve complex. This information may be triggered into conscious awareness at a later time by a preset stimulus-response signal in the environment, such as a sub-audio or visual signal. It might be noted here that not only do different alien groups use this technique, but modifications of this technique are used by ▓▓▓▓▓▓▓▓▓▓▓▓▓▓▓▓▓▓▓▓▓▓▓▓▓▓▓▓▓▓▓ Many of the ▓▓▓▓▓▓▓▓▓▓▓▓▓▓▓▓▓▓▓▓▓▓▓▓▓▓ in the United States were carried out in this manner. There are innumerable references to support that statement.

(handwritten right margin:) ASSUME 40 to 50 GHz. (Other specs unknown)

The carrier waves are usually emanations that will parallel the biological field freuqncy of the entity itself, or resonate upon it.

They are often sound-code symbols or visuals in facsimile form.

The Grey Species 2 (Reticulans) have an interesting variation in technique whereby the recipient sits fully aware facing a screen and computer console and interacts with images on a holographic display.

It is thought that the events during the Bentwaters incident in 1980 that took place underground to one of the military members was one of these processes. The subject was put before a similar screen, and even though there were others in chairs in the room, the screen was addressing him as an individual.

There is another process which occurs which involves the recipient lying on a table (or being suspended in the air) facing upwards where they can view a light bar of multi-colored flashing lights. It is here where billion-year-old psychological implants may be restimulated.

Some of these implants are responsible for humans not realizing their true nature and also for the system of self-imposed limitation that is rampant on earth. During this process, the recipient is re-programmed to perform other activities which can be triggered at a later moment. There is some evidence that many abductees over the past several years have been programmed with instructions, but we cannot determine the exact nature of the instructions - only that they are to be carried out in the next two to five years.

While these interactions serve to slow the evolution of humans, they do not bring anything to a halt. The Grey species in general will only gain a temporary interactive benefit from these actions, and eventually all Grey species will cease this type of interaction and will progress to other activties.

ORWELL 1984 1990?

PacificSun
Week of May 4, 1990

THE MARIN HUMANE SOCIETY

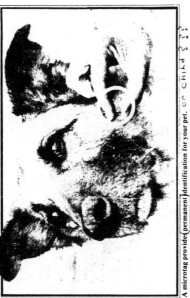

Sumner W. Fowler

An ID tag that won't get lost

By Mary Wright

When Tammy Adin of Novato found two collars half-buried in a muddy hole under her backyard fence, her heart dropped. Both of her dogs, Sandy, a five-year-old Shepherd mix and Buddy Holly, recently adopted from the Marin Humane Society, had dug a hole under the fence, squirming out of their collars in the process, and headed for the hills.

Adin searched everywhere, placed lost dog posters throughout the county, checked with the Marin and Sonoma Humane Societies every day, and even hired a private eye for pets to help track them down. After five days, Sandy showed up on his own, his pads bloody and worn. But Buddy Holly was nowhere to be found.

A few days later, a couple of hikers found a stray miniature pinscher roaming aimlessly on a fire road in the Novato hills. They brought the frightened dog to the shelter, where he was routinely scanned with an Infopet scanner. At the sound of a beep, a 10-digit number appeared on a screen identifying the *dog* as ~~MAN?~~ Buddy Holly.

For nearly a year, the Marin Humane Society has been implanting every dog and cat adopted from the shelter with an Infopet microchip I.D., a high-tech answer to the age-old problem of permanently identifying your beloved ~~pet~~ *neighbor* ? ? ?

The microchip, about the size of an uncooked grain of rice, is encased in biomedical grade glass. The chip is imprinted with a ten-digit alpha-numeric code and is implanted by simple injection between the animal's shoulder blades. With the wave of a hand-held scanner, the chip is activated to transmit the code to a computer which provides the owner's name and address, any relevant medical information and, most importantly, the owner's phone number.

Since May, the Marin Humane Society has recovered 16 animals with microchip I.D.'s. Some of the animals had no other form of identification, despite the fact that a few were wearing collars with both license and I.D. tags before being reported missing.

Thomas Fortmuller credits his brother-in-law, a Fremont veterinarian, and the Marin Humane Society with reuniting him with his cat, Meitzi, who wandered off while he was on a job site in Sausalito. If it weren't for the microchip implanted in Meitzi just days before she ran away, Fortmuller doubts she would be alive today.

"I kept thinking Meitzi would turn up on her own," said Fortmuller. "You know how cats are."

Unfortunately, shelters are all too familiar with the fact that people do not place I.D. tags on their cats and do not make a "dogged" effort to search for them when they are missing. In 1989 alone, 2,146 lost cats waited at the Marin shelter for owners who never came.

"It's a tragedy," says Humane Society executive director Diane Allevato. "While the percentage of dogs that are returned to their owners is nearly 80 percent at our shelter, the redemption rate for cats ranges from an abysmal 7 to 20 percent."

In the year and a half since Infopet began offering the service, 10,000 pets have been microtagged in California, Oregon, Missouri, Massachusetts, Arizona and Canada.

A microtag provides permanent identification for your pet. or child ? ? ?

In California, 160 veterinarians are currently implanting microchips for their clients' pets. Marin veterinarians who offer the service are Bel Marin Animal Hospital; Madera Hospital; the Marin Humane Society Spay and Neuter Clinic; Northbay Animal Hospital and Tamalpais Pet Hospital, Inc.

The microchip, its insertion and a year of registration cost $40. A small price to pay according to Liz Greenberg of Ignacio. Greenberg, whose purebred golden retriever, Beau, was purchased from a breeder for more than $500, decided to have Beau microtagged so that if he were to end up at the shelter without his collar, the Humane Society would know who to call.

Greenberg's instincts were proven right last September when Beau turned up at the shelter.

"I'm very glad that I did it," said Greenberg. "It's really a silly thing *not* to do."

Mary Wright is associate director of public relations for the Marin Humane Society.

BIG BROTHER'S COMING!

Revealed: Secret plan to tag every man, woman and child

CODED MICROCHIPS implanted in every person in the country would tie all of us into a master computer that could track anyone down at any moment, and plans for such a system are already under way whether you like it or not!

The secret scheme is being touted as a service for the protection of the people by high government officials, but some insiders who object to the move say it's just another way for Big Brother to control its cts.

Transmitters

Top-level national security agents are trying to convince sources in the Bush Administration to begin the project in which every man, woman and child will be implanted with a tiny transmitter," claims Davis Milerand, a critic of government intervention who says he has received leaked information from inside sources.

They're trying to say this will be a good way for authorities to quickly track down missing persons and children, as well as criminals and spies.

Injections

"But with the astounding technology of today, everything about you could be contained in one tiny microchip, which would be connected to a government computer.

"Any government agency will know what any person has done and is doing at any time."

Other sources say the tiny transmitters can be injected painlessly from a tiny gun in humans without them even knowing it ...ugh a nationwide nation" program.

...ll the government

> by JOE FRICK

would have to do is make up something like the swine flu vaccine," Milerand says.

"Imagine if they said there was a vaccine for AIDS. People would rush in droves to get shots.

The doctors themselves may not even know what they're injecting. They could be told the microchips are genetic implants that reprogram the body into fighting disease."

He adds: "The program would require all federal, state and local government workers to undergo the injections.

"It would only be a matter of time before everyone is implanted with a microchip, a slave to the government."

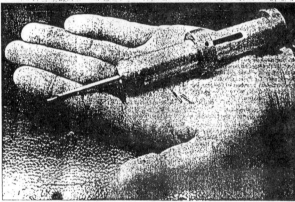

• TINY MICROCHIPS containing transmitters could be injected painlessly in humans with a small gun like this

No-sleep diet keeps you wide awake

IF YOU THINK there just aren't enough hours in the day, you can now get added time — thanks to a revolutionary new sleep method that helps people stay up nearly all night.

The new sleep system is called "Micro-Somnia," and it's billed as "The Entrepreneur's Guide to Sleep Reduction" by sleep management researcher Benjamin Plumb of Miami.

Plumb gets only 4½ hours of sleep each night and has a few

brief catnaps during the day.

He says that through Micro-Somnia he hopes to introduce short sleep "as a safe viable tool for people to use in increasing productivity."

Writes

The researcher cut red meat out of his diet, eats less gooey sweets, takes daily naps and avoids doing high-impact exercises in his leisure time.

He eats stuff like beans, rice and tofu, and does light exercises like walking and yoga.

Besides his prescribed diet and exercise regimen, the tireless sleep expert says he writes down his goals for the next day before retiring for the night — so he'll wake up excited the next morning.

Plumb says his brand of sleep management is only for "highly motivated, extremely goal-driven adults" because children and pregnant women require more sleep for health reasons.

Some super successful people like Winston Churchill, Napoleon and Thomas Edison worked won-

ders while catching only a few winks a night, he notes.

But they were born short sleepers and their nocturnal habits came naturally.

Now, however, Plumb says his program can make short sleepers out of sleepaholics who spend nine or 10 hours each night huddled under the covers.

He figures the best customers for his Micro-Somnia technique are corporate types who'd rather be awake pursuing their goals than wasting their time on sleep.

— KEN O'HARA

August 1, 1989 — SUN — 15

DEPARTMENT OF DEFENSE APPROPRIATIONS FOR 1970

UNITED STATES SENATE LIBRARY

HEARINGS

BEFORE A

SUBCOMMITTEE OF THE
COMMITTEE ON APPROPRIATIONS
HOUSE OF REPRESENTATIVES

NINETY-FIRST CONGRESS

FIRST SESSION

SUBCOMMITTEE ON DEPARTMENT OF DEFENSE

GEORGE H. MAHON, Texas, *Chairman*

ROBERT L. F. SIKES, Florida
JAMIE D. WHITTEN, Mississippi
GEORGE W. ANDREWS, Alabama
DANIEL J. FLOOD, Pennsylvania
JOHN M. SLACK, West Virginia
JOSEPH P. ADDABBO, New York
FRANK E. EVANS, Colorado [1]

GLENARD P. LIPSCOMB, California
WILLIAM E. MINSHALL, Ohio
JOHN J. RHODES, Arizona
GLENN R. DAVIS, Wisconsin

R. L. MICHAELS, RALPH PRESTON, JOHN GARRITY, PETER MURPHY, ROBERT NICHOLAS,
ROBERT FORTER, *Staff Assistants*

[1] Temporarily assigned

H.B. 15090

PART 5

RESEARCH, DEVELOPMENT, TEST, AND EVALUATION
Department of the Army
Statement of Director, Advanced Research Project Agency
Statement of Director, Defense Research and Engineering

Printed for the use of the Committee on Appropriations

U.S. GOVERNMENT PRINTING OFFICE

36-551

WASHINGTON : 1969

UNITED STATES SENATE LIBRARY

In 1969 (3 years before the World Health Organization's request) the United States Defense Department requested and got $10 million to make the AIDS virus in lab(s) as a political/ethnic weapon to be used mainly against Blacks. The Feasibility program & lab(s) were to have been compleated by 1974 - 1975, the virus between 1974 - 1979. The World Health Organization started to inject AIDS-laced smallpox vaccine (Vaccina) into over 100 million Africans (population reduction) in 1977. And over 2000 young white male homosexuals (Trojan horse) in 1978 with the hepatitis B vaccine through the Centers for Diease Control/New York Blood Center. And now the AIDS virus is on the streets IN THE DRUGS

PLEASE, WAKE UP!!

129 — Tuesday, July 1, 1969
SYNTHETIC BIOLOGICAL AGENTS

There are two things about the biological agent field I would like to mention. One is the possibility of technological surprise. Molecular biology is a field that is advancing very rapidly and eminent biologists believe that within a period of 5 to 10 years it would be possible to produce a synthetic biological agent, an agent that does not naturally exist and for which no natural immunity could have been acquired.

Mr. SIKES. Are we doing any work in that field?

Dr. MACARTHUR. We are not.

Mr. SIKES. Why not? Lack of money or lack of interest?

Dr. MACARTHUR. Certainly not lack of interest.

Mr. SIKES. Would you provide for our records information on what would be required, what the advantages of such a program would be, the time and the cost involved?

Dr. MACARTHUR. We will be very happy to.

(The information follows:)

The dramatic progress being made in the field of molecular biology led us to investigate the relevance of this field of science to biological warfare. A small group of experts considered this matter and provided the following observations:

1. All biological agents up to the present time are representatives of naturally occurring disease, and are thus known by scientists throughout the world. They are easily available to qualified scientists for research, either for offensive or defensive purposes.

✱ 2. Within the next 5 to 10 years, it would probably be possible to make a new infective microorganism which could differ in certain important aspects from any known disease-causing organisms. Most important of these is that it might be refractory to the immunological and therapeutic processes upon which we depend to maintain our relative freedom from infectious disease.

✱ 3. A research program to explore the feasibility of this could be completed in approximately 5 years at a total cost of $10 million.

4. It would be very difficult to establish such a program. Molecular biology is a relatively new science. There are not many highly competent scientists in the field, almost all are in university laboratories, and they are generally adequately supported from sources other than DOD. However, it was considered possible to initiate an adequate program through the National Academy of Sciences-National Research Council (NAS-NRC).

The matter was discussed with the NAS-NRC, and tentative plans were made to initiate the program. However, decreasing funds in CB, growing criticism of the CB program, and our reluctance to involve the NAS NRC in such a controversial endeavor have led us to postpone it for the past 2 years.

✱ It is a highly controversial issue and there are many who believe such research should not be undertaken lest it lead to yet another method of massive killing of large populations. On the other hand, without the sure scientific knowledge that such a weapon is possible, and an understanding of the ways it could be done, there is little that can be done to devise defensive measures. Should an enemy develop it there is little doubt that this is an important area of potential military technological inferiority in which there is no adequate research program.

AIDS Taking Heavy Toll of Children

L.A. Times 9/26/90

Acquired immune deficiency syndrome is striking many more children than previously thought, the World Health Organization reported. The U.N. agency said in Geneva that the HIV virus that causes AIDS will probably infect 10 million children by the year 2000. Already about 400,000 cases, or a third of the 1.2 million estimated cases of AIDS worldwide to date, are believed to have occurred in children under age 5.

I'm confused. Are we to believe that these 400,000 children are practicing homosexuals or IV drug users? Or that ≈400,000 (⅓) of their mothers transmit the disease? Or is it more likely that they are neither part of the high-risk group nor born of mothers with AIDS (Meaning, of course, that ⅓ babes + ⅓ moms = ⅔ of total AIDS population... no one is making this claim!) These data, if valid, come close to proving that AIDS is transmissible by casual contact and/or insects.

PROOFS

OF A

CONSPIRACY

AGAINST ALL THE

RELIGIONS AND GOVERNMENTS

OF

EUROPE,

CARRIED ON

IN THE SECRET MEETINGS

OF

FREE MASONS, ILLUMINATI,

AND

READING SOCIETIES.

(COLLECTED FROM GOOD AUTHORITIES,)

By JOHN ROBISON, (A. M.

PROFESSOR OF NATURAL PHILOSOPHY, AND SECRETARY TO THE
ROYAL SOCIETY OF EDINBURGH.

Nam tua res agitur paries cum proximus ardet.)

The THIRD EDITION.

(To which is added a POSTSCRIPT.)

PHILADELPHIA:

PRINTED FOR T. DOBSON, Nº. 41, SOUTH SECOND
STREET, AND W. COBBET, Nº. 25, NORTH
SECOND STREET.
1798.

****TOP SECRET****

Club of Rome Report

REGIONALIZED AND ADAPTIVE MODEL

OF THE GLOBAL WORLD SYSTEM

Report on the Progress in the

STRATEGY FOR SURVIVAL PROJECT

of the

Club of Rome

Mihajlo Mesarovic and Eduard Pestel, Directors

CONFIDENTIAL

September 17, 1973

****TOP SECRET****

1. Motivation and Objectives

The world *problematique* formulated by the CLUB OF ROME is not only global in nature, involving factors traditionally considered as unrelated, but also points to the crisis situations which are developing in spite of the noblest of intentions and, indeed, as their corollary. To point out the problematique and the spectrum of critical and traumatic situations it entails is not enough; the acceptance of the reality of the problematique MUST BE FOLLOWED BY CHANGES IF THE CONCERN IS NOT TO REMAIN PURELY ACADEMIC. It is necessary, therefore, to present the issues within the problematique in specific and relevant terms which requires regional interpretation of the global issues. Furthermore, a basis should be provided for the resolution of conflicts (inevitably accompanying the problematique-type situations) through cooperation rather than confrontation. These factors have provided the motivation for initiation of the *Strategy for Survival project* which calls for the construction of a regionalized and adaptive model of the total world system with the following specific objectives:

(1) TO ENABLE THE IMPLEMENTATION OF SCENARIOS FOR THE FUTURE DEVELOPMENT OF THE WORLD SYSTEM which represent visions of the world future stemming from different cultures and value systems and reflecting hopes and fears in different regions of the world.

(ii) To develop a planning and options-assessment tool for long-range issues, and thereby TO PROVIDE A BASIS FOR CONFLICT RESOLUTION by cooperation rather than confrontation.

2. Basic Structure of the Model

The basic characteristics of the model are:

(i) **THE WORLD SYSTEM IS REPRESENTED** in terms of interacting regions with provisions made to investigate any individual country or subregion in the context of regional and global development. Presently the world system is represented **BY TEN REGIONS: NORTH AMERICA, WESTERN EUROPE, EASTERN EUROPE, JAPAN, REST OF DEVELOPED WORLD, LATIN AMERICA, MIDDLE EAST, REST OF AFRICA, SOUTH AND SOUTH EAST ASIA, AND CHINA.**

(ii) **In order to be able to deal with the complex of factors involved in** *problematique* in a way which is sound, credible and systematic, a hierarchical structure has been adopted for the model in which each level in the hierarchy represents the evolution of the world system within a context defined by a given set of laws and principles. Specifically, the levels involved are:

GEO-PHYSICAL, ECOLOGICAL, TECHNOLOGICAL (MAN-MADE ENERGY AND MASS TRANSFERS), ECONOMIC, INSTITUTIONAL, SOCIO-POLITICAL, VALUE-CULTURAL AND HUMAN-BIOLOGICAL. Such an approach enables an optimal use of confirmed scientific knowledge and available data.

(iii) An adequate view of the conditions in which the *problematique* is emerging and under which the solutions must be found require the recognition of the purposive aspects of the human community and adaptiveness of human beings. The model of the world system will have, therefore, two parts:

(1) the so-called causal part, representing dynamical processes which follow historical patterns of development and (2) the so-called goal-seeking part which represents purposive changes under new conditions. The goal – seeking part in turn includes two

levels: the decision-making or actions level and the norms level; the former represents the purposive response of the system while the latter represents the values and norms which constrain and condition such a response.

3. Progress in the Model Construction

The construction of the model as described in Sec. 2 and with the objectives as specified in Sec. 1 is certainly a rather complex task and the research is organized to proceed in parallel in several directions. The overall assessment of the model status is the following:

The model has been developed up to the stage where it can be used for policy analysis related to a number of critical issues, such as: energy resources utilization and technology assessment; food demand and production; population growth and the affect of timing of birth control programs; reduction of inequities in regional economic developments; depletion dynamics of certain resources, particularly oil reserves; phosphorus use as fertilizer; regional unemployment; constraints on growth due to labor, energy or export limitation, etc.

Specific developments which enable use of the model as described above include the following:

1. **A COMPUTER MODEL OF THE WORLD ECONOMIC SYSTEM HAS BEEN DEVELOPED AND VALIDATED BY AN EXTENSIVE SET OF DATA.** The model has two levels - macro and micro. On the MACRO LEVEL the model of each region INCLUDES THE GROSS REGIONAL PRODUCT, TOTAL IMPORTS AND EXPORTS, CAPITAL AND LABOR PRODUCTIVITY AND VARIOUS COMPONENTS OF FINAL DEMAND SUCH AS PUBLIC CONSUMPTION, GOVERNMENT EXPENDITURE, AND TOTAL INVESTMENT. ON THE MICRO LEVEL EIGHT PRODUCTION SECTORS ARE RECOGNIZED: AGRICULTURE MANUFACTURING, FOOD PROCESSING, ENERGY, MINING, SERVICES, BANKING AND TRADE, AND RESIDENTIAL CONSTRUCTION. The input-output framework is used for the intermediate demands. **A FULL SCALE MICRO TRADE MATRIX ALSO HAS BEEN DEVELOPED.**

2. **A WORLD POPULATION MODEL HAS BEEN CONSTRUCTED IN TERMS OF THE SAME REGIONS AS THE ECONOMIC MODEL. The model has been validated by the data available. In each region the population structure is represented in terms of four age groups with appropriate delays which make possible assessment of population momentum and assessment of the effectiveness of implementation of various population control measures.**

3. **AN ENERGY MODEL HAS BEEN CONSTRUCTED which gives for each region the consumption and production of energy and interregional exchange of energy resources as a function of economic factors. Energy is treated both in composite terms and in reference to individual energy sources, namely solid fuel, liquid fuel, nuclear, gas and hydro.**

4. **A FOOD PRODUCTION AND ARABLE LAND USE MODEL HAS BEEN CONSTRUCTED which allows the assessment of a number of food related issues including: the need and availability of phosphorus required for intensive agriculture, AND THE CONSEQUENCES OF TIMING AND MAGNITUDES OF NATURAL DISASTERS SUCH AS DROUGHT, CROP FAILURE DUE TO DISEASE, ETC.**

5. A MAJOR CONCERN IN THE APPLICATION OF THE COMPUTER MODEL is its proper utilization so as to avoid dependence on the deterministic aspects of model operation. In order to avoid this an interactive method of computer simulation analysis has been developed. **THE METHOD REPRESENTS A SYMBIOSIS OF MAN AND COMPUTER IN WHICH THE COMPUTER PROVIDES THE LOGICAL AND NUMERICAL CAPABILITY WHILE MAN PROVIDES THE VALUES, INTUITION AND EXPERIENCE.** The method utilizes an option specification and selection program which enables the policy analyst or decision-maker to evaluate alternative options on various levels of the decision process, i.e., with respect to goals, strategies, tactical and implementational factors. SPECIAL ATTENTION IS PAID TO THE NORM CHANGING PROCESSES.

4. Progress in Application

THE MODEL HAS BEEN USED both for the assessment of alternative scenarios for future regional and global developments (under different regional conditions) as well as in the interactive mode selection of policy options (specifically for the energy crises issues in developed regions).

OUR EFFORTS IN THE IMMEDIATE FUTURE WILL BE CONCENTRATED ON FURTHER USE OF THE ALREADY DEVELOPED MODEL. THE PLANS INCLUDE EMPHASIS IN THE FOLLOWING THREE DIRECTIONS:

(i) Assessment in the changes over time of the span of options available to solve some major crisis problems.

(ii) IMPLEMENTATION *of the regional models in different parts of the world and their connection via a satellite communication network for the purpose of jo*int *assessment of the long term global future by teams from the various regions.*

(iii) Implementation of the vision for the future outlined by leaders from an underdeveloped region in order TO ASSESS *with the model* EXISTING OBSTACLES AND THE MEANS WHEREBY THE VISION MIGHT BECOME REALITY.

'KINGDOMS' : CLUB OF ROME'S TEN GLOBAL GROUPS

GROUP 1: North America

Canada

United States of America

GROUP 2: Western Europe

Andorra
Austria
Belgium
Denmark
Federal Republic of Germany
Finland
France
Great Britain
Greece
Iceland
Ireland
Italy
Liechtenstein

Luxembourg
Malta
Monaco
Netherlands
Norway
Portugal
San Marino
Spain
Sweden
Switzerland
Turkey
Yugoslavia

GROUP 3: Japan

GROUP 4: Rest of the Developed Market Economies

Australia
Israel
New Zealand

Oceania
South Africa
Tasmania

GROUP 5: Eastern Europe

Albania
Bulgaria
Czechoslovakia
German Democratic Republic

Hungary
Poland
Rumania
Soviet Union

****TOP SECRET****

GROUP 6: Latin America

Argentina
Barbados
Bolivia
Brazil
British Honduras
Chile
Colombia
Costa Rica
Cuba
Dominican Republic
Ecuador
El Salvador
French Guiana
Guatemala

Guyana
Haiti
Honduras
Jamaica
Mexico
Nicaragua
Panama
Paraguay
Peru
Surinam
Trinidad and Tobago
Uruguay
Venezuela

GROUP 7: North Africa and the Middle East

Adu Dhabi
Aden
Algeria
Bahrain
Cyprus
Dubai
Egypt
Iran
Iraq
Jordan
Kuwait

Lebanon
Libya
Masqat-Oman
Morocco
Qatar
Saudi-Arabia
Syria
Trucial Oman
Tunisia
Yemen

GROUP 8: Main Africa

Angola
Burundi
Cabinda
Cameroon
Central African Republic
Chad
Dahomey
Ethiopia
French Somali Coast
Gabon
Gambia

Ghana
Guinea
Ivory Coast
Kenya
Liberia
Malagasy Republic
Malawi
Mali
Mauritania
Mauritius
Mozambique

****TOP SECRET****

Niger
Nigeria
Portuguese Guinea
Republic of Congo
Reunion
Rhodesia
Rwanda
Senegal
Sierra Leone
Somalia
South Africa

South West Africa
Spanish Guinea
Spanish Sahara
Sudan
Tanzania
Togo
Uganda
Upper Volta
Zaire
Zambia

GROUP 9: South and Southeast Asia

Afghanistan
Bangladesh
Burma
Cambodia
Ceylon
India
Indonesia
Laos

Malaysia
Nepal
Pakistan
Philippines
South Korea
South Vietnam
Taiwan
Thailand

GROUP 10: Centrally Planned Asia

Mongolia
North Korea

North Vietnam
People's Republic of China

Ten Kingdoms . . . from: THE CLUB OF ROME

David Ben-Gurion — when prime minister of Israel forecast world rule from Jerusalem.

Look Magazine, January 16, 1962

David Ben-Gurion (Prime Minister of Israel): "The image of the world in 1987 as traced in my imagination: The Cold War will be a thing of the past. Internal pressure of the constantly growing intelligentsia in Russia for more freedom and the pressure of the masses for raising their living standards may lead to a gradual democratization of the Soviet Union. On the other hand, the increasing influence of the workers and farmers, and the rising political importance of men of science, may transform the United States into a welfare state with a planned economy. Western and Eastern Europe will become a federation of autonomous states having a Socialist and democratic regime. With the exception of the USSR as a federated Eurasian state, all other continents will become united in a world alliance at whose disposal will be an international police force. All armies will be abolished, and there will be no more wars. In Jerusalem, the United Nations (a truly *United* Nations) will build a Shrine of the Prophets to serve the federated union of all continents; this will be the seat of the Supreme Court of Mankind, to settle all controversies among the federated continents, as prophesied by Isaiah. Higher education will be the right of every person in the world. A pill to prevent pregnancy will slow down the explosive natural increase in China and India. And by 1987, the average life-span of man will reach 100 years."

The Associated Press

Military exchange *The Register 10/5/90*

Gen. Colin L. Powell, left, chairman of the US Joint Chiefs of Staff, shakes hands Wednesday with his counterpart, Gen. Mikhail A. Moiseyev, Soviet first deputy minister of defense. The two were honored in San Francisco before traveling to San Diego on Thursday, where they announced an agreement to extend until 1992 a military exchange program between the two nations.

S_T_A_T_E_M_E_N_T

From 1972 to 1974, I was stationed at Clark Air Base, Philippines. During
that time, when it appeared that then President Richard M. Nixon might be
impeached by Congress, the Base Commander received a message from the Chief
of the Joint Chiefs of Staff, Washington, D.C. This message was, at least
in part, reprinted in our daily base information publication, THE DAILY
BULLETIN. The portion published in THE DAILY BULLETIN stated that any messages
received by any base personnel directly from the White House, Washington, D.C.
were to be reported directly to the Base Commander immediately. Additionally,
the contents of these messages were to be ignored unless they were counter-
signed by the Chief of the Joint Chiefs of Staff and issued through the Base
Commander's Office. I discussed this item with several of the people with
whom I worked at the time. The people I can remember are:

              Staff Sergeant David Kasper
              Staff Sergeant Leah Aasen
              Mr. Conrado Barrera (Civilian Employee)
              Ms. Mercedes Grepo (Civilian Employee)

I recall that the reason this article was so interesting was that some of us
were trying to determine whether we believed that President Nixon would resign
rather than face possible impeachment. This was a very popular topic on the
base among people with whom I associated. Since no orders from the White House
were ever received, as far as I know, nothing more ever came of it.

I hereby declare that I make this statement freely without any reservations
and that it is the entire account of this incident according to my memory and
belief. I make this statement and declare that it is a true account under the
penalty of perjury.

Dennis E. Goce

6/18/90
Kathy Bennett
Comm Expires 10/23/93

William Cooper
1311 S. Highland Ave., Ste. 205
Fullerton, California 92632

December 8, 1989

Dear Mr. Cooper,

A friend who lives in Washington sent me a copy of your paper "The
Secret Government, the Origin, Identity, and Purpose of the (real)
MJ-12." I thought it was science fiction. As I read further into
the text the hair on the back of my neck stood on end. Your paper
contains information that I recognized as top secret. I will not
elaborate because the information may still be classified. From
that point on I read your paper with considerable interest.

I was surprised to say the least when I read your account of the
resignation of President Nixon and the message from the Joint Chiefs
that preceeded his departure. I too saw the message. I was a CT2
with a top secret crypto 14 clearance attached to the underground
command center (the tunnel) on Oahu. We received a specat message
from the Joint Chiefs stating, "Upon receipt of this message you
will no longer accept any orders from Top Hat. Acknowledge receipt."
Your paper says White House. You are correct but you must have seen
a transcribed message substituting White House for Top Hat.

What little I know tells me that you are a brave man. Please send
more information to my address listed below.

A new friend,

November 1, 1990

Hello Bill,

By way of introduction, I am a friend. I appreciate what you are doing and I want to help. When I run across information which may be of interest, I will send it along to you. You have a gift for finding, assembling and communicating vital information. I believe you are performing a great service for our country. Thankyou, and keep up the good work.

Very Sincerely

John Shemson

John Shemson

P.S. Please notice the last paragraph in the letter from
J. Edgar Hoover...."Mr. George Bush of the CIA".....1963.

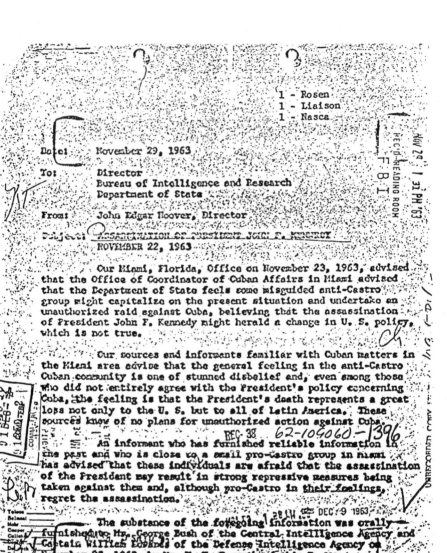

1 - Rosen
1 - Liaison
1 - Nasca

Date: November 29, 1963

To: Director
          Bureau of Intelligence and Research
          Department of State

From: John Edgar Hoover, Director

Subject: ASSASSINATION OF PRESIDENT JOHN F. KENNEDY
          NOVEMBER 22, 1963

Our Miami, Florida, Office on November 23, 1963, advised that the Office of Coordinator of Cuban Affairs in Miami advised that the Department of State feels some misguided anti-Castro group might capitalize on the present situation and undertake an unauthorized raid against Cuba, believing that the assassination of President John F. Kennedy might herald a change in U. S. policy, which is not true.

Our sources and informants familiar with Cuban matters in the Miami area advise that the general feeling in the anti-Castro Cuban community is one of stunned disbelief and, even among those who did not entirely agree with the President's policy concerning Cuba, the feeling is that the President's death represents a great loss not only to the U. S. but to all of Latin America. These sources know of no plans for unauthorized action against Cuba.

An informant who has furnished reliable information in the past and who is close to a small pro-Castro group in Miami has advised that these individuals are afraid that the assassination of the President may result in strong repressive measures being taken against them and, although pro-Castro in their feelings, regret the assassination.

The substance of the foregoing information was orally furnished to Mr. George Bush of the Central Intelligence Agency and Captain William Edwards of the Defense Intelligence Agency on November 23, 1963, by Mr. W. T. Forsyth of this Bureau.

1 - Director of Naval Intelligence

62-109060-1396

****TOP SECRET****

1 – Rosen
1 – Liaison
1 – Nasca

Date: November 29, 1963

To: Director
            Bureau of Intelligence and Research
            Department of State

From: John Edgar Hoover, Director

Subject: ASSASSINATION OF PRESIDENT JOHN F. KENNEDY
            NOVEMBER 22, 1963

Our Miami, Florida, Office on November 23, 1963, advised that the Office of Coordinator of Cuban Affairs in Miami advised that the Department of State feels some misguided anti-Castro group might capitalize on the present situation and undertake an unauthorized raid against Cuba, believing that the assassination of President John F. Kennedy might herald a change in U. S. policy, which is not true.

Our sources and informants familiar with Cuban matters in the Miami area advise that the general feeling in the anti-Castro Cuban community is one of stunned disbelief and, even among those who did not entirely agree with the President's policy concerning Cuba, the feeling is that the President's death represents a great loss not only to the U.S. but to all of Latin America. These sources know of no plans for unauthorized action against Cuba.

An informant who has furnished reliable information in the past and who is close to a small pro-Castro group in Miami has advised that these individuals are afraid that the assassination of the President may result in strong repressive measures being taken against them and, although pro-Castro in their feelings, regret the assassination.

The substance of the foregoing information was orally furnished to Mr. George Bush of the Central Intelligence Agency and Captain William Edwards of the Defense Intelligence Agency on November 23, 1963, by Mr. W. T. Forsyth of this Bureau.

1 - Director of Naval Intelligence

VHN:gci (12)

---

* * * *T O P   S E C R E T* * * *

1
DL 89-43
HJO:mvs

*James * Parrott*
1211 Parl
Houston, Tex

Re: JAMES MILTON PARROTT

Houston on November 22, 1963 advised that GEORGE
H. W. BUSH, a reputable businessman, furnished information to
the effect that JAMES PARROTT has been talking of killing
the President when he comes to Houston. A check with Secret
Service at Houston, Texas revealed that agency had a report
that PARROTT stated in 1961 he would kill President KENNEDY
if he got near him.

1 Xerox made 4 sent
WF: (in rr) in rr rr)
Lw, E.S.I.

213

The Report from Iron Mountain

62   THE REPORT

though not yet expressly put forth, is the development of a long-range sequence of space-research projects with largely unattainable goals. This kind of program offers several advantages lacking in the social welfare model. First, it is unlikely to phase itself out, regardless of the predictable "surprises" science has in store for us: the universe is too big. In the event some individual project unexpectedly succeeds there would be no dearth of substitute problems. For example, if colonization of the moon proceeds on schedule, it could then become "necessary" to establish a beachhead on Mars or Jupiter, and so on. Second, it need be no more dependent on the general supply-demand economy than its military prototype. Third, it lends itself extraordinarily well to arbitrary control.

Space research can be viewed as the nearest modern equivalent yet devised to the pyramid-building, and similar ritualistic enterprises, of ancient societies. It is true that the scientific value of the space program, even of what has already been accomplished, is substantial on its own terms. But current programs are absurdly and obviously disproportionate, in the relationship of the knowledge sought to the expenditures committed. All but a small fraction of the space budget, measured by the standards of comparable scientific objectives, must be charged *de facto* to the military economy. Future space research, projected as a war surrogate, would further reduce the "scientific" rationale of its budget to a minuscule percentage indeed. As a purely economic

****TOP SECRET****

SUBSTITUTES FOR THE FUNCTIONS OF WAR   63

substitute for war, therefore, extension of the space program warrants serious consideration.

In Section 3 we pointed out that certain disarmament models, which we called conservative, postulated extremely expensive and elaborate inspection systems. Would it be possible to extend and institutionalize such systems to the point where they might serve as economic surrogates for war spending? The organization of fail-safe inspection machinery could well be ritualized in a manner similar to that of established military processes. "Inspection teams" might be very like armies, and their technical equipment might be very like weapons. Inflating the inspection budget to military scale presents no difficulty. The appeal of this kind of scheme lies in the comparative ease of transition between two parallel systems.

The "elaborate inspection" surrogate is fundamentally fallacious, however. Although it might be economically useful, as well as politically necessary, during the disarmament transition, it would fail as a substitute for the economic function of war for one simple reason. Peace-keeping inspection is part of a war system, not of a peace system. It implies the possibility of weapons maintenance or manufacture, which could not exist in a world at peace as here defined. Massive inspection also implies sanctions, and thus war-readiness.

The same fallacy is more obvious in plans to create a patently useless "defense conversion" apparatus. The long-discredited proposal to build "total" civil defense

66　　　　THE REPORT

obvious destabilizing effect of any global social welfare surrogate on politically necessary class relationships would create an entirely new set of transition problems at least equal in magnitude.

Credibility, in fact, lies at the heart of the problem of developing a political substitute for war. This is where the space-race proposals, in many ways so well suited as economic substitutes for war, fall short. The most ambitious and unrealistic space project cannot of itself generate a believable external menace. It has been hotly argued[6] that such a menace would offer the "last, best hope of peace," etc., by uniting mankind against the danger of destruction by "creatures" from other planets or from outer space. Experiments have been proposed to test the credibility of an out-of-our-world invasion threat; it is possible that a few of the more difficult-to-explain "flying saucer" incidents of recent years were in fact early experiments of this kind. If so, they could hardly have been judged encouraging. We anticipate no difficulties in making a "need" for a giant super space program credible for economic purposes, even were there not ample precedent; extending it, for political purposes, to include features unfortunately associated with science fiction would obviously be a more dubious undertaking.

Nevertheless, an effective political substitute for war would require "alternate enemies," some of which might seem equally farfetched in the context of the current war system. It may be, for instance, that gross pollution of the environment can eventually replace the possibility of mass destruction by nuclear weapons as the principal

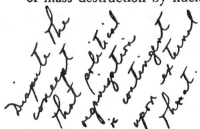

apparent threat to the survival of the species. Poisoning of the air, and of the principal sources of food and water supply, is already well advanced, and at first glance would seem promising in this respect; it constitutes a threat that can be dealt with only through social organization and political power. But from present indications it will be a generation to a generation and a half before environmental pollution, however severe, will be sufficiently menacing, on a global scale, to offer a possible basis for a solution.

It is true that the rate of pollution could be increased selectively for this purpose; in fact, the mere modifying of existing programs for the deterrence of pollution could speed up the process enough to make the threat credible much sooner. But the pollution problem has been so widely publicized in recent years that it seems highly improbable that a program of deliberate environmental poisoning could be implemented in a politically acceptable manner.

However unlikely some of the possible alternate enemies we have mentioned may seem, we must emphasize that one *must* be found, of credible quality and magnitude, if a transition to peace is ever to come about without social disintegration. It is more probable, in our judgment, that such a threat will have to be invented, rather than developed from unknown conditions. For this reason, we believe further speculation about its putative nature ill-advised in this context. Since there is considerable doubt, in our minds, that *any* viable political surrogate can be devised, we are reluctant to com-

Carnegie Endowment for International Peace
DIVISION OF INTERCOURSE AND EDUCATION
Foreword by Elihu Root
Publication No. 15

of the United States as to Central and South America and the enunciation of Japan's attitude toward China. In the first there is on the part of the United States no engagement or promise, while in the other Japan voluntarily announces that Japan will herself engage not to violate the political or territorial integrity of her neighbor, and to observe the principle of the open door and equal opportunity, asking at the same time other nations to respect these principles.

Therefore, gentlemen, you will mark the wide difference and agree with me, I am sure, that the use of the term is somewhat loose and misleading. I ask you to note this with no suggestion that I can or any one else does question the policy or attitude of your country, which we well know will always deal fairly and honorably with other nations.

As you must have noticed, I have persistently struck one note every time I have spoken. It has been the note of warning against German intrigue in America and in Japan—intrigue which has extended over a period of more than ten years. I am not going to weary you with a repetition of this squalid story of plots, conceived and fostered by the agents of Germany, but I solemnly repeat the warning here in this most distinguished gathering, so thoroughly representative of the highest ideals of American journalism.

In my speeches at various places I have endeavored to speak frankly on all points at issue or of interest at this time. There are, of course, some things which can not be openly discussed, because of a wise embargo upon unwise disclosures, but I am confident that from this time forward we will be able to effectively cooperate in all matters tending to secure a victory in this struggle which means so much for all of us, and that throughout all the years to come, differences of opinion or difficulties arising between our two countries will be settled, as all such questions and difficulties can be settled, between close friends and partners.

I thank you, sir, for your hospitality and for your courtesy. I assure you, gentlemen, again that we appreciate more than I can express the high consideration, the patriotism, and the broad and friendly spirit with which you have treated this Mission from Japan.

Comptroller William A. Prendergast was next called upon. He said in part:

Mr. Chairman, Viscount Ishii, gentlemen of the Commission, Your Excellency, and gentlemen: Our host has asked me to say a word of welcome to Viscount Ishii and associate members of the Commission in the name of the great city of New York.

It would seem to me that it is hardly necessary even to attempt to repeat the very great pleasure and honor and happiness that it gives New York to have you as its guests.

Now, Viscount Ishii, might I at this time sound a note which may be somewhat contrary to that which has been the dominant idea of our discussions upon these occasions? We have treated, and naturally, of war. That is the thought that is uppermost in our minds. It is the thing that is in the thought and the mind of man, woman, and child—war. I can say

THE IMPERIAL JAPANESE MISSION
1917
A Record of the Reception Throughout the United States
of the Special Mission Headed by Viscount Ishii

NEW YORK   105

detestable war, because war is detestable, and we are fighting this war today for the purpose of driving out war permanently. That is the great object of our entering this war, or one of the great objects, and I am sure that it is also one of yours. It was a great relief to us—a great relief to the civilized world—that when this war broke out you were in your position of primacy upon the Pacific, there to guard effectively and effectually against the diplomatic depredations that might have taken place if Germany had been permitted to do as she was disposed to do in China. For the service that you rendered in that respect the world is indeed your debtor. But the idea that I think we should also have in mind, as well as winning the war, as well as prosecuting it to a successful finish, is this: While we are engaged in this war, let us realize the ties that bind. Let us realize that brothers in war should be brothers in peace; that what we have at interest in the war we will also have at interest in times of peace; and during this struggle, when we are so close together, when we are fraternizing, as brothers should, when we are feeling toward each other as brothers should, let us lay the groundwork of a great commercial relation that no contingency or exigency will ever disturb in the future, the groundwork of a commercial relation that will draw us so close together that we will realize the genuine ties of brotherhood. That, I think, is one of the great desires of the American people, and that is one of the great desires that New York expresses to you, at the conclusion of your happy visit to us.

John Dewey, Professor of Philosophy in Columbia University, who was the next speaker, was listened to with great intentness. He said:

A {   Some one remarked that the best way to unite all the nations on this globe would be an attack from some other planet. In the face of such an alien enemy, people would respond with a sense of their unity of interest and purpose. We have the next thing to that at the present time. Before a common menace, North and South America, the Occident and Orient have done an unheard of thing, a wonderful thing, a thing which, it may well be, future history will point to as the most significant thing in these days of wonderful happenings. They have joined forces amply and intimately in a common cause with one another and with the European nations which were most directly threatened. What a few dreamers hoped might happen in the course of some slow coming century has become an accomplished fact in a few swift years. In spite of geographical distance, unlike speech, diverse religion, and hitherto independent aims, nations from every continent have formed what for the time being is nothing less than a world state, an immense cooperative action in behalf of civilization.

B.   It is safe to say that, with all its preparedness, Germany never anticipated *this* result. Even now the fact is so close to us that even we, who have been brought together, are too much engaged in the duties which the union imposes to realize the force of the new and unique creation of a union of peoples, yes, of continents. The imagination is not yet capable of taking it in.

C.   It has been more than once noted that Germany has exhibited an ex-

---

* * * *TOP SECRET* * * *

9453

106   THE IMPERIAL JAPANESE MISSION ·

traordinary spectacle to the world. It has stood for organization at home and disorganization abroad, for cooperative effort among its own people and for division and hostility among all other peoples. All through the earlier years of the war the intellectuals of Germany appealed for sympathy in this country because of what Germany had done in the way of social legislation and administration to promote the unity of all classes, because of its efficiency in organization, because of the intelligent efforts it had made to secure domestic prosperity. But, at the same time, as events have since only too clearly demonstrated, it was bending every energy of corrupt and hateful intrigue to disunite the American people among themselves and to incite suspicion, jealousy, envy, and even active hostility between the American nation and other nations, like Mexico and Japan, with whom we had every reason to live in amity and no reasons of weight for anything but amity. In the light of this exhibition, German love of organization and cooperative unity at home gains a sinister meaning. It stands convicted of falsity because born of a malicious conspiracy against the rest of the world. It loved unity and harmony, not for themselves, but simply as a means of bringing about that dominion of Germany over the world of which its remorseless and treacherous efforts to divide other peoples are the other half.

The rest of the world, of the once neutral world, was, it must be confessed, slow to awake to Germany's plots and purposes. They seemed fantastic, unreal, in their unbridled lust for power and their incredibly bad faith. It was especially hard for us in this country, who have never been trained to identify our loyalty to our own country with hatred of any other, to realize that Germany's genius for efficiency and organization had become a menace to domestic union and international friendliness over the world. But finally in North America, as in South America, and in Asia, when the case became too clear for further doubt, Germany's challenge was met. Against Germany's efforts to disunite there arose a world united in endeavor and achievement on a scale unprecedented in the history of this globe, a scale too vast not to endure and in enduring to make the future history of international relationships something very different from their past history. In struggling by cunning and corruption to separate and divide other peoples, Germany has succeeded in drawing them together with a rapidity and an intimacy almost beyond belief. Nations thus brought together in community of feeling and action will not easily fall apart, even though the occasion which brought them together passes, as, pray God, it will soon pass. The Germany which seems finally to be breaking up within has furnished the rest of the world with a cement whose uses will not easily be forgotten.

Formal alliances, set treaties, legal arrangements for arbitration and conciliation, leagues and courts of nations, all have their importance. But, gentlemen, their importance is secondary. They are effects rather than causes, symptoms rather than forces. You may have them all, and if nations have not discovered that their permanent interests are in mutuality and interchange, they will be evaded or overridden. They may be lacking, but if the vital sap of reciprocal trust and friendly intercourse is flowing through the arteries of commerce and the public press, they will come in due season

The Root-Takahira Understanding of 1908

AND

The Lansing-Ishii Agreement of 1917

NEW YORK   107

as naturally and inevitably as the trees put forth their leaves when their day of spring has come. It is our problem and our duty, I repeat, especially of you gentlemen of diplomacy and of what I shall venture to call the even more powerful instrument of good will and understanding, the public press, to turn our immediate and temporary relation for purposes of war into an enduring and solid connection for all of the sweet and constructive offices of that peace which must some day again dawn upon a wracked and troubled world.

Where diversity is greatest, there is the greatest opportunity for a fruitful cooperation which will be magnificently helpful to those who cooperate. This meeting this evening is a signal evidence of the coming together of the portions of the earth which for countless centuries went their own way in isolation, developing great civilizations, each in their own way. Now in the fulness of days, the Orient and the Occident, the United States and Japan, have drawn together to engage in faith in themselves and in each other in the work of building up a society of nations each free to develop its own national life and each bound in helpful intercourse with every other. May every influence which would sow suspicion and misunderstanding be accursed, and every kindly power that furthers enduring understanding and reciprocal usefulness be blest. May this meeting stand not only as a passing symbol, but as a lasting landmark of the truth that among nations as among men of good will there shall be peace, not a peace of isolation or bare toleration which has become impossible in this round world of ours, not a peace based on mutual fear and mutual armament, but a virile peace in which emulation in commerce, science, and the arts bespeaks two great nations that respect each other because they respect themselves.

Don C. Seitz, of the *New York World,* who has traveled in the Far East and studied its problems, caught the entire attention of the company as he responded to Mr. Villard's call:

I think the visit of the Japanese Commission has been the most impressive among all of those who have come to us from the other parts of the world as the outcome of the great war, and I think, too, it has a great purpose, and is bound to have a great result, because, if you will recall carefully, you will find that the other gentlemen all came to the United States to get something; but these gentlemen have come to give us something.

There is a great deal to be learned in the Orient, and I know it is a trite phrase to say that everything is upside down in the East, that all Oriental ideas are opposite those held by ourselves, but in some ways this is an improvement. There is also a perspicacity among Orientals which we lack ourselves. Only recently I had to sit for nearly an hour and listen to the efforts of a former Attorney General of the United States to explain and vindicate the Monroe Doctrine, and here Viscount Ishii, in the midst of many affairs, sizes it up in a few words, perceiving that our fundamental doctrine is that we will allow no one to lick our neighbors but ourselves.

The East has often been advertised as changeless. This is wrong.

I have stated again and again since 1984, that George Bush and others close to him, including the so-called "Pink Team" have been involved directly in the cocaine drug trade from Central America. In HOPE'S HUSBAND, I named the CIA-owned Costa Rican Corporations directly involved in this drug trade, using shrimp fishing boats with the cocaine frozen in with the shrimp. In that same book, still available for a mere $3.00, I told of the secret sailing course code that would insure that these CIA-owned fishing boats would not be intercepted by the U.S. Coast Guard. Former Military Intelligence Officers, risking their pensions and perhaps their freedom, have verified to me that these statements are correct and widely known among the professional Intelligence Community. I had often wondered where George Bush, and his relatives and friends, would be putting so much money for their own personal profit.

Panama Resists U.S. Pressure on Bank Laws

American law-enforcement officials said they had evidence that Panamanian banks were used to launder

In a recent interview, President Endara acknowledged that the success of Panama's financial center in

It would be hard to stash it in the United States banks, as someone who is unfriendly to them might leak the information. Well, as most sophisticated investors and financial people know, Panama was one of the best tax haven jurisdictions in the world prior to December 20, 1989. George Bush, with his friendship with Noriega assuring his privacy in financial affairs, would have left his millions in illegal drug profits right there in Panama both in secret bank accounts and in business and tourist properties.

We also know from the NEW YORK TIMES front page story of 2/6/90, by reporter Stephen Labaton, that in spite of the invasion supposedly to stop the international drug trade, Panama is not going to reveal those huge cash deposits in Panama banks, even when allegedly pressured to do so by the United States. Thus we see that Noriega's friends are still in full control in Panama.

Noriega's #1 economic advisor was Carlos Whitgreen. He "fled the country" and is somewhere in Western Europe according to my personal informant in Panama. Personally, I think Carlos has been given another assignment.

Senator John Kerry, (D Mass) has held extensive hearings into the money laundering and the use of Panamanian Banks for drug operations stated in the NEW YORK TIMES that he is "very concerned about it." However, he does not intend to do anything about it. Remember back in 1988 when the U.S. imposed economic sanctions in Panama to halt this money laundering? Well, after these 26 men gave their lives during the Panama Invasion, and Noriega is safely silenced, these sanctions have been suddenly cancelled! If the invasion was really to stop drug trafficking as well as illegal money laundering, the sanctions would have been increased not reduced. Yet, as of March 26th, the U.S. has released $480 million in funds which were frozen while Noriega was in power. Panama is in receipt of this money yet they have not informed the Panama citizens. Hundreds of government employees are not being paid on time, and some not at all.

One of the most important of the Noriega men is Panama Senator Mario Rognoni who has been up to his eyeballs in graft, drugs and theft. It therefore comes as no surprise that Senator Rognoni was scheduled to speak at HARVARD UNIVERSITY, Cambridge, MA. on Wednesday, April 4, 1990, right in John Kerry's back yard. He is to lecture on the violations of U.S. Treaties with Panama as to the sanctions and the invasion, and reportedly is now writing a book about his knowledge of what happened.

So, instead of increasing the economic pressure on Panama, your Congress has just approved the first payment of $42 million to be sent to Panama as part of a One Billion

- 3 -

U.S. Aid package. We have a hunch that some of this money is to protect the Bush Family investments in Panama, and to make the Panama tourist trade again popular so that the Bush string of hotels and resorts will start to make money as planned.

The George Bush hand-picked new President of Panama is Guillermo Endura. He is soon to marry his 24 year old mistress, and is on a special diet so as to lose some 150# for the wedding. However, all the Latin love stories aside, the fact remains that Endura is a Director of a Panamanian bank used exclusively by Columbia's Medellin drug cartel. Do not be so naive as to think that anything has changed with the sacrifice of 26 of our finest men in operation "Just Cause."

The George Bush hand-picked Vice President of Panama is Guillermo Ford, who is also the Chairman of the Banking Commission of Panama. As it happens, he is also part owner of the Dadeland Bank of Florida which was named in a court case two years ago as the central institution for the drug cartels.

The George Bush hand-picked new Attorney General of Panama is Rogello Cruz, and according to the NEW YORK TIMES is one of the bosses of the Cali drug cartel of Columbia. All this fits with what I wrote years ago in HOPE'S HUSBAND and other pamphlets, regarding George Bush and his Drug Connections. I make no apologies. What I saw in Central America and what I know and published from other sources has proven to be true and accurate. The U.S. Government under Bush command is making no effort whatever to rid the Panamanian Government of officials tied directly to drugs. Don't you see? If he did so, they would quickly give their stories to the world news media and bring down a scandal that would make Watergate and the Iran Contra Scandal seem insignificant by comparison. History may record that George Bush was the most dangerous man to ever serve as President of the United States. He must be impeached, and impeached quickly. I am not so naive as to suppose that it is going to happen in the near future.

On February 8, 1990, ABC Evening News carried a report regarding the Congressional Testimony by Senator Harry Reid (D NV) who complained that U.S. based oil companies were not being regulated in the shipment of chemicals necessary to the production of illegal drugs. Two of these chemicals are Acetone and Ethyl-Ether. The oil companies whose chemical affiliates are Exxon, Chevron and Shell, are sending these chemicals into Latin America with the full knowledge that this is its only commercial purpose there. George Bush has refused to sign an Executive Order prohibiting or limiting the shipment of these chemicals. We do know the reason why, don't we? The NEW YORK TIMES of 2/10/90 even carried a story by Robert Pear wherein it is stated that President Barco of Columbia demanded that Bush stop the shipment into his country of the "drug chemicals". The leaders of Peru and Bolivia have also demanded that these drug making chemicals, **originating in the United States**, be stopped. As of this writing, this has not been done.

As you can imagine, the Bush Administration does not appreciate the remarks in these pamphlets. The vultures are circling. We are knowingly placing ourselves in the cross-hairs of some very substantial firepower so that you can know the truth. This month we received two **consecutively** numbered Certified Letters from the Memphis, TN office of the Internal Revenue and they were returned unopened and refused. I continue to maintain that I am not under the jurisdiction of the Legislative Democracy of Washington, DC and thus not a "person" required to file returns or pay taxes. I ask that you pray for me, but that you not worry about me no matter what happens.

I include the foregoing paragraph

in this report on Bush, Drugs and the Panama treachery for a very good reason. I have mailed 350 copies of a fantastic report on the Bush Financial Investments in Panama to some of you whom I thought would be particularly interested. I simply could not afford to send out any more of them. This report, titled CRIMINAL POLITICS, is by my friend, Lawrence Patterson, PO Box 3812, Cincinnati, OH 45222. He is a financial advisor and normally his monthly reports cost $15.00. In my opinion they are well worth the money, even if you are not a millionaire. This particular issue, February 1990, he will send to you for only $1.00 per copy if you write to him and mention my name in doing so. However, he had what I see as a minor error in that issue regarding the law and a citizen's status. He may well know the truth and be writing for a particular educational level as to the law. In any event, what I respond to here is not intended to be critical of him, for in the case of most Americans, his statements are absolutely true as to how they apply.

Brother Patterson states on page 6 that "Drug Possession is now a CIVIL CRIME." He is quite correctly quoting an announcement by the Bush Administration Attorney General Thornburg's announcement of 12/2/89. In that announcement, Thornburg stated that possession of **no more than** an ounce of marijuana or **no more than** a gram of heroin or cocaine would be prosecuted as a "civil violation" -- not a criminal violation.

Remember I wrote in ENCORE!, the last 24 pages of HOPE'S HUSBAND!, that the government of the United States was formally inserted into a world government on January 19, 1989 without the knowledge of the American people! Since that is true, technically there are no longer any common law Rights guaranteed under the Constitution of the United States, such as those 4th and 5th Amendment protections.

I maintain that the World Government set up in secret during January, 1989 is *ultra vires*, that is, outside the Law and without legal standing. Therefore, I claim my common law Rights as a Citizen and am not a Subject who must submit to search of my home, person, papers and effects without a properly drawn 4th Amendment Warrant signed by a Judge in my County setting forth under oath the probable cause for believing there is a criminal activity on my part.

Here is the point. Read it carefully! Under American Constitutional Law, and the Laws of every one of the States, there is no such thing as a "civil crime." All crimes, even a humble traffic ticket, are legally criminal in nature and jurisdiction. The only jurisdiction wherein there can be a "civil crime", or where any Court can impose such a penalty, is under Admiralty/Maritime International Law. By what authority does an American, walking around with an ounce of Marijuana, come under the International Law of the Sea? Isn't he supposed to be under "the law of the Land?"

What is the only way that a citizen of the United States of America can be reduced to a "Person subject to Admiralty/Maritime Law" without Constitutional Rights? Only by Contract. By what contract has an American been forced into such jurisdiction? There may be a number of them which he is absolutely unaware of until it is too late to unravel his personal affairs and then **timely claim** his lawful rights. With all due respect to my friend Larry Patterson, no federal law can be passed that will do away with the 4th Amendment. For an American to be subject to search and seizure without a 4th Amendment warrant, he must have already waived those Rights by contract or he must have failed to object timely prior to the search.

I am not going to take time and space to list those typical contracts wherein many have waived, albeit inadvertently and perhaps through fraud, their common law rights. That has been published previously. However, with all due disrespect to Attorney General Thornburg, I am not a person subject to such searches without a warrant. I am not under the jurisdiction of any court who can impose such prosecution for "civil violations." Are you now beginning to see why I must write on so many seemingly different subjects and then show how they blend together?

Here is another thought that will be a shock to you but do not misunderstand me or draw conclusions beyond what I am teaching. It is not a violation of American Common Law or any of the common laws of any State, to possess marijuana or cocaine for your own personal use. Until there is a victim, there is no crime. Until you have deprived some other person of life, liberty or property, no crime has been committed, all the statutes and regulations to the contrary not withstanding. Most Americans these days, (because of the Social Security contract and other contracts that confer upon them maritime jurisdiction), are legally wards of the State. If you are a ward of the State, instead of a Freeman at law, then the State has the jurisdiction to compel you to perform according to contract and take good care of yourself and not smoke "pot". The State has the duty to take care of the property and chattel that it owns, including subjects and persons under contract for their care. Do you see that?

It has long been my position that the totalitarian socialists, which includes George Bush when the final truth is known, want the use of drugs going on as a means of softening up the next generation in prepara-

tion for the New World Order that they are now setting in place. If this were not so, they would stop the drug producing chemicals going to Latin America from American firms, and intercept the millions of dollars going through American banks to Panama, Israel, and other cooperating off-shore banking nations.

Here is how this works. There are no bank reporting requirements if money is **wired** off-shore. If you carry huge amounts of money through customs and fail to report it, and get caught, it is a crime punishable by a prison term. However, the built-in loophole for the drug dealers is that money **wired** off-shore need not be reported, and is not to be reported to the government by the banks either! A drug dealer can walk into any bank in America, lay down $200,000 in cash, and have it wired to a Panama Bank account that he has set up on his vacation there. He can then direct the same bank to wire the funds back to the same bank from which the money was initially sent and there are no reports required to be made. This is done all the time without breaking any U.S. Law. The funds are thus legally laundered and there is no record kept of the huge cash transactions. The Bush Administration wants to have it that way. Drugs can be stopped any time the American people get fed up enough to do something about it on the local scene and in

WC Author's Note: The following reproduction of the Northpoint Newsletter is included for your evaluation. Nord Davis claims that he has the proof that substantiates the information contained in this newsletter.

Please contact Mr. Davis directly if you want to obtain further information.

Northpoint Teams
P. O. Box 129
Topton, NC 28781

* * * * T O P   S E C R E T * * * *

the local courts.

THE BUSH SECRET EXPOSED

Exactly ten days after the illegal Bush invasion of Panama, the LOS ANGELES TIMES of December 30, 1989 ran a story which exposed the Bush Family deep involvement in the Panamanian financial affairs to the tune of hundreds of millions of dollars! Yes, the Bush Family has that kind of money. Yes, sweet grandmother Barbara Bush knows all about it for those of you who have written here asking about her.

As President, George Bush's time is pretty well occupied, the Bush Family investments are handled by his brother, Prescott S. Bush and their funds are laundered through a Japanese firm, which goes by the name Aoki Corporation. Prescott Bush, according to our sources, is a MAJOR PARTNER in Aoki Corporation, not just a minor stockholder. He is one of those who set the corporate policies of this Japanese firm. This Japanese firm, and their partners, have invested more than $350,000,000 in Panama, and their holdings include the famous Marriott Hotel around which firefights raged in the news not too long ago. They own a luxury resort on Contadora Island known as Caesar Park. You remember that resort, don't you? That was where the notorious "Peace Conferences for Central America" were held from which the pinko Oscar Arias, the former President of Costa Rica, won his Nobel Peace Prize. This Nobel Peace Prize has never been given to anyone who is not either a Communist or Totalitarian Socialist.

I pegged this story as a Bush Secret,

Bush's Brother Linked to Firm in Panama Deal

☐ Noriega: Prescott Bush is a partner in a venture with a Japanese firm accused of paying bribes to the ousted dictator.

Aoki's dealings with Noriega add another element of controversy as the Administration tries to ensure the stability of a post-Noriega government in the wake of last week's military invasion.

The allegations that Aoki paid

because he has never admitted a family commitment of capital to Panama. Financial disclosures are required by law, and this has never been done. More respectable politicians put their financial holdings into a blind trust so that there can be no accusations that they have used their political office or inside information for personal financial gain. In addition, the Bush Family having multiple millions invested in Panama, at the same time that extensive negotiations are going on regarding Noriega, is a serious breach of ethics sufficient to initiate impeachment proceedings against him.

Under normal circumstances, an independent prosecutor would certainly be called for to investigate the Bush involvement in Panamanian business ventures through his brother. Why has there been no investigation of the Bush Family investments in this world capital of drug dealing and money laundering? Can you understand the basic economic fact that valuable investment properties rise or go down in valuation de-pending upon the political climate of any nation, including Panama? Panama, unlike Costa Rica to the north, is not a beautiful country with a delightful climate. It is not one of those places normal people go to on their annual vacation. These resorts are there to supply the needs of the wealthy who go to Panama to handle international financial dealings, and the more money that flows through Panama, even drug money, the more valuable the properties there are going to be and the more money they will be making on investments.

I also pegged this story a Bush Secret

- 7 -

because while the LOS ANGELES TIMES did print the story as written by Doug Frantx and Jim Mann, their wire service did not publish the story, and the story did not appear in API, UPI, or the New York Times wire services. Someone with a lot of clout put a clamp on this story of the Bush Investments in Panama.

As a further insight into the Bush character, the same Japanese firm, Aoki Corporation, is now building the luxury resort facilities near Shanghai, in communist Red China. In that project, the Bush Family has invested $18 million, according to the LOS ANGELES TIMES. This is precisely why the U.S. Policy toward Red China has not changed one bit after the Tiananmen Square slaughter of freedom-loving Chinese students. Now you know why! Another major ethics violation by George Bush which normally would precipitate a Justice Department investigation.

DEEPER STILL!

In the January Letter, I mentioned a 4 million dollar bribe that was paid to Noriega by the Aoki Corporation for permits to build Panama's Hydroelectric Plants. I can now document that this bribe, by the Aoki Corporation, **was arranged by the Bush Family,** and paid to General Manuel Noriega for a special license for this power plant project. Then, according to the investigative staff of the LOS ANGELES TIMES, the bribe money was taken but the license/permit was not issued as promised. This forced a showdown between Aoki Corporation and Noriega, or stated more specifically, a test of wills between Noriega and the Bush Family. You must understand that Noriega is a "low class" person. He never learned any culture and did not understand the deeper workings of the world power elite. He thought that he could control what went on in Panama, and when push came to shove, it is believed that Noriega was about to "nationalize" some or all of the Aoki-Bush Family's $350,000,000 worth of investments in retaliation for the U.S. indictment of him in Florida. He looked upon this

as a betrayal of him by his friend George Bush. He did not understand that Bush had no control over that indictment and once it had been handed down, there was little he could do and still keep up the pretenses of being the "Leader of the War on Drugs."

I agree with Lawrence Patterson's assessment of this sinister situation when he writes:

"26 Men Died To Protect The Bush Investments in Panama!

The obvious fact is that the invasion of Panama was hatched by our President, not because he is concerned about the drug dealing going on in Panama, --but to protect his family's $350 million investment in the Marriott and other resorts in Panama...For this reason alone, the decision to invade Panama was made....Thus, we are left with the obvious conclusion: --that the 26 men who died in battle and the 324 men who were wounded in capturing Noriega for George Bush, were sent there on a personal mission to eliminate a potential threat to his presidency and to protect the Bush family investments, ---not to control the flow of drugs into the United States."

CRIMINAL POLITICS, February, 1990

So, what are we going to do about it?

I ask that each of you who receive this Month's Letter take it to your local printer and have at least 500 copies reprinted. I have printed it on white paper so that it will be "camera ready." It will be much less expensive for you to do this than for us to print **and pay the postage** to get them to you. Otherwise, 2 copies for $1.00 postpaid. Then make certain that a copy is provided to each officer of the local Democratic Party, the local newspapers, and to your state and federal congressmen. We must create enough political pressure so that Congress will order a Special Federal Prosecutor to investigate the Ethics Violations, or worse, of George Bush, the drug chemicals leaving America for Columbia, and the improper U.S. invasion of Panama for personal reasons.

Nord Davis, Jr., NORTHPOINT

The March Special Thank You Letter

Published by Nord Davis, Jr.
NORTHPOINT TEAMS
PO Box 129, Topton, N.C. 28781

There is a new military medal now being released for those of the Armed Forces who participated in numerous undeclared wars including the recent invasion of Panama known as **Operation Just Cause.** It is called the Armed Forces Expeditionary Medal and I have shown it here. It includes the operations against Libya, Grenada, Cambodia, Laos and the blockade of Cuba in 1962-1963. It includes such missions defined as "peace-keeping" as in the Congo in 1960-62 and Lebanon in 1963-1967. It includes all sorts of unusual operations from 1958 until 1989, some of which are long forgotten as the Naval Blockade off Red China from 1958-1963. I found the release of this new Expeditionary Medal, and the Ribbon that goes with it, a forboding of things to come where American Forces will be used to secure the global schemes of the international socialists and their New World Order.

Last December, on the day after the invasion of Panama, the international banker's mouthpiece, THE WALL STREET JOURNAL wrote that Manuel Noriega had "learned, and others like him should take note, that there are limits to the uncivilized behaviour that the United States will accept or endure."

I thought that quote was most interesting and I saved it for special comment this month. I wrote the first 8 pages for the general public to read as I hope that it will be reproduced widely. In this section, we will get down to some other things that you need to know about the criminal operations of the federal government that might not be as fitting in a general circulation pamphlet.

It is now about 3 months after that invasion where 26 of our finest men were killed, and American troops are still occupying the country. Panamanians are learning just what will and will not be tolerated. American Forces, with token Panamanian troops accompanying them, have openly raided newspaper offices and arrested anyone critical of the U.S. invasion, including a prominent newspaper publisher and the law professor who negotiated the 1977 Panama Canal Treaty. Hundreds of such dissidents have been rounded up and detained without charges at the United States Military Base or held in jails for "impeding the renewal of the powers of state."

Pickets parade daily with at least 100

people in front of President Endara's home demanding to be paid, and thus the U.S. Puppet Government is receiving less and less support. There are approximately 60 armed robberies daily in Panama City where my informant lives. They range from accosting customers in grocery stores and on the streets to open bank robberies. The Bush Government there is helpless to stop them. Local police, many of whom have been quietly rehired from the Noriega Regime cadre because of their experience, are stopping foreigners in automobiles and intimidating them into paying ficticious traffic violations "on the spot."

On January 29, 1990, the Associated Press ran a story about a writer and former CIA agent named Phillip Agee after a speech that Mr. Agee gave at Oregon State University at Corvallis, OR. Agee stated that Bush should be locked up along side Noriega, because he stated,

"Bush is up to his neck in illegal drug running on behalf of the Contras."

Agee spent 12 years with the CIA serving in various places in Central and South America. Then he left the CIA in 1969 and wrote a book on "The Company" and it is said that the CIA would like to see him very seriously dead. He made the unforgiveable mistake of naming currently operating CIA agents. Where do NORTHPOINT TEAMS know Phillip Agee from? Why he was working with the Sandinista Regime for years right there

in Managua, Nicaragua at the INTERNATIONAL HOTEL and even more specifically on the 5th floor. So, while he presents himself as a former CIA Agent, and says many of the right things, remember that his sympathies still lie with his Sandinista friends.

The next character you need to know about in the on-going saga of the Perfidy in Panama, is a secret Israeli Mossad Agent named Michael Harari. The NEW YORK TIMES said of this man on January 2, 1990:

"An Israeli reputed to be Gen. Manuel Antonio Noriega's closest associate may have eluded capture on the night of the United States invasion because he was warned to flee six hours before the American troops swept into the capital, the deputy commander of Panama's new police force said today...."
Story by David E. Pitt

I reported last month that my contact in Panama knew of the **exact time** of the invasion for almost two days, and now we are reading in the NEW YORK TIMES that the Israeli community in Panama was given at least a six hour warning to not be around when the Americans landed. Of the 26 men who died in Panama under combat conditions, it is known that at least 11 of these were U.S. Special Forces, a highly trained elite among our Armed Forces. For this many to have been

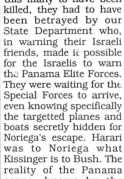

killed, they had to have been betrayed by our State Department who, in warning their Israeli friends, made it possible for the Israelis to warn the Panama Elite Forces. They were waiting for the Special Forces to arrive, even knowing specifically the targetted planes and boats secretly hidden for Noriega's escape. Harari was to Noriega what Kissinger is to Bush. The reality of the Panama scene, known by the whole world except America, is that Harari was the man that **Noriega** reported to, and it was Harari who was filling his pockets with the drug money. In the coming months, unless the Panama Invasion has been ordered out of the press speculation by the powers that be, there will be conflicting stories as to how the leak came about that alerted Israel and almost certainly the Noriega forces to the forthcoming invasion. No matter what happens, I want you to remember that these 11 Special Forces men died because they were

- 2 -

betrayed by an Israeli Mossad Hit Squad Chief named Michael Harari whose picture I have shown here. No apologies for the rather poor quality of reproduction. These photographs are often hard to get of such high-level covert operatives.

Michael Harari has a very interesting background of murder and sabotage. He holds the Rank of Colonel in the Israeli Mossad, and took over as the Central American Mossad Director in 1980. I saw him only once to my recollection, and it was in central San Jose, Costa Rica on the square in front of the Opera House. He was with two younger agents, and I did get a photograph of them. They were driving a late model brown four door Jeep Wagoneer. One or both of his men were seen by my people observing me on many occasions. Officially, Col. Harari was assigned to the Israeli Embassy in Mexico City, but in fact spent most of his time in Panama where he had a line of associates and contacts since as early as 1973. It was during that period that Noriega was strong man Omar Torrijos's Intelligence Chief, and double-dipping by getting a $200,000 per year salary as an informant for the CIA then under control of George Bush. He also worked for the MOSSAD as an informant. Isn't it a small world?

Noriega knew Col. Harari from his training in military intelligence in Israel. It is known that Noriega made five jumps with the Israeli Paratroopers and qualified for his Israeli Paratrooper wings, which he wore on his uniform for years. While Noriega was "bought and paid for by Bush's CIA" the fact remains that he was an Israeli creation as to his personal philosophy and military mind-set. Noriega was in his mind, a Zionist. He secretly wished that he was a Jew by birth instead of a Panamanian of uncertain origins. He bought a home in the Herzliya section of Tel Aviv. In Panama, he sent his children to the Jewish Alberto Einstein Day School instead of the Jesuit schools of his early days. He even sent his children to an Israeli Kibbutz one summer. The Panamanian Jewish community numbers around 5,000, but the Israelis control most of the Central Avenue business district. According to the WASHINGTON JEWISH WEEK of December 28, 1989, the Israelis in Panama:

"...do not reflect well on Israel or the Panama Jewish community....They are engaged in contraband and money·laundering. In general they engage in very aggressive and unfair business practices."

It was the Israeli business men, not the Panamanian Jews, who were looted during the confusion following the invasion with reported losses of around a billion dollars. Your government is now going to be taxing you to repay these Israeli businessmen for their losses.

The Associated Press of December 27th quoted a US Embassy official who stated that they had captured Col. Harari. Orders came down from Washington that Harari was to be released, and the next we heard concerning him was on an Israeli TV interview, from Israel, denying that he had anything to do with Noriega's affairs.

Our DEA intelligence sources reveal that Noriega had a mistress named Magdelena Kusmisk. She bore him an illegitimate son in Washington, DC in 1982. Mrs. Noriega, it seems, cast a "voodoo spell" on her, and Noriega had to bring in a Brazilian witch doctor to counter it. Noriega is not a true Catholic believer although he had been raised as one. The Vatican Embassy chose to take him in during "his hour of need". He was not Jewish by religion, only Zionist by international socialist politics. His actual religion is the Santeria Folk Theology imported into Brazil by the African slaves. Santeria is similar to Voodoo in that believers worship their gods with personal offerings and think that their magic can control and manipulate their enemies. Unfortunately, Santeria religious practices are commonly mixed in with the Catholic religion in Central and South America, and Noriega attended Catholic services but practiced Santeria in private. Santeria is what makes many Catholics so unpredictable

- 3 -

in Latin American countries. The Santeria uses ritual homicide and it is known that Noriega had a room in one of his luxury villas that was used for this purpose. There was an alter there to a Brazilian priestess, along with the other usual trappings of the Santeria, such as bottles, beads, candles and dried food offerings. Noriega, with the help of his Santeria gods, tried to influence people by putting handwritten lists of their names under a glob of wax or wrapped around a white candle. Our source is Chief Warrant Officer James Dibble, U.S. Army Specialist in the Occult, stationed at Fort Campbell, KY. Dibble was the man called to inspect the contents of the "ritual rooms" in the Noriega complex.

As you think of these things, remember that the ultimate goal of these international totalitarian socialists is to bring America down so that, as Kissinger wrote in FOREIGN AFFAIRS, "America can be comfortably merged with the Soviet Union." Toward that end, they are quite willing to be promoting the international drug trade for personal financial profit, and at the same time declaring a "war on drugs" for personal political profit. Some of my wonderful readers simply cannot imagine President Bush getting away with this duplicity for all these years. Therefore, they assume that all this cannot be true and that Nord Davis must have exaggerated the facts. Well, George Bush has not gotten away with it, for a number of us are adamantly exposing him with names, dates and places. We had to laugh, last month, when Bush set up his "drug summit", key to his "war on drugs", in Cartagena, Columbia of all places. Those of us who remember our history, know that Cartagena was the site of the greatest naval invasion defeat of America's pre-revolutionary Latin American escapades. In command of this invasion of Cartagena was an Admiral Vernon and under him in command was one Lawrence Washington, the brother of George, our first President. I do not recall the actual reason for the attack on Cartagena, but when the Yankees went ashore, the ladders they

carried were six feet too short to scale the walls of the Fort, and the Spanish defenders mowed them down by the thousands. Those who survived, with their immune systems not accustomed to the diseases of the tropics, came down with various diseases, and hundreds of them died. Lawrence Washington picked up one of these diseases, which finally took his life. However, Lawrence still named his home after this inept Admiral, calling it Mount Vernon. When Lawrence died, brother George inherited his lands, and today we think of Mount Vernon as being George Washington's home. Had it not been for the fiasco of Cartagena, George would have never lived there.

We can understand the folly of Admiral Vernon and his too short ladders. We can even understand the loyalty of Lawrence Washington to his friend in his final years of disgrace having lost thousands of men on the shores of South America. But the folly of the so-called war on drugs is quite another thing. The plan is to deliberately lose the war, as was done in Vietnam, to exploit inevitable political change in America. The no-win war on drugs serves the secret interests of the International Socialists by subverting the intent of the Bill of Rights that most Americans suppose still protects them from the tyranny of government. Under the pretext of rescuing people from the incalculable perils of rampaging mobs seeking their final fix, or the looting of their homes and ravaging their women by dope heads, the war on drugs is intended to claim for itself enormously enhanced powers of repression and control.

Here is the clue. Right after President Bush's speech in September, declaring the "war on drugs", an opinion poll is reported to show that 62% of all Americans were willing "to give up some freedoms" in order to rid America of the scourge of drugs. As the politicaly sophisticated know, "opinion polls" are used to **create** opinions, not monitor them. They are used to determine the effectiveness of the media propaganda. However in this case, it may be quite true that 62% of all Americans would be willing to give up some of

- 4 -

their freedoms to stop drugs, and the totalitarian socialists are certainly hoping you will ask that this be done. Isn't that the way that every dictatorship got started? Hitler controlled the German "Brown Shirts." The Brown Shirts were causing all sorts of civil upheavals. Hitler promised to stop the Brown Shirts and was quickly put in power.

George Bush is directly involved with the drug traffic, not only from Central and South America, but from the Golden Triangle of Northern Burma as well. The drugs are causing all sorts of civil upheavals. Bush promises to declare war on drugs. The people willingly give up freedom and liberty for what they believe will be peace and safety. Well, that is the plan. To prepare for that, we are hearing more and more about the need for more police, more judges, more jails, more prisons, more and longer punishments, and more people serving "serious time."

Along with the totalitarian socialist's zeal for coercion, the politicians of both parties are demanding longer prison terms, and harsher laws. Federal officers confiscate motor vehicles, boats and houses of suspected drug dealers even before these people have had their day in court. They are demanding, and it appears that they will get it, the right to invade almost anyone's privacy: search without a warrant anyone's car or boat; bend the rules of evidence, hire police spies, and monitor phone lines without a warrant. The Supreme Court has ruled that the police can stop, detain and question any person travelling through an airport whom the police say that they "see a resemblence to a drug dealer"---the very lowest level of our 4th Amendment Probable Cause Rights. In a recent ABC Poll it was reported that 55% of all Americans support mandatory drug testing for all Americans.

The enforcement of these "tougher laws" requires additional tiers of expensive government. Of the $7,900,000,000 dollars

($7.9 Billion) that Bush allotted to the war on drugs in September, the bulk of the money goes to swell the budgets of 58 federal agencies and 74 congressional committees already engaged in the "war on drugs." Each of these has its own agenda and armies to feed on the various fronts of the so-called campaign. The government agents have a talent for theft and fraud that is barely distinguishable from the talent for theft and fraud of the drug syndicates they insist that they are fighting.

Some of the statements on the CIA direct involvement with the importation of drugs from Central America are now coming out in the normal press. I know that there are a number of my friends who privately questioned my statements in HOPE'S HUSBAND, supposing, with love, that I must have spent too much time under the hot tropical sun. As I write, there is a Federal trial going on in Tulsa, Oklahoma. The defendant is Jose Abello-Silva who is charged with "conspiracy to import cocaine." A federal witness, a self-confessed drug smuggler named Fabio Ernesto Carrasco, testified that he worked for the defendant, thus proving the government's case of a conspiracy. However under cross-examination, Carrasco testified that he supervised two CIA-sponsored shipments of weapons to Costa Rica allegedly for the Nicaraguan Contras, and returned to the United States with cocaine for the Central Intelligence Agency! Two years ago, I even told you **where** these planes landed---John Hull's ranch in Northern Costa Rica, and **who** supervised these shipments both ways---Oliver North and his associates. I told you **where** the planes landed in the U.S. with the cocaine---Homestead Air force Base, Florida. I even know the official Pennsylvania owners of the aircraft used, and the amount of cocaine in the shipments: 1,000 Kilograms or just over one ton. The man who could testify that the drugs were picked up by Jeb Bush, the son of the then Vice-President, "committed suicide" in California a couple years ago, allegedly from a cocaine overdose. Nonsense! He was trained Special Forces.

- 5 -

There was a very revealing story, of all places, in the <u>U.S. News & World </u>Report, dated March 26, 1990 on page 16. Read it carefully:

"For more than a decade, Khun Sa, the warlord of opium, has flooded Washington with offers to end the poppy production within his Golden Triangle fiefdom in exchange for financial aid. The U.S. has not responded, and this year the region's crop could double from the levels of just a few years ago. Atty. Gen. Dick Thornburgh unsealed an indictment against the man considered responsible for 40 percent of the U.S. heroin supply. But Sa is not likely to be booked soon. In the remote hills of Burma, a private army of thousands protect him."

What the U.S. News & World Report states is that Gen. Khun Sa will stop his shipments amounting to 40% of the heroin supply if the U.S. will send his nation financial aid, and from other sources we know that he wants another agriculture crop that he can grow that the U.S. will buy from him so that his economy will function without drug money. What the story does **not** say is that the 1,200 metric tons of refined heroin per year, worth on the street an amount equal to 10% of America's Gross National Product, is being shipped from Thailand on U.S. Air Force cargo planes! One of my NORTHPOINT TEAM members recently finished his military tour of duty and told me that he was ordered to help load some of these shipments. What the story did **not** say is that the U.S. Army Corps of Engineers built a two lane road back into the North Burma mountains so that these shipments could be brought out on trucks instead of the backs of mules. We now know why the Bush Administration "has not reponded," don't we? The secret "CIA within the CIA" that Oliver North testified to, is using the millions of dollars in drug profits to push its worldwide covert operations of preparing the "third world nations" for international socialism in the new world government now being set in place. You might as well get used to the idea that personal privacy set forth in the 4th Amendment

is really a thing of the past. President Bush, with his "war on drugs" offers the nation the chance to deny its best principles, to corrupt its magistrates, and to repudiate its civil liberties. His deal is as shabby and unAmerican as is his tons of cocaine and heroin from Costa Rica and Northern Burma. ❏

Oliver North...Once Again

In an earlier monthly letter I stated that I would have some special questions for the former Admiral John Poindexter. I had an idea that the courts would do with him the same as it did with Oliver North---a mere slap on the wrist. Instead, Mr. Poindexter was convicted on all felony counts. I do not suppose that he will spend much, if any, time in prison. His sentencing is not due until later. However, since he was convicted, my questions, the kind one asks when he already knows the answers, need not be asked.

If one makes a study of the Iran-Contra Hearings, John Poindexter was the <u>only</u> witness that did not hang Oliver North out to dry. To an embattled retired Marine, caught in so many illegal activities and downright lies, Admiral Poindexter's testimony was a welcome relief. Oliver North, in his typical inept way, tried to do the same for his old friend and former boss. According to the U.S. NEWS & WORLD REPORT of March 19, 1990, North's testimony at the pretrial hearing was so favorable to Poindexter, in other words false, that even the Judge stepped out of his normally impartial role and called North's testimony "far-fetched." North was the first witness at the Poindexter trial and he stubbornly resisted saying anything that could aid in a conspiracy, obstruction of jus-

tice, or lying-to-congress conviction. Well North's intentions were foiled, and his perjury again uncovered, when the prosecutor confronted North with his own testimony during his trial wherein he implicated Poindexter as a key figure in the Iran-Contra scandal. North is now working with Joe Fernandez, the former CIA Agent we knew in Costa Rica as "Tomas Castillo", in the sale of light weight bullet-proof vests. See HOPE'S HUSBAND, page 65. ❏

BILLIONS UPON BILLIONS TO THE WORLD

In mid-March, George Bush called for $300,000,000 in aid to help rebuild Nicaragua. That, he told us, was only the first installment. If you remember, he called for some $570,000,000 in aid to Panama. This money, if the Bush plan succeeds, will come out of the Pentagon's budget and not out of the normal foreign-aid budget. We are not supposed to ask the obvious questions: "How does the expendature of almost a billion dollars rebuilding socialist Nicaragua and Panama help defend the United States? Where in the Constitution is there any authority for the Legislative Democracy of Washington, District of Columbia, [as an entity distinct from the Constitutional Republic of the United States of America], to spend any taxpayer money to rebuild or enrich non-American peoples and nations?" I can find no such authority. The foreign aid budget comes to $14 thousand million dollars, and $5 thousand million dollars, one third of the entire budget, is given to Israel and Egypt alone--both of which are anti-Christ nations. If you approve of these illegal expendatures, keep right on voting for the same set of politicians. Our philosophy remains as it has for years, don't re-elect anybody. Frankly we would have been better off with Dukakis and his drunken wife than with George Bush and his covert activities. ❏

SOME MORE ON THE IRS

On March 15th, the <u>Geraldo Riveria Show</u> devoted his entire hour-long show to the exposure of the bloody, inhumane and criminal brutality of the U.S. Treasury Agents in its supervision of the INTERNAL REVENUE SERVICE, Inc. a private Delaware Corporation. You mean you thought that the IRS was part of the Federal Government? No, they are part of, and in conspiracy with, the privately owned Federal Reserve Banking System. I am still trying to get a video copy of this Geraldo Riveria Show and would appreciate it if any of my Team Members have a copy that you can run one off for me. Those who can afford to do so, can purchase them from the Riveria Organization for $100 by calling (212) 265-8520. I saw only the tail end of it as I was called and advised to watch it -- but too late to see it all or to video tape it.

- 7 -

Cocaine seized on Air Force plane

2 arrested after flight from Panama arrives at base in Delaware

The Orange County Register 11/12/89
The Associated Press

DOVER, Del. — Authorities seized 66 pounds of cocaine that was flown aboard an Air Force cargo plane from Panama to Dover Air Force Base and arrested a 13-year Army veteran and his brother, who were to pick up the drugs, federal officials said Saturday.

The shipment, valued at $3 million, had been monitored from the time it was placed aboard the C-5 cargo plane at Howard Air Base in Panama, said Larry Whitfield, a Drug Enforcement Administration agent in Wilmington, Del.

DEA and Air Force investigators had learned of the shipment several months ago, he said.

Two men suspected of serving as couriers were arrested by undercover DEA agents and Air Force officials Saturday at a motel where they apparently were waiting for the shipment, Whitfield said.

Arrested were Nathan Thomas, 23, of New York and his brother, Victor M. Thomas, 32, an Army maintenance worker stationed at Fort Riley, Kan., and on leave from his job, Dover Air Force Base spokesman Walter Thorp said.

Both were held on suspicion of conspiracy and possession of cocaine with intent to deliver, Whitfield said.

They were being held at the Delaware Correctional Center near Smyrna pending arraignment Monday in US Magistrate Court in Wilmington.

Officials would not say who placed the drugs aboard the plane or what kind of tip authorities received because they did not want to jeopardize their investigation in Panama, Thorp said.

They also would not say whether any members of the Air Force were suspected of being involved in the smuggling operation. Whitfield said he was not aware of any arrests being made in Panama.

The cocaine — in 30 1-kilogram bricks — had a street value of about $3 million, Whitfield said. In addition, authorities seized $73,000 carried by the Thomas brothers, he said.

The C-5 crew was told it was carrying a top-secret cargo but not informed of the contents of the cardboard box holding the cocaine, Thorp said.

THE PRESS DEMOCRAT, WEDNESDAY, SEPTEMBER 19, 1990

IT'S NO VACATION

Remote island drug prisons part of plan in defense bill

By MARK BARNHILL
Los Angeles Daily News

WASHINGTON — Summoning visions of a modern-day Devil's Island, Congress is considering a plan to imprison drug-law offenders on "isolated and shark-surrounded islands" in the Pacific Ocean.

Supporters of the plan say it would help ease prison overcrowding and, as a bonus, help reduce the defense budget by using inmate labor for maintenance work on remote U.S. military outposts.

But critics say the proposal harkens back to a more brutal era of punishment in which inmates were carted off to places like Devil's Island, the infamous French penal colony off the coast of South America that was closed in 1938.

"This is the craziest thing I've ever heard," said Loren Siegel of the American Civil Liberties Union. "Deporting people to do slave labor on an island far out in the ocean is cruel and unusual punishment."

Under the plan, U.S. outposts on the World War II battlegrounds of Midway and Wake Island, tiny coral atolls, would be converted into penal colonies for Americans who are convicted of drug-related felonies.

The proposal is tucked away in an obscure section of the $283 billion defense authorization bill that is now being debated by the House of Representatives.

A four-paragraph section of the voluminous bill, approved by the House Armed Services Committee on July 31, asks the Pentagon to study the feasibility of island drug prisons and report back to Congress by next March.

"As an alternative to the shortage of available space for convicted drug offenders and as an effort to reduce the defense budget, utilizing some of these facilities for drug offenders should be considered," the bill says.

The feasibility study is not scheduled for debate and is expected to be approved as part of the full defense bill sometime this week.

Midway is a two-square-mile coral atoll about 1,500 miles northwest of Hawaii; Wake Island is a three-square-mile atoll about 2,300 miles west of Hawaii.

The two islands were focal points of Pacific operations during World War II, and Midway was the site of one of the U.S. Navy's most decisive victories.

Today, the atolls are maintained by the Defense Department as emergency airfields and communications stations.

Neither has any native inhabitants, but several hundred contract workers live on the islands year-round to maintain the U.S. facilities at a cost of about $8 million a year.

The proposal is the brainchild of Rep. Richard Ray, D-Ga., who called it a "keen idea" for cutting defense costs while at the same time saving money on prison construction costs.

"Using drug offenders to man these isolated and shark-surrounded islands would alleviate some of the overcrowding of federal prisons and save the Department of Defense some money," Ray said.

A28 The Orange County Register Sunday, November 19, 1989

Report links CIA, Pan Am bombing

CBS, lawmaker allege drug deal resulted in disaster

Reuters

NEW YORK — A CIA deal with a heroin smuggler might have played a crucial part in events leading to the bombing in December 1988 of Pan Am Flight 103 over Lockerbie, Scotland, which killed 270 people, CBS reported Saturday.

The bomb was smuggled onto the aircraft in a suitcase that was supposed to contain heroin, Rep. James Traficant, D-Ohio, said on CBS' "Saturday Night with Connie Chung."

He said he got his information from a confidential report by investigators hired by Pan Am's insurance underwriter.

CBS said Traficant plans to meet with Pan Am officials Monday to question them about the report. It said the CIA has dismissed the allegations as "nonsense".

CBS correspondent Chung and Traficant gave this description of the alleged deal: The CIA had allowed a man with terrorist connections to transport drugs to the United States in exchange for information about US hostages held in Lebanon.

Turkish baggage handlers at Frankfurt airport had been primed to substitute a suitcase containing drugs for a normal suitcase aboard the Pan Am flight. But Ahmed Jibril, allegedly hired by Iranian officials to place a bomb on a US carrier, knew of the drug run.

"Jibril knew of the drug run ... and he was able to orchestrate a situation where, instead of the drugs, he put the bomb on 103."

Traficant said on CBS. "And he was able to get a bomb on it because that thing was insulated by the CIA for a drug run."

According to CBS, West German intelligence, aware of the drug-running scheme, had placed the baggage for the Pan Am flight under video surveillance and reported to the CIA that the smuggler was not using his usual suitcase but had placed a brown Samsonite bag on the plane.

Traficant said the investigators found out that German intelligence notified the CIA. "They notified Washington and were told 'Disregard,'" he said.

Ex-CIA agent says diary referring to Kennedy assassination is hoax

Reuters *The Register*
9/21/90

HOUSTON — A diary claiming a Dallas policeman shot President John Kennedy was unveiled Thursday, but a leading assassination theorist immediately labeled it a hoax.

The diary included notations in which the late Dallas police officer Roscoe White supposedly confessed to participating in a Central Intelligence Agency plot to kill Kennedy, who was shot to death in Dallas on Nov. 22, 1963.

"They want me to kill the president. God help me. They say he's a threat to the United States," a line in the document said.

Private investigator Joe West showed copied pages from the diary at a news conference.

West said White's widow, Geneva White Galle, found the diary recently in the garage of her Midland, Texas, home.

She allowed him to make copies because she was dying and "wants to use the few days she has left to let the truth be known," he said.

But former CIA agent John Stockwell, who has written extensively on the possibility that Kennedy was killed by a government-led conspiracy, said at the same news conference that the diary appeared to be a fraud.

"I believe when analysis is done, it will show this document is a fabrication — and one that's fairly easy to expose," said Stockwell, who was allowed to view the actual document this week. He refused to speculate on who might have per-

petrated the alleged fraud.

He said the document refers to the Watergate break-in committed by the Nixon re-election campaign almost a year before it happened. It also appeared to have been written with a type of felt-tip pen that was not available during part of the time — from 1956 to 1971 — White supposedly wrote.

White died in a fire in 1971.

West, who has investigated the Kennedy assassination for two years, said he could not guarantee the veracity of the diary.

The document also talks about White's involvement with alleged Kennedy assassin Lee Harvey Oswald, Oswald murderer Jack Ruby and a Mafia gunman who supposedly also took part in the assassination.

****TOP SECRET****

APPENDIX G: KURZWEIL VS. HOPKINS

I originally became interested in the UFO subject by meeting Larry Lebelson, a writer for OMNI Magazine who told me about cattle mutilations and urged I attend an APRO meeting. I was not very impressed with the meeting but rather with an attractive woman named Joan Thompson who appeared to be one of the few non-strange looking people at the meeting. Ms. Thompson and her friends and later together we attended a MUFON meeting held in Boston. (This was about 1981.) Ms. Thompson explained that she was an employee of the CIA and urged that I work with Mr. Budd Hopkins to help with his research. (1982) Mr. Hopkins explained that he likewise was an employee of the CIA: "I'm the abduction specialist for them." He was extremely concerned that the cover-up be maintained lest "there be a revolution in this country". He fearfully told me that "alot" of people have been abducted: "we don't know what the UFOs did to them; I wrote the book to find out who had been abducted ("Missing Time"); the Gov't. has to get those people out of the military; they (ie., the CIA) thinks abductees may have been programmed." He was very upset about the amount of work required to investigate even one case. Mr. Hopkins said, "distrust the information passed on while obtained under hypnosis". He was shocked by the after effects of abductions; people frequently committed suicide FOLLOWING his "hypnotherapy"; many went on to become alcoholics or drug addicts such as Ms. Marcy Drexler. I asked him why he did the hypnosis if it caused the psychological and psychiatric problems! He could offer no reply whatsoever despite repeated questioning. I myself was appalled by the inhumane and medically indecent standards of "care" being applied to these victims of Nazi-like brutality. By all medical standards Mr. Hopkins was further causing injury to individuals already in distress. He made no provision for aftercare or follow-up. He displayed a complete lack of temperment and training (as well as a complete lack of compassion) for for these people. Once he obtained his "information", he would drop these people like hot potatoes and left them on their own. As a medical doctor I was disgusted; as an American I was sickened at this maltreatment of our own people. I refused to cooperate with Hopkins and reported him to the Medical Authorities as being involved in harmful and extremely questionable activities that were anti-humanitarian as well as anti-American. He threatened to get revenge by reporting me as "mentally impaired" since I believed in a government cover-up and reported harassment. This, he claimed, was evidence of paranoid delusion. "Steve, you had the nerve to tell me to F--- Myself" and "that's why I'm getting back at you". The New York State Office of Professional Conduct was told lies (1989) about my involvement in this subject. The State is required by law to investigate all reports (even by non-patients) of possible physician impairment. When the psychiatrist interviewed me I told him about the fact that the public knows nothing of this deplorable situation. He concluded that I was paranoid delusional (due to the telephone harassment) and that I was "grandiose" since I had "special knowledge". The psychiatrist is an 85 year old man who believes he knows all there is to know from his textbooks on psychiatry. My medical license is now on the line and hence my entire future career!! I would like to add that since I have been practising medicine since 1968 there has NEVER been even one case of any patient of mine who questioned my professional expertise, personal integrity or ethical standards. Since I originally reported Hopkins in 1983, I have received numerous telephone calls at all hours; notices from funeral parlors, interruption of my medical practise by "a third party" answering my line giving misinformation out to patients resulting in complete chaos to my office and grief to myself. This was told to me by Ms. Avonile Blackman, my telephone secretary (1984). An "extra-cross connection" or illegal tap was reported on my phone by Charles Lauretano of the NY Telephone Company. My life has been a nightmare ever since standing up

and speaking out for my rights as a patriotic American citizen!

I SWEAR UNDER PENALTY OF PERJURY THAT ALL OF THE ABOVE IS TRUE AND CORRECT TO THE BEST OF MY KNOWLEDGE.

Stephen J. Kurzweil, M.D.
936 Fifth Avenue
New York, NY 10021

STATE OF NEW YORK
COUNTY OF N.Y.
Sworn to before me this
_____ day of _____
19___

ZANDRA HENDERSON
Notary Public, State of New York
Qualified in New York County
Certificate Filed in New York County
Commission Expires

****TOP SECRET****

Practice Limited to Dermatology   (212) 628-1400

STEPHEN J. KURZWEIL, M. D.
936 FIFTH AVENUE
NEW YORK, N. Y. 10021

Attorney =
Amy Kulb
(516) 222-7330

CURRICULUM VITAE

Education:

New York University, B.A., 1965
State University of New York-Downstate
Medical Center, M.D., 1969
Metropolitan Hospital, Medical Internship, 1970
Mount Sinai Hospital, Residency in Psychiatry, 1971
Kings County Hospital, Residency in Dermatology,
                                              1974
Columbia University, Post-Graduate Training
in Clinical Hypnosis, 40 Credit Hours, 1982
Post-Graduate Courses:

(1) Nutrition
(2) Infectious Disease
(3) Medical Malpractise

Licensure:

Diplomate, National Board of Medical Examiners,
Certificate No. 103812, July, 1970

License to practise Medicine and Surgery
in the State of New York, No. 106198, July, 1970

Registration, The University of the State
of New York, State Education Department,
License No. 106198-1

Diplomate, International Academy of Cosmetic
Surgery, May, 1974

Medical Society Affiliations:

New York State Society of Dermatology
Medical Society of the County of New York
Medical Society of the State of New York
Pan American Medical Association

Other:

Phi Beta Kappa
Alpha Omega Alpha Honor Medical Society

****TOP SECRET****

```
STATE OF NEW YORK   :   DEPARTMENT OF HEALTH
STATE BOARD FOR PROFESSIONAL MEDICAL CONDUCT
-----------------------------------------------X
            IN THE MATTER           :    STATEMENT

                 OF                 :       OF

        STEPHEN J. KURZWEIL, M.D.   :    CHARGES
-----------------------------------------------X
```

STEPHEN J. KURZWEIL, M.D., the Respondent, was authorized
to practice medicine in New York State on July 1, 1970 by the
issuance of license number 106198 by the New York State
Education Department. The Respondent is currently registered
with the New York State Education Department to practice
medicine for the period January 1, 1989 through December 31,
1991.

FACTUAL ALLEGATIONS

1. From in or about 1980 to date, Respondent has maintained a
    private medical office at 936 Fifth Avenue, New York, N.Y.

2. From in or about 1981 to date, Respondent has held delusional
    beliefs.

3. Respondent suffers from a psychiatric disorder which was
    diagnosed on December 12, 1989 as a Delusional Disorder,
    grandiose and paranoid type, on Axis I; Premorbid Schizoid
    Personality Disorder on Axis II.

4. Respondent's insight and judgment are seriously impaired due
    to his psychiatric disorder.

SPECIFICATION OF CHARGES

PRACTICING WHILE IMPAIRED BY MENTAL DISABILITY

Respondent is charged with practicing the profession
while the ability to practice is impaired by mental disability
under N.Y. Educ. Law Section 6509(3)(McKinney 1985), in that
Petitioner charges the facts in paragraphs 1, 2, 3 and/or 4.

```
DATED:   February   , 1990
         New York, New York
```

```
                    CHRIS STERN HYMAN
                    Counsel
                    Bureau of Professional Medical
                    Conduct
```

* * * * TOP SECRET * * * *

Jacobson and Goldberg

ATTORNEYS AT LAW

585 Stewart Avenue
Garden City, New York 11530

———

(516) 222-2330

TELECOPIER (FAX)
(516) 222-2339

TELEX
80-4294 BARRISTER

November 15, 1990

Stephen J. Kurzweil, M.D.
340 East 80th Street
New York, New York 10021

   Re: In the Matter of Stephen J. Kurzweil, M.D.
     Our File No. 12310

Dear Dr. Kurzweil:

   Enclosed for your information and file, please find copy
of correspondence we have received with regard to the above matter.

     Very truly yours,

     JACOBSON AND GOLDBERG

     Amy T. Kulb

     Amy T. Kulb

ATK:ad
Enc.

(1) Ltr. of Marcia E. Kaplan w/enc.
(2) Ltr. of Judge Maureen J.M. Ely

DEPARTMENT OF HEALTH

8 East 40th Street,   New York, New York 10016

David Axelrod M.D
Commissioner

November 9, 1990

Hon. Maureen J.M. Ely, Esq.
Supervising Administrative Law Judge
New York State Department of Health
Corning Tower - Empire State Plaza
Albany, New York 12237

                              RE: In the Matter of Stephen J.
                                    Kurzweil, M.D.

Dear Judge Ely:

        I have enclosed Petitioner's Comments To The Report Of
The Hearing Committee in the Matter of Stephen J. Kurzweil, M.D.
Copies have been sent to Judge Smith and Ms. Kulb.

                         Very truly yours,

                         Marcia E. Kaplan
                         Associate Counsel
                         Bureau of Professional Medical Conduct

MEK/pdb

Enclosure

cc: Amy Kulb, Esq.
     Hon. Debra Smith

TOP SECRET

STATE OF NEW YORK : DEPARTMENT OF HEALTH
STATE BOARD FOR PROFESSIONAL MEDICAL CONDUCT
---X

       IN THE MATTER   :   PETITIONER'S
                                            COMMENTS TO
          OF   :   THE REPORT OF
                                            THE HEARING
   STEPHEN J. KURZWEIL, M.D.   :   COMMITTEE

---X

TO: HON. DAVID M. AXELROD, M.D.
     COMMISSIONER
     NEW YORK STATE DEPARTMENT OF HEALTH
     TOWER BUILDING
     EMPIRE STATE PLAZA
     ALBANY, NEW YORK 12237

       Having received the Hearing Committee Report ("Report")
in the above-captioned matter, the Petitioner submits the
following comments:

       Petitioner urges the Commissioner to adopt the Hearing
Committee's findings of fact, conclusions of law, and
recommendation that Respondent's license to practice medicine be
suspended until he successfully completes a course of therapy or
treatment for his psychiatric disorder by a psychiatrist or
treating facility, approved by the Department's Office of
Professional Medical Conduct (OPMC), which will make a definitive
diagnosis of the Respondent's psychiatric disorder and provide
appropriate treatment, and that the suspension should end when
the treating psychiatrist or facility, with the concurrence of
OPMC, has determined that the Respondent's ability to practice
medicine is no longer impaired by mental disability.

                                   Marcia E. Kaplan
                                   Associate Counsel
                                   Bureau of Professional
                                     Medical Conduct

DATED: November 9, 1990
       New York, New York

cc: Amy T. Kulb, Esq.
     Jacobson and Goldberg
     591 Stewart Avenue
     Garden City, New York 11530

****TOP SECRET****

STATE OF NEW YORK
DEPARTMENT OF HEALTH

Corning Tower   The Governor Nelson A. Rockefeller Empire State Plaza   Albany, New York 12237

David Axelrod, M.D.
Commissioner

October 26, 1990

FEDERAL EXPRESS

Amy T. Kulb, Esq.
Jacobson and Goldberg
585 Stewart Avenue
Garden City, New York 11530

Marcia E. Kaplan, Esq.
8 East 40th Street
Third Floor
New York, New York 10016

RE: In the Matter of
Stephen J. Kurzweil, M.D.

Dear Ms. Kulb and Ms. Kaplan:

Enclosed are the Report of the Hearing Committee and a **PROPOSED**
Commissioner's Recommendation which reflects the Hearing Committee's
conclusions. The proposed Recommendation is **not** a final decision. It is
subject to review by the Commissioner of Health and the Board of Regents.
The Commissioner may accept, modify or reject the report and the proposed
Recommendation. You will receive a copy of the Commissioner's
Recommendation after he has reviewed this matter.

Pursuant to 10 NYCRR §51.13, you may submit exceptions to the
report and alternative proposed recommendations if you wish to do so before
the matter is submitted to the Commissioner for review. Exceptions and
recommendations should be addressed to the Supervising Administrative Law
Judge. The Supervising Administrative Law Judge will submit all exceptions
and recommendations to the Commissioner of Health along with the record
of the hearing for review [§51.13(f)]. In addition, you must send a copy
of the exceptions and recommendations to all those who appeared in the
matter and the Administrative Law Judge [§51.13(c)].

Exceptions must be received in this office by close of business
November 20, 1990. Any request for an extension of the exception period
must be on notice to all those who appeared in the matter and must state
good cause for the granting of the extension.

A copy of 10 NYCRR §51.13 is enclosed.

Very truly yours,

Maureen J. M. Ely
Supervising Administrative Law Judge

ctt

Enclosure

****TOP SECRET****

Jacobson and Goldberg

ATTORNEYS AT LAW

585 Stewart Avenue

Garden City, New York 11530

(516) 222-2330

TELECOPIER (FAX)
(516) 222-2339

TELEX
80-4294 BARRISTER

November 15, 1990

VIA FEDERAL EXPRESS

Hon. Maureen J.M. Ely
Supervising Administrative Law Judge
State of New York
Department of Health
Corning Tower
Empire State Plaza
Albany, New York 12237

      Re: In the Matter of
          Stephen J. Kurzweil, M.D.
          Our File No. 12310

Dear Judge Ely:

     Enclosed please find the **Respondent's submission and
penalty proposal for the consideration of Commissioner Axelrod.**

     Thank you for forwarding it to the Commissioner.

               Very truly yours,

               JACOBSON AND GOLDBERG

               Amy T. Kulb

ATK:ad
Enc.
cc: Marcia Kaplan, Esq.
     Stephen J. Kurzweil, M.D.

****TOP SECRET****

Jacobson and Goldberg

ATTORNEYS AT LAW

585 Stewart Avenue

Garden City, New York 11530

(516) 222-2330

TELECOPIER (FAX)
(516) 222-2339

TELEX
80-4294 BARRISTER

November 15, 1990

Hon. David Axelrod
Commissioner,
NYS Department of Health
Tower Building
Empire State Plaza
Albany, New York 12227

      Re: Stephen Kurzweil, M.D.
          Our File No. 12310

Dear Dr. Axelrod:

Please accept this letter as our **comments** on behalf of Dr. Kurzweil for your consideration in issuing the Commissioner's recommendation to the Board of Regents in this matter.

It is uncontested that there is **no evidence of any patient harm** in this case. In all of the documentary evidence presented by BPMC never is any reference made therein by Dr. Kurzweil to patients or his medical practice. There is therefore no tangible evidence of or basis upon which any reasonable inference can be drawn of any potential for patient harm.

We urge you in reviewing the transcript to carefully consider the credible testimony of two expert witnesses, Dr. Schwartz, a psychiatrist and Dr. O'Rourke, a psychologist, who have extensive experience and training not just generally in psychiatry/psychology, but more specifically and relevantly to this case, in assessing the mental health of individuals directly and specifically as to its relationship to the individual's occupational fitness.

Dr. Schwartz carefully reviewed the entirety of the documentary evidence presented by BPMC, had two formal and several informal interviews with Dr. Kurzweil to assess his mental status generally and to question him about the extensive correspondence with Mr. Hopkins and telephone messages, and he ordered psychological testing as another mode of confirmation. Dr. O'Rourke administered the psychological tests and interpreted the tests and compared the results of the tests to the results of tests administered by another certified psychologist in 1981. There was no evidence of any major mental disorder; no substantiation of the

---

* * * *TOP SECRET* * * *

Jacobson and Goldberg

ATTORNEYS AND COUNSELLORS AT LAW

Hon. David Axelrod
Re: Stephen Kurzweil, M.D.
November 15, 1990
Page 2

diagnosis and assessment made by 1 PMC's psychiatrist, Dr. Bryt, on
the basis solely of one interview and nothing more; nor was there
any information elicited that demonstrated patient harm on any
potential whatsoever for patient harm.

        Dr. Kurzweil's relationship with Mr. Hopkins is certainly
unfortunate, irregardless of the conflicting psychiatric labels
attached to it, because it is that relationship, and nothing
whatsoever involving his medical practice, that was the predicate
for the instant proceedings. Mr. Hopkins in fact testified that
he actively solicited various medical specialists to participate
in his self-styled research by examining "abductees" but that Dr.
Kurzweil had never become so involved. It is Dr. Kurzweil's
concerns over Mr. Hopkins, a person with no medical or research or
any formal training other than as an artist, engaging in
potentially harmful hypnosis, experiments on individuals labeled
as abductees by Mr. Hopkins, that led him to report these
experiments, recently acknowledged by Mr. Hopkins in a "mystery'
show on prime time television, to the authorities. Dr. Kurzweil's
good faith inquiries as a physician to the Health Department and
New York State Medical Society about these uncontrolled experiments
by Mr. Hopkins are what led to an investigation of his relationship
Mr. Hopkins and the instant proceedings.

        As the record indicates, Dr. Kurzweil is certainly not
a wealthy man and his medical license is his only means of earning
a livelihood to support himself and his infirm mother. He does not
have a family and the ability to practice medicine is truly his
whole life. The fact that his license has been placed in jeopardy
by these proceedings has effectively served as a deterrent to his
continuing his relationship with Mr. Hopkins and generating the
emotional intensity of concern, in terms of its potential, to the
Hearing Committee. Dr. Kurzweil most importantly has demonstrated
that he has the capacity to modify his behavior appropriately in
that he has not contacted Mr. Hopkins since early May.

        The documentary evidence, relied upon exclusively by the
Hearing Committee in its report as the factual underpinnings, for
its conclusion and penalty recommendation was correspondence
directed to Mr. Hopkins or generated by his relationship with Mr.
Hopkins and Mr. Hopkins' work with "abductees". Thus, it is clear
that the conduct which resulted in the Hearing Committee's

Jacobson and Goldberg

ATTORNEYS AND COUNSELLORS AT LAW

Hon. David Axelrod
Re: Stephen Kurzweil, M.D.
November 15, 1990
Page 3

recommendation was unique to Dr. Kurzweil's involvement with Mr. Hopkins and that relationship has been concluded. The termination of Dr. Kurzweil's interest in Mr. Hopkins and his activities has thus eliminated the 'potential' of concern by the Hearing Committee. As importantly, by this long and troubled chapter in his life finally coming to a conclusion, Dr. Kurzweil has been able to again focus his energies entirely on his career and find ways to channel his energy productively and appropriately by building up his practice and/or finding appropriate employment in medicine.

It is respectfully requested that strong consideration be given to the assessment of Doctors Schwartz and O'Rourke, the fact that there is no evidence of patient harm nor is there any tangible evidence of or credible psychiatric basis for inferring any potential patient harm and the fact that conduct at issue was unique to Dr. Kurzweil's relationship with Mr. Hopkins and that Dr. Kurzweil has shown the capacity to appropriately modify his conduct by ending the relationship and moving forward with his life. We respectfully suggest that accordingly the Commissioner's Recommendation should be a modification of the Hearing Committee Recommendation as follows: That Dr. Kurzweil be limited to practicing in an institutional or other supervised setting until there has been assessment and treatment, if any, by an approved psychiatrist. This penalty recommendation would be a more appropriate response to the record as a whole while giving the Health Department and the Board of Regents assurance that any concerns about public health, safety, welfare would be adequately safeguarded.

Thank you for your consideration.

Very truly yours,

JACOBSON AND GOLDBERG

Amy T. Kulb

Amy T. Kulb

ATK:ad
cc: Marcia Kaplan, Esq.

THE CITIZENS AGENCY FOR JOINT INTELLIGENCE NEWSLETTER

SUBSCRIPTION ORDER FORM
(MAKE COPIES OF THIS ORDER FORM AND SEND IT TO EVERYONE YOU KNOW)

IF YOU WANT THE BEST NEWS

THE REAL FACTS

RESEARCHED AND EDITED

BY **WILLIAM COOPER**

EX-MEMBER OF THE CINCPACFLT NAVAL INTELLIGENCE BRIEFING TEAM

WHO WARNS YOU NOT TO BELIEVE HIM OR ANYONE ELSE
UNLESS IT CHECKS OUT IN YOUR OWN RESEARCH

WITH CONTRIBUTIONS FROM MANY OTHERS

MONTHLY

AT A COST THAT YOU CAN AFFORD
DELIVERED FIRST CLASS MAIL
TO YOUR PRIVATE MAIL BOX
**(A GUARANTEED RIGHT UNDER THE FIRST AMENDMENT OF THE
CONSTITUTION OF THE UNITED STATES OF AMERICA)**

Daily Update	1-900-535-9800 ext. 240
Computer BBS	(602) 567-6725
Hotline	(213) 281-8222
Orders	(602) 567-6109
Research Ctr.	(602) 567-6536

"Information, not money, is the power of the nineties."
William Cooper 1/7/90

SEND $35 FOR 1 YEAR'S SUBSCRIPTION CONSISTING OF 12 ISSUES
****

NAME _____   PHONE _____

ADDRESS _____

CITY _____ STATE _____ ZIP _____

**MAKE CHECK OR MONEY ORDER PAYABLE TO:
WILLIAM COOPER
P. O. BOX 3299
CAMP VERDE, AZ 86322**

Opinions and factual statements expressed herein are the
responsibility of the authors and are not
necessarily endorsed or verified by the publisher.